1994
The Supreme Court Review

1994
The

"Judges as persons, or courts as institutions, are entitled to
no greater immunity from criticism than other persons
or institutions . . . [J]udges must be kept mindful of their limitations and
of their ultimate public responsibility by a vigorous
stream of criticism expressed with candor however blunt."
—*Felix Frankfurter*

". . . while it is proper that people should find fault when
their judges fail, it is only reasonable that they should recognize the
difficulties. . . . Let them be severely brought to book,
when they go wrong, but by those who will take the trouble
to understand them."
—*Learned Hand*

THE LAW SCHOOL

THE UNIVERSITY OF CHICAGO

Supreme Court Review

EDITED BY

DENNIS J. HUTCHINSON

DAVID A. STRAUSS

AND GEOFFREY R. STONE

THE UNIVERSITY OF CHICAGO PRESS

CHICAGO AND LONDON

INTERNATIONAL STANDARD BOOK NUMBER: 0-226-36311-2

LIBRARY OF CONGRESS CATALOG CARD NUMBER: 60-14353

THE UNIVERSITY OF CHICAGO PRESS, CHICAGO 60637

THE UNIVERSITY OF CHICAGO PRESS, LTD., LONDON

© 1995 BY THE UNIVERSITY OF CHICAGO, ALL RIGHTS RESERVED, PUBLISHED 1995

PRINTED IN THE UNITED STATES OF AMERICA

The paper used in this publication meets the minimum requirements of American National Standard for Information Sciences—Permanence of Paper for Printed Library Materials, ANSI Z39.48-1984. ∞

TO D.

May it please the court

CONTENTS

RICHARD H. FALLON, JR.

SEXUAL HARASSMENT, CONTENT NEUTRALITY, AND THE FIRST AMENDMENT DOG THAT DIDN'T BARK

In *Harris v Forklift*,[1] one of the first two cases handed down during the 1993 Term, the Supreme Court decided with great speed and astonishing unanimity that an employee need not show serious psychological or other injury in order to prove sexual harassment prohibited by Title VII. Somewhat surprisingly, in light of increased publicity about collisions between speech and equality interests and despite briefing of free speech issues by both sides, the Court's opinion in *Harris* made no reference to the First Amendment.

Less than two years before *Harris*, in *R.A.V. v St. Paul*,[2] the Supreme Court invalidated a municipal ordinance that forbade the utterance of "fighting words" likely to "arouse anger, alarm, or resentment in others on the basis of race, color, creed, religion, or gender"[3] on First Amendment grounds. Title VII forbids harassment on similar bases. Moreover, the "hostile environment" cause of action involved in *Harris* frequently imposes liability based on speech and expressive conduct. Some observers therefore thought

Richard H. Fallon, Jr., is Professor of Law, Harvard Law School.

Author's note: I am grateful to Elena Kagan, Fred Schauer, Steve Shiffrin, and David Strauss, who provided exceptionally valuable comments on a prior draft, and to Melissa Hart, Jonathan Lotsoff, and Shon Morgan, who assisted ably with the research.

[1] 114 S Ct 367 (1993).

[2] 112 S Ct 2538 (1992).

[3] Id at 2541, quoting St. Paul, Minn Legis Code § 292.02 (1990).

that the Supreme Court might use *Harris* to clarify the bearing of the First Amendment on sexual harassment law and, in doing so, might cut back sharply on accepted theories of Title VII liability. Bereft of so much as a mention of the First Amendment, *Harris* is the jurisprudential equivalent of the dog that didn't bark[4]—a clue (but no more than that) to some of the First Amendment mysteries surrounding prohibition of sexually harassing speech.

In order to explore those mysteries, this essay begins with *Harris*, but then widens its focus to view the problem of sexually harassing speech in the broader context of First Amendment doctrine and theory. Within the domain of doctrine, I argue that the principle of content neutrality, which frequently is identified as the First Amendment's operative core, is neither so pervasive nor so unyielding as is often thought. More than is commonly recognized, First Amendment doctrine divides into distinctive spheres or categories; content-based regulation in one may sometimes be justified at least partly on the basis that unrestricted communication in others amply respects First Amendment values. Against this theoretical background, I suggest that *Harris* implicitly acknowledged that distinctive principles should apply to sexually harassing speech in the workplace, and I seek to identify appropriate principles in light of underlying concerns. I conclude with a brief discussion of *Harris*'s possible implications for the analogous First Amendment issues presented by regulation of sexually harassing speech on college campuses.

I. Harris v Forklift

A. THE FACTS

Teresa Harris worked as a manager for Forklift Systems, Inc., a company that sells, leases, and repairs forklift machines, from April 1985 until October 1987.[5] Her supervisor was Charles Hardy, Forklift's president and chief executive officer. According to testimony accepted by a U.S. magistrate judge, Hardy frequently insulted Harris because of her gender and subjected her to a stream of sexual comments. He asked Harris and other female employees to retrieve coins from his front pants pocket. He deliber-

---

[4] See Arthur Conan Doyle, *The Adventure of Silver Blaze*, Strand Mag (Dec 1892).

[5] See *Harris*, 114 S Ct at 369.

ately dropped things, asked women employees including Harris to pick them up, and remarked on their anatomy as they did so. Hardy delivered regular commentary on the dress of Harris and other female employees that was laced with sexual innuendo. Several times he told Harris, in the presence of others, that "We need a man as a rental manager" and "You're a woman, what do you know?"[6] At least once he ridiculed her as "a dumb ass woman."[7] Again in front of others, Hardy suggested on one occasion that he and Harris should "go to the Holiday Inn to discuss [her] raise."[8]

In mid-August of 1987, Harris complained to Hardy about his sexual commentary and sex-based ridicule. Hardy expressed surprise at her reaction, claimed to have been only joking, and apologized. Within a few weeks, however, Hardy resumed his prior ways. To cite one egregious example, when Harris later told him that she was optimistic about completing a multiple lease deal, Hardy retorted, in front of other employees, "What did you do, promise the guy . . . [sex] on Saturday night?"[9] After collecting her paycheck on October 1, Harris quit.

In a suit subsequently filed in federal district court, Harris alleged that Hardy's conduct created a hostile and abusive work environment in violation of Title VII and therefore amounted to a "constructive discharge." The claim was referred to a magistrate judge, who characterized Hardy as "a vulgar man" who "demeans the female employees at his workplace."[10] The magistrate judge also accepted Harris's testimony that she found Hardy's sexual comments to be demeaning and subversive of her authority as a manager. Nevertheless, the magistrate judge concluded that Harris had failed "to prove that Hardy's conduct was so severe as to create a hostile work environment" forbidden by Title VII.[11] The magistrate judge stated:

> In the Sixth Circuit, the test for whether or not sexual harassment rises to the level of a hostile work environment is whether the harassment is "conduct which would interfere with [the]

---

[6] Id.

[7] Id.

[8] Id.

[9] Id.

[10] App to Pet for Cert A24.

[11] Id at A26.

hypothetical reasonable individual's work performance and affect seriously the psychological well-being of that reasonable person under like circumstances." . . . Once the objective "reasonable person" test is met, the court must next determine if the victim was subjectively offended and suffered an injury from the hostile work environment.[12]

Applying this test, the magistrate judge found the case "a close one,"[13] but concluded that most of Charles Hardy's comments "cannot be characterized as much more than annoying and insensitive."[14] He noted that the other female employees at Forklift Systems "considered Hardy a joker"[15] and were not offended by his sexual comments, possibly because they were "conditioned to accept denigrating treatment."[16] According to the magistrate judge, several of Hardy's specific comments to Harris were "more objectionable"[17] than his usual barrage of sexual innuendo, but he concluded that even those remarks were not "so severe" as to violate Title VII. "A reasonable woman manager under like circumstances would have been offended by Hardy, but his conduct would not have risen to the level of interfering with that person's work performance,"[18] he concluded. The magistrate judge also determined that Harris was not "subjectively so offended that she suffered injury, despite her testimony to the contrary."[19]

The district court rejected Harris's objections, adopted the magistrate judge's report, and dismissed the action.[20] In an unpublished opinion, the Sixth Circuit summarily affirmed the district court's decision.[21] The Supreme Court granted certiorari to resolve a conflict among the circuits concerning whether a plaintiff bringing a hostile environment claim under Title VII must prove that the challenged conduct "seriously affect[ed]" her psychological well-being or led her to suffer other injury.[22]

---

[12] Id at A28–29, quoting *Rabidue v Osceola Refining Co.*, 805 F2d 611, 620 (6th Cir 1986).

[13] Id at A31.

[14] Id.

[15] Id.

[16] Id at 32.

[17] Id at 33.

[18] Id at A34.

[19] Id.

[20] See *Harris*, 114 S Ct at 369–70.

[21] See id at 370.

[22] Id.

B. LEGAL BACKGROUND

That issue seems simple enough, and, in the event, was simply enough resolved by the Supreme Court. It arose against a background that raised anticipations of more.

Title VII of the 1964 Civil Rights Act makes it "an unlawful employment practice for any employer . . . to discriminate against any individual with respect to . . . compensation, terms, conditions, or privileges of employment, because of such individual's race, color, religion, sex, or national origin."[23] Although this language does not refer expressly to sexual harassment, the courts have followed the Equal Employment Opportunity Commission in finding that it forbids sexual harassment of two types. "Quid pro quo" harassment involves the conditioning of employment benefits or opportunities on submission to sexual advances or provision of sexual favors.[24] The second kind of prohibited sexual harassment is "hostile environment" harassment.[25] Under the EEOC's Guidelines, "[u]nwelcome sexual advances, requests for sexual favors, and other verbal or physical conduct of a sexual nature" violate Title VII "when such conduct has the purpose or effect of unreasonably interfering with an individual's work performance or creating an intimidating, hostile, or offensive working environment."[26]

In *Meritor Savings Bank v Vinson*,[27] the Supreme Court upheld a Title VII claim based on a hostile environment theory. The Court quoted the EEOC Guidelines approvingly, noting that "the EEOC drew upon a substantial body of judicial decisions and EEOC precedent holding that Title VII affords employees the right to work in an environment free from discriminatory intimidation, ridicule, and insult."[28] The Court cautioned that "not all workplace conduct that may be described as 'harassment' affects a 'term, condition, or privilege' of employment within the meaning of Title VII."[29] Putting a gloss on the EEOC's interpretation, the Court ruled that, for sexual harassment to be actionable, it must be sufficiently severe

---

[23] 42 USC § 2000e-2(a)(1).

[24] See, for example, *Meritor Savings Bank v Vinson*, 477 US 57, 65 (1986).

[25] See id at 65–66.

[26] 29 CFR § 1604.11(a)(3) (1993).

[27] 477 US 57 (1986).

[28] Id at 65.

[29] Id at 67 (citations omitted) (alterations in original).

or pervasive 'to alter the condition of [the victim's] employment and create an abusive working environment.' "[30] Nonetheless, the Court was unanimous in accepting that speech or conduct creating a hostile work environment could violate Title VII.[31]

During the roughly seven years between *Meritor* and *Harris*, the lower courts generally agreed that a plaintiff must satisfy an objective test to establish that sexually harassing speech or conduct had created a hostile environment and thereby "alter[ed] the conditions of employment." But the circuits divided over whether a plaintiff must satisfy an additional, subjective test requiring proof of "psychological injury" or even a serious psychological effect on the victim's well-being.[32]

A second set of post-*Meritor* concerns looked past Title VII to the First Amendment. Many of the early hostile environment cases either ignored First Amendment concerns altogether or dismissed constitutional objections with surprising casualness.[33] In the years after *Meritor*, courts and commentators worried increasingly about

---

[30] Id at 67, quoting *Henson v Dundee*, 682 F2d 897, 904 (11th Cir 1982).

[31] *Meritor* included a number of subsidiary holdings that have attracted vigorous criticism for making the litigation of hostile environment claims difficult. See, for example, Susan Estrich, *Sex at Work*, 43 Stan L Rev 818, 825 (1991). First, the Court indicated that "[t]he gravamen of any sexual harassment claim is that the alleged sexual advances were unwelcome" and should have been perceived as such. *Meritor*, 477 US at 68. Second, the Court found that a plaintiff's "sexually provocative speech or dress" is "obviously relevant" to the question of "unwelcomeness." Id at 69. Third, the majority held that Title VII liability should not automatically be imposed on employers whose employees create a hostile environment. Although "declin[ing] . . . to issue a definitive ruling on employer liability," the Court said it "agree[d] with the EEOC that Congress wanted courts to look to agency principles for guidance in this area." None of these subsidiary holdings was revisited in *Harris*.

[32] The Sixth, Seventh, and Eleventh Circuits required that a plaintiff show psychological effects. See *Rabidue v Osceola Refining Co.*, 805 F2d 611, 620 (6th Cir 1986); *Brooms v Regal Tube Co.*, 881 F2d 412, 418–20 (7th Cir 1989); *Sparks v Pilot Freight Carriers*, Inc., 830 F2d 1554, 1561 (11th Cir 1987). The Ninth Circuit expressly rejected a psychological injury requirement. *Ellison v Brady*, 924 F2d 872, 878 (1991). The Third and Eleventh Circuits had not expressly addressed the question but had not required such a showing. See *Anderson v City of Philadelphia*, 895 F2d 1469 (3d Cir 1990); *Burns v McGregor Electronic Indus., Inc.*, 955 F2d 559 (8th Cir 1992).

By contrast, no circuit appears to have established a psychological injury requirement in cases in which a plaintiff attempted to prove hostile environment harassment based on race. See Brief for the United States and the EEOC in No 92-1168 at 19.

[33] See *United States v X-Citement Video, Inc.*, 982 F2d 1285, 1296 (9th Cir 1993), rev'd, 115 S Ct 49 (1994) ("Because First Amendment defenses were rarely raised, harassment law evolved with little concern for free speech, and some workplace harassment cases seem suspect on First Amendment grounds.").

the scope of the restrictions that Title VII, under the hostile environment theory, imposes on employee speech.[34]

C. THE HOLDING

The Court in *Harris* held, unanimously, that the hostile environment cause of action has both objective and subjective components. Objectively, the Court found, "[c]onduct that is not severe or pervasive enough to create an objectively hostile or abusive work environment—an environment that a reasonable person would find hostile—is beyond Title VII's purview."[35] Subjectively, the Court required the victim to perceive the environment as abusive, but rejected any further requirement of psychological injury. This rejection reflected the case's chief contribution to Title VII doctrine.

The contribution was modest. As Justice Scalia noted in concurrence, the Court did almost nothing to clarify the law's central standard—the requirement that "the challenged conduct must be severe or pervasive enough 'to create an objectively hostile or abusive work environment'—an environment that a reasonable person would find hostile or abusive."[36]

Nor did the Justices address the bounds imposed on the hostile environment cause of action by the First Amendment. Why were Hardy's sexual innuendos and his assertion that Harris was "a dumb ass woman"—crucial elements in Harris's case under Title VII—not protected instances of free expression? Why did the Supreme Court feel no compulsion even to address the issue?

---

[34] See, for example, *Robinson v Jacksonville Shipyards, Inc.*, 760 F Supp 1486, 1534 (M D Fla 1991); *Jenson v Eveleth Taconite Co.*, 824 F Supp 847, 884 n 89 (D Minn 1993); Kingsley R. Browne, *Title VII as Censorship: Hostile-Environment Harassment and the First Amendment*, 52 Ohio St L J 481 (1991); Marcy Strauss, *Sexist Speech in the Workplace*, 25 Harv CR-CL L Rev 1 (1990); Nadine Strossen, *Regulating Workplace Sexual Harassment and Upholding the First Amendment—Avoiding a Collision*, 37 Vill L Rev 757 (1992); Eugene Volokh, *Freedom of Speech and Workplace Harassment*, 39 UCLA L Rev 1791 (1992).

[35] 114 S Ct at 370.

[36] 114 S Ct at 372 (Scalia, J, concurring) (quoting the opinion of the Court, 114 S Ct at 370). But Justice Scalia could think of "no test more faithful to the inherently vague statutory language than the one the Court . . . adopts." Id at 372. Justice Ginsburg also wrote a concurring opinion, in which she rephrased the "critical issue" as whether "members of one sex are exposed to disadvantageous terms or conditions of employment to which members of the other sex are not exposed." Id at 372. She concluded that this reformulation was in harmony with the Court's opinion, however, and she did not claim that it would make the standard stated by the Court's opinion any easier to apply.

II. Hostile Environment Theory and the First Amendment

A. THE PROBLEM

The argument that Title VII offends the First Amendment by prohibiting speech and expression that create a hostile work environment can be stated succinctly.[37] Under the hostile environment theory, Title VII bans speech and expressive conduct based on its offensive content.[38] In the words of one commentator:[39]

> The terms complained of are primarily of two kinds . . . .: (1) the "hostility message" is conveyed by terms of derision, such as "broad," "bitch," and "cunt;" and the "sexuality message" is conveyed by terms of "endearment," such as "honey," "sweetie," and "tiger." The complained-of terms may refer to women in general, particular women other than the plaintiff, or they may refer to the plaintiff herself and be addressed either to her or to others while referring to her.

As applied to speech and expressive conduct, Title VII's "hostile environment" cause of action runs afoul of what the Supreme Court has often trumpeted as perhaps the central tenet of the First Amendment. To quote just one formulation, "[a]bove all else, the First Amendment means that government has no power to restrict expression because of its message, its ideas, its subject matter, or its content."[40] Emphasizing the principle requiring that government regulation of speech must be content neutral,[41] at least one com-

---

[37] Although Title VII is primarily enforced in civil suits by employees against their employers, the duty being enforced is imposed by federal statute and remedies are imposed by state and federal courts. First Amendment principles therefore apply. See *New York Times Co. v Sullivan*, 376 US 254, 265 (1964).

[38] The EEOC Guidelines define the prohibition as encompassing "verbal . . . conduct *of a sexual nature*" that has the "purpose or effect" of "creating an intimidating, hostile, or offensive work environment." 29 CFR § 1604.11(a) (1993) (emphasis added). For discussion of the legal categories of "content-based" regulation and content neutrality, see note 41 below.

[39] Browne, 52 Ohio St L J at 492 (footnotes omitted) (cited in note 34).

[40] *Police Dep't of Chicago v Mosley*, 408 US 92, 95–96 (1972). See also *Texas v Johnson*, 491 US 397, 414 (1989) ("If there is a bedrock principle underlying the First Amendment, it is that the government may not prohibit the expression of an idea simply because society finds the idea itself offensive or disagreeable."); *Street v New York*, 394 US 576, 592 (1969) (characterizing it as "firmly settled" that "the public expression of ideas may not be prohibited merely because the ideas are themselves offensive to some of their hearers").

[41] The concept of "content neutrality" is itself contested and inconsistently applied. See, for example, Susan Williams, *Content Discrimination and the First Amendment*, 139 U Pa L Rev 615 (1991); Geoffrey Stone, *Content Regulation and the First Amendment*, 25 Wm & Mary L Rev 189 (1983); Martin H. Redish, *The Content Distinction in First Amendment Analysis*, 34 Stan L Rev 113 (1981). The term is perhaps most typically defined negatively, by reference

mentator has concluded that Title VII's prohibition of speech that creates a hostile environment is radically overbroad and therefore unconstitutional.[42] Several others have striven to develop limiting constructions that sharply restrict the hostile environment prohibition.[43] The flaw in their logic is not obvious.

B. THE PUZZLE

After *Harris*, however, it is virtually inconceivable that the Supreme Court might hold that the First Amendment forbids the imposition of Title VII liability for a broad category of sexually harassing speech. Some trimming of the cause of action remains possible, but it is highly unlikely that workplace expressions of gender-based hostility and communications of explicitly sexual messages will receive categorical protection. Two bits of evidence support this conclusion.

First, the Supreme Court had clear notice in the briefs filed in *Harris* of First Amendment issues raised by the hostile environment cause of action. First Amendment objections were asserted by the defendant[44] and answered by the plaintiff.[45] Several amici also

---

to regulations that are content based and therefore presumptively impermissible. The literal scope of the content-based category seems to be very broad, encompassing a "family" of types of prohibitions. See Williams, 139 U Pa L Rev at 621. These include but are not limited to those based on message, subject matter, viewpoint, and verbal or symbolic form. See Stone, 25 Wm & Mary L Rev at 233–44. Sometimes, however, courts and commentators use the term more restrictively to refer only to regulations that are motivated by objection to the message being communicated. See Williams, 139 U Pa L Rev at 624–35. Geoffrey Stone suggests that the central concern of the legal category of content-based regulation is discrimination based on viewpoint. See Stone, 25 Wm & Mary L Rev at 197.

Although these disagreements are important for some purposes, prohibitions against sexually harassing speech would appear to count as "content based" even under the most restrictive definitions. The "hostile environment" prohibition depends on the presence of a message related to gender or sexuality, but not all messages related to gender or sexuality are forbidden—only those communicating particular attitudes or viewpoints that could be perceived by a reasonable person as creating a hostile or offensive environment. See Browne, 52 Ohio St L J at 492 (cited in note 34); Volokh, 39 UCLA L Rev at 1828 (cited in note 34).

[42] See Browne, 52 Ohio St L J at 491–98 (cited in note 34).

[43] See, for example, Volokh, 39 UCLA L Rev (arguing that harassing speech can be prohibited under the First Amendment only if it is intentionally directed at particular employees) (cited in note 34); Strossen, 37 Vill L Rev (arguing that the First Amendment requires a case-by-case balancing of speech against equality interests in sexual harassment cases) (cited in note 34).

[44] See Brief of Respondent at 31–33.

[45] See Reply Brief of Petitioner at 10–11.

briefed the First Amendment issue,[46] and at least one specifically urged the Court to narrow the scope of the "hostile environment" cause of action to accommodate constitutionally protected speech rights.[47] Against this background, the *Harris* Court pointedly declined to narrow the hostile environment theory to approximate the common law tort of intentional infliction of emotional distress.[48]

To establish intentional infliction of emotional distress as defined by § 46 of *The Restatement (Second) of Torts*, a plaintiff must demonstrate that the defendant's conduct (i) was extreme and outrageous, (ii) was intentional or reckless, and (iii) caused the plaintiff to suffer severe emotional distress.[49] Commentary emphasizes that "liability clearly does not extend to mere insults, indignities, threats, annoyances or other trivialities" that "plaintiffs must necessarily be expected and required to be hardened to."[50] Although *Hustler v Falwell*[51] held that the First Amendment sharply restricts the capacity of public officials and public figures to recover for intentional infliction of emotional distress, the Supreme Court's reasoning depended heavily on the need to avoid chilling speech "in the area of public debate about public figures."[52] Other Supreme Court decisions suggest that a different rule would apply to suits by private figures.[53] Several commentators have therefore concluded that, in suits by private figures, speech satisfying the requirements of the

---

[46] See Brief Amicus Curiae of the ACLU and the American Jewish Congress in Support of Petitioner; Brief of Amicus Curiae Feminists for Free Expression in Support of Petitioner.

[47] See Brief of Amicus Curiae Feminists for Free Expression in Support of Petitioner.

[48] The argument in this and the two following paragraphs draws heavily on an unpublished paper written by a third-year student at the Harvard Law School, Jonathan D. Lotsoff, *Title VII and the First Amendment: New Solutions to the Harassment Law Puzzle* (1994).

[49] The Restatement (Second) of Torts § 46 (1977).

[50] Id § 46 comment d.

[51] 485 US 46 (1988).

[52] Id at 53.

[53] See, for example, *Dun & Bradstreet, Inc. v Greenmoss Builders, Inc.*, 472 US 749 (1985) (holding that punitive damages may be awarded to private figures in cases involving matters of merely private interest upon a lesser showing of fault than would be required in a suit by a public figure or involving a matter of public interest); *Time, Inc. v Firestone*, 424 US 448, 460 (1976) (noting precedents establishing that states could permissibly base damages awards to private figures for "personal humiliation, and mental anguish and suffering" upon a showing of fault less than that required for libel judgments in favor of public figure defendants).

traditional cause of action for intentional infliction of emotional distress would not be protected by the First Amendment.[54]

By requiring the plaintiff to demonstrate personal psychological injury, the lower courts in *Harris* had maintained at least some affinity between Title VII's hostile environment cause of action and the common law tort. In considering whether to assimilate the Title VII to the common law cause of action, the Supreme Court possessed undisputed "power to adopt [a] narrowing construction[]," and indeed has recognized a "duty to avoid constitutional difficulties by doing so if such a construction is fairly possible."[55] Under these circumstances, the Court's failure to restrict the hostile environment cause of action, coupled with its central holding rejecting a psychological injury requirement akin to that of the tort of intentional infliction of emotional distress, supports the inference that the Justices thought no significant narrowing to be needed.[56]

Second, the Justices' discussion of Title VII in *R.A.V. v St. Paul*[57] appeared to indicate a general acceptance that at least the main elements of the hostile environment cause of action should survive First Amendment challenge. *R.A.V.* involved a municipal ordinance that, as authoritatively construed by the state's highest court,[58] prohibited "fighting words" likely to "arouse[] anger, alarm, or resentment in others on the basis of their race, color, creed, religion, or gender."[59] Assuming the category of "fighting words" to be constitutionally prohibitable,[60] the five Justices joining the majority opinion nonetheless found the ordinance unconstitutional. The ordinance's vice lay in its prohibition of some fighting

---

[54] See Lotsoff (cited in note 48); Robert Post, *The Constitutional Concept of Public Discourse: Outrageous Opinion, Democratic Deliberation, and Hustler Magazine v Falwell*, 103 Harv L Rev 601, 662 (1990). See, however, Nadine Strossen, *Regulating Racist Speech on Campus: A Modest Proposal?* 1990 Duke L J 484, 516 (reading *Falwell* as indicating that, under the First Amendment, "the intentional infliction of emotional distress should virtually never apply to words").

[55] *Boos v Barry*, 485 US 312, 330–31 (1988).

[56] In his concurring opinion, Justice Scalia commented specifically on the breadth of the hostile environment cause of action under Title VII in comparison with more familiar tort theories: "the class of plaintiffs seeking to recover for negligence is limited to those who have suffered harm, whereas under this statute 'abusiveness' is to be the test of whether legal harm has occurred, opening more expansive vistas of litigation." 114 S Ct at 372.

[57] 112 S Ct 2539 (1992).

[58] Id at 2542.

[59] Id at 2541, quoting St. Paul, Minn Legis Code § 292.02 (1990).

[60] See id at 2542.

words, but not others, based on a disapproval of the ideas expressed. According to Justice Scalia's majority opinion, this selectivity indicated that the city was "seeking to handicap the expression of particular ideas"[61] in contravention of the central First Amendment principle that government may not proscribe speech or expressive conduct "because of disapproval of the ideas expressed."[62]

Having rested the decision on this general principle, Justice Scalia responded specifically to the worry of four concurring Justices that "hostile work environment claims based on sexual harassment should fail First Amendment review" under the "broad principle" used to decide *R.A.V.*[63] According to Justice Scalia, "words can sometimes violate laws directed not against speech but against conduct," and if "the government does not target conduct on the basis of its expressive content, acts are not shielded from regulation merely because they express a discriminatory idea."[64] "Thus," Justice Scalia wrote, "sexually discriminatory 'fighting words,' *among other words*, may produce a violation of Title VII's general prohibition against sexual discrimination in employment practices."[65] When the majority and concurring opinions are viewed in conjunction, it appears that all nine Justices participating in *R.A.V.* assumed that the core Title VII prohibition against speech that creates a discriminatorily hostile work environment would pass constitutional muster. *Harris*, coming less than two years after the decision in *R.A.V.*, buttresses this impression.

C. FALSE STARTS

Still, questions remain: how, exactly, can a content-based prohibition of sexually harassing speech that creates a hostile work environment be justified under the First Amendment, and what bounds, if any, does the First Amendment place on Title VII liability?

1. *Speech beneath First Amendment concern.* A possible answer to

---

[61] Id at 2549.

[62] 112 S Ct at 2543.

[63] 112 S Ct at 2557 (concurring opinion of White, joined by Blackmun, Stevens, and O'Connor).

[64] 112 S Ct at 2546–47.

[65] 112 S Ct at 2546 (emphasis added).

the first of these questions, arguably suggested by the Supreme Court's failure even to discuss the First Amendment in *Harris*, would be that the Court regards sexually harassing speech as simply and obviously beneath constitutional concern. The First Amendment does not protect all speech, only "the freedom of speech," and the Supreme Court—along with nearly everyone else—has generally treated it as self-evident that some verbal acts get no protection.[66] Examples include speech used to make threats, demand bribes, solicit crimes, fix prices, conspire to rob or murder, and place bets.[67]

It is an interesting question why speech such as this is conventionally assumed to lie so far off the First Amendment map as to merit no notice at all,[68] whereas other categories of speech—including "obscenity," "child pornography," and "fighting words"—much more typically appear on lists of "exceptions" to the First Amendment. Background cultural understandings, which themselves are subject to change, would almost certainly loom large in any persuasive explanation. In any event, the existence of entire categories of "speech" that are almost universally assumed to have nothing to do with "the freedom of speech" raises the question whether sexually harassing speech that occurs in the workplace might fall into the latter domain. If so, the Supreme Court's failure to notice a First Amendment question would signal its unanimous view that there was no question to be noticed—a judgment that the prohibited category was so clearly unrelated to the First Amendment's purposes that it should not be dignified with an explanation as to why it constituted an "exception."

This hypothesis might explain the Court's response to some of the speech acts sometimes characterized as "sexual harassment," but not to all of them. The speech involved in quid pro quo sexual harassment seems as "obviously" outside the ambit of First Amendment concern as words used to utter a threat or solicit a prostitute. Even within the Title VII category of "hostile environment" sexual

---

[66] See Frederick Schauer, *Categories and the First Amendment: A Play in Three Acts*, 34 Vand L Rev 265, 267–71 (1981).

[67] See Kent Greenawalt, *Speech, Crime, and the Uses of Language* 6–7 (Oxford, 1989); Schauer, 34 Vand L Rev at 267–71 (cited in note 66).

[68] For an illuminating exploration of why some speech acts clearly lie beyond the ambit of First Amendment protection, see Greenawalt, *Speech, Crime, and the Uses of Language* at 6–7. See also Schauer, 34 Vand L Rev at 267–82 (cited in note 66).

harassment, the same analysis quite possibly applies to the direct solicitation of sexual favors. It might also extend to individually targeted, unwanted, and unreasonably persistent or recurring streams of comment that occur within the workplace and are sexually explicit or debasing.

Clearly, however, the set of speech acts that might plausibly be thought to constitute sexual harassment can be arrayed along a spectrum, not all of which could reasonably be thought to lie completely beyond First Amendment concern—even if some, most, or even all of those acts are ultimately determined to be constitutionally regulable.[69] Examples taken from the *Harris* case might include some of Hardy's gender-based criticisms of Harris's work performance, such as his rhetorical question, "You're a woman, what do you know?"[70] Clearer cases would be presented by expressions of opinion by some employees, not targeted at any woman in particular, that women lack the mental or physical capacity to perform particular jobs[71] and by the display of sexually explicit and demeaning pictures of women in the workplace.[72] At some point and in some form, a First Amendment question must be faced.

2. *General statutes and incidental restrictions.* If some sexually harassing speech at least implicates First Amendment concerns, but can nonetheless be prohibited in the workplace, an authoritative explanation might seem to come from *R.A.V. v St. Paul.*[73] In *R.A.V.*, Justice Scalia's majority opinion suggested that Title VII embodies a general prohibition against discriminatory conduct that only incidentally, and therefore permissibly, sweeps in some

---

[69] Professors Schauer and Greenawalt both distinguish between the First Amendment's "coverage"—the range of speech acts that come within its ambit of concern—and the class of speech acts that are ultimately protected by the First Amendment. See Schauer, 34 Vand L Rev at 267–71 (cited in note 66); Greenawalt, *Speech, Crime, and the Uses of Language* at 5 (cited in note 67). Within the terms of this distinction, speech used to effect a bribe is not even covered by the First Amendment, whereas fighting words and child pornography are covered, even though they are generally not protected.

[70] See *Harris*, 114 S Ct at 369.

[71] Compare *Lipsett v University of Puerto Rico*, 864 F2d 881, 887 (1988) (finding that assertions by one medical resident that women should not become surgeons could contribute to a hostile environment).

[72] "Pin-ups or 'girlie magazines' in the workplace have been the subject of innumerable sexual harassment claims." Browne, 52 Ohio St L J at 493 (cited in note 34).

[73] 112 S Ct 2538 (1992). See, for example, *Jensen v Eveleth Taconite Co.*, 824 F Supp 847, 884 n 89 (D Minn 1993) (rejecting a First Amendment challenge in a Title VII case on the basis of *R.A.V.*).

speech.[74] The predicate for this analysis lies in Justice Scalia's proposal that general statutes that only incidentally restrict speech or expressive conduct should not trigger heightened scrutiny under the First Amendment. Fortunately or unfortunately, this bold idea will not withstand analysis.

As a doctrinal matter, the argument that elevated First Amendment scrutiny should not apply to restrictions on expression arising from general prohibitions against harmful conduct is flatly rejected by one of the foundational cases of modern free speech doctrine, *United States v O'Brien*.[75] Under *O'Brien*, a regulation of this kind can permissibly be applied to speech or expressive conduct only "if it furthers an important or substantial governmental interest; if the governmental interest is unrelated to the suppression of free expression; and if the incidental restriction on alleged First Amendment freedom is no greater than is essential to that interest."[76] Scrutiny under *O'Brien* is elevated, even if not "strict."

There is a deeper problem, however, suggested by *O'Brien*'s requirement that the government's interest in regulation must be "unrelated to the suppression of free expression."[77] More or less obviously, the First Amendment has to limit the legislature's power to enact "general" statutes that aim at prohibitable conduct but sweep in speech that the legislature adjudges harmful only because of its content.[78] To take an example that Justice Scalia has used, Congress can prohibit treason, including treason effected through speech that divulges the nation's defense secrets to an enemy.[79] But Congress, in enacting a general prohibition against treason, cannot "incidentally" ban speech that gives aid and comfort to an enemy by criticizing public officials. It does not matter that the statute is a general one or that it aims mostly at treasonous conduct. Speech

---

[74] See 112 S Ct at 2546.

[75] 391 US 367 (1968).

[76] Id at 377.

[77] For a classic exposition of the problem to which *O'Brien* responded and the fundamental insight reflected in this formulation, see John Hart Ely, *Flag Desecration: A Case Study of the Roles of Categorization and Balancing in Constitutional Law*, 88 Harv L Rev 1482 (1975).

[78] It is not always easy to tell what counts as a general statute, since every statute will make some discriminations in terms of what does and does not prohibit. For example, a "general" antidiscrimination statute such as Title VII, see *R.A.V.*, 112 S Ct at 2546, does not prohibit all discrimination on all bases.

[79] See *R.A.V.*, 112 S Ct at 2546.

of this kind is protected by the First Amendment,[80] and heightened scrutiny is required to ensure that government does not purposely or off-handedly trample on speech rights without substantively adequate justification.[81]

A similar analysis should, and I am quite sure would, apply to at least some general prohibitions against race- and sex-based discrimination. Imagine that the city of St. Paul, in the *R.A.V.* case, had generally prohibited race- and sex-based discrimination throughout the city with respect to housing, public accommodations, education, membership in private clubs, and so forth, and that, as an aspect of this general prohibition, it had forbidden all public or private acts and utterances tending to create a racially or sexually hostile environment. A statute of this kind, which would restrict the press, political orators, and private citizens engaged in conversation in their homes, would surely offend the First Amendment.[82] Certainly Justice Scalia, who wrote the majority opinion in *R.A.V.*, does not believe otherwise.

If so, however, the case of Title VII's prohibition against speech that creates a hostile work environment must be distinguished, and the distinction must rest on some ground other than the "generality" of the statutes' prohibitions or the "incidental" character of their restrictions on speech.

3. *Imperfect analogies.* Commentators have combed First Amendment doctrine for a recognized exception to accepted free speech principles that would allow prohibition of sexually harassing workplace speech. Suggestive analogies emerge, but no currently established category quite fits.

a) Time, place, and manner regulation. At least one court has concluded that sexual harassment law can be justified as a "time, place, and manner" regulation that restricts sexually harassing speech in the workplace but not elsewhere.[83] The Supreme Court has stated

---

[80] See *New York Times v Sullivan*, 376 US 254 (1964).

[81] I do not mean to deny that government possesses broad authority to regulate speech under "general" statutes when the harm it wishes to prevent is unrelated to the content of the speech that it incidentally regulates. See Frederick Schauer, *Cuban Cigars, Cuban Books, and the Problem of Incidental Restrictions on Communications*, 26 Wm & Mary L Rev 779 (1985). In the hypotheticals discussed in text, however, the harm caused is closely linked to the content of the speech that causes the harm—the paradigmatic situation for which the *O'Brien* test was devised.

[82] Compare *American Booksellers Ass'n v Hudnut*, 771 F 2d 323 (7th Cir 1985), aff'd, 475 US 1001 (1986).

[83] See *Robinson v Jacksonville Shipyards, Inc.*, 760 F Supp 1486, 1535 (M D Fla 1991).

repeatedly, however, that time, place, and manner regulations must be content neutral in order to receive deferential judicial review.[84] Harassment law is explicitly content based: it prohibits sexually explicit and sexually demeaning speech.[85]

The Supreme Court has recognized a partial exception to the requirement that time, place, and manner restrictions must be content neutral for regulations justified by reference, not to the message that speech communicates, but to what the Court has termed "secondary effects." The generative case is *City of Renton v Playtime Theatres, Inc.*,[86] in which the Court permitted a city to apply special zoning regulations to purveyors of sexually explicit or "adult" but not legally "obscene" speech. According to the majority, the city's ordinance did not come within the rationale of the prohibition against content-based regulations, because it did not aim to suppress the message or communicative impact of the speech that it restricted. The city's purpose, rather, was to impose geographical limits on the availability of adult speech because of the activities, such as prostitution and drug use, that tend to cluster around adult theaters and bookstores. The Court characterized these activities as "secondary effects"[87] that provided a permissible basis for content-based regulation because, in the Court's view, they did not arise directly from any influence of the regulated expression on the mind of the listener; they were neither causally nor persuasively connected with either the regulated speech's offense-giving or its persuasive effects.

Despite occasional suggestions to the contrary, prohibitions against sexual harassment cannot be justified on the rationale that creation of a hostile environment is a prohibitable secondary effect. As the Supreme Court has made clear, the "direct impact that speech has on its listeners" is not a "secondary" but a primary effect.[88] Harassment law, which aims to afford protection against

---

[84] See, for example, *City of Cincinnati v Discovery Network, Inc.*, 113 S Ct 1505, 1514–16 (1993); *Pacific Gas & Electric Co. v Public Util. Comm'n*, 475 US 1, 20 (1986).

[85] See note 41 above.

[86] 475 US 41 (1986).

[87] 475 US at 47.

[88] *Boos v Barry*, 485 US at 321. Although the relevant section of Justice O'Connor's opinion was joined only by Justices Stevens and Scalia, Justices Brennan and Marshall endorsed this analysis in a concurring opinion. See id at 334 (concurring opinion of Brennan, J). Significantly, even the three dissenting Justices did not dispute that the regulation involved in the case was content based. See id at 338 (Rehnquist, C J, concurring in part and dissenting in part).

sexually explicit and sexually demeaning messages because of their harmful content, "focus[es] on the direct impact of speech on its audience"[89] and therefore cannot qualify for the "secondary effects" exception to the content-neutrality principle.

b) Captive audience. Several commentators have argued that prohibitions against sexual harassment in the workplace are constitutionally permissible because employees constitute a "captive audience."[90] At least one court has also endorsed this analysis.[91] The captive audience argument is hard to assess, because the doctrine is inchoate. In several cases the Supreme Court has invoked an audience's "captive" status to justify content-based regulation,[92] and it has suggested in dictum that the doctrine might have general sweep.[93] But the dictum is misleading.

In cases involving the home, the Supreme Court has upheld regulation of broadcast speech[94] and of the content of the mail,[95] even though the purported captives could easily have avoided exposure by turning the dial or discarding a mailer. Outside of the home, the Court has refused to apply the captive audience rationale to permit the prohibition of offensive speech in a school board meeting[96] and in a courthouse,[97] both situations in which escape might have been costly if not impossible. When the so-called captive audience cases are read in conjunction, the character of the place seems more important than the degree of audience "captivity" in explaining the applications of captive audience doctrine.[98]

---

[89] Id at 321.

[90] See J. M. Balkin, *Some Realism About Pluralism: Legal Realist Approaches to the First Amendment*, 1990 Duke L J 375, 423; Strauss, 25 Harv CR-CL L Rev at 36 (cited in note 34).

[91] *Robinson v Jacksonville Shipyards, Inc.*, 760 F Supp 1486, 1535–36 (M D Fla 1991) (quoting Balkin, 1990 Duke L J at 423).

[92] See, for example, *FCC v Pacifica Foundation*, 438 US 726, 748–50 (1978); *Lehman v Shaker Heights*, 418 US 298 (1974); *Rowan v United States Post Office Dep't*, 397 US 728, 737–38 (1970).

[93] See *Erznoznik v City of Jacksonville*, 422 US 205, 209 (1975).

[94] See *Pacifica Foundation*, 438 US at 726 (1978).

[95] See *Rowan*, 397 US at 728 (1970). But see *Bolger v Youngs Drug Products Corp.*, 463 US 60, 72 (1983).

[96] See *Rosenfeld v New Jersey*, 408 US 901 (1972).

[97] See *Cohen v California*, 403 US 15 (1971).

[98] This conclusion is consistent with the very few cases in which the Supreme Court has relied on a captive audience rationale to uphold content-based restrictions not aimed at protecting the home. See, for example, *Bethel School Dist. No. 403 v Fraser*, 478 US 675, 683–84 (1986) (citing audience captivity as one justification for regulating the content of a

Just as the Supreme Court clearly believes that special characteristics of the home justify restrictions to exclude unwanted speech
from the outside, so it may have concluded that special characteristics of the workplace warrant content-based regulation. If so, however, the analytical weight is not borne by a general doctrine applicable whenever "captive audiences" are present, but must rest on
distinctive features of the workplace.

c) Existing workplace speech doctrine. No opinion of the Supreme
Court has explicitly recognized a "workplace speech doctrine" permitting the government to engage in content-based regulation of
employee speech in private workplaces. Without pretense of origi-
nality on this point,[99] I believe that a doctrine responding to distinctive features of the workplace ought to be developed. Indeed, I
think it may be necessary to posit such a doctrine to reconcile the
sexual harassment cause of action framed by *Meritor* and *Harris*
with the First Amendment. If so, however, *Harris* foreshadows a
significant innovation.

In *NLRB v Gissell Packing Co.*,[100] the Supreme Court held that
interests in fair and peaceful labor relations justify limited restrictions on employers' speech in the context of labor disputes. Somewhat more specifically, the Court upheld restrictions on speech
likely to be perceived as containing a " 'threat of reprisal or force
or promise of benefit.' "[101] Outside of this limit, however, the Court
affirmed that "an employer's free speech right to communicate his
views to his employees is firmly established and cannot be in-
fringed."[102]

---

student speech to a school assembly, but also relying on the schools' educational mission);
Lehman v Shaker Heights, 418 US 298 (1974) (plurality opinion) (invoking a captive audience
rationale to justify the exclusion of political advertising from municipal buses). Compare
Volokh, 39 UCLA L Rev at 1833 (cited in note 34) (distinguishing these cases and maintaining that the Supreme Court "has never upheld" a content-based restriction aimed at
protecting a captive audience "outside the home").

[99] As will become abundantly clear, my own thinking on this subject is deeply influenced
by the work of Robert Post. See, for example, Robert C. Post, *Racist Speech, Democracy, and
the First Amendment*, 32 Wm & Mary L Rev 267, 289 (1991) Robert Post, *The Perils of
Conceptualism: A Response to Professor Fallon*, 103 Harv L Rev 1744, 1746 (1990) (denying the
necessity that "speech that is appropriately protected when it occurs in public discourse is
also appropriately regulated when it occurs within the context of an employment relationship"). See also Volokh, 39 UCLA L Rev at 1819–20 (cited in note 34).

[100] 395 US 575, 616–20 (1969).

[101] Id at 618 (quoting 29 USC § 158(c)).

[102] Id at 617.

Commentators have suggested that sexually harassing speech is inherently threatening and that its prohibition comes within the rationale of *Gissell*.[103] But *Gissell* involved the speech of employers; the Title VII cause of action for "hostile environment" sexual harassment more often focuses on the speech of employees. Moreover, although some sexually harassing speech is undeniably threatening, the hostile environment prohibition does not require proof that any threat was either intended or perceived. Insistence that all harassment is "inherently threatening" requires a far broader concept of a "threat" than *Gissell* adopted.

In another effort to justify prohibitions against sexually harassing speech, Rodney Smolla has argued that First Amendment decisions implicitly permit government to engage in content-based regulation in what he calls "transactional settings."[104] The underlying idea is that, because government can permissibly regulate the terms on which "transactions" such as sales, leases, and trades are effected, it can also regulate the speech—including threats, bribes, offers, and counteroffers—that produces or constitutes the transactional process. But even if Smolla is right about the regulability of "transactional speech," he fails to "explain why the presence of such transactional speech in the workplace justifies the suppression of *non*transactional workplace speech, which includes the great majority of harassing speech" prohibited by Title VII.[105]

In short, the regulation of workplace speech that creates a sexually hostile environment seems to presuppose some new category of regulable speech under the First Amendment that depends on the character of the workplace, the nature of sexually harassing speech, or both. This makes it the more surprising that a Supreme Court that has enshrined a "content neutrality" requirement as the central principle of the First Amendment could have decided *Harris v Forklift* without so much as a word about free speech doctrine. Or does it?

---

[103] See Comment, *Of Supervision, Centerfolds, and Censorship: Sexual Harassment, the First Amendment, and the Contours of Title VII*, 46 U Miami L Rev 403, 431–32 (1991). Compare Mari Matsuda, *Public Response to Racist Speech: Considering the Victim's Story*, 87 Mich L Rev 2320, 2336–37 (1989) (suggesting that "hate speech" is inherently threatening).

[104] See Rodney A. Smolla, *Rethinking First Amendment Assumptions About Racist and Sexist Speech*, 47 Wash & Lee L Rev 171 (1990).

[105] Volokh, 39 UCLA L Rev at 1824 (cited in note 34).

III. Sexual Harassment in First Amendment Context

Although the Supreme Court talks often about its general commitment to content neutrality, the commitment is much more limited than the Court appears to grasp. Instead of being governed by a single, master principle, First Amendment doctrine is contextual and, in Steven Shiffrin's term, "eclectic."[106] Somewhat more specifically, the jurisprudence divides into a number of distinct categories or spheres, each subject to distinctive rules.[107] Contrary to what the Supreme Court has suggested, permitting content-based regulation in one sphere, when opportunities for uncensored expression remain in others, is neither particularly novel nor necessarily disturbing under the First Amendment.

Even if departures from content neutrality are accepted in some contexts, however, it does not follow that prohibitions against sexual harassment in the workplace are unproblematically justifiable. Guiding norms must be established, at least partly by reference to underlying First Amendment values. In short, the free speech issues raised by the Title VII prohibition against "hostile environment" sexual harassment cannot be considered in isolation. Analysis requires critical immersion in First Amendment doctrine and theory, with special reference to the principle of content neutrality.

A. THE TWO-LEVEL THEORY AND ITS LIMITS

A purported rule requiring content neutrality in regulation is the natural and historical complement of what Harry Kalven dubbed the "two-level theory" of the First Amendment.[108] According to the two-level theory, all categories of speech are either protected (level one) or unprotected (level two). Protected, level-one status constitutes the norm. Only a few, narrowly defined categories—such as obscenity, fighting words, and child pornogra-

---

[106] See Steven H. Shiffrin, *The First Amendment, Democracy, and Romance*, 132–39 (Harvard, 1990); Steven Shiffrin, *The First Amendment and Economic Regulation: Away from a General Theory of the First Amendment*, 78 Nw U L Rev 1212, 1251–53 (1983).

[107] See Richard Pildes, *Avoiding Balancing: The Role of Exclusionary Reasons in Constitutional Law*, 45 Hastings Const L Q 711 (1994) (arguing that government action within identifiable spheres of action should be required to respect values appropriate to those spheres).

[108] See Harry Kalven, *The Metaphysics of the Law of Obscenity*, 1960 Supreme Court Review 1, 11.

phy—are relegated to level two. After these disfavored categories have been excluded, the prohibition against content-based regulation ensures that all speech on level one receives the same degree of First Amendment protection.

The allure of a two-level theory emerges from history. At least since the Warren Court, judges and theorists have aspired to avoid the ad hoc, balancing approach that prevailed in earlier eras, notably under the "clear and present danger" test.[109] As John Ely has emphasized, the defendants in the three cases in which that test was introduced[110] "all ended up going to prison for quite tame and ineffectual expression" on matters of political concern.[111] For Ely, as for a generation of First Amendment theorists, the challenge became one of devising categorical rules to preclude such travesties and, more generally, to bar governmental distortion of public debate.[112] The master rule on which judges and theorists predominantly converged was the requirement of content neutrality,[113] conceived largely as the antithesis of ad hoc balancing of free speech interests on the one hand against the interests favoring regulation on the other.[114]

Although the underlying motivation is laudable, the conceptual space covered by the First Amendment is too vast to yield to a general rule of content neutrality, a categorical prohibition of ad hoc balancing, or any other single formulation. However much the ideal of content neutrality may be trumpeted by courts and commentators, analysis of the free speech issues presented by verbal sexual harassment should begin with a clear-eyed recogni-

---

[109] See, for example, *Schenck v United States*, 249 US 47 (1919).

[110] The cases were *Schenck*, 249 US at 47 (1919); *Frohwerk v United States*, 249 US 204 (1919); and *Debs v United States*, 249 US 211 (1919).

[111] John Hart Ely, *Democracy and Distrust: A Theory of Judicial Review* 107 (Harvard, 1980).

[112] For similarly categorical, although otherwise distinctive, approaches, see, for example, Melville Nimmer, *Nimmer on Freedom of Speech* (Mathew Bender, student ed, 1984); Laurence Tribe, *American Constitutional Law* 789–94 (Foundation, 2d ed 1978).

[113] Partly because "content neutrality" may mean different things to different people at different times, see note 41 above, "[d]eciding whether a particular regulation is content based or content neutral is note always a simple task." *Turner Broadcasting System, Inc. v FCC*, 114 S Ct 2445, 2459 (1994).

[114] See, for example, J. Ely, *Democracy and Distrust* at 110–16.

tion that existing doctrine almost inevitably reflects a complex effort to balance competing interests, to promote a multiplicity of values, and to reach practically and symbolically acceptable results.[115]

1. *Speech acts outside the First Amendment.* As I have suggested already, some speech acts—notably including those involved in threats, bribes, wagering, price fixing, fraud, and criminal conspiracy—lie wholly outside the coverage of the First Amendment.[116] As explained by leading commentators, speech of this kind is so far removed from the values associated with freedom of speech that its regulation triggers no First Amendment issue.[117]

2. *Definitions of unprotected categories.* Among the categories of speech that implicate First Amendment values and therefore fall within the amendment's coverage, not all are ultimately protected from categorical, content-based prohibition.[118] Obscenity, fighting words, and child pornography are well-known examples of generally unprotected categories. Although the content-neutrality principle presupposes the division of speech into protected and unprotected categories, judgments about which categories are unprotected are content-based and reflect a balancing of interests.

3. *Intermediate categories.* During the years since the Warren Court, if not before, the Supreme Court has explicitly recognized several categories within which content-based regulation is sometimes permitted, often on a relatively ad hoc basis.

a) Commercial speech. The Supreme Court has developed a four-part test to determine whether particular content-based regulations

---

[115] The argument that follows is pervasively indebted to the work of Steven Shiffrin. See, for example, Shiffrin, *The First Amendment, Democracy, and Romance* (cited in note 106); Shiffrin, *The First Amendment and Economic Regulation*, 78 Nw U L Rev at 1212 (cited in note 106).

[116] See note 66 above and accompanying text.

[117] See note 67 above (citing works by Professors Greenawalt and Schauer).

[118] For example, obscenity is regulable, even though the Supreme Court has rejected the view that speech is obscene and therefore unprotected only if it is "utterly without redeeming social value." See *Miller v California*, 413 US 15 (1973). Similarly in *New York v Ferber*, 458 US 747, which established the category of regulable child pornography, "the Court never determine[d] that child pornography, in isolation, is totally beyond the normative functions of the First Amendment," but instead emphasized "the particularly overwhelming nature" of the state's regulatory interest. Frederick Schauer, *Codifying the First Amendment: New York v Ferber*, 1982 Supreme Court Review 285, 304.

of commercial advertising are permissible.[119] In some cases, the test requires relatively ad hoc balancing judgments.[120]

b) Adult speech. As noted already, Supreme Court decisions countenance some forms of content-based regulation of "adult" or "sexually explicit" speech that is not technically "obscene" and therefore receives some First Amendment protection.[121]

c) Labor speech. "Labor speech" may define a third category in which content-based regulation is permitted under less exacting standards than "strict scrutiny."[122] In the context of a live labor dispute, the Supreme Court has upheld content-based prohibitions in order to protect employees from the fact or perception of employer coercion.[123]

4. *Libel.* Prior to *New York Times v Sullivan*,[124] libelous speech appeared entirely unprotected by the First Amendment. In the *New York Times* case, however, the Supreme Court held that even false and defamatory speech about public officials is constitutionally protected unless uttered with "actual malice."[125] *Gertz v Robert Welch*[126] extended the "actual malice" test to libel actions brought by public figures. Even in the case of false and defamatory statements about private persons, modern doctrine holds that liability may not be imposed without a showing of fault.[127] Cases establishing constitutional protections of libelous speech do not fit easily into a two-level theory of the First Amendment and are similarly

---

[119] See *Central Hudson Gas & Elec. Corp. v Pub. Serv. Comm'n*, 447 US 557, 566 (1980).

[120] The Supreme Court seems to have decided categorically that commercial speech may not be restricted under the otherwise applicable four-part test if it poses no special dangers not posed by other, nonregulated speech. See *City of Cincinnati v Discovery Network, Inc.*, 113 S Ct 1505, 1514–16 (1993).

[121] See *City of Renton v Playtime Theatres, Inc.*, 475 US 41 (1986); *Young v American Mini Theatres*, 427 US 50 (1976).

[122] See James Pope, *The Three-Systems Ladder of First Amendment Values: Two Rungs and a Black Hole*, 11 Hastings Const L Q 189 (1984).

[123] See *NLRB v Gissell Packing Co.*, 395 US 575 (1969).

The Supreme Court also appears to have developed a somewhat murky category of "private speech" subject to special rules, including rules permitting content-based regulation. For citations to cases and relevant literature, see William Lockhart et al, *Constitutional Law Cases and Materials* 863–69 (West, 7th ed, 1991).

[124] 376 US 254 (1976).

[125] Id at 279–80.

[126] 418 US 323 (1974).

[127] See id at 347.

difficult to reconcile with the rule that government may not regulate speech on the basis of content.

Geoffrey Stone has argued that "libel," in common with the other categories of content-based regulation that I have discussed so far, should be regarded as "low value" speech.[128] According to his interpretation, content-based regulation is permissible with respect to low-value, but not "level one" or high-value expression. Although plausibly capable of rationalizing libel and certain other categories, this theory cannot account adequately for the First Amendment doctrine bearing on the categories that follow.

5. *Broadcast media.* Although the rationale has varied from case to case, the Supreme Court has established that the categorical prohibition against content-based regulation does not apply to radio and television.[129] In the leading case,[130] the Court dismissed the broadcaster's claim to freedom from content-based regulation with the assertion that the interests of viewers and listeners, not the interests of broadcasters in speaking as they chose, were paramount.[131]

6. *Nonregulatory functions.* The content-neutrality rule was crafted for contexts in which government functions in a traditionally coercive, regulatory capacity. Sometimes explicitly and sometimes implicitly, the Supreme Court has found the rule inapplicable when the government performs functions other than regulating private conduct.

---

[128] See Stone, 25 Wm & Mary L Rev at 194–96 (cited in note 41).

[129] Compare *Red Lion Broadcasting Co. v FCC*, 395 US 67 (1969) (basing justification on spectrum scarcity) and *Turner Broadcasting System, Inc. v FCC*, 114 S Ct 2445 (1994) (same) with *FCC v Pacifica Foundation*, 438 US 726 (1978) (relying on the broadcast media's accessibility to children and intrusion into the home).

[130] *Red Lion Broadcasting Co. v FCC*, 395 US at 67 (1969).

[131] Similarly differentiating among media, the Supreme Court has permitted licensing requirements for films that would not be permitted under the prior restraint rules applied to more traditional media. See, for example, *Times Film Corp. v Chicago*, 365 US 43 (1961), quoting *Joseph Burstyn, Inc. v Wilson*, 343 US 495 (1952) (reasoning that, because motion pictures tend to present distinctive problems, they are " 'not necessarily subject to the precise rules governing any other particular method of expression' ").

There is also at least one area in which cable broadcasting may be subject to differential treatment. Although the Supreme Court held in *Turner Broadcasting System, Inc.*, 114 S Ct 2445 (1994), that the scarcity rationale justifying content-based regulation of the broadcast media does not apply to cable television, *Leathers v Medlock*, 499 US 439 (1991), upheld a tax levied on cable television but not other information sources, notwithstanding precedents forbidding any differential taxation of different elements of the print media. See, for example, *Arkansas Writers' Project v Ragland*, 481 US 221 (1987); *Minneapolis Star & Tribune v Minnesota Comm'r of Revenue*, 460 US 575 (1983).

a) Speech of government employees. A complex body of doctrine has developed concerning government's authority to impose content-based regulations on the speech of its employees.[132] For present purposes, only two points are essential. First, content-based restrictions are often permissible,[133] sometimes based on a relatively ad hoc balance of competing interests. Second, from the perspective of the employee threatened with dismissal, content-based limits on permissible speech will often be experienced as both regulatory and coercive.

b) Student speech. Although public school students do not check their First Amendment rights at the schoolhouse door,[134] speech occurring in the classroom and under school sponsorship can be regulated for any reasonable pedagogical purpose.[135] Within the structure of the curriculum, students can be rewarded or penalized based on the judged quality of the ideas that they express. Students may have broader freedom on the playground, but even there content-based restrictions can be imposed to avert disruption.

c) Speech in non-public fora. Government can likewise employ content-based standards in regulating rights of access to public facilities not designated as a public forum.[136] In cases of this kind, the Supreme Court has sometimes said that regulation must be "reasonable and not an effort to suppress expression merely because public officials oppose the speaker's view."[137] But the latter restriction is hard to take seriously. It seems doubtful at best that a local government launching an antismoking campaign cannot share a press conference with health experts opposed to smoking while excluding representatives of the tobacco industry.

d) Government-sponsored speech. Sometimes, at least, the government may permissibly fund some but not other private speech based on judgments about the desirability of content or even viewpoint.[138] To take an example cited by the Supreme Court in *Rust*

---

[132] For an introduction, see Toni Massaro, *Significant Silences: Freedom of Speech in the Public Sector Workplace*, 61 So Cal L Rev 1 (1987). For a recent exhibition of some of the complexities, see *Waters v Churchill*, 114 S Ct 1878 (1994).

[133] See, for example, *Connick v Myers*, 461 US 138, 142 (1983).

[134] *Tinker v Des Moines Ind. Sch. Dist.*, 393 US 503, 506 (1969).

[135] See *Hazelwood School Dist. v Kuhlmeier*, 484 US 260, 270 (1988).

[136] See, for example, *Perry Educ. Ass'n v Perry Local Educators' Ass'n*, 460 US 37 (1983).

[137] Id at 46.

[138] Compare *Rust v Sullivan*, 111 S Ct 1759 (1991) (holding that government may fund organizations advocating some, but not other, means of family planning) with *FCC v League of Women Voters*, 468 US 364 (1984) (invalidating a statutory provision that forbade any

v Sullivan,[139] the government can establish the National Endowment for Democracy to support advocacy in favor of democracy without being required to "encourage competing lines of political philosophy." The bounds of governmental discretion in this area are much controverted.[140] Clearly, however, the controlling principle is not that government may not discriminate based on content, even when government's decision to fund preferred but not dispreferred content may be experienced by some speakers as coercive.[141]

7. *Overbreadth.* A long line of Supreme Court cases has established that "substantially overbroad" statutes must sometimes be deemed judicially unenforceable under the First Amendment.[142] The Court has occasionally suggested that calculations of overbreadth reflect a geometric proportion, "judged in relation to the statute's plainly legitimate sweep."[143] In fact, however, it is impossible to apply the overbreadth doctrine sensibly without a context-sensitive inquiry into the value as well as the quantity of the constitutionally protected speech that an overbroad statute is likely to chill.[144] In at least some cases, the Supreme Court has explicitly acknowledged as much.[145] In others, the Court's assessment of value and weighing of competing interests are nearly transparent.[146]

---

noncommercial radio or television station receiving public funds to engage in editorializing) and *Arkansas Writers' Project, Inc. v Ragland*, 481 US 221 (1987) (invalidating a state sales tax scheme that exempted some classes of publications but not others).

[139] 111 S Ct 1759, 1773 (1991).

[140] Among the most useful contributions to the debate are Kathleen M. Sullivan, *Unconstitutional Conditions*, Harv L Rev 1415 (1989); Steven Shiffrin, *Government Speech*, 27 UCLA L Rev 565 (1980); Cass R. Sunstein, *Why the Unconstitutional Conditions Doctrine Is an Anachronism (With Particular Reference to Religion, Speech, and Abortion)*, 70 BU L Rev 593 (1990).

[141] See generally Elena Kagan, *The Changing Faces of First Amendment Neutrality: R.A.V. v St. Paul, Rust v Sullivan, the Problem of Content-Based Underinclusion*, 1992 Supreme Court Review 29 (arguing that funding of expression of some viewpoints but not others raises many of the same issues of constitutional principle as viewpoint-based prohibitions against speech).

[142] See, for example, *Osborne v Ohio*, 110 S Ct 1691 (1990); *City of Houston v Hill*, 482 US 451 (1987). The First Amendment overbreadth doctrine traces to *Thornhill v Alabama*, 310 US 88, 105 (1940). The requirement that overbreadth be "substantial" in order to trigger the doctrine's application emerged more recently. See *New York v Ferber*, 458 US 747, 770–71 (1982).

[143] See, for example, *Osborne*, 110 S Ct at 1697 (quoting *Broaderick v Oklahoma*, 413 US 601, 615 (1973)).

[144] See, for example, Richard H. Fallon, Jr., *Making Sense of Overbreadth*, 100 Yale L J 853, 894–95 (1991); Martin H. Redish, *The Warren Court, The Burger Court and the First Amendment Overbreadth Doctrine*, 78 Nw U L Rev 1031 (1983).

[145] See, for example, *Young v American Mini Theatres, Inc.*, 427 US 50 (1976).

[146] See Fallon, 100 Yale L J at 895 (cited in note 144).

8. *Variable strict scrutiny of content-based regulations.* The two-level theory of the First Amendment postulates that content-based regulation of protected speech can be justified only if it can survive the most exacting scrutiny. Sometimes, however, "strict scrutiny" turns out not to be very strict at all.

In *Burson v Freeman*,[147] for example, the Supreme Court upheld a content-based prohibition against the solicitation of votes or the display or distribution of campaign materials within 100 feet of the entrance to a polling place. The plurality reasoned persuasively that the state had a compelling interest in averting voter intimidation and election fraud, but demanded little or no concrete evidence that a content-based prohibition against political advocacy was a necessary safeguard. Indeed, in a reversal of the usual burden of proof, the plurality suggested that it would be unreasonable to force the state to prove that a smaller zone, of perhaps 25 feet, would not suffice.[148]

In *Buckley v Valeo*,[149] the Supreme Court found "closest scrutiny" appropriate to determine the constitutionality of restrictions on campaign contributions and expenditures. Having done so, however, the Court then applied a less exacting test than is usually associated with the alternative standard that it purported to reject.[150]

B. FIRST AMENDMENT VALUES

In light of this partial list of departures from the First Amendment's content-neutrality principle and of doctrinal balancings of competing values and interests, it would be easy to craft a relatively ad hoc argument for the regulability of sexually harassing speech in the workplace. To do so, however, would omit a crucial step. Although arguing that First Amendment doctrine is far from consistent in demanding that government may regulate only in content-neutral ways, I have not denied that there are important domains in which content neutrality is strictly required. Nor have I

---

[147] 112 S Ct 1846 (1992).

[148] See id at 1857.

[149] 424 US 1, 25 (1976).

[150] As one commentator has observed, "the degree of scrutiny employed in *Buckley* varies from paragraph to paragraph." Shiffrin, *The First Amendment, Democracy, and Romance* at 32 (cited in note 106).

looked behind the content-neutrality principle to examine its foundations. Identification of underlying concerns may help to explain
when the content-neutrality principle should be enforced and when
departures are appropriate.

The strongest arguments in favor of the content-neutrality principle typically involve an affirmative value, most plausibly democracy or autonomy; an argument that government officials should
not be trusted with content-based regulatory power; and a demand
for firm "rules," rather than mere standards or presumptions, restricting government's regulatory authority. Upon close examination, I shall argue, these values and concerns prove less than is
often thought. They provide a justification for requiring content
neutrality in some doctrinal contexts but not in all.

1. *Democracy and the political process.* John Ely stands prominent
among those who have staked their case for content neutrality on
the imperatives of democratic politics.[151] The supporting argument is alluringly simple. For the people to be self-governing,
they must have access to a very broad range of ideas and information. When government attempts to prohibit speech on the
basis of content, it violates the central democratic principle that
the people should be deemed competent to decide for themselves
what to believe, what values to hold, and how to arrange their
affairs.

Notoriously, however, the contours of "politics," "political
speech," and the kind of speech relevant to politics may be defined
either narrowly or broadly. If the terms are used narrowly, only
speech specifically addressing issues of public policy would deserve
protection.[152] There would be neither need nor justification for a
general presumption that government must observe a requirement
of content neutrality.

It is possible, of course, to take a broader view, under which
virtually all speech may have an indirect effect on political outlooks. Many First Amendment theorists have done so.[153] But this

---

[151] See Ely, *Democracy and Distrust* (cited in note 111 above). The great progenitor of
contemporary, democracy-based theories is Alexander Meiklejohn. See Alexander Meiklejohn, *Political Freedom* (Harper, 1960).

[152] See, for example, Robert Bork, *Neutral Principles and Some First Amendment Problems*,
47 Ind L J 1, 20 (1971) (adopting a narrow view of protected political speech).

[153] See, for example, Alexander Meiklejohn, *The First Amendment Is an Absolute*, 1961
Supreme Court Review 245 (taking a very broad view).

position demands the denial of intuitively powerful differences of kind between, for example, the advocacy of candidates or legislation on the one hand and image-based advertising of beer and cigarettes on the other. When a theory begins by asserting the primacy of political speech and ends by denying the distinction (between political and nonpolitical speech) that provided its point of departure, its argument is unlikely to convert those not already committed to the conclusion.

A further issue deserves mention. Beginning with the premise that the First Amendment aims to protect political democracy, some theorists have argued that the First Amendment should impose no impediment to regulatory legislation designed to promote equally effective political participation and to ensure an informed electorate.[154] On this view, the First Amendment should sometimes tolerate content-based regulation even of core political speech. Those who oppose governmental regulation must rely, not just on the value of political democracy, but also on a distrust of government—a somewhat distinct concern that I shall discuss further below.

2. *Autonomy-based theories.* Autonomy is a contestable and sometimes protean concept, two main conceptions of which dominate the First Amendment literature. According to ascriptive conceptions, autonomy is the metaphysical presupposition of personhood.[155] On this view, autonomy does not denote any empirical quality or condition that, beyond some minimum threshold, is subject to measurement or comparative assessment.[156] Rather, autonomy is something ascribed to persons as the foundation not only of their capacity, but also of their right, to exercise personal sovereignty in matters of thought, expression, and primarily self-regarding choice.[157] Ascriptive autonomy also implies personal responsibility for personal choice.[158] Conceived as an ascriptive con-

---

[154] See, for example, Owen M. Fiss, *Free Speech and Social Structure,* 71 Iowa L Rev 1405 (1986); Cass R. Sunstein, *The Partial Constitution* 213–25 (Harvard, 1993).

[155] See Richard H. Fallon, Jr., *Two Senses of Autonomy,* 46 Stan L Rev 875 (1994).

[156] See id at 891.

[157] See, for example, Joel Feinberg, *Harm to Self* 47–97 (Oxford, 1986) (defining and defending a conception of autonomy as sovereignty).

[158] On the connection between autonomy and responsibility, see Lloyd L. Weinreb, *Natural Law and Justice* 200–23 (Harvard, 1987).

cept, autonomy is often associated with freedom of the will from causal determinism.[159]

Ascriptive conceptions of autonomy tend to support a First Amendment principle requiring content neutrality in many contexts, but not in all. For government to silence someone based on the content of her speech would normally infringe her autonomy. To censor speech on the ground that the listener could not be trusted to evaluate its content would equally affront the listener's autonomy in most cases.[160] Exceptions are possible, however, when the private speech that government wishes to regulate itself constitutes an affront to or infringement of autonomy. For example, a number of theorists have followed Kant in maintaining that lies and manipulative speech disrespect the autonomy of their targets by treating them merely as means to the attainment of some goal rather than as autonomous ends in themselves.[161] Coercive speech that alters the conditions of choice by communicating a threat is similarly regulable under principles rooted in ascriptive conceptions of autonomy.[162] On the other hand, regulation of speech that is hateful or hurtful but does not communicate a situation-altering threat is often thought not to be regulable under an ascriptive conception of autonomy. If ascriptive autonomy implies freedom of the will, hateful speech cannot be "causally" efficacious in, for example, shaming someone into silence or causing someone to withdraw, be silent, or fail to pursue a job, opportunity, or benefit. To be regulable, speech must either disrespect another's autonomy, constitute a threat, or inflict a harm, and defenders of ascriptive autonomy have generally denied that mere words can satisfy the "harm principle."[163]

Although an ascriptive conception of autonomy may be foundational of much of our moral thought, it fails to accommodate a fact

---

[159] See Fallon, 46 Stan L Rev at 892 (cited in note 155).

[160] See T. M. Scanlon, *A Theory of Freedom of Expression*, 1 Phil & Pub Aff 204, 215–22 (1971); Charles Fried, *The New First Amendment Jurisprudence: A Threat to Liberty*, 59 U Chi L Rev 225, 233–37 (1992).

[161] See, for example, Fried, id at 233; Christine Korsgaard, *The Right to Lie: Kant on Dealing with Evil*, 15 Phil & Pub Aff 325, 330–37 (1986); David Strauss, *Persuasion, Autonomy, and Freedom of Expression*, 91 Colum L Rev 334 (1991).

[162] See Fried, 59 U Chi L Rev at 241–42 (cited in note 160).

[163] For a further discussion, see text accompanying notes 240–44 below.

too important to be ignored in all contexts: We are empirical beings, shaped by our histories and determined at least in part by
causal forces. From an empirical perspective, our autonomy may
be undermined when we are dominated by others, when we are
the slaves of addiction or impulse, when our wants are unreflec-
tively shaped by fads or commercial advertising, or when our views
reflect the uncritical acceptance of messages conveyed by mass media.[164] Taking an empirical view, we can hardly help viewing our
own autonomy and that of others as partial and contingent—
dependent on such factors as our critical and self-critical capacities,
our awareness of the range of options open to us, our self-awareness
when confronted with wants and impulses, our freedom from addiction, and our competence to act effectively.[165]

When autonomy is conceived descriptively, it is a variable, not
a constant, and content-based regulation of speech might sometimes help to promote autonomy. For example, if image-based cigarette advertising manipulates some of its targets into states of addiction, regulation might do more to promote than to frustrate
descriptive autonomy.[166] More controversially, some have argued
that race- and gender-based hate speech diminishes descriptive autonomy by coercively preempting or silencing its targets,[167] by
appealing to irrational beliefs and thereby subverting critical awareness and self-awareness,[168] or both.

3. *Distrust of government.* As the discussion above has tried to
make clear, neither commitment to democracy nor respect for individual autonomy—taken by itself—dictates an across-the-board requirement of content neutrality. Even after a particular conception
of democracy or autonomy is adopted, a premise of distrust of
governmental regulation must be introduced in many cases.[169]

---

[164] See, for example, Joseph Raz, *The Morality of Freedom* 372–73 (Oxford, 1986) (identifying "conditions of autonomy" that are typically realized to greater or lesser degree).

[165] See id at 369–90; Cass R. Sunstein, *Democracy and Shifting Preferences*, in David Copp,
Jean Hampton, & John E. Roemer, eds, *The Idea of Democracy* 196 (Cambridge, 1993).

[166] See Fallon, 46 Stan L Rev at 490 (cited in note 155).

[167] See, for example, Richard Delgado, *Words That Wound: A Tort Action for Racial Insults,
Epithets, and Name-Calling*, 17 Harv CR-CL L Rev 133, 143–49 (1982); Charles R. Lawrence,
If He Hollers Let Him Go: Regulating Racist Speech on Campus, 1990 Duke L J 431, 452–55.

[168] See, for example, Lawrence, id at 466–72. For a structurally similar argument about
the impact of pornography on women, see Cass R. Sunstein, *Pornography and the First
Amendment*, 1986 Duke L J 589, 592–602.

[169] See Frederick Schauer, *Free Speech: A Philosophic Inquiry* 73–86 (Cambridge, 1982).
Schauer concludes that "freedom of speech is based in large part on a distrust of the ability

a) Democracy and distrust. To justify a content-neutrality require-ment under a democracy-based theory of the First Amendment requires not only a very broad conception of political speech, but also a strong and pervasive distrust of government as a regulator.[170] In the absence of such distrust, there might often be good reason to enforce content-based regulations aimed, for example, at im-proving the quality of political debate. Prudence surely requires distrust of some types of governmental regulation, but it is far from obvious that a general prohibition should be imposed.[171]

b) Autonomy and distrust. In principle, even an ascriptive concep-tion of autonomy imposes no barrier to content-based regulation of manipulative and coercive speech. There is no short or easy answer, however, to the question of how the categories of coercive and manipulative speech ought to be defined.[172] For some theorists, distrust of governmental regulation becomes the determining fac-tor: the less that government is trusted to regulate, the more nar-rowly the categories of manipulative and coercive (and therefore regulable) speech are defined.

Under a descriptive conception of autonomy, a great deal of speech may have autonomy-reducing effects, and regulation, in principle, might frequently help to enhance the critical awareness on which autonomy partly depends. As under theories linking the First Amendment to the requirements of political democracy, the proposition that governmental regulation might sometimes have desirable effects does not establish that regulation ought to be al-lowed. Plainly, government could regulate in ways that would di-minish, rather than enhance, descriptive autonomy. Again, how-ever, it seems doubtful that distrust of government should be broad and deep enough to mandate a stringent, across-the-board rule against governmental regulation based on content.

4. *Values and rules.* The most forceful argument for a content-neutrality requirement and against relatively ad hoc First Amend-ment decision making ultimately relies on a distinction between "rules," which the doctrine has aspired to achieve, and "standards,"

---

of government to make the necessary distinctions, a distrust of government determinations of truth and falsity, an appreciation of the fallibility of political leaders, and a somewhat deeper distrust of governmental power in a more general sense." Id at 86.

[170] See, for example, Ely, *Democracy and Distrust* at 110–16 (cited in note 111).

[171] See Frederick Schauer, *The Calculus of Distrust*, 77 Va L Rev 653 (1991).

[172] See Strauss, 91 Colum L Rev at 361–70 (cited in note 161).

which more nearly invite all-things-considered balancing judgments.[173] A rule that government may not regulate speech on the basis of content must be supported by background justifications— for example, that this rule is necessary or appropriate to protect political democracy or individual autonomy. The rule presumably has certain costs. For example, it may stop government from preventing harm that may result from painful, embarrassing, and possibly untrue statements about people's private lives. Indeed, the rule may even bar regulation that would enhance democracy or autonomy. In framing a rule, costs such as these may be taken into account and balanced against the benefits that the rule is expected to confer. Once the rule is adopted, however, further case-by-case reference to background interests is at least presumptively barred. As Frederick Schauer has pointed out, a "rule" must preclude a decision maker from all-things-considered reference to background interests in order to function as a rule at all.[174]

In the context of First Amendment history, the allure of a content-neutrality requirement lies in its ruleness, its purported capacity to block legislatures and judges from engaging in ad hoc, all-things-considered judgments about the value of and harm occasioned by particular speech acts. Too often, judges have responded to radical and iconoclastic speech with the same fear and loathing as legislatures have shown.[175]

It is one thing, however, to accept that First Amendment doctrine should be rulelike in some aspects, and quite another to maintain that the doctrine should be organized around a single, nearly exceptionless rule of content neutrality. The latter position seems to depend on a premise made explicit by Harry Kalven: "Freedom of speech is indivisible; unless we protect it for all, we will have it for none."[176] To this empirical and predictive argument, existing

---

[173] For discussion of the distinction between rules and standards, see, for example, Duncan Kennedy, *Form and Substance in Private Law Adjudication*, 89 Harv L Rev 1685, 1687–89 (1976); Kathleen M. Sullivan, *The Supreme Court, 1991 Term—Foreword: The Justices of Rules and Standards*, 106 Harv L Rev 22, 57–59 (1992). But compare Frederick Schauer, *Playing by the Rules: A Philosophical Examination of Rule-Based Decision-Making in Law and in Life* 115–18 (Oxford, 1991) (arguing that rules are also susceptible of being overcome by supervening factors of sufficient weight).

[174] See Schauer, *Rules*, id at 77–78.

[175] See, for example, Ely, *Democracy and Distrust*, at 107–09 (cited in note 111).

[176] Harry Kalven, *Upon Rereading Mr. Justice Black on the First Amendment*, 14 UCLA L Rev 428, 432 (1967).

doctrine provides the best retort. As I have argued already, the freedom of speech that we now have is not that which would be mandated by an across-the-board commitment to content neutrality. The arguments supporting such a commitment are simply not strong enough.

5. *Summary*. To sum up, the most important values and concerns that are commonly cited to justify a content-neutrality requirement in fact provide only equivocal support. Beginning with those values and concerns, anyone is not led inexorably to a demand for content neutrality in all or nearly all contexts.

C. FIRST AMENDMENT VALUES AND DOCTRINAL OUTLINES

It takes little imagination to see that the values and concerns advanced to justify a prohibition against content-based regulation actually help to explain—even though they fall far short of uniquely determining—the kind of eclectic, multifaceted doctrinal structure that actually exists under the First Amendment.[177]

1. *Democracy*. To protect the integrity of political self-government, existing doctrine ensures a wide sphere of essentially unregulated debate about politics and matters of public interest. Broad privileges exist to criticize public officials and public figures.[178] Prior restraints on political comment are virtually per se prohibited.[179] Public forum doctrine similarly helps to ensure opportunities for uncensored political debate. Content discrimination is prohibited, and only narrow classes of utterances occurring within a public forum can be punished, except in the few places in which strict scrutiny is less than entirely strict.

We are not, however, totally political beings,[180] and the First Amendment has been construed to permit government to protect private spaces in which people, if they wish, can take refuge from

---

[177] This characterization of the doctrine follows Shiffrin, *Democracy* at 132–39 (cited in note 106).

[178] See, for example, *New York Times Co. v Sullivan*, 376 US 254 (1964); *Gertz v Robert Welch*, 418 US 323 (1974).

[179] See, for example, *New York Times Co. v United States*, 403 US 713 (1971).

[180] For an illuminating discussion of the balance between "private" and "public" citizenship that the Constitution presupposes, see 1 Bruce Ackerman, *We the People: Foundations* (Harvard, 1991).

politics.[181] *Frisby v Schultz*,[182] which upheld a prohibition against targeted picketing of individual residences, epitomizes government's capacity to constitute the home as a sanctuary from unwanted political bombardment. The concept of a "captive audience," though doctrinally inchoate,[183] reflects a similar intuition that there are places in which people should not have to be subjected to intrusive political messages.

With a broad sphere of unregulated "public discourse" established, the doctrine is also able to acknowledge that the interest in protecting political speech need not always predominate above all other interests even when protection of privacy is not the underlying concern.[184] Sometimes, at least, government may engage in content-based censorship of political speech in contexts—such as those of the public schools and public employment—in which unregulated talk about politics could interfere with the performance of significant governmental functions.

2. *Autonomy.* Although ascriptive and descriptive conceptions of autonomy are mutually incompatible at some deep level, I have argued elsewhere that both are fundamental to our understanding of human personhood.[185] If this claim is accurate, it should not be surprising that some areas of First Amendment law reflect the primacy of ascriptive autonomy, whereas others are better explained by reference to descriptive autonomy.

To cite just a few examples, the claims of ascriptive autonomy predominate in First Amendment doctrines dealing with the public forum, with governmental regulation of the traditional media, and with people's use of their homes and similarly private facilities to express themselves uninhibitedly. Ascriptive autonomy posits a "heroic" self,[186] capable of speaking freely but also of resisting the

---

[181] See Post, 103 Harv L Rev at 675–84 (cited in note 99).

[182] 487 US 474 (1988).

[183] See Marcy Strauss, *Redefining the Captive Audience Doctrine*, 19 Hastings Const L Q 85, 88 (1991) (showing that the case law is "riddled with inconsistency and ambiguity").

[184] See Post, 103 Harv L Rev at 680 (cited in note 99) (noting that "[t]he boundaries of [constitutionally protected] public discourse . . . define . . . the point at which our commitments shift from one set of goals to another").

[185] See Fallon, 46 Stan L Rev at 899–901 (cited in note 155).

[186] See Mary Ellen Gale, *Reimagining the First Amendment: Racist Speech and Equal Liberty*, 65 St John's L Rev 119, 129–31 (1991).

efforts of others to achieve autonomy-reducing "causal" influence or domination. When an ascriptive conception prevails, the selection of idiom, as much as adoption of viewpoint, is a matter of individual prerogative.

Hard to explain by reference to ascriptive autonomy are cases upholding government's authority to regulate commercial advertising of lawful products and activities. So is the doctrine of *Austin v Michigan Chamber of Commerce*,[187] which allows governmental regulation of political expenditures to prevent corporate domination of the political process. *Austin* reflects the worry that political advertising achieves causal dominance, not rational persuasion. This conclusion is plausible only under a descriptive conception of autonomy.

3. *Distrust.* First Amendment doctrine is more trusting of content-based regulation in some areas, and on some bases, than others. In part, at least, current doctrine reflects two plausible intuitions about the appropriateness of trust and distrust. First, the values underlying political democracy require less distrust of government when government regulates commercial advertising, for example, than when government regulates political speech. Second, governmental regulation may be trusted in some contexts precisely because the distrust manifest in others virtually guarantees free, robust, and effective criticism of any abuses of regulatory authority. To take just one example, Lee Bollinger has argued that content-based regulation of the broadcast media, which current doctrine permits, is tolerable partly because the print media, which are largely exempt from content-based regulation, are available to spotlight any abuse of power.[188]

4. *Rules and standards.* With respect to rules and standards, the doctrine again reveals a mixture. In some areas, governmental regulation based on content is indeed ruled out. In others, balancing tests reign. Balancing tests generally reflect relative trust of government, typically to protect or promote descriptive autonomy or to enhance political democracy. Rules prohibiting governmental regu-

---

[187] 110 S Ct 1391 (1990).

[188] Lee Bollinger, *Freedom of the Press and Public Access: Toward a Theory of Partial Regulation of the Mass Media*, 75 Mich L Rev 1 (1976). Similarly, regulation of speech in public schools may be acceptable at least partly because of the potential for public criticism in cases of abuse.

lation more typically signal respect for ascriptive autonomy and for democratic self-government by ascriptively autonomous citizens.

D. CONTEXTS AND COMPROMISE

It is not, I hope, belaboring the point to note that existing doctrine frequently attempts to accommodate a diverse set of values and concerns through distinctions based not only on subject matter, but also on places, times, and contexts. The presence of a content-neutrality requirement in some domains—and the resulting contribution to or protection of democracy or autonomy—may help to rationalize, or at least minimize the dangers of, content-based restrictions in others.[189] A few examples may illustrate the kind of contextualization that I have in mind.

Adult speech. Under the "secondary effects" doctrine, businesses predominantly trafficking in adult films, books, and similar material may be zoned—confined to areas where they are least troublesome, offensive, or harmful—even though sexually explicit but nonobscene speech could not be prohibited entirely. In short, the doctrine recognizes a crucial distinction between prohibiting adult speech in particular places and prohibiting it altogether.

Broadcast indecency. A similar rule applies to the broadcast of "dirty words" over the public airwaves. Even if not subject to ban on grounds of obscenity, offensive language may be "channeled" to late-night hours.[190]

Commercial advertising. Claims that would be absolutely protected if uttered in some contexts may be prohibited in others. As part of general public discourse, the assertion that "vitamin C cures cancer" would merit absolute protection. In an advertisement for vitamin C tablets, it would not.

Messages targeted at the home. Communication targeted at the home may be regulated to protect privacy interests associated with the home, even if similar communication would be protected if directed elsewhere.

The public workplace. Public employees enjoy only limited protection against sanction based on speech occurring in the work-

---

[189] But compare *Consolidated Edison Co. v Public Serv. Comm'n*, 447 US 530, 541 n 10 (1980) ("we have consistently rejected the suggestion that a government may justify a content-based prohibition by showing that speakers have alternative means of expression").

[190] See *FCC v Pacifica Foundation*, 438 US 726 (1978).

place,[191] while restrictions of off-duty speech outside the workplace trigger more stringent review.[192]

The public school. In order educate effectively, schools must be empowered to sanction disruptive student speech, even if similarly disruptive speech would be protected in a public forum.

Private communication. Words vilifying a public figure might constitute legally sanctionable intentional infliction of emotional distress if spoken directly to their target in a late-night telephone call, yet attain First Amendment protection as a contribution to public discourse if disseminated to a public audience.[193]

"Spheres of neutrality." I have emphasized, and indeed perhaps overemphasized, doctrines under which messages that would be constitutionally protected in some contexts may be regulated in others, on the basis of content, due to some peculiarity of a place, environment, or audience. As David Cole has noted, however, there are some doctrinal domains in which government generally need not behave in content-neutral ways, but must nonetheless maintain some relatively isolated "spheres of neutrality."[194] The government is generally free to subsidize or not to subsidize speech based on content, but it must provide equal benefits to all who wish to use a public forum.[195] Neither may government condition funding to universities in ways that compromise academic freedom.[196] In public schools, where government is generally authorized to attempt to inculcate values, the Supreme Court's decision in *Board of Education v Pico*[197] establishes the school library as a distinct sphere from which school boards may not remove books for "partisan" reasons.[198] Whether successful or not, the aim of a spheres-of-neutrality approach is to limit governmental power and

---

[191] See *Connick v Myers*, 461 US 168 (1983) (First Amendment protects workplace speech of public employees only if it involves matters of public concern, and even speech of this type may be sanctioned pursuant to a balancing test).

[192] See, for example, *Pickering v Board of Education*, 391 US 563 (1968); *Keyishian v Board of Regents*, 385 US 589 (1967).

[193] See Post, 103 Harv L Rev at 675 (cited in note 99).

[194] See David Cole, *Beyond Unconstitutional Conditions: Charting Spheres of Neutrality in Government-Funded Speech*, 67 NYU L Rev 675 (1992).

[195] Id at 717–23.

[196] See *Rust v Sullivan*, 111 S Ct 1759, 1776 (1991); Cole, 67 NYU L Rev at 678, 723–29 (cited in note 194).

[197] 457 US 853 (1982).

[198] See Cole, 67 NYU L Rev at 729 (cited in note 194).

influence, to foster opportunities for independent thought and criticism, and to ensure that abuses of power can be criticized effectively.

E. IN DEFENSE OF CONTEXTUALIZATION

The governing philosophy of First Amendment eclecticism may not be elegant, but neither is it shallow. As T. M. Scanlon has pointed out, the discourse of rights occurs on several levels.[199] At the foundational level, philosophical inquiry can identify the values that free speech doctrine ought to serve.[200] After the foundational values are identified, the specification of protected rights depends on further calculations of whether specific "limit[s] or requirement[s] on policy decisions [are] *necessary* if unacceptable results are to be avoided," and of whether any particular "limit or requirement is a *feasible* one, that is, [whether] its acceptance provides adequate protection against such results and does so at tolerable costs to other interests."[201]

As I have suggested, democracy and autonomy number among the most important foundational values of free speech doctrine. In the transition from foundations to arguments about necessity and feasibility, the hard if not "paradoxical"[202] fact is that governmental regulation, governmental speech, and governmental funding of speech can be powerful tools for the promotion of democracy and autonomy, but they also can be used to squelch, buy up, or drown out dissent, to establish orthodoxy, and to stifle freedom of mind. With affirmative potential paired against danger in this way, many commentators have assumed that the protection of these values requires cabining government's authority as narrowly as possible —as, for example, by forbidding government to regulate speech on the basis of content.[203] By contrast, some recent writers have argued that the government should act affirmatively to promote democracy and autonomy and that the First Amendment should

---

[199] See T. M. Scanlon, *Freedom of Expression and Categories of Expression*, 40 U Pitt L Rev 519, 535–37 (1979).

[200] Id at 535.

[201] Id.

[202] Cole, 67 NYU L Rev at 682 (cited in note 194).

[203] See, for example, Ely, *Democracy and Distrust* (cited in note 111 above) (democracy); Fried, 59 U Chi L Rev at 225 (autonomy) (cited in note 160).

not restrict governmental regulation, including content-based regulation of speech, that is designed to do so.[204] It is both imprudent and unnecessary, however, to embrace either position in uncompromised form. As current doctrine implicitly recognizes, what is necessary to protect democracy and autonomy in some spheres may not be necessary, feasible, or appropriate in all.

The definition of spheres, and the specification of governing principles within them, can be informed by philosophical values but ultimately requires practical, historical, and prudential judgment. Celebrations of situation sense and practical reason frequently dissolve into philosophical mush, and I shall therefore say no more, except to make clear that I by no means approve of everything, or even nearly everything, that the Supreme Court has done. The point is only that, as Aristotle suggested in a famous passage of the *Nichomachean Ethics*, it is a mistake to demand more theoretical elegance than the nature of the subject matter permits.[205]

IV. SEXUAL HARASSMENT IN THE WORKPLACE

When the mosaic of First Amendment doctrine is seen for what it is, *Harris*'s First Amendment insouciance loses some, but not all, mystery. Under the most sensible interpretation, *Harris* implicitly recognizes a category of constitutionally regulable speech defined by (i) an understanding of the content of sexually harassing expression as characteristically possessing little First Amendment value, (ii) a view of the workplace as a context apt for regulation, and (iii) a conception of reasonableness (or a set of objective standards) designed to mediate between interests in freedom from harassment on the one hand and legitimate speech interests on the other. A category defined in such terms would represent a sensible accommodation of First Amendment doctrine to the harms occasioned by sexual harassment, but should be tailored carefully to protect fundamental First Amendment values.

---

[204] See, for example, Fiss, 71 Iowa L Rev at 1405 (cited in note 154); Gale, 65 St John's L Rev at 154–58 (cited in note 186).

[205] See Aristotle, *Nichomachaen Ethics*, 308, 309 in R. McKeon, ed, *Introduction to Aristotle* (Mod Lib, 1947) ("Our discussion will be adequate if it has as much clearness as the subject-matter admits of, for precision is not to be sought alike in all discussions. . . .").

A. THE REGULATED CATEGORY

1. *The concept of sexual harassment.* As defined by the EEOC Guidelines, sexual harassment involves speech or conduct of a sexual nature that is by definition unwelcome[206] and that creates an unequal work environment based on gender. As the Supreme Court has recognized repeatedly, the government has a compelling interest in eradicating discrimination of this kind.[207]

Within the workplace, sexual harassment occurs paradigmatically, albeit not exclusively, in face-to-face encounters. Even when harassment is not targeted at particular individuals face-to-face—as, for example, when a workplace is pervaded by sexually demeaning pictures, or when women are routinely referred to (rather than addressed by) hostile or degrading epithets—the forced, ongoing intimacy of the workplace creates an almost inevitable association between harassing words or pictures and the physical presence of known or unknown harassers.

Narrowly targeted, face-to-face expression has often received less constitutional protection than words and expressive conduct in other contexts. Speech of this kind is less likely to have public or political value than speech directed to larger audiences. Even more important, individually targeted, face-to-face speech is especially likely to have the purpose of being,[208] and to be experienced as, invasive, threatening, or coercive. To cite just two familiar examples, lawyers may be forbidden to solicit clients in person,[209] even if they might have a right to do so by mail,[210] and vilification that would be constitutionally protected in public debate might constitute prohibited harassment if it occurred in a late-night telephone call.[211]

---

[206] According to Judge Posner, " 'Welcome sexual harassment' is an oxymoron." *Carr v Allison Gas Turbine Div., General Motors Corp.* 1994 US App Lexis (7th Cir 1994).

[207] See *Roberts v Jaycees*, 468 US 609, 623 (1984) (finding that the state has a "compelling interest in eradicating discrimination against its female citizens"); *Board of Directors of Rotary International v Rotary Club of Duarte*, 481 US 537, 549 (1987) (same).

[208] See Kent Greenawalt, *Insults and Epithets: Are They Protected Speech?*, 42 Rutgers L Rev 287, 292–93 (1990).

[209] See *Ohralik v Ohio State Bar Ass'n*, 436 US 447 (1978).

[210] Compare *In re Primus*, 436 US 412 (1978) (holding that the state could not discipline an ACLU "cooperating lawyer" for soliciting a prospective client by mail).

[211] See Post, 103 Harv L Rev at 675 (cited in note 99).

2. *Features of the workplace.* Characteristic features of the workplace provide additional reasons for allowing a legal prohibition against sexually harassing speech and expressive conduct.[212] For many if not most, employment is a practical necessity, and the economic and other costs of changing jobs would often be prohibitive.[213] As I noted earlier, the Supreme Court has hesitated to apply the "captive audience" doctrine wherever the label would fit descriptively, but the case for extending the designation to the workplace is strong. Not only is it typically infeasible to flee the workplace in order to escape sexual harassment; most working people spend more hours per week on the job site than anywhere else except their homes[214]—the place to which the "captive audience" label has most regularly been applied. Moreover, even more than at home, many people at work are ill-equipped to protect themselves effectively. Harassment frequently occurs within the structure of authority relationships;[215] even when it does not, a victim may have

---

[212] The American Civil Liberties Union has emphasized the "unique characteristics of the workplace" in propounding its recommended standard for constitutionally proscribable sexual harassment:

> Where conduct or expression is sufficiently pervasive or intense that its effect on a reasonable person in those particular circumstances would be to hinder significantly a person from functioning as an employee or significantly adversely affect mental, emotional, or physical well-being on the basis of sex. Conduct that meets this definition is actionable because of the unique characteristics of the workplace— including the existence of authority relationships, the economic necessity to remain, and the limited opportunity to respond—even though it might not be actionable in other settings.

ACLU, *Policy Guide of the American Civil Liberties Union* (rev ed 1992), at Policy No 316, quoted in Strossen, 37 Vill L Rev at 765 (cited in note 34).

[213] In addition to the direct costs of finding a new job, leaving an established position often involves forfeiting important benefits such as longer vacations, larger pension contributions, and greater security against layoffs. Lloyd G. Reynolds, Stanley H. Masters, and Colletta H. Moser, *Labor Economics and Labor Relations* 6 (Prentice-Hall, 9th ed 1986). Various studies have also noted the psychic costs of a job change, such as disruption of familiar routines and the necessity of forming new social relationships. See Clark Kerr, The Social Economics Revisionists: The "Real World" Study of Markets and Institutions, in *Labor Economics and Industrial Relations* 77–81 (Harvard, 1994) (discussing several such studies).

[214] See generally Juliet B. Schor, *The Overworked American*, passim (Basic Books, 1991) (citing numerous studies of the way Americans spend their time).

[215] See, for example, Catharine A. MacKinnon, *Sexual Harassment of Working Women* 87 (Yale, 1979) ("The often uncontested facts in sexual harassment complaints, the indications in empirical studies, and women's experience . . . document over and over again the same basic pattern of advances from a man to a subordinate woman or women, together with impact or reprisals on the job."); *ACLU Policy Guide* at Policy No 316 (cited in note 212).

little opportunity to respond effectively to those who dominate the environment.[216] In light of these considerations, protection against workplace harassment appears as essential both to human dignity and to equal employment opportunity as prohibitions against discriminatory hiring and unsafe working conditions. As the Supreme Court suggested in *Meritor* and *Harris*, no one should have to endure a gauntlet of discriminatory insult or ridicule or suffer discriminatorily demeaning sexualization as a condition of employment,[217] nor should the threat or perpetuation of hostile work environments be permitted to deter women from entering traditionally male-dominated occupations or workforces."

3. *Reasonableness standards.* In *Harris* as in *Meritor*, the Supreme Court emphasized that "hostile environment" claims must meet an "objective" standard: to violate Title VII, speech or expressive conduct must be sufficiently "severe or pervasive to create an *objectively* hostile or abusive work environment—an environment that a *reasonable person* would find hostile."[218] This formulation seems designed to play a crucial, mediating role in the effort to accommodate equality and dignitary interests without trampling on free speech values.

In a brief filed in *Harris*, the National Organization for Women Legal Defense and Education Fund, Catharine MacKinnon, and others argued that hostile environment claims should not include an objective test of whether harassing speech is harmful.[219] Under ordinary tort principles, they asserted, people engaging in wrong-

---

[216] See Reynolds, Masters, and Moser, *Labor Economics and Labor Relations* at 7 (observing that under nonunion conditions, a worker's bargaining power effectively means only her ability to quit); *ACLU Policy Guide* at Policy No 316 (cited in note 212). For a discussion of distinctive features of the labor market that make it difficult for workers to protect their interests through individual bargaining, see Paul C. Weiler, *Governing the Workplace: The Future of Employment Law* 63–71, 140–42 (Harvard, 1990).

[217] See *Meritor*, 477 US at 67, quoting *Henson v Dundee*, 682 F2d 897, 902 (11th Cir 1982); *Harris*, 114 S Ct at 370–71. See, e.g., Martha Chamallas, *Structuralist and Cultural Domination Thoeries Meet Title VII: Some Contemporary Influences*, 92 Mich L Rev 2370, 2381–2408 (1994).

[218] *Harris*, 114 S Ct at 370 (emphasis added).

[219] See Brief of Amici Curiae NOW Legal Defense and Education Fund, Catharine A. MacKinnon, The American Jewish Committee, American Medical Women's Ass'n, Inc., Asian American Legal Defense and Education Fund, Association for Union Democracy, The Center for Women Policy Studies, Chicago Women in Trades, The Illinois Coalition Against Sexual Assault, National Organization for Women, Inc., National Tradeswomen's Network, Northern New England Tradeswomen Inc., Puerto Rican Legal Defense and Education Fund, and the Women's Law Project in support of the petitioner at 10–11, 15–22.

ful conduct must take their victims as they find them,[220] and the amici saw no reason to subject sexual harassment cases to a different rule.[221] Although the Court failed to address this argument directly, the general thrust of its opinion almost surely signals a deserved rejection. Even under ordinary tort principles, only "wrongful" conduct will support liability.[222] For sexual harassment law and the First Amendment, it is therefore a crucial question which expressive acts should be considered wrongful—all sexual or sexist utterances that have adverse effects on others in the workplace, or only those that create an "objectively hostile or abusive work environment." As a matter of First Amendment principle,[223] speech should not be adjudged "wrongful" conduct unless it meets an objective standard of wrongfulness, nor should objective standards of wrongfulness be divorced from reasonable judgments and expectations about what is and is not harmful. For symbolic reasons among others, it is vital that the First Amendment protect against regulation that could reasonably be perceived as establishing a governmentally enforced orthodoxy in matters of thought and opinion. Mere expression of viewpoint must not be regulable— only the objective conditions that certain forms of expression may create.[224] In cases alleging purely verbal sexual harassment, the prevailing objective standard should be viewed, not as a measure of remediable harm, but as a constitutionally mandated limitation on the statutory prohibition.

How the "objective" test should be formulated is a further question. Citing psychological literature as well as anecdotal evidence, commentators have argued that "men regard conduct, ranging from

---

[220] See id at 19–22 & n 22.

[221] See id.

[222] To establish "the contours" of what constitutes a prohibited "assault," for example, analysis focuses "on the perception of the reasonable victim." Ronna Greff Schneider, *Sexual Harassment and Higher Education*, 65 Tex L Rev 525, 536–37 (1987).

[223] Although I have treated democracy and autonomy as perhaps the most important First Amendment values, I have not meant to imply that they are the only ones, and an appeal to first amendment principle properly reaches more broadly.

[224] See generally Laurence H. Tribe, *The Mystery of Motive, Private and Public: Some Notes Inspired by the Problems of Hate Crime and Animal Sacrifice*, 1993 Supreme Court Review 1 (distinguishing between constitutionally permissible punishment of antisocial acts and impermissible inquiring into or punishment of the unorthodox belief systems that produce such acts).

sexual demands to sexual innuendo, differently than women do,"[225] and a number of courts have held that objectivity and reasonableness should be measured from the perspective of a reasonable person of the plaintiff's gender.[226] A "reasonable woman standard" should survive First Amendment scrutiny. Men can fairly be asked to take into account, and substantially adapt their behavior to, the understanding of reasonable women that speech is sufficiently threatening, abusive, demeaning, or unreasonably recurring to create a hostile and unequal work environment.

A reasonableness standard by no means obviates all problems. A reasonableness test of any kind may imply more consensus than actually exists[227] and may require normative judgments at least in close cases.[228] A reasonable woman standard, in particular, may also have some tendency to incorporate norms that developed during a long history of male dominance[229] and to reinforce stereotypes.[230] Nevertheless, a reasonableness standard seems crucial to the Supreme Court's understanding of the sphere of permissible regulation, and a "reasonable victim" test provides the best mechanism yet proposed for accommodating the conflicting values at stake. It is common ground among nearly everyone involved in this debate that, in light of First Amendment values, Title VII must "not serve 'as a vehicle for vindicating the petty slights of the hypersensitive.'"[231]

---

[225] Kathryn Abrams, *Gender Discrimination and the Transformation of Workplace Norms*, 42 Vand L Rev 1183, 1202 (1989).

[226] See, for example, *Andrews v Philadelphia*, 895 F2d 1469, 1482 (3d Cir 1990); *Ellison v Brady*, 924 F2d 872, 879 (9th Cir 1991). This is also the standard endorsed by the EEOC. See EEOC, *Policy Guidance on Sexual Harassment*, 8 FEP Manual (BNA) 405:6681, 6690 (March 19, 1990).

[227] See, for example, Nancy S. Ehrenreich, *Pluralist Myths and Powerless Men: The Ideology of Reasonableness in Sexual Harassment Law*, 99 Yale L J 1177, 1204 (1990).

[228] Id at 1117–18.

[229] To ameliorate this problem, Professor Abrams proposes that a plaintiff should be able to make out a prima facie case of Title VII liability based on a subjective experience of "feelings of coercion or devaluation." Abrams, 42 Vand L Rev at 1209 (cited in note 225). She then moves part but not all the way back toward an objective standard, by suggesting that the prima facie case could be rebutted "if the defendant can demonstrate that . . . the plaintiff's response was idiosyncratic." Id at 1211.

[230] See, for example, Lucinda M. Finley, *A Break in the Silence: Including Women's Issues in a Torts Course*, 1 Yale J L & Fem 41, 62–64 (1989).

[231] EEOC, *Policy Guidance on Sexual Harassment*, 8 FEP Manual (BNA) 405:6681, 6689 (March 19, 1990).

B. FIRST AMENDMENT BOUNDARIES

If the Supreme Court's insistence on a reasonableness or objective standard defines one important boundary on permissible regulation of workplace harassment, it remains to consider whether First Amendment values require others.

1. *Sexual harassment and political speech.* In view of the First Amendment value of political democracy and especially the concern about viewpoint-based censorship of political expression, an exception to Title VII liability ought to be recognized for any speech or expressive conduct that is "reasonably designed or intended to contribute to reasoned debate on issues of public concern."[232] This exception would provide breathing space for First Amendment freedoms and, in particular, would guard against actual and imagined[233] abuses of the hostile environment cause of action that have agitated critical commentators.[234] Among other things, a First Amendment defense for reasoned contributions to political debate would provide a shield for nonabusive workplace discussions of charged political issues such as affirmative action and appropriate gender roles in which some views could plausibly be experienced as inherently hostile. On the other hand, prohibitions could be enforced under this standard against gratuitously offensive or abusive but nontargeted speech (such as public displays in the workplace of pornography that depicts women in demeaning ways);[235] against individually targeted harassment, even about political matters, that is so persistent or patently harassing that it could not be reasonably designed to contribute to reasoned debate; and against the use of derogatory epithets that are not reasonably

---

[232] This "free speech proviso" is adapted from the draft Guidelines Concerning Sexual Harassment developed by the Harvard Law School Committee on Sexual Harassment Guidelines and presented to the Harvard Law School faculty in May 1994. I should acknowledge my role as chair of that committee. No action has yet been taken on the draft guidelines.

[233] Critics of the hostile environment cause of action have offered surprisingly few examples of what they would take to be First Amendment violations. See, for example, Browne, 52 Ohio St L J at 483 (cited in note 34) (footnote omitted) (acknowledging that, "with only one apparent exception no reported harassment decision has imposed liability solely on the basis of arguably protected expression").

[234] The following discussion responds directly to arguments raised by Volokh, 39 UCLA L Rev at 1843–63 (cited in note 34).

[235] See, for example, *Andrews v City of Philadelphia*, 895 F2d 1469, 1485–86 (3d Cir 1990); *Robinson v Jacksonville Shipyards, Inc.*, 760 F Supp 1486, 1535 (MD Fla 1991).

designed or intended to contribute to reasoned debate and that can give an abusive character even to political discussion.

Some commentators have urged that considerations associated with political democracy require even further limitations on Title VII liability. In their view, the workplace provides many people with their primary forum for political communication about issues of gender, sex, and race,[236] and it is unacceptable for government to handicap those on one side of a political debate, no matter how crude or offensive their mode of expression.[237] The answer to this complex objection is largely implicit in what I have argued already. If the protected status of reasoned political debate were acknowledged, the political value of speech appropriately subject to the hostile environment cause of action would be marginal at best—as, for example, when someone claims that characterizations such as "dumb-ass woman" reflect a political point of view. Given the harm that the pervasive presence of speech such as this can cause in the workplace, it is not unreasonable to ask that viewpoints articulated there should be cast in less abusive terms. As Robert Post has argued, political democracy requires a broad space for unrestricted "public discourse," but that space need not be boundless.[238] Not all contexts are equal from the perspective of the First Amendment. It should suffice that opportunities remain for more untrammeled discourse in places that are more public, such as the public forum, and more private,[239] such as homes or other places of more voluntary congregation.

Even if the workplace is special, the value of suppressed speech is marginal, and other fora for uncensored communication are open, the argument that the sexual harassment prohibition bears unequally on particular viewpoints remains troubling. This consid-

---

[236] See Volokh, 39 UCLA L Rev at 1849 (cited in note 34).

[237] See, for example, Browne, 52 Ohio St L J at 492 (cited in note 34); Volokh, 39 UCLA L Rev at 1828 (cited in note 34).

[238] See Post, 103 Harv L Rev at 675–84 (cited in note 99).

[239] I do not mean to imply that individually targeted, patent, and persistent sexual harassment could not under any circumstances be prohibited in more "public" settings such as streets and parks—only that the terms of constitutionally permissible prohibitions, if any, would need to be narrower in order to respect differences of context. For provocative discussions of the legal norms appropriately applied to sexual harassment in public spaces, see Deborah M. Thompson, *"The Woman in the Street:" Reclaiming the Public Space from Sexual Harassment*, 6 Yale J L & Feminism 313 (1994); Cynthia Grant Bowman, *Street Harassment and the Informal Ghettoization of Women*, 106 Harv L Rev 517 (1993).

eration should not be dispositive, however. Contrary to what is sometimes suggested, viewpoint-based regulation is not a total anomaly under current doctrine. Regulations of commercial and labor speech, for example, forbid the assertion of some but not other views about what people have good reason to do; in schools and public workplaces, expressions of some viewpoints (but not others) may be held disruptive and therefore subject to sanction. Perhaps even more important is that, although the Title VII prohibition is not exactly viewpoint-neutral, neither does it take aim at particular ideas. The restriction of sexually harassing speech extends to messages that run the gamut from threats to professions of love or longing to ridicule to assertions of hatred. In addition, any of these messages that has a political component can be expressed in reasoned terms. So limited a prohibition against speech of such scant political value is not dangerously or disturbingly dissonant with either an already eclectic doctrinal structure or with First Amendment principle.

2. *Sexual harassment and autonomy.* If objection to regulating sexual harassment in the workplace rests not on democracy but on autonomy, analysis should start with recognition that interests in "descriptive" autonomy may actually support the prohibition of sexual harassment. Face-to-face utterances that constitute sexual harassment are particularly likely to be coercive and hurtful in both purpose and effect. Speech of this kind contributes nothing to the critical awareness and self-awareness on which descriptive autonomy depends, and it may diminish the range of attractive options experienced by its targets.

Relying on a conception of ascriptive autonomy, opponents of regulation sometimes deny that harassing speech that falls short of an explicit threat or a common law assault could actually cause the "harm" necessary to justify regulation.[240] On this view, the (ascriptive) autonomy interest in being free to speak or act as one will should yield only when speech or action causes harm.[241] But "harm" requires more than hurt feelings, the argument continues, and most harassment should be deemed to produce no more. As I have argued elsewhere, arguments such as these are the predictable

---

[240] See, for example, Fried, 59 U Chi L Rev at 250 (cited in note 160).

[241] In principle, the rights entailed by ascriptive autonomy are limited by the harm principle. See, for example, Feinberg, *Harm* at 61–62 (cited in note 157).

concommitants, though not the entailments, of an ascriptive conception of autonomy.[242] To stop the domain of protected autonomy rights from shrinking to triviality, champions of ascriptive autonomy frequently invoke an ascriptive theory of harm and nonharm[243] and simply deny that speech could be harm-producing outside of traditional, common law torts. But this position requires a virtual blindness to empirical effects.[244] Refusing to count psychic pain as a reason for suppressing speech may be justified in some contexts—in the public forum, for example, with the Nazi march in Skokie furnishing a case in point—but not in all. When a broad ambit for ascriptive autonomy is protected elsewhere, regulation of harassment in the workplace does no violence to First Amendment values and indeed may help to promote the (nonexclusive) value of descriptive autonomy.

   3. *Sexual harassment and protected categories.* If prominently or pervasively displayed in a workplace, sexually explicit and hostile materials that are not legally obscene or otherwise prohibitable in other contexts could contribute to a hostile work environment under Title VII.[245] Yet if an employee of a producer or distributor of such materials could claim that their display violates Title VII, the hostile environment cause of action could become the engine of suppression reaching far beyond the workplace. To prevent this result, a partial exception to the hostile environment prohibition is probably needed for the workplaces of producers and disseminators of constitutionally protected materials that might, in other contexts, create or contribute to a prohibited hostile environment.

---

[242] See Fallon, 46 Stan L Rev at 896–98 (cited in note 155).

[243] See Frederick Schauer, *The Phenomenology of Speech and Harm*, 103 Ethics 635, 652 (1993).

[244] See Dara A. Charney & Ruth C. Russell, *An Overview of Sexual Harassment*, 151 Am J Psychiatry 10, 13–14 (1994):

> Surveys have shown that over 90% of victims suffer from a significant degree of emotional distress . . . . They describe not only psychological effects but also physiological sequelae, such as headaches, decreased appetite, weight loss, decreased sleep, and an increased frequency of respiratory or urinary tract infections . . . . Victims' initial reactions to sexual harassment are typified by self-doubt and confusion. They often feel guilty and wonder if they might have caused the behavior . . . . Later, their anxiety tends to shift to depression, and self-confidence may erode to a point of crisis.

On the harms inflicted by racist epithets, see Delgado, 17 Harv CR-CL L Rev at 133 (cited in note 167).

[245] See, for example, *Andrews*, 895 F2d at 1485–86; *Robinson*, 760 F Supp at 1535; Abrams, 42 Vand L Rev at 1212 n 118 (cited in note 225).

C. HARRIS'S FUTURE

Although this survey of First Amendment boundary issues is far from complete, the basic conclusion should be clear. If *Harris* implicitly recognizes an exception to the content-neutrality principle for sexually harassing speech in the workplace, some accommodations will be needed, notably for expressly political speech aimed to contribute to reasoned political debate. For the most part, however, the constitutionally mandated adjustments of Title VII doctrine should be minor. The hostile-work-environment cause of action, as shaped by the Supreme Court in *Harris* and *Meritor* before it, fits more comfortably into the tapestry of existing First Amendment doctrine than its critics have imagined.

V. Toward a Law of the Campus?

If the Supreme Court's decision in *Harris* foreshadows recognition of a First Amendment category of sexual harassment in the workplace, there are possible though by no means necessary implications both for the thorny issues surrounding campus speech codes[246] and for the burgeoning cause of action for "hostile environment" sexual harassment under Title IX.[247] In particular, a doc-

---

[246] For insightful and disparate analyses, see, for example, Charles Lawrence, 1990 Duke L J at 431 (cited in note 157); Post, 32 Wm & Mary L Rev at 267 (cited in note 99); J. Peter Byrne, *Racial Insults and Free Speech Within the University*, 79 Georgetown L J 399 (1991); Strossen, 1990 Duke L J at 484 (cited in note 54); Frank Michelman, *Universities, Racist Speech and Democracy in America: An Essay for the ACLU*, 27 Harv CR-CL L Rev 339 (1992).

To date, the courts have responded to such codes with hostility. See, for example, *Doe v University of Michigan*, 721 F Supp 852 (ED Mich 1989); *UWM Post, Inc. v Board of Regents of the Univ. of Wisconsin*, 774 F Supp 1163 (ED Wis 1991). See also *Chapter of Sigma Chi Fraternity v George Mason Univ.*, 993 F2d 386 (4th Cir 1993) (nullifying sanctions imposed based on performance of a skit with racist and sexist overtones).

[247] Title IX, 20 USC § 1681(a) (1988) provides in pertinent part that "[n]o person in the United States shall, on the basis of sex, be excluded from participation in, be denied the benefits of, or be subjected to discrimination under any education program or activity receiving Federal financial assistance." Although the statute does not refer specifically to sexual harassment, the Supreme Court's landmark decision in *Franklin v Gwinnett County Pub. Sch.*, 112 S Ct 1028 (1992), established both that the prohibition against discrimination encompasses sexual harassment, id at 1037, and that the prohibition may be enforced through suits for damages. Although *Franklin* has spawned a number of lawsuits asserting hostile environment theories of sexual harassment, the controlling legal principles have not yet crystallized. See Tamar Lewin, *Students Seeking Damages for Sex Bias*, The New York Times (July 15, 1994), at B7, col 1 (noting that "the first round of cases are nearing trial" and that "there is still widespread uncertainty about how offensive the behavior must be before a student has a right to damages, how a school should respond to complaints of harassment or discrimination and when a school is responsible for one student harassing another").

trine allowing regulation based on the distinctive character of the workplace and the characteristic features of sexually harassing speech would invite arguments that college campuses are distinctive environments that deserve to be governed by their own distinctive First Amendment principles.

Mari Matsuda has argued that uniquely powerful reasons justify the regulation of harassing speech on university campuses:

> Universities are special places, charged with pedagogy, and duty-bound to a constituency with special vulnerabilities. Many of the new adults who come to live and study at major universities are away from home for the first time, and at a vulnerable stage of psychological development. Students are particularly dependent on the university for community, for intellectual development, and for self-definition.[248]

Students may find it hard to avoid their harassers on campus, may be distracted or deterred by harassment from enjoying equal educational opportunities,[249] and may be constrained from transferring to another school.[250]

On the other hand, the Supreme Court has repeatedly characterized universities and especially their classrooms as paradigmatic marketplaces of ideas.[251] This metaphor reflects the university's important social role of promoting the critical spirit on which descriptive autonomy and political democracy ultimately depend. According to one recent formulation, the university is an institution charged with the search for truth, in which no idea or viewpoint can claim immunity from challenge.[252] University students may feel as "captive" as employees in the workplace,[253] but easy analogies between the two contexts should be resisted.[254]

---

[248] Matsuda, 87 Mich L Rev at 2370–71 (cited in note 103). See also Mary Becker, *Conservative Free Speech and the Uneasy Case for Judicial Review*, 64 U Colo L Rev 975, 1040 (1993); Richard Delgado & David H. Yun, *Pressure Valves and Bloodied Chickens: An Analysis of Paternalistic Objections to Hate Speech Regulation*, 82 Cal L Rev 871, 887 (1994).

[249] See Schneider, 65 Tex L Rev at 590 (cited in note 222).

[250] See Note, *Racist Speech on Campus: A Title VII Solution to a First Amendment Problem*, 64 So Cal L Rev 105, 126 (1990).

[251] See, for example, *Keyishian v Board of Regents*, 385 US 589, 603 (1967); *Healy v James*, 408 US 169, 180 (1972).

[252] See J. Peter Byrne, *Academic Freedom: A "Special Concern of the First Amendment,"* 99 Yale L J 251 (1989).

[253] See Note, 64 So Cal L Rev at 124–27 (Cited in note 250).

[254] See David F. McGowan & Ragesh K. Tangri, *A Libertarian Critique of University Restrictions on Offensive Speech*, 79 Cal L Rev 825, 901–03 & n 377 (1991); Subcommittee of American Association of University Professors Committee A on Academic Freedom and Tenure, *Academic Freedom and Sexual Harassment*, 80 *Academe* 64 (September-October 1994).

Given the distinctive character of the university, I could not hope to sketch the full range of First Amendment issues raised by campus speech codes, or even by more limited prohibitions against sexual harassment. With respect to the latter, however, a crucial distinction would greatly advance analysis. As developed by the courts, the Title VII cause of action for "hostile environment" sexual harassment encompasses two logically distinct types of claim. One involves sexual advances, requests for sexual favors, and other speech and conduct that I shall hereinafter describe as "inherently sexual"—speech and conduct conveying what one commentator has called a "sexuality message."[255] A second type of sex-based harassment is not inherently sexual, but instead communicates a "hostility message,"[256] targeted at others based on their gender. Because the Supreme Court clearly regards Title VII as creating rights to freedom from both, the courts' use of the term "sexual harassment" to include both has been wholly understandable.[257] In a university, however, the analytical distinction between harassment that is "inherently sexual" and harassment that conveys sex-based hostility may clarify which free speech values are implicated and to what degree in different kinds of cases.[258]

With only rare exceptions, a narrowly worded prohibition against harassment through inherently sexual speech—sexual advances, sexual innuendo, and so forth—would neither implicate nor threaten any special function of the university. The "hostile environment" standards developed under Title VII could therefore be extended to campus settings under Title IX without damage to academic freedom or the First Amendment in cases involving "inherently sexual" harassment.

---

[255] Browne, 52 Ohio St L J at 492 (cited in note 34).

[256] Id.

[257] Interestingly, the EEOC drew almost precisely this distinction in a set of proposed, but subsequently withdrawn, Guidelines on Harassment Based on Race, Color, Religion, Gender, National Origin, Age, or Disability. In the proposed guidelines, the EEOC characterized its Guidelines on Discrimination Because of Sex as dealing only with "sex-based harassment that is sexual in nature," and offered for comment standards prohibiting, among other things, sex-based harassment that is not inherently sexual. See 58 Fed Reg 51266, 51266-67 (1993). The EEOC withdrew the proposed guidelines roughly a year after they were offered for comment with the cryptic explanation that "they did not achieve the stated goal of 'consolidat[ing], clarify[ing] and explicat[ing]' existing law relating to harassment" on the relevant bases. 59 Fed Reg 51396 (1994).

[258] "Some words, primarily those relating to female sexual anatomy, may actually convey a dual message by showing contempt for women by equating them with their sex organs." Browne, 52 Ohio St L J at 492 (cited in note 34).

By contrast, any broad interpretation of the prohibition against "sex-based" harassment—harassment that communicates a sex-based message of hostility or inferiority—would be much more likely to chill debate at the heart of the university's critical, discursive, truth-seeking, and pedagogical missions. Some forms of sex-based harassment barred under Title VII—notably epithets aimed at individuals or small groups of individuals that are commonly understood to convey direct, visceral hatred or contempt on the basis of gender—are not plausibly related to those missions, and indeed may frustrate their accomplishment. Such epithets, which also have no necessary role in political democracy and can damage the descriptive autonomy of their targets, should therefore be prohibitable.[259] But a wide breathing space should be given to protect free, robust, provocative, and occasionally offensive exchanges of views even about charged subjects. As elsewhere, the First Amendment should establish an express protection for any speech or combination of speech and conduct that is reasonably designed or intended to contribute to education, including public education, academic inquiry, or reasoned debate on issues of public concern. In addition, the prohibition against gender-based harassment by hostility messages should be limited to speech that: (i) is intended to insult or stigmatize on the basis of gender, (ii) is addressed to or targeted at an individual or small group of individuals whom it insults or stigmatizes, (iii) makes use of words or symbols that are commonly understood to convey direct, visceral hatred for human beings on the basis of their gender, and (iv) has the purpose or reasonably foreseeable effect of unreasonably interfering with an individual's work or academic performance or of creating a seriously intimidating, hostile, demeaning, degrading, or otherwise egregiously offensive working or educational environment.[260]

---

[259] See, for example, Byrne, 79 Georgetown L J at 418–27 (cited in note 246).

[260] This formulation largely follows the recommendations of the Harvard Law School Committee on Sexual Harassment Guidelines, see note 232 above, which is much influenced by (even though it departs in some respects from) the controversial Stanford University hate speech regulation whose drafters included Professor Thomas Grey. The Stanford regulation is printed as an appendix to Thomas C. Grey, *Civil Rights vs. Civil Liberties: The Case of Discriminatory Harassment*, 8 Soc Phil & Pol 81 (1992). A state court enjoined enforcement of Stanford's regulation on free speech grounds Feb 27, 1995, and the university announced it would not appeal the ruling. *Corry v Stanford Univ.*, No 740309, Cal Superior Ct (Santa Clara Co).

The Department of Education has recently issued a "notice of investigative guidance" to be followed by its officials in investigating alleged violations of Title VI of the Civil Rights Act of 1964, which prohibits discrimination on the basis of race, color, or national origin in any program receiving federal funds. This notice is not limited in the way outlined in

Both this formulation and the arguments offered in its defense invite objections directed at my repeated reliances on concepts of "reason," reason-giving, and contribution to "reasoned" debate. These are value-laden constructs. In some contexts, the First Amendment undoubtedly protects expression designed to arrest, to shock, and to destabilize conventional notions of reason and reasonableness.[261] Even and perhaps especially on college campuses, not all caustic rejections of conventional notions of reason and reasonableness lie beyond the constitutional pale. I mean only to suggest that hate-charged epithets, targeted at individuals or small groups of individuals with the purpose or predictable effect of interfering with their work or education, need not be constitutionally immune from regulation in every context even if they are properly protected in a public forum, and that this particular form of unreasoning speech has no plausible claim of consistency with the central purposes of a university.

Eloquent protests have sounded that efforts to legitimate content-based suppression of racist and sexist speech are tactically misguided. Kathleen Sullivan has argued that:[262]

> Bans on hate speech may have perverse effects; they may replicate the very marginalization that they are meant to subvert, carrying a subtext that victims cannot talk back for themselves. They may stifle in the name of civility and reason the most empowering responses, which sometimes consist of shouting back angrily in like kind. They may backfire by turning the haters into martyrs, giving their hate speech magnified publicity and effect.

Concerns such as these should give pause to policymakers, but neither policymakers nor judges should be taken in by the different, misleading argument that traditional victims of discrimination should embrace the neutral and ubiquitous First Amendment norm of content neutrality as their own best hope in the long term. This argument is misleading, because its premise is at best only partly correct. The norm of content neutrality has always admitted nu-

---

the text. See 59 Fed Reg 11448 (1994). Instead, its "hostile environment analysis" draws heavily on Title VII cases, without considering whether speech might deserve more constitutional protection in the university than in the workplace.

[261] See, for example, Kenneth Karst, *Boundaries and Reasons: Freedom of Expression and the Subordination of Groups*, 1990 U Ill L Rev 95.

[262] Kathleen M. Sullivan, *The First Amendment Wars*, The New Republic (Sept 28, 1992), at 35, 40.

merous exceptions. The space occupied by the First Amendment, both conceptually and in practical effect, is simply too diverse for the reality to be otherwise.

VI. Conclusion

The imperatives of principled yet sensible governance have spawned different First Amendment rules for different areas. Surprisingly, the Supreme Court has often seemed unaware of the variety of its own handiwork—especially in its aggrandized estimates of the territory governed by the principle barring content-based regulation. *Harris v Forklift Systems, Inc.* appears to reflect a departure from that principle and a step toward the development of distinctive First Amendment norms governing sexual harassment in the workplace. In this essay, I have tried to show that a special doctrine for workplace speech would fit comfortably into the tapestry of First Amendment law, the complexity of which is often unappreciated. I have also identified the principles by which the doctrine that *Harris* appears to foreshadow should be defined and limited. It bears emphasis, however, that the attribution of a First Amendment theory to *Harris* does not rest on what the Court said, but rather on what it failed to mention at all. For now, at least, *Harris* and Title VII's hostile environment cause of action remain attended by mystery—the mystery of the First Amendment dog that didn't bark.

C. EDWIN BAKER

TURNER BROADCASTING: CONTENT-BASED REGULATION OF PERSONS AND PRESSES

In response to the virtual gatekeeper control that cable systems exercise over access to local broadcasting, Congress in 1992 gave local commercial and public television broadcasters the right to demand that cable systems carry their over-the-air broadcast channels without charge. In largely rejecting the cable systems' First Amendment challenge to these must-carry rules, the Supreme Court in *Turner Broadcasting v FCC*[1] gave the government and local broadcasters a significant victory. Although the decision was not as sweeping as the district court's grant of summary judgment for the government, the Court's remand to determine whether the legislation meets *O'Brien*'s[2] mid-level scrutiny requirements of being adequately designed to further important governmental purposes[3] should not place a serious constitutional obstacle to approval of the must-carry rules.

C. Edwin Baker is Nicholas F. Gallichio Professor of Law, University of Pennsylvania Law School.

Author's note: I wish to thank Michael Madow, Sue Sturm, and Seth Kreimer for helpful comments on earlier drafts and to thank Howard Lesnick for a discussion of several important issues covered here.

[1] 114 S Ct 2445 (1994).

[2] *United States v O'Brien*, 391 US 367 (1968).

[3] I will not discuss the Court's conclusion that, under its legal framework, a more extensive factual record was needed nor discuss what factual findings will be relevant. Justice Blackmun's concurrence emphasized the significance to be given Congress's predictive judgments but agreed that a remand was appropriate because "the standard for summary judgment is high" and because the government had not yet even introduced the complete record developed by Congress. Justice Stevens indicated a preference for affirming without remand because under the majority's framework no current factual showing, only experience, could undermine the government's position. Unsurprisingly given the tremendous economic stakes, cable interests consistently assert that the government will not be able to meet its burden and the remand is producing extensive and expensive discovery.

I. The Decision

As analyzed by the Court, the case turned on two issues. First was determination of the constitutional standard to be applied to government regulation of cable. The leading press-access case has long been *Miami Herald v Tornillo*,[4] a unanimous decision cited to say, roughly, that the government should keep its hands off the press (a more precise description becomes important later). The conventional wisdom is that broadcasting is the one communication medium in which the First Amendment permits government regulation. Indeed, in *Red Lion Broadcasting v FCC*,[5] the Court unanimously upheld a right-to-reply requirement applied to broadcasting that was in relevant respects identical to the law directed at newspapers that was unanimously invalidated in *Tornillo*. Seemingly, the permissibility of regulation of cable would turn on whether cable is more like broadcasting or newspapers. Lower courts have long struggled with this issue, to which the Supreme Court has studiously avoided speaking.[6]

In *Turner*, the Court stated that whereas physical scarcity provided the rationale for regulatory intervention in broadcasting, no such scarcity exists in cable. Rather than then making the predicted move of following *Tornillo* and applying strict scrutiny,[7] the Court said that the "analogy to *Tornillo* ignores an important technological difference between newspapers and cable television."[8] The "cable operator exercises far greater control over access to the relevant medium" because "the physical connection between the television set and the cable network gives the cable operator bottleneck, or gatekeeper, control . . . ."[9] Observing the "potential for abuse of [cable's] private power over a central avenue of communication,"

---

[4] 418 US 241 (1974).

[5] 395 US 367 (1969).

[6] See, e.g., *Los Angeles v Preferred Communications*, 476 US 488 (1986).

[7] Commentators and lower courts have routinely assumed the two alternatives in First Amendment challenges to cable are to apply the broadcast model represented by *Red Lion* and apply a mid-level *O'Brien* scrutiny or to follow the print model represented by *Tornillo* and apply strict scrutiny. Interestingly, and, as I will suggest in Part IV, refreshingly, *Tornillo* did not adopt strict scrutiny and *Red Lion* did not adopt *O'Brien* or any explicit form of mid-level scrutiny. These characterizations came later. Both decisions were written without reference to tests or levels of scrutiny but rather directly evaluated the arguments.

[8] 114 S Ct at 2466.

[9] Id at 2466.

the Court relied on *Associated Press v United States*[10] for the proposition that the First Amendment "does not disable the government from taking steps to ensure that private interests not restrict . . . the free flow of information and ideas."[11] That is, after rejecting the broadcasting analogy, the Court also rejected *Tornillo's* government-hands-off philosophy by relying on a different newspaper case, *Associated Press*, to assert the legitimacy of broad governmental power over cable. Interestingly, the four dissenters did not dispute any of this.

The second issue treated, as apparently crucial by both the majority and dissent, was whether the must-carry rules are content-based. Of course, on their face the rules are speaker-based, not content-based—only "local" broadcasters get the benefit. But the majority and dissent agreed that a law can be content-based not only on its face but because of its purpose. Although the only clear holding that the Court cited for this proposition was the most recent flag-burning case,[12] where the law could easily have been interpreted as facially content-based, the Court's view seems unexceptional. A content-based purpose, at least if it relates to suppressing expression, places a law outside the ubiquitous *O'Brien* test. And since *O'Brien* now applies to content-neutral time, place, and manner regulations, those excluded from this category on the basis of the content-based purpose are presumably treated more severely—with the obvious alternative being to treat them like facially content-based laws. In any event, that alternative gathered unanimous approval in *Turner*.

The Court split 5–4 on whether the must-carry rules were content-based, a split that perfectly reflected the vote on whether to invalidate the law.[13] According to the majority, the law was content-neutral. Its admirable, anti-trust type purpose was to provide a fair playing field for television in order to prevent cable from using its control over the communication bottleneck to undermine

---

[10] 326 US 1, 20 (1945).

[11] 114 S Ct at 2466.

[12] *United States v Eichman*, 496 US 310 (1990) (punishing anyone who "mutilates, defaces, physically defiles, burns, maintains on the floor, or tramples upon" but not one who disposes of a worn or soiled flag).

[13] The five consisted of Justices Kennedy, Souter, Stevens, Blackmun, and Chief Justice Rehnquist—although Stevens only concurred in the disposition, favoring an outright affirmance.

the economic viability of (or to injure in somewhat less serious ways) local broadcasting. The law also helped preserve free (over-the-air) television, a service that many people value and that may be especially valuable for those who cannot afford cable. The dissent argued that the majority "cannot be correct."[14] It quoted findings, which Congress enacted as a section of the law, that consistently emphasized Congress's concern with content. The findings asserted that "local news and public affairs programming and other local broadcast services [are] critical to an informed electorate" and that "educational and informational programming" provided by public television serves "the Government's compelling interest in educating its citizens."[15]

The majority, in addition to emphasizing the content-neutral purposes, argued that the law does not fit the purpose the dissent identified. When forced to carry an over-the-air broadcast station, even if it has minimal local content, a cable station could drop a cable channel (if one exists) that emphasized local news. Nevertheless, quarrel with the majority is more than possible.[16] It is difficult to imagine that Congress would justify the must-carry rules except in part on grounds that the content of local television is expected characteristically to differ from that on cable and that this different content has value.[17] Certainly, Congress's concerns in structuring

---

[14] 114 S Ct at 2478.

[15] 114 S Ct at 2476 (quoting Cable Act of 1992, § 2(a)(11) and § 2(a)(8)(A)). The question of whether a law supported by a content-based purpose would be saved if it also had a content-neutral purpose becomes important here. The dissent said no such position has ever been approved, and that the Court has "often struck down statutes as being impermissibly content based even though their primary purpose was indubitably content neutral." Id at 2478. However, in support the dissent only cited cases with content lines on the face of the statute. In no case did a purpose unrelated to content explain the content discrimination. The proper analogy would seem to be whether a law that was content-neutral on its face would be invalidated if supported by both content and noncontent reasons. A careful reading of both *O'Brien* and *Eichman* indicates that a purpose entirely independent of the expressive act's communicative impact arguably would suffice to save the law—which is what *Arlington Heights v Metropolitan Housing Dev. Corp.*, 429 US 252, 271 n 21 (1977), suggests in the analogous equal protection context.

[16] In one possibly important respect, however, must-carry is clearly content neutral. Cable companies complained primarily that they had limited carriage capacity and the must-carry rules would require them to exclude other material. And the sole compliant of cable programmers was that must-carry made it more difficult for them to get their productions on cable. The must-carry rules were entirely content-neutral in indicating what material would be displaced—that choice was left entirely to the cable operators. This point gains significance if First Amendment concerns distinguish between government suppression of content and its promotion of content.

[17] Political and cultural participatory values might justify local people's involvement in programming decisions, maybe local people talking on local talk shows, even if the speech content, even if the words on the talk show, were the same as those carried on a national

the broadcast industry, which it was here attempting to preserve, have consistently related to content.[18]

In defined circumstances, the Cable Television Consumer Protection and Competition Act of 1992[19] even gives the FCC authority to order a cable system to carry an otherwise ineligible station on the basis of the FCC's findings that the station would provide content which Congress specially valued—that is, programming that "would address local news and informational needs which are not being adequately served" or "news coverage of issues of concern to such community . . . or coverage of sporting and other events of interest to the community."[20] Recognizing that these appear facially content-based, the majority in a footnote indicated that the District Court, which had not addressed these particular provisions in its original decision, "may do so on remand."[21] But even if technically severable, the point ignored by the majority is that these grants of authority provisions illustrate the most obvious justification for must-carry provisions as a whole—to promote local content by safeguarding local broadcasting. Congress believed that local broadcasters are more likely than their competitive alternatives, especially national cable channels, to provide content that the FCC and Congress have traditionally considered and continue to consider especially valuable—local content. Or, at least, that these stations provide a content element that should not be lost.

In this article, I will defend three points. Most centrally, Part IIC argues that, although the dissent probably got the best of the question of whether the must-carry rules are content-based, both the majority and dissent were wrong to assume that a content-motivation is objectionable here. Safeguarding local broadcast television because of a concern for local content is perfectly appropriate. This content aim should be applauded rather than being a basis for a more exacting scrutiny.

---

cable channel. Whether from this participatory perspective the same words said by different people should be viewed as the "same content" is unclear. In any event, those holding this participatory vision are likely to predict and hope that the textual content will be different as well as being local.

[18] See, e.g., Jonathan Weinberg, *Broadcasting and Speech*, 81 Cal L Rev 1101 (1993); Donald W. Hawthorne and Monroe E. Price, *Rewiring the First Amendment: Meaning, Content and Public Broadcasting*, 12 Cardozo Arts & Enter L J 499 (1994).

[19] Pub L 102-385, 106 Stat 1460.

[20] 47 USC §§ 534(h)(2)(B), (h)(1)(C)(III).

[21] 114 S Ct at 2460 n 6. Justice Stevens's preference for affirming without any reconsideration suggests that he may not have been troubled by this content-based element.

Leading up to this critique of the Court's treatment of content discrimination, Parts IIA and IIB argue that for First Amendment purposes there is a fundamental difference between individuals and various legally created collective entities including media entities. My claim is that law has little role in structuring individuals (except maybe in defining and protecting the borders between one individual and another), and any law censoring or directed at suppressing individual speech is presumptively objectionable. In contrast, Congressional conceptions of the public good ought to inform the inevitable choices in the manner of structuring legally created entities and, often, those conceptions will include content-oriented judgments about how the entities will best serve a democratic communications order. Part III will show that, historically, acceptance of content-based governmental involvement with the communications order has been a constant and that courts have routinely upheld the governmental involvement on the few occasions when the communications industries challenged it on First Amendment grounds. And, most importantly here, that this difference between individuals and legally created entities should affect the question of when content-based laws are objectionable.

Finally, Part IV sketchily suggests that problems with the Court's analysis in *Turner* reflect a generally undesirable but increasingly common preoccupation with mechanical "tests," "scrutinies," and rigid categories that are too disconnected from the normative commitments underlying constitutional law.

II. Critique

A. INDIVIDUALS AND ARTIFICIAL ENTITIES

With the dissent's approval,[22] the Court began its substantive discussion with the statement: "There can be no disagreement on an initial premise: Cable programmers and cable operators engage in and transmit speech, and they are entitled to the protection of the speech and press provisions of the First Amendment."[23] Yes, maybe. But the question here is whether being cable operators rather than gossiping colleagues, anti-abortion demonstrators, or

---

[22] Id at 2475.

[23] Id at 2456.

schoolchildren during a flag ceremony should matter for purposes of the form (or degree) of constitutional protection the "speaker" should receive against government imposition of "must-carry" tasks.

Nongovernmental cable operators are typically business enterprises that take a corporate form; they inevitably deduct the costs of their speech as business expenses. Speech is their business. In these ways, they differ from individuals who speak as an aspect of (or who listen in order to aid in) making personal choices for themselves. Even identification of the "speaker" differs in the context of cable (or other business enterprises) from the personal context. In the latter, the speaker is the person speaking. Of course, outside forces greatly influence people's speech choices. Nevertheless, the dominant conception of the person attributes speech to the speaker who is normally treated as having authority and responsibility to control her own speech content. In contrast, with artificial, legally created entities, determining who has authority to control speech decisions requires examination of laws (and often other customary presumptions). When the Court says the cable operator engages in speech, to whom does it refer? Does it mean the owner(s) (often thousands of stockholders), the board or chief executive officer, some subordinate who is not overruled when she actually makes a particular choice, or the entity itself?[24] Despite these differences, perhaps the nature of the speaker does or should make no difference. Certainly, the Court's "initial premise" disregards any distinction between individuals and these legally created entities. On closer examination, however, the Court's reasoning proceeds in two directions.

In discussing general First Amendment principles, especially issues concerning content-based laws, the Court relied indiscriminately on cases involving individual speakers and those involving collective entities. In contrast, the identity of the speaker seemed relevant when the Court argued that cable is not like broadcasting

---

[24] See Meir Dan-Cohen, *Freedoms of Collective Speech: A Theory of Protected Communications by Organizations, Communities, and the State*, 79 Cal L Rev 1229 (1991) (arguing that it makes sense to refer to the speech of the collective entity). Although sometimes emphasizing different points, for the most part, Dan-Cohen's overall argument is consistent with those developed in C. Edwin Baker, *Human Liberty and Freedom of Speech* 194–271 (Oxford, 1989), on which much of the discussion here is based, and with Victor Brudney, *Business Corporations and Stockholders' Rights Under the First Amendment*, 91 Yale L J 235 (1981).

but also is not like newspapers because of a "technological difference"—the "bottleneck or gatekeeper control" that cable has over the television programming channeled into the subscriber's home that results from "the physical connection between the television and the cable network."[25] The Court followed precedent in explaining that "[e]ach medium of expression . . . must be assessed for First Amendment purposes by standards suited to it, for each may present its own problems."[26] In addition to distinguishing among media, this directive seems very policy oriented, more like a point that is addressed to a legislature designing industrial policy than to a forum of principle.

The question of whether differing constitutional standards do or should apply to differing media entities is left until Part III. I first examine the Court's other major analytic turn. In considering the applicability of more general doctrines like those concerning content discrimination, are, as the majority and dissent both seemed to think, all speakers analogous?

Reasons for flattening First Amendment precedent into a single matrix applied to all cases of speech are not hard to find. First, any other approach might appear to abandon the claim that the constitutional order involves fundamental principles and to admit instead that constitutional law merely involves unprincipled judicial social engineering. For some audiences, the force of constitutional argument relates directly to the generality of its crucial principles. (Of course, the opposite view—that justifiability relates directly to the sensitivity of the analysis to context—also has devotees.[27]) Second, the source of speech should not matter from the perspective of the marketplace of ideas. "The inherent worth of

---

[25] 114 S Ct at 2466. This reliance on a "technology-based" bottleneck may be unfortunate and doctrinally destabilizing. Already the technological basis for removing this bottleneck exists and already the FCC has approved phone company "video dialtone," which allows delivery of video programs and possibly of multiple competing cable systems over telephone lines utilizing video dialtone. *In the Matter of Telephone Company–Cable Television Cross-Ownership Rules*, 7 FCC Rcd 5781 (1992). Economic and policy reasons, mostly related to the desirability of creating a more open and diverse communications order, will continue to support regulating cable differently from newspapers. See C. Edwin Baker, *Merging Phone and Cable*, 17 Hastings Comm/Ent L J 97 (1994). But the Court's rationale creates an easy target for opponents of useful media policies in the same way that the scarcity doctrine has in the broadcast context.

[26] 114 S Ct at 2466 (quoting *Southeastern Promotions v Conrad*, 420 US 546, 557 (1975)).

[27] C. Steven Shiffrin, *The First Amendment, Democracy, and Romance* (Harvard, 1990) (advocating that courts accept and engage in social engineering in favor of dissenting speech).

the speech in terms of its capacity for informing the public does
not depend on the identity of the source . . . ."[28] Of course, sometimes the Court rejects this premise. Many listeners find that the
identity of the source affects the worth or at least their evaluation
of the speech. Not surprisingly, a major policy reason for laws
requiring sources to identify themselves is the belief that the source
does matter. In the interest of listeners, the Court has upheld these
laws, striking them only when it could reasonably conclude that
the law will restrict speakers' expressive freedom.[29] In any event,
the Court's episodic doctrinal indifference to the source, especially
in its examination of content-based laws, can be criticized both
analytically and normatively.

The dominant Enlightenment conception of personal identity
would treat any law that gives someone other than the speaker
herself an original power to dictate her self-expressive speech as an
overt interference with her autonomy or liberty. Whatever insights
are involved in the postmodernist portrayal of the disappearance
of the subject, virtually everyone in her personal interactions treats
what the other says and does as central to how she should judge,
value, relate to, or feel about the other. Except under special institutionally bounded circumstances, few people will fail to object if
explicitly denied the right to make their own expressive choices.
Ascribing speech to the speaker is implicit in the pragmatics of
everyday communicative action. This ascription probably provides
the best explanation for "the principle" that lies "at the heart of
the First Amendment . . . that *each person* should decide for him
or herself the ideas and beliefs deserving of expression, consideration, and adherence."[30]

Groups into which a person is born plus those with whom the
person becomes associated largely determine the person's beliefs.
Associational relations likewise greatly influence a person's speech.
Nevertheless, "[o]ur political system and cultural life rest upon

---

[28] *First Natl. Bank v Bellotti*, 435 US 765, 777 (1978).

[29] Compare *Brown v Socialist Workers*, 459 US 87 (1982) and *Talley v California*, 362 US
60 (1960) with *Buckley v Valeo*, 424 US 1 (1976) and *Lewis v Morgan Publishing*, 229 US 283
(1913). See Geoffrey R. Stone and William P. Marshall, *Brown v Socialist Workers: Inequality
as a Command of the First Amendment*, 1983 Supreme Court Review 583, 626 (arguing that
even content-based exemptions from otherwise justified disclosure laws are justified "when
the commitment to neutrality conflicts with the commitment to preservation of ideas in the
political marketplace").

[30] *Turner*, 114 S Ct at 2458 (emphasis added, cites omitted).

[the] ideal"[31] that the speaker is the natural or appropriate locus of choice for a speaker's expressive acts. Even when a person is expected to repeat another person's words, as in a marriage ceremony where the person "repeat[s] after me," in a legal proceeding where a person takes an oath, or in a ceremonial pledge of allegiance, the premise is that the repeated words manifest the speaker's own commitments. Surely, this was the constitutional basis for objecting to the mandatory flag salute in *West Virginia Board of Education v Barnette*.[32]

In contrast, a corporate entity is a person only within some legal fictions. Analytically, the law does not impinge personal identity or autonomy but rather helps structure and maintain power relationships when it recognizes one rather than another person's authority to determine the content of some communication from a particular division of Time-Warner, a company owned by thousands and an employer of thousands more. Law provides the framework within which people create corporate structures that then relate various people to various corporate choices, including expressive choices. Within these legally structured entities, law inevitably either provides for one person's (or role's or office's) authority rather than another's or prohibits particular exercises of authority of one over another, but this does not compromise anyone's autonomy in any obvious sense. As long as autonomy—or at least the constitutionally protected form of autonomy—does not imply any inherent right to exercise power over another, the law does not abridge autonomy if it fails to give one person or group within the corporation the power to order an actual "speaker," for example, a writer or programmer or actor, either to say or not say particular things or to be fired for refusal.

Often the locus of authority within these collective entities is structured by generally applicable instrumentally justified corporate, contract, or other regulatory laws—as opposed to speech or media specific laws. The policy bases of these general laws seldom focus on the communications order. Nevertheless, any legitimate societal objective can presumably provide their justification. Once the quality of the communications order is recognized as a proper subject of government attention, reasons related to furthering a

---

[31] Id.

[32] 319 US 624, 638, 640–42 (1943).

better or more inclusive "public debate" should justify adoption of "structural" rules that determine whose speech prevails. Certainly, this concern would explain requiring shopping centers to allow for expressive opportunities.[33] Government ought to be praised rather than condemned if its reason for opening up shopping centers was not merely pro-speech but was content-based—namely, if its reason was that opening up this arena provides needed opportunities especially for dissident speech or for those espousing unpopular views.

Thus, my claim is that our most fundamental, deeply rooted practices treat the mind/body integration and moral agent conception of an individual as basic—a natural default position.[34] Even though countless influences operate on the person, the person typically claims control over and others hold her responsible for her speech. From this perspective, law that mandates a person's speech on a basis other than the person's choice impinges on individual autonomy. (Autonomy, however, may be consistent with speech-related conditions on grants or benefits, like conditions of employment—a point to which I will return below.)

On the other hand, legal frameworks that determine whose speech choices prevail within collective entities are inevitable. Whatever framework is adopted necessarily favors some and disfavors other speakers and content. In a sense, here there are no non-politically or non-socially created, natural default positions. As the Court explained in *West Coast Hotel v Parrish*,[35] given this lack of a default position, a structural choice merely sets the framework in which people exercise their autonomy. "The liberty safeguarded is liberty within a social organization . . . ."[36] Thus, a social structure that requires businesses to pay minimum wages

---

[33] *Pruneyard Shopping Center v Robins*, 447 US 74 (1980).

[34] I do not claim that this view is nonideological—only that the ideology is so deeply rooted that consistent deviation is practically untenable. Wittgenstein famously argued that although giving grounds comes to an end, "the end is not an ungrounded presupposition: it is an ungrounded way of acting." Ludwig Wittgenstein, *On Certainty* § 110. Possibly Wittgenstein's best image for how some of our presuppositions are less subject to change is: "And the bank of that river consists partly of hard rock, subject to no alteration or only to an imperceptible one, partly of sand, which now in one place now in another gets washed away, or deposited." Id at § 99. Jurgen Habermas, for example, could argue that the communicative action aimed at agreement is not a practice we could easily give up—it is like the hard rock of the river bank.

[35] 300 US 379 (1937).

[36] Id at 391.

need not be understood as suppressing the employers' freedom. Rather, the absence of a minimum wage requirement can be understood as a subsidy for profiteering employers.[37] Likewise, the inevitable regulation of collective entities will disfavor some speakers or some content; however, these regulations need not be interpreted as suppressing their speech or limiting their autonomy. They merely set a favorable baseline for other speakers or content.

Even though the autonomy ascribed to individuals does not normally apply to legally created collective entities, distinctions among regulations of collective entities' speech will sometimes be relevant to free speech concerns. Many of these regulations—for example, a law providing a candidate a right to purchase "reasonable amounts of time for use of a broadcasting station . . . in behalf of his candidacy,"[38] or a law giving various nonprofits reduced-rate postage—can be understood to establish baselines or to provide subsidies for favored speakers or content. Likewise, law necessarily determines whether (or the extent and the circumstances in which) the stockholders, the board of directors, the CEO, a lower-level employee, the union, or some other person or group has the right to determine the company's advertising strategy. These unproblematic baseline or subsidy laws (hereafter called "structural" rules) differ in two respects from a second category—laws that prohibit various collective entities from communicating certain content or that purposively burden such communications (hereafter called "prohibitory" laws). First, these prohibitory laws suppress speech; they limit the expressive role of the restricted collective entities. Second, unlike structural rules whose allocative function is to determine whose private expressive decision will prevail, the existence of prohibitory laws is not inevitable. Bans on the publication or broadcast of a rape victim's name, restrictions on casinos' truthful advertising, limits on corporate participation in political campaigns, or prohibitions on or channeling of indecent expression within the media illustrate such prohibitions. These two differences provide a basis of constitutional challenge to these prohibitory laws, although I will suggest below that the success of the

---

[37] "The exploitation of a class of workers . . . casts a direct burden for their support upon the community. . . . What these workers lose in wages the taxpayers are called upon to pay. . . . [The community] is not bound to provide what is in effect a subsidy for unconscionable employers." Id at 399.

[38] 47 USC § 312(a)(7) (1988), upheld against First Amendment challenge in *CBS v FCC*, 453 US 367 (1981).

challenge should and usually does depend on the category of collective entities to which prohibition applies.

The inevitability of structural rules helps explain why this first category poses few constitutional problems. In *Turner*, the dissent asserted that "the government may subsidize speakers that it thinks provide novel points of view, [but] it may not restrict other speakers on the theory that what they say is more conventional."[39] Subsidizing governmentally identified "novel points of view" is surely content-based.[40] Thus, the dissent apparently accepts content-based laws in the context of subsidies. The difficult analytic problem becomes distinguishing "subsidies" from "restrictions."

The dissent in *Turner* did not argue, but apparently merely assumed, that must-carry rules restrict rather than subsidize.[41] Here, its blindness to distinctions between individuals and collective entities became important. Clearly, the "must-carry" flag salute in *Barnette* counts as a restriction—but the "must-carry" rule for the shopping center in *Pruneyard* is, following the logic of *West Coast Hotel* and given California's interpretation of its property law, a baseline allocation of property rights. First Amendment analysis generally should treat allocations of rights relating to institutional entities as establishing baselines or creating subsidies and as creating little constitutional problem, as in *Pruneyard*, unless the government's purpose was to suppress speech. Even when suppression of a collective entity's speech is the government's goal, whether this suppression raises a constitutional issue depends on the normative theory of the First Amendment. I will suggest below that the suppression is a problem only for certain categories of collective entities, that is, for media enterprises and "solidarity" or expressive associations—the first because of the special, instrumental role of the press in a democratic society and the second because of their derivative status as embodiments of individual liberty.

In contrast, structural regulation of individuals—giving anyone

---

[39] 114 S Ct at 2478.

[40] Even though content-based, maybe a subsidy does not count as content-based "regulation." Often the Court's language implies that regulations are restrictive while subsidies are enabling. Nevertheless, the majority in *Turner* found it necessary to defend must-carry rules as " 'unrelated to the suppression of free expression,' " citing *O'Brien*, 391 US at 377, "*or to the content of any speakers' messages.*" 114 S Ct at 2469 (emphasis added).

[41] In their role as restrictions, the must-carry rules are indisputably content neutral because the cable operator, not the rule, determines what content is not delivered. The dissent's argument that the rules are content-based only applies to the speech they benefit. See note 16.

other than the individual authority over her speech—is presumptively suppressive. For individuals, distinguishing subsidies from restrictions is usually easy except in the perplexing case of conditional grants of government benefits.[42] Arguably, if the condition is reasonably understood as furthering a legitimate governmental purpose in providing the benefit, the benefit merely subsidizes that government project and the speech-restrictive condition should be upheld; but without this connection (or if the governmental project is itself impermissibly suppressive), the condition unconstitutionally suppresses speech.

The above distinctions between legally created collective entities and individuals and between structural and prohibitory regulation of entities were analytic. Given deeply entrenched conceptions of personhood, individual autonomy is normally at issue in regulation aimed at individual speech but not, or at least not in the same way, in regulation aimed at the speech of legally created collective entities. Still, the relevance of this analytic point depends on the normative concerns that animate First Amendment interpretation. If the marketplace of ideas or, maybe,[43] if "undistorted" public debate were the central normative premise, the source of the speech is irrelevant. Any law aimed at suppressing any (protected) speech, especially on a content basis, is presumptively unconstitutional censorship.

In contrast, the source of the suppressed expression is crucial if the central normative value is individual expressive liberty—the value emphasized by the dissent in *First National Bank v Bellotti*[44] but now said by the majority in *Turner* to be the "heart" of the First

---

[42] "Copyright" also presents a curious case. This "structural" regulation gives copyright holders authority to restrict nonholding individuals' speech; but copyright's purpose is clearly to subsidize the original author and to do so as a means of improving the communications order, that is, "[t]o promote the progress of science and useful arts." US Const, Art I, § 8, cl 8. Possibly a broad noncommercial "fair use" provision is constitutionally required in order to take the "autonomy," as opposed to the commercial, sting out of the restriction.

[43] "Maybe" because in some notions of undistorted public debate, the government must restrict sources that have already had their share of speech opportunities in order to prevent their dominance from "distorting" debate. More generally, the meaning of "distortion" is very much derivative of the nature of debate that the commentator favors for independent normative reasons.

[44] Corporate communications do not further "what some have considered to be the principal function of the First Amendment, the use of communication as a means of self-expression, self-realization and self-fulfillment." 435 US 765, 804 (1978). The dissenting position has arguably prevailed given the questionable current validity of *Bellotti*. Compare *Austin v Michigan State Chamber of Commerce*, 494 US 652 (1990).

Amendment. On this view, the difference between individuals and collective entities is basic. Respect for individual autonomy requires respect for individuals' expressive choices. But in a secular age, the same does not follow for the choices of legally created entities like governments or business enterprises or most other artificial entities.

The important exception is that respect for individual autonomy requires protection for expressive or solidarity associations. People create and join expressive or solidarity associations in part to embody or further their values. These collectivities draw their normative significance from their role in people's lives and from the voluntary allegiance of its members.[45] This voluntary basis means that these associations could (even if they often do not) exist even independent of coercive power or of legal structuring. Unlike either governmental or market-oriented entities, functioning of these collective entities does not inherently depend on exercising legally based instrumental power over others—for example, their internal functioning does not necessarily depend on the purely instrumental use of property within exchange transactions.

Of course, often even these associations employ corporate forms and various other legally established options—for instance, in their tax treatment. Arguably, respect for autonomy requires that those institutional forms that society makes generally available must also be available for use by these autonomy-based associations—except where the associations are exercising instrumental power over others. Thus, regulations aimed at controlling their expression when they take a corporate form or restrictions imposed on other legal benefits received by these expressive or solidarity associations should normally be viewed as unconstitutional conditions restric-

---

[45] The Court, speaking through Justice Brennan, made this distinction in striking down regulations of voluntary, noncommercial associations' political speech, *FEC v Massachusetts' Citizens for Life*, 479 US 238 (1986), despite later upholding similar regulations of commerce-related entities. *Austin v Michigan State Chamber of Commerce*, 494 US 652 (1990). See also *FEC v Nat'l. Right to Work Comm.*, 459 US 197 (1982). The dissents in *Austin* can be read in part to object to the Court's unwillingness to adopt a marketplace-of-ideas understanding of the First Amendment. But in line with Brennan's distinction, the Court has never suggested that the constitutionally based freedom of association applies to the typical commercial entity.

Elsewhere, I defended a theoretical justification for this distinction—and also argued that autonomy is not at stake in most definitions or regulations of property rights, especially when the law restricts instrumental uses of property oriented toward market transactions. C. Edwin Baker, *Property and Its Relation to Constitutionally Protected Liberty*, 134 U Pa L Rev 741 (1986).

tive of individuals' expressive freedom. Nevertheless, the normative differences between these collectivities and those entities
addressed by this article and the borders of the category are
complexities that are beyond the scope of this discussion.[46] I flag
the category here only to emphasize that they are not covered by
this article's discussion of legally created collective entities.

In its many, varied discussions of free speech, the Court invokes
both the premise of individual liberty and of the marketplace of
ideas. A plausible view is that the Court treats the two as overlap-
ping, nonexclusive bases for constitutional protection of speech. If
so, possibly the first premise could lead to basically absolute protection when it is truly at stake, while the second only justifies a
weighing of values.[47] This is not the place to make an extensive
defense of the liberty conception.[48] However, some recent judicial
trends arguably reveal a willingness to allow the political process,
itself ideally an embodiment of liberty, to prevail over challenges
based only on the marketplace of ideas. This explains, for example,
rejection of constitutional claims to access to governmentally controlled information and reduced protection of corporate speech
both in the political arena[49] and the commercial realm.[50]

The perspective of people's *autonomy as speakers* views regulation
of individuals, for whom autonomy is directly at stake, differently
than regulation of collective entities. But government can also disrespect *listeners' autonomy*, for example, by paternalistically concluding that people should not receive certain information. Many
of the best First Amendment scholars who have treated autonomy

---

[46] Many of these issues are discussed in Baker, *Human Liberty* (cited in note 24); Baker, 134 U Pa L Rev 741 (cited in note 45); Dan-Cohen, 79 Cal L Rev 1229 (cited in note 24).

[47] When the dissent in *Bellotti* claimed that "[i]deas that are not a product of individual choice are entitled to less First Amendment protection," 435 US at 807, it significantly said "less," not "no," protection. This fairly accurately summarizes existing judicial precedent. Among recent members of the Court, Justice Brennan has been perhaps most explicit in defending this two-level approach. See, e.g., *Herbert v Lando*, 441 US 153, 183–87 (1979) (Brennan dissenting).

[48] See Baker, *Human Liberty* (cited in note 24).

[49] *Austin v Michigan State Chamber of Commerce*, 494 US 652 (1990); *FEC v Massachusetts' Citizens for Life*, 479 US 238 (1986).

[50] *Posadas de Puerto Rico Associates v Tourism Company*, 478 US 328 (1986), faithfully followed the dicta in *Central Hudson v Public Service Comm'n*, 447 US 557 (1980). There, the Court approved suppressing a corporation's truthful speech, i.e., about use of electrical power, if its promotional speech conflicted with the government's important interest in energy conservation. See also *United States v Edge Broadcasting*, 113 S Ct 2696 (1993).

as normatively central have had listener autonomy in mind—and this easily leads to the conclusion that the source of the speech is irrelevant.[51] However, why these theorists focus on the listener's autonomy is not immediately clear. After all, speech is what *speakers* do. Often speakers and writers engage in verbal activities without any concern for an audience. Some diarists are even distressed to have an audience—especially if the audience turns out to be the FBI or a Congressional committee. And certainly without speakers, listeners' autonomy is irrelevant. Moreover, the listener's desire to hear something seldom gives her the right to hear it unless some speaker has both the right (or bureaucratically defined duty) and desire to talk.[52]

Of course, the marketplace-of-ideas paradigm emphasizes the listener perspective. Sometimes an emphasis on listener autonomy may reflect an unthinking acceptance of the primacy of the marketplace paradigm of the value of speech. Alternatively, the emphasis on the listener could reflect an attempt to identify something special about speech. From the speaker's "actor" perspective, arguably speech is not especially different from other exercises of self-expressive liberty. But from the listener's second-party perspective, a communication has a relatively unique manner and type of impact. The listener is typically affected only through mental

---

[51] The best example is T. M. Scanlon, Jr., *A Theory of Freedom of Expression*, 1 Phil & Pub Aff 204 (1972).

[52] Some cases (of which I approve) may seem to hold the contrary. Most obviously, in *Board of Education v Pico*, 457 US 853 (1982), the Court, without a majority opinion, held that under some circumstances a school's removal of books from its library could violate the First Amendment. See also note 62. Elsewhere I have argued that *Pico* is better understood as based on the notion that school suppression of speech is impermissible than on any free-standing right to receive information, although both were suggested in Justice Brennan's plurality opinion. Baker, *Human Liberty* 171 (cited in note 24). But the principle asserted in the text generates a different issue: whether any "speaker" had a right not to have their speech suppressed. There are at least three constitutionally relevant ways to answer this question and to distinguish this suppression from, for example, the suppression of a casino's advertising. First, certainly the author (even if dead) had a right to speak and presumably, if she published her book, had a desire to reach any willing audience—that is, there is (or was) a willing speaker with a right to speak. Second, below, collective entities that are part of the press will be distinguished from other commercial entities such that suppression of speech of the former is impermissible—so that suppression of books would in any circumstances be presumptively unconstitutional. Finally, there may be entities created by the government for purposes related to expression or culture or education in which decisions as to what expression to favor or promote are and must be made but in which the purpose of suppression of ideas is sufficiently contrary to the function of the institution that it should be found impermissible in that context. Compare *FCC v League of Women Voters*, 468 US 364 (1984).

assimilation. And the listener receives something crucial for meaningful exercises of her own autonomy—information, arguments, and viewpoints. Intuitively, from the listener's perspective, these qualities distinguish the actor's speech from the actor's other activities and give listeners as a group a more general interest in the existence of freedom for communicative activity.

From the premise of listener autonomy, David Strauss derives the principle that it is presumptively impermissible for the government to suppress speech because of the bad consequences that may result if the speech persuades people.[53] The objection to suppressing persuasion is similar to the objection to lying.[54] Both attempt to manipulate listeners by denying them the information or argument that they presumably would want in order to decide how to act or what to believe. Both try to "control the audience's mental processes"—both "interfere with a person's control over her own reasoning processes."[55]

Granting the significance of listener autonomy and, for its purpose, the relevance of the speakers' identity, the question remains whether the premise of listener autonomy or the principle Strauss derives from it can do adequate constitutional work without reliance on an even more basic commitment to speaker autonomy. My suggestion is that, by itself, the premise of listener autonomy leads to too little—or to too much.

First, honoring listener autonomy could impose too great a restriction on government if it means that the government must not base a decision not to disclose information on the ground that the disclosed information would inform or persuade various listeners.

---

[53] David A. Strauss, *Persuasion, Autonomy, and Freedom of Expression*, 91 Colum L Rev 334 (1991). Since persuasion is something speakers do, it might not immediately be clear that Strauss's focus is on listener autonomy. However, Strauss argues that not allowing the listener to decide the violation of autonomy involved in suppressing speech—the violation "is taking over [listeners'] thinking processes." Id at 356. He reports that his Kantian conception of autonomy "focuses on what is happening to the listener." Id at 356 n 62. Moreover, when considering a government suppression of speech, Strauss never considers whether the speaker has autonomy rights at stake.

[54] Moreover, Strauss's conception of autonomy only encompasses persuasion as a rational process. Thus, his principle not only does not protect speech involving a false statement of fact, but it also does not protect speech that uses nonrational means of influence, sometimes not protecting speech that precipitates ill-considered reactions.

[55] Strauss, 91 Colum L Rev at 354. Interestingly, many of the less controversial exceptions to constitutional protection of speech involve lying—for example, fraud, perjury, false or misleading advertising, defamation that is knowingly (or recklessly) false. See Baker, *Human Liberty* 34, 55–68 (cited in note 24).

Certainly, private individuals often do not tell another person various things because of a concern of how the person will act—the listener might reject the speaker's job application or romantic proposal. The listener might decide to act in a manner that the speaker believes is bad for the listener or for the speaker or a third person whom the speaker cares about. Private individuals often do not disclose merely because of a fear that hearers will take the information out of context or without full consideration of its relevance, or because of an expectation that their enemies will use the information against them.

The government likewise often does not divulge information for similar reasons—sometimes even acting almost as an agent of a private person whom the information describes and whom the government suspects would not want the information disclosed. But still a potential listener may want this governmentally held information—for example, information about other people's employment or medical records, police records containing the rape victim's name, current Federal Reserve Board minutes, secret military research, Cabinet meeting notes. Strauss accepts the propriety of governmental refusals to provide some of this information, for example, to protect someone's privacy.[56] But it is difficult to see this interest in privacy, whether it is the interest of the government or the private person on whose behalf the government does not divulge, as involving much other than a fear of the consequences (either attitudinal or behavioral) of the listener having the information. Strauss's acceptance of the privacy concern amounts, I think, to a wise rejection of complete allegiance to listener autonomy. But if properly rejected here, the question becomes when and why listener autonomy should be accepted. Specifically, if government is not constitutionally required to give up information, why can it not legislatively require nondisclosure by those entities that have no autonomy rights and over which government has legitimate power.

Strauss as well as others conclude that respect for listener autonomy requires protection of commercial speech—tobacco advertising, for example.[57] Assume, however, that a commercial speaker

---

[56] Strauss, 91 Colum L Rev at 358 (cited in note 53).

[57] Id at 343–45. This conclusion follows for anyone who treats listener autonomy as central to the rationale for free speech. When Scanlon explained backing away from full allegiance to the Millian principle, which had amounted to an interpretation of listener

or other collective entity has no autonomy rights as a speaker—
Strauss does not argue otherwise and the Court has implicitly
accepted the view that they do not.[58] Then, restrictions on the
commercial entity's speech might be even easier to justify than
restrictions on access to government-held employment or medical
records. The government's rationale for restrictions could reflect
objections to the tobacco company's participation in the persuasion
process. Thus, unlike refusals to disclose government-held information, the prohibition of the corporate entity does not require a
judgment that the listener should not be persuaded to smoke or to
vote for corporate interests. This follows if the government's content restriction applies only to some speaker's, that is, to corporations' product advertising or political message. The government

autonomy, he gave as an example the benignness of regulation of tobacco and liquor advertising. T. M. Scanlon, Jr., *Content Regulation Reconsidered*, in Judith Lichtenberg, ed, *Democracy
and the Mass Media* 331, 344–52 (Cambridge, 1990). Whether Scanlon would have found his
retreat necessary if speech were protected as an aspect of speaker autonomy is less clear.

Richard Fallon suggests similar concerns. Richard H. Fallon, Jr., *Two Senses of Autonomy*,
46 Stan L Rev 875 (1994). First, Fallon distinguishes descriptive and ascriptive autonomy—
with descriptive meaning, roughly, people's actual empirical autonomy and ascriptive as a
capacity they are assumed to have for purposes of how they are to be treated. (The notion
of autonomy that I have long argued provides that the foundational premise of free speech
is, in Fallon's terms, "ascriptive," although I have also argued that respect for ascriptive
autonomy, at least for adults, will in the long run turn out to contribute meaningfully to
promotion of descriptive autonomy.) Then Fallon also argues that ascriptive autonomy (but
not descriptive) favors protecting cigarette advertising or other forms of commercial speech.
Id at 878, 901. Unless he holds the surprising view that ascriptive autonomy is something
that tobacco companies can claim, he too here apparently adopts a listener-based conception
of autonomy. Without any notion of inconsistency, however, Fallon clearly identifies ascriptive autonomy with the speaker in other places. Id at 897.

Many practices further (or undermine) descriptive autonomy—good education, nurturing
communities, availability of resources. Debates about most public policies could be styled as
presenting contrasting views about which policy better contributes to descriptive autonomy.
Thus, the concept is inevitably too contested and too comprehensive to serve usefully as a
source of constitutional principle even if it is an appropriate aim of governmental policy.
On the other hand, ascriptive autonomy refers to a type of respect the government must
accord the individual as it adopts policies that pursue, among other things, descriptive
autonomy. Respect for ascriptive autonomy would not be at stake in most governmental
choices but, when it is, it could operate as a principled side constraint on democratic choice.

Of course, this does not imply that ascriptive and descriptive autonomy are entirely
unrelated. Possibly, only a society of descriptively relatively autonomous people would
want or be able to establish a society that respected ascriptive autonomy. Likewise, the
appeal of ascriptive autonomy as a constraint on government action would lose considerable
force as doubts arise about its long-term contribution to a form of social life in which
descriptive autonomy flourishes.

[58] In cases where commercial speakers received constitutional protection, the Court eschewed any speaker autonomy justification and premised protection on a marketplace-of-
ideas or a listener-oriented "public debate" rationale. See, e.g., *Virginia State Bd. of Pharmacy
v Virginia Citizens Consumer Council*, 425 US 748 (1976); *First Natl. Bank v Bellotti*, 435 US
765 (1978).

could explain that it did not want "that" self-interested entity to participate in the process of persuasion. This justification, however, must fail if applied to speakers (even if self-interested) whose autonomy, whose freedom of speech, the government must respect.

Unfortunately, this analysis of listener autonomy is tricky. The restrictions do reflect the government's concern with consequences of persuasion. The government concludes that legitimate interests are furthered if the listener does not receive the information or advocacy. The government, however, argues that its attempt to influence "the audience's mental process" is equivalent to an attempt improve the communications environment with which the audience engages. And, of course, sculpting the communications environment is something the government often does—by promoting education, by engaging in speech itself, by subsidizing both popular discourse and scholarly research, which also are intended to influence audience's mental processes. All these activities (as well as government's refusal to disclose certain information and its regulation of commercial speech) reflect the judgment that the set of communications people receive will influence their choices.

Since there is no natural set of communications to receive, the government will inevitably influence and ought to self-consciously and wisely influence the communications that people receive. Although both refused disclosure and restrictions on commercial speech deny the audience information out of concern for consequences, in neither case does the government prohibit the listener's receipt of the information. Rather, the government judges that the likelihood of negative consequences justifies exercising control over itself and entities without their own basis to claim autonomy and restricting the participation of both in creating the information environment that contributes to these bad consequences. Nevertheless, if individuals (or media entities) have the information or maintain the viewpoint that the government or corporations do not supply, they still can speak. They can publish drug price information[59] or advocate smoking their favorite brand. Or they can disclose to any interested listener the name of the rape victim, the content of the Pentagon papers, or the content of nonadmissible confessions.

But if respect for listener autonomy allows government nondis-

---

[59] *Virginia Bd. of Pharmacy*, 425 US at 782–83 (Rehnquist dissenting).

closure and regulation of commercial speech because of concern with the consequences and allows the government to provide public education and support for culture out of hopes for consequences, what does respect for listener autonomy rule out? It could mean that the government cannot justify preventing a listener from receiving communications that the government, despite its structuring responsibilities, has no right to stop even if it fears bad consequences. But what would those communications be? The obvious answer would be communications that reflect speakers' autonomy (or media communications, which, I will argue below, receive special constitutional protection).

The above discussion does not disavow the necessity of respect for listener autonomy. Rather, it claims that if the premise of listener autonomy means that the government can never make choices on the basis of predictions of negative (or positive) consequences flowing from certain information or advocacy, then the premise leads to too much and too indeterminate protection of speech. That is, this broad conception of respect for listener autonomy would prevent the government from denying the listener information even if on balance it concludes that the speech does not contribute to the good and even if it is acting either as a speaker[60] or as a regulator of entities that have no autonomy rights.

Instead, in its more defensible, modest form, listener autonomy must be respected but doctrinally adds very little to speaker autonomy. It combines with speaker autonomy to require that government not block speech from an (ascriptively[61]) autonomous speaker to an (ascriptively) autonomous listener out of fear of the consequences of persuasion. In this account, however, listener autonomy offers very little protection without prior invocation of speaker autonomy.[62] And speaker autonomy usually would require the pro-

---

[60] This does not mean that government secrecy is generally acceptable. Often governments refuse to provide information for "corrupt" or illegitimate reasons—such as fear that disclosures will reveal their misfeasance or malfeasance. More often, bureaucracies' almost instinctual attempts to maintain secrecy are practically unwarranted—not because bad on principle but because the secrecy reflects typical bureaucratic distortions in the calculation of the beneficial and harmful effects of disclosure. Laws like the Freedom of Information Act, 5 USC § 552, are appropriate responses to this problem.

[61] See note 57.

[62] If the speaker did not have protected rights, the notion of listener autonomy might require that the government regulate the speaker, not the listener. See, e.g., *Lamont v Postmaster General*, 381 US 301 (1965); cf *Meese v Keene*, 481 US 465 (1987). Although the

tection on its own. Moreover, not only does the premise of listener autonomy add little, it also is surely inadequate by itself for First Amendment theory. It does not, for example, protect speakers from forced avowals such as mandatory flag salutes.[63]

In sum, analytically, structural regulation of the individual, to the extent the notion is meaningful, is usually objectionable except in the sense of recognizing a person's authority over her self, her mind and body. In contrast, structural regulation of instrumentally created, collective entities in ways that affect their speech is unavoidable. When this regulation purposely influences speech, it should be seen as little different from establishing baselines or providing subsidies for favored communications or favored communicators. Its inevitability means that this regulatory structural intervention cannot be automatically problematic from a normative perspective. A marketplace-of-ideas perspective, however, might object to intervention that has the purpose of suppressing some expression (as opposed to regulation that has that effect in the context of promoting something else). In contrast, from a perspective that emphasizes either speaker autonomy or (more controversially) an appropriately limited listener autonomy, even regulatory suppression of communication by collective entities is usually unproblematic.

For example, neither a ban on corporate political speech nor a targeted restriction on casino advertising prevents autonomous individuals from speaking or autonomous individuals from hearing these speakers. Rather, these bans represent policy judgments concerning the appropriate role of these legally created corporate entities. The judgment is that, just as society sometimes benefits from government not providing certain information, society sometimes benefits from restricting these entities' informational and advocacy roles. At least since the demise of *Lochner*, the government can decide that a commercial entity serves society only on certain con-

---

area is unsettled, the Court in *Pearson v Dodd*, 410 F2d 701 (DC Cir 1969), in effect protected the listener when it denied liability for publication of information *received* from a speaker who had tortiously obtained the information. Also, whether the First Amendment permits regulation of the speech of an ascriptively autonomous speaker assumed not to have standing to object is a separate issue. See *Kleindienst v Mandel*, 408 US 753 (1972). Cf *Lamont v Woods*, 948 F2d 825 (2d Cir 1991).

[63] *West Virginia Bd. of Ed. v Barnette*, 319 US 624 (1943).

ditions. These policies embody structural judgments about the appropriate role in social life of collective entities created and given power under collectively established rules.

B. MEDIA ENTITIES

If the First Amendment only minimally restrains regulation of collective entities, what about media entities? The "press" is the only business to receive explicit constitutional protection.[64] Although some constitutional issues require a choice among theories of the constitutional role of the press, all these theories include the view that the press should provide the public with information and opinion uncensored by government. This distinguishes the press from other legally created collective entities.

In accord with an autonomy-focused interpretation of free speech, current doctrine allows the government to restrict the speech of most commercial entities in order to improve the wisdom of individual decision making or the quality or fairness of public debate. In contrast, the government cannot suppress press communications on this rationale.[65] Laws aimed at restricting either the press' expression or an individual's autonomously chosen expression should be, even if for different reasons, equally impermissible. In this respect, constitutional doctrine radically distinguishes the press from other collective entities.[66]

In contrast, media entities are like other commercial entities and unlike individuals in being inevitably structured by law.[67] These structural choices often reflect policies unrelated to the communications order, such as efficiency in capital structures, fairness in employee relations, preservation of the environment, or maintenance

---

[64] See, e.g., Justice Potter Stewart, *"Or of the Press,"* 26 Hastings L J 631 (1975).

[65] See, e.g., *Mills v Alabama,* 384 US 214 (1966).

[66] There is plenty of language, usually in dissents or concurrences, rejecting this dichotomy, but this rejection is uniformly made in support of greater protection for commercial entities rather than to favor reduced protection of the press. See, e.g., *Austin v Michigan Chamber of Commerce,* 494 US 652, 691–92 (1990) (Scalia dissenting); *First Natl. Bank v Bellotti,* 435 US 765, 795-802 (1978) (Burger concurring).

[67] Any suggestion that the choice of structures can be left entirely to private actors arranging their affairs on the basis of contract ignores that both the content of contract law and the availability of the option to enter obligatory or legally enforceable contracts reflect policy choices and that these choices cannot be justified on any neutral or abstract economic grounds. Compare Duncan Kennedy and Frank Michelman, *Are Property and Contract Efficient?* 8 Hofstra L Rev 711 (1979–1980).

of ethics. Nevertheless, the government has also always engaged in regulation to advance its conception of a desirable communications order—a conception that includes promotion of viewpoint diversity, quality of discourse, education, and ease of participation. A democracy concerned with promoting collective conceptions of the good arguably requires this form of regulation.

The question is whether it is proper to advance these policies with media-specific laws.[68] As I show in Part III, structural choices aimed specifically at the media, typically motivated and justified on the basis of content concerns, have been common in American history. On the rare occasions when these structural rules have been challenged, they have consistently been upheld by the Court. The legitimacy of a democracy's concern with the effective functioning of the communications order offers prima facie support for media-specific regulation. Moreover, two features that typically prompt objection to content regulation of individuals—first, that choices and speech of individuals can plausibly be thought to have intrinsic value and, second, that individuals are conceptualized as significant entities independent of legal structuring—are both absent in institutions that are valued only instrumentally in relation to how they contribute to human flourishing and that are inevitably subject to legal structuring.

Of course, attempts to undermine press performance are invalid under any regime of freedom of the press. Still, media-specific laws could support the press in performing its constitutional roles.[69] Since only instrumental arguments could be the basis of objecting to media-specific structural regulation, presumably the argument must be that an appropriate distrust of government's motives or wisdom in enacting structural regulation combined with a sufficient lack of confidence in courts' ability to identify cases where the law undermines rather than aids press performance outweigh the

---

[68] In response to the claim that the must-carry rules should be upheld as industry-specific antitrust regulations, the Court commented that the cases cited by the government involved laws of general application and "that laws that single out the press, or certain elements thereof, for special treatment 'pose a particular danger of abuse' . . . and so are always subject to at least some degree of heightened First Amendment scrutiny." 114 S Ct 2458 (citations omitted). But the Court also said: "As Leathers illustrates, the fact that a law singles out a certain medium, or even the press as a whole, "is insufficient by itself to raise First Amendment concerns." Id at 2468 (citation omitted).

[69] See C. Edwin Baker, *Private Power, the Press, and the Constitution*, 10 Const Comm 421 (1993).

potential gains to media performance from media-specific laws. Although such a conclusion is possible, neither American history nor prior judicial judgments supports such a negative view.

Before elaborating on these claims in Part III, I want to turn to the principle that both the majority and dissent believed could be determinative in *Turner*—that must-carry rules would be substantially discredited if content-based.

C. CONTENT QUESTIONS

The Court in *Turner* began its account of the normative basis of the content-based/content-neutral doctrine by asserting: "At the heart of the First Amendment lies the principle that *each person should decide* for him or herself the ideas and beliefs deserving of expression, consideration, and adherence."[70] Despite the Court's assumption to the contrary, my claim is that the Court's individual-choice notion of the "heart" of free speech does not support objections to content-motivated structural regulation of media enterprises.

The "heart" is fundamental. Apparently, both the First Amendment and the special objection to content-based laws somehow embody or support the principle of each person deciding for herself about matters of expression, reflection, and commitment. They might do so in either or both of two ways: directly by empowering speakers or indirectly by empowering listeners. The constitutional guarantee protects the speaker's choice to speak and may aid listeners in obtaining the information that will make their subsequent expression and commitments meaningful.

First, if the government mandates or prohibits speech, it violates speaker's free choice. The Court's citation to *Barnette* and *Cohen* as support for personal choice being at the heart of the First Amendment was apt.[71] Personal choice is central to why a person cannot be forced to swear allegiance to the flag. And as the Court said in relation to the person wearing a jacket emblazoned with "Fuck the Draft": "[the constitutional right of free expression] put[s] the decision as to what views shall be voiced largely into the hands of each of us, . . . in the belief that no other approach would comport

---

[70] 114 S Ct at 2458 (emphasis added, citing *Barnette* and *Leathers* citing *Cohen*).
[71] Id.

with the premise of individual dignity and choice upon which our political system rests."[72]

Analytically, the individual choice central to *speaker* autonomy could not be offended by content-based or any other structural regulation of legally created collective entities. The Court's theoretical introduction to its First Amendment discussion even used some language that might suggest that it recognized that this concern for speaker choice does not automatically extend to media entities. It began with "each person" deciding. After elaborating for three sentences, the Court started the next paragraph with: "For these reasons, the First Amendment . . . does not countenance governmental control over the content of messages expressed by private *individuals*."[73]

The Court, however, added to this emphasis on individual speaker choice another concern that might relate more to listeners' decision making. It referred to the "risk that the Government seeks . . . [to] manipulate public debate through coercion rather than persuasion;" to " 'the specter that the Government may effectively drive certain ideas or viewpoints from the marketplace;' " and to the "risk of excising certain ideas or viewpoints from the public dialogue."[74] These references might explain objections to content-based laws that are directed at collective entities, especially media entities.

These statements could be forced into the mold of a concern for speaker autonomy, for example, if the normatively relevant conception of public debate and dialogue were equated with the unconstrained dialogic participation of individuals in an attempt to reach agreement. Then, any regulation of speakers that risked "driving out" or "excising" *their* viewpoints from public dialogue would deny them their participation rights as well as undermine the legitimacy of conclusions reached through public dialogue. Still, these references, as well as the Court's uncritical application of content-discrimination doctrine to the issue of must-carry rules, suggest a concern with the listener benefiting from an undistorted public debate. Moreover, as asserted in the last section, special

---

[72] *Cohen v California*, 403 US 15, 24 (1971).

[73] 114 S Ct at 2458 (emphasis added).

[74] Id (the second statement quoting *Simon & Schuster v New York State Crime Victims Bd.*, 502 US 105 (1991)).

protection of press enterprises exists precisely to provide listeners with information and ideas. Thus, maybe the concern with content-based laws represents a First Amendment theory focused on the listener as well as (or rather than) the speaker. If so, maybe content-based laws directed at collective entities, or at least at media entities, should be treated the same as laws concerning individuals. Content discrimination would be equally objectionable in both cases.

In this listener perspective, the evil would be that content-based laws distort public debate. This view has substantial support. Geoffrey Stone, in the classic article on the content-based/content-neutral doctrine, defends the doctrine because, "properly defined and understood," it sufficiently serves several fundamental First Amendment values.[75] Stone credits three of the four considerations that he identifies as possible explanations of the constitutional problem with content- (or least viewpoint) based laws.[76] The third, distortion of public debate, might apply irrespective of the speaker to any content-based laws, and, thus, apply to the must-carry rules.[77]

Stone repeatedly refers to distortion—for example, arguing that the First Amendment is concerned with distortion of "public debate" perhaps "more fundamentally" than with "the total quantity of communications."[78] Initially, this concern with distortion seems to offer little justification for special treatment of content-based

---

[75] Geoffrey R. Stone, *Content Regulation and the First Amendment*, 25 Wm & Mary L Rev 189, 251 (1983).

[76] Despite the attention it had received, Stone observed that the notion of equality standing alone could not justify the content discrimination doctrine. Id at 201–07. Roughly, the point is that laws always make distinctions. The issue must be what substantive equality norm does a law offend. See C. Edwin Baker, *Neutrality, Process, and Rationality: Flawed Interpretations of Equal Protection*, 58 Tex L Rev 1029 (1980). This means the objection to the content discrimination must lie in the offense to some substantive norm, which leads to Stone's other three concerns.

Other than distortion of public debate, discussed above, Stone's two other justifications for the content discrimination doctrine are that content discrimination often reflects paternalistic concerns with speech's communicative impact, which is usually an objectionable basis for a restriction, and that it often reflects an improper motive to restrict speech with which the government disagrees.

[77] Stone's category of content-based laws are those that are content-based on their face and, thus, does not immediately apply to must-carry rules. He describes content-neutral laws that have a content-based purpose as raising separate issues that result in their sometimes but not always generating serious first amendment concerns. Stone, *Content Regulation* at 234–39 (cited in note 75).

[78] Id at 198. See also id at 200, 212.

laws because content-neutral laws often have significant content-differential effects. Moreover, many content-based laws leave plenty of channels open for the disfavored content and, therefore, have only modest content-based effects. Stone suggests, however, that content-based laws pose a greater danger of being used improperly to distort. Eventually, he argues that this danger and the significant difficulty of identifying objectionable content-based laws provide support for the doctrine.[79] Nevertheless, he never explained, but merely assumed (as do the courts and many other commentators), that distortion of public debate is a "fundamental" First Amendment evil and that the concept has sufficient content to justify judicial intervention.

There is no "natural" version of public dialogue that the First Amendment could prohibit the government from distorting. The content and quality of public dialogue depend on many factors, including the overall legal order and legally established resource allocations. It reflects the societal resources devoted to education or to places of dialogue and the wealth legally placed into the hands of people who do or do not wish to engage in particular ways in public dialogue. The government even participates, massively and purposefully, in the debate itself.

A critic of content discrimination cannot reply that the government's huge impact on public dialogue is unfortunate and should be avoided to the extent possible. Democratic theory requires a government role. Since all laws inevitably favor some conceptions of the good over others, rationality virtually requires that the choice of laws turn in part on collective notions of the good. Indeed, one purpose of democratic government is to provide for collective means to promote conceptions of the good in contexts where individual decision making would be inadequate for realizing the chosen conceptions. (Of course, the legitimacy of collective promotions of favored conceptions does not justify suppressing dissenting views and alternative conceptions.) In this regard, government ought to promote—that is, structure institutions in a manner that would promote—a collectively valued communications order. And

---

[79] Id at 217–27. Arguably, Stone portrays avoidance of distortion as weaker than other supports for the doctrine. But he repeatedly refers to it both here and in other treatments of content discrimination. See, e.g., Geoffrey R. Stone, *Restrictions of Speech Because of Its Content: The Peculiar Case of Subject-Matter Restrictions*, 42 U Chi L Rev 81, 101–03, 107 (1978).

it should participate in the communications order to noncoercively advance collective conceptions of the good.

Of course, the appropriate content and manner of government participation is always politically contested. After reflection, however, virtually no one argues that government participation should be entirely eliminated. The government selects what information to develop in government studies, to foster with government research grants, and to publicize in government publications. It also often promotes specific viewpoints. Public schools teach, or at least claim to teach, community values—and often carefully avoid teaching marxism or fascism.[80] Schools may even be constitutionally required to be partisan on the issue of racism. The Surgeon General advances the view that smoking is bad. The Defense Department promotes enlistment, while other government agencies sometimes advocate conservation.[81] Sometimes the government simplistically participates on the side of "just say[ing] no."

Government's recognized role in structuring society in ways that affect public dialogue and its discretionary participation in that dialogue make it unclear why anything called "distortion" could be constitutionally objectionable. These facts also mean that there can be no standard with which to compare the effect of governmental policies in order to describe these effects as "distortions." But if distortion cannot lie merely in the fact or the effect of government involvement, it is unclear how distortion of "public dialogue" can be identified.[82] Certainly, if it is to be more than a constitutional

---

[80] All members of the Court apparently agree that it is proper for schools to teach community values. See, e.g., *Hazelwood School District v Kuhlmeier*, 484 US 260 (1988). I put aside here the question of the Constitutional basis of the principle of academic freedom as well as its content and the possible variable application depending on level of instruction or other contextual factors.

[81] Surely all these examples involve the government is promoting particular viewpoints. Moreover, although a court held that during the Vietnam War enlistment was not a controversial issue, *Green v FCC*, 405 F2d 1082 (DC Cir 1971), other governmental viewpoints, like conservation, are quite controversial. See David Helvarg, *The War on Greens*, The Nation 646 (Nov 28, 1994).

[82] In defending the view that distorting public debate is the prime evil the First Amendment should be interpreted to prevent (the Distortion model) and that the First Amendment requires "a rigidly enforced official government neutrality," Lillian BeVier never explains how such distortion can be identified (or why it is bad). Lillian R. BeVier, *Rehabilitating Public Forum Doctrine: In Defense of Categories*, 1992 Supreme Court Review 79, 102. She rules out most of the obvious, but as she recognizes, "naive" notions of neutrality. Id at 103 n 96. Certainly, once the permissibility (and desirability) of government speech is recognized, the notion of improper distortion will either become vacuous or, as I argue below, turn on an independent normative basis (involving commitments BeVier seeks to avoid) for objecting to certain ways in which the government affects public debate.

epithet, there must be some way to distinguish "distortion" from "purposefully influence." It is hardly obvious that this distinction will turn on whether the government's intervention was content-based.

The above discussion understood "distortion" as an objectionable "effect" the government action has on public dialogue. This view is logical if the concern is with listeners' opportunities to make intelligent, some might say, "autonomous" decisions. Ideally the issue should be the government's effect on listeners getting the information and viewpoints they need. Undistorted communications could be complete information and all viewpoints—or, at least, all the information and viewpoints the listener would find relevant and could reasonably assimilate. Any government action that detracts from this information set could be called distortion. More modestly, recognizing that complete or even adequate information is impossible, distortion might be any *government* influence on the information that people receive—although it is not clear why this "distortion" is always bad. In any event, neither conception can be the referent for a constitutional critique. Completeness of information is never possible, and virtually everything the government does will affect the information available to listeners— often in ways that aid some listeners but that confuse others.

The primary alternative to the "mere effects" conception of distortion is to identify distortion with objectionable *methods* of or *reasons* for affecting dialogue. This alternative, however, makes distortion a derivative concept. The primary norm is the theory that identifies "bad" methods or reasons. Given that democratic theory suggests that government often ought to be concerned with content, the government's intent to influence content cannot in itself be objectionable. However, its effect on dialogue can be called bad, hence distortive, if its method of acting violates someone's expressive rights or its purpose is to undermine a democratic press. The violated expressive right obviously cannot be the listener's right to a nondistorted communications realm because that would make the analysis overtly circular. The violated right could, however, be people's (or other entities') expressive right to participate in public debate. Any attempt to suppress this participation would be "distortion." Here the two key concepts become "people or entities with speech rights" and "suppress."

This derivative notion of distortion leads back to the earlier discussion. From the perspective of individual autonomy, suppression of expression of most legally created collective entities is usually unproblematic—except that media entities are different because of their special constitutional role. Suppression of media entities' content is objectionable—as is structural regulation aimed at undermining their constitutional role[s]. However, structural regulation of the media is not only inevitable but it should be praised when wisely designed to enhance the quantity or quality of their participation. That is, content-motivated structural regulation of the media is generally permissible and will often be affirmatively desirable. Finally, any suppression of individuals' expression is clearly impermissible.

This emphasis on speakers' rights explains the constitutional objection in paradigm content discrimination cases. The Court early concluded that grants of discretionary power to officials to permit or license expressive activities in streets, parks, or public facilities create a danger of restricting individuals' speech choices on the basis of the officials' censorial preferences. Next, given a presumption that people ought to be able to use public spaces for their expressive activities, the Court suggested that only those narrowly designed restrictions on expression necessary to prevent direct interference with government programs or other private people's activities ought to be allowed.[83] Any permission given to people presenting some content but not another, such as labor picketing in *Mosley*,[84] strongly suggests that expressive activity at that place and time does not seriously interfere with other uses of the space. And the government cannot persuasively argue that it is using its property to subsidize favored speech rather than to suppress people's expression, given that people have a right to be present at the location and to express themselves if doing so does not interfere with the location's dedicated use. Thus, permission for particular content generally means that the prohibition of other content violates the rights of those whose expression is suppressed. Hence this content discrimination is unconstitutional.

The general conceptual problem is to evaluate a government claim that it is not suppressing speech but rather that any content discrimination merely reflects some other legitimate undertaking. The government asserts that having flexibility allows it to make the

---

[83] See, e.g., *Grayned v Rockford*, 408 US 104 (1972).

[84] *Police Dept. of Chicago v Mosley*, 408 US 92 (1972).

best use of public spaces; or that it is subsidizing labor picketing, maintaining the draft registration system or the park facilities in the nation's capital,[85] trying to ensure good job performance by its employees, restraining those with a demonstrated inclination for violence at abortion clinics, or using the school's mail system for its dedicated use. Sometimes the Court allows content-discriminatory conditions. Without unraveling the unconstitutional conditions doctrine, a possible interpretation is that if the condition relates to the government's legitimate reasons for its use of its resources, the condition should be acceptable. Likewise, announcements that some facilities are "nonpublic" fora have been most legitimately used as shorthand for the conclusion that the public's general expressive use of the facility would interfere with the purposes to which the government had dedicated the facility while the permitted expressive uses specifically relate to those purposes.

One puzzle in content-discrimination doctrine is why (and whether) a law that is facially content-neutral should be treated as content-based if it has a content-based purpose. *O'Brien* may help explain the move. Although the prohibition on burning draft cards facially did not relate to expression at all, the *O'Brien* test later became the standard test for content-neutral laws.[86] But *O'Brien* scrutiny applies only to laws that are not related to the "suppression of free expression."[87] When they purposefully suppress it will typically be a content-related suppression (as was the ban on burning draft cards, according to critics of *O'Brien*'s application of its own test). And although *O'Brien* did not say explicitly what to do with such laws, presumably they normally should be struck down. In effect, they are treated just like facially content-based laws. Thus, *O'Brien* establishes the treatment for facially content neutral laws that have a content-based purpose.

The only missing step is that *O'Brien* treats the nonfacially content-based law as content-based only if it aims at *suppressing* expression. In contrast, existing doctrine, at least as described by both

---

[85] From an effects perspective and, more controversially, a speaker's rights perspective, *O'Brien* and *Clark v Community for Creative Non-Violence*, 468 US 288 (1984), involve content discrimination. See Susan H. Williams, *Content Discrimination and the First Amendment*, 139 U Pa L Rev 615 (1991).

[86] Williams, 139 U Pa L Rev 615 (cited in note 85) (criticizing the logical slippage of conflating the tests for content-neutral laws with laws not directed at expression).

[87] 391 US at 377.

the majority and dissent in *Turner*, applies even when the law is directed at favoring particular content.[88] Nevertheless, the many cases that uphold content-related conditions on protected speech show that this claim cannot be quite right.[89] Possibly, the content-discrimination doctrine is properly used only when the government's claim to be merely "subsidizing" the favored expression seems implausible; then the laws are seen as really suppressing the unfavored speech.

---

[88] Both the majority and the dissent in *Turner* emphasized that the objection to content discrimination exists whether the distinction relates to hostility or favoritism toward the content. 114 S Ct at 2458–59, 2477. Between them, they cited nine cases for the proposition that government favoritism or agreement with a message would not support content discrimination. Id. Nevertheless, support for the proposition that government favoritism for a message is objectionable is quite weak. The two cases cited by the majority merely provided dicta. In the first, *Ward v Rock Against Racism*, 491 US 781 (1989), the cited language could only be dicta since the challenged law was treated as content neutral and upheld. In the second, *R.A.V. v St. Paul*, 112 S Ct 2538 (1992), despite the statement that "[t]he government may not regulate [speech] based on hostility—or favoritism—towards the underlying message," id at 320, the challenged government practice can only be understood as suppression of a category of racist communications, not a benefit for preferred speech. In the one of the seven additional cases cited by the dissent, *Arkansas Writers' Project v Ragland*, 481 US 221, 231–32 (1987), the Court referred to pages where the Court rejected the states' purported explanation that the discriminatory tax was a subsidy for justifiably favored "fledgling publications" as so ill-fitting that the explanation was implausible. The implication was that the Court instead viewed the tax exemption as the baseline for the media and that the tax imposed a suppressive burden on a few; but it also implied that coherently structured content-based tax subsidy, for example, for "fledgling publications," might be upheld. Likewise, in the other six cases, the content discrimination should be viewed as suppression since the normal baseline ought to be free speech. Surely the normal assumption is the right to photograph, so the limitation on photographing currency was clearly suppressive. *Regan v Time*, 468 US 641, 648–49 (1984). As noted, the normal assumption is that people are free to use streets and parks (and arguably many other public facilities) for expressive purposes, so that when content-based limitations are imposed, they should be interpreted as suppressing what is not allowed rather than favoring that which is permitted. This point explains the other cited cases. *Metromedia v San Diego*, 453 US 490, 514–15 (1981) (plurality); *Carey v Brown*, 447 US 455, 466–68 (1980); *Police Dept. of Chicago v Mosley*, 408 US 92, 96 (1972); *Cox v Louisiana*, 379 US 536, 581 (1965) (Black concurring).

[89] *Hazelwood School District v Kuhlmeier*, 484 US 260 (1988) (principal censored content of paper written in connection with journalism class); *Meese v Keene*, 481 US 465 (1987) (government identification of some foreign films as "political propaganda"); *Bethel School District v Fraser*, 478 US 675 (1986) (student punished for content of his speech); *Connick v Myers*, 461 US 138 (1983) (content evaluation of employees' speech); *Perry Educ. Ass'n v Perry Local Educators' Ass'n*, 460 US 37, 48 (1983) ("[i]mplicit in the concept of the nonpublic forum is the right to make distinctions . . . on the basis of subject matter); *Lehman v Shaker Heights*, 418 US 298 (1974) (favoring commercial over political advertising on public bus). All these cases are controversial—I would argue with the result in each. My objection, however, would not be that they involved content discrimination, which I believe must be viewed as uncontroversial in the context of many government endeavors and many cases of government subsidy, but rather with the majority's characterization of what was occurring in each case. Generally, the strategy would be to show that, properly characterized, the government engaged in suppression rather than merely avoidance of support.

Thus, the real objection to laws properly invalidated as content-based should be that those laws were aimed at suppressing the expression of people who have a right of free speech or at restricting the communications of media enterprises. If this is right, the traditional doctrine needs revision. Specifically, properly interpreted, the First Amendment does not outlaw content-based subsidies of speech or content-based laws needed to make proper use of government resources or most content-based laws regulating the expression of legally created commercial entities. More relevantly here, the First Amendment allows content-*motivated* structural laws directed at the media unless the law is designed to undermine the media's functioning. It should also, although somewhat more controversially, allow even facially content-*based* laws imposed on the media as long as the law does not suppress expression or undermine the media's integrity but, rather, supports a desirable communications order. For example, the government could require broadcasters to include children-oriented programming or to cover controversial issues.

Although the above formulations summarize the analysis in this and the previous section, the scope of permitted content discrimination may seem troublingly broad. I want to note two possible modifications of the above formulations involving the arguably special category of viewpoint discrimination[90]—and tentatively approve one modification and reject the other. First, permitted content regulation or even content subsidies should arguably be limited to subject matter discriminations. Second, in any event, the government arguably should not be permitted to engage in strictly political party partisanship. The first point validly observes that viewpoint discrimination is often much more objectionable than subject matter discrimination. The second point refers to the way commentators often drive home the first point—they argue that the government surely should not be permitted to explicitly subsidize Democrats and exclude Republicans.

Of course, many laws—franking privileges, for example—favor incumbents over challengers. In practice such a law subsidizes the "view" that incumbents are worthy, a view currently at odds with

---

[90] Of course, the distinction between viewpoint and subject matter is never precise given that by stepping back the choice to consider or exclude a particular subject matter can amount to a very partisan viewpoint. See Stone, 42 U Chi L Rev 81 (cited in note 79).

the tendency for electorates to impose term limitations. Likewise, a law that private employers must pay employees for time taken off on election day may be permissible even if Democrats supported the law (in part) because of a viewpoint-based belief that the benefited workers will tend to use the time to vote Democratic.[91] And although many states do restrict local governments' support of particular positions in referendums, it is very doubtful that this is a requirement of the First Amendment as opposed to state policy choices. Should the First Amendment be understood to prohibit local school boards from promoting favorable votes in referendums on their proposed budget or local governments from lobbying their state legislature for benefits for the city? If allowed, however, the government will have purposively favored obviously controversial viewpoints. Moreover, even though it seems unacceptable for the government to require private employers to give out leaflets saying, "Vote Republican—Vote for Jones," it may be very appropriate to require that they pass out literature discussing fair employment practices or environmentally sound operating procedures, even though in both cases the literature may represent viewpoints, in fact, viewpoints with which the corporate managers or owners and some other members of the public strongly disagree.

These observations lead to the following suggestion. Just as many imaginable regulations are not only economically stupid but sometimes politically offensive without being unconstitutional, most viewpoint-oriented subsidies and viewpoint regulation of non-media entities that cannot claim autonomy rights as speakers should be constitutionally permissible.

As for media entities, the argument becomes somewhat more complicated. Arguably, none of the many content-motivated regulations and only some of the content-based regulations of the media (for example, a requirement that television include children-oriented programming), some of which I will discuss in the next section, have been overtly viewpoint-based. The requirement that structural or nonsuppressive content regulation of the media is proper only if it does not undermine the media's democratic functions permits regulations designed to improve the communications order, but, it could be persuasively argued, viewpoint regulation will never (or seldom) pass this test. Thus, for the media, content

---

[91] Compare *Day-Brite Lighting v Missouri*, 342 US 421 (1952).

regulation not only must not be aimed at suppression, but also must not be viewpoint-based.[92]

Finally, the narrower objection to overt, narrowly partisan, candidate-oriented subsidies or regulation seems right. However, the difference between this objectionable viewpoint regulation and the regulations and subsidies that I have argued should be allowed seems solely that objectionable regulation relates to partisan candidate support within the electoral process, not to any general principle about speech or government's viewpoint favoritism. Thus, arguably the First Amendment is the wrong text from which to object. The most obvious problem with government providing partisan support for its own entrenchment is that this violates any plausible conception of republican government. Of course, the Guarantee Clause has been generally assumed to raise only nonjusticiable political questions.[93] If this doctrine continues, the partisanship may still be a denial of equal protection—it violates a fundamental right of electoral fairness.[94] However, even if the objection is located in First Amendment–based requirements on the electoral process,[95] it hardly represents a general objection to viewpoint discrimination.

III. The Grand Tradition: Content-Motivated Structural Regulation of the Communications Order

Often discussion of the constitutionality of media-specific structural regulation narrowly limits itself to invoking *Tornillo* (and occasionally the newspaper tax cases[96]). It then concludes that structural regulation, especially content-based regulation, is unconstitutional. Finally, *Red Lion* (and sometimes a few other broadcast regulation cases[97]) is cited for the proposition that, as long as physi-

---

[92] Of course, the government can pay to have a viewpoint included in the media as an advertisement, but in that case it is clearly the government's speech that is being circulated.

[93] See *Pacific States Telephone & Telegraph v Oregon*, 223 US 118 (1912); *Luther v Borden*, 7 How 1 (1849).

[94] Compare *Williams v Rhodes*, 393 US 23 (1968).

[95] Compare *Anderson v Celebreeze*, 460 US 780 (1983).

[96] E.g., *Grosjean v Am. Press Co.*, 297 US 233 (1936); *Minneapolis Star and Tribune Co. v Minn. Comm'r Revenue*, 460 US 575 (1983).

[97] E.g., *NBC v United States*, 319 US 190 (1943) (upholding the chain broadcasting rules against constitutional attack). Since scarcity obviously cannot justify restricting what is broadcast, *FCC v Pacifica Foundation*, 438 US 726 (1978) (upholding regulation of indecency), is seldom cited in this context. *Pacifica*, whatever the merits of the decision, is best analogized to *Young v Am. Mini Theatres*, 427 US 50 (1976), rather than other broadcast cases.

cal scarcity is accepted as distinguishing broadcasting from other media, broadcasting will be treated as different. This approach is summarized as presenting a dominant newspaper model and a secondary broadcasting model.

In this section I develop three points in challenging this conventional view and argue that the United States has consistently and properly engaged in content-motivated structuring of the communications realm. First, the conventional view encompasses too narrow a conception of communications media; given a broader conception, the ubiquity of content-oriented regulation becomes apparent and, despite often especially benefiting politically powerful industrial interests, it has usually also benefited the nation. Second, broadcasting regulation is not unique, and the conventional view's interpretation of its constitutional basis is misleading. Third, the conventional view is also wrong to assert that structural regulation of newspapers is impermissible.

A. TELEPHONE AND MAIL

Even adding magazines, books, music productions, cable, and theater to the usual focus on newspapers and broadcasting leaves too narrow an image of the communications order. The telephone and postal systems, for example, are major communications industries. Their function is communication. Their usage creates culture, generates public opinion, and provides personally and politically salient communications. And unlike noncommercial, face-to-face speech between individuals, the telephone and mail systems are institutionally structured media that normally sell their services.

Of course, the telephone and postal systems are usually conceived as strictly conduits of others' speech—but it need not be this way. Both enterprises could assert "editorial" power to "censor" the speech they deliver. Historically, the postal system usually denies mail privileges for speech considered illegal—that is, obscene or treasonous material—but it has also claimed the right to restrict mailing privileges to other speech or material of which the government disapproves.[98] Likewise, the phone company recently as-

---

[98] Compare *Hannegan v Esquire*, 327 US 146, 150 (1946) (rejecting postmaster's claim to deny second-class mailing privileges to nonobscene material because it did not "contribute to the public good and the public welfare").

serted an interest in control of messages delivered over its lines. The Court of Appeals upheld the company's decision to exclude constitutionally protected "adult entertainment."[99] Of course, the most profitable use of their facilities will generally favor allowing anyone who will pay the charge to use the facility for their speech.[100]

Whether any media will seek to exercise editorial control is a historically contingent matter. In the initial stages, AT&T expected broadcasting to develop without editorial control. As an operator of radio stations AT&T planned "to provide no programs" but rather to create a phone booth of the air. "Anyone who had a message for the world or wished to entertain was to come in and pay their money as they would upon coming into a telephone booth . . . ."[101] Similarly, some accounts of eighteenth-century press ideology suggest that the press thought it had an essentially common carrier obligation under which it would be inconsistent with freedom of the press not to print all views.[102] Essentially, these providers of a communication service gave a different answer to the question, "freedom for whom?" than do modern newspaper corporations.[103] Freedom of broadcasting or the press would be for anyone who had something to say (and would pay the charge) over the medium. Certainly, law as well as economic conditions that are themselves reflective of law will influence the form these historically contingent developments will take.

Thus, telephone companies, like newspapers, could argue that

---

[99] *Carlin Communications v Mountain States Telephone & Telegraph*, 827 F2d 1291, 1294 (9th Cir 1987). The Court allowed the telephone company to accede to the heckler's veto, concluding that the exclusion did not violate common carrier obligations because done for business reasons. See also *Carlin Communication v Southern Bell Telephone & Telegraph*, 802 F2d 1352 (11th Cir 1986).

[100] Although newspapers' acceptance of advertising resembles this pattern, newspapers as currently constituted also find it profitable to engage in reporting, story writing, and editing—and they use their editorial power to exclude some advertising, and these exclusions are often economically advantageous.

[101] Erik Barnouw, *A Tower in Babel: A History of Broadcasting in the United States* 106 (Oxford, 1966) (quoting AT&T's Lloyd Espenschied). See also Robert W. McChesney, *Telecommunications, Mass Media, & Democracy* 12–15 (Oxford, 1993). McChesney noted that AT&T's success was undermined by other stations giving away time.

[102] "Newspapers were to be open channels of public communication, and 'publick printers' were to be just that: printers, not editors. This impartiality was itself one meaning of the term *liberty of the press*." John Nerone, *Violence Against the Press: Policing the Public Sphere in U.S. History* 22 (Oxford, 1994).

[103] Compare Jerome A. Barron, *Freedom of the Press for Whom?* (Indiana, 1973).

their business is communications and that they therefore should have full First Amendment rights.[104] Certainly some regulations of the telephone or mail systems can violate the First Amendment. The Court has indicated wariness of any ban of constitutionally protected expression in either.[105] Nevertheless, usually the constitutional objection, even the regulation of privately owned telephone systems, is that the restriction violates users' speech rights rather than the speech or editorial rights of the medium.

Once telephone and mail are seen as important communications media, it becomes apparent that government policy significantly and purposefully shapes the communications order. An examination of regulatory policies relating to these media can test any thesis concerning the propriety of content-based regulation. Here, I merely note a few aspects of government regulation, often reflecting implicit or explicit content concerns, that favor various categories of communications or communicators.

Both telephone and mail have complicated, governmentally imposed or approved rate structures. These structures purposefully promote (subsidize) some users' expression, usually by imposing higher than cost fees on other users' expression. Telephone has seen various rate preferences.[106] Historically, regulation promoted universal service.[107] At times, urban users have subsidized rural and, with less egalitarian justification, suburban users. Business and long distance users have subsidized residential local users. Non-poor users have subsidized life-line service for the poor. Telephone rate regulation may merely reflect government's choice to favor politically significant categories of users—just as Congress's

---

[104] Patrick O'Neill, *Editorial Rights of Telephone Carriers*, 71 Journalism Q 99 (1994). Telephone companies' increasing claims of First Amendment rights have begun to receive somewhat critical attention. See, e.g., Angela J. Campbell, *Publish or Carriage: Approaches to Analyzing the First Amendment Rights of Telephone Companies*, 70 NC L Rev 1071 (1992); Daniel Brenner, *Telephone Company Entry into Video Services: A First Amendment Analysis*, 67 Notre Dame L Rev 97 (1991).

[105] See *Sable Communications v FCC*, 492 US 115 (1989); *Lamont v Postmaster General*, 381 US 301 (1965); *Hannegan v Esquire*, 327 US 146 (1946).

[106] One critical review claims the current system's subsidies favor local over long distance, residential over business, heavy over light, and rural over urban users. David L. Kaserman and John W. Mayo, *Cross-Subsidies in Telecommunications: Roadblocks on the Road to More Intelligent Telephone Pricing*, 11 Yale J Reg 119, 131 (1994).

[107] This was one of various concerns that led government regulators to turn telephone into a monopoly business early in the century. See Warren G. Lavey, *The Public Policies That Changed the Telephone Industry Into Regulated Monopolies: Lessons from Around 1915*, 39 Fed Comm Bar J 171 (1987).

must-carry cable rules might realistically be described as Congress favoring politically powerful local broadcasters over others. But publicly defensible policies, including content preferences, also seem implicit. For example, government apparently considers local telephone usage to be especially important in people's lives. Similarly, the name of the heavily subsidized "life-line" service implicitly indicates a high value placed on reports of emergencies or calls for help.

Because the postal system is governmentally owned, it cannot make claims analogous to newspapers' asserted right to exclude on the basis of content. Indeed, the First Amendment might require the converse. Access to the postal system might be like access to a public forum.[108] Any content-based exclusion (of a protected category of speech) would be impermissible censorship.

Nevertheless, even without imposing exclusions, postal policy has continuously favored some users and some content. In a policy that existed from the beginning of the Republic until at least the 1970 Postal Reorganization Act, the postal service has charged some mail more than its share in order to subsidize favored mail. For the first time in 1970, Congress established the principle that each category of mail, with some notable exceptions, should pay its own way, and not more than its own way, phasing out the subsidies that newspapers and magazines had enjoyed throughout American history.[109] The remaining exceptions, however, show Congress's continued determination to favor some speakers, in part because of favorable judgments concerning content. For example, the most high-minded justification for the franking privilege is the content-based concern to promote knowledge of governmental affairs.[110]

---

[108] This view goes back to dissents by Holmes and Brandeis in *United States ex rel Milwaukee Social Democratic Publishing Co. v Burelson*, 255 US 407, 417, 436 (1921) that are now cited as authoritative. In *Blout v Rizzi*, 400 US 410, 416 (1971), the Court found the postal system procedures for excluding obscenity "violate the First Amendment unless they include built-in safeguards against curtailment of constitutionally protected expression." This contrasts with people's mailboxes, which are not public forums—at least, a person must use the postal system in order to gain access. *U.S. Postal Service v Greenburgh Civic Assns*, 453 US 114 (1981).

[109] Richard B. Kielbowicz and Linda Lawson, *Reduced-Rate Postage for Nonprofit Organizations: A Policy History, Critique, and Proposal*, 11 Harv J L & Pub Pol 347, 348, 367 (1988). The burden placed on users charged the higher rates is even more overt during the periods when the postal service operated without a deficit. In those times not only did those favored receive a subsidy but the subsidy was clearly being paid by the disfavored mail.

[110] Content limitations are imposed on the use of the frank. Roughly, federal elected officials can use the frank for communications related to their representative role but not for personal or campaign purposes. 39 USC § 3210(a)(4), (5) (1988). Although categorization is difficult, in some circumstances courts have been willing to enforce these content exclu-

Likewise, the 1970 Act continued the policy of subsidizing the mail of certain broad, but limited, categories of nonprofit organizations.[111]

Historically, newspapers were the largest beneficiaries of postal subsidies. In 1792, Congress's first major legislation on postal service charged rates for newspapers that, depending on the size of the paper and the distance sent, were from one-sixth to one-fiftieth the rate set for letters.[112] These beneficial rates continued throughout our history. In 1912, the government reported that first-class mail produced a $70 million profit, while second-class postage entailed a $70 million loss, with letter mail paying a rate eighty times that charged newspapers.[113]

These subsidies have been important for the print medium. The post office carried about 4 million of the roughly 22.5 million papers printed in 1810 and roughly 500 million of the 1.5 billion periodicals (newspapers plus magazines) published in 1870.[114] Moreover, the subsidies have always reflected content concerns. When Congress in 1879 created the modern four-class system of mail, it for the first time gave magazines the same beneficial treatment as newspapers, apparently in part because magazines often had "the very best class" of content.[115]

This early cheap rate for newspapers, supported by the high rates for letters that were disproportionately sent by merchants,[116] reflected the great value placed on newspaper content. Federalists believed in the nationalizing effects of newspapers, and Republicans thought that access to public information encouraged the type

---

sions. See, e.g., *Rising v Brown*, 313 F Supp 824 (CD Cal 1970). Interestingly, almost the opposite content restraints are imposed on its use by former presidents and their spouses— they can send only "non-political mail." 39 USC § 3214 (1988).

[111] See Kielbowicz and Lawson, 11 Harv J L & Pub Pol 347 (cited in note 109).

[112] Richard B. Kielbowicz, *News in the Mail: The Press, Post Office, and Public Information, 1700–1860s* 34 (Greenwood, 1989).

[113] *Lewis Publishing v Morgan*, 229 US 288, 304 (1913).

[114] Kielbowicz, *News in the Mail* at 43 (cited in note 112); Richard B. Kielbowicz, *Origins of the Second-Class Mail Category and the Business of Policymaking, 1863–1879*, 96 Journalism Monographs at 6 (1986).

[115] Id at 19–20. Newspapers were charged not by the item but by weight at 2 cents a pound. Congress adopted this extension despite Representative Joseph Cannon's objection that second-class mail already cost the Post Office $18 million a year while producing only $1 million in revenue. Id.

[116] Kielbowicz, *News in the Mail* at 180 (cited in note 112). Of course, these postal subsidies also represent the political power of newspapers as compared to letter-mailers' lack of effective interest-group lobbying power.

of nation they favored—with the result that subsidies received bi-
partisan support.[117] Some of the new nation's leaders argued that
even these subsidies were insufficient. History has enshrined James
Madison's view that a person should not be forced to pay even
three pence to support any religion.[118] But the press was different.[119] Both Madison, a central author and sponsor of the First
Amendment, and George Washington argued that the established
low postage for newspapers was too high.[120] Their advocacy was
related to content. Washington emphasized the value of "political
intelligence and information."[121] Madison argued that, given a government such as ours, the "easy and prompt circulation of public
proceedings is peculiarly essential."[122]

Thus, both telephone and postal policy illustrates a continual
practice of subsidizing favored speech, often favored in part on
content grounds, and a continual practice of burdening other constitutionally protected expression to help pay the cost of realizing
the government's communications preferences.

B. RED LION: THE BROADCASTING ANOMALY

Both courts and commentators commonly view physical scarcity
of broadcast frequencies as providing the original constitutional
basis for upholding Congressional regulation of broadcasting. Both
also seem largely unpersuaded by the justification, either because
attribution of scarcity was always conceptually misguided or because it is now empirically inaccurate.

Conceptually, the only reason scarcity in broadcast properties
differs from scarcity in newspaper properties is that broadcast licenses are given away for free, at least by the government.[123] Of
course, there is a physical limit of frequency space—but there are
also a limited number of trees in the world; scarcity of wood pulp

---

[117] Id at 179.

[118] *Everson v Board of Education*, 330 US 1, 65–66 (1947) (appendix to Rutledge, dissenting)
(quoting James Madison, Memorial and Remonstrance). The dissent continually referred to
the three-pence language, id at 40 n 29, 49 n 41, 57; the majority also adopted Jefferson's
related metaphor of a "wall of separation between church and state." Id at 16.

[119] But see Randall P. Bezanson, *Taxes on Knowledge in America* (Penn, 1994).

[120] Kielbowicz, *News in the Mail* at 35 (cited in note 112).

[121] Id.

[122] Id.

[123] Licenses are, however, less scarce but more expensive if sought from current holders.

would likely result if wood pulp (and other inputs into newspapers) were given away for free. Moreover, the two reasons that the "physically limited" frequency space does not presently accommodate many more broadcaster channels are FCC regulations and insufficient money-backed demand for more channels. Only greater demand would justify the added cost of the technological refinements needed to provide more broadcasting capacity. Thus, the only real limit is economic. Of course, the experienced physical scarcity is not surprising. Whenever a limited but valuable resource, whether a broadcast license, printing press, plot of land, or wood pulp, is offered for free, demand will exceed supply. But given a market, supply will just meet demand at the market-clearing price.

Empirically, scarcity also seems doubtful. The number of broadcasting licenses has continually expanded. Today, many more broadcast stations exist than at the time of *Red Lion*.[124] Likewise, many more exist than daily newspapers.[125] Moreover, the main constraint on greater expansion is economic, not physical or technological.

Without scarcity, the constitutionality of regulation appears to hang by a slender thread. Commentators argue that broadcast regulation "conflicts, starkly and gratuitously, with conventional [individualistic] free-speech philosophy."[126] In a superb article, Jonathan Weinberg observes in detail the collective-good or communitarian orientation of broadcast regulation, which responds situationally, recognizes the pervasive role of government in structuring the private order, and is consistently content-oriented. He shows that this regulatory regime is utterly inconsistent with standard free speech principles.[127] But Weinberg argues that deviation

---

[124] *Syracuse Peace Council v FCC*, 867 F2d 654, 661 (1990) (FCC found that between 1974 and 1985 the number of radio stations had increased by 30%, FM stations had increased by 60%, and the proportion of households receiving nine or more TV signals had increased from 21% to 64%).

[125] In 1989, there were 10,600 radio stations and 1,424 television stations on the air. In addition, there were 624 lower-power television stations operating, and construction permits had been issued for an additional 1,284 radio stations, 257 television stations, and 1,713 low-power television stations. Marc A. Franklin & David A. Anderson, *Mass Media Law* 761 (1990). In contrast, there were 1,586 daily newspapers operating in 1992. C. Edwin Baker, *Advertising and a Democratic Press* 16 (Princeton, 1994).

[126] Weinberg, 81 Cal L Rev at 1205 (cited in note 18).

[127] Id. See also, Matthew L. Spitzer, *The Constitutionality of Licensing Broadcasters*, 64 NYU L Rev 990 (1989).

is justifiable.[128] He concludes that broadcast regulation and conventional free-speech philosophy embrace different, competing, probably irreconcilable worldviews, but that both contain an element of truth and we must live with both.[129]

In contrast to conventional wisdom, I suggest that the foundational broadcast cases, especially *Red Lion*, embody an analysis that differs little from that which is appropriate and has historically prevailed in respect to other media. Moreover, in contrast to Weinberg's conclusions, both *Turner* and most[130] broadcast regulations are consistent with a coherent First Amendment analysis that explains the distinction between regulation of individuals and regulation of the structure of collective entities.

Various passages certainly invite reading *Red Lion* to be based on "scarcity."[131] The penultimate sentence announcing the holding begins: "In view of the scarcity of broadcast frequencies. . . ." Even this sentence, however, continues with two additional elements: "[in view of] the Government's role in allocating those frequencies, and the legitimate claims [of possible users]."[132] This list could be taken as a temporal progression—scarcity is a "state of nature," creating the necessity of the government adopting a method of allocation; then the government's chosen method of allocation created legitimate claims, for which the government finally provides. Seen as describing such a progression, the argument is coherent but not unique to broadcasting.

---

[128] Lee Bollinger has long argued for a similar conclusion on only slightly different grounds. See Lee C. Bollinger, *Images of a Free Press* (Chicago, 1991). But cf Geoffrey R. Stone, *Imagining a Free Press*, 90 Mich L Rev 1246 (1992).

[129] This view illustrates Duncan Kennedy's notion of the "fundamental contradiction." Weinberg relies heavily on Critical Legal Studies literature, especially Duncan Kennedy, *Form and Substance in Private Law Adjudication*, 89 Harv L Rev 1685 (1976).

[130] Possibly the most troubling aspect of traditional broadcast regulation is not Congressional or FCC content-motivated rule-making but the broad discretion put into official hands, creating the danger that the Commission will suppress protected expression or that the existence of this discretion will stimulate self-censorship. This problem, however, is not limited to broadcasting. Discretion continually raises problems when postal officials must place items within categories for purposes of postal rates. Arguably the greatest constitutional evil of an unwise but still otherwise constitutionally defensible Newspaper Preservation Act is the authority it gives to the Attorney General, who decides with only the vaguest statutory restrictions whether to approve a proposed JOA. Lucas A. Powe, Jr., *The Fourth Estate and the Constitution: Freedom of Press in America* 219 (California, 1991); James D. Squires, *Read All About It! The Corporate Takeover of America's Newspapers* 123–24 (Times, 1993).

[131] The analysis of *Red Lion* here and the analysis of cases involving newspaper structural regulation in the next section roughly parallel discussion in my article, *Merging Phone and Cable*, 17 Hastings Comm/Ent L J 97 (1994) (forthcoming).

[132] *Red Lion*, 395 US at 400.

Certainly, the first point is right. Scarcity exists initially. Essentially, broadcast frequencies present the problem of the commons. In the paradigm commons, "scarcity" of pasture exists in the absence of cooperative or governmental structural regulation. Regulation solves the problem—whether regulation takes the form of defining property rights, creating rules of queuing, creating licenses, or some other response and whether regulation relies on custom or law. Broadcast frequencies merely present a commons where some government definition of rights is necessary.

Justice White's analysis in *Red Lion* began by recognizing this point. "Before 1927, the allocation of frequencies was left entirely to the private sector, and the result was chaos."[133] He then correctly observed that under these circumstances frequencies were a scarce resource, and noted that "[w]ithout government control, the medium would be of little use because of the cacophony of competing votes, none of which could be clearly and predictably heard."[134] This is precisely the commons—the limited availability of a valuable resource (scarcity of land or broadcast frequencies), combined with the absence of some form of governmental (or social) allocation of usage rights, results in overuse, making the resource worthless to everyone.

The government responded with a licensing regime. The Court would be mistaken if it thought this were the only possible government response. But the Court was not so naive. A major premise of White's opinion was that Congress was not so limited in its structural choice. For example, he noted that, rather than the licensing scheme actually adopted, "the Government could surely have decreed that each frequency should be shared among all or some of those who wish to use it, each being assigned a portion of the broadcast day or the broadcast week."[135]

Still, some commentators assert that the First Amendment requires that Congress create private property rights in broadcast frequencies much like the rights that exist in printing presses.[136] The Court, at least implicitly, noted this possibility but found that Congress had permissible reasons for rejecting it. Making broadcast

---

[133] Id at 375.

[134] Id at 376.

[135] Id at 390–91.

[136] See Spitzer, 64 NYU L Rev 990 (cited in note 127).

frequencies into the equivalent of private property would have created a potential problem that the Court said Congress could choose to avoid. "Station owners and a few networks would have unfettered power to make time available only to the highest bidders."[137] Arguably, the market creates this problem in the world of print. Refusing to decide a question not before it, the Court expressed no view on whether, in general, the government could "multiply voices and views presented to the public through . . . devices which limit or dissipate the power of those who sit astride the power of the channels of communication with the general public."[138]

Although private property rights were presumably a possibility, Justice White quoted a sponsor of the original legislation to prefer a different route. Congressman White argued that if the Radio Act of 1927 were enacted, "the broadcasting privilege will not be a right of selfishness," a fair characterization of what private property and commercial interests were understood to mean in the context of the broadcast debate.[139] Twice, the Court noted broadcasters' claim to have unlimited choice in respect to the use of their license, which would effectively treat the license like private property, and then responded by citing the portion of *Associated Press* which asserted that the "First Amendment does not sanction repression of that freedom by private interests."[140] That is, the Court recognized the possibility but rejected the necessity of creating traditional exclusionary private property rights in broadcasting.

---

[137] 365 US at 392.

[138] 395 US at 401 n 28 (citing *Citizen Publishing v United States*, 394 US 131 (1969)). An interesting feature of the Court's analysis here is its reliance on print media cases as precedent that might justify restrictions in broadcasting. Thus, in raising this possibility of dispersing the power of media entities, the Court referred to a decision that, itself relying on *Associated Press*, rejected a newspaper's claim that structural (antitrust) regulation by the government had violated its First Amendment rights.

[139] 395 US at 377 n 5. Joy Elmer Morgan, the Chairperson of the National Committee on Education by Radio, to which she was the National Education Association representative, repeatedly used the language of "selfishness" to characterize the commercial interests. Morgan talked of the "censorship maintained by powerful private interests who are responsible to no one but their own selfish interests" and, in the early 1930s, posed the legislative reform issue as "whether broadcasting be used as a tool of education or as an instrument of selfish greed." See McChesney, *Telecommunications* 48, 94 (cited note 101). Despite the public interest rhetoric coming from Congress, which misleadingly suggested that Congress had resisted the interests of commercial broadcasters, the licensing regime adopted was a victory for the private commercial broadcasters, at least as long as they could control the regulatory agency. Thus, they blocked the public interest lobby at almost every step with the adoption of the Communications Act of 1934. See generally, id.

[140] 395 US at 386–87, 392.

Congress's choice to give out licenses for free inevitably created a second scarcity. When any valuable good is given away for free, there are, as the Court said of broadcast licenses, always "substantially more individuals who want [the good] than there are [goods] to allocate."[141] But the legitimate reason for choosing a free license scheme rather than a private property regime was that Congress wanted allocations to reflect considerations of the public good rather than mere purchasing power. That is, as the Court seemed to realize, this second form of scarcity does not justify regulation—it results from regulation. Then, given Congress's rationale for "creating" scarcity, the FCC acted properly when it took account of "legitimate claims" of those who otherwise would not get access.[142]

In this reading of *Red Lion*, the Court recognized the government's need to respond to the natural scarcity that exists without legal definition of rights, recognized that the government had discretion in how to respond, and implicitly concluded that Congress was not bound to adopt a private property regime, which would allow economic power and commercial market forces to prevail. Finally, given the scarcity created by Congress's chosen structural form, the Court concluded that the government acts properly in making structural decisions that address the legitimate expressive claims of otherwise excluded portions of the public.

Rather than relying on an assertedly unique but ultimately incoherent notion of scarcity, the Court in *Red Lion* is better understood to have developed a more tenable general principle. Relying most heavily on a case coming from the print realm (*Associated Press*), the Court essentially held that the government has the power to structure the media in a manner that the government thinks will promote the best communications environment. Of course, this general principle does not mean that the First Amendment imposes no limits. As the Court explained, "[t]here is no question here of the Commission's refusal to permit the broadcaster to carry a particular program or to publish his own views . . . [or] of government censorship of a particular program contrary to § 326."[143] And a different First Amendment issue would be presented if the chal-

---

[141] Id at 388.

[142] Id at 400.

[143] Id at 396.

lenged regulation had "the net effect of reducing rather than enhancing the volume and quality of coverage. . . ."[144] The Court
approved content-oriented structural regulation while clearly treating suppression as a different issue.

C. NEWSPAPERS: STRUCTURAL AND CONTENT INTERVENTIONS

Above I considered how the postal system favored some generic
categories of speech, especially newspapers. This section examines
how the government has used the postal system to favor particular
categories of newspapers and newspaper content and disfavor others. Then I will consider some more direct governmental regulation
of the structure of the newspaper industry.

The politics of postal rates in the eighteenth and nineteenth centuries was animated by the conflict between the interests of local
"country" and potentially national "city" papers.[145] Presumably in
response to transportation costs, Congress in 1792 created nine
distance gradations for letters ranging from 6 cents per sheet for
delivery within 30 miles to 25 cents for distances over 450 miles.
Zoned rates for newspapers, however, were more controversial.
Those who favored a heavily subsidized flat rate for newspapers
argued that everyone ought to have equal access to the information—this equality protected liberty. However, low flat rates were
seen especially to benefit city, often mid-Atlantic papers. These
rates helped these papers invade other regions, especially the territory of local "country" papers. Congressional supporters of zoned
rates maintained that postage for greater distances should reflect
the greater expense. But even more vigorously, they asserted that
low flat rates would unfairly advantage city newspapers in their
competition with their small rural counterparts. The claim of these
supporters of zoned rates—that "country papers are important on
many accounts, and ought to be encouraged"—virtually duplicates
the content-based concerns of those who today favor must-carry
cable rules in order to help preserve the strength of local television
stations. But in 1792, those favoring nationalizing content arguably
got the best of a compromise—newspapers, typically three sheets,
paid 1 cent for the first 100 miles and 1.5 cents if sent farther.

---

[144] Id at 393.

[145] This paragraph is based on Kielbowicz, *News in the Mail* at 33–34 (cited in note 112).

Debate about how low postal rates should be for newspapers might pragmatically be seen as turning on competing financial interests. Nevertheless, the question was surely also influenced and certainly fought on the ground of competing content-inspired principle. During the Jackson period, Jackson's opponents argued that democratization of information and dissemination of knowledge among all classes required eliminating postage for newspapers. Senator George Gibb even invoked the First Amendment as affirmatively requiring postal subsidies.[146] But others feared that rates that were too low would cause the small-town press to succumb to eastern urban papers. For example, Senator Isaac Hill, a former publisher, argued that lower postage would " 'annihilate at least one-half of our village newspapers.' "[147] When in 1832 Jackson's opponents attempted to abolish all postal charges for newspapers, the proposal failed in the Senate vote, 23 to 22, with no Jackson supporter voting for free postage.[148]

Another policy innovation favored local knowledge. Legislation in 1845 provided free postage for newspapers within thirty miles of where they were published. This was changed to free delivery for weekly papers in their home county in 1851, a privilege briefly withdrawn in 1873 but quickly restored for all in-county newspapers in 1874.[149] The entirely subsidized, free in-county postage that benefited local content partly balanced the heavily subsidized, virtually flat rate that benefited nationalizing content. Richard Kielbowicz observes, however, that the flat rate also may have unintentionally promoted local reporting because many rural or country editors, who otherwise primarily printed nonlocal information "stripped" from outside papers, responded to the competitive challenge by printing more local content, which distinguished their papers from the city press.[150]

Since before the Revolution, the government also provided free postage for "exchange" papers. Benjamin Franklin and William Hunter, deputy postmasters for the colonies, issued a formal direc-

---

[146] Id at 59–60.

[147] Id at 61.

[148] Id.

[149] Id at 84, 86–87; Kielbowicz, *Origins* (cited in note 114) at 9, 11. Free in-county postage for weekly newspapers was finally ended in 1962, although other in-county preferences remained.

[150] Kielbowicz, *News in the Mail* at 63 (cited in note 112).

tive in 1758 (itself continuing earlier practice) that newspapers could send a copy of each issue for free to any other paper, a policy Congress reaffirmed in its 1792 law. This practice had both clear content effects and, presumably, a broad content-based purpose of spreading nonlocal news and opinion. At least until the dominance of the telegraph—and even then for more wordy reporting—papers depended heavily on other papers for their nonlocal news. Newspapers merely copied and reprinted news or commentary from elsewhere.

These "free exchanges" were a significant economic benefit as well as a major stimulus for carrying nonlocal content.[151] For example, during one month in 1843, 16.5% of all papers mailed were free exchanges; each publisher, mostly of weekly papers, received an average of 364 exchanges.[152] Of the 40,000 papers coming into New York during a week in 1850, 35,000 were postage-free exchanges—while 28% of those arriving in New Orleans fell into this category.[153] Free exchanges directly increased the circulation and local republication of nonlocal news and opinion. They also may have indirectly supported local news by adding to local papers' financial viability. Of course, these huge subsidies are hardly comprehensible outside the great value Congress or the postal authorities placed on nonlocal "intelligence"—a clear content concern.

The subsidies described above furthered implicit content-based goals. Congress also has used explicitly content-based postal rate provisions to advance its conception of a good communications order. The content-based purpose of second-class postal rates was to encourage "the dissemination of current intelligence."[154] Thus, when Congress created the second-class postage in 1879, it granted the rate only to newspapers "published for the dissemination of information of a public character, or devoted to literature, the sciences, arts or some special industry."[155] It also carefully attempted

---

[151] Id at 17–18, 142.

[152] Id at 149.

[153] Id at 151.

[154] *Lewis Publishing v Morgan*, 229 US 288, 302 (1913) (quoting the Commission on Second-Class Mail Matter).

[155] Post Office Act of March 3, 1879, 20 Stat 355. The Court rejected an attempt by the post office to give this categorization real evaluative content. *Hannegan v Esquire*, 327 US 178 (1946).

The parallels between the legitimate purposes and the content limitations of second-class postage provided for the "fourth estate" provocatively resemble the announced purposes

to avoid support of advertising. Congress specifically denied the second-class rate to "regular publications designed primarily for advertising purposes, or for free circulation, or for circulation at nominal rates." To further distinguish journals with reader-valued news content from advertising sheets that might have some news attached, Congress required that to qualify for the subsidized rates a publication must have "a legitimate list of subscribers"—a requirement recently upheld against First Amendment attack.[156]

A major Progressive era reform required that newspapers using second-class postage, other than "religious, fraternal, temperance, [or] scientific, or other similar publications," publish twice a year information chosen by the government, not the editor—specifically, the names and addresses of the editors, publishers, and owners.[157] The law exhibited a substantive concern with content. Supporters of the requirements wanted to aid the public in learning, for example, whether powerful and self-interested commercial and industrial interests controlled the news they received.[158]

An additional provision of the Act had the same "evil" that the Court found in the right-to-reply law invalidated in *Tornillo*. The Act restricted second-class mail to publications that meet a requirement that only comes into play given an initial publication decision. A relatively common industry practice had been to print paid advertisements disguised as news stories or editorials. In response, the Act required that material published for "money or other valuable consideration . . . be plainly marked 'advertisement.'" The required "speech" would either deter the publication decision (the paper would not publish the "advertorial") or would give the public access to arguably relevant information.[159] Again, Congress attempted to shape the content of newspapers to reflect Congress's preferences.

Partly in pursuit of broadly defined content-based concerns,

---

and content limitations on the frank provided for government communications. See note 110.

[156] *Enterprises v United States*, 833 F2d 1216 (6th Cir 1987).

[157] *Lewis Publishing v Morgan*, 229 US 288 (1913) (upholding § 2 of Post Office Appropriation Act, 37 Stat 539, 554 (1912). This statute also required daily newspapers to publish their average circulation for the past six months. The Court reasoned that these publication requirements were acceptable conditions on the grant of a privilege.

[158] The best account of this legislation is Linda Lawson, *Truth in Publishing: Federal Regulation of the Press's Business Practices, 1880–1920* (So Ill, 1993).

[159] Later regulation imposed similar requirements on broadcasting.

Congress also has directly regulated newspapers in ways that advantage some papers and disadvantage others. In *Associated Press v United States*,[160] the Court required the Associated Press to speak regularly to those to whom it would prefer not to speak. That is, it approved the lower court's remedy for Associated Press' monopolistic limitation on membership and access to its news. As interpreted by the Court, the decree meant "that AP news is to be furnished to competitors of old members without discrimination."[161]

Of course, *Associated Press* applied generally applicable antitrust laws. Therefore, its precedential value for media-specific regulations can be reasonably disputed. Nevertheless, courts have invoked it to uphold such structural regulation. For example, *Red Lion* relied heavily on *Associated Press* at three crucial points in its First Amendment analysis.[162] This reliance is understandable. The Court in *Associated Press* explained itself with media-specific language. Most dramatically, it asserted that the command "that the government itself shall not impede the free flow of ideas does not afford non-governmental combinations a refuge if they impose restraints upon that constitutionally guaranteed freedom. . . . Freedom of the press from governmental interference under the First Amendment does not sanction repression of that freedom by private interests."[163] Thus, the Court forcefully rejected the press' attempt to use the First Amendment as a shield against governmental structural regulation designed to give greater voice to those otherwise disadvantaged by the distribution or form of private media ownership.

When at least one competing paper is in danger of financial failure, the Newspaper Preservation Act overrides the antitrust laws and allows the competing papers to form a joint operating agreement (JOA) in which various business functions are merged, but the editorial functions are kept separate. As should be expected, given that the antitrust laws are intended to protect competition, this exemption from antitrust constraints advantages the exempted

---

[160] 326 US 1 (1945).

[161] 326 US at 21. The Court, however, noted that this did not require AP to say things that it did not want to say.

[162] 395 US at 387, 390, 392.

[163] 326 US at 20.

papers, disadvantaging their present or potential competitors. Unsurprisingly, some papers, especially suburban competitors of metro papers, opposed the Newspaper Preservation Act both in Congress and before the courts.[164] Likewise, some members of Congress argued that the Act "will preserve certain newspapers but will stifle competition in ideas by crippling the growth of small newspapers and preventing successful establishment of competing dailies."[165] Nevertheless, the courts have upheld this media-specific structural law because of its permissible purpose of keeping alive independent editorial voices that might otherwise have been silenced by competition. The Court also has upheld a labor law exemption for newspapers published weekly or semiweekly with a circulation, primarily within the county of publication, of less than 3 thousand, in part because the exemption was "not a 'deliberate and calculated device' to penalize a certain group of newspapers."[166]

Like other FCC regulations, the FCC's cross-ownership restrictions are often treated as First Amendment anomalies limited to the special category of broadcasting. Physical scarcity means that there cannot be any "unbridgeable First Amendment right to broadcast" and that not everyone can own a broadcast station.[167] However, a prohibition on *newspapers* holding a broadcast license in their own community burdens newspaper publishing. Generally the government cannot impose a burden on the exercise of a constitutional right—that is, on operating a newspaper. But in *National*

---

[164] See, e.g., *Committee for an Independent P-I v Hearst Corp.*, 704 F2d 467 (9th Cir 1983).

[165] HR Rep No 1193, 91st Cong, 2d Sess (1979), reprinted in 1970 *USCCAN* 3547–91, 3558, quoted in *Committee for an Independent P-I*, 704 F2d at 481.

[166] *Mabee v White Plains Publishing Co.*, 327 US 178, 184 (1946).
A major method of government influence on media content is to provide the media with easy, inexpensive access to government-favored information. By discriminating between types of media granted access, the government favors some type of media entities over others. Thus, although the Court of Appeals upheld the principle that once the government provides press facilities in the White House it cannot deny use of the facilities to "bona fide Washington-based journalists" for "arbitrary or less than compelling reasons," the Court seemed unconcerned that the government limited usage rights to Washington-based journalists, which clearly distinguishes between papers. *Sherrill v Knight*, 569 F2d 124 (DC Cir 1977). More controversially, lower courts in California upheld the Los Angeles county sheriff's and city police's denial of press cards to specialized publications such as trade or college papers or to members of the media "who perform functions other than those directly connected with the regular gathering and distributions of hard core news." *Los Angeles Free Press v Los Angeles*, 9 Cal App 3d 448, 452, 88 Cal Rptr 605, 608 (1970), cert denied, 401 US 982 (1971) (Black, Douglas, and Brennan dissenting).

[167] *FCC v National Citizens Committee for Broadcasting (FCC v NCCB)*, 436 US 775, 799 (1978) (quoting *Red Lion*, 395 US at 388).

Citizens Committee for Broadcasting, the Court unanimously upheld this structural regulation that specifically imposed a limit on newspapers—a limit that the rule did not impose on individuals or even the ordinary corporation.

The Court justified this structural regulation on the basis of the government's purpose "to enhance the diversity of information heard by the public"[168]—a content-based concern. Or at least this characterization is urged by the dissent in *Turner:* "the Court is mistaken in concluding the interest in diversity . . . is content neutral. Indeed, the interest is not 'related to the suppression of free expression,' . . . but that is not enough for content neutrality. . . . The interest . . . is directly tied to the content of what the speakers will likely say."[169] The problem for the dissent in *Turner*, assuming it is right in its characterization, is that *NCCB* apparently says that rather than raising constitutional doubts, this content-based purpose helps justify a regulation of newspapers. And if it does that, why not justify a regulation of cable too? Surely cable should not receive greater protection.

D. THE ABERRATION: TORNILLO

Both history and legal precedent demonstrate that government often regulates media structure. This brings me to *Miami Herald v Tornillo*,[170] possibly the only Supreme Court decision that supports the proposition that the government cannot regulate press structure in order to improve the press' contribution to a robust communications environment.[171] Of course, many decisions hold that the government cannot suppress communications by the press.[172] The gov-

---

[168] Id at 801 (quoting with approval the Court of Appeals decision, 555 F2d 938, 954 (DC Cir 1977)). Language from *Associated Press*, a newspaper case, is routinely cited for a similar proposition, often in the context of structural regulation cases. Specifically, *Associated Press* asserts that "the widest possible dissemination of information from diverse and antagonistic sources is essential to the welfare of the public." 326 US 1, 20 (1945).

[169] 114 S Ct at 2477.

[170] 418 US 241 (1974).

[171] Probably the case most problematic from the perspective taken here is *Pacific Gas & Electric Co v Public Utilities Com'n*, 475 US 1 (1986). Both the opinion there and the Court's treatment of the case in *Turner* found that it involved the same issues as *Tornillo*, leaving open the possibility that it will be limited in the same way *Turner* limited *Tornillo*.

[172] The press tax cases were mostly suppressions—the tax usually imposed special burdens on the press. None are plausibly interpreted as government initiatives to improve the communications order (except by the impermissible means of suppression). Moreover, in characterizing the taxes, the Court notes that there is never any revenue need to impose a tax on just the press because revenue can be even better obtained from a broader tax. Generally

ernment cannot constitutionally suppress such communications because the communications are scandalous; it cannot prohibit the press from editorializing on election day; and it cannot prevent public broadcasting from editorializing.[173] Suppression is barred. But like all subsidies, structural regulation aimed at promoting affirmative performance generally is permitted.

But is *Tornillo* really to the contrary—at least as interpreted by *Turner Broadcasting?* In *Tornillo*, the Court advanced both a narrow and broad basis for invalidating a statute that provided political candidates a right of reply to newspaper attacks. Broadly, the Court said that the Constitution forbids the government from compelling newspapers "to publish that which " 'reason" tells them should not be published' . . . ."[174] It explained that "[t]he choice of material to go into a newspaper . . . constitute[s] the exercise of editorial control and judgment."[175] The statute failed "because of its intrusion into the function of the editors."[176] These statements support a broad prohibition of any government action that mandates inclusion of any content in a newspaper—and if applied to cable, would dispose of the law in *Turner* without even considering the content-discrimination issue.[177]

---

these special taxes on the press seem like intentional burdens on the exercise of a constitutional right. Tax exemptions are a different matter. *Leathers v Medlock*, 499 US 439 (1991), applied little serious scrutiny to an exemption for some but not other portions of the media. However, earlier in *Arkansas Writers' Project v Ragland*, 481 US 221 (1987), the Court struck down an exemption that made distinctions among the press. *Arkansas Writers* is not contrary evidence to the assertion that the government can act or regulate to structure the press as a means to improve press performance. The breadth of the exemption in *Arkansas Writers* and the narrowness of the tax's application to only one to three publications suggest that the baseline for magazines should be seen as exemption. At least this is so given that the government could not persuasively explain the differential treatment as an attempt to promote the government's view of an ideal press. In fact, the Court recognized that a state interest in encouraging fledgling publications might be compelling, but found the exemption here could not be rationally seen to promote that end.

[173] *Near v Minnesota*, 283 US 697 (1931); *Mills v Alabama*, 384 US 214 (1966); *FCC v League of Women Voters*, 468 US 364 (1984).

[174] 418 US at 256 (quoting *Associated Press*, 326 US at 20 n 19).

[175] Id at 258.

[176] Id.

[177] Even this broad reading of *Tornillo* leaves unexamined questions that could leave a major role for governmental structural regulation. Only forced content seems ruled out. I have argued that the First Amendment protects press freedom but does not identify who the press is. Baker, *Human Liberty* ch 11 (cited in note 24). In the United States, most commentators without reflection identify the press with owners, although in some Western democracies this makes no more (and maybe less) sense than identifying the press with the editors and journalists. Even in this country, courts recognize a limited constitutional testimonial privilege for "reporters," not owners. Despite the majority opinion in *Branzburg*

More narrowly, the Court in *Tornillo* emphasized that under the challenged statute the duty to print was triggered only by the newspaper's initial decision to print criticism. This duty, the Court explained, improperly "exacts a penalty on the basis of content."[178] "Punishing" a newspaper for its communicative choices is directly contrary to basic First Amendment principle. In addition, the threat of this "penalty" could deter editors from printing critical commentary, with the result that "political and electoral coverage would be blunted or reduced."[179] This narrower rationale rules out only laws that "penalize" or "deter" the publication of particular content.

The broad and narrow rationales differ significantly. If cable were treated like newspapers, the must-carry rules are obviously impermissible under the broad reading of *Tornillo*. In contrast, the narrow rationale poses no problem for most structural regulation. It does not speak to the question of whether the government can mandate, even for content-motivated reasons, access opportunities that do not turn on the newspaper's own constitutionally protected behavior.[180] Of course, various structural regulations might pose other constitutional problems. But the narrow rationale in *Tornillo* does not itself rule out laws that compel newspapers to accept noncommercial ads on a common carrier basis, to publish statements by all candidates for office, to publish ownership or circulation information, or to identify advertisements as such.

In *Turner*, the Court distinguished the right-to-reply in *Tornillo*

---

v Hayes, 408 US 665 (1972), most courts read the dissenting and concurring opinions in *Branzburg* together to recognize this right. Franklin & Anderson, *Mass Media Law* 600 (cited in note 125). Likewise, the Court's precise language in *Tornillo* refers to the "function of editors." Imagine an editor asserting that the owner cannot stop her from printing that which she chooses. What is required of law in order to protect the "exercise of editorial control and judgment" or to avoid "intrusion into the function of the editors"? Even if the government cannot intrude on editors, *Tornillo* leaves open the possibility that the government by statute could protect their role from intrusions by owners, at least if the purpose of intervening on the editor's rather than the owner's side was to support rather than undermine the integrity and constitutional role of the press.

[178] 418 US at 256.

[179] Id at 257.

[180] If *Tornillo* does not make editorial control sacrosanct but only prohibits punishment for constitutionally protected publication decisions, then the government should be able to require publication of governmentally specified content as a remedy for a law violation (that is, for behavior that the First Amendment does not protect). This possibility could explain the concurrence of Justices Brennan and Rehnquist in *Tornillo*, where they asserted that *Tornillo* left open the question of mandatory publication as a remedy for libel. 418 US at 258 (Brennan and Rehnquist concurring).

from the must-carry rules on two grounds.[181] The Court noted
the "technological differences between newspapers and cable," the
importance of which apparently lies in the potential cable technology creates "for abuse [by] this private owner over a central avenue
of communication."[182] Here it cited the portion of *Associated Press*,
emphasized above, for the proposition that the government can
intervene to prevent "private interests" from restricting "the free
flow of information and ideas."[183]

More relevantly here, the Court only credited the narrow rationale in *Tornillo*. It explained that, unlike the right-to-reply law, the
must-carry rules "exact no content-based penalty," and there is no
suggestion that they "will force cable operators to alter their own
messages" or "cause a cable operator or cable programmer to conclude that 'the safe course is to avoid controversy,' . . . and by so
doing diminish the free flow of information and ideas." To the
extent *Tornillo* applies to cable, this narrow reading was essential
to the holding in *Turner*. And given this reading of *Tornillo*, there
is scant Supreme Court precedent for restricting content-based
structural regulation of the media.

IV. DOCTRINAL DOGMAS

Turner reached a sensible result. Thus, I might limit my
objections to its analysis of content discrimination in the media
context. But *Turner* may illustrate a deeper problem with constitutional doctrine. The force and legitimacy of constitutional law depend on it embodying normative commitments that restrict government's choice of ends and of means. Increasingly prevalent,
relatively mechanical constitutional "tests" often abstract too much
from underlying constitutional normative commitments. My claim
is that *Turner* illustrates this failure. More generally, it illustrates
that the further judicial tests and doctrine move from embodying
prohibitions of precisely identified normative evils, the more likely
the analysis will lead to error.

---

[181] It also mentioned a third point, that the must-carry rules will not force a change in
cable's own messages to respond to the must-carry programming. 114 S Ct at 2466. I treat
this point as merely an aspect of the narrow interpretation of *Tornillo*, which emphasizes
that the government should not influence or penalize the newspaper's own speech.

[182] Id at 2466.

[183] Id.

Doctrinal tests often permit quick and easy application of constitutional mandates. Doctrinal analysis identifies factors that in the most familiar cases lead to the "right" constitutional result. Courts can then use these factors within tests and announced levels of scrutiny to enhance predictability and to guide their audiences. In addition, some doctrines serve useful analytic tasks, especially in contexts where a court can more acceptably label another branch of government "confused" than call it "immoral." For example, a court may "know" that an objectionable governmental purpose exists (e.g., to suppress speech or invidiously deny equality). Ordinarily the court can still judiciously examine the law, accept any governmental suggestion of a benign purpose at face value, but strike the law for not relating sufficiently to that purpose. Although the point usually is unspoken, the court will convincingly have shown that the benign purpose does not really explain the law. The court thus invalidates the law without drawing the bottom line—that is, without announcing that the law is best understood as having a normatively unacceptable purpose. In order to do this, however, the court must manipulate levels of scrutiny in order to pick out those laws with impermissible purposes. Use of factors that correlate with objectionable purposes aid this task—although it is obviously a mistake to confuse the correlation with the evil.

Other, less defensible influences probably contribute to the prevalence of these doctrinal devices. First is ideology. Most constitutional tests purport to structure a constrained balancing. This balancing easily harmonizes with a commitment to a utilitarian or some similar pragmatic accounting in which judicial rationality appears triumphant despite a world in which the alleged subjectivity of values has stripped rationality to its instrumental surface.[184]

Institutional forces also press toward mechanically applying apparently discrete factors within a relatively value-free doctrine. Tests focus and organize lawyers' arguments. Analytic and rhetorical skills often rewarded in law school can be brought to bear on fact situations when applying these tests. Dispassionate arguments then focus on empirical and logical matters, often avoiding except by implication the key ethical issues. Finally, after narrowing the dispute to nonideological matters and apparently giving both sides

---

[184] Baker, 58 Tex L Rev 1029 (cited in note 76).

their due, the tests permit "reasoned" conclusions.[185] In *Turner*, for example, the lawyers can heartily agree that content discrimination is bad and then quarrel over whether it is present.

The above diagnosis is at best suggestive. Here, I briefly offer two related but speculative points: First, the Court often completely ignores established and obviously applicable tests if they would lead to the substantively wrong result—a practice that suggests the tests' substantive bankruptcy. Second, when taken seriously, these judicial tests can confuse analysis and deflect discussion from the real issues—as did the emphasis in *Turner* on whether must-carry rules are content-based.

Because I think this doctrinal focus of *Turner* represents a general problem in constitutional law and because I think one of the unfortunate developments in First Amendment analysis over the last twenty years is its increasing resemblance to Equal Protection doctrine, I will illustrate these points with examples drawn from both Equal Protection and First Amendment case law. Of course, a few examples will be inadequate to establish my speculative claims, both because advocates of these tests will be able to contest the interpretation of any example and because few will argue that the tests are always adequately sculpted. Moreover, most advocates of these tests will concede that occasionally normative constitutional concerns will conflict with and ought to prevail over the test.[186] Still, illustrations of the doctrinal failures can be suggestive. They can support the claim that, at best, these tests provide useful, rule-of-thumb indications of what a proper normative analysis would show in commonly considered contexts. But the illustrations also support the claim that these tests can misguide analysis if they are used to substitute for normative analysis.

As developed over that last dozen years, the Court's widely criticized public forum doctrine illustrates a rush from substance to more mechanical doctrine, with the resulting doctrine then being either ignored or misdirecting inquiry.[187] Of course, any desirable

---

[185] A superb critique of this doctrinal stupidity is presented in another review of *Turner*. Hawthorne and Price, 12 Cardozo Arts & Enter L J 499 (cited in note 18).

[186] "The simple lesson of [*Brown v Socialist Workers' 74 Campaign Committee*, 459 US 87 (1982)] is that when the commitment to neutrality conflicts with the commitment to preservation of ideas in the political marketplace, the latter will prevail." Stone & Marshall, 1983 Supreme Court Review 583, 626 (cited in note 29).

[187] There have been many effective critiques of the Court's public forum analysis. See, e.g., Daniel A. Farber & John E. Nowak, *The Misleading Nature of Public Forum Analysis:*

conception of government will recognize government's authority to use its resources to carry out public purposes. It follows that the First Amendment's restriction on government's power to suppress speech cannot mean that government must never stop a speaker from using the government property she chooses to speak. The government must be allowed to restrict the speech that interferes with its chosen uses of public resources. Linguistically, the government's choice to use its property for various public purposes does not "abridge" speech freedom even if, in a sense, it "limits" speech freedom. Justice Marshall's formula for the Court in *Grayned v Rockford*[188] sums up these observations. "The crucial question is whether the manner of expression is basically incompatible with the normal activity of a particular place at a particular time."[189] This formula directly embodied crucial constitutional values. Nevertheless, as the Court faced claims of speech rights in a widening variety of circumstances, it changed its focus into a "forum" categorization. Constitutional review would be severe if the challenged regulation applied within a traditional public forum, like streets and parks, or a designated public forum—places "opened [by the government] for use by the public as a place for expressive activity."[190] All other property constituted nonpublic forums in which regulation of speech was subjected to the more relaxed reasonableness review.

In the progression I describe, public forum doctrine illustrates the tendency to generate legal categories that distance normative constitutional concerns. The results are predictably bad. The most obvious problem in this doctrine is that the category of "designated public forums" was presumably intended to provide significant protection of speech in many contexts other than traditional public forums. However, as long as the government can remove the designation at will, and as long as government intent is determinative, a governmental restriction that someone challenges will itself constitute the basis for the challenge to fail—the restriction shows that

---

Content and Context in First Amendment Adjudication, 70 Va L Rev 1219 (1984); Lawrence Tribe, *American Constitutional Law* 986–997 (Foundation, 2d ed 1988). For an alternative to this public forum approach, see Baker, *Human Liberty* chs 7 & 8 (cited in note 24).

[188] 408 US 104 (1972).

[189] Id at 116.

[190] *Perry Educ. Ass'n v Perry Local Educators' Ass'n*, 460 US 37, 45 (1983).

the government does not wish the arena to be a public forum.[191] More generally, the public forum analysis diverts attention from the real issues—most prominently, whether the restriction is needed in order for the government to achieve its purposes in the use of the property in question.

The doctrine's bankruptcy is evident in the Court's finding that a ban on the distribution of literature in an airport violates the First Amendment. In *Lee v International Society for Krishna Consciousness*,[192] four Justices concluded that the airport was a public forum and the ban was invalid, four others disagreed on each point, and the ninth, Justice O'Connor, created two separate majorities by concluding that the airport was not a public forum but that the ban on leafletting was unconstitutional. For the majority, rejection of the traditional public forum categorization seemed mandated since tradition hardly covers these new facilities. Moreover, the government, as illustrated by its rule challenged in the litigation, certainly did not wish to designate airports as public forums. Four of the Justices who reached this formalistic conclusion effectively used the analysis to distance themselves from the normative issues that should be controlling; they voted to uphold the restriction.

Justice O'Connor, the fifth Justice to find the airport was not a public forum, proceeded to examine the airport, reporting that the government had made it into a shopping mall.[193] She relied on authority that " '[t]he reasonableness of the Government's restriction . . . must be assessed in light of the purpose of the forum and all the surrounding circumstances,' "[194] and concluded that the regulation was not "reasonably related to maintaining the multipurpose environment that the Port Authority has deliberately cre-

---

[191] See *Cornelius v NAACP Legal Defense & Educ. Fund*, 473 US 788, 813 (1985) (Blackmun, joined by Brennan, dissenting); id at 833 (Stevens). Blackmun argued: "If the Government does not create a limited public forum unless it intends to provide an 'open forum' for expressive activity, and if the exclusion of some speakers is evidence that the Government did not intend to create such a forum, no speaker challenging denial of access will ever be able to prove that the forum is a limited public forum. The very fact that the Government denied access . . . indicates that the Government did not intend to provide an open forum . . . . " The circularity here resembles that of Justice Rehnquist's "bitter with the sweet" approach to procedural due process, *Arnett v Kennedy*, 416 US 134 (1974) (plurality opinion), later rejected by the Court. See, e.g., *Cleveland Bd. of Educ. v Loudermill*, 470 US 532 (1985).

[192] 112 S Ct 2701, 2709 (1992).

[193] 112 S Ct at 2713.

[194] Id at 2712 (quoting *Cornelius*, 473 US at 809).

ated."[195] She explained that this followed because she could find
no "problems intrinsic to the act of leafletting that would make it
naturally incompatible with [the forum here]."[196] In other words,
under the reasonableness label, O'Connor got awfully close to
Grayned's normatively based principle of looking to see if "the expression is basically incompatible with the normal activity of [the
place]." Essentially, she had accepted forum doctrine only then
wisely to ignore it. Her opinion was persuasive on the question of
whether leafletting must be allowed, but her analysis was not aided
by calling the airport a nonpublic forum.

Both the majority and dissent in *Cohen v Cowles Media Co.*[197] too
quickly resorted to general First Amendment principles, which had
been descriptively useful in paradigmatic cases, before considering
the principles' applicability to the normative issues at stake. Dan
Cohen had provided several reporters information under a promise
of confidentiality, but the newspapers published his name after
editors at two papers independently decided Cohen's identity as
the source was an important element of the story. Because of the
central principle that " '[t]he publisher of a newspaper has no special immunity from the application of general laws,' "[198] in a 5–4
decision, the Court found that the First Amendment does not block
Cohen's promissory estoppel suit against the papers. Justice Blackmun's dissent effectively responded to this asserted principle with
the invocation of *Hustler Magazine v Falwell.*[199] There, the Court
protected speech that constituted an "intentional infliction of emotional distress" under a state tort " 'law of general applicability'
unrelated to suppression of speech."[200] Blackmun argued that the
determinative principle was, instead, that "a State may not punish
the publication of lawfully obtained, truthful information 'absent

[195] Id at 2713.

[196] Id at 2714.

[197] 501 US 663 (1991).

[198] Id at 630 (quoting *Associated Press v NLRB*, 301 US 103, 132–33 (1937)). Unsurprisingly,
in the dissent in *Cowles Media* joined by Justice O'Connor, Justice Souter cited O'Connor's
rejection of an analogous principle recently asserted in the free exercise area. 111 S Ct at
2522 (citing *Employment Div., Dept. of Human Resources of Oregon v Smith*, 494 US 872, 901
(1990) (O'Connor concurring)). Although a Court could consistently apply either principle,
both principles are contrary to precedent and both undervalue the constitutional values at
stake—free speech, an effective and robust press, and religious freedom.

[199] 485 US 46 (1988).

[200] 501 US at 675.

a need to further a state interest of the highest order.' "[201] The majority, however, properly cited copyright laws to show that sometimes the state can punish publication of truthful statements.

Emphasis on these competing general principles unnecessarily confused the analysis. Certainly, *Hustler* shows that the majority's general principle was inadequate. From the perspective of speakers for whom the prohibited activity is integral to their expression, laws of general applicability that are unrelated to speech can even amount to a form of (usually unintentional) content discrimination.[202] For example, from the perspective of the antiwar protestors, the law prohibiting burning draft card laws amounted to discrimination against their speech.[203] The Court's willingness to accept "as applied" challenges suggests that a court could refuse to apply a law to a particular expressive activity rather than strike down all applications.[204]

The majority in *Cowles Media* may be on better ground arguing that civil liability is appropriate because the information was not lawfully obtained[205] or because the restriction on publication was "self-imposed."[206] In cases relied on by the dissent, the sole alleged wrong committed by the press was publication. In the case of promissory estoppel, the wrong was not merely publishing but publishing after promising not to. Surely the First Amendment does not allow a person to ignore with impunity all nondisclosure agreements between private individuals, for example, in court settlements[207] or employment contracts.[208]

---

[201] Id at 673 (citing *Smith v Daily Mail Publishing Co.*, 443 US 97, 103 (1979)).

[202] Williams, 139 U Pa L Rev at 659–61, 719–21 (cited in note 85).

[203] Note that the Court in *O'Brien* imposed First Amendment scrutiny even after it found that the law, which was of general applicability, was unrelated to the suppression of speech.

[204] Williams defends this approach. 139 U Pa L Rev at 709–14 (cited in note 85).

[205] But cf *Nebraska Press Association v Stuart*, 427 US 539, 572 (1976) (Brennan, with Stewart and Marshall, concurring in the judgment) (indicating that a prior restraint would be improper "no matter how shabby the means by which the information is obtained"). Moreover, the concept of "not lawfully obtained" must be formulated with care to avoid circularity. For example, it is different to prohibit a reporter from directing someone else to steal files to obtain information than to make it unlawful to receive information that someone had unlawfully obtained. Arguably, the second should not count as "not lawfully obtained" in that the only "wrong" in obtaining is "listening," an activity arguably protected by the First Amendment. See *Pearson v Dodd*, 410 F2d 701 (DC Cir 1969).

[206] 501 US at 671.

[207] Compare *Seattle Times Co. v Rhinehart*, 467 US 20 (1984).

[208] Compare *Snepp v United States*, 444 US 507 (1980).

Even if the retreat from the two general principles led to balancing, as recommended by Justice Souter's dissent, and even if the normative analysis favored a robust communications environment over the interests of the injured sources (as constitutional law has favored robust speech over the interests of libeled and emotionally distressed individuals), it is not clear which result best furthers First Amendment values. The ability of the press to bind itself contractually to confidentiality might aid it in gathering information from various sources.[209] In fact, the need to make its promise of confidentiality believable was the basis of the press' attempt to justify a constitutional reporters' privilege not to be forced to expose their sources in judicial proceedings.[210] Thus, whether application of or exemption from contract rules would best support the press' performance of its role of informing the public is an empirical question. The answer is unclear and may vary with historical circumstances.

The flaws in the dissent's general principle—that the government cannot punish lawfully obtained, truthful information—may be similar to those in the principle accepted in *Turner* that content discrimination is always presumptively bad. The paradigm cases representing each principle involved suppression of speech. In some circumstances, however, punishment for a truthful publication, like structural regulation of the media designed to further content concerns, can serve the goal of increasing the capacity of

---

[209] Note, *Damages for a Reporter's Breach of Confidence*, 105 Harv L Rev 277–87 (1991). A focus on which rule leads to greatest "quantity" or the greatest "overall stock of information," id at 280, is too simplistic. The press-source relationships that lead a source to give information to a reporter are sufficiently various and complex that any hypotheses concerning if and when the possibility of contractual enforcement of promises of confidentiality rights will aid the press in generating *useful* information must be developed with care. Contractual rights might lead primarily to greater leakage of inaccurate or, as in *Cowles Media*, truthful but inflammatory and misleading, information. If lack of contractual rights reduced press access to this information, it might improve the media's contribution to democracy. Moreover, whether individuals merit the protection of contractual promises varies. The times when responsible editors are most likely to choose to expose a confidential source because the source is itself newsworthy may, as in *Cowles Media*, be precisely the contexts where the source least deserves protection and, thus, least merits the benefits of contractual protection. These issues are carefully developed in Lili Levi, *Dangerous Liaisons: Seduction and Betrayal in Confidential Press-Source Relations*, 43 Rutgers L Rev 609 (1991).

[210] *Branzburg v Hayes*, 408 US 665 (1972). Of course, sources may rely heavily on their impression of the reliability of the reporter and little on some potential contractual right, meaning empirically that recognizing contractual rights will do more to restrain publication than to impede newsgathering. On the other hand, sources may have considerable fear of the government so that a testimonial privilege here would be beneficial.

the communications order to perform its democratic functions. The constitutional justification for copyright, which allows for punishment of certain truthful publications, is "to promote the progress of science and the useful arts."[211] Basically, this instrumental justification assumes that overall copyright will increase the social availability of information and insight. The enforceability of contracts about confidentiality, like copyright, may restrict publication of some truthful information while serving to improve the overall set of communications. Of course, the First Amendment may require "fair use" limits on copyright. This suggests the question whether there must be "fair use" exemptions from contractual obligations.

Certainly, the claim that enforcement of promises of confidentiality benefits the communications order is contestable. Persuaded of the merits of the press' argument in *Cowles Media*, a state might completely exempt media entities from liability for violation of this type of promise. If it did, could a newspaper, frustrated by this limit on its news-gathering capacities, succeed with a First Amendment claim that the government had unconstitutionally adopted a media-specific law that denied it a generally available, valuable legal right, a right to enter into certain binding contracts? Surely, a state should be able to do what four Justices in *Cowles Media* thought was constitutionally compelled. Should not the answer be the same as with the constitutional challenge to the Newspaper Preservation Act—that the government can adopt media-specific laws to structure the media, even if they disadvantage some media entities, as long as the laws do not suppress speech or attempt to undermine press functioning?

Equal protection doctrine periodically becomes similarly dysfunctional. When it becomes analytic rather than normative, it is often wisely ignored or else it creates confusion. For example, a male-only selective service registration requirement, that is, a "classification by gender," did not "serve important governmental objectives" and was not "substantially related to *achievement* of those objectives," as required by mid-level scrutiny,[212] since the government's possible objective of drafting only men could be as easily achieved whether or not women were also registered (assuming registration forms that had people check a box identifying them-

---

[211] US Const, Art I, § 8, cl 8.

[212] The language of mid-level scrutiny is taken from *Craig v Boren*, 429 US 190, 197 (1976) (emphasis added).

selves as either male or female). Thus, the classification quickly flunks mid-level scrutiny.[213] But both the majority and dissents in *Rostker v Goldberg* rejected this mechanical application of mid-level scrutiny because the analysis would lead to a decision creating only "superficial equality,"[214] a result that is "essentially useless"[215] or arguably "pointless."[216]

The real issue in *Rostker* was whether the majority was right that this classification "is not invidious"[217] or whether Marshall was correct that "[t]he Court today places its imprimatur on one of the most potent remaining public expressions of 'ancient canards about the proper role of women.'"[218] Here is not the place to address that substantive argument. Rather, the point is that both the majority and dissents recognized that the crucial issue was substantive— not a mechanical application of mid-level scrutiny.

Palmore v Sidoti[219] exemplifies the opposite spectacle—the Court unanimously invalidated a use of race that strict scrutiny should have upheld. Florida had denied a white mother custody of her child because the woman's new husband was black. The Court agreed that the "best interests of the child" is a "substantial government interest."[220] It did not, although it could,[221] dispute the trial

---

[213] The Court claimed that the classification "is not only sufficiently but also closely related to Congress's purpose in authorizing registration." *Rostker v Goldberg*, 453 US 57, 79 (1981). Although my comment feels uncomfortably like a semantic distinction, exemption of women does seem "closely related" to the majority's conception of Congress's purpose, but the gender classification is not related at all "to achievement" of that purpose, as required by *Craig*, in that universal registration would equally advance the purpose.

[214] Id at 79.

[215] Id at 84 (White and Brennan dissenting).

[216] Id at 96 (Marshall and Brennan dissenting).

[217] Id at 79.

[218] Id at 86 (quoting *Phillips v Martin Marietta* 400 US 542, 545 (1971)). In addition, there was a factual quarrel about whether Congress had recognized that conscripted women would be useful in the wartime military. The dissent could also argue that the male-only registration system treats women invidiously by structuring future decision making in a manner which biases consideration of the value of women's military involvement. At the time of an emergency draft, the country can only effectively look to the registrant pool. Any law that unnecessarily restricts consideration at that time of a legally imposed gender difference and that thereby locks women into current roles should be understood as invidious.

[219] 466 US 429 (1984).

[220] Id at 433.

[221] Given the vagaries of character development, even if the prevalent but inevitably not universal social reaction in the child's community would be stigmatization, the placement's full consequences for the child's development will be varied and could even be profoundly beneficial. In contrast, the lesson that promotion of racial homogeneity is properly determinative of the family in which a child should be raised could profoundly damage the child's ethical development.

court's factual premise—that the child would inevitably "suffer from the social stigmatization" if custody were granted to an interracial couple. Accordingly, considering race directly advances the best interests of the child, one of the state's highest interests.[222] That is, this use of race apparently passes strict scrutiny. But the Court refused to permit it, explaining:

> The question . . . is whether the reality of private biases and the possible injury they might inflict are permissible considerations for removal of an infant child from the custody of its natural mother. We have little difficulty concluding that they are not. . . . Private biases may be outside the reach of the law, but the law cannot, directly or indirectly, give them effect. . . . The effects of racial prejudice, however real, cannot justify a racial classification removing an infant child from the custody of [its mother].[223]

The Court ignored scrutiny analysis because to apply it would allow the state to be involved in giving invidious effect to, rather than opposing, the reality of private prejudice.[224]

Rostker and *Sidoti* both properly ignored the directives of scrutiny review just as the majority in *Turner* ignored content-based reasons for the must-carry rule. Like the dissent's use of content discrimination analysis in *Turner*, taking equal protection scrutiny seriously can perhaps generate greater problems. This is possibly most obvious in the affirmative action context. Focus on determining what level of scrutiny to apply and then applying it misses the point. The challenge is to identify the substantive value at stake, to explain the value's constitutional significance, and to determine whether the challenged practice offends the value.[225] Not only is this inquiry

---

[222] The case surely did not turn on treating the "best interests of the child" as only a "substantial" rather than a "compelling" interest.

[223] 466 US at 433–34.

[224] *Sidoti* is obviously relevant to the heckler's veto issue raised in *Feiner v New York*, 340 US 340 (1951). Likewise, if a generally legitimate reason for closing a swimming pool is its cost, but if the high cost per person results because racial integration leads to reduced attendance due to some people's racist attitudes or to higher policing costs due to the danger of interracial turmoil, *Sidoti* suggests that closure would unconstitutionally give effect to private prejudice. Cf *Palmer v Thompson*, 403 US 217 (1971).

[225] A common but highly partisan view is that color blindness is a moral imperative—that taking race into account is inherently bad and that only its use to avoid a greater evil can justify the sin. An alternative view is that people can and do value race in various positive ways—as a person might value her own or others' ethnicity, sexual identity, family history, or any distinguishing feature. And, likewise, that the state can make unobjectionable instrumental use of race, for example, in promoting a more egalitarian society. What the state cannot do, even if doing so would advance important goals, is to stigmatize or subordinate

necessary to sound constitutional analysis, but its careful completion makes the added question of what level of scrutiny to apply
irrelevant.

Metro Broadcasting v FCC[226] illustrates the befuddlement of traditional doctrine. The Court upheld affirmative action by avoiding
mechanical application of doctrine. Several methods of obtaining
broadcast licenses were open *only* to particular minorities. To uphold these programs, the Court emphasized that broadcast cases
are different from other speech cases, and that a lower-level equal
protection scrutiny governs Congressionally mandated programs.

An easy application of doctrine, however, would hold that the
law was doubly unconstitutional. The program was explicitly race-
based,[227] violating Equal Protection, and its main justification was
content-based (promoting minority-oriented programming), violating the First Amendment. Nevertheless, the Court held that the
law's content-based purpose was sufficiently compelling to avoid
equal protection invalidation. And apparently the equality-based
interests in diversity were so obviously appropriate that no First
Amendment challenge was considered—although presumably the
race-based purpose of promoting a more racially diverse spectrum
of voices would be sufficient to satisfy First Amendment scrutiny.[228] Each presumptive constitutional offense apparently has a
sufficient affirmative value to save the law from invalidation on the
basis of its other constitutional offense. The critical features, which
the traditional doctrinal tests obscure, are that the FCC program
was a structural regulation, was not suppressive of speech, and was
not racially invidious (although the dissent disputed this last point).

Often, however, scrutiny doctrine seems functional. Applying
strict scrutiny when a law uses race as a criterion historically has
appeared unproblematic for the same reason that most doctrinal

---

on the basis of race. Although both views can be elaborated with considerable sophistication
and rhetorical power, my own conclusion is that the second is so clearly right that what
lies in most need of explanation is the power and influence of the first view.

[226] 497 US 547 (1990).

[227] Of course, Brennan's majority opinion did not apply strict scrutiny. My claim is that
mechanical versions of the doctrine would require its application and that avoidance of
strict scrutiny will actually reflect substantive reasons that are believed to explain why the
challenged use of race does not offend constitutional values.

[228] The dissent emphasized that the interest was not merely with diversity but with
promoting "distinct views . . . associated with particular ethnic and racial groups," id at
621, but did not raise a First Amendment objection to viewpoint discrimination.

tests often appear useful. Tests develop when they identify and turn on features that past judicial experience has shown usually correlate with constitutional offense. American history seldom shows race being used, especially by government, except in an invidious or subordinating manner. These uses should be blocked—but not because they fail strict scrutiny but because they are subordinating or invidious.

Occasionally, judicial tests aid thought. Even informed, intelligent, decent people bring their class or social backgrounds to their understandings. Ingrained conformity to conventional ways can obscure the invidiousness of seemingly inoffensive practices. Thus, government use of race (or sex), especially when not closely related to a legitimate governmental purpose, rightly raises the suspicion that the use embodies prejudice or stigmatization or should be understood as reflecting a subordinating purpose. But, still, this suspicion is just that—it should not substitute for normative analysis.

Problems with equal protection doctrine resemble problems with the content-discrimination doctrine in *Turner*. Historically, legal challenges to content discrimination often took place in situations involving censorship. The challenged law usually either suppressed disfavored expression or gave officials such unconstrained discretion that it effectively allowed censorship.

Mosley[229] provides an illustration. Even when majorities (or those in power) prefer a more serene life to the robust world of public controversy, some influential interests may gain a right to engage in self-expression. If the First Amendment requires government to permit speech where the speech does not interfere with the use to which government has devoted its property, or more moderately, generally requires government to permit speech in facilities like parks and streets, the baseline is free expression. Although occasionally circumstances require that expression be limited in order to serve some other interest, given that the baseline is free expression, a restriction that permits one content-defined category of speech demonstrates that the facility can tolerate expression. Therefore, the restriction must generally be interpreted as suppressing speech, not as subsidizing the permitted speech. It would be unconvincing, for example, to argue that the government's pur-

---

[229] *Chicago Police Dept. v Mosley*, 408 US 92 (1972).

pose in maintaining streets and sidewalks is to subsidize labor picketing.

The evil in *Mosley*, however, was suppression, not content discrimination. More recent cases have faced content discrimination
that does not seem properly characterized as suppression. Various
doctrinal moves have developed to allow these discriminations.
One is to find that the content-based condition was not an unconstitutional condition. Another, as noted above, was to develop the
non-public forum label, the legitimate function of which is to identify situations in which the permitted speech involves the government using its property to achieve non-speech-suppressive, public
ends.

Thus, like the early cases involving the use of racial criteria, the
early content-discrimination cases embodied impermissible purposes and were properly struck down. But in both the race and
speech cases, the reason for invalidation was that the laws offended
substantive values. Later, cases arose in which these substantive
values were not at stake—or in which the substantive values even
supported the use of race (affirmative action) or of content (diversity
of voices or local information). These legitimate uses of race or
content typically involve resource allocations or structural regulation. In the speech context, many of these content-based subsidies
or content-motivated structural regulations are not constitutionally
problematic. *Turner* is such a case. The invocation of standard
content-discrimination doctrine in *Turner* only muddied the inquiry.

*   *   *

My claim has been that the Court in *Turner* failed to pay attention to the value basis of the First Amendment and that doing so
would have led to treating media entities very differently from
individual speakers. Specifically, it would have led the Court to
see that content-motivated structural regulation of the media is
often perfectly proper. Rather than being a call for a radical rethinking, my conclusion on this point is in accord with our historical tradition, often considered and approved by the Court, of
government structural interventions directed specifically at the media. The Court seemed to forget this history as it analyzed the
must-carry rules in terms of whether they were content-based. My
immediate claim is that this content-discrimination analysis is the

wrong approach and is not a faithful application of prior media law precedent. My deeper claim, only suggestively supported by the analysis of *Turner* and illustrations from other cases, is that the approach used in *Turner* reflects an increasingly common dysfunctional fixation on doctrinal tests and avoidance of normative analysis in constitutional analysis.

CRAIG M. BRADLEY

NOW v SCHEIDLER: RICO MEETS THE FIRST AMENDMENT

It is customary for articles in the *Supreme Court Review* to begin by pointing out that the case about to be discussed is, or at least would have been if the Court had handled it right, one of the "most important" cases of the last Term.[1] This is as it should be since the *Review*, limited as it must be to a discussion of six or seven out of a hundred or so decisions, necessarily focuses on those that really are the "most important."

Judging by the outcry that attended the Court's decision in *National Organization of Women (NOW) v Scheidler*,[2] in which the Court held that RICO could apply to anti-abortion protesters, one would assume that it, too, should be included on any list of the most significant cases of the last Term. For example, Randall Terry, the founder of Operation Rescue, one of the defendants in the suit, termed the holding "a vulgar betrayal of over 200 years of tolerance

Craig M. Bradley is James Louis Calamaras Professor of Law, Indiana University (Bloomington) School of Law.

AUTHOR'S NOTE: I wish to thank Dan Conkle, Joe Hoffmann, Jim Lindgren, and John Garvey for their helpful comments on earlier drafts of this article.

[1] For example, "Consider two cases—the most debated as well as the most important, First Amendment cases decided by the Supreme Court in the past two Terms." Elena Kagan, *The Changing Faces of First Amendment Neutrality: R.A.V. v St. Paul, Rust v Sullivan, and the Problem of Content-Based Underinclusion* 1992 Supreme Court Review 29; "In recent years, two major decisions—*Employment Division v Smith*, and *Lee v Weisman*—have effected a significant shift in our religion clause jurisprudence." Suzanna Sherry, *Lee v Weisman: Paradox Redux*, 1992 Supreme Court Review 123. "In the companion cases of *International Society for Krishna Consciousness v Lee* and *Lee v International Society for Krishna Consciousness*, The Supreme Court finessed an important opportunity to chart a clear future course for public forum doctrine." Lillian R. Bevier, *Rehabilitating Public Forum Doctrine: In Defense of Categories*, 1992 Supreme Court Review 79.

[2] 114 S Ct 798 (1994).

toward protest and civil disobedience."[3] An attorney for the
America Center for Law and Justice complained that "the court's
opinion today clearly and unequivocally would have applied to
the lunch counter sit-ins in Selma, Alabama."[4] A spokesman for
ACT-UP, a gay rights organization, declared that not only his
organization but animal rights activists, environmentalists, and
even feminist organizations would now be vulnerable to RICO
suits.[5]

NOW v Scheidler may thus have been the most controversial unanimous decision by the Supreme Court since *Brown v Board of Education.*[6] But from a lawyer's point of view, the unanimity was emi-
nently justified, for the Court did nothing more than hold that a
federal statute meant exactly what it said.

But if *Scheidler* was an unimportant case itself, by allowing a
civil RICO suit by pro-choice groups against pro-life activists to
proceed, it paved the way for a number of difficult issues to be
raised in the future. These involve the applicability of RICO and
other statutes to suits and prosecutions against political advocacy
organizations that may also engage in criminal activity.

As will be seen, the reassurance offered by Patricia Ireland of
NOW that her group will use RICO "only when violence erupts"[7]
does not wash away these concerns. This is because NOW's and
other potential plaintiffs' views of when violence has "erupted" and
who is responsible for it will differ radically from the views of
prospective defendants. This article will briefly discuss the Court's
decision in *NOW v Scheidler.* However, the bulk of the article will

---

[3] *Abortion Clinics Upheld by Court on Rackets Suits*, New York Times (Jan 25, 1994), p 1,
col 4. Mr. Terry, a veritable Vesuvius of vitriol toward the Court, was also quoted, on the
same day, as declaring the Court's ruling "the iron heel of government crushing protest and
dissent," USA Today, p 1A, and that "the Supreme Court has told civil protest to go to
hell." American Political Network, *Abortion Report* (Jan 25, 1994).

[4] Jay Sekulow quoted on American Political Network, Jan 25, 1994. Another representative of the same group declared that "through this technically limited court opinion, the
death crowd can brand peaceful protesters, authors, publishers and ardent advocates 'racketeers.' " Keith Fournier, The Houston Chronicle (Jan 28, 1994), p 15.

[5] "Ruling on RICO exposes activists to costly lawsuits," Washington Times (Jan 26, 1994),
p A4. In a similar vein, an editorial in the Chicago Sun-Times declared that "[e]veryone who
passionately holds unpopular political . . . views will now have to think twice about the
dire financial consequences of engaging in militant protest."

[6] 347 US 483 (1954).

[7] USA Today, supra note 3. "Patricia Ireland of NOW says her group will use RICO
only when violence erupts. 'What we're talking about are extortion and bombings and acts
of violence.' "

be devoted to considering the various hurdles—arising from RICO itself, the predicate crimes that must be alleged in a RICO suit, and the First Amendment—that plaintiffs/prosecutors must overcome before a RICO case can be won against anti-abortion protesters. As will be seen, notwithstanding *NOW v Scheidler*, those hurdles are high.

I. NOW v SCHEIDLER

The plaintiffs, including the National Organization for Women and women's health centers that perform abortions, sued a coalition of anti-abortion groups, including the Pro-Life Action Network (PLAN), Operation Rescue, and various individuals associated with these groups, including the named respondent Joseph Scheidler. The suit alleged violations of the Sherman Act and of §§ 1962 (a), (c), and (d) of RICO[8] in that the defendants were

---

[8] The Racketeer Influenced and Corrupt Organizations Statute, 18 USC § 1961 et seq, provides in pertinent part:

   1961(1): "racketeering activity" means (A) any act or threat involving murder, kidnapping, gambling, arson, robbery, bribery, extortion . . . which is chargeable under State law and punishable by imprisonment for more than one year; (B) any act which is indictable under any of the following provisions of Title 18, United States Code: . . . Section 1951 (relating to interference with commerce, robbery or extortion). . . .

* * * *

   1961(4) "enterprise" includes any individual, partnership, corporation, association, or other legal entity, and any union or group of individuals associated in fact although not a legal entity.
   1961(5) pattern of racketeering activity" requires at least two acts of racketeering activity. . . .

* * * *

   1962 (a) It shall be unlawful for any person who has received any income derived directly or indirectly, from a pattern of racketeering activity . . . to use or invest, directed or indirectly (in) any enterprise which is engaged in or the activities of which affect, interstate or foreign commerce.
   1962(b) It shall be unlawful for any person through a pattern of racketeering activity . . . to acquire or maintain, directly or indirectly, any interest or control of any (interstate) enterprise.
   1962(c) It shall be unlawful for any person employed by or associated with any enterprise engaged in, or the activities of which affect, interstate or foreign commerce, to conduct or participate, directly or indirectly, in the conduct of such enterprise's affairs through a pattern of racketeering activity. . . .
   1962(d) It shall be unlawful for any person to conspire to violate any of the provisions of subsection (a), (b), or (c) of this section.

* * * *

   1964(c). . . . Any person injured in his business or property by reason of a (RICO) violation may sue . . . and shall recover threefold the damages he sustains. . . .

members of a nationwide conspiracy to shut down abortion clinics through a pattern of extortionate acts that violated the Hobbs Act. Examples of this "conspiracy" included various allegations of trespass, threats, physical attacks, arson, theft of fetuses, and a variety of other activities.[9]

The Sherman Act and the RICO claims were all dismissed by the District Court, and these dismissals were affirmed by the court of appeals.[10] Of these, the Supreme Court only considered plaintiffs' claim under § 1962(c) of RICO,[11] that defendants operated their anti-abortion "enterprises" through a "pattern of racketeering activities," that is, extortion under the Hobbs Act.

As to this claim, the Seventh Circuit had issued an unusual decision in which it claimed to be ruling against plaintiffs "reluctantly," and then seemed to belie that claim by reading RICO more narrowly than was justified by the terms of the statute.

The dispute focused on the meaning of the term "enterprise," which is defined by the statute as "includ(ing) any individual, partnership, corporation, or other legal entity, and any union or group of individuals associated in fact, although not a legal entity." The Supreme Court had previously held, in *United States v Turkette*,[12] that RICO was not limited to "legitimate" organizations:[13] "There is no restriction upon the associations embraced by the definition [of enterprise]."[14]

Nevertheless, in *Scheidler*, the Seventh Circuit concluded that the term "enterprise" was limited to entities that had a "financial purpose."[15] The court's decision was based on a Second Circuit case, *United States v Ivic*.[16] *Ivic* had held that a Croation terrorist

[9] See Jt App pp 66–70, 95.

[10] *National Organization for Women v Scheidler*, 765 F Supp 937 (ND Ill 1991), aff'd 968 F2d 612 (7th Cir 1992). The Sherman Act claim was dismissed under the doctrine of *Eastern Railroad Presidents Conference v Noerr Motor Freight*, 365 US 127 (1961) because the defendants' activities had political, not economic, objectives and hence did not violate antitrust laws. 114 S Ct at 802. The § 1962(a) RICO claim was dismissed because voluntary contributions received by the defendants did not constitute income derived from racketeering activity. Id. The RICO conspiracy claim was dismissed because there were no substantive sections left on which to base the RICO conspiracy. Id.

[11] The Supreme Court also held that petitioners had standing to sue. 114 S Ct 802–03.

[12] 452 US 576 (1981).

[13] Id at 580.

[14] Id.

[15] 968 F2d 628.

[16] 700 F2d 51 (2d Cir 1983).

organization could not be prosecuted under RICO because the "enterprise" element of RICO was limited to "organized profit-seeking venture(s)."[17] The *Ivic* court reasoned that RICO was, as its legislative history showed, aimed at the "evil corruption of our commerce and trade" by organized crime, and not aimed at politically motivated acts. Furthermore, the term "enterprise" as used in §§ 1962(a) and (b) of RICO seemed to be limited to commercial organizations, and therefore the same understanding should be applied as to § 1962 (c). Finally, the phrase "enterprise engaged in, or the activities of which affect, interstate or foreign commerce" suggested to the court that the enterprise must be commercial in nature.

The Supreme Court, following a generally admirable series of cases in which it has carefully read RICO as covering no more and no less than the statutory language suggests,[18] made short work of the Seventh and Second Circuits' holdings. In a unanimous opinion by Chief Justice Rehnquist, the Court noted that the definition of "enterprise" in the statute could have been limited to individuals or groups that had an "economic motive," but was not.[19] Rather, as § 1961(4) declares, "enterprise includes *any* individual . . . or group of individuals. . . . "The Court further observed that, while the statute may have had " 'organized crime as its focus, [it] was not limited in application to organized crime.' "[20] Third, the Court recognized that it is not necessary to be a profit-seeking organization in order to "affect interstate commerce" under the statute.[21]

As to the "reading like terms alike" argument of the *Ivic* court, the Supreme Court held that "[t]he term 'enterprise' in subsections (a) and (b) plays a different role . . . than it does in subsection (c):"[22]

> The enterprise in [(a) and (b)] is the victim of unlawful activity and may very well be a "profit-seeking" entity that represents

---

[17] Id at 60.

[18] See, e.g., *Reves v Ernst and Young*, 113 S Ct 1163 (1993); *Sedima, S.PR.L. v Imrex*, 473 US 479 (1985); *United States v Turkette*, 452 US 576 (1981). But see *H.J. Inc. v Northwestern Bell Telephone Co.*, 492 US 229 (1989), where the Court's requirements for proving the "pattern" under RICO seemed to be based more on a statement in the legislative history rather than on the words of the statute.

[19] 114 S Ct 805.

[20] 114 S Ct 805, quoting *H.J. Inc. v Northwestern Bell Telephone Co.*, 492 US 229, 248 (1989).

[21] 114 S Ct 804, quoting 18 USC § 1962(c).

[22] Id at 804.

a property interest that may be acquired. But the statutory language in subsections (a) and (b) does not mandate that the enterprise be a "profit-seeking" entity; it simply requires that the enterprise be an entity that was acquired through illegal activity or the money generated from illegal activity.

By contrast, the "enterprise" in subsection (c) connotes generally the vehicle through which the unlawful pattern of racketeering activity is committed. . . . Since the enterprise in subsection (c) is not being acquired it need not have a property interest that can be acquired nor an economic motive for engaging in illegal activity; it need only be an association in fact that engages in a pattern of racketeering activity.[23]

Indeed, it seems clear that the premise of the *Ivic* court, as well as its conclusion, was incorrect. If a group of terrorists robbed banks to raise money to "buy out" a competing terrorist group, or used a pattern of arson and murder to take over such a group, it would violate §§ 1962(a) and (b), respectively, as long as it could be shown that the activities of the target group affected interstate commerce. Since terrorist and other political action groups may "affect commerce" in various ways without being "profit-seeking," it follows that they may qualify as "enterprises" under all of the RICO subsections.

Finding the statutory language "unambiguous" and " 'no clearly expressed legislative intent to the contrary' "[24] the Court unanimously overruled the dismissal of the plaintiff's RICO action and allowed the suit to proceed.

Obviously, this conclusion does not strike a "death blow" or any kind of blow to the First Amendment because the question of how this lawsuit may affect the First Amendment rights of political advocacy organizations was explicitly not considered by the Court.[25] However, it is natural and appropriate to anticipate this issue now that this case is to go forward, especially in view of the fact that many of the specific allegations in NOW's complaint involve conduct that appears to be protected speech.[26] Indeed, when

---

[23] Id.

[24] 114 S Ct 806, quoting *Reves v Ernst & Young*, 113 S Ct 1163 (1993).

[25] 114 S Ct 806 n 6. However, one of the concerns expressed after the decision was that the very existence of such causes of action will allow harassing suits against political advocacy organizations even if those suits prove unsuccessful. For example, "The kinds of money pro-lifers have spent defending themselves ($1 million and climbing) by itself will cool other protesters." Dennis Byrne, Chicago Sun-Times (Jan 25, 1994), p 19.

[26] For a discussion of this issue, see text at note 111.

a case stirs up as much concern and controversy among diverse elements of society as this one did, it is wise for one or two Justices to issue a concurring opinion that, while not undercutting the majority opinion, indicates that at least some members of the Court are concerned about, and will be watching, how future developments may affect constitutional rights.

This is exactly what Justice Souter, joined by Justice Kennedy, did. Justice Souter first expressed strong support for the Court's interpretation of RICO.[27] However, he went on to stress that "nothing in the Court's opinion precludes a RICO defendant from raising the First Amendment in its defense in a particular case."[28] In particular, citing *NAACP v Claiborne Hardware*,[29] he noted that "conduct alleged to amount to Hobbs Act extortion, for example, or one of the other, somewhat elastic RICO predicate acts may turn out to be fully protected First Amendment activity. . . ."[30] He added that "even in a case where a RICO violation has been validly established, the First Amendment may limit the relief that can be granted against an organization otherwise engaging in protected expression."[31] The remainder of this article will discuss the two types of cases raised by Justice Souter: a lawsuit where criminality, or at least criminality for the purposes of RICO, is unclear, and a suit where criminality is clear but the responsibility of the group for the criminal acts must be established.

II. RICO Criminality Unclear: The Next Phase of NOW v Scheidler

Having survived the challenge in the Supreme Court, the litigation in this case has been returned to the District Court for further proceedings. These should prove interesting. Though the defendants' and their supporters' reaction to the Supreme Court's decision was overblown, their concerns about the impact on First Amendment rights if plaintiffs were to prevail on the complaint filed in this case were not exaggerated.

---

[27] Id at 806–07 (Souter, J, concurring).

[28] Id at 807.

[29] 458 US 886 (1982).

[30] Id.

[31] Id.

The complaint named four organizations[32] and seven individuals[33] as defendants. As noted above, the sole predicate crime charged as the basis for the RICO suit was the Hobbs Act. The plaintiffs charged that the "defendants have attempted, conspired, or actually (sic) threatened or used actual force, violence or fear to induce or attempt to induce the employees of affected clinics to give up their jobs . . . doctors . . . to give up their economic right to practice medicine . . . patients . . . to give up their right to obtain services, etc."[34] Although the plaintiffs attached an appendix to the complaint listing a series of crimes such as arson and bombing committed by various people against abortion clinics in the last fifteen years, none of the arson and bombing crimes, for example, were committed by the named defendants.[35] Nor does the complaint suggest what the connection of the arsonists and bombers to the named defendants might be.

Instead, the complaint details a lengthy catalog of activities, many of which are clearly protected by the First Amendment and none of which appears to be a violation of the Hobbs Act. For example, among the "predicate acts" listed in the complaint are "Attempts, conspiracies to commit and commission of extortion against the Women's Awareness Clinic, its employees, doctors, patients and prospective patients in Ft. Lauderdale, Fla. by persons attending the 1984 National Pro-Life Conference, at which defendant Scheidler presented a workshop."[36] However, earlier in the complaint, where the activities of this workshop are spelled out, "extortionate" conduct is not alleged:

> Defendant Scheidler presented a conference workshop on "Effective Confrontation: A 'How To' of Picketing, Leafletting, Sit-ins and Blitzes." He also spoke at a "Ready for Action" rally. As part of their training, approximately 200 conference participants were taken by bus from the convention to the Women's Aware-

---

[32] Vita-Med Laboratories; Pro-Life Action League (PLAL); Pro-Life Direct Action League (PDAL); Operation Rescue; and Project Life. Jt App 43–44.

[33] Joseph Scheidler, John Ryan, Randall Terry, Andrew Scholberg, Conrad Wojnar, Timothy Murphy, and Monica Migliorino. Jt App pp 42–43.

[34] RICO Case Statement, id at 91.

[35] For example, the "Exhibit" lists bombings and arson by Peter Burkin, Michael Bray, Don Benny Anderson, and Curtis Beseda, Jt App at 162–64, but the complaint does not otherwise mention these people.

[36] Jt App p 66.

ness Clinic, a clinic that offers abortion services. They surrounded the clinic, blocking all entrances and exits.[37]

Elsewhere, the complaint charges the defendants with "trying to gain media attention,"[38] and "setting out guidelines to ensure better control of PLAN demonstrations in order to improve public perception."[39] More to the point, the defendants are charged with "criminal trespass,"[40] "storm[ing] a clinic" and "ransacking a medical procedures room, destroying surgical supplies,"[41] and shipping stolen laboratory specimens in interstate commerce.[42] In short, plaintiffs' charge that the defendants employed these tactics in order to force clinics to close, thus affecting commerce.

Some of the activities specified are clearly crimes, and others, though they may constitute protected speech on their face, may also be used to establish a conspiracy.[43] However, none of these activities constitutes "extortion" under the Hobbs Act. Since Hobbs Act violations were the sole predicate for the RICO case, it follows that, unless more can be shown, the RICO case must fail.

A. PROBLEMS WITH THE HOBBS ACT CHARGE

A Hobbs Act charge based on extortion contains four elements: (1) in any way or degree affecting commerce, (2) obtaining property from another (3) with his consent (4) induced by wrongful use of actual or threatened force, violence, or fear, or under color of official right.[44]

---

[37] Id at 48–49.

[38] Id.

[39] Id at 53.

[40] Id at 51.

[41] Id at 50.

[42] Id at 48.

[43] *Yates v United States*, 354 US 298, 334 (1957) (overt act in indictment need not be criminal).

[44] 18 USC § 1951(a) provides:

> Whoever, in any way or degree obstructs, delays or affects commerce or the movement of any article or commodity in commerce by robbery or extortion or attempts or conspires so to do, or commits or threatens physical violence to any person or property in furtherance of a plan or purpose to do anything in violation of this section shall be fined, etc.
>
> ***
>
> (b)(2) The term extortion means the obtaining of property from another, with his consent, induced by wrongful use of actual or threatened force, violence or fear, or under color of official right.

The difficulty with NOW's complaint is that it fails to allege that the defendants "obtained property" or attempted to obtain property from the plaintiffs. But NOW asserts that this doesn't matter: "Extortion does not require that the extorter receive anything."[45] Since this goes against the clear language of the Hobbs Act, the burden is on the plaintiffs to support this assertion.

They cite four cases. In the first, *United States v Green*,[46] the Supreme Court held that the Hobbs Act covered a union representative's threatening violence in order to obtain payment for "imposed, unwanted, superfluous and fictitious services" by union members.[47] That is, it was not necessary that the defendant attempt to "obtain property" *for himself*[48]; it was sufficient that he sought to obtain it for the union members. *Green* in no way suggests that the "obtaining property" requirement can be read out of the Hobbs Act. The other cases cited by the plaintiffs are to similar effect.[49] The plaintiffs can point to nothing in the legislative history that suggests that Congress intended that the clear words of the statute be ignored.

The plaintiffs are on somewhat stronger ground when they correctly point out that "intangible property such as the rights to vote, assemble and speak in a union setting and to make business decisions free of coercion" have been covered by the Hobbs Act.[50] Since these rights cannot be "received" by another person, they reason, it must follow that loss to victims is sufficient to establish the crime. Thus, plaintiffs argue that, in this case, the loss of and interference with the legitimate business of the abortion clinics is sufficient to satisfy the Hobbs Act even though the defendants neither experienced nor sought economic gain from their actions.[51]

---

[45] Reply Brief of Petitioners (Filed Nov 1, 1993), pp 11–12.

[46] 350 US 415 (1956).

[47] Id at 417.

[48] Id at 420.

[49] In *United States v Frazier*, 560 F2d 884, 887 (8th Cir 1977), cert den 435 US 968, the Court held that, where the defendant never attempted to pick up the money he had extorted, the Hobbs Act was nevertheless violated. In *United States v Lance*, 536 F2d 1065, 1068 (5th Cir, 1976), the court rejected the defendant's claim that, in seeking to obtain a "loan" from the victim by threats, he had not sought to "obtain property." The court held that use of money even for a short period of time is a "property" interest. Id at 1068. In *United States v Santoni*, 585 F2d 667 (4th Cir 1978) cert den 440 US 910 (1979), the defendant, a public official, sought to obtain a subcontract for his designee from an unwilling contractor/victim by promising future government contracts to the contractor. Obviously, the defendant sought to "obtain property" for the subcontractor here.

[50] Reply Brief of Petitioners, supra note 45, at p 12, and cases cited therein.

[51] Id.

The problem with this argument is that, in the cases cited by the plaintiffs, even though the loss to the victim may have been intangible, the defendant nevertheless sought to obtain property, that is, *economic advantage*. For example, in *United States v Tropiano*,[52] one of the leading cases on this topic, the defendant threatened the victim company with unlawful force unless the victim stopped competing for business that the defendant wanted for himself. The court held that the victim's loss was "the [intangible] right to solicit business free of territorial restrictions wrongfully imposed by its competitors."[53] Property included "any valuable right considered as a source or element of wealth."[54] Obviously, though, the reason for the extortionate threats was that the defendant wanted to take business, or the right to solicit business, away from the victim—that is, he sought to obtain property.[55]

Similarly, in *United States v Local 560*,[56] the defendants sought to take over a union through acts of extortion and murder. While the victims' loss was characterized as an intangible right of union members to participate in the affairs of the union, nevertheless, the defendants were again plainly seeking "property," that is, control of the union, and the economic benefits that would bring.[57] Even the cases cited by NOW in which the defendants' primary motivation may have been political, such as *United States v Anderson*,[58] in which the defendant kidnapped an abortion clinic doctor, all included demands for economic advantage as well.[59]

---

[52] 418 F2d 1069 (2d Cir 1969) cert den 397 US 1021.

[53] Id at 1075–76.

[54] Id at 1075.

[55] The Model Penal Code takes the same approach as the Hobbs Act, limiting "Extortion" to the obtainment of property and calling threats made "with purpose unlawfully to restrict another's freedom of action" "Criminal Coercion." II American Law Institute, Model Penal Code and Commentaries (Official Draft 1980) § 223.4 p 203.

[56] 780 F2d 267 (3d Cir 1985) cert den 476 US 1140.

[57] In *United States v Debs*, 949 F2d 199 (6th Cir 1991), also cited by Petitioners, the defendant employed threats and violence to induce potential opponents not to oppose him for the union presidency. The court quite rightly held that "property" under the Hobbs Act included a union presidency. Id at 201.

[58] 716 F2d 446 (7th Cir 1983).

[59] For example, in *Anderson*, id, the court noted that "during the first two days of captivity, the abductors spoke only of the victims' money and how it could be obtained." Id at 447. Nothing in the case suggests that defendant's motive to obtain economic advantage need not be shown. Similarly, in *United States v Mitchell*, 463 F2d 187 (8th Cir 1972), the defendant, a representative of the Congress of Racial Equality, threatened violence against a company if the company didn't make a $1000 contribution to CORE and rehire a discharged black employee. Id at 189.

The only case to have expressly held that a defendant who lacked any intent to gain could commit "extortion" under the Hobbs Act is *Northeast Women's Center, Inc. v McMonagle*, a case that is virtually identical to *NOW v Scheidler*.[60] In *McMonagle*, the Third Circuit, citing the same inapposite precedents discussed in the preceding two paragraphs, concluded that deprivation of the victim's property interest was sufficient to satisfy the "obtaining property" requirement in the Hobbs Act.[61] This ignores the clear words of the statute.[62]

The Hobbs Act was drawn from New York's Field Code.[63] Under that code, it was well settled that extortion required an unlawful taking. As the New York cases cited by the Supreme Court in *United States v Enmons*[64] make clear, an accused could not be guilty of extortion unless he "was actuated by the purpose of obtaining a *financial benefit* for himself. . . ."[65] The crime described by the plaintiffs in this case, to the extent that they have described a crime

---

[60] 868 F2d 1342 (3d Cir 1989). In *NOW v Scheidler*, the Seventh Circuit "agree[d] with the Third Circuit's interpretation of the Hobbs Act . . . " on this point. 968 F2d at 629 and n 17.

[61] Id at 1350. See also *Town of West Hartford v Operation Rescue*, 915 F2d 92 (2d Cir 1990). In that case, the *town* where anti-abortion violence had occurred brought a civil RICO suit against the protestors, based on Hobbs Act violations. The court vacated an injunction against the defendants on the ground that the defendants had not obtained or attempted to obtain any property from the town: "the term 'property' cannot plausibly be construed to include altered official conduct." Id at 102. It could similarly be said that the requirement of "obtaining property" is not satisfied by altering the behavior of clinic personnel, but, since the court assumed, arguendo, that "interference with the Center's operations constituted extortion of the Center," id, it did not consider this issue.

[62] The court also ignored an earlier Third Circuit case, *United States v Nedley*, 255 F2d 350, 355–58 (1958). *Nedley* held that merely beating up a truck driver during a labor dispute, and thus interfering with commerce by violence, did not constitute "robbery" under the Hobbs Act because there was no "obtaining of property" by the defendants. *Nedley* did not consider whether this could have been a violation of the third, "interference with commerce by force" clause of the Hobbs Act discussed in text at notes 77–80.

[63] *Evans v United States*, 112 S Ct 1881, 1886 (n 9) (1992). "The definitions in this bill are copied from the New York Code substantially." 91 Cong Rec 11900 (1945). (Statement of Cong Hobbs.)

[64] 410 US 396 (1973).

[65] Id at 406, n 16, quoting *People v Adelstein* (emphasis added, citation omitted). Accord, *People v Ryan*, 232 NY 234, 235, 133 NE 572, 573 (1921) (intent to extort requires intent to "gain money or property"); *Field Code*, chap IV, § 584 (extortion "include[s] the criminal acquisition of the property of another). See also *United States v Nedley*, supra note 62, and New York cases cited therein, 255 F2d 355. The Supreme Court recently reiterated that extortion under the Hobbs Act covers "acts by private individuals by which property is obtained by means of threats, force or violence." *Evans v United States*, 112 S Ct 1881, 1885 (1992).

at all, is, under the Model Penal Code and the laws of most states, the crime of "criminal coercion."[66] Unfortunately for the plaintiffs, this is not one of the pattern crimes listed in RICO. Thus, although RICO itself does not require a financial motivation, as *Scheidler* held, if the pattern crime charged is extortion under the Hobbs Act, an economic motive must be proved.

The issue is virtually identical to that decided by the Supreme Court with regard to the mail fraud statute, 18 USC § 1341, in *McNally v United States*[67] and *Carpenter v United States*.[68] Section 1341 forbids anyone who, "having devised . . . any scheme or artifice to defraud, or for obtaining money or property by means of false or fraudulent pretenses," to use the mails in furtherance of such scheme. Even though the first clause, prohibiting "fraud," does not expressly mention "money or property," the *McNally* Court concluded that the mail fraud statute was "limited in scope to the protection of property rights," as the second clause illustrated.[69] *Carpenter* went on to hold that these property rights could be intangible, such as business information, and, as I read the cases, the defendant's gain need not be identical to the victim's loss.[70] Nevertheless, even in the first clause of the statute, where "obtaining property" was not specifically mentioned, the Court read it in. Clearly in the Hobbs Act, where Congress specifically stated that *"extortion means the obtaining of property"* the Court will not read the economic gain element out.[71]

---

[66] American Law Institute, *Model Penal Code and Commentaries* (Official Draft, 1980) § 223.4 p 203: "Criminal coercion punishes threats made 'with purpose unlawfully to restrict another's freedom of action to his detriment' while extortion is . . . limited to one who 'obtains property of another by' threats."

[67] 483 US 350 (1987).

[68] 484 US 19 (1987).

[69] 483 US 360.

[70] Craig Bradley, *Foreward: Mail Fraud After McNally and Carpenter: The Essence of Fraud*, 79 J Crim Law & Criminol 573, 602 (1988). Thus, I concluded that the statute requires proof of a "scheme in which the defendant, through knowingly deceitful behavior, intends an economic gain and is at least negligent as to economic harm to the victim." Id. *McNally* dealt with a situation where the defendant's gain was clear; it was the loss to the victim that was in doubt. Therefore, it is the converse of this case. However, as the above summary of the *McNally* and *Carpenter* holdings shows, both potential economic harm to the victim *and* economic gain to the defendant must be shown before mail fraud can be found.

[71] "[W]here there are two rational readings of a criminal statute, one harsher than the other, we are to choose the harsher only when Congress has spoken in clear and definite language." *McNally*, supra note 67, 483 US at 359–60. The Hobbs Act was based on the Anti-Racketeering Act of 1934 (48 Stat 979) HR No 238, 79th Cong, 1st Sess (Feb 27, 1945), p 1. That statute was even more explicit in its property requirement. It prohibited

Another problem raised by defendants is that "extortion" under the Hobbs Act requires the "*wrongful* use of actual or threatened force, etc."[72] In *United States v Enmons*,[73] the Supreme Court held that the Act did not apply to threats of violence to achieve legitimate union objectives, but only to demands for under-the-table payoffs to union officials, superfluous employees, and the like. Threats of violence to achieve higher wages, for example, were not "wrongful" threats.[74] Since defendants' use of violence in this case is similarly to achieve the "legitimate" end of closing down abortion clinics,[75] they argue that it is also not a "wrongful" threat of force. However, *Enmons* is heavily influenced by specific legislative history indicating that threats or acts of *labor* violence were not covered by the act,[76] and does not hold generally that any ultimately "legitimate" goal excuses violence under the Hobbs Act.

B. A POSSIBLE SOLUTION

In any event, there is more to the Hobbs Act than the plaintiffs, or anyone else, seem to have realized. The statute forbids obstructing, delaying, or affecting commerce by robbery or extortion, or attempting or conspiring so to do. As discussed, "obtaining property" by the defendant is an element of extortion (and of robbery). But, the statute goes on to forbid "committ[ing] or threaten[ing] physical violence to any person or property in furtherance of a plan or purpose to do anything in violation of this section." No "obtaining property" qualification applies to this portion of the statute.

This rather confusing clause is susceptible of two interpretations. First it may simply forbid committing or threatening violence in furtherance of a plan to obstruct commerce by robbery or extortion. But this interpretation makes no sense! Robbery and extortion

"any person who [affecting commerce] (a) obtains or attempts to obtain, by the use of [force, etc.], the payment of money or other valuable considerations, or the purchase or rental of property [etc.] or (b) obtains the property of another with his consent [etc.]." Id.

[72] Brief of Respondent Migliorino, pp 32–34.

[73] Note 64 supra.

[74] Id at 410.

[75] In *Bray v Alexandria Women's Health Clinic, et al*, 113 S Ct 753 (1993), the Court observed that "it cannot be denied that there are common and respectable reasons for opposing [abortion] other than hatred of or condescension toward [or indeed any view at all concerning] women as a class." Id at 760.

[76] Id at 406 (quoting Cong Hobbs asserting that assaults that occurred during a strike would not be covered by the Act).

frequently involve the commission (robbery) or threat (extortion) of violence, though "extortion" covers other threats as well. Moreover, the "robbery and extortion" clauses also forbid "attempts" and conspiracies. Thus, under this reading, the "physical violence" clause would be less inclusive, and hence would add nothing, to the preceding "robbery" and "extortion" clauses. One who commits violence in furtherance of a plan to commit robbery or extortion has either committed, attempted, or conspired to commit robbery or extortion and thus has violated the first clause, rendering the third clause nugatory.[77]

The other possible reading is more sensible. It forbids threatening or committing physical violence in furtherance of a plan to "obstruct delay or affect commerce" (other than through robbery or extortion). The Hobbs Act was first proposed during World War II, and a major concern of Congress at that time was that interstate shipments of commodities and war material not be interfered with.[78] Contrary to the common assumption that the Act prohibits interference with commerce only by robbery or extortion, both of which require an economic motive, a third sort of activity is also prohibited on the face of the Act: "obstruct[ing], delay[ing] or affect[ing]" (e.g., sabotaging) interstate shipments through the commission or threat of violence, regardless of any obtainment of property motive on the defendant's part. Thus, Nazi saboteurs who blew up interstate shipments or delayed them

---

[77] It is possible to imagine a case in which one threatens violence in furtherance of a personal plan to rob a bank (or commit extortion) without conspiring or attempting to rob the bank. For example, calling a bank guard the day before the planned robbery and saying, "If you interfere with me when I rob the bank, I'll kill you," but then taking no further steps to rob the bank is, arguably, such a threat without yet being an attempt. However, such a case seems far-fetched and unlikely. Ordinarily such threats, even if the robbery never occurred, would constitute an attempt or be part of a conspiracy. Surely Congress did not add a special clause to the Hobbs Act to deal with such a remote possibility.

[78] "The purposes of this bill are (1) to prevent interference with interstate commerce by robbery or extortion, as defined in the bill, and (2) to prevent interference during the war with the transportation of troops, munitions, war supplies, or mail in interstate or foreign commerce." HR No 238, 79th Cong, 1st Sess (Feb 27, 1945), p 1. (Submitted by Cong Hobbs.) However, the Committee's reference to the war effort apparently applied to another portion of the bill than what was to become the Hobbs Act. Id at p 9. This second portion (Title II) was never enacted, presumably because the war ended. Nevertheless, the quoted passage shows Congress's concern with interference with commerce by threats and violence that may not constitute extortion. As another congressman put it, "The so-called Hobbs bill is designed to make assault, battery and highway robbery unpopular. Its purpose is to protect commerce against interference by violence, threats, coercion, or intimidation." 91 Cong Rec H11907 (Dec 12, 1945) (statement of Cong Fellows).

through bomb threats (true or false) would be guilty under this reading of the statute.[79] So too would anti-abortion protesters who, with no economic motive, interfered by threats or violence with the abortion business, at least if we leave aside First Amendment concerns, which are discussed below.[80]

C. PROBLEMS WITH EXTORTION AS A PREDICATE ACT

Another possible approach for the plaintiffs is simply to charge extortion under state law, which is a separate RICO predicate offense. Although many states limit "extortion" to property offenses as the Hobbs Act does (calling the activities of the defendants here "criminal coercion," which is not a RICO pattern crime), "a number of states leave the realm of property altogether and cover threats made to induce the [victim] to do 'any act against his will.' "[81] The difficulty with this approach is that the plaintiffs will be limited to charging activities that occurred in the states that do not require an economic motive for extortion.[82]

Another obstacle must be overcome if state law extortion is charged.[83] Unlike the Hobbs Act, the typical extortion statute re-

[79] Congress was well aware that Nazi saboteurs had in fact been landed by submarine on American shores to carry out such activities. United States Department of Justice, *Annual Report of the Attorney General to Congress* (1942), p 13; Leslie Thomas, *Orders for New York* (Penguin Books, 1990) is a novel devoted to this episode. See also 2 *German-Born Men Held for Espionage*, New York Times (Jan 22, 1943), p 9, referring to another, 32-agent spy ring, headed by a Gestapo agent.

[80] That the Hobbs Act covers three, rather than two, means of interfering with commerce is supported by dictum in *Stirone v United States*, 361 US 212, 215 (1960): "The Act speaks in broad language, manifesting a purpose to use all the constitutional power Congress has to punish interference with commerce by extortion, robbery or physical violence" (in *Stirone*, extortion was charged). Quoted with approval, *United States v Culbert*, 435 US 371, 373 (1978).

[81] 2 Wayne LaFave and Austin Scott, *Substantive Criminal Law* (1986) § 8.12 p 460.

[82] According to LaFave and Scott, id at 460, the only such states are Alaska, Colorado, Kansas, New Mexico, Ohio, and Wyoming. However, other states may simply call extortion "criminal coercion." Under the reasoning of *United States v Nardello*, 393 US 286 (1969), as long as the defendant's activities fall under what *Congress* would have considered extortion, it doesn't matter that state law may "label" it something else. Id at 293–94. But *Nardello* was based on the fact that "extortion" under the Travel Act clearly included "blackmail" as that term was used in Pennsylvania law. By contrast, "extortion" under the Hobbs Act is limited to "obtaining property." Thus, plaintiffs may have a hard time arguing that when Congress referred to "extortion . . . chargeable under state law" in RICO, it had in mind a crime that is not called extortion by either the state or the US Code.

[83] In contrast to the usual extortion statute, the Hobbs Act does not require a threat. Violence or fear will also suffice. The federal courts are agreed that, "as long as a defendant exploits his victim's fear, it is not necessary that the defendant make any threat, nor that he have created the fear." Norman Abrams and Sara Sun Beale, *Federal Criminal Law* (2d ed 1993), p 203 and cases cited therein.

quires that certain *threats* be used to obtain the property in question.[84] These include threats to inflict bodily injury on the victim, to accuse him of a criminal offense, to expose a secret, and so on.[85] But when one examines the complaint in *NOW v Scheidler*, it does not clearly set forth such threats. Rather, it simply lists a series of demonstrations, trespasses, and other efforts by the defendants to discourage or prevent abortions. The nearest thing to an extortionate threat in the complaint is ¶ 44, which states that

> Scheidler told the then-clinic administrator that he had come to "case the place" because he and his followers intended to force DWHO to close. . . . *He threatened Conner with reprisals should she refuse to quit her job.* Conner subsequently left her job. . . . [86]

If these "reprisals" were that she would be subjected to violence or exposure of secrets, then it would qualify as an extortionate threat in most states (leaving aside the "obtaining property" problem). But if by "reprisals" Scheidler merely meant further demonstrations and harassment, then there will be problems with the definition of "extortion" in most or all states, since there is neither a threat of bodily harm nor of exposure of secrets.[87] Where the

---

[84] Under the Hobbs Act, to establish extortion, the obtainment of property may be achieved by use of "actual or threatened force, violence or fear." It has been held that the fear need not be a consequence of a direct or implied threat by the defendant. *United States v Billups*, 692 F2d 320 (4th Cir 1982) cert den 464 US 820.

[85] See, e.g., Model Penal Code, supra note 55, § 223.4. See also LaFave and Scott, supra note 81 at § 8.12.

[86] Jt App pp 50–51. Another of what plaintiffs call a "threat" appears in ¶ 45: "Scheidler threatened that anti-abortionists 'will get rid of' [clinics such as DWHO]. I proclaim Delaware is going to become the first state in the union to be free of abortion facilities." Id. This is clearly a political, not an extortionate, "threat." See Kent Greenawalt, *Criminal Coercion and Freedom of Speech*, 78 Nw L Rev 1081 (1984) for a detailed discussion of the various types of extortionate threats.

Beyond this, there are several references to implied threats to unidentified victims such as ¶ 74: "The public statements of defendant Scheidler and the local co-conspirators implied that the clinics were not following proper procedures in disposing of medical waste. They carried the clear threat to suppliers, landlords, doctors and others who provide goods or services to the clinics that they too could be targeted by defendants for theft and other illegal activity as well as harassment and public controversy." Jt App p 60. See also ¶¶ 75 and 77. Any prosecutor who attempted to base an extortion prosecution on such a vague charge would be subject to prompt dismissal of his case.

[87] See LaFave and Scott, supra note 81, at § 8.12, discussing the kinds of threats that qualify as extortion under various state laws. It is also possible to violate the extortion laws of some states, as well as the Hobbs Act, by threatening concerted action, such as strikes or picketing, if the threatener is not paid off by the victim, but this is limited to under-the-table payoffs to the threatener, not satisfaction of the group's demands. Model Penal Code and Commentaries, supra note 56, p 219; *United States v Enmons*, 410 US 396, 406 n 16 (1973).

threat is of unlawful but nonviolent behavior, such as trespassing on the clinic's property, interfering with patient access, etc., it is unlikely to qualify under state extortion statutes. The additional First Amendment problems with criminalizing such threats are discussed in Part IV below.[88]

III. A RICO CASE WHERE CRIMINALITY IS CLEAR

Thus far, the discussion has focused on the *NOW v Scheidler* case itself where, in my view, the plaintiffs have failed to adequately allege the pattern crimes that must be the basis of the RICO civil action. Assume, however, that the commission of pattern crimes that are clearly outside the protection of the First Amendment can be established. This portion of the article discusses the difficulties a plaintiff would face in tying the organization, from which they wish to recover treble damages, to those crimes.

Imagine an anti-abortion organization called "Save Our Babies" (Sob). Sob is a nonprofit organization formed for the purpose of engaging in "all legitimate means to prevent the destruction of unborn children." Its charter limits the organization's activities to lobbying, picketing, testifying before legislative committees, taking out ads in newspapers, and "engaging in all legitimate forms of vigorous political protest." However, its members have frequently gone beyond the charter by trespassing on abortion clinic property and disrupting operations there by interfering with access by doctors and patients. Their activities have included grabbing and hitting clinic employees, throwing rocks through clinic windows, and stealing discarded fetuses as well as other property that was of value to the clinics. Moreover, the board of directors has endorsed all of the above activities.

So far, while a variety of local laws, as well as the new federal Freedom of Access to Clinic Entrances Act, have been violated, none of these acts are included within the listed pattern crimes of RICO,[89] as those crimes have, up to now, been viewed.[90] Conse-

---

[88] Plaintiffs also assert that they can prove other RICO predicate offenses such as theft from interstate shipments, 18 USC § 659 and the Travel Act, 18 USC § 1952. Petitioner's Reply Brief (Nov 1, 1993), p 14. Since these claims are not developed in the complaint, they are not dealt with here.

[89] See 18 USC § 1961(1), note 8 supra.

[90] As discussed above, under my interpretation of the Hobbs Act, some of these acts could be regarded, not as extortion, but as interference with commerce by the commission or threat of physical violence.

quently, any RICO civil suit or prosecution against Sob or the individuals involved in these various crimes must be dismissed, without regard to any special concerns about the First Amendment.[91]

However, two members of Sob, Bakunin and Molotov, conclude that these methods are too tame. Accordingly, on two successive weeks, they firebomb two different abortion clinics. On the third week they are arrested, and assorted bomb-making equipment is seized—evidence that they are planning further firebombings. They, the board of directors of Sob, and Sob itself are indicted for RICO violations as well as sued under RICO by the clinics in question. In addition to fines and imprisonment, removal of the board of directors under § 1964(a) will be sought by the government upon conviction. Treble damages are sought by the civil plaintiffs under § 1964(c).

The RICO indictment, which is also the basis for the civil suit, charges that Molotov, Bakunin, and the board conducted Sob through a pattern of racketeering activities (two counts of arson in violation of state law), in violation of 18 USC § 1962(c), and conspired to do so in violation of § 1962(d). Since "arson" is one of the crimes listed in RICO's definition of racketeering activity, the first hurdle to a successful RICO prosecution/civil suit has been surmounted. Furthermore, Sob is clearly an "enterprise" after *Scheidler*.

A. THE "PATTERN" ISSUE

There is a good deal more that must be proved to make out a RICO case against all named defendants. The first issue is whether a "pattern" of racketeering activity has been committed as defined by *H.J. Inc. v Northwestern Bell Telephone Co.*[92] In *H.J. Inc.*, the Court was concerned that the definition of "pattern" in § 1961(5) states only that a pattern "requires at least two acts of racketeering activity." The Court concluded that, while two acts are thus necessary to establish a "pattern," they are not sufficient.[93] Rather, the

---

[91] Many of the allegations in the complaint in *NOW v Scheidler* involve similar acts. Recognizing that these acts alone could not be the basis of a RICO suit, NOW's attorneys couched these charges as examples of a "conspiracy to commit extortion," which, on its face, would constitute a RICO violation. The First Amendment issues raised by such a complaint are discussed in Part IV.

[92] 492 US 229, 239 (1989).

[93] Id.

term "pattern" suggests something more than just two unrelated events. Thus, they turned to the legislative history to determine that "pattern" requires both a showing that "the racketeering predicates are related and that they amount to or pose a threat of continued criminal activity."[94]

Since these crimes were carried out by the same two people who belonged to the same organization and for the same purpose, the "relatedness" prong has been satisfied.[95] Indeed, in the context of attacks on abortion clinics, relatedness is unlikely to be a problem since the crimes will all have similar purposes and victims.[96]

Establishing "continuity" is a more difficult task. In *H.J. Inc.*, the Court required that the predicate crimes must either occur, or have threatened to occur, over a

> substantial period of time. Predicate acts extending over a few weeks or months and threatening no future criminal conduct do not satisfy this requirement: Congress was concerned with long-term criminal conduct.[97]

This seems to impute a more limited meaning to the term "pattern" than it would ordinarily have, and it is a meaning that is not justified by the legislative history, as Justice Scalia, concurring in the result, pointed out.[98]

Nevertheless, this is now the law, and the "continuity" requirement will pose a substantial barrier to any RICO suit or prosecution.[99] In the Sob case, the evidence of two bombings a week apart would not, after *H.J. Inc.*, establish a pattern. However, the additional evidence found during the search that showed that the sus-

---

[94] Id.

[95] "Criminal conduct forms a pattern if it embraces criminal acts that have the same or similar purposes, results, participants, victims, or methods of commission, or otherwise are interrelated by distinguishing characteristics and are not isolated events." Id at 240 quoting 18 USC § 3575(e).

[96] However, two such crimes will have to be committed by members of the same enterprise in order to qualify under RICO at all. It is surely sufficient, however, that *any* two of the RICO pattern crimes be committed—there need not be two of the *same* crime.

[97] 492 US at 242.

[98] 492 US at 253. As Justice Scalia noted, the majority seemed to be holding that "at least a few months of racketeering activity (and who knows how much more?) is generally for free, as far as RICO is concerned." Id at 254.

[99] Since *H.J. Inc.*, a number of cases have been lost due to a failure to satisfy this "continuity" requirement. For example, *Brode v Cohn*, 966 F2d 1237 (8th Cir 1992); *River City Markets, Inc. v Fleming*, 960 F2d 1458 (9th Cir 1992); *Aldridge v Lily-Tulip, Inc. Salary Retirement Plan Benefits Comm.*, 953 F2d 587 (11th Cir 1992).

pects were planning future bombings would be enough to show a "specific threat of repetition extending indefinitely into the future,"[100] and thus to satisfy the "continuity" requirement.[101]

B. THE "CONDUCT OR PARTICIPATE" ISSUE

Even though it has now been established that Bakunin and Molotov have committed a "pattern of racketeering activity" and that Sob is a "enterprise" under RICO, the RICO case is far from complete. It must now be established that the bombers "conducted or participated, directly or indirectly, in the conduct" of Sob's affairs "through" the pattern of bombings.

In *Reves v Ernst & Young*,[102] an accounting firm misrepresented the value of certain assets of an agricultural co-op to hide the fact that the co-op was insolvent, to the disadvantage of the co-op's creditors. The accountants, as far as the record reflected, were acting without the knowledge of the co-op's board.[103] The RICO suit was brought by the trustee in bankruptcy, Reves, against the accounting firm, claiming that the defendant had "conducted or participated in the conduct" of the *co-op's* (not the accounting firm's) affairs through a pattern of securities fraud in violation of 18 USC § 1962(c).

The Supreme Court concluded that the "conduct or participate" element of RICO had not been satisfied—that to violate RICO one must "participate in the operation or management of the enterprise itself."[104] Since the accounting firm was an independent auditor

---

[100] 492 US at 242.

[101] See also *United States v Indelicato*, 865 F2d 1370 (2d Cir 1989), cited with approval in *H.J. Inc.*, 492 US at 235 n 2, finding "continuity" in a triple murder that occurred in a matter of a few minutes, because the purpose of the murder, a Mafia power struggle, posed the threat of ongoing criminal activity.

It is not entirely clear from *H.J. Inc.* whether the "ongoing criminal activity" must also be RICO predicate crimes or whether other crimes, such as battery or trespass, might establish "continuity" by combining with predicate crimes that are too close in time to establish a "pattern" by themselves. However, since RICO requires a "pattern of racketeering activity" and since the Court has said that "pattern" requires continuity, it is likely that continued racketeering offenses and not just any offenses would be required.

[102] 113 S Ct 1163 (1993).

[103] Id at 1167. Just why Ernst and Young did this is unclear. For an interesting discussion of the economic consequences of *Reves* and other RICO cases, see Daniel Fischel and Alan Sykes, *Civil RICO After Reves: An Economic Commentary*, 1993 Supreme Court Review 153 (1994).

[104] Id at 1173.

that was not acting by direction of, or even with the knowledge of, the co-op's board of directors, it could not be said to have "conducted or participated in the conduct" of the co-op's affairs.[105] Having taken this clear, but restrictive,[106] view of RICO, the Court then backed off from it somewhat:

> We agree that liability under § 1962(c) is not limited to upper management. . . . An enterprise is "operated" not just by upper management but also by lower-rung participants in the enterprise who are under the direction of upper management. An enterprise also might be "operated" or "managed" by others "associated with" the enterprise who exert control over it as, for example, by bribery.[107]

While the limits of *Reves* are thus unclear, it is obvious that the plaintiff/prosecutor must show considerably more connection between the bombers and the Sob leadership than that the bombers were members of Sob, and were generally trying to advance its agenda. Either the bombers must have been acting at the direction of the leadership, or the leadership must have been sufficiently connected to the bombings that individual officers would be guilty, at least as accessories or conspirators,[108] of arson under state law. If this were shown, then the officers themselves could be found to have conducted the enterprise through a pattern of arson with no

---

[105] Id at 1167. Another approach that the plaintiff might have taken would have been to denominate the accounting firm as the "enterprise" and attempt to show that that firm was conducted through a pattern of securities fraud, but this was not charged.

[106] Prior to *Reves*, the broadest view of RICO, held by the Second Circuit, was that one could be guilty under § 1962(c) if "the predicate offenses are related to the activities of the enterprise." *United States v Scotto*, 641 F2d 47, 54 (2d Cir 1980) cert den 452 US 961. Compare *Bennett v Berg*, 710 F2d 1361, 1364 (8th Cir 1983) cert den 464 US 1008, requiring "some participation in the operation or management of the enterprise itself," a very narrow reading of the statute that the Court also rejected.

[107] 113 S Ct 1173. The Court declined to decide "how far § 1962(c) extends down the ladder of operation because it is clear that Arthur Young [Respondent's predecessor] was not acting under the direction of the Co-op's officers or board." Id at n 9. But the Court rejected the narrow reading of some circuits that the defendant must exercise "significant control over or within an enterprise." Id at 1170 n 4.

[108] The definition of "racketeering activity" in § 1961(1) includes "any act or threat involving . . . arson under state law. . . . " Thus co-conspirators and accessories, including, apparently, accessories after the fact, would be covered. See Norman Abrams and Sara Sun Beale, *Federal Criminal Law* (2d ed 1993), p 511, and cases cited therein (conspiracy to commit pattern crimes enough). Solicitation to commit a crime would also apparently be covered by this section.

need to show participation of Bakunin and Molotov in the operation or management of Sob.[109]

Another way to get around the "operation or management" problem is to define the "enterprise" differently. If, for example, Bakunin and Molotov had no position in the national organization but were in charge of the Kalamazoo branch of Sob, then that branch could be the "enterprise."[110] However, this would mean that the national organization, its directors, and assets would be exempt from prosecution and suit.

IV. First Amendment Issues

A. THE PROTECTION OF POLITICAL ADVOCACY GROUPS

So far, this article has been devoted to a basic discussion of RICO, and the underlying pattern crimes of Hobbs Act and extortion, that would be applicable to any prosecution or civil suit directed at an organization under the RICO statute. It has taken no account of the special problems posed when the defendant organization is a political advocacy group and, as such, entitled to the highest level of First Amendment protection:

> At the heart of the First Amendment is the recognition of the fundamental importance of the free flow of ideas and opinions on matters of public interest and concern. . . . We have there-

---

[109] RICO also requires that the enterprise must be conducted "through," that is, by means of, the racketeering activity. Thus if the managers of an enterprise merely committed pattern crimes on the premises of the enterprise, this is not a RICO violation. For example, *United States v Nerone*, 563 F2d 836 (7th Cir 1977) (a trailer park that was a front for a gambling operation was not operated "through" the pattern of racketeering activity absent proof that gambling proceeds were used by or channeled into the park). This is unlikely to be a problem in the anti-abortion context where the crimes are committed to advance the purposes of the organization.

[110] It is important to recognize, however, that the enterprise must have an existence *independent* from the mere association of people necessary to commit the pattern crimes. *Turkette*, note 18 supra, 452 US at 583: "The 'enterprise' is not the 'pattern of racketeering activity'; it is an entity separate and apart from the pattern of activity in which it engages. The existence of an enterprise at all times remains a separate element which must be proved by the government." Such factors as the existence of a physical location where the enterprise is situated and the conduct of other business, or crimes, beyond the pattern crimes may be used to establish the enterprise.

fore been particularly vigilant to ensure that individual expressions remain free from governmentally imposed sanctions.[111]

Group expression on matters of public concern is, if possible, entitled to even greater protection:

> Effective advocacy of both public and private points of view, particularly controversial ones, is undeniably enhanced by group association, as this Court has more than once recognized by remarking upon the close nexus between the freedoms of speech and assembly.[112]

As Justice Souter recognized in his concurrence in *Scheidler*, the case that is most pertinent to his First Amendment concerns is *NAACP v Claiborne Hardware Co.*[113] In that case, a boycott of white merchants was organized by the NAACP to secure compliance with a list of demands for equality and racial justice. The merchants successfully sued the NAACP and 144 individuals in state court on the ground of malicious interference with business, among other charges. The Mississippi Supreme Court upheld the judgment because the petitioners "had *agreed* to use force, violence and threats to effectuate the boycott" (against blacks who violated the boycott), and that "the agreed use of illegal force . . . to achieve a goal [is not protected by the First Amendment]."[114] Several instances of violence and threats of violence were established.[115]

After recognizing the importance of associating to express political views, the Court further observed that peaceful picketing and boycotting were also protected.[116] "Speech does not lose its pro-

---

[111] *Hustler Magazine v Falwell*, 485 US 46, 50–51 (1988). Accord, *N.A.A.C.P v Claiborne Hardware*, supra, at note 29 p 913: "This Court has recognized that speech on public issues 'has always rested on the highest rung of the hierarchy of First Amendment values.' . . . 'Speech concerning public affairs is more than self-expression; it is the essence of self-government' " (citations omitted).

[112] *NAACP v Alabama ex rel. Patterson*, 357 US 449, 460 (1958).

[113] 458 US 886 (1982).

[114] 458 US at 895 (emphasis the Court's; citations omitted).

[115] For example, Charles Evers, Field Secretary of the NAACP, stated, "If we catch eny of you going in any of them racist stores, we're gonna break your damn neck." Id at 902. Four incidents of actual violence were proved to have occurred "because the victims were ignoring the boycott." Id at 904. In none of these incidents was anybody hurt. Id.

[116] Id at 909.

tected character . . . simply because it may embarrass others or coerce them into action."[117]

On the other hand, the Court noted that the "First Amendment does not protect violence. . . . No federal rule of law restricts a State from imposing tort liability for business losses that are caused by violence and by threats of violence."[118] But, "the presence of activity protected by the First Amendment imposes restraints on the grounds that may give rise to damages liability and on the persons who may be held accountable for those damages."[119]

In particular, two limitations were placed on tort liability where First Amendment protected activity is combined with illegal or tortious behavior. First, damages must be limited to "the direct consequences of violent conduct."[120] Second,

> [f]or liability [of an individual] to be imposed by reason of association alone, it is necessary to establish that the group itself possessed unlawful goals and that the individual held a specific intent to further those illegal aims.[121]

These two limitations are not directly relevant to the hypothetical case, but they are pertinent to the actual litigation in *Scheidler* and to other similar cases where the damages, especially treble damages sought under RICO, may not be readily tied to the illegal behavior[122] or where the responsibility of certain members of the group may not be clearly established.

Finally, and directly relevant to the Sob case, the Court discussed the liability of the organization for the acts of individual members:[123] "The NAACP—like any other organization—may be held liable for the acts of its agents that are undertaken within the

---

[117] Id at 910.

[118] Id at 916.

[119] Id at 916–17.

[120] Id at 918 (citations omitted). This probably would eliminate the treble damage option under RICO, even if an organization's liability under that statute could otherwise be established.

[121] Id at 920.

[122] In a RICO case, damages are limited to those "proximately caused" or "flowing from" the pattern of racketeering activity. *Sedima S.PR.L. v Imrex*, 473 US 479, 497 n 15 (1985). Accord, *Holmes v Securities Investor Protection Corp*, 112 S Ct 1311 (1992).

[123] Since the Court had already found that the imposition of liability on Charles Evers was improper, it concluded that liability could also not be imposed "on his principal [i.e. the NAACP]." Id at 930. Accordingly, the following discussion of organizational liability is dictum.

scope of their actual or apparent authority" and for "other conduct of which it had knowledge and specifically ratified."[124] Later, the Court noted that "[t]o impose liability without a finding that the NAACP authorized—either actually or apparently—or ratified unlawful conduct would impermissibly burden the rights of political association that are protected by the First Amendment."[125] Lastly, the Court observed that to "equate the liability of the national organization with that of a branch" required proof that "the national authorized or ratified the misconduct in question. . . ."[126]

Unfortunately, these various statements express somewhat contradictory tests for when the organization may be held responsible for the acts of its members. The first statement, that the NAACP "like any other organization may be held liable for the acts of its agent, etc." does, indeed, state the general rule of corporate liability:

> Courts [have] easily concluded that public policy considerations required that the corporation be held accountable for crimes committed or authorized by officers and directors at the policy-making level of the corporate hierarchy. . . . Similarly, courts [have] rationalized the imposition of criminal liability upon corporations for the conduct of managers and supervisors. . . . subject to the limitation that the agents must act "within the scope of their employment." It should be noted, however, that criminal conduct may occur within the scope of employment even though the agent is not authorized to commit crimes and despite good faith efforts to prevent their commission.[127]

Nor is corporate liability limited to supervisory personnel. " 'The corporation may be criminally bound by the acts of subordinate, even menial, employees.' Corporations accordingly may be held accountable for criminal acts of low level employees such as salesmen, clerical workers, truck drivers and manual laborers."[128] The "only limitation" is that such workers be acting within the scope of their employment.[129] The mens rea necessary to hold the corpo-

---

[124] Id at 930.

[125] Id at 931.

[126] Id (citations omitted).

[127] Kathleen Brickey, *Corporate Criminal Liability* (2d ed 1992), p 100 (citations omitted). Accord, American Law Institute, Model Penal Code (Official Draft, 1985) § 2.07.

[128] Id at 100–01 (citations omitted).

[129] Id at 105 (citations omitted). In fact, Prof. Brickey goes on to note that such liability is found even if the agent is violating an express corporate policy. Id at 109.

ration responsible for the crimes of its agents will be imputed to the corporation if the agent acted with an "intent to benefit the corporation." Thus, "managerial inattention to ongoing patterns of criminal conduct" or "neglect of supervisory responsibilities may provide a basis for holding a corporation guilty of a knowing violation of the law."[130]

If the NAACP in *Claiborne Hardware*, or Sob in our case, is treated "like any other organization," as the Court suggested, there would seem to be extensive organizational liability for the acts of individual members. Molotov and Bakunin were members of the organization acting generally within the scope of the organization's goal of shutting down abortion clinics. Moreover, they were obviously acting with an intent to benefit Sob. Thus, Sob would be liable, notwithstanding any official policies against violence or lack of knowledge of the bombers' activities. At most, as Professor Brickey suggests, negligence on the part of supervisors suffices for corporate liability and perhaps strict liability (without any fault on the part of supervisors) may be imposed as long as the agents were acting within the scope of their employment.

But the Court's later statements in *Claiborne Hardware* clearly undercut such a result. The thrust of the *Claiborne* opinion is that political advocacy organizations may *not* be treated like "any other organization." This leads to the Court's second observation that the NAACP may be found liable "for other conduct of which it had knowledge *and* specifically ratified."

If the Court is still referring to the acts of agents here, which subsequent discussion suggests it is,[131] then it is surely extending too much protection since, if the leadership had knowledge of its agents' illegal conduct, it would hardly be necessary that they also "specifically ratify" it.[132]

---

[130] Id at 131. Prof. Brickey continues: "[A] corporate culpable mental state may be established by imputing to the corporation the collective knowledge of its employees as a group, notwithstanding the absence of proof that any single agent intended to commit the offense or even knew of the operative facts that led to the violation." Id. The Model Penal Code would only hold the corporation liable if "the offense was authorized, requested . . . or recklessly tolerated by a high managerial agent acting in behalf of the corporation within the scope of his employment." § 2,07(1)(c). However, Prof. Brickey observes that the Code's restrictive approach has not been followed by the federal courts. Brickey, supra note 127, at p 95.

[131] "[T]here is no evidence here that the NAACP ratified—or even had specific knowledge of—any of the acts of violence or threats of discipline [by its agent] associated with the boycott."

[132] The Court's reference to "other" conduct also may be read as suggesting that Sob could even be responsible for acts of nonmembers if it had knowledge of, and ratified, that conduct. Thus, if the President of Sob heard about bombings committed by another

Third, the Court stated that liability could not be imposed without a finding that "the NAACP authorized—either actually or apparently—or ratified unlawful conduct. . . ." Assuming that this liability is limited to the acts of members of Sob, this standard seems closest to the mark.

The Court's formulation is similar to the Model Penal Code's general provision for imposing liability on corporations for the criminal acts of it agents. The Code provides that the

> corporation may be convicted for the commission of an offense if:
> (c) the commission of the offense was authorized, requested, commanded, performed or recklessly tolerated by the board of directors or by a high managerial agent acting on behalf of the corporation within the scope of his office or employment.[133]

Thus, if the officials of the organization "authorized, requested, commanded or performed" the offense, the organization would clearly be responsible. Moreover, "recklessly tolerated" means essentially the same thing as apparent authorization. If the board members were "reckless," in that they "disregarded a substantial and unjustifiable risk"[134] that members of the organization were going to commit bombings in furtherance of organizational goals— such as by ignoring the fact that bottles filled with gasoline with rags stuffed in the top were being stored at corporate headquarters—the organization should be liable. Similarly, if the leadership created a climate in which violent behavior seemed to be encouraged, then it is also appropriate to hold Sob responsible. This would be "reckless toleration" under the Model Penal Code and "apparent authorization" under *Claiborne Hardware*.

As noted above, negligence on the part of the board, that is,

---

organization and publicly stated his approval, the Court seems to be saying that Sob would now be criminally liable. But again, this is surely not the Court's intent. Neither foreknowledge nor subsequent ratification of planned violent activity by Organization B should not subject Organization A to civil liability unless some further connection between the organizations can be established.

[133] Model Penal Code, supra note 55, § 2.07(1)(c). The Code originally included a similar provision for unincorporated associations, but, in the final draft, it was eliminated "in favor of an approach that invited specific legislative consideration of each expansion of liability as may from time to time appear desirable." 1 Model Penal Code and Commentaries (Official Draft, 1985) § 2.07, p 343.

[134] Model Penal Code, supra note 55 at § 2.02(2)(c). The Code goes on to explain that the disregard of the risk "involves a gross deviation from the standard of conduct that a law abiding person would observe in the actor's situation." Id.

failing to perceive a risk of which it should have been aware, would also ordinarily give rise to corporate liability.[135] However, the need to err on the side of First Amendment protections—to provide "breathing space"[136] for Sob's First Amendment rights—must be considered. If negligence is the ordinary standard for corporate liability,[137] then it cannot be the standard for the liability of a political advocacy organization, even when certain members of that organization commit serious crimes. Otherwise, no "breathing space" would have been afforded the advocacy group. This is consistent with the *Claiborne Hardware* test since no "apparent authority" could be found in the board's failure to even perceive a risk that bombings might occur, even if that failure was negligent. Thus, in the above hypothetical, if the board members could convince a jury that they had no clue as to the potential uses of bottles filled with gasoline, neither Sob nor its board would be liable, despite the fact that a "reasonable person" would have perceived this risk.

A recklessness standard is further supported by the Court's holdings in the field of libel. There, liability may be imposed on both the original speaker and on the media that publish his speech, for a statement about a public figure made "with knowledge that it was false or with reckless disregard of whether it was false or not,"[138] but not when the statement was merely false in fact, or even negligently false.

It seems appropriate to create a "political advocacy organization"

---

[135] Some readers may be wondering why I am not discussing § 2.06, "Culpability for the Acts of Another." This is accomplice liability and is, in general, more difficult to prove than is organizational responsibility for the acts of members. In order to establish that the board members were "accomplices" to the bombing, it would be necessary to prove that, "with a purpose of promoting or facilitating the commission of the offense," they either "solicited [another] person to commit it" or "aid[ed] or agree[d] to aid such other person in planning or committing it." § 2.06(3)(a). As discussed earlier, if it can be can be shown that Sob's directors were accomplices in the bombings, then Sob's responsibility as an "enterprise" under RICO would be established with no need to prove that Molotov and Bakunin had any ties to Sob at all.

[136] *Hustler Magazine v Falwell*, 458 US 46, 52 (1988) (citations omitted).

[137] As Prof. Brickey observes, the Model Penal Code "greatly restrict[s]" corporate liability compared to how the law has actually developed. Brickey, supra note 127 at p 96.

[138] *New York Times v Sullivan*, 376 US 254 (1964). As the Court has more recently explained, "actual malice mean[s] only knowledge of falsity or reckless disregard as to truth or falsity, the latter not being satisfied by mere negligence." Frederick Schauer, *Constitution Law and Individual Rights in Constitutional Law (1994 Supplement to Gerald Gunther)* 188, characterizing, *Masson v New Yorker Magazine, Inc.*, 501 US 496 (1991). This is comparable to the Model Penal Code requirement that the actor must "disregard a substantial and unjustifiable risk that the material element exists or will result from his conduct."

category that mirrors, in the criminal law, the special protections that are afforded to speakers and the media in libel law when they discuss "public figures." Libel is not regarded with as much opprobrium by society as criminal behavior, but this fact cuts both ways. On the one hand, one could argue that if a reckless organization is held responsible for libel, it is only fair to also hold it responsible for more serious wrongs. On the other hand, since the damage to the organization, and to its ability to get out its message, would be even greater in case of a criminal conviction and/or a RICO treble damage suit, a higher standard of mens rea should perhaps be required. This is consistent with the Supreme Court's approval of strict liability (i.e., no level of mens rea need be proved) only for relatively nonserious, administrative violations, whereas some higher level of culpability is required for more serious crimes.[139]

In my view, a reckless attitude by the leadership should be sufficient to hold the leadership and the organization responsible for crimes committed by the membership. Recklessness is sufficient, in a homicide case, to subject a defendant to serious criminal penalties (for manslaughter) and, in the libel area, to make the defendant responsible for major damages, despite the limitations imposed by the First Amendment.

A recklessness standard gives political advocacy groups sufficient "breathing space" that they need not fear that vigorous espousal of their cause will lead to criminal prosecution. But if the leadership consciously disregards known risks that the membership is committing or planning particular crimes (felonies in a RICO case), it is appropriate to subject the organization to criminal and civil penalties when those crimes are carried out.[140] This captures the spirit of the "apparent authority" limitation of *Claiborne Hardware*.

Another fundamental question is, What is a "political advocacy organization" and do we really want to give it any special protection? Should groups such as the KKK, the Aryan Brotherhood, and certain extremist anti-abortion groups, which combine political advocacy and a political message with violent criminal behavior, be

---

[139] *Morissette v United States*, 342 US 246, 252–53 (1952).

[140] It will be necessary for the plaintiff/prosecutor to establish that the organization, formally or informally, explicitly or implicitly, endorsed both the ends and the means adopted by the actors. Thus, Sob would not incur organizational liability merely because the board knew that its anti-abortion policies would attract certain fanatics who were willing to commit murder to advance the organization's stated goal of eliminating abortion.

entitled to any special consideration by the law when the criminal behavior of the organization leads to prosecution or civil suit?

The answers are, first, that a "political advocacy organization" is any group that has a political message to convey. If that message is merely a front for criminal activity, then it will not be difficult to satisfy the limited additional protections that the First Amendment provides, for such an organization will, by definition, be purposeful or knowledgeable, or at least reckless, as to the criminal conduct of its members. Second, as the Court reiterated in *Claiborne Hardware*, " 'blanket prohibition of association with a group having both legal and illegal aims' would present 'a real danger that legitimate political expression or association would be impaired.' "[141] Consequently, limited First Amendment protection for such groups, whose tactics may be both abhorrent and illegal, is simply the price that must be paid for freedom of speech and association.

Up to this point, the discussion has assumed that the criminal actors were "members" of a formal organization. However, many of the most serious crimes might well be committed by people who never were, or no longer are, officially on the membership rolls, or by groups that have no formal membership. To hold the organization liable for crimes or treble damages for acts committed by nonmembers might allow hostile outsiders to destroy the organization by committing crimes in its name. On the other hand, organizations should not be allowed to escape liability simply because they have no formal "members" (or officers or board of directors) or because the perpetrators of the crime have "resigned" prior to committing criminal acts.

There is no blanket resolution to this class of problems. Courts will simply have to decide case by case whether it is appropriate to charge the organization with the acts of people who act like "members" or "officers" even though they may not be formally designated as such. Conspiracy law has frequently faced the problem of who is a "member" of a conspiracy, and RICO's "operation or management" test will be useful in ascertaining who the leaders of an organization may be. RICO's definition of "enterprise" clearly includes groups of people that have no formal organization.

It must, however, be reemphasized that in order to make out a RICO case it is necessary to establish the existence of an "enter-

---

[141] 458 US at 919, quoting *Scales v United States*, 367 US 203, 229 (1961).

prise," formal or informal, legal or illegal, with an existence *independent* of the pattern crimes. Two people who agree to commit a series of bombings do not, by that agreement alone, commit a RICO conspiracy. Rather, the prosecution/plaintiff must show that there was an "enterprise" (e.g., an organized crime "family") that had an existence separate from the bombing scheme, and that the defendants conducted, or planned to conduct, that enterprise "through" the bombings. Thus it must be shown that Sob was conducted through a pattern of bombings before Sob can be a RICO defendant.

To summarize: In order to hold a political action organization liable under *any* theory or statute, it is necessary to show that the leaders of that organization had a mens rea of "purpose," "knowledge," or "recklessness" toward criminal activity performed by members, or people who acted like members. As the Court put it in *Claiborne Hardware*, the member-perpetrators must act with "actual or apparent authorization" of the leadership or the leadership must ratify their acts. Frequently, the evidence will show that the leadership's involvement in the crimes was sufficient to charge them with aiding and abetting. But it is easy to imagine cases where the leadership creates a climate in which criminal behavior is encouraged, without any leadership planning of specific crimes. This is sufficient for organizational liability if it can be shown that the leadership "apparently authorized," including recklessly tolerating, such acts.

The statutory limits on a RICO case seem to be similar to these First Amendment limits, but, unlike ordinary civil liability, a RICO case may only be based on proof of the serious felonies listed in the statute. The only issue is whether the Court's observation in *Reves* that, under RICO, lower-level personnel must be acting "under the direction" of upper management is co-extensive with *Claiborne*'s First Amendment admonition that organizational liability is limited to cases where the leadership "actually or apparently" authorized the unlawful conduct. Arguably, "direction" is a more limited term than "apparent authorization," and consequently RICO may prohibit fewer activities than the First Amendment would allow it to. However, if the Supreme Court were ever to consider this issue, I suspect it would extend RICO's coverage to those who were acting with the "apparent authority" of management, as well as those who were "directed" by management. That is, a mens rea of "recklessness" by management toward criminal behavior of members should satisfy the requirements of both RICO and the First Amendment.

B. THE PROTECTION OF POLITICALLY MOTIVATED CRIMES

We have seen that the First Amendment offers some protection to political advocacy organizations when they are attacked on the ground that their members have committed crimes. But does it also limit those crimes for which a politically motivated actor may be charged (and hence for which he may be sued under RICO)? I believe that it does.

For example, it is well settled that inducing fear of economic loss satisfies the "extortion by fear" element of the Hobbs Act.[142] Thus, if a public official states that he will not approve a construction project unless he is paid off, he induces "fear" in the victim and violates the Hobbs Act.[143] This is so despite the fact that disapproval of the project is perfectly legal.[144] By this reasoning, if Operation Rescue threatens an abortion clinic with picketing unless it closes down, and in so doing creates fear of economic loss, the Hobbs Act has, on its face, been violated (assuming *arguendo* that this constitutes "obtaining property" as NOW urges).[145]

But despite the fact that this threat has violated all of the elements of the Hobbs Act, this *cannot* be a criminal violation because the threat is protected by the First Amendment. In *Organization for a Better Austin v Keefe*,[146] a civil rights group demanded that the respondent cease his "blockbusting" real estate sales practices or they would distribute pamphlets critical of him. The Court struck

---

[142] For example, *United States v Lisinski*, 728 F2d 887, 890–91 (7th Cir 1984) and cases cited therein.

[143] *United States v Williams*, 952 F2d 1504, 1513 (6th Cir 1991) and cases cited therein. As discussed above, the only exception to this principle seems to be a limited one, based on Congress's intent in enacting the Hobbs Act, that labor leaders who threaten violence do not violate the Hobbs Act as long as their demands are "legitimate," that is, for wages and benefits, rather than for under-the-table payments or featherbedding.

[144] It is the "paradox of blackmail" that threatening legal behavior, such as reporting a crime to the police unless one gets something he is legally entitled to request, such as a job, is nevertheless the crime of extortion or blackmail. See James Lindgren, *Unraveling the Paradox of Blackmail*, 84 Col L Rev 670 (1984) for a full discussion of this paradox and the reasons for it.

[145] As noted, supra text at notes 44–71, this is an assumption with which I disagree.

[146] 402 US 415 (1971).

down an injunction on the pamphleteering and, in the process, seemed also to validate the original threat to the respondent: "The claim that the expressions were intended to exercise a coercive effect on respondent does not remove them from the reach of the First Amendment."[147]

This is not extortion, but not because the threat is to perform some legitimate activity since, as noted above, threats to perform legitimate acts may nevertheless be the basis of an extortion charge. Nor is it that the act threatened is constitutionally protected. Thus, if X threatens a merchant that CORE will picket, legally, outside his store and drive away business unless he contributes $500 to CORE, this is probably extortion as well.[148] Rather, the reason must be, as in *Keefe*, that the threat is to perform a legal act, *and* the goal is to achieve a political end, rather than to obtain property from a particular victim.[149]

On the other hand, the Court has frequently held that "the First Amendment does not protect violence (or). . . . threats of violence."[150] To the extent that violent acts occur, it seems correct that society's interest in preventing, and protecting victims from, acts of violence completely overcomes First Amendment interests.

---

[147] Id at 911. On the other hand, it is clear that threats of *violence* on behalf of a public interest organization, either to influence behavior, or to receive contributions, *is* extortion. For example, *United States v Mitchell*, 463 F2d 187, 191 (8th Cir 1972).

[148] The facts of the hypothetical are drawn from *United States v Mitchell*. However, in *Mitchell*, there was a threat of violence if the victim did not contribute to CORE. Id at 191–92. Accord, *United States v Starks*, 515 F2d 112 (3d Cir 1975). It is also clear that extortion of political contributions by a threat that the victim will not receive a government job or contract violates the Hobbs Act. See, e.g., *United States v Cerilli*, 603 F2d 415, 420 (3d Cir 1979) cert denied 444 US 1043, and cases cited therein. However, no case seems to have dealt with a threat to picket or engage in other First Amendment activity in order to obtain money except the labor cases which, as noted above, are outside the coverage of the Hobbs Act. In my view such demands are "commercial speech" and, as such, not fully protected by the First Amendment. Consequently, a threat to engage in First Amendment activity that would cause economic harm to the victim, *coupled with* a demand for money, does constitute extortion.

[149] This is a tentative conclusion that is somewhat undercut by the Supreme Court's further observation in *Keefe* that "'[S]o long as the means are peaceful, the communication need not meet the standards of acceptability.'" However, the Court was not concerning itself with demands for money or property in *Keefe*. See Edwin Baker, *Scope of the First Amendment Freedom of Speech*, 25 UCLA L Rev 964, 1003 (1978): "Since whistle blowing, but not blackmailing, involves using speech directly to make the world correspond to the speaker's substantive values rather than merely to increase the speaker's wealth . . . " (it is entitled to First Amendment protection). For a thorough discussion of the clash between the crime of criminal coercion and First Amendment values, see Kent Greenawalt, *Criminal Coercion and Freedom of Speech*, 78 Nw L Rev 1081 (1984).

[150] For example, *Claiborne* at p 916.

Thus, no special First Amendment considerations should apply to violent crimes, or threats of violence, other than the limitations on organizational liability discussed above.

Similarly, it is clear that nonviolent crimes, such as trespass or violations of the new federal statute on freedom of access to abortion clinics, can be charged even as to political protest activities. In *Adderly v Florida*,[151] civil rights protestors were arrested when they trespassed on the property of the county jail, blocked the entrances (at least in the sheriff's opinion),[152] and appeared to be attempting to enter. The Supreme Court, by a 5–4 vote, upheld their convictions for trespass despite the fact that no violence occurred: "Nothing in the Constitution of the United States prevents Florida from even-handed enforcement of its general trespass statute. . . . "[153]

Though the dissenters in *Adderly* strongly disagreed with this holding, their disagreement was based on the fact that the jail was public property. They conceded that trespass on private property, even to advance First Amendment goals, could constitutionally be prohibited.[154]

The only issue remaining, and the one that is directly pertinent to the extortion charges leveled in *NOW v Scheidler*, is whether *threats* to commit nonviolent crimes may also be punished. (Threats to commit violent crimes are clearly unprotected because of society's need to intervene *before* the defendant has a chance to carry out his threat, or even to attempt it.) When an anti-abortion protester calls the abortion clinic and says, "If you open your doors tomorrow, we're going to picket and harass employees and patients who come there," is this extortion? The issue is especially troubling when the nonviolent crime itself may be a petty misdemeanor, such as trespass, but the threat to commit it may be the felony of extortion or, more usually (because of the absence of the "obtaining of property" element), criminal coercion.

Such a threat is potentially eligible for triple First Amendment

---

[151] 385 US 39 (1966).

[152] The majority says that the sheriff "claim(ed) that they were blocking the entrance." Id at 45. The dissent says, "it is undisputed that the entrance to the jail was not blocked." Id at 52.

[153] Id at 47.

[154] Id.

protection since it is speech about associational activities that are political in nature. Moreover, at the time it is uttered, it is nothing more than speech. To make the utterer liable for arrest at the time that the threat is made is akin to a prior restraint on expression. There is no clear and present danger unless the threat is of immediate criminal action. The appropriate response of the victim of the threat is to threaten back: "If you trespass on my property, or interfere with my staff or patrons, I'll have you arrested."

It is a part of the threatener's constitutional rights to test the victim's resolve by making a threat of nonviolent illegality and seeing if the victim is prepared to invoke the law. Where the "victim" is, for example, a utility company, it may well be that the victim would prefer to accommodate the threatener's demands rather than appear on the news ordering hundreds of protesters to be dragged off of its property by police. If the victim is not interested in negotiating, then he can have the police standing ready to arrest the protesters as soon as they break the law.

Beyond this, allowing a crime (and hence, an arrest) to occur at the time of the threat would deprive the threatener of the *opportunity to be arrested at the scene of the protest*. As nonviolent protesters such as Gandhi and Martin Luther King were well aware, the public arrest of hundreds or thousands of protesters can be the most potent arrow in the protester's quiver.[155] Moreover, to allow the leadership to be arrested for threatening a protest (also known as "negotiating") would likely kill off the protest altogether. This would be similar to the injunction of the protest (which began with a threat) that the Court struck down in *Keefe*.

By contrast, even an *implicit* threat of conduct that may result in injury to people is a crime.[156] Suppose an anti-abortion group

---

[155] "Since nonviolent action has entered the scene, however, the white man has gasped at a new phenomenon. He has seen Negroes, by the hundreds and by the thousands, marching toward him, knowing they are going to jail, wanting to go to jail, willing to accept the confinement and to risk the beatings and the uncertain justice of the southern courts.

"There were no more powerful moments in the Birmingham episode than during the closing days of the campaign, when Negro youngsters ran after white policemen, asking to be locked up. There was an element of unmalicious mischief in this. The Negro youngsters, although perfectly willing to submit to imprisonment, knew that we had already filled up the jails, and that the police had no place to take them." Martin Luther King, *Why We Can't Wait* 29–30 (New American Library 1963).

[156] But not, as discussed, extortion, because the "obtaining property" element is missing. This would, however, be the crime of criminal coercion in most states as well as a violation of the Hobbs Act for interfering with commerce by threats of violence.

calls an abortion clinic and threatens, "If you open your doors tomorrow there's going to be trouble." This could be a crime if, based on the past behavior of the defendant, a jury could conclude that the defendant, "with purpose unlawfully to restrict another's freedom of action threatened to commit a crime of violence."[157] Threats to throw rocks at, or physically blockade, the clinic would likely put staff and patrons in fear of bodily injury[158] and would also be criminally punishable.[159]

Threats to throw eggs at the clinic, by contrast, or to otherwise trespass on clinic property in ways that do not threaten bodily injury would be immune from prosecution. But the actual throwing of the eggs or trespassing would be criminal, and the protesters could be arrested for an attempt as soon as they arrived at the clinic because, at this point, a clear and present danger of crime is present.[160]

If the threatener is not guilty of extortion when he makes a nonviolent threat with a political goal, then the problem of a threat to trespass being a more serious crime, extortion, than the trespass itself, is also taken care of. Finally, if there is no extortion, there can be no RICO civil suit.

The above formulation is consistent with the Supreme Court's recent holding in *Madsen v Women's Health Center*.[161] In *Madsen*, the Court upheld, in part, an injunction that limited the range of anti-abortion protesters' demonstrations outside a clinic. As such, it did not consider the limits of the constitutional right, posited here, to threaten nonviolent protest. After *Madsen*, in my view,

---

[157] Model Penal Code § 212.5 (Criminal Coercion). The Code prohibits threats to "commit any criminal offense." My proposal is narrower to accommodate the First Amendment. I would further use a "recklessness" mens rea as to such threats. Thus if the threatener consciously disregarded a known risk that his threat would be taken as a threat of violence, then he is guilty. However, he would not be guilty for negligence, that is, even though a reasonable person might have construed his threat as a threat of violence.

[158] However, as discussed in note 161, infra, if the threat to blockade makes it clear that the proposed blockade will not lead to injury to people, it is protected by the First Amendment, and also not covered by the Freedom of Access to Clinics Act of 1994.

[159] So, too, would advocacy of violence toward people at the clinic, so long as it was "directed to inciting or producing imminent lawless action and . . . likely to incite or produce such action." *Brandenburg v Ohio*, 395 US 444, 447 (1969). Advocacy of nonviolent conduct would similarly not be punishable until it rose to the level of an attempt, a concept that is slightly closer to the actual commission of a crime than the *Brandenburg* standard.

[160] I am not troubled by using their threat as evidence against them to show intent once an actual attempt has occurred. However, this may be a matter for further debate.

[161] 114 S Ct 2516 (1994).

anti-abortion protesters could still threaten nonviolent breaches of the injunction with impunity. If they actually violated the injunction, they could be prosecuted, as in *Madsen*.

This formulation is also consistent with the Freedom of Access to Clinics Act of 1994, which forbids interfering with clinics by "force or threat of force or by physical obstruction" and "intentionally damaging or destroying property" of a clinic but does not forbid threats of trespass or property damage.[162]

C. SPECIAL PROBLEMS IN CONSPIRACY CASES

Since ordinarily, any enterprise, and certainly an anti-abortion organization, will involve cooperative action by more than one person, a RICO conspiracy may also be charged,[163] as was done in *Scheidler*. An extended discussion could be devoted to the issues raised by the RICO conspiracy statute,[164] but for the purposes of this article, two issues must be raised, if not resolved. The first is that the terms "conspiracy" (a crime) and "association" (a protected First Amendment right) may mean the same thing. Courts must be especially careful in applying a conspiracy statute to a political advocacy organization. In *Claiborne Hardware*, the Court held that liability may be imposed only if "the group itself possessed unlawful goals and the individual held a specific intent to further those illegal goals."[165] However, it is not clear that the Court really intended to restrict liability to those who "specifically intended" illegality, as opposed to those who were knowing or reckless as to such activity. Second, as discussed above, intending *any* illegal activity, as opposed to violent illegality, is not

---

[162] The wording of the statute, "by force or threat of force or by physical obstruction," suggests that threats of physical obstruction are not covered by the statute, so long as they don't also constitute a threat of force. This is consistent with the First Amendment right posited here. While most threats of physical obstruction will also be threats of force, if a protester threatens, for example, to chain the doors of the clinic shut at night, such that no use force is threatened to clinic patients or employees, this is a "threat of physical obstruction" which would not violate the statute and could not be punished under the First Amendment.

[163] 18 USC § 1962(d) provides: "It shall be unlawful for any person to conspire to violate any of the provisions of subsections (a), (b), or (c) of this section."

[164] For a discussion of some of the problems and possibilities raised by § 1962(d), see Gerard Lynch, *RICO: The Crime of Being a Criminal*, 87 Colum L Rev 661, 945–55 (1987); Craig Bradley, *Racketeers, Congress and the Courts*, 65 Iowa L Rev 837, 876–88 (1980).

[165] *Claiborne Hardware* (note 113 above) at 920.

sufficient for conspiracy liability when the purpose of the conspiracy is to achieve First Amendment goals.[166]

These problems are especially troubling when a RICO conspiracy is charged since the defendants may now be responsible for the doubly inchoate offense of agreeing to form an enterprise that will commit the pattern crimes,[167] rather than simply agreeing to commit a crime. Yet, despite the fact that the RICO charge is more removed from actual harm than ordinary conspiracy, the penalties are much greater.[168]

V. CONCLUSION

To summarize: Although NOW was rightly victorious in the Supreme Court on the issue of whether political organizations can fall within the prohibitions of RICO, its complaint, at least in the form that it appears in the Joint Appendix in the Supreme Court, is defective. First, it does not adequately plead extortion under the Hobbs Act, since one of the elements of Hobbs Act extortion, "obtaining property," is missing. However, this problem may be solved by the argument that the third clause of the Hobbs Act, forbidding interfering with commerce by force or violence, does not require proof of the "obtaining property" element. Also, there may be other crimes mentioned in the complaint, such as interstate transportation of stolen property—18 USC § 2314—that can be adequately tied to the named defendants and will suffice as pattern crimes under RICO.

Second, the complaint also fails to establish extortion under most state laws because there is no extortionate threat, that is, a threat of violence, exposure of secrets, etc. if defendant's demands are

---

[166] In *Scales v United States*, 367 US 203, 229 (1961), on which the Claiborne Court relied, the Court only approved conspiracy prosecutions when the defendant intended to accomplish the aims of the organization by "resort to violence." In *Claiborne*, the Court speaks as if "unlawful" behavior and "violent" behavior are synonymous. 458 US at 920.

[167] There is, at least, generally agreement that each defendant must have personally agreed to at least two pattern crimes (but not necessarily all of the crimes that are the object of the conspiracy). For example, *United States v Rastelli*, 870 F2d 822, 828 (2d Cir 1989) and cases cited therein.

[168] Five years for a violation of 18 USC § 371; twenty years, forfeiture, and treble damages for RICO violations.

not met, as well as the "obtaining property" problem discussed above.

Even if the members of a defendant organization have clearly committed two RICO predicate offenses, such as arson, it still must be proved that these crimes constituted a "pattern" and that the organization was "conducted through" that pattern of crimes if a RICO case is to be established under § 1962(c).

Assuming that plaintiffs can establish all of the elements of a RICO offense, the political nature of the defendants' acts means that the First Amendment will make it more difficult to render the organization responsible for the acts of its members than would otherwise be the case.

Finally, the First Amendment will not allow the plaintiffs to make out a RICO case based on "extortion" if the defendants' only threat was to engage in nonviolent (*even if illegal*) protest activities. Rather, plaintiffs' only recourse will be to demand enforcement of the state and federal laws protecting against the *actual* trespass and blockading of abortion clinics, plus state law civil suits based on such conduct. If, however, violence or threats of violence can be shown, the Hobbs Act will have been violated and the RICO case should proceed. However, the *Claiborne Hardware* limitation of damages to "the direct consequences of violent conduct"[169] will likely eliminate the treble damage remedy.

---

[169] See note 113 above, at p 918.

WILLIAM P. MARSHALL

AND SUSAN GILLES

THE SUPREME COURT, THE FIRST

AMENDMENT, AND BAD JOURNALISM

INTRODUCTION

The First Amendment's guarantees of freedom of the press and freedom of speech do not purport to set standards for the news media. In interpreting the First Amendment, however, the Supreme Court has played a significant role in setting the legal framework for journalistic practice. Everything from the reporter's use of confidential sources to the protection of her files from police search, from her access to government proceedings and institutions to her potential liability for infringing upon rights of privacy and reputation have been the subject of the Court's First Amendment jurisprudence. Indeed, the Court's decisions have covered much of the full range of the journalistic enterprise.[1]

Despite this extensive involvement, the Court generally has not considered how its decisions affect the standards of journalistic practice. At one level, this is perfectly understandable—the Court

William P. Marshall is Galen J. Roush Professor of Law, Case Western Reserve University Law School. Susan Gilles is Visiting Professor of Law, Washington and Lee Law School, Assistant Professor of Law, Capital University Law School.

AUTHORS' NOTE: We wish to express our appreciation to Jack Doppelt, Jonathan Entin, Christopher Harper, Roslyn Mazer, Brian Murchison, and James Tierney. We would also like to thank Kellie McIvor, Louis Lyons, and Lee Berlik for their research assistance.

[1] See also Brian C. Murchison, John Soloski, Randall P. Bezanson, Gilbert Cranberg, and Roselle L. Wissler, *Sullivan's Paradox: The Emergence of Judicial Standards of Journalism*, 73 North Ca L Rev 7 (1994) (noting that, under the actual malice standard of *Sullivan*, the lower courts have created a system of journalistic norms which cover all three stages of news reporting—research, writing, and editing).

is in the business of crafting constitutional law, not a code of professional standards. At another level, however, the way in which
journalism is practiced has significant implications for First
Amendment theory. The viability of the First Amendment's goals
of fostering self-governance and checking the power of the state,
for example, depends upon the existence of a news media that is
engaged in serious coverage and investigation of issues of public
import. Therefore, the extent to which the Court creates incentives
and disincentives for journalists to act in furtherance of these goals
is of considerable First Amendment interest.

In this article, we examine the potential impact of the Supreme
Court's decisions on journalistic practice. Specifically, we ask
whether these decisions encourage a public interest style of journalism involving serious investigation and reporting of issues of public
import or whether they encourage a nonanalytical and/or celebrity-
oriented style of journalism consisting of little or no sound journalistic practice and a minimal concern for serious issues.[2] For purposes of convenience, we term the first style of journalism "serious
journalism" and the second "superficial journalism."[3] Our contention is that the Court's decisions, taken as a whole, tend to

---

[2] The two categories inherent in this definition (sound journalistic practices and concern
for issues of public import) are not interdependent. One can employ shoddy journalistic
techniques, such as forgoing independent verification, in the coverage of serious issues.
Conversely, one can apply sound journalistic practices such as investigative reporting to the
pursuit of trivial stories.

[3] The terms "serious" and "superficial" journalism are admittedly amorphous. We do,
however, take some comfort that our terms mirror those of a number of authorities who
have suggested that the functions of investigating and reporting on matters of public import
are the attributes of a "good" and responsible press. Perhaps most important in this regard
was the report published in 1947 by the Commission on the Freedom of the Press that
asserted that a good press would provide "first, a truthful, comprehensive, and intelligent
account of the day's events in a context which gives them meaning; second, a forum for the
exchange of comment and criticism; third, a means of projecting the positions and attitudes
of the groups in the society to one another; fourth, a method of presenting and clarifying
the goals and values of the society; and, fifth, a way of reaching every member of the society
by the currents of information, thought, and feeling which the press supplies." Commission
on Freedom of the Press, *A Free and Representative Press* 20–21 (1947). The Commission
found that the United States, sadly lacking a good press, was saddled instead with news
"twisted by the emphasis on firstness, on the novel and sensational . . . a miscellaneous
succession of stories and images which have no relation to the typical lives of real people
anywhere." Id at 68. See also Lee C. Bollinger, *Images of a Free Press* 30–31, 44 (University
of Chicago Press, 1991) (noting the attributes of a "good" and a "bad" press). As Bollinger
indicates, the Court has at times indicated that it too understood the difference between
"good" and "bad" journalism. Id at 44.

create significant incentives for superficial journalism and disincentives for serious journalism.[4]

Two important caveats are in order. First, the normative judgment inherent in the terms "serious" and "superficial" journalism is intended only as an appraisal of journalistic merit. It is not intended as a statement of First Amendment value. Although we note that serious journalism is more in line with the Court's own exposition that one of the primary goals of the First Amendment is to foster an informed electorate,[5] we do not argue that superficial journalism is without First Amendment value.[6] Rather our premise is that both superficial and serious journalism are entitled to equal constitutional weight.[7]

Second, our analysis is not based upon empirical data. Although we begin with the likely assumption that the Court's decisions will affect how media lawyers advise their clients,[8] the question to what extent the absence of legal protection actually results in press abandonment of serious journalism in favor of celebrity or noninvestigative stories is beyond the scope of our study.[9]

[4] The Court's decisions encouraging serious journalism are discussed in notes 56–68 and accompanying text.

[5] See notes 12–19 and accompanying text.

[6] For differing views on the relative First Amendment worth of serious and superficial journalism, contrast Cass R. Sunstein, *Democracy and the Problem of Free Speech* (Free Press, 1993) with Robert Post, *Meiklejohn's Mistake: Individual Autonomy and the Reform of Public Discourse*, 64 U Colo L Rev 1109 (1993).

[7] Constitutional protection of superficial journalism might be justified on grounds other than the fostering of an informed electorate. See C. Edwin Baker, *Scope of the First Amendment Freedom of Speech*, 25 UCLA L Rev 964 (1978) (value of self-expression); Martin H. Redish, *The Value of Free Speech*, 130 U Pa L Rev 591 (1982) (value of self-realization). Additionally, superficial journalism cannot be fully discounted as a valid vehicle in promoting self-governance. Post, 64 U Colo L Rev at 1109 (cited in note 6).

[8] See Martin Garbus, *New Challenges to Press Freedom*, New York Times Magazine § 6 (Jan 29, 1984) ("Press spokesmen routinely deny that they kill articles because of the risk of libel, but the chilling effect is well known to lawyers who work with the media."); Lili Levi, *Challenging the Autonomous Press*, 78 Cornell L Rev 665, 681–82 (1993) ("perhaps the greatest influence of the judicial image of the press is on the lawyers and First Amendment scholars who deal with these matters.").

[9] Many of the negative effects of Supreme Court decisions on journalistic practices noted in this article are documented in Clark R. Mollenhoff, *25 Years of New York Times v Sullivan*, The Quill (Mar 1989). Empirical studies of the impact of Court decisions on the press, however, have yielded conflicting results. Contrast James Bow and Ben Silver, *Effect of Herbert v Lando on Small Newspapers and TV Stations*, 61 Journalism Q 414, 415 (1984) (survey of editors found that 61% denied that a recent libel ruling had an effect on their ability to gather news) and Russell L. Weaver and Geoffrey Bennett, *Is The New York Times "Actual Malice" Standard Really Necessary? A Comparative Perspective*, 53 La L Rev 1153 (1993) (reporting that in interviews reporters, editors, and defamation lawyers generally asserted that professional standards, not fear of libel suits, controlled the editorial process) with

In Part I, we explore the Court's vision of the press.[10] We show that although the Court has a clear vision of the constitutional role of the press, it rarely has considered how the press functions or the potential impact of its decisions on press practices. In Part II we analyze the Court's decisions in terms of their potential effect on journalistic practice, with particular attention to those decisions that discourage serious journalism and encourage superficial journalism. In Part III we ask why the case law has evolved in this manner and identify some of the turns taken by the Court that may have been in error. Our conclusion is straightforward. The First Amendment should not be interpreted to prefer superficial, over serious, journalism.

I. THE SUPREME COURT'S VISION OF THE PRESS

A. THE CONSTITUTIONAL VISION

The Court has consistently offered a constitutional vision of the role of the press in the American political system.[11] According to

---

David A. Barrett, *Declaratory Judgments for Libel: A Better Alternative*, 74 Cal L Rev 847, 860 (1986) (reporting statements by publishers that they withheld controversial stories for fear of libel), and Richard E. Labrunski and John V Pavlik, *The Legal Environment of Investigative Reporters: A Pilot Study*, 6 Newspaper Res J 13, 15 (1985) (survey of journalist organization's members concluded that 65% felt that some stories were not covered because of libel decisions). See also Note, *Reporting the Truth and Setting the Record Straight: An Analysis of U.S. And Japanese Libel Laws*, 14 Mich J Intl L 871 (1993) ("media executives cannot agree whether libel litigation has actually reduced news coverage of controversial topics."). For other empirical studies, see Vince Blasi, *The Newsman's Privilege: An Empirical Study*, 70 Mich L Rev 229, 246 (1971); John E. Osborn, *The Reporter's Confidentiality Privilege: Updating the Empirical Evidence After a Decade of Subpoenas*, 27 Colum Hum Rts L Rev 57, 64–67 (1985); Douglas Anderson and Marian Murdock, *Effects of Communication Law Decisions on Daily Newspaper Editors*, Journalism Q 525 (1981).

[10] The term "press" as used in this article refers to both the print and broadcast media.

[11] The Court has made clear, after some debate, that the importance of the press' role does not mean that it enjoys a preferred position in the constitutional system. See, for example, *First National Bank v Bellotti*, 435 US 765, 802 (1978) (Burger concurring) ("I can see no difference between the right of those who seek to disseminate ideas by way of a newspaper and those who give lectures or speeches and seek to enlarge the audience by publication and wide dissemination. . . . In short, the First Amendment does not 'belong' to any definable category of persons or entities. It belongs to all who exercise its freedoms."); *Pennekamp v Florida*, 328 US 331, 364 (1946) (Frankfurter concurring) ("[T]he purpose of the Constitution was not to erect the press into a privileged institution but to protect all persons in their right to print what they will as well as to utter it. [T]he liberty of the press is no greater and no less that the liberty of every citizen of the Republic"); but see *Pell v Procunier*, 417 US 817, 840 (1974) (Douglas dissenting) ("The press has a preferred position in our constitutional scheme"); and Potter Stewart, *Or of the Press*, 26 Hastings L J 631 (1975) ("Most of the other provisions in the Bill of Rights protect specific liberties or specific rights of individuals. . . . In contrast, the Free Press clause extends protection to an institu-

the Court, the press helps create and foster an informed public which, in turn, is necessary to effective democracy.[12] It is through the information the press provides that the electorate is able to "intelligently discharge [its] political responsibilities."[13] As the Court has stated:

> Enlightened choice by an informed citizenry is the basic ideal upon which our open society is premised. . . . Our society depends heavily on the press for that enlightenment. Though not without its lapses, the press has been a mighty catalyst in awakening public interest in governmental affairs, exposing corruption among public officers and employees and generally informing the citizenry of public events and occurrences.[14]

The Court also has indicated how the press might fulfill this vision. Echoing what we have termed "serious" journalism, the Court has noted that the press should report and investigate, fully and accurately,[15] on matters of public concern.[16] "A free press," the Court has observed, "cannot be made to rely solely upon the sufferance of the government to supply it with information."[17] Finally, in order to serve its function, the press must be indepen-

---

tion. The publishing business is, in short, the only organized private business that is given explicit constitutional protection.").

The Court has suggested that the media may enjoy some enhanced protection when they act as the public's surrogate. *Richmond Newspaper, Inc. v Virginia*, 448 US 555, 572–73 (1980).

[12] *Minneapolis Star and Tribune Co. v Minnesota*, 460 US 575, 585 (1983) (observing that "[an] untrammeled press [is] a vital source of public information . . . and an informed public is the essence of working democracy") (citations omitted).

[13] *Gannet Co. v DePasquale*, 443 US 368, 397 (1979) (Powell concurring) (citations omitted).

[14] *Houchins v KQED*, 438 US 1, 17 (1978) (citations omitted). See also *Mills v Alabama*, 384 US 214, 219 (1966) ("The Constitution specifically selected the press . . . to play an important role in the discussion of public affairs. Thus the press serves and was designed to serve as a powerful antidote to any abuses of power by governmental officials and as a constitutionally chosen means for keeping officials elected by the people responsible to all the people whom they were selected to serve.").

[15] See, for example, *Cox Broadcasting Co. v Cohn*, 420 US 469, 492 (1975) ("the news media [should] report fully and accurately. . . . ").

[16] *Landmark Communications, Inc. v Virginia*, 435 US 829, 839 (1978) ("The article . . . provided accurate factual information about a [public issue] and in so doing clearly served those interests in public scrutiny and discussion of public affairs which the First Amendment was adopted to protect.").

[17] *Smith v Daily Mail Publ. Co.*, 443 US 97, 103–04 (1979). See also *Branzburg v Hayes*, 408 US 665, 729 (1972) (Stewart dissenting) ("If it is to perform its constitutional mission, the press must do more than merely print public statements or publish prepared handouts"); id at 722 (Douglas dissenting) ("The function of the press is to explore and investigate events. . . . ").

dent;[18] accordingly, it must be scrupulously protected from any form of government control.[19]

B. THE PRACTICAL UNDERSTANDING

Although the Court has articulated a coherent vision of the constitutional role of the press, it has failed to develop any coherent underlying assessment of the reality of the press. It therefore seldom understands, or even attempts to understand, the impact of its decisions on the press as an institution or on specific journalistic practices. Rather, what is striking is that the Court has developed its constitutional vision almost entirely in the abstract. It has rarely seriously considered the actual nature of the press or how the press actually functions.

Indeed, the Court's view of the nature of the press as an entity is notable primarily for its inconsistency. At times, the Court draws an image of the press as a lonely pamphleteer fighting an overpowering government. In *New York Times v Sullivan*,[20] for example, the Court described the press as vulnerable and easily intimidated by adverse verdicts:

> Whether or not a newspaper can survive a succession of such judgments, the pall of fear and timidity imposed upon those who would give voice to public criticism is an atmosphere in which the First Amendment freedoms cannot survive.[21]

---

[18] See, for example, *Leathers v Medlock*, 499 US 439, 446 (1991) ("The press plays a unique role as a check on government abuse. . . . "); *Grosjean v American Press Co.*, 297 US 233, 250 (1936) ("A free press stands as one of the great interpreters between the government and the people. To allow it to be fettered is to fetter ourselves."); *Mills v Alabama*, 384 US 214, 219 (1966) ("the press serves and was designed to serve as a powerful antidote to any abuses of power by governmental officials. . . . ").

[19] The Court has repeatedly rejected efforts by the government to control the press or dictate the content of its publications. See, for example, *Landmark Communications, Inc.*, 435 US at 839 ("If the constitutional protection of a free press means anything, it means that government cannot take it upon itself to decide what a newspaper may and may not publish"); *Miami Herald v Tornillo*, 418 US 241, 261 (1974) (White concurring) ("[It is an] elementary First Amendment proposition that government may not force a newspaper to print copy which, in its journalistic discretion it chooses to leave on the newsroom floor"); *CBS v Democratic National Committee*, 412 US 94 (1973).

The Court has relaxed this rule somewhat in the case of the regulation of the broadcast and cable media. See *Red Lion Broadcasting v FCC*, 395 US 367 (1969); *Turner Broadcasting System v FCC*, 114 S Ct 2445 (1994).

[20] 376 US 254 (1963).

[21] *Sullivan*, 376 US at 278. See also id at 294 (Black concurring) ("The half-million-dollar verdict does give dramatic proof . . . that state libel laws threaten the very existence of an American press vital enough to criticize the conduct of public officials."). The Court's assessment was apparently on target. See Anthony Lewis, *Make No Law* 35 (Random House, 1991) ("The *Times* was financially vulnerable in those days. James Goodale, later its general

In other cases, however, the Court has summoned a vision of a press of a far different nature.[22] In *Zurcher v Stanford Daily*,[23] for example, the Court described the press as being "not easily intimidated."[24] And in *Miami Herald v Tornillo*,[25] the Court, having come full circle from *Sullivan*, depicted the press as an institution wielding awesome influence and power:

> Newspapers have become big business. . . . Chains of newspapers, national newspapers, national wire and news services, and one-newspaper towns are the dominant features of a press that has become noncompetitive and enormously powerful and influential in its capacity to manipulate popular opinion and change the course of events.[26]

Such inconsistency does little to promote a coherent analytic approach to cases involving the press. In fact, the Court's varied descriptions of the press seem to be only rhetorical devices designed to justify particular results reached on other grounds and not serious efforts to develop a workable understanding of the press as an institution.[27]

---

counsel, said of the 1960 libel cases: 'Without a reversal of those verdicts, there was a reasonable question of whether the *Times* then racked by strikes and small profits, could survive.' ").

[22] The Court has of course recognized the corporate nature of the press when reviewing business regulations affecting the press. See, for example, *Associated Press v United States*, 326 US 1 (1945) (antitrust legislation); *Associated Press v NLRB*, 301 US 103 (1937) (labor law); *Grosjean v American Press Co.*, 297 US 233, 244–45 (1936) (taxes).

[23] 436 US 547 (1978).

[24] Id at 566.

[25] 418 US 241 (1974).

[26] Id at 254.

[27] Geoffrey R. Stone, *Imagining a Free Press*, 90 Mich L Rev 1246, 1251 (1992). For instance, in the libel cases, where the description of the press as weak and vulnerable predominates, the Court has extended protections to the press so it can have breathing space to publish. See, for example, *Gertz v Robert Welch*, 418 US 323, 340 (1974) (actual malice standard essential to avoid "inducing a cautious and restrictive exercise of the constitutionally guaranteed freedoms of speech and press"); *Philadelphia Newspapers, Inc. v Hepps*, 475 US 676, 777 (1986) (private figure required to show falsity as any lesser standard would deter the media from publishing); *Hustler Magazine v Falwell*, 485 US 46, 56 (1988) (extension of actual malice standard necessary to ensure political cartoons had adequate breathing space to survive). On the other hand, in the newsgathering cases, where the Court has repeatedly denied press claims for protection, the Court has employed an image of a strong commercial press with little need for protection from the Court. *Zurcher Stanford v Daily*, 436 US 547, 566 (the characterization of the press in *Zurcher* as not easily intimidated is particularly ironic given that the case concerned a student newspaper—hardly an economic giant of immense social influence); *Branzburg*, 408 US at 706 (the press is "far from helpless to protect itself from harassment or substantial harm."). *Tornillo* is the exception. Despite the Court's description of the press in that case as all-powerful, the Court refused to uphold a

It is even more unusual for the Court to inquire into how the press actually functions.[28] There are, of course, exceptions. The Court has occasionally been sensitive to deadline concerns[29] and matters of journalistic license.[30] More often, however, the Court has relied upon assumptions as to how the press operates, and even those assumptions are often contradictory. For example, in *Miami Herald v Tornillo*,[31] the Court assumed that a compelled right of reply would force editors not to cover controversial issues.[32] And in *Time, Inc. v Hill*, the Court assumed that not protecting the press with the actual malice standard would discourage it from publishing.[33] In neither case was proof of actual impact required.

On the other hand, in cases such as *Branzburg v Hayes*,[34] the Court refused to recognize a constitutional privilege authorizing reporters to maintain the confidentiality of their sources, despite testimony that the absence of such a privilege would inhibit press coverage by deterring informants from coming forward. Characterizing the testimony as "uncertain" and "unclear," the Court indicated that without more certain data demonstrating that informants were "actually deterred," it would not assume that press coverage would be impaired.[35]

---

statute which would have required a newspaper to grant a right of reply to persons against whom it had editorialized. *Tornillo*, 418 US 241.

[28] Compare Todd F. Simon, *Libel as Malpractice: News Media and the Standard of Care*, 53 Fordham L Rev 449, 461 (1984) ("The Supreme Court has frequently indicated that consideration of industry and professional practices of newsgathering and dissemination is appropriate in libel cases.").

[29] See *Curtis Publ. Co. v Butts* and *Associated Press v Walker*, 388 US 130, 158–59 (1967) (deadline considerations relevant to determination of whether reporter acted with actual malice). See also *New York Times v United States*, 403 US 713 (1971) (implicitly recognizing the press' competitive need to be the first to break a news story).

[30] In *Masson v New Yorker Magazine, Inc.*, 501 US 496 (1991), for example, the Court took into account journalistic norms in holding that a reporter's deliberate misquotation of a source did not automatically constitute actual malice unless the substance of the quotation was altered. Interestingly, the Court offered this holding without citation to any testimony. Compare notes 36–47 and accompanying text. For a further account of *Masson*, see Note: *Malice in Wonderland: Fictionalized Quotations and the Constitutionally Compelled Substantial Truth Doctrine*, 41 Case W Reserve L Rev 1271 (1991).

[31] 418 US 241 (1974).

[32] Id at 257.

[33] 385 US 374, 389 (1967). See also cases cited in note 27.

[34] 408 US 665 (1972).

[35] Id at 690, 693–95. The Court's change of assumption was not lost on the *Branzburg* dissent:

The impairment of the flow of news cannot, of course, be proved with scientific precision, as the court seems to demand. . . . We have never before demanded

In light of the Court's penchant to draw random assumptions about how the press actually operates, it is not surprising that there are barely a handful of cases in which the Court has acknowledged evidence of what reporters actually do. Even in these cases, reliance on this evidence occurs only in dissents. In his dissent in *Zurcher v Stanford Daily*,[36] for example, Justice Stewart relied on the affidavits of numerous reporters in concluding that newsroom searches would have a negative impact on the press.[37] The Court majority, however, was uninterested.[38] Similarly, in *Saxbe v Washington Post*,[39] Justice Powell noted in dissent that the district court had received testimony from both journalists and journalism professors who "agreed [that] personal interviews are crucial to effective reporting in the prisons context."[40] The Court again ignored the evidence. And in his dissenting opinion in *Branzburg v Hayes*,[41] Justice Douglas noted that "the record in this case [was] replete with weighty affidavits from responsible newsmen, telling how important is the sanctity of the sources of information."[42] The Court responded that this evidence was biased,[43] inconclusive,[44] and insufficient.[45]

---

that First Amendment rights rest on elaborate empirical studies demonstrating beyond any conceivable doubt that deterrent effects exist; we have never before required proof of the exact number of people potentially affected by governmental action, who would actually be dissuaded from engaging in First Amendment activity. Id at 733 (Stewart dissenting).

[36] 436 US 547 (1978).

[37] Id at 573–74 (noting that "[o]ne need not rely on mere intuition to reach this conclusion. The record in this case includes affidavits not only from members of the staff of the Stanford Daily but also from many professional journalists and editors, attesting to precisely such personal experience.").

[38] Id at 566 ("Whatever incremental effect there may be in this regard . . . it does not make a constitutional difference in our judgment.").

[39] 417 US 843 (1974).

[40] Id at 853.

[41] 408 US 665 (1972).

[42] Id at 723 (Douglas dissenting).

[43] Id at 694–95 ("[S]urveys of reporters on this topic are chiefly opinions of predicted informant behavior and must be viewed in the light of the professional self interest of the interviewees.").

[44] Id at 694 (available data is "unclear").

[45] Id at 690–91 ("On the records now before us, we perceive no basis for holding that the public interest in law enforcement and in ensuring effective grand jury proceedings is insufficient to override the consequential, but uncertain burden on news gathering that is said to result from insisting that reporters like other citizens respond to relevant questions put to them in the course of a valid grand jury investigation or criminal trial.").

Finally, although the Court has occasionally made passing references to ethical codes that govern journalism[46] and has sporadically noted newspapers' own codes of conduct,[47] it has not relied upon the ethical standards (or proposed ethical standards) of the press in crafting its decisions. Rather, it has declined to consider such standards, arguing "it is not the function of this Court to write a code."[48]

The Court's reluctance to develop a practical vision of the press may be intentional.[49] Indeed the Court's resistance to creating norms of the press as an institution or to imposing standards of journalistic practice has been quite explicit.[50] On the other hand, this aversion, whether deliberate or not, has led to some curious results if the Court's goal is to foster a press that acts in conformity with the Court's own constitutional vision.

II. The Reality—The Incentives for Superficial Journalism Created by the Court's Decisions

No assessment of the relative incentives created for superficial, as opposed to serious, journalism can be fairly offered without first acknowledging that, as a whole, the protections the Court has granted to the press are substantial. The Court has effectively abolished seditious libel.[51] It has consistently protected the press

---

[46] *Gannet v DePasquale*, 443 US 368, 390 n 23 and 433 n 13 (1979) (citing ABA Standards for Criminal Justice, Fair Trial and Free Press); *Branzburg*, 408 US at 731 n 10 (Stewart dissenting) (citing to American Newspaper Guild's code of ethics for journalists on source disclosure); *Nebraska Press Association v Stuart*, 427 US 539, 542 (1976) (citing Nebraska Bar-Press voluntary guidelines on reporting criminal cases).

[47] See *New York Times v Sullivan*, 376 US 254, 287 (1964) (noting that in accepting the advertisement, the *New York Times* complied with its own advertising standards as set out in its "Advertising Acceptability Standards"); *Florida Star v BJF*, 491 US 524, 528 (1989) (noting that the newspaper violated its own internal policy when it published a rape victim's name).

[48] *Nebraska Press Ass'n.*, 427 US at 551. See also id at 550 (noting the "practical difficulties of managing such guidelines").

[49] Bollinger, *Images* at 39 (cited in note 3) (suggesting the Court in its First Amendment decisions has elected to apply a "romantic" rather than an accurate view of the press).

[50] As Chief Justice Burger has explained, "[a] responsible press is an undoubtedly desirable goal, but press responsibility is not mandated by the Constitution and like many other virtues it cannot be legislated." *Miami Herald*, 418 US at 256. See also, for example, *Rosenbloom v Metromedia*, 403 US 29, 51 (1971) ("[while in] an ideal world, the responsibility of the press would match the freedom and public trust given it . . . from the earliest days of our history, this free society dependent as it is for its survival upon a vigorous free press has tolerated some abuse.").

[51] *New York Times v Sullivan*, 376 US 254 (1964); *Garrison v Louisiana*, 379 US 64 (1964).

against prior restraints, whether justified by claims of state secrecy,[52] fair trial,[53] or public order.[54] It has protected the press from discriminatory taxes.[55]

The Court has also been solicitous of the press in other respects. It has recognized the importance of deadlines and the necessity of journalistic license,[56] and has created at least a limited First Amendment right of access to judicial proceedings.[57] It has defended the press against right of reply legislation on grounds that the press enjoys the essential right to exercise "control and judgment" over the content of its publications.[58] It has been steadfast in protecting the editorial role of the press. Editorial opinion, whether expressed in text[59] or by caricature,[60] has been accorded virtually absolute First Amendment protection.[61] The Court's decisions, in sum, do provide substantial support for the maintenance of an independent and free press.

The Court's record in cases that create differing incentives between serious and superficial journalism is more problematic, but even here the record is not wholly one-sided. There are some instances in which the Court has provided important incentives for serious journalism. For example, the Court has created some strong

---

[52] *New York Times v United States*, 403 US 713 (1971).

[53] *Nebraska Press Ass'n.*, 427 US at 539.

[54] *Near v Minnesota*, 283 US 697 (1931).

[55] *Grosjean v American Press Co.*, 297 US 233 (1936). See also *Minneapolis Star and Tribune Co. v Minnesota*, 460 US 575 (1983).

[56] See notes 93–96 and accompanying text.

[57] See *Richmond Newspapers v Virginia*, 435 US 829 (1978).

[58] *Miami Herald*, 418 US at 258. But see *Red Lion Broadcasting v FCC*, 395 US 367 (1969) (upholding the fairness doctrine which required broadcast media to afford reasonable opportunity for the discussion of conflicting issues of public importance).

[59] *Mills v Alabama*, 384 US 214 (1966). See also *Greenbelt Cooperative Publ. Ass'n. v Bresler*, 398 US 6 (1970).

[60] *Hustler Magazine v Falwell*, 485 US 46 (1988).

[61] The decisions protecting editorial content do comport with the constitutional vision the Court has ascribed to the media. The press' editorial role, like the informative function that is the subject of this article, is of vital constitutional interest; democratic decision making requires not only the dissemination of information but also the airing of different perspectives. See Sunstein, *Democracy* at 19–22 (cited in note 6).

Some have argued, however, that even in this area the Court has not done enough to assure that a divergence of perspectives is actually aired. Id at 23. Contrast *Miami Herald*, 418 US at 241 (striking down mandatory right of reply statute) with *Metro Broadcasting v FCC*, 497 US 545 (1990) (upholding a broadcast license regulation designed to promote broadcast diversity) and *Red Lion Broadcasting*, 395 US at 367 (upholding the fairness doctrine).

incentives for accuracy. In its libel cases, for example, the Court has declared that the press is absolutely protected if it publishes the truth.[62] Conversely, the Court's actual malice decisions make it quite clear that deliberate or reckless falsifications are not protected;[63] and in its implicit adoption of the common law republication rule, the Court has indicated that the press will not be protected if it simply repeats the lies of others.[64]

The Court has also created some incentives for the reporting of serious issues of public import. This is most evident in the Court's approach to matters involving news reporting on government. The Court has consistently held that reports about the activities of government and its officials are entitled to the broadest and most stringent protections,[65] thus directly encouraging press attention to serious issues affecting the polity. It has also provided incentives for the discussion of serious issues in its privacy[66] and private figure

---

[62] *Sullivan*, 376 US at 279–80. The Court has also required a private plaintiff suing the media on a matter of public concern to prove falsity. *Philadelphia Newspapers, Inc. v Hepps*, 457 US 767, 776 (1985). The Court has further encouraged the reporting of the truth by holding that retractions cannot be treated as evidence of actual malice, thus encouraging the press to correct its errors. See *Sullivan*, 376 US at 286–87 (neither the *New York Times*'s issuance of a retraction to the governor, nor its refusal to offer one to the plaintiff, were evidence of actual malice).

The Court, however, has so far refused to extend the absolute protection of the truth to privacy cases. See notes 115–16 and accompanying text.

[63] See, for example, *Gertz v Robert Welch, Inc.*, 418 US 323, 339 (1974) ("There is no constitutional value in false statements of fact."). See also *Garrison v Louisiana*, 379 US 64, 75 (1964) (no protection for deliberate falsehoods); *Ocala Star-Banner v Damron*, 401 US 295, 301 (1971) (White concurring) ("The First Amendment is not so construed, however, to award merit badges for intrepid but mistaken or careless reporting. Misinformation has no merit in itself; standing alone it is antithetical to the purposes of the First Amendment as the calculated lie").

[64] See, for example, *Sullivan*, 376 US 254 (1964) (implicitly adopting republication rule); *St. Amant v Thompson*, 390 US 727 (1968) (speaker liable for repeating statement of another); *Pittsburgh Press Co. v Pittsburgh Commn. on Human Rels.*, 413 US 376, 386 (1973) ("The newspaper may not defend a libel suit on the ground that the falsely defamatory statements are not its own."). But see discussion of cases protecting the press when it reports from government sources in notes 107–13 and accompanying text. See also *Edwards v National Audubon Society, Inc.*, 556 F2d 113 (2d Cir), cert denied, 434 US 1002 (1977) (creating First Amendment privilege of "neutral reportage" protecting the publication of another's serious charges against a public figure when those charges are newsworthy and are reported accurately and in good faith); cf. *Harte-Hanks v Connaughton*, 419 US 567, 694–95 (1989) (Blackmun concurring) (suggesting that the Court might have been willing to recognize a neutral reportage principle).

[65] See, for example, *Sullivan*, 376 US 254; *Mills v Alabama*, 384 US 214 (1966); *Landmark Communications v Virginia*, 435 US 829 (1978); *Time, Inc. v Pape*, 401 US 279 (1971); *Cox Broadcasting Corp. v Cohn*, 420 US 469 (1975).

[66] *Cox Broadcasting Corp.*, 420 US 469 and *Florida Star v BJF*, 491 US 524 (1989).

libel cases,[67] holding that press exposure may be more limited when it reports on matters of public concern than when it reports on only private affairs.[68]

Nevertheless, although the cases may offer an occasional encouragement to serious reporting, far more potent incentives have been created for engaging in superficial journalism. We discuss six examples of this phenomenon.

A. COVER PERSONALITIES, NOT ISSUES

The Court's public/private distinction in its libel and emotional distress decisions creates an important incentive for superficial journalism. In both areas, the Court has held that when the press reports on public officials or public figures, plaintiffs can recover only if they prove actual malice.[69] If the press reports about private figures, a lower level of protection is applied.[70] Thus, it is safer for the press to cover public officials and public figures than it is to report on private figures.

On its face, this would seem to promote serious journalism. The press is encouraged to report on public officials and public figures—thus informing the electorate of the conduct of those in power. But, the distinction has a number of negative consequences. First, not all reports about public issues receive the higher level of constitutional protection—rather only those reports which involve a public person. Because it is the status of the plaintiff, rather than

---

[67] See *Gertz*, 418 US 332; *Dun & Bradstreet, Inc. v Greenmoss Builders, Inc.*, 472 US 749 (1984).

[68] As we shall see, however, even a public concern/private concern dichotomy may not necessarily encourage serious journalism. It may simply encourage the press to report on stories that have already come to the public's attention. See notes 128–31 and accompanying text.

In any event, the Court's early returns in defining what constitutes matters of public concern, however, are not encouraging. In the privacy cases, public concern has thus far been defined as what the government indicates is of public concern. See notes 121–22 and accompanying text (discussing cases holding a rape victim's name is of public concern). Meanwhile, the Court has indicated in its libel law cases that the financial condition of a construction company was not a matter of public concern. *Dun & Bradstreet, Inc.*, 472 US at 749.

[69] *Sullivan*, 376 US at 254; *Curtis Publ. Co. v Butts*, 388 US 130 (1967). Accord *Hustler Magazine v Falwell*, 485 US 46 (1988) (as to emotional distress claims).

[70] *Gertz*, 418 US at 323. However, private figure plaintiffs in suits concerning matters of public concern must meet a higher burden to recover punitive or presumed damages. Id.

the issue involved,[71] that determines the level of protection, many reports on matters essential to an educated citizenry do not receive the highest level of scrutiny.[72] A classic illustration is *Hutchinson v Proxmire*,[73] in which the Court refused to apply the actual malice standard because no public figure was involved, despite the fact that the publication concerned the wasteful spending of government funds.

Second, the decision to correlate the degree of protection with the notoriety of the plaintiff encourages the press to focus on the person rather than the issue. In assessing its potential for liability in running a particular story, the press is encouraged to examine the fame of the person and not the importance of the issue involved.[74]

---

[71] The nature of the issue does have a secondary role in the constitutional analysis. A private figure libeled in a matter involving a public issue must show at least some degree of fault on behalf of the press. *Hepps*, 475 US at 775; *Gertz*, 418 US at 323. If no public issue is involved, the standard may be strict liability. *Dun & Bradstreet, Inc.*, 472 US at 755–60.

The nature of the issue is also relevant to the Court's determination of "limited public figures," that is, persons who, because they have assumed a prominent role in a particular public controversy, may be treated as public figures for a "limited range of issues" related to that specific involvement. *Gertz* at 345 and 351. Importantly, unlike the true public figure about whom virtually all news reporting is protected, reports about limited public figures must be carefully confined to their involvement on particular issues in order to receive the benefits of the actual malice standard.

[72] The Court for a short period did toy with extending protection to all public issues, regardless of the status of the plaintiff. Thus, in *Rosenbloom v Metromedia*, 403 US 29 (1971), Justice Brennan, writing for a plurality, advocated that the actual malice standard should attach whenever the press reported on a public issue, regardless of whether a public or private plaintiff was involved. In his words:

> If a matter is a subject of public or general interest it cannot suddenly become less so merely because a private individual is involved or because in some sense the individual did not "voluntarily" choose to be come involved. The public's primary interest is in the event; the public focus is on the conduct of the participant and the content effect and significance of the conduct, not the participant's prior anonymity or notoriety. Id at 43.

However, only three years later, in *Gertz*, 418 US 323, a majority of the Court explicitly rejected the public issue approach of *Rosenbloom*, and re-instated the public/private figure distinction. Thus, under the Court's current media jurisprudence, press reports on public issues not concerning public officials or figures do not merit the highest level of First Amendment protection.

[73] 443 US 111 (1979).

[74] As Justice Brennan forewarned in his *Rosenbloom* opinion, the public/private figure distinction "could easily produce the paradoxical result of dampening discussion of issues of public or general concern because they happen to involve private citizens while extending constitutional encouragement to discussion of aspects of the lives of 'public figures' that are not in the area of public or general concern." *Rosenbloom*, 403 US at 48.

Third, the message that the press is safer reporting the life-styles of the rich and famous than covering issues more directly affecting the polity has been augmented by another factor. Although the Court initially seemed to suggest that actual malice might only apply to comments on "official conduct,"[75] it has subsequently made clear that the standard is instead triggered by coverage of "anything which might touch on" an official or public figure's conduct.[76] Thus, so long as the press focuses on a public figure or official, it receives a high level of protection, whether it reports on her economic policy or sexual habits.[77] As one commentator has observed, the Court's approach, "by eliminating most of the risks associated with the journalism of scandal, at least when directed at public officials or public figures . . . throws the weight of the law on the side of the public appetite for scandal. This tilt encourages even those in the press who would prefer another direction to gravitate toward scandal."[78]

B. DON'T REVIEW YOUR STORIES

The Court's decisions undermine sound journalism by discouraging the press from internally reviewing its news stories. The prime example is *Herbert v Lando*.[79] In *Lando* the Court held that the thought processes of a reporter, her colleagues, and her editor were subject to judicial inquiry in order to determine the newspaper's knowledge of probable falsity under the actual malice standard.[80] This discourages critical comments by editors and colleagues who may fear that their questions or suggestions to investigate further could later be used against the reporter as evi-

---

[75] *Sullivan*, 376 US at 279.

[76] *Monitor Patriot Co. v Roy*, 401 US 265 (1971).

[77] Id at 274 (in *Roy* the purportedly defamed person was a candidate for public office).

[78] David A. Anderson, *Is Libel Law Worth Reforming?* 140 U Pa L Rev 487, 534 (1991). *Time, Inc. v Firestone*, 424 US 448 (1975), might signal some limitation on the unfettered protection of reporting on scandal. In *Firestone* the Court held that a prominent socialite's divorce was not sufficient to make her a public figure because she was not involved in a public issue: "Dissolution of marriage through judicial proceedings is not the sort of 'public controversy' referred to in *Gertz*, even though the marital difficulties of extremely wealthy individuals may be of interest to some portion of the reading public." Id at 454.

[79] 441 US 153 (1979).

[80] *Herbert v Lando*, 441 US 153, 160 (1979).

dence of actual malice.[81] Indeed, *Lando* implies that liability may best be avoided if the reporter does not share her story with her colleagues at all. As the dissent in *Herbert v Lando* recognized:

> The possibility of future libel judgments might well dampen full and candid discussion among editors of proposed publications. . . . Those editors who have doubts might remain silent; those who prefer to follow other investigative leads might be restrained; those who would otherwise counsel caution might hold their tongues.[82]

This result can only harm the journalistic product, as the absence of editorial and collegial review will diminish "the accuracy, thoroughness and profundity of consequent publications."[83] This result also has implications for the press's constitutional role in informing the public. As the dissent recognized, "[t]o the extent the accuracy, effectiveness and thoroughness of such coverage is undermined, social values protected by the First Amendment suffer abridgment."[84]

C. DON'T INVESTIGATE

The Court's decisions deter investigative reporting, arguably the most important informative function of a serious press. This result is in part a product of the "actual malice" rule first announced in *New York Times v Sullivan*.[85] The Court has held that under this standard a public official or figure cannot recover for libel unless she proves that the media acted with knowing falsity or reckless

---

[81] Anderson, 140 U Pa L Rev at 516–17 (cited in note 78) (expressions of skepticism or calls for more investigation can be used as evidence of actual malice).

[82] See *Herbert*, 441 US at 194 (Brennan dissenting).

[83] Id.

[84] Id. A related disincentive for responsible reporting practice was created in *Zurcher v Stanford Daily*, 436 US 547 (1978). In *Zurcher*, the Court, by allowing searches of newspaper offices and reporter's files, created a major incentive for reporters to either not create files in the first place and/or destroy notes or other documentation as soon as possible. As will be noted, the effect of *Zurcher* has been mitigated by the passage of the Privacy Protection Act of 1980, which effectively overturned the *Zurcher* decision. Privacy Protection Act, 42 USC § 2000aa (1980). See also discussion in note 100.

[85] 376 US 254 (1964). As we shall see, the disincentive to investigate is not solely a product of actual malice, but is also the result of a series of decisions concerning stories originating from government sources. See notes 107–26 and accompanying text.

disregard for the truth[86]—a requirement that is not satisfied by proof of gross negligence or extreme departure from professional standards.[87] Accordingly, actual malice will not be found merely because the press relies upon only one source to the exclusion of others likely to know[88] or deliberately fails to check a story with the person about whom it was written.[89] The press, in other words, is under no obligation to investigate, even when a reasonable person would do so.[90]

The actual malice standard not only holds that there is no need to investigate; it suggests that it often is better not to investigate. This is so because the actual malice test turns on whether the newspaper has "a high degree of awareness of probable falsity."[91] For example, if a newspaper has one reliable source for a story and

---

[86] *Sullivan*, 376 US at 279–80. The actual malice standard also applies to private figure libel law plaintiffs involved in issues of public concern who attempt to recover punitive or presumed damages. *Gertz*, 418 US at 349; *Dun & Bradstreet, Inc.*, 472 US 749. Actual malice has also been applied to plaintiffs suing for intentional infliction of emotional distress, *Hustler Magazine*, 485 US 46; and false-light privacy, *Time Inc. v Hill*, 385 US 374, 388 (1967), *Cantrell v Forest City Publ.*, 419 US 245, 250–51 (1974). *Cantrell* left open, however, the question of whether a lesser standard might apply in the case of a private figure plaintiff. Id.

[87] *Harte-Hanks Comms. Inc. v Connaughton*, 491 US 657, 666 (1989) (noting that "there is no question that public figure libel cases are controlled by the New York Times standard and not by [a] professional standards rule.").

For example, although their codes of ethics demand that journalists act without bias or personal hatred (see Society of Professional Journalists, *Code of Ethics*, Standard 1 (1987); Radio-Television News Directors Association, *Code of Ethics*, Standard 2; American Society of Newspaper Editors, *Statement of Principles*, Article IV (1975)), the Court's definition of actual malice contains no such limitation. Evidence that an article is written out of spite or hatred is not proof of actual malice and does not trigger liability. See *Garrison v Louisiana*, 379 US 64, 73 (1964) (ill will is not evidence of actual malice); *Greenbelt Cooperative Publ. Assn. v Bresler*, 398 US 6, 10–11 (1970) (publisher's dislike of subject of article is not proof of actual malice); *Harte-Hanks*, 491 US at 666 (1989) (ill-will is not actual malice).

[88] See *St. Amant v Thompson*, 390 US 727, 732 (1968), but see *Harte-Hanks*, 491 US at 692, discussed in note 92.

[89] *Rosenbloom v Metromedia*, 403 US 29, 55–56 (1971) (no actual malice despite one reporter's failure to interview the subject of the story and a part-time reporter's hanging up on the plaintiff when he telephoned to complain of the inaccuracy).

[90] *St. Amant*, 390 US at 731 and 733 (press need not investigate to avoid liability under actual malice standard); *Beckley Newspapers Corp. v Hanks*, 389 US 81 (1967) (actual malice standard not met where paper failed to investigate); *Gertz*, 418 US at 332 ("mere proof of failure to investigate, without more, cannot establish reckless disregard for truth"); *Harte-Hanks*, 491 US at 692 (1989) ("failure to investigate will not alone support a finding of actual malice. . . . "). In *Sullivan* itself the Court found no liability even though no one at the newspaper "made an effort to confirm the accuracy of the advertisement, either by checking it against recent *Times* news stories relating to some of the described events or by any other means." 376 US at 261.

[91] *St. Amant*, 390 US at 731.

proceeds to print, there is no "awareness" of probable falsity. But, if the press investigates further, the picture may get murkier—there may be contradictions and denials. The more the press investigates, the more it may become aware of possible falsity. The investigated story is undoubtedly a better one—more complete, more well-rounded, and more informative. But it is also more risky. Ironically, by investigating and becoming aware of the possibility of falsity, the newspaper increases the risk that it will be found to have acted with actual malice. As the Court itself has conceded: "[i]t may be said that [the actual malice] test puts a premium on ignorance [and] encourages the irresponsible publisher not to enquire."[92]

The disincentive to investigate created by the actual malice rule is further demonstrated by the Court's willingness to apply a less stringent standard if the reporter is on a shorter rather than a longer deadline. The Court's rationale is straight-forward—reporters with tight deadlines are less able to ensure accuracy than those with more time to perfect their reports.[93] In one sense, this view accommodates legitimate journalistic concerns.[94] On the other hand, by making immediate (inaccurate) coverage relatively cost free, the Court renders more thorough investigations unnecessary and potentially more risky.[95] The message to the press is that if it covers immediate events, it will enjoy the benefit of a more lenient standard of review. If it decides to invest the resources for an in-depth

---

[92] Id at 731.

To be fair, the Court has indicated that when the press has reasons to doubt the veracity of its sources, it cannot elect to remain deliberately ignorant. *Harte-Hanks*, 491 US at 692. In *Harte-Hanks* the Court found actual malice when a newspaper ran a story reporting an ex-employee's allegation of improper offers, but failed to interview a key player and failed to listen to the tape (which the paper had in its possession) of the conversation in which the improper offers were allegedly made. Such evidence of "purposeful avoidance of the truth" was held to amount to actual malice. Id.

[93] Contrast *Curtis Publ. Co. v Butts*, 388 US 254 (1964) with *Associated Press v Walker*, 388 US 130, 157–59 (1967) (finding that the reporter in *Butts* who was working with a relatively relaxed schedule violated the actual malice standard, but the reporter in *Walker* who was on a tight deadline did not). See also *Masson v New Yorker Magazine, Inc.*, 501 US 496, 521 (1991) (noting that the reporter "had the tapes in her possession and was not working under a tight deadline. Unlike a case involving hot news, [the reporter] cannot complain that she lacked the practical ability to compare the tapes with her work in progress.").

[94] See note 56 and accompanying text.

[95] Market forces also appear to have some effect in pressuring the press to cover the most immediate news. See Tom Rosenstiel, *The Myth of CNN*, New Republic 27, 28 (Aug 22, 1994).

examination of the issues, it will have to meet a higher standard.[96]
The result again is to encourage superficial reporting to the detriment of serious investigation.

The Court's refusal to extend constitutional protection to newsgathering also discourages investigation.[97] In *Branzburg v Hayes*,[98] for example, the Court held that the First Amendment does not entitle the press to a qualified privilege when it refuses to disclose its confidential sources to grand juries. This refusal to protect sources makes investigation harder, more protracted, and more expensive—sources who otherwise would have provided information may refuse to come forward because of fear of exposure,[99] and others may be unwilling to provide verification.[100]

The newsgathering decisions discourage investigative reporting

---

[96] Id at 33 ("Breaking news is not always hard news").

[97] *Branzburg v Hayes*, 408 US 665 (1972); *Zurcher v Stanford Daily*, 436 US 547 (1978). The Court's reluctance to extend constitutional protection to the newsgathering process is also evident in the media access cases, discussed in notes 125–26 and accompanying text, and in the editorial review case discussed in notes 79–84 and accompanying text.

[98] 408 US 665 (1972).

[99] As Justice Douglas put it in dissent, "[a] reporter is no better than his source of information." *Branzburg*, 408 US at 721 (Douglas dissenting). See also Osborn, 27 Colum Hum Rts L Rev at 64–67 (cited in note 9) (demonstrating that 5%–50% of tips on "hot" leads reporters would not have discovered themselves come from confidential sources); Blasi, 70 Mich L Rev at 246 (cited in note 9). Although it conceded that its refusal to protect sources could adversely effect the flow of news, the Court characterized any impact as not "significant." *Branzburg*, 480 US at 694–95.

[100] One study of Pulitzer Prize–winning reporters revealed the important role confidential sources play in story verification. The study, although allowing that many reporters might have been able to verify the information themselves, showed that 86% of reporters use sources for story verification. Osborn, 27 Colum Hum Rts L Rev at 79 (cited in note 9).

Similar concerns were also raised, and rejected, in *Zurcher v Stanford Daily*, 436 US 547 (1978), where the Court upheld the government's right to search the newsroom, rejecting the press' claim that without protection "confidential sources will disappear." Id at 566. According to the Court, "[w]hatever incremental effect there may be [on news gathering] if search warrants . . . are permissible . . . does not make a constitutional difference." Id. Again, as the dissent pointed out, the Court may have underestimated the effect of its decision on newsgathering.

It requires no blind leap of faith to understand that a person who gives information to a journalist only on condition that his identity will not be revealed will be less likely to give that information if he knows that, despite the journalist's assurance, his identity may in fact be disclosed. Id at 572–72 (citations omitted).

As with *Branzburg*, the potential of *Zurcher* is to chill press coverage of controversial issues and impair its pursuit of accuracy. Congress itself has acted to alleviate some of the concerns created by *Zurcher* in the Privacy Protection Act of 1980 (42 USC § 2000aa) (protecting from government search and seizure "any work product material possessed by a person reasonably believed to have a purpose to disseminate to the public a newspaper, book, broadcast, or other similar form of public communication.").

in other ways. Investigative reports relying on confidential sources will often attract the attention of government subpoenas,[101] and may also trigger government searches of newsrooms.[102] The press, accordingly, may be deterred from reporting investigative stories that rely on confidential sources in order to avoid the institutional costs of defending and responding to subpoenas and searches.

Finally, the failure to protect source confidentiality deters investigation by increasing the personal risks of the reporter. In the absence of a statutory privilege, reporters who refuse to disclose the identity of their sources face the threat of going to jail.[103] Or, if they do reveal their sources, they risk both harm to their professional credibility and possible civil liability for breach of promise.[104] Denial of privilege, moreover, may also discourage the investigation of stories that could place the reporter at personal risk in the absence of a guarantee of source confidentiality.[105]

In sum, while the Court may describe the press as having the role of serving as an independent informer of the citizenry, it has not used the cases dealing with investigative journalism as an opportunity to facilitate press fulfillment of this role.[106] Rather, its

---

[101] *Branzburg*, 408 US at 721 (Douglas dissenting) ("forcing a reporter before a grand jury will have two retarding effects upon the ear and pen of the press. Fear of exposure will cause dissidents to communicate less openly to trusted reporters. And, fear of accountability will cause editors and critics to write with more restrained pens.").

[102] *Zurcher*, 436 US at 566 ("the press will suppress news because of fears of unwarranted searches.").

[103] For a recent incident of a reporter going to jail rather than reveal his sources, see *Roche v Florida*, 589 S2d 978 (Fla App 1991). The reporter spent 18 days in jail despite offer by governor to commute sentence to community service. See Marc A. Franklin and David A. Anderson, *Mass Media Materials* 93 (Foundation Press, Supp 1993).

[104] *Cohen v Cowles Media Co.*, 501 US 663 (1991), discussed further in note 106.

[105] In *Branzburg* itself, for example, the reporter's story, for which he claimed privilege, concerned his observations of an illegal drug operation. *Branzburg*, 408 US 665.

[106] The Court's only other ruling concerning sources, *Cohen*, 501 US 663 (1991), seems neutral in its impact on serious reporting. In *Cohen*, the Court held that the First Amendment did not immunize the press from liability where it breached a promise of confidentiality to a source. Id.

On one hand the Court's ruling that the press must keep its promises of confidentiality can be viewed as enhancing investigative journalism. The knowledge that the press is bound by its promises should encourage future sources to come forward, thus aiding investigative journalism. See Lili Levi, *Dangerous Liaisons: Seduction and Betrayal in Confidential Press-Source Relations*, 43 Rutgers L Rev 609, 662 (1991) ("[N]onenforcement of promises of confidentiality may discourage sources from sharing information with the press, thereby limiting the information available to the public.").

The facts in *Cohen*, however, illustrate the counterargument. In that case, Cohen, a Republican activist, requested and obtained a promise that he would not be identified as the source of a report on the opposing democratic candidate's criminal record. *Cohen*, 501 US at 665. The purpose of obtaining the promise was obviously to avoid the charge of negative campaigning and muckraking which inevitably followed the revelation that the

rules of liability and constitutional protection tend to discourage
the investigative function.

D. RELY ON OFFICIAL ACCOUNTS

The Court's decisions suggest that when a story involves the
government, the press should repeat the government's version
rather than engage in independent review. For example, in the libel
area, the Court generally has held that under the republication
rule, the press is liable for publishing the defamatory statements
of others.[107] The Court has wavered from this understanding, however, when the initial speaker is the government. Rather, relying
on the importance of press coverage of government activities, the
Court has protected the press when it simply repeats what the
government has announced.[108] In *Time, Inc. v Pape*,[109] for example,
the Court held that the press was not liable when it summarized a
Justice Department report and omitted the word "alleged" when
describing an incident of police brutality. Noting that the publication was a "news report of a particular government publication,"
the Court held that the omission could not trigger liability. The
Court indicated that when the press repeats government "reports,
speeches and press conferences," a more relaxed definition of falsity
must apply.[110]

---

information came from the Republican camp. When two of the newspapers broke their
promises of confidentiality, the resulting stories gave a fuller and more complete picture to
the public. The citizenry learned both the Democratic candidate's record and the Republican's mode of campaigning. As Justice Souter noted in dissent: "There can be no doubt
that the fact of Cohen's identity expanded the universe of information relevant to the choice
faced by Minnesota voters in that State's 1982 gubernatorial election." *Cohen*, id at 678
(Souter dissenting). Thus, by breaking its promise, the press avoided being manipulated
and provided a fuller report to the public.

Of course, if the press had not been so willing to extend the promise, it would not have
had to breach it. As one commentator observed, "[i]t may be that the only real effect of
permitting recoveries in source contract suits would be to cause journalists to use confidential
sources more carefully—with more specific understandings of the sources' motives, the
terms of the confidentiality agreement, and the reporter's own authority, as well as more
explicit disclosures to the sources as to what they can expect." Levi, 43 Rutgers L Rev at
662.

[107] *Sullivan*, 376 US 254 (1964) (newspaper liable for republishing the advertisement of
another); *St. Amant v Thompson*, 390 US 81 (1967) (speaker liable for repeating statement of
another).

[108] See *Time, Inc. v Pape*, 410 US 279 (1970); *Greenbelt Cooperative Publ. Assn. v Bresler*,
398 US 6 (1970). But see *Time, Inc. v Firestone*, 424 US 448, 456 ("Our decisions should
make it clear that no such blanket privilege for reports of judicial proceedings is to be found
in the Constitution.").

[109] 401 US 279 (1970).

[110] *Pape*, 401 US at 285–86. But see *Firestone*, 424 US 448 (rejecting a blanket privilege
for reports of judicial proceedings).

On this basis, the Court has thus expressly distinguished press stories repeating government announcements from press attempts to report the "historic facts"[111] or "other direct accounts of events."[112] Such "other direct accounts" are not entitled to the same protection.[113] The lesson, then, is that it is safer to simply report what the government has announced than to investigate what is actually going on.

The Court has adopted a rule of similar effect in the private facts torts cases.[114] In these cases, the Court has declined to hold the press immune from liability when it publishes the truth,[115] instead declaring the narrower principle that liability will not attach if the information was received from government sources.[116] Thus, while the press is fully protected when it reports information received from a government source, it may not be protected if it publishes the same information from a nongovernment source.[117] Press protection is most secure when it simply "reproduce[s], with no substantial change, the government's rendition of the event in question."[118] The press's own "rendition of the event" is not similarly protected.

---

[111] *Pape*, 410 US at 290 (1970).

[112] Id at 285.

[113] Id at 285–86.

[114] *Cox Broadcasting Corp. v Cohn*, 420 US 469 (1975), and *Florida Star v BJF*, 491 US 524 (1989).
The publication of private facts version of the privacy tort is distinct from libel and false light in that it seeks compensation for the publication of true information, while the latter complain of falsity.

[115] *Cox*, 420 US at 490–91 (Court refuses to decide the broader issue of whether true speech is always protected); *Florida Star*, 491 US at 532 ("Nor need we accept appellant's invitation to hold broadly that truthful publication may never be punished consistent with the First Amendment. Our cases have carefully eschewed reaching this ultimate question. . . .").

[116] See *Cox*, 420 US at 469: "Once true information is disclosed in public court documents open to public inspection, the press cannot be sanctioned for publishing it." See also *Florida Star*, 491 US 524 (holding a newspaper could not be liable for the publication of a rape victim's name where it had copied its story from a police press release). The Court has reached similar results in other contexts addressing liability for the publication of truthful facts. See *Landmark Communications, Inc. v Virginia*, 435 US 829 (1978) (reversing conviction for publication of truthful information regarding an inquiry into judicial misconduct being conducted by a state commission), and *Smith v Daily Mail Publ. Co.*, 443 US 97 (1979) (reversing conviction for the accurate publication of the name of juvenile defendant).

[117] See notes 110–13 and accompanying text. The Court has, it is true, indicated that it will protect a story that reports true information that is "lawfully obtained," *Florida Star*, 491 US at 541. And, that this definition might extend beyond information received directly from the government. *Smith*, 443 US at 103–04 (indicating the fact that in *Cox* the press' receipt of the information from a government source was not controlling). Nevertheless, the Court has so far only actually protected the publication of true information when it has been received, at least in part, from government sources.

[118] *Florida Star*, 491 US at 536.

Press reliance on government accounts is also encouraged by another aspect of the Court's privacy decisions—their definition of what issues are of "public significance," a standard that must seemingly be satisfied before constitutional protection will accrue.[119] As noted previously, this focus on the public importance of a story might be promising in that it encourages the press to cover serious issues.[120] The problem, however, is that the Court has held that the "public significance" requirement is met by virtue of the published information being found by the government to be significant[121] rather than by any independent evaluation of the importance of the information in question.[122] The press, in short, is encouraged to defer to the government's selection of what is significant.

At first glance, these decisions may seem to reflect sound policy. Press coverage of government and government records is of critical First Amendment concern.[123] The Court's libel and privacy decisions thus encourage the press to report stories of public import—one of the major goals of serious journalism. But, on further exami-

---

[119] Although the Court has never explicitly held that only speech of public significance will be protected in the privacy cases, it has strongly implied such a rule. Thus, it has stated that "if a newspaper lawfully obtains truthful information *about a matter of public significance* then state officials may not constitutionally punish publication of the information absent a need to further a state interest of the highest order." *Smith*, 443 US at 103 (emphasis added). See also *Florida Star*, 491 US at 533.

[120] See notes 66–68 and accompanying text.

[121] *Cox Broadcasting*, 420 US at 495 ("by placing the information in the public domain on official court records, the state must be presumed to have concluded that the public interest was thereby being served."). See also *Florida Star*, 491 US at 536 (public issue was involved because the article discussed a crime "which had been reported to authorities.").

[122] For example, in neither *Cox Broadcasting*, 420 US 469, nor *Florida Star*, 491 US 524, did the Court independently weigh whether the published information was a matter of legitimate public concern. This was so, moreover, although in both cases the published information was the name of a rape victim, the "public significance" of which is a matter of considerable dispute. See, for example, Paul Marcus and Tara L. McMahon, *Limiting Disclosure of Rape Victims' Identities*, 64 S Cal L Rev 1019 (1991); Deborah W. Denno, *Essay: Perspective on Disclosing Rape Victims' Names*, 61 Fordham L Rev 1113 (1993).

[123] See, for example, *Sullivan*, 376 US at 269 ("[I]t is a prized American privilege to speak one's mind, although not always with perfect good taste, on all public institutions") (citations omitted). See also *Cox Broadcasting*, 420 US at 495 ("Public records by their very nature are of interest to those concerned with the administration of government, and a public benefit is performed by the reporting of the true contents of the records by the media. The freedom of the press to publish that information appears to us to be of critical importance to our type of government in which citizenry is the final judge of the proper conduct of public business.").

The common law doctrine of fair and accurate report also protects reports from government documents and proceedings. See Rodney A. Smolla, *Law of Defamation* § 8.01[3] at 8-4 (Clark Boardman Co., 1992 ed).

nation, the decisions may also be seen as encouraging the press to cover the issues only superficially—to merely repeat government accounts rather than present all sides of the story. Moreover, not only is simply repeating government accounts shoddy journalism, it is particularly troublesome from a constitutional perspective. Rather than checking government power, it allows the government to set the news agenda. As Justice Stewart has stated, "If it is to perform its constitutional mission, the press must do more than merely print public statements or publish prepared handouts."[124]

In this respect, the Court's decisions in the newsgathering[125] and media access[126] area are also significant. In both circumstances, the Court has declined to protect press access to sources of information which might enable the press to independently assess the government's assertions.[127] The result is that the press's safest, and in many cases, only readily accessible, story is that which the government chooses to provide.

E. COVER WHAT HAS ALREADY ATTRACTED ATTENTION

The Court encourages the press to report on stories that already are widely disseminated. Part of this stems from Court's definition of public/private figure distinction. As we have seen, the Court

---

[124] *Branzburg v Hayes*, 408 US 665, 729 (1972) (Stewart dissenting). Accord *Branzburg*, 408 US at 722 (Douglas dissenting) ("If what the Court sanctions today becomes settled law, then the reporter's main function in American society will be to pass on to the public the press releases which the various departments of government issue.").

[125] *Branzburg*, 408 US 665; *Zurcher v Stanford Daily*, 436 US 547 (1978).

[126] See *Houchins v KQED*, 438 US 1 (1978); *Pell v Procunier*, 417 US 817 (1974) (prisons); *Saxbe v Washington Post*, 417 US 843 (1974) (same). See also *United States DOJ v Reporter Comm. for Freedom of the Press*, 489 US 749 (1989) (limiting press rights of action to government documents under the Freedom of Information Act).

The only area where the Court has found a right of access is judicial proceedings. See *Richmond Newspaper, Inc. v Virginia*, 448 US 555 (1980) (criminal trial); *Globe Newspaper Co. v Superior Court for Norfolk*, 457 US 596 (1982) (criminal trial); *Press-Enterprise Co. v Superior Court of California for Riverside*, 464 US 501 (1984) (voir dire examination of jurors); *Press-Enterprise Co. v Superior Court*, 478 US 1 (1986) (preliminary hearing); *El Vocero De Puerto Rico v Puerto Rico*, 113 S Ct 2004 (1993) (preliminary hearing).

The Court's test in determining whether a right of access exists, however, appears designed not to apply beyond the judicial proceeding context. See, for example, *Press Enterprise II*, 478 US 1 (1986) (access right applies to proceedings which have "historically been open to press and the general public" and where "public access plays a significant positive role in the functioning of the particular process in question"). On this basis, for example, the Court has consistently denied the press access to prisons on grounds that "penal institutions do not share the long tradition of openness." *Richmond*, 448 US at 576 n 11.

[127] See notes 170–84 and accompanying text.

extends its highest level of protection, the actual malice standard, to cases in which the plaintiff is a public figure. But the very definition of public figure encourages the press to play "copy cat." Public figures are those who have already achieved "pervasive fame and notoriety."[128] If a newspaper reports on the same set of characters that everyone else is covering, be it O. J. Simpson, Tonya Harding, or the media's current fixation, it is assured that it will be protected by the actual malice standard. If it reports on a less celebrated person, there is no such protection.

This incentive is also created, though less clearly, by the Court's "limited purpose public figure" doctrine. According to this doctrine, an individual who thrusts herself into a particular controversy may be deemed a "limited public figure," thus triggering the actual malice standard for stories addressing that controversy.[129] In other words, once there is a debate raging on an issue, its participants will be deemed to be limited public figures. The fifth paper to cover the issue can therefore easily satisfy the first prong of the test by claiming that there is an ongoing controversy. The first paper to break the story, however, runs a greater danger.[130] The lesson for the press, once again, is jump on the bandwagon and be protected, report on a new issue and risk liability.[131]

F. AVOID ASSERTIONS OF FACT

The final incentive to superficial journalism is the Court's willingness to accord greater protection to hyperbole and exaggeration than it accords to factual reports. In a series of cases starting with *Greenbelt Cooperative Publishing Ass'n. v Bresler*[132] and *National Ass'n. of Letter*

---

[128] *Gertz*, 418 US at 351.

[129] Id at 351.

[130] The Court has held that a newspaper cannot create a public figure through its own coverage. See *Hutchinson v Proxmire*, 443 US 111, 135 (1984) ("Clearly those charged with defamation cannot, by their own conduct create their own defense by making the claimant a public figure.").

[131] Curiously, the market incentive to cover sensationalist issues combined with efforts of the "serious press" efforts to retain its reputation may also be pushing newspapers to rehash old news. See, for example, Anna Quilden, *The Media: Out of Control*, New York Times Magazine 26, 29 (June 26, 1994) (quoting Barbara Ehrenreich, an essayist for *Time*) ("There's a new standard. It used to be, get the scoop and be first. Now you want to be 14th or 23d: 'No, I didn't do it until after NBC did it and ABC did it.' You have to be the last one to do these stories and wear the badge of purity.").

[132] 398 US 6 (1970).

Carriers v Austin,[133] the Court has held that exaggeration and rhetoric cannot form the basis of a libel action because no reasonable reader could consider such statements to be assertions of fact.[134]

Under this doctrine, the greater the exaggeration, the greater the protection. Thus if a newspaper intends to allege wrongdoing, it has an incentive to use particularly inflammatory language. In criticizing an individual for declining to join a union, it is safer to call him a "scab" and a "traitor" than to publish a factual account of how his actions.[135] There is a risk of liability only if the rhetoric verges on an assertion of fact.[136]

This incentive to avoid factual assertions was reinforced in *Hustler Magazine v Falwell*, a case which addressed potential media liability for intentional infliction of emotional distress.[137] The claim in *Hustler* was based on a satirical advertisement that depicted the plaintiff, Reverend Falwell, as a drunkard whose first sexual liaison was with his mother in an outhouse. The Court held that a public figure could not recover on the intentional infliction of emotional distress claim absent proof of falsehood and actual malice. Because the jury had found that "the parody could not reasonably be understood as describing actual facts or actual events in which [Falwell] participated," the Court held that recovery was precluded.[138] The Court concluded that the publication of a "caricature" could not, consistent with the First Amendment, form the basis of an award of damages.[139]

The decision is an important safeguard of free speech.[140] As the

---

[133] 418 US 264 (1974).

[134] *National Ass'n. of Letter Carriers*, 418 US at 285 (no liability for language which is "merely rhetorical hyperbole, a lusty and imaginative expression of the contempt"). See also *Milkovich v Lorain Journal Co.*, 497 US 1, 20 (1990) ("the *Bresler-Letter Carriers-Falwell* line of cases provides protection for statements that cannot 'reasonably be interpreted as stating actual facts' about an individual . . . . [T]his provides assurance that public debate will not suffer for lack of 'imaginative expression' or the 'rhetorical hyperbole' which has traditionally added much to the discourse of our Nation.").

[135] *National Ass'n. of Letter Carriers*, 418 US 264.

[136] *National Ass'n. of Letter Carriers*, 418 US at 286–87 (rhetorical language will only trigger liability if "used in a way as to convey a false representation of fact.").

[137] 485 US 46 (1988).

[138] *Hustler Magazine*, 485 US at 57.

[139] Id.

[140] For an in depth analysis of the impact of the *Hustler* case on public discourse, see Robert Post, *The Constitutional Concept of Public Discourse: Outrageous Opinion, Democratic Deliberation and Hustler Magazine v Falwell*, 103 Harv L Rev 601 (1990).

Court explained, American politics has long been illuminated by the skill of the satirist, a voice that would be chilled if protection were denied.[141] But the flip side of the message is that, when in doubt, the press should satirize rather than report. If the magazine had reported erroneous facts indicating that Falwell did not practice the virtues he preached, the article would receive less protection. It is only because the magazine eschewed the facts and engaged in extreme fictionalization and exaggeration that the protection was guaranteed.[142]

III: WHY HAVE THE CASES EVOLVED AS THEY HAVE? A PARTIAL EXPLANATION

As the previous discussion illustrates, the Court's decisions significantly differ from its constitutional vision of the role of the press. Although the Court maintains that the First Amendment is designed to foster an informed electorate, its decisions often discourage the press from covering matters of public import and from thoroughly and accurately reporting on the serious issues that they do choose to cover. Rather the press is encouraged to cover personalities rather than issues, abandon review and investigation, rely on government announcements, report on what is already widely known, and avoid factual representations.

Moreover, the incentives created by the Court exacerbate existing nonlegal incentives that also tend to dissuade the press from the pursuit of serious journalism. Independent investigations are significantly more expensive than publishing information readily available from other sources;[143] and stories on serious issues are not apparently the best way to sell papers or increase viewership.[144] If constitutional

---

[141] Id at 53–55.

[142] Id at 57.

An even more cynical lesson of the media law cases is that a newspaper which develops a reputation for accurate factual reporting may be penalized for its efforts. In *Masson v New Yorker Magazine, Inc.*, 501 US 496, 513 (1991), the Court held that in determining whether the use of altered quotes could be actionable, it was relevant that the work at issue "was published in the New Yorker, a magazine which at the relevant time seemed to enjoy a reputation for scrupulous factual accuracy." 115 L Ed 2d at 470. Accordingly, its quotations could be held to a higher standard of accuracy. The message is that a newspaper is most at risk when it has a reputation for accuracy and thorough reporting.

[143] Bollinger, *Images* at 56 (cited in note 3); Walter Goodman, *Are Newspapers Pushing to Do Less?* New York Times (Feb 8, 1990).

[144] *Anderson*, 140 U Pa L Rev at 534 (cited in note 78).

rules add still further to the existing incentives to engage in superficial journalism, it is no wonder the press seems to be increasingly lured to tabloid and press-release styles of journalism.

Why, then, have the decisions evolved as they have? Are the incentives for superficial journalism the inevitable result of accept ed First Amendment principles,[145] or may they be explained,at least in part, as wrong turns taken within the existing structure?[146]

Some of the results probably are inevitable. For example, the cases creating greater protection for hyperbole and exaggeration than for verifiable assertions of fact follow from a straightforward application of sound First Amendment principles.[147] These cases reflect the well-settled and well-founded First Amendment position that ideas are entitled to the most stringent constitutional protection.[148] Indeed, even from a journalistic perspective, the protection of ideas furthers the press's essential editorial role as a purveyor of differing opinions and commentary.[149]

Nevertheless, these decisions may also discourage serious, informative journalism.[150] The absolute protection of ideas in the form

---

[145] *Miami Herald v Tornillo*, 418 US 241, 256 (1979) ("press responsibility is not mandated by the Constitution").

[146] There is also another possibility, namely, that the media law cases are but one example of a fundamentally flawed jurisprudence that, as currently constituted, necessarily leads to results counterproductive to the goal of fostering an informed electorate. See, for example, Owen Fiss, *Free Speech and Social Structure*, 71 Iowa L Rev 1404 (1986); Sunstein, *Democracy* (cited in note 6). In a similar vein, it might be contended that the fundamental flaw within the jurisprudence rests with the actual malice rule announced in *New York Times v Sullivan*, 376 US 254 (1963). See, for example, Richard Epstein, *Was New York Times v Sullivan Wrong?* 53 U Chi L Rev 782 (1986); Brian Murchison et al, 73 North Ca L Rev (cited in note 1). As the reader has undoubtedly observed, many of the incentives for shoddy journalism stem directly from the actual malice standard. See, for example, notes 69–78, 79–84, 84–92, and 127–30 and accompanying text.

Whether the whole of First Amendment jurisprudence, or one of its central decisions, should be entirely overhauled is beyond the scope of this article. But see William P. Marshall, *Free Speech and the Problem of Democracy*, 89 Nw L Rev 191 (1994) (disagreeing with the contention that the essential First Amendment understanding should be reformed).

[147] See, for example, *National Ass'n. of Letter Carriers v Austin*, 398 US 6 (1970); *Greenbelt Cooperative Publ. Ass'n. v Bresler*, 398 US 6 (1970); *Hustler Magazine*, 485 US 46; *Milkovich v Lorain Journal Co.*, 497 US 1, 20 (1990).

[148] See, for example, *Police Dept. of the City of Chicago v Mosely*, 408 US 92, 95–96 (1972) (the government may not restrict expression because of its ideas); *Gertz v Robert Welch, Inc.*, 418 US 323, 339 (1974) ("under the First Amendment there is no such thing as a false idea. However pernicious an opinion may seem we depend for its correction not on the conscience of judges and juries but on the competition of other ideas.").

[149] See notes 58–61 and accompanying text.

[150] See notes 137–41 and accompanying text.

of exaggerations and hyperboles, while perhaps furthering the First Amendment goal of promoting diversity of perspective, leads to results that are perverse for the purpose of informing the electorate of the facts underlying particular issues.[151] The citizenry may hear a wide range of opinions on a public controversy, but unless they are exposed to the underlying facts, they will be ill-equipped to form conclusions on their own.[152]

This of course does not mean that the idea/fact distinction should be discarded. Given the importance of protecting editorial comment,[153] this may be an area where some discouraging of serious journalistic practice is justified by overriding First Amendment concerns.[154] In other circumstances, however, the Court's

[151] This result may be consistent, however, with the role of the press during the founding period. During that time, newspapers were not purveyors of news as that term is understood now. Rather, they were more opinion tracts than they were publications of factual information. See, for example, Michael Schudson, *Discovering the News: A Social History of American Newspapers* 18 (Basic Books, 1978); Gerald J. Baldasty, *The Nineteenth-Century Origins of Modern American Journalism*, in John B. Hench, ed, *Three Hundred Years of the American Newspaper* 407, 408–09 (1991) ("Partisan advocacy was the central content of these newspapers, and what we would call editorials today constituted the form of newspaper writings."); Comment, *The Reporter as Citizen: Newspaper Ethics and Constitutional Values*, 141 U Pa L Rev 221, 224–30 (1992) (charting the move from activism to neutrality in American newspapers).

[152] See Rosenstiel, New Republic (cited in note 95) (lamenting the journalistic trend to "sensationalism and an emphasis on punditry and interpretation at the expense of old-fashioned reporting"). Rosenstiel attributes this trend, not to judicial decisions, but to the availability of instant coverage of news events. Id.

[153] Conversely, there are important reasons why factual reporting, when inaccurate, should be subject to sanction. Incorrect factual assertions presumably add little to public awareness, and for the purposes of promoting an informed electorate are therefore of little constitutional value. See, for example, *Dun & Bradstreet, Inc. v Greenmoss Builders, Inc.*, 472 US 749, 767 (1985) (White concurring) (the ability of the people to govern themselves and to assess the performance of public officials is not served by false statements of fact). But see *Sullivan*, 376 US at 279 n 19 ("Even a false statement may be deemed to make a valuable contribution to public debate, since it brings about 'the clearer perception and livelier impression of truth, produced by its collision with error.' Mill, *On Liberty* (Oxford: Blackwell, 1947), at 15; see also Milton, *Areopagitica*, in *Prose Works* (Yale, 1959), Vol II, at 561.").

[154] It is possible, however, that the disincentive to serious journalism created by the absolute protection of ideas might have been at least mitigated without compromising the First Amendment principle at stake. In *Milkovich v Lorain Journal*, 497 US 1 (1990), for example, the Court, after refusing to adopt a blanket opinion privilege in libel cases (a holding that might at first seem to further the cause of factual reporting by ostensibly countering the incentive to publish only opinion), rejected the lower court's distinction between the editorial and reporting functions of a newspaper. Rather, the Court appeared to hold that in reviewing a claim for libel, the context of the allegedly defamatory remarks was of no consequence. Statements made in an editorial column were to be treated the same as statements on the front page—they were to be searched for factual content and if the "facts" in the story were false, liability might attach. The message that the editorial and reporting functions are indistinguishable, however, means that there is no particular incentive for the news reporter to be precise. Rather, the reporter is best protected by adopting the style of the editorial writer—a result that may have been avoided had the Court taken

decisions may not be as clearly compelled.[155] We offer three examples.

A. THE RELIANCE ON A "NOTORIETY" PRINCIPLE

Some of the decisions appear to be guided by a principle that reporting on what is "notorious" is entitled to heightened constitutional protection. This "notoriety" principle explicitly appears in the public/private figure distinction of the libel decisions,[156] but also has a surprising role in the access cases. In both circumstances the Court has taken the position that reporting about a matter that captures the attention of the community will generate heightened First Amendment protection.[157]

The notoriety theme is most intriguingly developed in *Richmond Newspapers*,[158] the case in which the Court found a First Amendment right of access to trials. The Court in *Richmond Newspapers* employed an historical test—a right of access would be allowed if a similar right existed at common law. But instead of relying solely on the ground that open trials serve an educative function and promote the fairness of the proceedings[159] (rationales that could equally be applied to support access to other government activities and institutions), the Court highlighted the trial's historical role as

---

into account the difference between the reporting and editorial functions. For whatever its worth, it is also notable that the division of the news and editorial functions is mandated by journalistic ethics. American Society of Newspaper Editors, *Statement of Principles*, Article 5 (1975); Radio-Television News Directors Association, *Code of Ethics*, Standard 1E; Society of Professional Journalists, *Code of Ethics*, Rule IV5 (1987).

[155] Another example in which a disincentive for serious journalism follows logically from a settled First Amendment principle is *Herbert v Lando*, 441 US 153 (1979), allowing inquiry into a reporter's discussions with her editor ("*New York Times* and its progeny made it essential to prove liability that plaintiff focus on the conduct and state of mind of the defendants. . . . Inevitably, unless liability is to be completely foreclosed, the thoughts and editorial process of the alleged defamer would be open to examination."). Id at 160. Assuming the actual malice inquiry is itself sound, the disincentive for editorial review created by *Lando* may be unavoidable. But see *Harlow v Fitzgerald*, 457 US 800, 818 (1982) (applying an objective standard in determining whether a public official is entitled to official immunity in order to avoid "excessive disruption of government."); *Malley v Briggs*, 475 US 335, 341 (1986) (same).

[156] *Gertz v Robert Welch*, 418 US 320, 351 (1974) (defamation of person of "pervasive fame or notoriety" subject to actual malice standard). Accord *Masson v New Yorker Magazine, Inc.*, 501 US 496, 115 L Ed 2d 447, 470 (docudramas and histories are less at risk from libel than journalistic writing). But see *Time, Inc. v Firestone*, 424 US 448 (1975).

[157] See notes 71–78 and 126, and accompanying text.

[158] 448 US 555 (1980).

[159] *Richmond*, 448 US at 570, 572.

a "mode of passing time"[160] and as a purveyor "of real life drama."[161] The Court also stressed the "therapeutic value"[162] of the trial, including its role as a vehicle for release of the public's feelings of outrage by satisfying the "fundamental, natural yearning to see justice done."[163] As the Court stated:

> When a shocking crime occurs, a community reaction of out-rage occurs and public protest often follows. Thereafter the open processes of justice serve an important prophylactic pur-pose providing an outlet for community concern, hostility and emotion. Without an awareness that society's responses to crim-inal conduct are underway, natural human reactions of outrage and protest are frustrated and may manifest themselves in some form of vengeful "self-help," as indeed they did regularly in the activities of the vigilante "committees" on frontiers.[164]

Trials, in short, are vehicles for a community's entertainment and catharsis.[165] For these reasons, the Court recognized a First Amendment right of access to trials even though no right of access existed to other governmental institutions or activities.[166]

---

[160] *Richmond*, 448 US at 572.

[161] *Richmond*, 448 US at 572. It is perhaps no coincidence that the judicial access cases before the Court all involved high profile cases. See, for example, *Richmond*, 448 US 559 (murder); *Globe Newspaper Co.*, 457 US 596 (sexual assault on minor victims); *Press Enterprise I*, 464 US 501 (rape); *Press Enterprise II*, 478 US 1 (mass murder by nurse of his patients).

[162] *Richmond*, at 569.

[163] 448 US at 572. The Court has repeated this rationale in other access cases. See, e.g., *Gannet Co. v DePasquale*, 443 US 368, 443 (1979) (Blackmun dissenting) ("There should be no need for a representative of the public to demonstrate that the public interest is legitimate or genuine, or that the public seeks access out of something more than mere curiosity. Trials and suppression hearing by their nature are events of legitimate public interest, and the public need demonstrate no threshold respectability in order to attend."); *Press Enterprise II*, 478 US at 13 (denial of access to preliminary hearing would have frustrated the commu-nity therapeutic value of openness).

[164] 448 US at 571 (citations omitted).

[165] The Court does balk when it perceives that judicial proceedings are being used simply for the purpose of getting a story. Thus in *Seattle Times Co. v Rhinehart*, 467 US 20 (1984), the Court refused to allow the press to utilize discovery in a civil suit to obtain and publish sensitive information. Equally, in *Nixon v Warner Communications, Inc.*, 435 US 589 (1978), the Court refused to provide copies of the Nixon White House tapes on grounds that there would be no "safeguard . . . against the distortion though cutting, erasing and splicing of tapes [and] [t]here would be strong motivation to titillate as well as to educate listeners." Id at 601.

[166] As noted previously (note 159 and accompanying text), the *Richmond* Court recognized that open trials also served the goals of ensuring a fair proceeding and in educating the public. However, these rationales do not distinguish trials from other government institu-tions, activities, or records. Thus, if the Court was sincere in promoting the education and fairness goals, its failure to extend the right of access to other government activities which would be equally educative is inexplicable. Indeed, the interest in assuring fairness through openness rationale may have a lesser importance with respect to trials than with respect to other government activities and institutions because, as the Court had noted in *Gannet Co.*,

The notoriety principle is not easily reconciled with sound First Amendment theory. Why should the fact that an activity is cathartic and entertaining be of particular First Amendment interest? There is no reason why an activity that is cathartic or entertaining should be of any special value if the goal is to foster an informed citizenry. There is little to suggest, for example, that the electorate would be more able to engage in sound political decision making upon watching the O. J. Simpson trial than it would be if it watched a city council debate on tax rebates for an influential corporation or witnessed a warden administering the state prison.[167]

This is not to say that there is no First Amendment interest in the values of an open trial recognized in *Richmond Newspapers*. Besides the education and fairness functions, the catharsis value is substantial.[168] Gossip and entertainment also have important functions in educating and in forging community bonds.[169] But, it is significant to note that the particular need the Court yields to in *Richmond Newspapers* stems from humanity's irrational side. The Court is concerned that, without the public trial, the human emotions of revenge and frustration would lead to social disturbance.[170] This, of course, is an interesting contrast to what the Court does not yield to in the other access cases—the public's need to be informed so it can make rational political choices. One would think that both needs would be deemed equally deserving of constitutional attention.

B. THE INADEQUATE RELIANCE ON THE "REPORTING ON
   GOVERNMENT" PRINCIPLE

Some of the disincentives for serious journalism result from the principle that First Amendment protection is at its most stringent

---

443 US 368, the ability of the defendant and the prosecution to demand openness in a criminal trial usually ensures fairness.

[167] It is notable, in this respect, that the California Secretary of State requested that the O. J. Simpson trial be recessed on Election Day so that people will get out and vote rather than stay home and watch the trial on television. Michael Janofsky, *Simpson Trial's Allure Puts State Politicians on the Spot*, New York Times A28 (Aug 13, 1994).

[168] Compare Thomas I. Emerson, *The System of Freedom of Expression* 7 (Random House, 1970) (articulating the "safety valve" value in freedom of expression).

[169] See, for example, Diane L. Zimmerman, *Requiem for a Heavyweight: A Farewell to Warren and Brandies' Privacy Tort*, 68 Cornell L Rev 291, 326–37 (1983) (arguing that both historically and in contemporary life gossip serves several constructive functions); Susan M. Gilles, *All Truths Are Equal, But Are Some Truths More Equal Than Others?* 41 Case W Reserve L Rev 699 (1991).

[170] *Richmond*, 448 US at 571.

when the press criticizes and reports on matters involving government.[171] As an abstract matter, this principle is unassailable. Reporting on government is essential to an informed electorate because it provides a check on those in power and an insight into the activities, performance, and possible abuses of public officials and government institutions. The problem is that the Court does not take this principle far enough. The result is to undercut the press's ability to fulfill this role.

First, the Court's emphasis on government activity ignores the fact that many of the most critical decisions affecting the social and economic fabric of a community are the product of private corporations and individuals rather than only of those who formally hold public office.[172] The community, accordingly, needs to be exposed to information about private as well as governmental power centers in order to determine when political action is necessary or appropriate.[173] The Court's libel jurisprudence, however, although nodding to the importance of information about private power,[174] nevertheless provides greater protection to the press when it reports on government. The press is more clearly protected, for example, when it reports on the activities of a mayor's assistant, no matter how powerless she may be, than when it reports on the activities of private citizens who wield far greater

---

[171] See, for example, *Sullivan*, 376 US 254. Cf. Vincent A. Blasi, *The Checking Value in First Amendment Theory*, 1977 Am Bar Found Res J 521.

[172] Frederick Schauer, *Defamation and the First Amendment: New Perspectives: Public Figures*, 25 Wm & Mary L Rev 905, 916 (1984) ("[I]n innumerable cases, a nominally private person exercises as much, if not more, influence on the determination of public policy issues as do many public officials."); Cass R. Sunstein, *Hard Defamation Cases*, 25 Wm & Mary L Rev 891, 901 (1984) (First Amendment concerns are "raised when one is dealing with nominally private citizens exercising significant power or involved in issues of public importance—a possibility that suggests that the court seriously misstepped in the Gertz case. Those not formally associated with the government, of course, often play an important part in formulating public policy."). The Court itself recognized this point in *Curtis Publ. Co. v Butts*, 388 US 130, 163 (1967) ("[I]ncreasingly the distinction between governmental and private sectors are blurred. In many situations, policy determinations which traditionally were channelled through formal political institutions are now originated and implemented through an array of boards, committees, commissions, corporations and associations, some only loosely connected with the government. This blending of positions and power had also occurred in the case of individuals so that many who do not hold public office at the moment are nevertheless intimately involved in the resolution of important public questions. Our citizenry has a legitimate and substantial interest in the conduct of such persons, and freedom of the press to engage in uninhibited debate about their involvement in public issues and events is as crucial as it is in the case of 'public officials.' ").

[173] Schauer, 25 Wm & Mary L Rev at 916–17 (cited in note 172).

[174] *Curtis Publ. Co.*, 388 US at 163.

influence on the matters affecting the community.[175] The Court's decisions thus work to steer even the serious investigative press away from reporting about significant private malfeasance in favor of relatively trivial stories about minor public official wrongdoing.[176]

Second, even if the private/public distinction is supportable in this context,[177] the Court runs afoul of First Amendment concerns

---

[175] Although the Supreme Court has not directly addressed the issue, the lower courts have generally held that mere prominence in business is not enough to trigger the public figure classification. *Tavoulareas v Piro*, 817 F2d 762, 773 (DC Cir), cert denied, 484 US at 870 (1987) (stating that "[b]eing an executive within a prominent and influential company does not by itself make one a public figure," although finding that the plaintiff in that instance was a public figure given his role in "spearheading a public counterattack" on efforts to reform the oil industry). Accord *Wilson v Scripps-Howard Broadcasting*, 642 F2d 371 (6th Cir), cert granted, 454 US 962, cert dismissed, 454 US 1130 (1981) (cattleman is private figure); *Dixson v Newsweek*, 562 F2d 626 (10th Cir 1977) (former airline vice-president found private figure); *Mead Corporation v Hicks*, 4498 S2d 308, 311 (Ala 1983) (businessman involved in garbage collection, waste disposal for nuclear power plant, landfill, grocery, and cattle concerns held a private figure). See also Rodney Smolla, *The Law of Defamation* at § 2.218 (cited in note 123) ("From a sheerly numerical perspective, there seem to be more cases holding such persons to be private figures than public figures. . . . ").

An alternative to the public figure analysis, that is, to extend protection based on the issue, not the status of the plaintiff, is not without difficulty. First, if "public issue" is descriptive, the result is circular. What is in the public interest is what the public has shown an interest in. See also Cynthia L. Estlund, *Speech on Matters of Public Concern: The Perils of an Emerging First Amendment Category*, 59 Geo Wash L Rev 1, 30 n 181 (1990). Second, as Estlund points out, the "public concern" inquiry runs counter to central First Amendment principles in that it requires the development of "an approved list of legitimate topics for public debate, a prospect that offends basic principles of democracy and freedom of expression." Id at 31.

The Court, however, has continued to experiment with the public concern test in the private figure defamation law and privacy tort area. See *Dun & Bradstreet, Inc.*, 472 US 749 (defamation); *Cox Broadcasting v Cohn*, 420 US 469 (1975) (privacy); and *Florida Star v BJF* 491 US 524 (1989) (privacy). See also *Connick v Meyers*, 461 US 138 (1983) (public employee speech).

[176] The authors are indebted to Christopher Harper for offering this point.

[177] The Court has offered two rationales purportedly justifying its public – private figure distinction. The first is that a public figure can resort to a form of self-help by using her prominence to gain a forum in which she may respond to the defamatory attack. The private figure, on the other hand, may not have access to such a forum. *Gertz*, 418 US at 344 ("Public officials and public figures usually enjoy significantly greater access to the channels of effective communication and hence have a more realistic opportunity to counteract false statements than private individuals normally enjoy."). The Court's second reason is that public figures have assumed the risk of their notoriety—a risk which presumably includes the likelihood that they may be held up to personal attack. Private figures, on the other hand, have presumably not assumed this risk. Id at 345 ("the communications media are entitled to act on the assumption that public officials and public figures have voluntarily exposed themselves to increased risk form injury from defamatory falsehood concerning them.").

Whether either of these rationales is persuasive is debatable. It is unclear, for example, if public figures truly possess the type of access to the media that would make self-help potentially effective. Responses to charges seldom receive the attention and prominence of the charges themselves. See also *Rosenbloom*, 403 US 29, 46–47 (Brennan plurality) (the ability to respond depends not on fame but on "the unpredictable event of the media's continuing interest in the story"). Moreover, there is significant question as to whether self-help would be effective even if there were meaningful opportunities to respond. Denials, unfortunately, often serve only to add credence to allegations. Even the *Gertz* Court has acknowledged this weakness. Id at 344 n

by not going far enough in its commitment to fostering the media's ability to serve as an independent source of information about government affairs. Specifically, the Court has failed to grapple with the reality that protecting the press when it reports on government is only part of what is necessary if the press is to serve as an effective check on government power.

This is so because of the government's power to manage the news.[178] Because whatever the government says is news, government is able to dominate the news agenda. It is thus able to determine the issues that will be perceived by society as important.[179] Moreover, because government is able to control the timing of its actions, it is able to gain the power of immediacy in augmenting its message.[180] As a result, the press, in the hands of an effective government public relations effort, can be turned from a check on government to an agent of government.[181]

The Court, however, has made it difficult for the press to counteract the government's ability to manage news. Instead, in a variety of decisions, the Court has discouraged the press from basing its stories on sources other than those that the government selects.

---

9 ("Of course an opportunity for rebuttal seldom suffices to undo hard of defamatory falsehood. Indeed, the law of defamation is rooted in our experience that the truth rarely catches up with a lie.").

The assumption of risk rationale is equally flimsy. To begin with, the idea that one who achieves prominence can be said to have voluntarily assumed the risk of having her name and persona dragged through the tabloids seems a stretch. Second, the Court's rationale presumes that the individuals who strive for success in arts, football, etc. should be held to the knowledge that success necessarily involves the risk of defamatory attacks. This stretches to breaking point the traditional definition of assumption of the risk in tort law. As Prosser observes, "the defense of assumption of risk is in fact quite narrowly confined and restricted by two or three elements of requirements: First the plaintiff must know that the risk is present, and he must further understand its nature; and second, his choice to incur it must be free and voluntary." W. Page Keeton, Dan B. Dobbs, Robert E. Keeton, and David G. Owen, *Prosser and Keeton on the Law of Torts* 487 (West Publishing Co., 5th ed 1984). Since "knowledge of the risk is the watchword of assumption of the risk," id at 487, the plaintiff must "not only know of the facts which create the danger, but must comprehend and appreciate the nature of the danger he confronts." Id at 487. Can we honestly say that a public figure while pursuing a career comprehends and appreciates the danger of defamatory stories, just like a fan at a baseball game comprehends the danger of fly balls? The public figure's lack of knowledge of the specific risk that eventually injures her goes far beyond the tort law's concept of assumption of the risk. See Anderson, 140 Pa L Rev at 527–28 (cited in note 87) (the self-help and assumption of risk rationales are "unconvincing" and "riddled with fallacies").

[178] Schudson, *Discovering the News* at 160–76 (cited in note 151).

[179] Shanto Iyengar and Donald R. Kinder, *News That Matters: Television and American Opinion* 16–33 (University of Chicago Press, 1987).

[180] Schudson, *Discovering the News* at 170–72 (cited in note 151).

[181] Id. See also David Strauss, *Persuasion, Autonomy, and Freedom of Expression*, 91 Colum L Rev 334, 357–58 (1991).

For example, the Court's libel and privacy decisions encourage the press to take the government at its word by imposing a greater risk of liability on the press when it deviates from government accounts.[182] Similarly, the decisions denying a right of press access to government information and institutions allow the government to package its news releases without oversight.[183] And the Court's decisions discouraging investigating reporting, in turn, inhibit the ability of the press to generate its own sources from which it can independently evaluate the government's reports.[184] The Court's decisions, in short, protect the press more when it carries, than when it questions, the government's message; they thus tend to facilitate, rather than curb, government manipulation of public opinion.

C. THE RELUCTANCE TO DISTINGUISH BETWEEN MEDIA AND NON-MEDIA

The disincentives for serious journalism also result from the Court's refusal to recognize any significance in the distinction between media and non-media.[185] The Court has not explicitly articulated the basis of this refusal, but it appears influenced by the speech equality principle that pervades much of current First Amendment jurisprudence[186] and by a reluctance to define who the media is.[187]

---

[182] *Time, Inc. v Pape*, 410 US 279 (1970); *Florida Star v BJF*, 491 US 524 (1989). See also notes 107–24 and accompanying text.

[183] Strauss, 91 Colum L Rev at 357 (cited in note 181) ("the first amendment is not generally thought to forbid the government from manipulatively denying information in the government's own possession," citing to *Houchins v KQED*, 438 US 1 (1978)).

[184] See notes 85–106 and accompanying text.

[185] *Cohen v Cowles Media*, 501 US 663 (1991); *Houchins*, 438 US 1; *Dun & Bradstreet Inc. v Greenmoss Builders, Inc.*, 472 US 749 (1985); *Branzburg v Hayes*, 408 US 665 (1972). But see *Richmond Newspapers v Virginia*, 448 US 555, 572–73 (1980) (recognizing the press' role as agent of the public).

[186] The speech equality principle maintains that the state may not restrict speech because "of its message, its ideas, its subject matter, or its content." *Police Dept. of the City of Chicago v Mosely*, 408 US 92, 95 (1972). See, for example, Kenneth L. Karst, *Equality as a Central Principle in the First Amendment*, 43 U Chi L Rev 20 (1975); Geoffrey R. Stone, *Content Regulation and the First Amendment*, 25 Wm & Mary L Rev 189 (1983).

Justice Brennan has explicitly relied on the speech equality principle in denying special protection for the media: "The free speech guarantee gives each citizen an equal right to self-expression and to participation in self-government. . . . Accordingly . . . the rights of the institutional media are no greater and no less than those enjoyed by other individuals or organizations engaged in the same activities." *Dun & Bradstreet Inc.*, 472 US at 783–84 (Brennan dissenting) (citing inter alia *Police Dept. of the City of Chicago*, 408 US 82).

[187] See, for example, *Branzburg*, 408 US at 703–05.

The failure to distinguish between media and non-media has its price. As the cases involving reporter's privilege and rights of access attest,[188] it prevents the Court from providing special protection to the press consistent with its constitutional function of informing the electorate and providing a check on government.[189] Moreover, on the other side, the refusal to admit media/non-media distinctions has led the Court to overprotect the press in circumstances where a particular protection may not only be unjustified, but may be affirmatively detrimental to First Amendment goals. The classic examples of this are the actual malice decisions involving the failure to investigate.[190] In those decisions the Court, as we have seen, has created a rule in which the media is more vulnerable to liability when it follows settled journalistic practice designed to promote accuracy than when it acts less diligently. By imposing the same standards of verification (or, more accurately, nonverification) on media and non-media, the Court, while perhaps protecting lay individuals who are not trained in journalistic techniques, effectively dissuades the media from using professional standards that further First Amendment goals.

It is questionable, however, whether the Court's refusal to acknowledge media/non-media differences is warranted.[191] And,

---

[188] *Branzburg*, 408 US 665 (privilege); *Houchins v KQED*, 438 US 1 (1978) (access).

[189] Contrast Alexander Meiklejohn, *Free Speech and Its Relation to Self-Government* (Harper, 1948) with David Strauss, *Rights and the System of Freedom of Expression*, 1993 U Chi Legal F 197, and with Blasi, 1977 Am Bar Found Res J 521 (cited in note 171.

[190] See notes 85–96 and accompanying text.

[191] While a full examination of the constitutionality of a media and non-media distinction is beyond the scope of this article, it may preliminarily be noted that such a distinction does not appear to violate speech equality concerns. First, any distinction between media and non-media would be in the nature of a non-viewpoint, speaker-based restriction and thus subject to a lesser standard of review than would a content-based restriction that more directly implicates equality concerns. See, for example, *Leathers v Medlock*, 499 US 439, 452 (1991); *Regan v Taxation with Representation*, 461 US 540 (1983); *Perry Educ. Ass'n. v Perry Local Educators' Ass'n.*, 460 US 37 (1983); Stone, 25 Wm & Mary L Rev at 244–51 (cited in note 186) (discussing speaker-based restrictions). Second, the Court itself has engaged in comparable distinctions in its media law cases. For example in *Masson v New Yorker*, 501 US 496 (1991), the Court distinguished between media with a "scrupulous reputation for accuracy" and media that does not enjoy this reputation; and, in a number of cases the Court has relaxed speech equality requirements between speech that is and is not a matter of public concern. See Estlund, 59 Geo Wash L Rev at 31 (cited in note 175); David A. Logan, *Tort Law and the Central Meaning of the First Amendment*, 51 U Pitt L Rev 493, 534 (noting that the public issue/private issue distinction in libel and privacy cases is inconsistent with a strict reading of content neutrality).

The Court's reluctance to distinguish between media and non-media also appears to rest on its unwillingness to define who the media is. *Branzburg*, 408 US at 703–05. This definitional concern, however, may be exaggerated. Numerous state shield laws and the Federal Privacy Protection Act of 1980 provide special protection for persons "engaged in newsgathering" and for "mediums of communication to the public" without creating unduly difficult problems in interpretation. See generally Carl C. Monk, *Evidentiary Privilege for Journalists'*

even if special protection for the media as an institution is constitutionally problematic,[192] there is no constitutional requirement that the Court ignore that differing functions and practices may appropriately have differing legal ramifications.[193] For example, the reason why it might be appropriate to subject the professional reporter, and not the lay individual, to a greater duty to investigate is because journalistic practice in evaluating information normally differs from that of the lay person.[194] Similarly, the justification for protecting the reporter and not the lay person from searches and seizures and/or compelled testimony when the reporter has obtained the information by active involvement in the enterprise of newsgathering is that she has not become aware of the information via the happenstance of the casual observer. The reporter's interests in protecting that information, accordingly, raise an entirely different set of concerns than that raised by the lay witness[195]—concerns, it might be added, that have been recognized by legislatures in the form of state shield laws[196] and the Federal Privacy Protection Act of 1980.[197]

Sources: Theory and Statutory Protection, 51 Mo L Rev 1 (1986). See also Paul Marcus, *The Reporter's Privilege: An Analysis of the Common Law, Branzburg v Hayes, and Recent Statutory Developments*, 25 Ariz L Rev 815, 860–64 (1984).

[192] See, for example, *First National Bank v Bellotti*, 435 US 765, 802 (1978) (Burger concurring).

It has been argued that conferring a preferred constitutional status on the media may be troublesome from a press freedom perspective in that special protection may imply special obligation. See Bollinger, *Images* at 58 (cited in note 3); William Van Alstyne, *The Hazards to the Press of Claiming a "Preferred Position,"* 28 Hastings L J 761 (1971).

[193] Contrast *Curtis Publishing, Inc.* with *Associated Press v Walker*, 388 US 130 (1967) (recognizing that the exigencies of journalistic practice, at least in the form of deadlines, may have differing legal implications).

[194] Todd F. Simon, *Libel as Malpractice: News Media Ethics and the Standard of Care*, 53 Fordham L Rev 449 (1984) (comparing a reasonable person standard with a reasonable journalist standard).

[195] For example, in addition to adding to the disincentive to investigate, see notes 97–105 and accompanying text, the Court's denial of press protection from compelled testimony and search and seizure also undercuts press independence by allowing the government to conscript the press as an enforcement agent. Allowing the government to compel reporters' testimony and search reporters' files, in effect, puts the institution of the press in the service of the government.

[196] See, generally, Monk, 51 Mo L Rev 1 (cited in note 191), and Marcus, 25 Ariz L Rev 815 (cited in note 191).

[197] See Privacy Protection Act, 42 USC § 2000aa (1980) (prohibiting government search and seizure of "any work product material possessed by a person reasonably believed to have a purpose to disseminate to the public a newspaper, book, broadcast, or other similar form of public communication.").

The Court's refusal to acknowledge media/non-media differences is thus not required by First Amendment concerns and is ultimately counterproductive. Rather than reflecting a sound First Amendment principle, the Court's failure to acknowledge the particular exigencies of newsgathering and news dissemination only leads to a jurisprudence that is out of touch with the reality that it purports to guide.

IV. CONCLUSION

It is not news that the media seldom act as an idealized fourth estate, watchfully protecting the public from the abuses of government and vigilantly researching and reporting on matters necessary for the fostering of an informed electorate. What is news is that the media's reluctance to aspire to this ideal may be encouraged not only by market forces and the media's own lack of conviction but also by the decisions of the Supreme Court. The Court has created a jurisprudence that too often encourages a trivial, lax, and sensationalist press over a press that is devoted to the thorough and accurate investigation and reporting of matters of public import.

This result does not appear to be intentional. To the contrary, the Court in its rhetoric continues to assert the importance of an idealized press vigilantly fulfilling its constitutional role. The incongruity between the Court's articulated vision of the press and its creation of a jurisprudence antagonistic to that vision appears to be a consequence of the Court's application of First Amendment doctrine to the press without understanding, or attempting to understand, the realities of what the press actually is and how it actually functions.[198]

The First Amendment, however, does not work well in a vacuum. Ignoring journalistic concerns has led not only to the creation of disincentives to serious journalism but in some instances to the misapplication of First Amendment principles. The First Amendment does not have a special solicitude for coverage of the notorious; it does not suggest that concerns over private power are irrelevant nor that the government's power of news management is of

---

[198] See Bollinger, *Images* at 39 (cited in note 3).

only peripheral import; it does not require that all media/non-media distinctions be ignored.

It may be that sound First Amendment considerations may, at times, have effects that inadvertently encourage superficial over serious journalism. If these results occur, however, it should be because they are required by considered application of First Amendment principles and not because the Court has unintentionally accorded serious journalism secondary constitutional status.

BERNARD SCHWARTZ

HOLMES VERSUS HAND: CLEAR AND PRESENT DANGER OR ADVOCACY OF UNLAWFUL ACTION?

In his just-published biography of Learned Hand,[1] Gerald Gunther discusses the differences between Judge Hand and Justice Oliver Wendell Holmes on one of the most important First Amendment issues—that of the constitutional protection accorded to speech that may lead to unlawful action. That was the issue dealt with in Justice Holmes's Clear and Present Danger test, his most famous contribution to our public law. Not long before Holmes enunciated his test, Judge Hand had confronted the same issue in the *Masses* case.[2] According to Gunther, the "standard Hand articulated in the *Masses* case was far more speech-protective than, and preferable to, the 'clear and present danger' standard."[3]

Because Gunther's book fills the long-felt need for a comprehensive biography of Learned Hand and because of the prestige of its author, there is a danger that the Gunther estimate of the Holmes versus the Hand standard will take over the field. Why do I call this a "danger"? Because, as this article will attempt to show, the Hand *Masses* test, as modified by a later Hand opinion on the subject, represents not an improvement on, but a significant dilution of, the Holmes Clear and Present Danger test. Indeed, adoption

Bernard Schwartz is Chapman Distinguished Professor of Law, The University of Tulsa, College of Law, Tulsa, Oklahoma.

[1] Gerald Gunther, *Learned Hand: The Man and the Judge* (Knopf, 1994) ("Gunther").

[2] *Masses Pub. Co. v Patten*, 244 Fed 535 (SDNY 1917), reversed, 246 Fed 24 (2d Cir 1917).

[3] Gunther at 599 (cited in note 1). Compare Harry Kalven, Jr., *A Worthy Tradition: Freedom of Speech in America* 125 (Harper & Row, 1988).

of the Holmes, rather than the Hand, standard has been the foundation of our law's protection of First Amendment rights during the present century.

I. Hand's Masses Test

After only eight years on the federal bench, Judge Learned Hand was presented with *Masses Publishing Co. v Patten*[4]—the case in which Hand laid down his test to determine when speech that may lead to unlawful action is not protected by the First Amendment. Gunther states the issue presented in *Masses* as follows: "When, if at all, may the state penalize political dissenters—those who criticize government leaders and their policies?"[5] But more than mere dissent was involved in the case. The government had argued that the speech at issue urged violations of the law contrary to the prohibitions in the Espionage Act of 1917.

The Espionage Act was the first Congressional attempt to curb freedom of expression since the Sedition Law of 1798.[6] The 1917 law made it a crime to make "false statements with intent to interfere with the operation or success of the military or naval forces of the United States," to "cause or attempt to cause insubordination, disloyalty, mutiny, or refusal of duty, in the military or naval forces," or to "obstruct the recruiting or enlistment service of the United States." It also provided that any publication containing material that violated the statute "is hereby declared to be non-mailable."

Acting under the Espionage Act, the postmaster of New York had refused to accept *The Masses*, "a monthly revolutionary journal," in the mails. The magazine sought an injunction and the case came before Judge Hand in the district court. The defense was based on cartoons and articles in the magazine which allegedly violated the Espionage Act. The cartoons were, in Judge Hand's phrase, "intended to rouse detestation for the draft law" and to show that the war was being continued "for purposes prejudicial to true democracy." The articles expressed admiration for draft

---

[4] 244 Fed 535.

[5] Gunther at 151 (cited in note 1).

[6] The best books on the 1798 law are James M. Smith, *Freedom's Fetters* (Cornell, 1956) and John C. Miller, *Crisis in Freedom* (Little, Brown, 1951).

resisters and were "designed to arouse animosity to the draft and to the war."[7]

In granting the requested injunction, Judge Hand conceded "that Congress may forbid the mails to any matter which tends to discourage the successful prosecution of the war."[8] But, Hand concluded, the cartoons and articles in *The Masses* did not come within the Espionage Act's prohibitions.

Hand discussed the three types of acts made criminal by the statute. As far as the first was concerned, he found that the attacks in *The Masses* on the draft and the war could not be considered "a willfully false statement." According to Judge Hand, "That phrase properly includes only a statement of fact which the utterer knows to be false, and it cannot be maintained that any of these statements are of fact, or that the plaintiff believes them to be false. They are all within the range of opinion and of criticism; they are all certainly believed to be true by the utterer."[9]

The cartoons and articles, according to Hand, "fall within the scope of that right to criticize either by temperate reasoning, or by immoderate and indecent invective, which is normally the privilege of the individual in countries dependent upon the free expression of opinion." To "class [attacks on existing policies and laws] as a false statement of facts [is] to raise [the statute] into a means of suppressing intemperate and inflammatory public discussion, which was surely not its purpose."[10]

The allegation that *The Masses* was "willfully causing insubordination, disloyalty, mutiny, or refusal of duty in the military" was based on defendant's claim "that to arouse discontent and disaffection among the people with the prosecution of the war and with the draft tends to promote a mutinous and insubordinate temper among the troops." To Judge Hand, this was stretching the concept of "cause" too far. Indeed, he asserted, "to interpret the word 'cause' so broadly would . . . involve necessarily as a consequence the suppression of all hostile criticism, and of all opinion except what encouraged and supported the existing policies."[11]

---

[7] *Masses*, 244 Fed at 536–37.

[8] Id at 538.

[9] Id at 539.

[10] Id.

[11] Id.

Nor, in Hand's view, could the published material come within the prohibition against obstructing recruiting or enlistment. To the contrary, "the most that can be said of that is that it may breed such animosity to the draft as will promote resistance and strengthen the determination of those disposed to be recalcitrant. There is no intimation that, however hateful the draft may be, one is in duty bound to resist it, certainly none that such resistance is to one's interest."[12]

The *Masses* decision was thus made on the basis of statutory construction:[13] the published material did not come within the prohibitions enacted by Congress. If this was all that Judge Hand wrote about the matter, his *Masses* opinion would scarcely be worthy of consideration today. The opinion did not, however, limit itself to the holding that *The Masses* publication did not come within the statutory language. It also stated the test that should be followed in determining whether such material might be prohibited: "Could any reasonable man say, not that the indirect result of the language might be to arouse a seditious disposition, for that would not be enough, but that the language directly advocated resistance to the draft?"[14]

This test concentrates exclusively upon the speaker's *words*, for, as Hand put it, "Words are not only the keys of persuasion, but the triggers of action." It follows that words "which have no purport but to counsel the violation of law cannot by any latitude of interpretation be a part of that public opinion which is the final source of government in a democratic state." As Hand emphasized, "One may not counsel or advise others to violate the law."[15]

The Masses, Hand conceded, may have been engaged in "political agitation." "Yet to assimilate agitation, legitimate as such, with direct incitement to violent resistance, is to disregard the tolerance of all methods of political agitation which in normal times is a safeguard of free government." To Hand, this was a fundamental distinction. It "is not a scholastic subterfuge, but a hard-bought acquisition in the fight for freedom."[16]

---

[12] Id at 541.

[13] Kalven at 125 (cited in note 3).

[14] *Masses*, 244 Fed at 542.

[15] Id at 540.

[16] Id.

The Hand *Masses* test, then, is a "content-focused inquiry";[17] it considers only the words used. If the words "directly advocated" violation of the law, they might be prohibited. But, "If one stops short of urging upon others that it is their duty or their interest to resist the law, it seems to me one should not be held to have attempted to cause its violation." Otherwise, "I can see no escape from the conclusion that under this section every political agitation which can be shown to be apt to create a seditious temper is illegal."[18]

As Judge Hand explained in a later opinion, under his *Masses* test the "limits [on speech are] determined by the character of the words themselves."[19] What words would come within the Hand test? According to Hand, "the words uttered must amount to counsel or advice or command to commit the forbidden acts"[20]—that is, acts that violate the law. Hence, a pamphlet which "undertakes to show that America's entrance into the war was the result of capitalist intrigue" did not violate the Espionage Act, even though "It is obviously inflammatory to the feelings of such readers as believe themselves unjustly treated by the existing order, which it presents as . . . proper only for immediate destruction."[21] Hand emphasized that, in application of his test, "The meaning of words" was the key. But since "the terms, 'counsel' or 'advice' have a content which can be determined objectively, [they] do not depend upon the subjective intent of their author."[22] That, wrote Hand, was what he had tried to suggest in *Masses*.

The *Masses* test, its author stressed, was an *objective* test. As such, it could deal with "our old friend Marc Antony's speech [which] is continually thrown at me in discussion."[23] The later Hand opinion recognized "That there may be language, as, for instance, Marc Antony's funeral oration, which can in fact counsel violence while it even expressly discountenances it." Yet the Hand test would not

[17] *Jones v Key West*, 679 F Supp 1547, 1557 (SD Fla 1988).

[18] *Masses*, 244 Fed at 540.

[19] *United States v Nearing*, 252 Fed 223, 227–28 (SDNY 1918).

[20] Id.

[21] Id at 223.

[22] Id at 227.

[23] Zechariah Chafee, Jr., to Learned Hand, March 28, 1921, reprinted in Gerald Gunther, *Learned Hand and the Origins of Modern First Amendment Doctrine: Some Fragments of History*, 27 Stan L Rev 719, 773 (1975).

exempt such speech, since it "raises only the situation, familiar enough everywhere in the law, . . . of the actual meaning of words to their hearers." The Hand test turns on "the meaning of words" and "the meaning of words comprises what their hearers understand them to convey."[24]

II. HOLMES AND CLEAR AND PRESENT DANGER

The *Masses* test focused on the words used because, in Judge Hand's striking phrase, "Words are . . . triggers of action."[25] What happens, however, if the words "amount to counsel or advice or command to commit the forbidden acts,"[26] but, in the circumstances in which they are uttered, are not "triggers of action"?

Such is the case with John Stuart Mill's famous example: "An opinion that corn-dealers are starvers of the poor, or that private property is robbery, ought to be unmolested when simply circulated through the press." At the same time, "speech that would be innocuous if addressed to an audience of divines might produce an entirely different result in quarters where a light breath would be enough to kindle a flame." Hence, according to Mill, stating "that corn-dealers are starvers of the poor may justly incur punishment when delivered orally to an excited mob assembled before the house of a corn-dealer, or when handed about among the same mob in the form of a placard."[27]

The great contribution of Justice Holmes to First Amendment law was to recognize, with Mill, that it was not the words alone but also the circumstances in which they were uttered that had to be considered in the *Masses* type of case. Such recognition was the foundation of the Clear and Present Danger test that Holmes developed soon after Judge Hand delivered his *Masses* opinion.

Justice Holmes also enunciated his test in an Espionage Act case—*Schenck v United States.*[28] Schenck, an official of the Socialist Party, had mailed 15,000 leaflets to draftees, calling the draft unconstitutional and declaring, "A conscript is little better than a

---

[24] *Nearing*, 252 Fed at 227.

[25] *Masses*, 244 Fed at 540.

[26] *Nearing*, 252 Fed at 227.

[27] John Stuart Mill, *On Liberty* 56 (Cambridge, 1989).

[28] 249 US 47 (1919).

convict . . . ASSERT YOUR RIGHTS!" Schenck was convicted of violating the Espionage Act by mailing the leaflet with intent to obstruct the draft.

Justice Holmes wrote the opinion for a unanimous Court affirming the conviction. More important than the decision was Holmes's reasoning. The Justice himself wrote that the opinion was "one that I hoped the Chief would give me,"[29] and that Chief Justice White chose him because White believed that Holmes "would go farther probably than the majority in favor" of free speech.[30] If this was, in fact, the Chief Justice's expectation, it was borne out by Holmes's *Schenck* opinion, which took a major step forward in First Amendment jurisprudence.

The Schenck opinion starts by rejecting the absolutist interpretation of the First Amendment. Despite Holmes's deep faith in the free interchange of ideas, Justice Frankfurter tells us, "he did not erect even freedom of speech into a dogma of absolute validity nor enforce it to doctrinaire limits."[31]

His rejection of First Amendment absolutism placed Holmes in the mainstream of jurisprudence on the matter. As the Supreme Court has summed it up, "the prohibition on encroachment of First Amendment protections is not an absolute. Restraints are permitted for appropriate reasons."[32] Holmes's famous example in his *Schenck* opinion of the man falsely shouting "fire!" in a theater[33] is simply an obvious example of speech than can be controlled.

It may well be true that "*Schenck*—and perhaps even Holmes himself—are best remembered for the example of the man 'falsely shouting fire' in a crowded theater."[34] But the "fire" example is so extreme that it scarcely adds to our understanding of the *Masses-Schenck* type of case. The same is not true of the remainder of the *Schenck* opinion, which states the Clear and Present Danger test as the standard for reviewing restrictions on speech such as that in *Masses* and *Schenck*.

---

[29] Mark DeWolfe Howe, ed, 1 *Holmes-Laski Letters* 186 (Harvard, 1953).

[30] Liva Baker, *The Justice from Beacon Hill* 521 (Harper Collins, 1991). See similarly Mark de Wolfe Howe, ed, 2 *Holmes-Pollock Letters* (Harvard, 1941).

[31] Felix Frankfurter, *Mr. Justice Holmes and the Supreme Court* 76 (Belknap Press, 1938).

[32] *Elrod v Burns*, 427 US 347, 360 (1976).

[33] *Schenck*, 249 US at 52.

[34] Kalven at 133 (cited in note 3).

When, according to Holmes, may such speech be restricted? He gave his answer in another case. "Only the emergency that makes it immediately dangerous to leave the correction of evil counsels to time warrants making any exception to the sweeping command, 'Congress shall make no law . . . abridging the freedom of speech.'"[35] But when does such an "emergency" arise? Holmes replied in *Schenck:* When "the words are used in such circumstances and are of such a nature as to create a clear and present danger that they will bring about the substantive evils that Congress has a right to prevent."[36]

Under this Clear and Present Danger test, speech may be restricted only if there is a real threat—a danger, both clear and present, that the speech will lead to an evil that the legislature has the power to prevent. The Holmes concept of speech is a relative one. The stress is not, as in the Hand *Masses* test, on the words themselves, but on their relation to the circumstances in which they are used. But the words must bear a direct relation to those circumstances.[37] It is not enough that the words used could be Judge Hand's "triggers of action." There must be a direct nexus between the words and the action; more specifically, there must be a clear and present danger that the words *will* trigger action that is unlawful.

In a letter to the Justice some years after *Schenck*, Zechariah Chafee asked Holmes whether the test stated in the case had been an original one or whether he had gotten it somewhere else. Holmes replied that it was original—"not helped by any book that I know of." Instead, Holmes wrote, "I did think hard on this matter . . . in my *Common Law*."[38]

The *Schenck* reasoning was based on an example that Holmes himself had given over a quarter century earlier in his seminal *Common Law*. Discussing the law of criminal attempts then, Holmes had given the case of "lighting a match with intent to set fire to a haystack." It "has been held to amount to a criminal at-

---

[35] *Abrams v United States*, 250 US 616, 630–31 (1919).

[36] *Schenck*, 249 US at 52.

[37] Compare Max Lerner, ed, *The Mind and Faith of Justice Holmes* 293 (Transaction Publishers, 1989).

[38] G. Edward White, *Justice Oliver Wendell Holmes* 430 (Oxford, 1993); Baker, at 524 (cited in note 30).

tempt to burn it, although the defendant blew out the match on seeing that he was watched." Holmes explained this result: "The reason for punishing any act must generally be to prevent some harm which is foreseen as likely to follow that act under the circumstances in which it is done." Though the act committed was itself harmless, "the otherwise innocent act [was rendered] harmful, because it raises a probability that it will be followed by such other acts and events as will all together result in harm."[39] Holmes had actually applied this reasoning in a 1901 case decided when he had been Chief Justice of the highest Massachusetts court.[40]

The Clear and Present Danger test was thus based on the analogy of the law of criminal attempts. Just as a criminal attempt must come sufficiently near completion to be of public concern, so there must be an actual danger that speech will bring about an unlawful act before it can be restrained. In both cases, the question how near to the unlawful act itself the attempt or speech must come is a question of degree to be determined upon the special facts of each case.[41] In both cases, as Holmes had put it in the 1901 case, "the degree of proximity held sufficient may vary with circumstances."[42]

Thus, if I gather sticks and buy some gasoline to start a fire in a house miles away and do nothing more, I cannot be punished for attempting to commit arson. However, if I put the sticks against the house and pour on some gasoline and am caught before striking a match, I am guilty of a criminal attempt. The fire is the main thing, but when no fire has occurred, it is a question of the nearness of my behavior to the outbreak of a fire. So under the Constitution, according to the Holmes test, lawless acts are the main thing. Speech is not punishable as such, but only because of its connection with lawless acts. But more than a remote connection is necessary, just as with the attempted fire. The fire must be close to the house; the speech must be close to the lawless acts. So long as the speech is remote from action, it is protected by the Constitution.[43] But if

[39] Oliver Wendell Holmes, *The Common Law* 67–68 (Little, Brown, 1938). Compare Baker, at 523 (cited in note 30); White, at 430 (cited in note 38).

[40] *Commonwealth v Peaslee*, 177 Mass 267 (1901).

[41] See Joseph Beale, *Criminal Attempts*, 16 Harv L Rev 491, 501 (1903).

[42] *Commonwealth v Peaslee*, 177 Mass 267, 272 (1901).

[43] Compare Zechariah Chafee, *Thirty Five Years with Freedom of Speech* 7 (Baldwin Civil Liberties Foundation, 1952).

the speech will result in action that government can prohibit, then, Holmes tells us, the speech itself can constitutionally be reached by governmental power, provided there is a clear and present danger that the action will result from the speech.

III. Hand-Holmes Debate

The Holmes speech test came after an exchange on the subject that took place between the Justice and Judge Hand. The exchange began by chance in June 1918 when the two judges met on the train from New York to Massachusetts. There are no notes on what the two talked about, but, according to Gunther, "They talked about the majority's right to suppress dissent. Holmes insisted that the majority had a legal right to prevail in this area as in all others; Hand objected that the courts must curb the majority when the minority's free-speech interests were at stake, difficult as that might be when, for example, majoritarian wartime hysteria was squelching antiwar dissidents."[44]

"Echoes of their conversation"[45] are preserved in a letter written by Judge Hand from his New Hampshire summer home a few days later. Hand wrote that he "gave up rather more easily than I now feel disposed" in their train meeting. Hand restated his view that "we must be tolerant of opposite opinions." That was true because "Opinions are at best provisional hypotheses, incompletely tested." They "are never absolutes"; hence, tolerance was the proper posture, not "the sacred right to kill the other fellow when he disagrees."[46]

Holmes's letter in reply stated, "I agree with it [Hand's letter] throughout," though he still refused to accept the view that freedom of speech stood in any preferred position. Instead, his letter to Hand asserted, "My only qualification . . . would be that free speech stands no differently than freedom from vaccination . . . if for any reason you did care enough [to stop it] you wouldn't care a damn for the suggestion that you were acting on a provisional hypothesis and might be wrong."[47]

---

[44] Gunther at 162 (cited in note 1).

[45] Id.

[46] Gunther, 27 Stan L Rev at 755–56 (cited in note 23).

[47] Id at 756–57.

After he had read the *Schenck* opinion, Judge Hand tried to persuade Justice Holmes that the *Masses* test was preferable. In what he termed his "last appearance in the role of liberator," he wrote to Holmes urging that it was the words, not their probable consequences, that should be determinative. "Speech," Hand conceded, may lead to an unlawful act "by its influence on others' conduct. . . . but responsibility does not go pari passu. I do not understand that the rule of responsibility for speech has ever been that the result is known as likely to follow. It is not . . . a question of responsibility dependent upon reasonable forecast, with an excuse when the words, had another possible effect." Rather, "The responsibility only began when the words were directly an incitement."[48] The Holmes test, on the contrary, might well be "a dangerous test"; it might "serve to intimidate,—throw a scare into,—many a man who might moderate the storms of popular feeling."[49]

Holmes replied with what Gunther terms "this remarkable comment":[50] "I don't see how you differ from the test as stated by me [in] *Schenck*."[51] It is, however, probable that the Justice was only engaged in a diplomatic effort to placate his judicial critic. In the end, neither Holmes nor Hand had his mind changed by the exchange between them. Hand continued to assert, as he later wrote, "I still prefer that which I attempted to state in my first 'Masses' opinion."[52] Holmes, on his side, seized the opportunity, after his exchange with Hand, to reaffirm his Clear and Present Danger test. The opportunity came in *Abrams v United States*.[53]

IV. ABRAMS—FREE TRADE IN IDEAS

In *Abrams*, as will be seen in the next section, Justice Holmes applied his Clear and Present Danger test to reach what he considered the correct decision. But Holmes's *Abrams* opinion involved more than that. Holmes used *Abrams* as the occasion for

---

[48] Id at 758.

[49] Id at 759.

[50] Gunther at 166 (cited in note 1).

[51] Gunther, 27 Stan L Rev at 760 (cited in note 23).

[52] Id at 763.

[53] 250 US 616 (1919).

delivering what has been called "the greatest utterance on intellectual freedom by an American, ranking in the English tongue with Milton and Mill."[54]

There is no doubt that his exchange with Judge Hand had led Holmes to think about the whole subject of freedom of expression. The Justice may have started with the view in his first letter to Hand "that free speech stands no differently than freedom from vaccination."[55] But Holmes soon moved to the protective approach to speech adopted in his Clear and Present Danger test. Then, in *Abrams*, as he wrote to Albert J. Beveridge, he thought it was his "duty" and his "right" to explain more broadly what he "thought the limits were to the doctrine that condemned [Schenck] and some others."[56]

The explanation came at the end of Holmes's *Abrams* opinion, when, as he put it in a later letter, "I had my whack on free speech."[57] As set forth in his *Abrams* opinion, the Holmes concept of freedom of speech is a direct descendant of John Milton and John Stuart Mill. Milton's *Areopagitica* argues for "a free and open encounter" in which "[Truth] and Falsehood grapple."[58] Holmes in *Abrams* sets forth the foundation of the First Amendment as "free trade in ideas,"[59] which through competition for their acceptance by the people would provide the best test of truth. Or, as the Justice put it in a letter, "I am for aeration of all effervescing convictions—there is no way so quick for letting them get flat."[60]

Like Milton and Mill, Holmes stressed the ability of truth to win out in the intellectual marketplace. For this to happen, the indispensable sine qua non was the free interchange of ideas.[61] The crucial passage of the Holmes opinion states, "when men have realized that time has upset many fighting faiths, they may come to believe even more than they believe the very foundations of their own conduct that the ultimate good desired is better reached by

---

[54] Lerner at 306 (cited in note 37) (italics omitted).

[55] Cited in note 47. See *Jacobson v Massachusetts*, 197 US 11 (1905).

[56] Baker at 538 (cited in note 30).

[57] Richard A. Posner, *The Essential Holmes* 322 (Chicago, 1992).

[58] Lerner at 290 (cited in note 37).

[59] *Abrams*, 250 US at 630.

[60] 1 Howe at 153 (cited in note 29).

[61] Frankfurter at 51 (cited in note 31).

free trade in ideas—that the best test of truth is the power of the
thought to get itself accepted in the competition of the market, and
that truth is the only ground upon which their wishes safely can
be carried out."[62]

According to Holmes, those who govern too often seek to "express [their] wishes in law and sweep away all opposition," including "opposition by speech." They forget that time may also upset
their "fighting faiths" and that, in the long run, "truth is the only
ground upon which their wishes safely can be carried out." Governance, Holmes explained, is an experimental process. Indeed, the
Constitution itself "is an experiment, as all life is an experiment."
To make the experiment successful, room must be found for new
ideas which will challenge the old, for "the ultimate good desired
is better reached by free trade in ideas."[63]

The Holmes concept, like those of Milton and Mill, is not limited
to free trade in ideas that are approved. "The prevailing notion
of free speech," Holmes wrote to his English correspondent, Sir
Frederick Pollock, "seems to be that you may say what you choose
if you don't shock *me*."[64] This was emphatically not Holmes's view.
When he wrote, in a passage to be quoted,[65] that the constitutional
principle that imperatively called for attachment was the principle
of free thought, he added "not free thought for those who agree
with us but freedom for the thought that we hate."[66] Or, as he put
it in another letter, "the usual notion is that you are free to say
what you like if you don't shock *me*. Of course the value of the
constitutional right is only when you do shock people."[67]

Judge Posner tells us that, in *Abrams*, Holmes not only "laid the
foundations . . . for the expansive modern American view of free
speech"; he also did so "for the double standard in constitutional
adjudication that is so conspicuous a feature of modern constitutional law: laws restricting economic freedom are scrutinized much
less stringently than those restricting speech and other noneco-
nomic freedoms. Here . . . , we again find Holmes seeming to

---

[62] *Abrams*, 250 US at 630.

[63] Id. Compare Lerner at 306 (cited in note 37).

[64] 2 Howe at 163 (cited in note 31).

[65] See note 75.

[66] *United States v Schwimmer*, 279 US 644, 655 (1929).

[67] Posner at 322 (cited in note 57).

work both sides of the street—rejecting the protection of economic freedom in *Lochner*,[68] insisting upon the protection of freedom of expression in *Abrams*."[69]

Holmes's inconsistency in this respect is, however, more apparent than real. It is true that Holmes was the prime architect of the judicial restraint doctrine that has taken over the field in cases involving challenges restricting economic rights. Nevertheless, the theme of judicial restraint was overridden by another Holmes theme in cases involving the freedom of expression guaranteed by the First Amendment. In a characteristic letter Holmes wrote, "at times I have thought that the bills of rights in Constitutions were overworked—but . . . they embody principles that men have died for, and that it is well not to forget in our haste to secure our notion of general welfare."[70]

Justice Frankfurter has shown that there was no real inconsistency in Holmes's abandonment of his basic rule of restraint in First Amendment cases. Restraint was the proper posture in cases like *Lochner v New York*,[71] where economic regulation was at issue. "The Justice deferred so abundantly to legislative judgment on economic policy because he was profoundly aware of the extent to which social arrangements are conditioned by time and circumstances, and of how fragile, in scientific proof, is the ultimate validity of a particular economic adjustment. He knew that there was no authoritative fund of social wisdom to be drawn upon for answers to the perplexities which vast new material resources has brought. And so he was hesitant to oppose his own opinion to the economic views of the legislature."[72]

A different situation was presented in First Amendment cases. Here, says Frankfurter, history had taught Holmes that "the free play of the human mind was an indispensable prerequisite"[73] of social development. "Since the history of civilization is in considerable measure the displacement of error which once held sway as official truth by beliefs which in turn have yielded to other truths,

---

[68] *Lochner v New York*, 198 US 45 (1905).

[69] Posner at xii (cited in note 57).

[70] Lewis M. Dabney, ed, *The Portable Edmund Wilson* 533 (Penguin, 1983).

[71] 198 US 45 (1905).

[72] Frankfurter at 75 (cited in note 31).

[73] Id.

the liberty of man to search for truth was of a different order than some economic dogma defined as a sacred right because the temporal nature of its origin had been forgotten. And without freedom of expression, liberty of thought is a mockery."[74]

The Bill of Rights itself, Holmes recognized, specifically enshrines freedom of speech as its core principle. "If there is any principle of the Constitution that more imperatively calls for attachment than any other it is the principle of free thought," he asserted in a 1928 dissent.[75] "Naturally, therefore, Mr. Justice Holmes attributed very different legal significance to those liberties of the individual which history has attested as the indispensable conditions of a free society from that which he attached to liberties which derived merely from shifting economic arrangements."[76] Because freedom of speech was basic to any notion of liberty, "Mr. Justice Holmes was far more ready to find legislative invasion in this field than in the area of debatable economic reform."[77] Thus, Holmes was not, despite Judge Posner's characterization, walking "a crooked path"[78] in *Abrams*.

It is true, as Edmund Wilson points out, that, "In the matter of free speech, [Holmes] was perhaps somewhat inconsistent."[79] In *Schenck*, Holmes enunciated the Clear and Present Danger test. But he used it to uphold a conviction where there was no real danger that the leaflets mailed would obstruct the draft. The same was true in the *Frohwerk*[80] and *Debs*[81] cases, decided a week after *Schenck*, where Holmes also wrote opinions upholding convictions for speech urging draft resistance. In both cases, the Justice found that the words used tended to obstruct recruiting and that that was enough even though there was no showing that there was any danger—clear and present or otherwise—that any actual resistance to the draft would result.

Had Holmes followed his *Schenck-Frohwerk-Debs* approach, he

---

[74] Id.

[75] *United States v Schwimmer*, 279 US 644, 654–55 (1929).

[76] Frankfurter at 51 (cited in note 31).

[77] Id.

[78] Posner at xii–xiii (cited in note 57).

[79] Dabney at 553 (cited in note 70).

[80] *Frohwerk v United States*, 249 US 204 (1919).

[81] *Debs v United States*, 249 US 211 (1919).

would have reached the same result in *Abrams* as the majority. But the earlier cases troubled the Justice. "I greatly regretted," he wrote to Harold J. Laski soon after the decisions, "having to write them—and (*between ourselves*) that the Government pressed them to a hearing."[82] By the time of *Abrams*, eight months later, Holmes's thinking had evolved and he urged a result different from those he had reached in *Schenck*, *Frohwerk*, and *Debs*.

The *Abrams* opinion remains the seminal one in Holmes's First Amendment jurisprudence, for in it the Justice not only stated his concept of free speech; he also showed for the first time how his Clear and Present Danger test was more protective of speech than the then-prevailing Supreme Court approach, as well as the Hand *Masses* test. We can see this by comparing the decision Holmes reached in *Abrams* with that which Judge Hand would have made under his *Masses* test.

V. ABRAMS—HOLMES OR HAND?

Early one morning in 1918, the air above passersby at the corner of Houston and Crosby streets in New York City was filled with leaflets thrown from a loft window. Written in lurid language, they contained a bitter attack against the sending of American soldiers to Siberia and urged a workers' general strike in support of the Russian Revolution and as a "reply to the barbaric intervention" by the United States. Six Russian factory workers who had printed and distributed the leaflets were arrested by the police and were convicted under the Espionage Act of 1917 for the publishing of language which incited resistance to the American war effort by encouraging "curtailment to cripple or hinder the United States in the prosecution of the war."

That was the fact pattern in the *Abrams* case. The Supreme Court affirmed the convictions, holding that, even though the defendants' primary intent had been to aid the Russian Revolution, their plan of action had necessarily involved obstruction of the American war effort against Germany.

Justice Holmes issued a strong dissent. To Holmes, the facts in *Abrams* did not justify the convictions. Again Holmes restated his Clear and Present Danger test, saying that "the United States constitutionally may punish speech that produces or is intended to

---

[82] Howe at 190 (cited in note 29).

produce a clear and imminent danger that it will bring about forthwith certain substantive evils that the United States constitutionally may seek to prevent."[83]

In *Abrams*, however, according to Holmes, the necessary nexus
did not exist. Instead, the "silly" leaflets thrown by obscure individuals from a loft window presented no danger of resistance to
the American war effort. Not enough, Holmes contended, "can be
squeezed from these poor and puny anonymities to turn the color
of legal litmus paper."[84]

The Hand *Masses* test, on the other hand, would have resulted
in a different decision than that urged in Holmes's dissent. Judge
Hand himself welcomed Holmes's broad discussion of free speech
in *Abrams*. "[N]othing," he wrote, "could be more needed than
Justice Holmes's opinion. I am delighted that it appeared."[85] After
all, as Gunther put it, the eloquent passages in Holmes's opinion
"indeed respond to Hand's sense of the values of free speech."[86]

Judge Hand's delight at the *Abrams* dissent did not, however,
extend to Holmes's reasoning and result. To the contrary, soon
after *Abrams*, Hand repeated his disagreement with the Holmes
test and his preference for his own *Masses* approach: "I do not
altogether like the way Justice Holmes put the limitation. I myself
think it is a little more manageable and quite adequate a distinction
to say that there is an absolute and objective test to language. I
daresay that it is obstinacy, but I still prefer that which I attempted
to state in my first 'Masses' opinion, rather than to say that the
connection between the words used and the evil aimed at should
be 'immediate and direct.' "[87]

The *Masses* objective focus on the words used alone, without
consideration of "the connection between the words used and the
evil aimed at," would lead to the same decision as that reached by
the *Abrams* majority. Hand himself wrote about *Abrams*, "I must
say . . . that on the facts it seems to me very questionable whether
the decision was not correct."[88] That was true because, as already
stressed, the *Masses* test protects speech only "so long as the utter-

---

[83] *Abrams*, 250 US at 627.

[84] Id at 629.

[85] Gunther, 27 Stan L Rev at 763 (cited in note 23).

[86] Gunther at 166 (cited in note 1).

[87] Gunther, 27 Stan L Rev at 763 (cited in note 23).

[88] Id.

ance, objectively regarded, can by any fair construction be held to fall short of counselling"[89] unlawful action. The *Abrams* leaflets could by a fair construction be held to counsel resistance to the war effort by urging a strike designed to interfere with war production. As such, the words used met the Hand criterion of "counsel . . . to violate the law."[90]

That is the result if, as *Masses* requires, we look only to the words used. An entirely different situation is presented if we require a clear and present "connection between the words used and the evil aimed at."[91] It may be reasonable to conclude that the words used in the *Abrams* leaflets met the Hand test of counseling or even inciting curtailment of war production.[92] But "nobody can suppose that the surreptitious publishing of a silly leaflet by an unknown man, without more, would present any immediate danger that its opinions would hinder the success of the Government arms or have any appreciable tendency to do so."[93] Under the Holmes test, "nothing less than that would bring these papers within the scope of this law."[94]

The *Abrams*-type case is a crucible for the testing of the Holmes and Hand standards. Under the Hand *Masses* approach, "enough can be squeezed from [the *Abrams*] poor and puny anonymities"[95] to convict them of counseling unlawful action, even though there was no danger, clear and present or otherwise, that their "silly leaflets" would lead to action on anyone's part. What it comes down to is that the *Masses* test in a case such as *Abrams* means a decision in which "defendants are to be made to suffer not for what the indictment alleges but for the creed that they avow."[96] Perhaps, in Holmes's characterization, it is "a creed that I believe to be the creed of ignorance and immaturity when honestly held, as I see no reason to doubt that it was held here."[97] But it is one that "no

---

[89] Id at 766.

[90] Cited in note 15.

[91] Gunther, 27 Stan L Rev at 763 (cited in note 23).

[92] Though, according to Holmes, they did not show "an intent to bring it about"—that is, the "substantive evils that the United States constitutionally may seek to prevent." *Abrams*, 250 US at 628, 627.

[93] Id at 628.

[94] Id.

[95] Id at 629.

[96] Id.

[97] Id.

one has a right even to consider in dealing with the charges before the Court."[98] Under the majority decision in *Abrams*, in Judge Hand's phrase during his exchange with Justice Holmes, "the merry sport of Red-baiting goes on."[99] But the same result would have been reached under Hand's *Masses* test.

In his exchange with Holmes, Hand stressed, "I do say that you may not cut off heads . . . because the victims insist upon saying things which look against Provisional Hypothesis Number Twenty-Six."[100] Such a result is, however, required when "the rule of responsibility for speech . . . does not go pari passu [with] the causal sequence."[101] That is true because, as Hand once put it, his test does not make "responsibility dependent upon reasonable forecast, with an excuse when the words, had another possible effect."[102] Instead, Hand would "prefer a test based upon the nature of the utterance itself. If, taken in its setting, the effect upon the hearers is only to counsel them to violate the law, it is unconditionally illegal." There is no tolerance for such speech, "notwithstanding the [lack of] probability that it may produce a violation of law" or "may have some other result than to produce the evil against which the law is directed."[103]

VI. HAND AND SEDITIOUS LIBEL

"It puzzles me also, I confess," Sir Frederick Pollock wrote to Justice Holmes after he had read the *Abrams* opinions, "that a special Act of Congress should be necessary to make seditious . . . incitements to rebellion, in time of war, offences of some kind."[104] To which Holmes replied, "your puzzle as to a special act of Congress being necessary is answered by the consideration that there are no crimes against the U.S. except by statute."[105]

The Pollock puzzlement stems from the fact that, in England, seditious libel has been a common-law crime since at least the

---

[98] Id at 630.

[99] Gunther, 27 Stan L Rev at 761 (cited in note 23).

[100] Id at 756.

[101] Id at 758.

[102] Id.

[103] Id at 765.

[104] 2 Howe at 31 (cited in note 30).

[105] Id at 32.

beginning of the seventeenth century.[106] Seditious libel has not only been a common-law crime in England, it is one that has been widely used to suppress speech. As stated by the leading modern English authority, "Every person commits a misdemeanour who publishes (orally or otherwise) any words or any document with a seditious intention. Now a seditious intention means an intention to bring into hatred or contempt, or to excite disaffection against the King or the government and constitution of the United Kingdom as by law established, or either House of Parliament, or the administration of justice, or to excite British subjects to attempt otherwise than by lawful means the alteration of any matter in Church or State by law established, or to promote feelings of illwill and hostility between different classes."[107]

The danger in such a conception is obvious: "any one will see at once that the legal definition of a seditious libel might easily be so used as to check a great deal of what is ordinarily considered allowable discussion, and would if rigidly enforced be inconsistent with prevailing forms of political agitation."[108]

Though the crime of seditious libel has all but disappeared in the modern English practice,[109] the danger referred to in the previous paragraph was very real at the time the Constitution was adopted. During the eighteenth century, says the leading constitutional historian of the period, "To speak ill of the government was a crime. . . . Every one was a libeller who outraged the sentiments of the dominant party."[110] The crime of seditious libel was virtually used to prohibit criticisms of government.

In his *Abrams* dissent, Justice Holmes declared, "I wholly disagree with the argument of the Government that the First Amendment left the common law as to seditious libel in force. History seems to me against the notion."[111] Though this Holmes position has been challenged,[112] it has been confirmed by *New York Times*

---

[106] *The Case de Libellis Famosis, or of Scandalous Libels*, 5 Co Rep 125a (1606).

[107] A. V. Dicey, *Law of the Constitution* 243–44 (Macmillan, 9th ed 1939).

[108] Id at 244.

[109] During the present century only two seditious libel prosecutions have taken place in England: *The King v Aldred* (1909), 2 Cox CC 1 and *Rex v Caunt*, discussed in Note, 64 L Q Rev 203 (1948).

[110] T. Erskine May, 2 *The Constitutional History of England since the Accession of George Third* 106–07 (A. C. Armstrong, 3d ed 1863).

[111] *Abrams*, 250 US at 630.

[112] See Leonard W. Levy, *Legacy of Suppression* vii–ix (Harvard, 1960); Leonard W. Levy, *The Legacy Reexamined*, 37 Stan L Rev 767 (1985).

Co. v Sullivan.[113] "For good reason," stated the Court in that case, " 'no court of last resort in this country has ever held, or even suggested, that prosecutions for libel on government have any place in the American system of jurisprudence.' "[114] More than that, the *Times* Court declared (over a century and a half after that ill-starred law itself was enacted) that the 1798 Sedition Act was unconstitutional: "Although the Sedition Act was never tested in this Court, the attack upon its validity has carried the day in the court of history. . . . the Act, because of the restraint it imposed upon criticism of government and public officials, was inconsistent with the First Amendment."[115]

Constitutional commentators today agree with the conclusion of Justice Black "that under our Constitution there is absolutely no place in this country for the old, discredited English Star Chamber law of seditious criminal libel."[116] Nevertheless, it should be emphasized that the common-law crime of seditious libel, to the extent that it still exists in England, is not at all like what it was at the time of the founding of the American Republic. It is not helpful to quote the precedents of the eighteenth and early nineteenth centuries for an understanding of the scope of the offense today.[117] As it has been interpreted during the present century, seditious libel in England is actually more protective of speech than Judge Hand's *Masses* test.

During this century, there have been only two English prosecutions for seditious libel. In the first of them, the 1909 case of *The King v Aldred*,[118] there is to be found in the charge of Coleridge, J., to the jury a virtual "summary of the law of seditious libel which represents the modern [English] attitude to this offence."[119] According to the charge, if the defendant "makes use of language calculated to advocate or to incite others to public disorders, to wit, rebellions, insurrections, assassinations, outrages, or any physical force or violence of any kind, then . . . there would be evidence on which a jury might, on which I think a jury ought, to decide that he is guilty of a seditious publication."[120]

---

[113] 376 US 254 (1964).

[114] Id at 291.

[115] Id at 276.

[116] Concurring, in *Garrison v Louisiana*, 379 US 64, 80 (1964).

[117] Dicey at 580 (cited in note 107).

[118] (1909) 2 Cox CC 1.

[119] Dicey, at 580 (cited in note 107).

[120] Id at 579.

As thus stated, the English law on the subject is not far removed from the *Masses* test. If anything, the test stated by Justice Coleridge is more protective of speech than the *Masses* test, for it includes only speech that "advocates" or "incites." The Hand test, as we saw, includes speech that "may . . . counsel or advise others to violate the law."[121]

In addition, unlike the *Masses* test, the English law on seditious libel, as stated in *Aldred*, does not focus upon the words used alone. "You are entitled," Justice Coleridge charged, "to look at all the circumstances surrounding the publication with a view to seeing whether the language used is calculated to produce the results imputed."[122]

As thus stated, the modern English law on the subject is closer to the Holmes than the Hand test. If there is no "clear and present danger" in view of "the circumstances surrounding the publication," it cannot be said that the language used was "calculated to produce the results imputed." And whether there is a real danger of such result being brought about depends upon the particular fact pattern in each case—in Justice Coleridge's words, "that is to say you are entitled to look at the audience addressed, because language which would be innocuous, practically speaking, if used to an assembly of professors or divines might produce a different result if used before an excited audience of young and uneducated men. You are entitled to take into account the state of public feeling. Of course there are times when a spark will explode a magazine."[123]

Paradoxical though it may seem in view of Gunther's laudatory estimate, Hand's *Masses* test is even less protective of speech than the modern English law of seditious libel. As put in an English law review, "a major difficulty with the Hand test is that words which may be apt to incite are punishable even if they were delivered to a pre-school class or a senior citizens' church group."[124] Such a "harmless inciter, the speaker explicitly urging law violation but with little realistic hope of success,"[125] would be exonerated

---

[121] Cited in note 15.

[122] Dicey at 580 (cited in note 107).

[123] Id.

[124] James G. Boasberg, *Seditious Libel v Incitement to Mutiny: Britain Teaches Hand and Holmes a Lesson*, 10 Oxford J Legal Stud 106, 113 (1990).

[125] Gunther, 27 Stan L Rev at 729 (cited in note 23).

under English law today and, even more so, under Holmes's Clear and Present Danger test.

VII. Dennis—Hand Dilutes Holmes

Harold J. Laski wrote to Justice Holmes that "a clever young lawyer . . . who has been reading your dissenting opinions" told him that he was "amazed that you were not speaking for the Court in the [*Abrams*] case." To which, stated Laski, "I explained that you were speaking for the Court of the next decade."[126]

And so it turned out, though Laski was somewhat overoptimistic on the time it would take for the Holmes view to be adopted. Over the next three decades, the Clear and Present Danger test did become accepted Supreme Court doctrine. By 1943, the Court could declare, "It is now a commonplace that censorship or suppression of expression of opinion is tolerated by our Constitution only when the expression presents a clear and present danger of action of a kind the State is empowered to prevent and punish."[127] A few years later, Chief Justice Vinson stated, "The rule . . . is that . . . a conviction relying upon speech or press as evidence of violation may be sustained only when the speech or publication created a 'clear and present danger' of attempting or accomplishing the prohibited crime, *e.g.*, interference with enlistment."[128]

The Vinson statement was made in *Dennis v United States*[129]—the most important case in which the Court ostensibly applied the Holmes test. It was, however, an alloyed version of the Clear and Present Danger test that was applied in *Dennis* and the dross was largely the handiwork of Judge Hand, whose lower court version of the Holmes test was adopted by Chief Justice Vinson's opinion.

Dennis arose out of a criminal prosecution for violation of the Smith Act of 1940—the first peacetime sedition law enacted by Congress since the Sedition Act of 1798. Defendants in *Dennis*, ten of the principal leaders of the Communist Party in this country, were indicted for violating the Smith Act by wilfully and knowingly conspiring (1) to organize as the Communist Party of the

---

[126] 2 Howe at 1219 (cited in note 29).

[127] *West Virginia Board of Education v Barnette*, 319 US 624, 633 (1943).

[128] *Dennis v United States*, 341 US 494, 505 (1951).

[129] 341 US 494 (1951).

United States of America a society, group, and assembly of persons who teach and advocate the overthrow and destruction of the Government of the United States by force and violence, and (2) to advocate and teach the duty and necessity of overthrowing the Government of the United States by force and violence. The case was tried at great length. The trial extended over nine months, six of which were devoted to the taking of evidence, resulting in a record of 16,000 pages. The jury brought in a verdict against all the defendants, and they were sentenced in accordance with the criminal penalties provided in the Smith Act.

In evaluating the Supreme Court's disposition of the appeals, it is important to bear in mind that the Court's reviewing function was essentially limited to questions of law. For purposes of the appeal, the Supreme Court had to assume the correctness of the findings of fact made by the two lower courts. These findings, based on the lengthy record of the evidence presented at the trial, included the following basic propositions: the policies of the Communist Party, in the postwar period covered in the indictment, were changed from peaceful cooperation with the United States and its economic and political structure to a policy which had existed before the United States and the Soviet Union were fighting a common enemy, namely, a policy which worked for the overthrow of the American Government by force and violence; the Communist Party is a highly disciplined organization, adept at infiltration into strategic positions, uses of aliases, and double-meaning language; the party is rigidly controlled; the Communists, unlike other political parties, tolerate no dissension from the policy laid down by the guiding forces, and the approved program is slavishly followed by members of the party; the literature of the party and the statements and activities of its leaders advocated— and the general goal of the party was, during the period in question, to achieve—a successful overthrow of the existing order by force and violence.

On these findings, the jury could, without a doubt, return its verdict that defendants had violated the Smith Act. But the sufficiency of the evidence to support the jury's determination was not the matter with which the Supreme Court was concerned. At issue before the Court was the question whether the Smith Act, inherently or as construed and applied in the particular case, violated the First Amendment.

Both the court of appeals and the Supreme Court answered this question in the negative. The court of appeals opinion was by Judge Learned Hand. Under his *Masses* test, *Dennis* would be an easy case, since "the utterances of these defendants . . . would have lost [First Amendment] protection, coupled as they were with the advocacy of the unlawful means."[130] But Hand had to concede that his *Masses* emphasis upon the words used alone was not determinative. As a lower court judge, Hand had to recognize that the Supreme Court had adopted the Holmes, rather than the Hand test. Thus, his *Dennis* opinion conceded, "it is not always enough that the purpose of the utterer may include stirring up his hearers to illegal conduct,"[131] and "The phrase, 'clear and present danger,' has come to be used as a shorthand statement of those . . . utterances which the Amendment does not protect."[132]

But Hand's opinion in *Dennis* did not simply follow the Clear and Present Danger test as it had been stated by Holmes and applied in prior cases. Instead, Hand rephrased the Holmes test: "In each case [courts] must ask whether the gravity of the 'evil,' discounted by its improbability, justifies such invasion of free speech as is necessary to avoid the danger."[133]

In the Supreme Court, Chief Justice Vinson stated for a plurality, "In this case we are squarely presented with the application of the 'clear and present danger' test, and must decide what that phrase imports."[134] After repeating the test as interpreted by Judge Hand in the passage quoted in the last paragraph, Vinson said, "We adopt this statement of the rule. As articulated by Chief Judge Hand, it is as succinct and inclusive as any other we might devise at this time. It takes into consideration those factors which we deem relevant, and relates their significances."[135]

With the Hand gloss on Holmes the determining criterion, the *Dennis* case was as easy as it would have been under the *Masses* test. As Judge Hand summarized his version in a later portion of his *Dennis* opinion, " 'clear and present danger' depends upon whether

---

[130] *United States v Dennis*, 183 F2d 201, 207 (2d Cir 1950).

[131] Id at 212.

[132] Id.

[133] Id.

[134] *Dennis*, 341 US at 508.

[135] Id at 510.

the mischief of the repression is greater than the gravity of the evil, discounted by its improbability."[136] Such a test means that speech such as that in *Dennis* will always be held beyond First Amendment protection.

What Judge Hand did in *Dennis* was to substitute a balancing test under which, as the gravity of the evil increased, the nexus required would become proportionately less and less definite. Since no substantive evil which government may prevent is greater than its own overthrow by force and violence, the requirement that there be danger that the advocacy actually will lead to the evil is all but eliminated: "under this rule any talk of revolution, however unlikely, must weigh as a requisite danger."[137]

Justice Brandeis once explained that the Holmes nexus requirement was intended to avoid the anomaly of finding a clear and present danger of an insubstantial evil:[138] "even advocacy of violation however reprehensible morally, is not a justification for denying free speech where . . . there is nothing to indicate that the advocacy would be immediately acted on."[139] Justice Holmes himself never suggested that the gravity of the evil was to be weighed against the likelihood of the danger. Yet, as Harry Kalven tells us, "that is the effect of the Hand-Vinson restatement."[140] Kalven explains this comment: "fastening on the gravity requirement the *Dennis* Court is able to loosen the imminence requirement and thereby to remove the obstacle to conviction which the clear and present danger test would otherwise have presented."[141]

Under the Hand restatement of Holmes, *Dennis* involves a virtual per se application of the Clear and Present Danger test. In fact, however, the American Communist Party at the time did not really pose any substantial threat to our established system of government. How could such an inconsequential group, whose doctrines had been so utterly rejected by the American people, be seriously considered a "clear and present" danger to government in this country?

---

[136] *Dennis*, 183 F2d at 215.

[137] Kalven at 198 (cited in note 3).

[138] Id.

[139] Concurring, in *Whitney v California*, 274 US 357, 376 (1927).

[140] Kalven at 198 (cited in note 3).

[141] Id.

Historical perspective has given added weight to Justice Douglas's *Dennis* dissent: "Communists in this country have never made a respectable or serious showing in any election. I would doubt that there is a village, let alone a city or county or state, which the Communists could carry. Communism in the world scene is no bogeyman; but Communism as a political faction or party in this country plainly is. Communism has been so thoroughly exposed in this country that it has been crippled as a political force. Free speech has destroyed it as an effective political party. . . . How it can be said that there is a clear and present danger that this advocacy will succeed is, therefore, a mystery."[142]

Judge Hand's *Dennis* restatement has been well characterized as "the discounted [Holmes] test."[143] Since it all but does away with the nexus requirement in *Dennis*,[144] it means that, in such a case, there must always be a finding that the requisite danger existed. When the gravity of the evil is as great as that in *Dennis*, the requirement of "immediate injury to society that is likely if [the] speech is allowed,"[145] has been virtually eliminated.

Despite Gunther's disclaimer,[146] Judge Hand's *Dennis* opinion contributed directly to what is now rightly viewed as "a debacle for the First Amendment."[147] When *Dennis* was decided, Hand still adhered to his view on the inadequacy of the Holmes test. Soon after the Supreme Court decision, Hand wrote to Justice Frankfurter, "As res integra, I think that Holmes—nomen clarrisima et venerabilissime—for once slipped his trolley on 'clear and present.' "[148]

A year later, Hand reiterated his preference for his *Masses* test in a letter to a former law clerk: "I dissent from the whole approach to the problem of Free Speech which the Supreme Court has adopted during the last thirty-five or forty years. . . . I would make the purpose of the utterer the test of his constitutional protec-

---

[142] *Dennis*, 341 US at 588.

[143] Kalven at 198 (cited in note 3).

[144] Justice Brennan goes further and cites *Dennis*, among other cases, to support the statement that "[t]he Court long ago departed from 'clear and present danger' as a test for limiting free expression." *Greer v Spock*, 424 US 828, 863 (1976).

[145] Douglas, J, dissenting, in *Dennis*, 341 US at 585.

[146] Gunther at 599–604 (cited in note 1).

[147] Id at 599.

[148] Id at 604.

tion. Did he seek to bring about a violation of existing law? If he did, I can see no reason why the constitution should protect him, however remote the chance may be of his success."[149]

In his *Dennis* dilution of the Holmes test, Judge Hand came closer to his *Masses* test. Under the Hand discounted test, the emphasis was placed on the words used and the gravity of the evil advocated, "however remote the chance may be of . . . success."[150] The Hand *Dennis* test did not, however, take over the field for long, since the Court rejected the *Dennis* standard in *Brandenburg v Ohio*.[151]

VIII. Brandenburg—Hand, Holmes, or Neither?

The Hand *Dennis* test has not had a baneful effect upon First Amendment law because it has been replaced by the test laid down in *Brandenburg v Ohio*.[152] That case arose out of the conviction of a Ku Klux Klan leader for violating an Ohio law that prohibited "advocat[ing] . . . the duty, necessity, or propriety of crime, sabotage, violence or unlawful methods of terrorism as a means of accomplishing industrial or political reform."[153]

The evidence was the film of a Klan meeting that showed twelve hooded figures, guns, and a burning cross. Words were heard about "burying the nigger" and "sending the Jews back to Israel." Defendant made a speech, in which he said, "We're not a revengent organization, but if our President, our Congress, our Supreme Court, continues to suppress the white, Caucasian race, it's possible that there might have to be some revengeance taken." He also urged "Marching on Congress . . . four hundred thousand strong."

The Court reversed the conviction. The governing principle, according to its opinion, was "that the constitutional guarantees of free speech and free press do not permit a State to forbid or proscribe advocacy of the use of force or of law violation except where

---

[149] Id at 604–05.

[150] Id at 605.

[151] 395 US 444 (1969).

[152] Id.

[153] Id at 444–45. A similar statute had been upheld in *Whitney v California*, 274 US 357 (1927).

such advocacy is directed to inciting or producing imminent lawless action and is likely to incite or produce such action."[154]

Measured by this test, the Ohio statute could not be sustained. Its "bald definition of the crime [was] in terms of mere advocacy not distinguished from incitement to imminent lawless action." Defendant was convicted only for "assembly with others merely to advocate the described type of action."[155] Under the test stated by the Court, that could not be done without violating the First Amendment.

Brandenburg was assigned to Justice Fortas. The draft opinion that he circulated stated a modified version of the Clear and Present test. Under it, advocacy of unlawful action might be proscribed only where it was "directed to inciting or producing imminent lawless action and is attended by present danger that such action may in fact be provoked."[156] Justice Fortas refused to accept Justice Black's suggestion to strike any reference to the Clear and Present Danger test from his draft.[157]

As it turned out, *Brandenburg* did not come down as a Fortas opinion. Though the Justice had circulated his draft opinion in April 1969 and quickly secured the necessary votes, he followed Justice Harlan's suggestion to delay its announcement.[158] Before then, the events occurred that led to Justice Fortas's forced resignation from the Court. The *Brandenburg* opinion was then redrafted by Justice Brennan,[159] who eliminated all references to the Clear and Present Danger test and substituted the present *Brandenburg* language: "where such advocacy is directed to inciting or producing imminent lawless action and is likely to incite or produce such action."[160] The Brennan redraft was issued as a per curiam opinion.

Brandenburg as redrafted by Justice Brennan made for "a new standard of speech protection,"[161] which replaced both the original

---

[154] 395 US at 447.

[155] Id at 448–49.

[156] *Brandenburg v Ohio*, draft opinion of Justice Fortas, April 11, 1969, p 5. Thurgood Marshall Papers, Library of Congress.

[157] See Bruce A. Murphy, *Fortas: The Rise and Ruin of a Supreme Court Justice* 543 (Morrow, 1988).

[158] Id at 544.

[159] Id.

[160] *Brandenburg*, 395 US at 447.

[161] Gunther at 603 (cited in note 1).

Holmes test[162] and what Justice Douglas called the "free-wheeling" Hand *Dennis* version.[163] Under the new *Brandenburg* test, only speech that *incites* "imminent lawless action and is likely to . . . produce such action" may be punished.

In an article twenty years ago, Gunther asserted that "*Brandenburg* combines the most protective ingredient of the *Masses* incitement emphasis with the most useful elements of the clear and present danger heritage."[164] According to Gunther, *Brandenburg*'s "incitement emphasis is Hand's, and "the language-oriented incitement criterion, so persistently urged by Hand in *Masses*, has become central to the operative law of the land."[165] On the other hand, according to Gunther, the Holmes nexus requirement is no longer a crucial element. "Under *Brandenburg*, probability of harm is no longer the central criterion for speech limitations. The inciting language of the speaker—the Hand focus on 'objective' words—is the major consideration."[166]

Under *Brandenburg*, the "magic words are now 'incitement to imminent lawless action.' "[167] Gunther is wrong to assume, however, that under the Hand *Masses* test "*incitement* to lawless action" was the "central prerequisite."[168] Although it is true that Judge Hand contrasted "agitation . . . with direct incitement to violent resistance"[169] in his *Masses* opinion, his test was whether the words used "counsel or advise others to violate the law"—whether "the language . . . can be thought directly to counsel or advise"[170] a violation. As Hand explained his test in a case decided soon after *Masses*, "the words uttered must amount to counsel or advice or command to commit the forbidden acts."[171] This is quite different

---

[162] Though courts in the hinterland still may not realize this. See, e.g., *Price v State*, 873 P2d 1049, 1051 (Okla Crim App 1994).

[163] *Brandenburg*, 395 US at 454.

[164] Gunther, 27 Stan L Rev at 754 (cited in note 23).

[165] Id at 755.

[166] Id.

[167] Kalven at 124 (cited in note 3).

[168] Gunther, 27 Stan L Rev at 754 (cited in note 23). This has become the accepted interpretation even though it can be argued that the *Brandenburg* opinion itself does not make "incitement" a constitutional requirement. It merely says that even incitement cannot be punished unless "it is likely to produce . . . [imminent lawless] action." 395 US at 447.

[169] 244 Fed at 540.

[170] Id at 540–41.

[171] *United States v Nearing*, 252 Fed 223, 227 (SDNY 1918).

from a requirement of "incitement," which implies immediacy. Gunther thus reads an important gloss into Judge Hand that was not contained in his *Masses* opinion.

Interestingly, it was Justice Holmes, not Judge Hand, who moved toward what was to be the *Brandenburg* test in some of his post-*Schenck* opinions. In his *Abrams* dissent, Holmes rephrased his test to reach speech "intended to produce a clear and *imminent* danger that it will bring about *forthwith* certain substantive evils."[172] Here was a statement of the requirement of imminence that was to be crucial in *Brandenburg*.

In *Gitlow v New York*,[173] Justice Holmes also dealt with the need for "incitement." The *Gitlow* Court upheld a conviction for publication of a pamphlet entitled "Left Wing Manifesto" advocating the overthrow of capitalism by "mass political strikes and revolutionary mass action" on the ground that "it is the language of direct incitement."[174] Holmes, dissenting, countered with the now-famous aphorism, "Every idea is an incitement."[175] In a letter soon after *Gitlow*, Holmes wrote that, in his *Gitlow* dissent, he "did no more than lean to [his *Abrams* dissent] and add that an idea is always an incitement. To show the ardor of the writer is not a sufficient reason for judging him. I regarded my view as simply upholding the right of a donkey to drool."[176]

But, even though Holmes recognized in *Gitlow* that an incitement "may set fire to reason,"[177] and thus seek more directly to induce the result, he still insisted upon the nexus between "enthusiasm for the result"[178] and the likelihood of its occurrence. In *Gitlow* itself, Holmes asserted that the required nexus did not exist. To the contrary, there was "doubt whether there was any danger that the publication could produce any result." The *Gitlow* manifesto, like the *Abrams* leaflets, was "futile and too remote from possible consequences."[179]

---

[172] *Abrams*, 250 US at 627 (italics added).

[173] 268 US 652 (1925).

[174] Id at 665.

[175] Id at 673.

[176] Posner at 322 (cited in note 57).

[177] *Gitlow*, 268 US at 673.

[178] Id.

[179] Id.

Under *Brandenburg*, the speaker must seek the result in the manner covered by the "term of art"[180] *incitement;* there must be a likelihood that the speech will produce "imminent lawless action." Thus, *Brandenburg* requires three things: (1) express advocacy of law violation; (2) the advocacy must call for *immediate* law violation; and (3) the immediate law violation must be *likely* to occur. The result is that *Brandenburg* is even more protective of freedom of expression than the Holmes test. Rare will be the speech that not only advocates lawless action, but is likely to accomplish that result imminently. Under *Brandenburg*, it is much more difficult to show the required nexus between given expression and imminent lawless action.

The original *Brandenburg* draft by Justice Fortas had stated that advocacy of unlawful action could be proscribed where it incited "imminent lawless action and is attended by present danger that such action may in fact be produced."[181] The Brennan redraft, which became the final *Brandenburg* per curiam, changed this to require the advocacy to be "likely to incite or produce such [imminent lawless] action."[182] Only speech like the incitement before the corn-dealer's house in Mill's example[183] will meet the *Brandenburg* test.

In particular, it is most unlikely that any publication by the press can come within the *Brandenburg* test. No matter how fiery the advocacy in a newspaper, magazine, book, or pamphlet, it is hard to see how it can meet the *Brandenburg* requirement that imminent lawless action is likely to result. We can refer again to the Mill example. No matter how extreme a newspaper statement on corn dealers as starvers of the poor may be, it can scarcely have the impact of the same statement by a rabble-rouser to a mob before a corn dealer's house. Only the latter incites to imminent lawless action that is likely to be produced by the agitator's arousing. Even the most extreme advocacy in the press is now shielded by *Brandenburg*, since print alone is hardly likely to produce imminent lawless action.

---

[180] But see Kalven at 124 (cited in note 3).

[181] *Brandenburg v Ohio*, draft opinion of Justice Fortas, April 11, 1969. Thurgood Marshall Papers, Library of Congress.

[182] 395 US at 447.

[183] See note 27 and accompanying text.

One may, indeed, wonder whether the Holmes test is not preferable in some cases, for *Brandenburg* may immunize speech that
should not be protected by the First Amendment. Consider, for
example, a variation on the death sentence pronounced by the Aya-
tollah Khomeini against Salman Rushdie for his authorship of *The
Satanic Verses*.[184] Hand's approach would permit the speech to be
punished, as would Holmes's understanding of clear and present
danger. The *Brandenburg* test, however, probably would require a
different result. It is hard to see how such advocacy could meet
the *Brandenburg* requirement of *imminent* unlawful action. Yet in
the years since that sentence was pronounced, a number of transla-
tors and publishers connected to the Rushdie book have been killed
or wounded.[185]

IX. BIOGRAPHY OR HAGIOGRAPHY?

Throughout his life, Judge Hand continued to believe that
his *Masses* test was superior to the Holmes Clear and Present Danger test. Not long before his death, in his Holmes lectures at Harvard, Hand referred to the Holmes doctrine: "I doubt that the
doctrine will persist, and I cannot help thinking that for once
Homer nodded."[186]

Some years earlier, Judge Hand wrote to Zechariah Chafee: "I
am not wholly in love with Holmesy's test and the reason is this.
Once you admit that the matter is one of degree, while you may
put it where it genuinely belongs, you so obviously make it a matter
of administration, i.e., you give to Tomdickandharry, D.J., so
much latitude that the jig is at once up."[187] Instead of the Holmes
"matter . . . of degree," which would fluctuate with the particular
fact pattern, Judge Hand sought a more "absolute and objective
test" focusing on "language."[188]

Gunther tells us that Hand was particularly concerned by the
fact that the Holmes "matter . . . of degree" would give broadside
discretion, not "to Tomdickandharry, D.J.," but to "impassioned

---

[184] N.Y. Times (Feb 15, 1989), p A1, col 5.

[185] N.Y. Times (Nov 25, 1993), p A1, col 4.

[186] Learned Hand, *The Bill of Rights* 59 (Harvard, 1958).

[187] Gunther, 27 Stan L Rev at 770 (cited in note 23).

[188] Id at 725 (cited in note 1).

juries."[189] "My own objection to the rule," Hand wrote to Chafee, "rests in the fact that it exposes all who discuss heated questions to an inquiry before a jury."[190]

"All I say," Hand stated in one of his letters to Justice Holmes, "is that since the cases actually occur when men are excited and since juries are especially clannish groups, . . . it is very questionable whether the test of motive is not a dangerous test. Juries wont much regard the difference between the probable result of the words and the purposes of the utterer."[191] Or, in Gunther's phrase, "even if predictions about the consequences of words were thought to be appropriate court business, the task would ordinarily fall not to the judge but to the jury, a body reflecting majoritarian sentiments unlikely to be conducive to the protection of dissent."[192]

It is, however, not true that, as Chafee said of the Holmes test, "The Jury would go over it rough shod."[193] *Dennis* not only diluted the clear and present danger requirement. It also decided that the question of whether clear and present danger existed was one of law for the court, which was to be decided by the trial judge, not a matter for submission to the jury.[194]

Yet, even if the danger that the Holmes test would leave juries too much at large has been removed by the *Dennis* transference of decision power to the judge, that does not affect the Hand criticism that, under the Clear and Present Danger Test, "you give [the judge too] much latitude."[195] Indeed, Hand wrote, even "their Ineffabilities, the Nine Elder Statesmen, have not shown themselves wholly immune from the 'herd instinct' and what seems 'immediate and direct' to-day may seem very remote next year even though the circumstances surrounding the utterance be unchanged."[196]

Instead of a test that depends on differences of degree, Judge Hand went on, "I own I should prefer a qualitative formula, hard,

---

[189] See Gunther at 165 (cited in note 1).

[190] Gunther, 27 Stan L Rev at 766 (cited in note 23).

[191] Id at 759.

[192] Id at 725.

[193] Id at 773.

[194] *Dennis*, 341 US at 515. See also Douglas, J, dissenting, id at 587.

[195] Gunther, 27 Stan L Rev at 770 (cited in note 23).

[196] Id.

conventional, difficult to evade."[197]—this was the "absolute and objective test to language" that he had stated in *Masses*.[198]

It may be that by stating his test as a broad standard, Justice Holmes "loses the great administrative advantages of Judge Hand's test."[199] But ease in application is not necessarily the crucial criterion in jurisprudence. Holmes once wrote that the "objection to . . . 'guessing at motive, tendency and possible effect' is an objection to pretty much the whole body of the law, which for thirty years I have made my bretheren [sic] smile by insisting to be everywhere a matter of degree."[200]

In a 1913 opinion, Justice Holmes stated, "the law is full of instances where a man's fate depends on his estimating rightly, that is, as the jury subsequently estimates it, from matters of degree."[201] The objection that the Holmes test vests too much discretion in the judge proves too much, for it might with equal validity be directed against a large part of the law. What is applied under the Clear and Present Danger test is a broad standard rather than a closely defined precept. The same thing is done in most of the important areas of modern law. Indeed, it is in its application of such standards, instead of only mechanical rules, that a developed legal system differs most from a formative one.

Early law, unable to differentiate between varying degrees of the same type of conduct, brands all equally and metes out similar consequences to those concerned. As the law grows more mature, distinctions get made and a judge is allowed to elaborate differences of degree instead of simply punishing with society's vengeance the visible source of any evil result. Thus, to take an obvious example, the mechanical rule of absolute liability for torts, characteristic of the formative period of a legal system, gives way to liability only for culpability, with culpability in each case being judged by the standard of the reasonable man. Certainly the standard of the reasonable man applied in the modern law of torts leaves much to the inclinations and idiosyncrasies of the individual judge or jury; yet

---

[197] Id.

[198] Id at 763.

[199] Zechariah Chafee, *Free Speech in the United States* 82 (Harvard, 1941).

[200] 1 Howe at 203 (cited in note 29).

[201] *Nash v United States*, 229 US 373, 377 (1913).

few suggest replacing it (except in certain special fields) with the unmoral rule (mechanical though it may be) of liability regardless of the culpability of the actor. Justice Holmes himself tells us that the whole law depends upon differences of degree as soon as it is civilized. Between the differences of degree in a standard such as that of the reasonable man or that of due process, "and the simple universality of the rules in the Twelve Tables or the Leges Barbarorum, there lies the culture of two thousand years."[202]

In the end, however, it all comes down to the question of which test—the Hand or the Holmes test—is more protective of free expression. The Gunther biography comes down emphatically in favor of Hand. If this article has shown anything, it is that Gunther's estimate is erroneous. By focusing on the words alone, the Hand *Masses* test permits punishment for speech advising or counseling a violation of the law even though the speech is by a harmless inciter who urges law violation but with little realistic hope of success.[203] Under such a test, the "silly" leaflets thrown by the "puny anonymities" in *Abrams* would come within governmental punitive power. The same would be true of the almost pathetic Klan rally in *Brandenburg*, though there was no likelihood, or even possibility, that the call for "revengeance" there would lead to any action.

Under the Holmes test, on the other hand, the *Abrams* and *Brandenburg* speech would fall within the scope of First Amendment protection. As Gunther himself puts it, under the Hand "test based on the nature of the utterance itself . . . if the words constituted solely a counsel to violate the law, solely an instruction that it was the listener's duty or interest to violate the law, they could be forbidden."[204] According to the Holmes test, the words may be made criminal only because of their relation to violation of the law, and that relation must be so close that the words constitute "a clear and present danger" of actual law violation.[205] "This is a rule of reason [that] will preserve the right of free speech both from sup-

---

[202] *LeRoy Fibre Co. v Chicago, Mil. & St. P. Ry.*, 232 US 340, 354 (1914).

[203] Gunther, 27 Stan L Rev at 729 (cited in note 23).

[204] Gunther at 157 (cited in note 1).

[205] Chafee at 82 (cited in note 199).

pression by tyrannous well-meaning majorities and from abuse by irresponsible fanatical minorities."[206]

Which is more protective of free speech—the Hand or Holmes test? The biographer's admiration for his subject—particularly when the subject is perhaps the greatest judge who never sat on the Supreme Court—is understandable. All the same, to come down on the side of Hand, as Gunther does, smacks less of biography than of hagiography.[207]

---

[206] Brandeis, J, dissenting, in *Schaefer v United States*, 251 US 466, 482 (1920).

[207] Perhaps I am guilty of the same fault in my (some might say) overpraise of Holmes. I trust, however, that the current revisionism on Holmes will not change the estimate of his seminal contribution to First Amendment jurisprudence.

PAUL FINKELMAN

STORY TELLING ON THE SUPREME COURT: PRIGG v PENNSYLVANIA AND JUSTICE JOSEPH STORY'S JUDICIAL NATIONALISM

Few scholars dispute Justice Joseph Story's enormous significance for American law. He was unquestionably "one of our greatest jurists and legal theorists."[1] His numerous *Commentaries* on various subjects became fundamental textbooks and reference tools for a generation of lawyers and helped create a national legal system. His vast legal scholarship made him a "one-man West Publication Company."[2] As a Harvard professor he helped train an important segment of the antebellum elite bar and, moreover, set the stage

Paul Finkelman is Visiting Associate Professor of Law, Chicago-Kent College of Law.

AUTHOR'S NOTE: I thank Raymond O. Arsenault, Bruce Dudley, Charles Geyh, James O. Horton, Allison Lindsey, Michael McReynolds, Wayne Moore, Sharleen Nakamoto, Emily Van Tassel, and Peter Wallenstein for their input on this article, and the staffs of the Harford County Historical Society, the York County Historical Society, the Maryland Hall of Records, the Maryland Historical Society, and the State Archives of Pennsylvania for their help. The research for this article was partially funded by grants from the National Endowment for the Humanities, the American Philosophical Society, and the History Department of Virginia Tech.

[1] Kent Newmyer, *Supreme Court Justice Joseph Story: Statesman of the Old Republic* 282 (University of North Carolina Press, 1985). This does not, however, make him the most accurate judicial scholar. For a discussion of the weakness of Story's scholarship, see Alan Watson, *Joseph Story and the Comity of Errors: A Case Study in the Conflict of Laws* (University of Georgia Press, 1992).

[2] Newmyer, *Justice Joseph Story* (cited in note 1).

for the development of serious legal education in America. He is on everyone's all time hit parade of Supreme Court justices.[3]

Story was something of a "lawyer's" justice, whose opinions, as well as his learned treatises, helped revolutionize American law. Most of his important opinions involved technical issues of procedure or commercial law, rather than great issues of statecraft. For better or worse, he spent most of his career on the bench with Chief Justice John Marshall, who assigned most decisions affecting major public policy issues to himself.[4] After Marshall's death, Story usually fared no better when it came to writing politically important opinions. In his last decade on the bench, under Chief Justice Roger B. Taney, Story often found himself in the minority on major policy questions,[5] but was still chosen to write the opinion of the court in major technical cases, such as *Swift v Tyson*,[6] the most important procedure case of the nineteenth century.[7]

One critical exception, where Story wrote a majority opinion on an issue of politics and statecraft, was *Prigg v Pennsylvania*.[8] To understand Story, and mid-nineteenth-century law and politics, one has to come to terms with *Prigg*. This is true whether one likes Story,[9] dislikes him,[10] or is simply ambivalent about him.[11] In coming to terms with Story's *Prigg* opinion, we are faced with a

---

[3] A. Leon Higginbotham, *An Open Letter to Clarence Thomas from a Federal Judicial Colleague*, 140 U Pa L Rev 1007, citing Albert P. Blaustein and Roy M. Mersky, *The First One Hundred Justices: Statistical Studies in the Supreme Court of the United States* 35–36 (Archon Books, 1978).

[4] Professor David Currie's iconoclastic statement makes the point: "[T]hanks to John Marshall's insistence on writing everything himself, the Supreme Court was popularly known as 'John Marshall and the Six Dwarfs.'" David Currie, *The Most Insignificant Justice: A Preliminary Inquiry*, 50 U Chi L Rev 466, 469 (1983).

[5] For example, *Proprietors of the Charles River Bridge v Proprietors of the Warren Bridge*, 11 Peters (36 US) 420, 581 (1837) (Story dissenting).

[6] 16 Peters (41 US) 1 (1842).

[7] Tony Freyer, *Harmony and Dissonance: The Swift and Erie Cases in American Federalism* (New York University Press, 1981). Without *Swift*, first year procedure professors would be unable to subject students to weeks of understanding the *Erie* doctrine. See *Erie Railroad Co v Tompkins*, 304 US 64 (1938).

[8] 16 Peters (41 US) 539 (1842).

[9] Christopher L. M. Eisgruber, *Joseph Story, Slavery, and the Natural Law Foundations of American Constitutionalism*, 55 U Chi L Rev 273 (1988).

[10] Robert M. Cover, *Justice Accused: Antislavery and the Judicial Process* (Yale University Press, 1975); see more recently Barbara Holden-Smith, *Lords of the Lash, Loom, and Law: Justice Story, Slavery and Prigg v Pennsylvania*, 78 Cornell L Rev 1086 (1993).

[11] Newmyer, *Justice Joseph Story* (cited in note 1).

case in which an otherwise scholarly, judicious, and apparently humane jurist wrote an opinion that was intellectually dishonest, based on inaccurate historical analysis, judicially extreme when it need not have been, and inhumane in its immediate results and in its long-term consequences. Furthermore, we face an extreme proslavery opinion written by a man who, at least on the surface, opposed slavery.[12] Moreover, in looking at the aftermath of *Prigg* we find that either Story, or his filiopietistic son, William Wetmore Story, sought to cast the decision as subtly antislavery, while the justice himself was working hard behind the scenes to help implement the proslavery implications of the decision.[13]

Story's primary goal in *Prigg* was to enhance the power in the national government. Story was willing to accomplish this at the expense of civil liberties, fundamental notions of due process, and accepted concepts of antebellum federalism.

In analyzing *Prigg* it is important to remember that the nationalization of power in the 1840s meant strengthening southern slaveholders and their proslavery northern doughface allies.[14] Story lived in a Union dominated by slaveholding presidents,[15] a proslav-

---

[12] Holden-Smith, 78 Cornell L Rev (cited in note 10), challenges the conventional wisdom of Story's opposition to slavery. I think it is clear the Story disliked slavery and found it morally offensive, the way virtually all northerners did. However, this seems to have had little affect on his jurisprudence after the 1820s.

[13] See Story to John Macpherson Berrien, April 29, 1842, in John Macpherson Berrien Papers, Southern Historical Collection, University of North Carolina (hereafter cited as Story to Berrien Letter [cited in note 13]), quoted at length in James McClellan, *Joseph Story and the American Constitution* 262n–63n (University of Oklahoma Press, 1971). This is discussed at note 23.

[14] The term was an insult to describe "northern men with southern principles." In essence, a "doughface" had a face of dough that southern politicians shaped as they wished. "Doughface Democrats" were northern Democrats who voted to support proslavery positions.

[15] By 1842, when Story wrote *Prigg*, the United States had only had three northern presidents—all one-term presidents—and only two—John Adams and John Quincy Adams—had been even mildly antislavery. Martin Van Buren, although a New Yorker, was a classic "doughface." Six presidents (Washington, Jefferson, Madison, Monroe, Jackson, and Tyler)—including all five antebellum two-term presidents—had been slaveowners during their term of office; Harrison, a native of Virginia, had been a slaveowner for much of his adult life, and only ceased owning slaves when he failed, as territorial governor of Indiana, to get Congress to allow slavery in the old Northwest. On Harrison's attempts to bring make slavery legal in the old Northwest, see Paul Finkelman, *Evading the Ordinance: The Persistence of Bondage in Indiana and Illinois*, 9 J Early Republic 21–52 (1989), and Paul Finkelman, *Slavery and the Northwest Ordinance: A Study in Ambiguity*, 6 J Early Republic 343–70 (1986).

ery Supreme Court,[16] and more often than not a Congress controlled by southern politicians.[17] Similarly, states rights in antebellum America often meant the right of northern states to free visiting slaves,[18] to protect free blacks from kidnapping,[19] to prevent the extradition to the South of whites or blacks who helped slaves escape,[20] and even the right of northerners to interfere in the rendition of fugitive slaves, if it could be done under the color of state law.[21] Thus, we must not look at Story's nationalizing jurisprudence through the lens of a late twentieth-century Constitution, with three Civil War amendments (and various other amendments and statutes) that allow or obligate the national government to protect civil rights and civil liberties. On the contrary, Story lived in an age when federal power meant federal support for a proslavery Constitution[22] implemented by a proslavery national regime. Story not only knew all this, but saw ways that the national government

---

[16] As of 1842, when the Court heard *Prigg*, 19 of the 29 men appointed to the Supreme Court had been southerners. Cumulatively, up to 1842 southern justices had served a total of 209 years on the court, while northerners had served only 149 years. From 1800 to 1861, southerners outnumbered northerners in every term, except for the short period from 1830 to 1837. Significantly, the Court heard no major cases involving slavery during that period. In 1842, Story served on a court with five southerners and four northerners.

[17] From 1789 to 1842, there were 16 northern and 25 southern Presidents Pro Tempore of the Senate; more significantly, from 1801 to 1842, 20 Presidents Pro Tempore were southern, and only 5 were northern. Similarly, before 1801 all 5 Speakers of the House were from the North. But from 1801 until 1842, there were 11 southern Speakers and only 3 northern speakers.

[18] Paul Finkelman, *An Imperfect Union: Slavery, Federalism, and Comity* (University of North Carolina Press, 1981).

[19] Thomas D. Morris, *Free Men All: The Personal Liberty Laws of the North, 1780–1861* (Johns Hopkins University Press, 1974).

[20] Paul Finkelman, *States Rights North and South in Antebellum America*, in Kermit Hall and James W. Ely, Jr., eds, *An Uncertain Tradition: Constitutionalism and the History of the South* 125–58 (Athens, Ga, 1989); Paul Finkelman, *The Protection of Black Rights in Seward's New York*, 34 Civ War History 211–34 (1988); and Paul Finkelman, *States' Rights, Federalism, and Criminal Extradition in Antebellum America: The New York-Virginia Controversy, 1839–1846*, in Hermann Wellenreuther, ed, *German and American Constitutional Thought: Contexts, Interaction, and Historical Realities* 293–327 (Berg, 1990).

[21] See, for example, *In Re Booth*, 3 Wis 1 (1854); *Ex parte Booth*, 3 Wis 145 (1854); *In re Booth and Rycraft*, 3 Wis 157 (1855); Jenni Parrish, *The Booth Cases: Final Step to the Civil War*, 29 Willamette L Rev 237 (1993). For an earlier example, see *Norris v Newton*, 18 F Cases 322 (CCD Ind, 1850); Paul Finkelman, *Fugitive Slaves, Midwestern Racial Tolerance, and the Value of Justice Delayed*, 78 Iowa L Rev 89–141 (1992).

[22] Paul Finkelman, *Slavery and the Constitutional Convention: Making a Covenant with Death*, in Richard Beeman, Stephen Botein, and Edward C. Carter II, eds, *Beyond Confederation: Origins of the Constitution and American National Identity* 188–225 (University of North Carolina Press, 1987). On the antislavery analysis of the Constitution, see William M. Wiecek, *The Sources of Antislavery Constitutionalism, 1760–1848* (Cornell University Press, 1977).

might use his *Prigg* opinion to further implement the proslavery aspects of the Constitution.[23]

In the end Story favored national power over any other value, even if it meant strengthening slavery. His *Prigg* opinion showed indifference to the civil liberties of northerners and to the fate of free blacks (as well as fugitive slaves) living in the North.

One final caveat is in order. It might be easy to cast this analysis of Story and his *Prigg* opinion as anachronistic—as trying to hold Story to the standards of the late twentieth century. In an age when most scholars have only recently rediscovered the importance of race for American history, it is important to understand that the following analysis is not based on our own contemporary notions of what is either important or correct. Rather, this analysis begins with the assumption that to understand or criticize *Prigg* we must view it within the context of the mid-nineteenth century. In doing so we find that Story's contemporaries and friends condemned the opinion, and that the opinion ran counter to the conclusions of distinguished state judges. The facts of the case, contemporary concepts of justice, and the language of the Constitution itself offered Story an opportunity to write a different opinion. That he chose not to do so—that he shaped both constitutional history and the "facts" of the case to support and even compel the opinion he wrote—suggests that his opposition to slavery, whatever it might once have been,[24] had withered away to a theoretical abstraction that denied the reality of mid-century America.

Despite *Prigg*, it is possible to remain in awe of Story's scholarly productivity, his skills as a mentor, and his significance as a great

---

[23] Shortly after the Court decided *Prigg*, Story wrote to Senator John Macpherson Berrien of North Carolina to discuss a draft bill on federal jurisdiction that he had sent to Berrien. He reminded Berrien that he had suggested in that proposed bill

> that *in all cases*, where by the Laws of the U. States, powers were conferred on State Magistrates, the same powers might be exercised by Commissioners appointed by the Circuit Courts. I was induced to make the provision thus general, because State Magistrates now generally refuse to act, & cannot be compelled to act; and the Act of 1793 respecting fugitive slaves confers the power on State Magistrates to act in delivering up Slaves. You saw in the case of Prigg . . . how the duty was evaded, or declined. In conversing with several of my Brethren on the Supreme Court, we all thought that it would be a great improvement, & would tend much to facilitate the recapture of Slaves, if Commissioners of the Circuit Court were clothed with like powers.

Story to Berrien Letter (cited in note 13).

[24] See Newmyer, *Justice Joseph Story* (cited in note 1), and Eisgruber on how Story was antislavery in the beginning of his life.

Supreme Court justice. *Prigg*, however, forces us to reevaluate Story and his nationalistic jurisprudence as well as the role of the antebellum court in shaping the politics of slavery a decade and a half before *Dred Scott*.[25]

I. A PROSLAVERY DECISION

In 1837, Nathan S. Beemis, Edward Prigg, and two other men traveled to Pennsylvania, where they seized as fugitive slaves Margaret Morgan and her children. They then brought the blacks back to Maryland without first complying with all of the requirements of an 1826 Pennsylvania law regulating the return of fugitive slaves.[26] This statute, known as a personal liberty law, required that anyone removing a black from the state as a fugitive slave first obtain a certificate of removal from a state judge, justice of the peace, or alderman.

The York County prosecutor immediately sought indictments against the four men for kidnapping and failing to follow the Pennsylvania law. After protracted negotiations between Maryland and Pennsylvania, the governor of Maryland agreed to allow the extradition of one of the four slave catchers, Edward Prigg. Prigg was subsequently convicted of kidnapping for removing Margaret Morgan and her children from Pennsylvania without obtaining a certificate of removal from a state magistrate. Prigg appealed to the U.S. Supreme Court, and in 1842 the Court overturned his conviction.

In his Opinion of the Court, Justice Joseph Story reached five major conclusions: (1) that the federal fugitive slave law of 1793[27] was constitutional; (2) that no state could pass any law adding additional requirements to that law which could impede the return of fugitive slaves; (3) that the Constitution provided a common law right of recaption—a right of self-help—which allowed a slave-

---

[25] *Dred Scott v Sandford*, 19 How (60 US) 393 (1857).

[26] "An Act to give effect to the provisions of the constitution of the United States relative to fugitives from labor, for the protection of free people of color, and to prevent Kidnapping," ch L, Pennsylvania Session Law, 1826 150 (1826) (hereafter Pennsylvania Personal Liberty Law); on the passage of the act itself, see William R. Leslie, *The Pennsylvania Fugitive Slave Act of 1826*, 13 J Southern History 429 (1952), reprinted in Paul Finkelman, ed, 6 *Articles on American Slavery: Fugitive Slaves* 211 (Garland, 1989).

[27] "An Act Respecting Fugitives from Justice and Persons Escaping from the Service of Their Masters," 1 Stat 302 (1793) (Hereafter cited as Fugitive Slave Act).

owner (or an owner's agent) to seize any fugitive slave anywhere and bring that slave back to the master without complying with the provisions of the federal fugitive slave law, and that no state law could interfere with such a removal; (4) that state officials ought to, but could not be required to, enforce the federal law of 1793; (5) that no fugitive slave was entitled to any due process hearing or trial beyond a summary proceeding to determine if the person seized was the person described in the affidavit or other papers provided by the claimant. However, a claimant did not have to comply with even this minimal procedure if he exercised a right of common law recaption, under Story's notion of self-help.

This sweeping opinion undermined the security of free blacks living in the North, endangered the liberty of fugitive slaves who had escaped to freedom, and threatened the public peace and stability of northern society. These results stemmed from two prongs of Story's opinion. First, by striking down Pennsylvania's Personal Liberty Law, and by extension the personal liberty laws of other states, Story left the northern states without the weapons or the legal authority to prevent the kidnapping of blacks. Second, Story further endangered blacks in the North by asserting that the Constitution gave a master a right of self-help, "to seize and recapture his slave" anywhere in the nation regardless of state or federal statutory law.[28]

Story claimed that the fugitive slave clause "manifestly contemplates the existence of a positive, unqualified right on the part of the owner of the slave, which no state law or regulation can in any way qualify, regulate, control or restrain."[29] Story declared:

> we have not the slightest hesitation in holding, that under . . . the constitution, the owner of a slave is clothed with entire authority, in every state in the Union, to seize and recapture his slave, whenever he can do it, without any breach of the peace or any illegal violence. In this sense, and to this extent this clause of the constitution may properly be said to execute itself, and to require no aid from legislation, state or national.[30]

This conclusion was extraordinary. It meant that any southerner could seize any black and remove that person to the South without

---

[28] *Prigg* at 613.

[29] Id at 612.

[30] Id at 613.

any state interference or even a hearing before either a state or federal magistrate. This removal without any judicial superintendence or the need to show any proof of the slave's status to anyone was legal as an act of self-help, as long as no "breach of the peace" occurred. One might presume that a "breach of the peace" would always occur when a black, especially a free one, was seized as a fugitive slave. However, for both logical and practical reasons, this was not always the case.

In his dissent, Justice McLean pointed out the theoretical problems of limiting Story's right of self-help to instances in which there was no breach of the peace. McLean noted that under Story's opinion, "the relation of master and slave is not affected by the laws of the state, to which the slave may have fled, and where he is found." Thus, McLean reluctantly concluded that "[i]f the master has a right to seize and remove the slave, without claim, he can commit no breach of the peace, by using all the force necessary to accomplish his object."[31] In other words, McLean feared that under Story's opinion no amount of violence against an alleged slave would be illegal. Using Story's logic, it would never be a breach of the peace for a master to take his slave by brutal force, nor could this force be considered "illegal violence" as long as it was directed against a slave or an alleged slave.

There was also a practical problem. Seizures at night or in isolated areas could be accomplished without anyone observing a breach of the peace. Once a black was shackled, intimidated, and perhaps beaten into submission, travel from the North to the South could be accomplished without any obvious breach of the peace. If state officials could not stop a white transporting a black in chains, then kidnapping of any black could always be accomplished. Under such a rule anyone, especially children, might be kidnapped and enslaved. Kidnappings of this sort had led to the enactment of Pennsylvania's 1826 Personal Liberty Law.[32] By requiring state judicial supervision of fugitive slave rendition, Pennsylvania hoped to prevent such abuses. But by striking down Pennsylvania's law, and by extension similar laws in other states, Story

---

[31] Id at 668 (McLean dissenting).

[32] Leslie, 13 J Southern History at 429 (cited in note 26). Leslie notes that shortly before the adoption of this law, five black children were kidnapped in Philadelphia and sold as slaves. Three were eventually returned to their families, but two died.

left the North powerless to prevent this type of kidnapping. More-over, by deciding that masters had a right of self-help, Story al-lowed whites to seize any blacks and bring them south without any proof of their status as slaves.

Story's opinion effectively made the law of the South the law of the nation. In the South, race was a presumption of slave status,[33] and by giving masters and slave hunters a common law right of recaption, Story nationalized this presumption. As a result, slave catchers could operate in the North without having to prove the seized person's slave status. The consequences for the nearly 175,000 free blacks in the North could have been dire.

In *Prigg*, Justice Story shaped both the history of the Constitu-tion, relevant precedents, and the facts of the case to justify his opinion. He created a mythological origin of the fugitive slave clause that legitimized his harsh interpretation of it. He misstated the existing case law, or ignored it, to bolster his opinion. Simi-larly, he ignored or misstated important facts about Margaret Mor-gan and her children that might have compelled a different result in the case. These were the stories the justice from Massachusetts told. By examining these tales, we see there were viable alternatives to Story's sweeping opinion upholding the 1793 Fugitive Slave Law and simultaneously striking down Pennsylvania's 1826 Personal Liberty Law.

II. The First Story: The Fugitive Slave Clause and the Bargain of 1787

After summarizing its procedural history, Story acknowl-edged the importance of the case. "Few questions which have ever come before this Court" he wrote "involve more delicate and im-portant considerations; and few upon which the public at large may be presumed to feel a more profound and pervading interest."[34] For Story the greatest danger of this constitutional minefield was its potential for disruption of the Union. His lifetime goal as a jurist, scholar, teacher, and politician was to preserve national harmony and to strengthen the national government.

In *Prigg* he could accomplish both goals if he could give the

[33] See generally, Paul Finkelman, *The Crime of Color*, 67 Tulane L Rev 2063 (1993).
[34] *Prigg* at 610.

South a result it wanted and somehow convince the North that the Constitution dictated this result. The result was a creative, but historically inaccurate, original intent analysis of the Constitution's Fugitive Slave Clause.

A. STORY'S HISTORY OF THE FUGITIVE SLAVE CLAUSE

Story hoped to persuade the North that his opinion was correct by elevating the Fugitive Slave Clause to a matter of the highest constitutional order. To do this, he made two important historical arguments. First, he asserted that the Fugitive Slave Clause was central to the compromises over slavery necessary for the adoption of the Constitution. Second, Story argued that this was well understood during the debates over ratification. In fact, both of these arguments are historically suspect. But, before considering what actually happened at the Convention and during the ratification process, it is necessary to examine Story's arguments.

1. *Story's history of the drafting of the clause.* With a tone of authority Story wrote:

> Historically, it is well known, that the object of this clause was to secure to the citizens of the slaveholding states the complete right and title of ownership in their slaves, as property, in every state in the Union into which they might escape from the state where they were held in servitude. The full recognition of this right and title was indispensable to the security of this species of property in all the slaveholding states; and, indeed, was so vital to the preservation of their domestic interests and institutions, that it cannot be doubted that it constituted a fundamental article, without the adoption of which the Union could not have been formed.[35]

He then elaborated on this argument. He compared the Fugitive Slave Clause to the Three-Fifths Clause and the protection of the African slave trade as one of the fundamental bargains over slavery at the Convention. Story argued that at the Convention "several" of the states "required as a condition, upon which any constitution should be presented to the states for ratification, a full and perfect security for their slaves as property, when they fled into any of the states of the Union."[36] He asserted that the southern demand

---

[35] Id at 611.

[36] Id at 638–39.

for a Fugitive Slave Clause, along "with an allowance of a certain portion of slaves with the whites, for representative population in Congress, and the importation of slaves from abroad, for a number of years; were the great obstacles in the way of forming a constitution."[37] The compromises on these issues, Story asserted, were central to the constitutional bargain, and "without all of them . . . it was well understood, that the Convention would have been dissolved, without a constitution being formed."[38] Story offered this, not as interpretation, but as inconvertible fact: "I mention the facts as they were. They cannot be denied. . . . I am satisfied with what was done; and revere the men and their motives for insisting, politically, upon what was done. When the three points relating to slaves had been accomplished, every impediment in the way of forming a constitution was removed."[39] Thus, according to Story's history, the Fugitive Slave Clause was both essential to the writing of the Constitution and the work of men who Story "revere[d]."

2. *Story's history of ratification.* Tied to his history of the Convention was Story's briefer history of ratification. First he asserted that the "provision in respect to fugitives from service or labour" was "a guarantee of a right of property in fugitive slaves, wherever they might be found in the Union." This simple statement seemed to preclude any analysis that might have led to a more subtle and complex interpretation of the clause. Then Story asserted that this was well understood at the time of ratification.

> The Constitution was presented to the states for adoption, with the understanding that the provisions in it relating to slaves were a compromise and guarantee; and with such an understanding in every state, it was adopted by all of them. Not a guarantee merely in the professional acceptation of the word, but a great national engagement, in which the states surrendered a sovereign right, making it a part of that instrument, which was intended to make them one nation, within the sphere of its action.[40]

3. *The implications of Story's history.* These arguments—that the Fugitive Slave Clause was "a fundamental article" of constitutional

---

[37] Id.
[38] Id.
[39] Id.
[40] Id at 638–39.

compromise and that this was well known during the ratification struggle—set the stage for the rest of Story's opinion. If the clause was indeed *fundamental*, then perhaps it required extraordinary— and exclusive—enforcement by the federal government. Thus Story continued and extended his original intent analysis to assert that the framers must have intended not only federal enforcement of the clause, but exclusive federal jurisdiction. Story argued that if the clause allowed state legislation on the subject,"The right" of the master to capture a runaway slave "would never, in a practical sense be the same in all the states. It would have no unity of purpose, or uniformity of operation. The duty might be enforced in some states; retarded, or limited in others; and denied, as compulsory in many, if not in all."[41] Story argued that "It is scarcely conceivable that the slaveholding states would have been satisfied with leaving to the legislation of the non-slaveholding states, a power of regulation, in the absence of that of Congress, which would or might practically amount to a power to destroy the rights of the owner."[42] If Congress did not have exclusive jurisdiction, then each state would have the power "to dole out its own remedial justice, or withhold it at its pleasure and according to its own views of policy and expediency."[43] This, Story believed, could not have been in the intentions of the framers.

Story's argument about the historic importance of the clause and the intentions of its framers deviated somewhat from his analysis of a decade earlier. In *Commentaries on the Constitution of the United States*[44] he had asserted—erroneously—that the Convention had considered the clause necessary because the lack "of such a provision under the [Articles of] confederation was felt, as a grievous inconvenience by the slave-holding states, since in many states no aid whatsoever would be allowed to the masters; and sometimes indeed they met with open resistance."[45] There was little truth to this position. In 1787 no state prevented southern masters from recovering runaways. But when writing his *Commentaries*, Story

---

[41] Id at 624.

[42] Id.

[43] Id.

[44] Joseph Story, *Commentaries on the Constitution of the United States* (Hilliard, Gray & Co., 1833).

[45] Id at § 952.

had not considered the clause a key part of the constitutional bargain. In the *Commentaries*, he noted only that the clause was a boon "for the benefit of the slaveholding states" to indicate northern good will toward the "peculiar interests of the south."[46] He thought the clause was evidence that the South "at all times had its full share of benefits from the Union."[47] Significantly, Story did not argue in *Commentaries* that the clause was part of a bargain, was a quid pro quo for something in the Constitution that the North wanted.[48] Nor did he argue that it was a "a fundamental article, without the adoption of which the Union could not have been formed."[49]

B. THE REAL HISTORY OF THE FUGITIVE SLAVE CLAUSE

Story's assertion that the clause was an essential element of the constitutional bargain of 1787, and that it was equivalent to the three-fifths compromise or the slave trade compromise, was his first "story" in the *Prigg* decision. It was a strong argument in favor of his proslavery opinion, but it was also an argument that did not comport with the available evidence from Madison's *Notes of the Federal Convention*.[50]

Late in the Constitutional Convention, Pierce Butler and Charles Pinckney of South Carolina proposed that a fugitive slave clause be added to the article requiring the interstate extradition of fugitives from justice. James Wilson of Pennsylvania objected to the juxtaposition because "This would oblige the Executive of the State to do it, at the public expence." Butler discreetly "withdrew his proposition in order that some particular provision might be made apart from this article." A day later the Convention, without debate or formal vote, adopted the fugitive slave provision as a separate

---

[46] Id.

[47] Id.

[48] Without any evidence to support his position, Mr. Jonathan Meredith, counsel for Prigg, argued before the Supreme Court that "it is well known" that "the fugitive slave clause was the result of mutual concessions in reference to the whole subject of slavery. On the one hand the south agreed to confer upon Congress the power to prohibit the importation of slaves after the year 1808. On the other, the north agreed to recognise [sic] and protect the existing institutions of the south." *Prigg* at 565.

[49] Id at 611.

[50] See note 48 supra.

article of the draft constitution.[51] Eventually the two clauses emerged as succeeding paragraphs in Article IV, Section 2 of the Constitution.[52]

The paucity of debate over the Fugitive Slave Clause is remarkable because by the end of August 1787, when the Convention adopted the clause, slavery had emerged as one of the major stumbling blocks to a stronger union. While morally offensive to a number of the northern delegates, some southerners defended slavery with an analysis that anticipated the "positive good" arguments of the antebellum period. Nevertheless, unlike the debates over the slave trade, the Three-Fifths Clause, the taxation of exports, and the regulation of commerce, the proposal for a fugitive slave clause generated no serious opposition.[53] Story made much of this. He noted that the clause "was proposed and adopted by the unanimous vote of the Convention."[54] This unanimity should have alerted Story to the relative unimportance of the clause. Every other slavery-related clause at the Convention led not only to debate but opposition. Story's elevation of the importance of the Fugitive Slave Clause is not supported by the Convention debates. Some of the longest and most acrimonious debates at the Convention occurred over the Three-Fifths Clause and the slave trade provision. On the other hand, the Convention delegates barely discussed the Fugitive Slave Clause, not because there was generally agreement on what the clause meant or on its necessity, but more likely because the northern delegates simply failed to appreciate the legal problems and moral dilemmas that the rendition of fugitive slaves would pose.

The relationship between slavery and the Constitution generated

---

[51] The only other response to Butler's proposal was Roger Sherman's sarcastic observation that he "saw no more propriety in the public seizing and surrendering a slave or servant, than a horse." Max Farrand, ed, 2 *The Records of the Federal Convention of 1787* (Yale University Press, 1966) 443, quotations at 453–54. The history of this clause is discussed in Finkelman, *Slavery and the Constitutional Convention* at 219–24 (cited in note 22). See also William M. Wiecek, *The Witch at the Christening: Slavery and the Constitution's Origins*, in Leonard W. Levy and Dennis J. Mahoney, eds, 167–84 *The Framing and Ratification of the Constitution* (Macmillan, 1987).

[52] The clause reads: "No person held to Service or Labour in one State, under the Laws thereof, escaping into another, shall, in Consequence of any Law or Regulation therein, be discharged from such Service or Labour, but shall be delivered up on Claim of the Party to whom such Service or Labour may be due."

[53] Finkelman, *Slavery and the Constitutional Convention* at 219–24 (cited in note 22).

[54] *Prigg* at 638–39.

a great deal of debate during the ratification struggle. Northerners objected to the Three-Fifths Clause and the migration and importation clause, which prevented Congress from ending the slave trade before 1808. Some of this debate was extremely emotional and vivid. For example, "A Countryman from Dutchess County" thought that Americans might become "a happy and respectable people" if the Constitution were "corrected by a substantial bill of rights" and, among other changes, the states were forced into "relinquishing every idea of drenching the bowels of Africa in gore, for the sake of enslaving its free-born innocent inhabitants."[55] In the New Hampshire Convention Joshua Atherton complained:

> The idea that strikes those, who are opposed to this clause, so disagreeably and so forcibly, is, hereby it is conceived (if we ratify the Constitution) that we become consenters to, and partakers in, the sin and guilt of this abominable traffic . . . .
> We do not think ourselves under any obligation to perform works of supererogation in the reformation of mankind; we do not esteem ourselves under any necessity to go to Spain or Italy to suppress the inquisition of those countries; or of making a journey to the Carolinas to abolish the detestable custom of enslaving the Africans; but, sir, we will not lend the aid of our ratification to this cruel and inhuman merchandise, not even for a day. There is a great distinction in not taking a part in the most barbarous violation of the sacred laws of God and humanity, and our becoming guaranties for its exercise for a term of years.[56]

Similarly, "A Friend of the Rights of People" asked, "Can we then hold up our hands for a Constitution that licences this bloody practice? Can we who have fought so hard for Liberty give our consent to have it taken away from others? May the powers above forbid."[57]

Yet, despite the vigorous attacks on the slave trade provision and complaints about the Three-Fifths Clause, no antifederalists seem

---

[55] "Letters from a Countryman from Dutchess County" (letter of Jan 22, 1788), in Herbert Storing, ed, 6 *The Complete Anti-federalist* 62 (University of Chicago Press, 1981).

[56] Fragment of Debate at New Hampshire Convention, in Jonathan Elliot, ed, 2 *The Debates in the Several State Conventions on the Adoption of the Federal Constitution* 203–04 (J. B. Lippincott, 1881).

[57] "A Friend to the Rights of the People," in Storing, 4 *The Complete Anti-federalist* (cited in note 55), 234, 241.

to have publicly discussed the fugitive slave provision.[58] They did not see it as obligating either themselves, or the federal government, to become involved in the dirty business of capturing runaway slaves. The authors of *The Federalist* discussed the three-fifths provision and the slave trade, but ignored the Fugitive Slave Clause.[59] Contrary to Story's telling, if the Fugitive Slave Clause was an important provision of the Constitution, few in the North, on either side of the ratification debate, seemed to notice it.

In the South, supporters of the Constitution pointed to the Fugitive Slave Clause as a boon to their interests, but not as either a major component of the constitutional bargain or as something that would lead to federal enforcement.

In the Virginia Ratifying Convention, for example, the antifederalist George Mason complained that the Constitution might threaten slavery. James Madison replied by defending the various clauses that protected slavery. He asserted that the Fugitive Slave Clause "was expressly inserted to enable owners of slaves to reclaim them."[60] Madison noted that under the Articles of Confederation if a slave escaped to a free state "he becomes emancipated by their laws. For the law of the States are uncharitable to one another in this respect." But under the Fugitive Slave Clause this could not happen, and this was "a better security than any that now exists."[61] Had Madison believed the clause guaranteed federal enforcement, he probably would have made this point because it would have

---

[58] The only northern opposition to this clause that I have encountered is found in correspondence from and to the Rhode Island merchant and Quaker abolitionist Moses Brown. In private correspondence, Brown expressed concern that the Fugitive Slave Clause was "designd to Distroy the Present Assylum of the Massachusets from being as a City of Refuge for the poor Blacks, many of whom had resorted there on Acc[oun]t of their Constitution or Bill of rights declaring in the first Article 'That all men are born free & Equal &c.' and there being no Laws in that State to support slavery, the Negroes on Entering that state are as free as they are on Entering into Great Brittain and the southern people have not been able by Applycation of the Governour, Judges or other Authority to Recover those they had held as Slave, who Chose to Stay there." Moses Brown to James Pemberton, 17 Oct 1787, reprinted in John P. Kaminski and Gaspare J. Saladino, eds, 14 *The Documentary History of the Ratification of the Constitution by the States: Commentaries on the Constitution, Public and Private* 506–07 (State Historical Society of Wisconsin, 1983). See also William Rotch, Sr. to Brown, 8 Nov, 1787, in id at 521; Brown to James Thornton, Sr., 13 Nov 1787, in id at 522–23; Edmund Prior to Brown, 1 Dec 1787, in id at 526.

[59] Federalist 42 and Federalist 54.

[60] James Madison, in the Virginia Ratifying Convention, 17 June 1788, in John P. Kaminski and Gaspare J. Saladino, eds, 10 *The Documentary History of the Ratification of the Constitution by the States: Virginia [3]* 1339 (State Historical Society of Wisconsin, 1993).

[61] Id.

strengthened his argument in favor of ratification by Virginia. But, he did not make such a point because he did not believe it accurate. Similarly, when Patrick Henry asserted that the Constitution would lead to an abolition of slavery, Edmund Randolph, who had been at the Philadelphia Convention, pointed to the Fugitive Slave Clause to prove that this was not so. He said that under the clause "authority is given to owners of slaves to vindicate their property."[62]

In other states the debate was much the same. The North Carolina delegates told their governor that "the Southern States have also a much better Security for the Return of Slaves who might endeavour to Escape than they have under the original Confederation."[63] Similarly, Charles Cotesworth Pinckney told the South Carolina House of Representatives, "We have obtained a right to recover our slaves in whatever part of America they may take refuge, which is a right we had not before."[64]

None of the supporters of the Constitution who at been at the Convention intimated that the Fugitive Slave Clause was a fundamental part of the bargain. Rather, they pointed to it as a plus for the South, but not as a major clause. Similarly, none of these framers anticipated that the federal government would enforce the clause. The structure of the Constitution supported this interpretation of the clause.[65]

C. JUSTICE STORY'S HISTORY AND THE PROSLAVERY CONSTITUTION

Story's history of the origin of the Fugitive Slave Clause does not comport with either the records of the Constitutional Convention or with the discussion of the clause during the ratification process. Significantly, both sources were available to him in 1842 when he wrote the decision. The history he gave did, however,

---

[62] Edmund Randolph in the Virginia Ratifying Convention, June 24, 1788, in Kaminski and Saladino, 10 *Documentary History* 1484 (cited in note 60).

[63] North Carolina Delegates [William Blount, Rich'd D. Spaight, Hugh Williamson] to Governor Caswell, Sept 1787, reprinted in Farrand, ed, 3 *Records* 83 at 84 (cited in note 51).

[64] Charles Cotesworth Pinckney, Speech in South Carolina House of Representatives, Jan [17], 1788, reprinted in 3 Farrand, *Records* 252 at 254.

[65] The Fugitive Slave Clause is in Art IV, § 2 of the Constitution. Sections 1, 3, and 4 of Art IV all give specific enforcement powers to the federal government. Because § 2 is the only part of that article which *does not* explicitly grant authorize federal implementation, it is reasonable to argue that the framers did not intend to grant Congress such power.

support his goal of nationalizing the law. By reshaping the clause into a fundamental part of the bargain over the Constitution, he could argue for exclusive federal jurisdiction over the return of fugitive slaves.

At another level, the *Prigg* opinion brought Story's jurisprudence closer to the true meaning of the Constitution, if not to the meaning of this particular clause. It seems clear that one goal of the Constitutional Convention was to protect the South's interest in slavery. Throughout the Convention, southerners explicitly demanded such protection. They gained it in a variety of clauses dealing with representation, taxation, the slave trade, and the power of the national government to suppress rebellions and insurrections. Most important of all, from the perspective of slaveowners, was the limited nature of the national government, which precluded a general emancipation. As General Charles Cotesworth Pinckney of South Carolina told his state's house of representatives:

> We have a security that the general government can never emancipate them, for no such authority is granted and it is admitted, on all hands, that the general government has no powers but what are expressly granted by the Constitution, and that all rights not expressed were reserved by the several states.[66]

Significantly, at the Convention and in its aftermath, no one considered the Fugitive Slave Clause to be a particularly important part of the constitutional bargain over slavery. But, by the 1830s, southerners felt that their peculiar institution was under attack. In his *Commentaries on the Constitution of the United States*,[67] Story tried to assuage the South by describing the clause as a gift from the North to the South; then in *Prigg* Story tried to further please the South by elevating the Fugitive Slave Clause to a central part of the constitutional bargain, and then protecting expanded southern claims under this elevated clause.

In *Commentaries on the Constitution of the United States*, published a decade before *Prigg*, Story had erroneously asserted that the Fugitive Slave Clause was necessary because the lack "of such a provision under the [Articles of] confederation was felt, as a grievous

---

[66] Charles Cotesworth Pinckney, Speech in South Carolina House of Representatives, Jan [17], 1788, reprinted in 3 Farrand, *Records* 252 at 254–55 (cited in note 51).

[67] Story, *Commentaries on the Constitution* (cited in note 44).

inconvenience by the slave-holding states, since in many states no aid whatsoever would be allowed to the masters; and sometimes indeed they met with open resistance."[68] There was only a little truth to this position. Had the lack of such a clause been "felt as a grievous inconvenience" it would not have taken southerners until late August to propose the clause. Indeed, the stumbling nature of Pierce Butler's initial proposal of the clause suggests that he had not thought of it until just that moment. This record of the Convention (which was not available to Story in 1833 but was in 1842) surely undermines Story's contentions. So too did the state statutes existing at the time of the Convention. These statutes were of course available to Story in 1833.

In 1787, no state specifically prevented southern masters from recovering runaways. Only in Massachusetts does it appear that runaway slaves found asylum.[69] Pennsylvania, Connecticut, and Rhode Island recognized the right of a master to recover a fugitive slave even while they were dismantling slavery themselves.[70] New York and New Jersey were still slave states, and willing to participate in the return of runaways. But, in his *Commentaries* Story ignored this history because it suited his nationalistic purpose to elevate the fugitive slave provision to a key constitutional clause, in order to prove that the Constitution gave the South special protection for its most important social and economic institution. For Story the clause was a boon "for the benefit of the slaveholding states" to indicate northern good will toward the "peculiar interests of the south."[71] Thus in his *Commentaries*, Story had offered the Fugitive Slave Clause "to repress the delusive and mischievous notion, that the south has not at all times had its full share of benefits from the Union."[72]

---

[68] Id at § 952.

[69] See the correspondence of Moses Brown on this issue. Moses Brown to James Pemberton, 17 Oct 1787, reprinted in Kaminski and Saladino, eds, 14 *Documentary History* 506–07 (cited in note 58); William Rotch, Sr. to Brown, 8 Nov, 1787, in id at 521; Brown to James Thornton, Sr., 13 Nov 1787, in id at 522–23; Edmund Prior to Brown, 1 Dec 1787, in id at 526. There is no evidence of runaway slaves reaching New Hampshire and the putative state of Vermont at this time. Recovery of slaves from those regions would have been difficult, but it would have been even more difficult for southern slaves to reach them.

[70] On the rights of masters in those states, see Finkelman, *An Imperfect Union* (cited in note 18).

[71] Story, *Commentaries* at § 952.

[72] Id.

In *Prigg*, Story expanded and shifted the argument. The U.S. government would guarantee the interests of the South, prevent the North from interfering with the rendition of fugitive slaves, and even allow masters to seize and remove alleged fugitives without any due process procedure at all. All this was necessary, Story argued in *Prigg*, because the Constitution required it.

There is an obvious explanation for the difference between Story's analysis of the Fugitive Slave Clause in his *Commentaries* and his later analysis of it in *Prigg*. In the *Commentaries*, Story was trying to provide a nationalistic interpretation of the Constitution that would be accepted in all sections of the country. Story was writing just after the emergence of the militant abolitionist movement, in the wake of the Webster-Hayne debate, and at the time of the nullification crisis. The South was the section most likely to reject his nationalist interpretation of the Constitution. Thus, his assertion that the Fugitive Slave Clause was inserted in the Constitution solely "for the benefit of the slaveholding states"[73] was designed to garner support in the South for Story's constitutional nationalism. The result of this would be to renew southern faith in the fundamental spirit of the Constitution—that the Constitution protected slavery. In *Prigg*, however, Story did not have to appeal to the South. The opinion was overwhelmingly favorable to the interests of slavery. Rather, Story had to convince the North to accept his proslavery opinion. Thus, he put a new spin on his constitutional history, arguing that the Constitution required both the federal law of 1793 and his harsh interpretation of it in *Prigg*. Story doubtless hoped the North would accept *Prigg* because he asserted it was dictated by the Constitution itself and because the Fugitive Slave Clause was an essential part of the constitutional bargain of 1787. In effect, Story accepted a proslavery interpretation of the Constitution as a vehicle for strengthening the federal government. Although Story's son would later argue that the opinion was antislavery because it localized slavery, in fact, the opinion was significantly proslavery because it actually nationalized slavery.[74]

---

[73] Id.

[74] For a discussion of the "localization" argument, see Part V, A, of this article. Ironically, by nationalizing the return of fugitive slaves, and making the Fugitive Slave Clause a central part of the constitutional bargain, Story gave support to the antinationalist position of William Lloyd Garrison and Wendell Phillips that the Constitution was a proslavery "covenant with death."

III. The Second Story: The Relevant Precedents

In upholding all aspects of the Fugitive Slave Law of 1793, Story naturally looked for precedents to support his position. Story argued that the existing case law, consisting of three state cases, totally supported his position. In doing so, the justice and legal scholar created his second story. In fact, one of the cases he cited for authority held the opposite of what Story claimed it held. Furthermore, Story ignored two state cases that did not support his position.

Although the Fugitive Slave Act had been in force for a half century when the Supreme Court heard *Prigg*, the existing case law on the issue was hardly noticeable. A few lower federal courts had heard cases under the law, but the district judges offered little guidance or intellectual support of Story.[75] While riding circuit, Justice Henry Baldwin had delivered one opinion on the law.[76] Although offering perfunctory support for the constitutionality of the law, Baldwin did not analyze it. The case was a suit for damages against Pennsylvanians who helped a slave escape, and Baldwin easily found for the plaintiff slave owner.[77]

More important than any federal cases were the discussions of the 1793 law in the state courts. By the time *Prigg* reached the Supreme Court, there were five state precedents involving the Fugitive Slave Law of 1793.[78] Three, from Pennsylvania, Massachusetts, and New York, had been officially reported. A case from New Jersey was not officially reported, but the case and the opinion by Chief Justice Joseph Hornblower were widely reported in

---

[75] In re Susan, 23 F Cases 444 (US DC, Ind, 1818) (Fugitive slave Susan returned to slavery with no opinion of the court); Case of Williams, 29 F Cases 1334 (US DC, Pa, 1839) (court discharges a black (Williams) seized by professional slave catcher because court determines that Williams is not a fugitive slave); In re Martin, 16 F Cases 881 (US DC, NY, 1827–1840) (in this case of an unknown date, the Federal District Judge in New York declared that the act of 1793 was constitutional and a New York official then issued a certificate of removal under the law).

[76] *Johnson v Tompkins et al.*, 13 F Cases 840 (US C C Pa, 1833) (Justice Baldwin, riding circuit, upholds damages for a fugitive slave rescued by Tompkins).

[77] Id. The fact that Baldwin was an extremely weak justice undermined the value of any opinion he wrote. More importantly, perhaps, many observers believed Baldwin was insane. Carl B. Swisher, *History of the Supreme Court of the United States: The Taney Period, 1836–64* 51 (Macmillan, 1974). His opinion in *Prigg* supports both observations.

[78] *Wright v Deacon*, 5 Serg & Rawle 62 (Pa 1819); *Commonwealth v Griffith*, 19 Mass (2 Pick) 11 (1823); *Jack v Martin*, 14 Wend 507 (NY 1835); *State v Sheriff of Burlington*, No 36286 (NJ 1836); *Pennsylvania v Prigg* (unreported, Pa, 1841) reversed, *Prigg v Pennsylvania*, 16 Peters (41 US) 1 (1842).

newspapers and cited by an important Ohio abolitionist lawyer a few years before *Prigg*.[79] The fifth case was the Pennsylvania Supreme Court's opinion in *Prigg*, which had not been reported. But of course Story had the full benefit of the view of that Court.

A. THE JUSTICE'S STORY ABOUT THE RELEVANT CASE LAW

Despite the mixed response of state courts to the 1793 law, Justice Story argued that all states supported his position. Story wrote that the law had:

> naturally been brought under adjudication in several states in the Union, and particularly in Massachusetts, New York, and Pennsylvania, and on all these occasions its validity has been affirmed. The cases cited at the bar . . . are directly in point.[80]

He noted in passing that no federal court had ever denied the validity of the law, although he did not examine any federal opinions.[81]

Story used this sweeping assertion of support from state cases to bolster his assertion that the 1793 act was "clearly constitutional in all its leading provisions."[82] Story argued that if the interpretation of the Fugitive Slave Clause and the law of 1793 "were one of doubtful construction, such long acquiescence in it, such contemporaneous expositions of it, and such extensive and uniform recognition of its validity, would in our judgment entitle the question to be considered at rest."[83] To the extent that constitutional interpretation was designed to give Americans certainty, then following

---

[79] *State v Sheriff of Burlington*, No 36286 (NJ 1836) (also known as *Nathan, Alias Alex. Helmsley v State*). For newspaper accounts of the case, see "Upholding Slavery," 20 Friend 281–82 (June 11, 1836). Portions of this article are reprinted as *Important Decision*, Liberator (July 30, 1836), at 124. *Important Decision*, Newark Daily Advertiser (Aug 18, 1836). The case was cite by Salmon P. Chase in *Salmon P. Chase, Speech of Salmon P. Chase in the Case of the Colored Woman, Matilda* 18–19 (Pugh and Dodd, 1837), reprinted in Paul Finkelman, ed, 2 *Southern Slaves in Free State Courts* 1 (Garland, 1988). For a discussion of the Hornblower decision, see Paul Finkelman, *State Constitutional Protections of Liberty and the Antebellum New Jersey Supreme Court: Chief Justice Hornblower and the Fugitive Slave Law of 1793*, 23 Rutgers L J 753 (1992).

[80] *Prigg* at 621.

[81] Id. "So far as the judges of the Courts of the United States have been called upon to enforce it, and to grant the certificate required by it, it is believed that it has been uniformly recognised as a binding and valid law; and as imposing a constitutional duty." Id.

[82] Id at 622.

[83] Id at 621.

the state cases supported that goal. Story argued that the alternative
was that "the interpretation of the Constitution is to be delivered
over to interminable doubt throughout the whole progress of legislation, and of national operations."[84]

B. THE REAL CASE LAW

Story's use of state cases to bolster his opinion was logical and
constitutionally sound. However, it was neither historically correct nor jurisprudentially honest. There were five important state
decisions on the Fugitive Slave Law by 1842. Two supported
it,[85] two did not.[86] The fifth case, the Pennsylvania Supreme
Court's decision in *Prigg* itself, did not question the constitutionality of the 1793 law, but also did not support Story's other conclusions.

This division is not simply a 2–2–1 split among state jurists.
The supportive opinions were short, analytically weak, and decided *before* the northern states began to pass personal liberty laws
in the mid-1820s. On the other hand, the state opinions attacking
the federal law and upholding state authority to legislate on the
subject were newer and analytically stronger than either of the
cases upholding the 1793 law.

In 1819, Pennsylvania's Chief Justice, William Tilghman, enforced the federal law while denying that a fugitive slave had the
right to a jury trial. However, he did not otherwise examine the
constitutionality of the federal act.[87] In 1823, Chief Justice Isaac
Parker of Massachusetts also upheld the 1793 law but limited his
analysis to "a single point: whether the statute of the United States
giving power to seize a slave without a warrant is constitutional."[88]
Parker upheld this warrantless seizure because "slaves are not parties to the constitution, and the [Fourth] [A]mendment has [no]
[*sic*] relation the parties."[89] Parker noted, without any citation or

---

[84] Id.

[85] *Wright v Deacon*, 5 Serg & Rawle 62 (Pa 1819); *Commonwealth v Griffith*, 19 Mass (2 Pick) 11 (1823).

[86] *Jack v Martin*, 14 Wend 507 (NY 1835); *State v Sheriff of Burlington*, No 36286 (NJ 1836) (also known as *Nathan, Alias Alex. Helmsley v State*).

[87] *Wright*, 5 Serg & Rawle at 62.

[88] *Griffith*, 19 Mass (2 Pick) at 11, 18.

[89] Id at 19.

reference to a specific constitutional provision, that "[t]he constitution does not prescribe the mode of reclaiming a slave, but leaves it to be determined by Congress."[90]

Parker might have reached a different conclusion if he had bothered to analyze the 1793 law or the Fugitive Slave Clause of the Constitution. A structural analysis of the Constitution might have led Parker to conclude that because the Fugitive Slave Clause was placed in Article IV, Section 2, the clause was in fact not subject to Congressional enforcement. Sections 1, 3, and 4 of the Article have specific provisions giving Congress enforcement power. For example, in Section 1 Congress was specifically authorized to "proscribe the Manner in which" acts, records, and court decisions in one state might be proved in another.[91] Similarly, Section 3 empowered Congress to admit new states to the Union and "to dispose of and make all needful Rules and Regulations" for the Territories.[92] Indeed, Section 2 was the only part of Article IV that did not empower the national government to enforce its provisions. Logically, fugitive slave rendition was part of the comity provisions of this section of Article IV, and should have been left to the states to enforce as a matter of comity.[93]

The opinions of Chancellor Reuben Walworth of New York and Chief Justice Joseph C. Hornblower stand in marked contrast to the meager analysis of Tilghman and Parker. Both judges offered a careful analysis of the constitutional issues involved in the 1793 law and Fugitive Slave Clause. Both opinions were relatively recent, and reflected concepts of federalism as they were understood in Jacksonian America. Moreover, both judges thought the 1793 law was unconstitutional.

Hornblower's opinion was unreported, and although Story prob-

---

[90] Id.

[91] US Const, Art IV, § 1, "Full Faith and Credit shall be given in each State to the public Acts, Records, and judicial Proceedings of every other State. An the Congress may by general Laws prescribe the Manner in which such Acts, Records and Proceedings shall be proved, and the Effect thereof."

[92] US Const, Art IV, § 3. Section 4 of this Article empowered "The United States" to guarantee a "Republican Form of Government" in every state. Thus, Congress, along with the other branches of government, could act to enforce this clause. See generally, William M. Wiecek, *The Guarantee Clause of the U.S. Constitution* (Cornell University Press, 1972).

[93] See the discussion in note 95.

ably had access to it,[94] it is possible he was either unaware of the decision or felt that because it was unreported he could ignore it.[95]

Chancellor Reuben Walworth's decision in *Jack v Martin*,[96] however, was well known to Story and was cited in argument. Speaking for New York's highest court, Walworth found the Fugitive Slave Act unconstitutional because Congress lacked the power to pass such a law. Walworth had

> looked in vain among the powers delegated to congress by the constitution, for any general authority to that body to legislate on this subject. It is certainly not contained in any express grant of power, and it does not appear to be embraced in the general grant of incidental powers contained in the last clause of the constitution relative to the powers of congress.[97]

After careful consideration of the Constitution's text and the state statutes existing in 1787, Walworth applied a version of original intent analysis to conclude that the 1793 law was unconstitutional.

> It is impossible to bring my mind to the conclusion that the framers of the constitution have authorized the congress of the United States to pass a law by which the certificate of a justice of the peace of the state, shall be made conclusive evidence of

---

[94] Ohio attorney Salmon P. Chase had cited it while arguing a case in 1837. Chase, *Speech of Salmon P. Chase* at 18 (cited in note 79).

[95] In his analysis of Article IV, Hornblower compared the Full Faith and Credit Clause, which explicitly gives Congress the power to pass laws, with the Fugitive Slave Clause. Since no such explicit language exists in § 2, the court concluded that "no such power was intended to be given" to Congress for implementation of the clauses in that section of the Constitution. Indeed, Hornblower argued that Congressional legislation over the Privileges and Immunities Clause or over interstate rendition "would cover a broad field, and lead to the most unhappy results." Such legislation would "bring the general government into conflict with the state authorities, and the prejudices of local communities." Hornblower asserted that Congress lacked the "right to prescribe the manner in which persons residing in the free states, shall be arrested, imprisoned, delivered up, and transferred from one state to another, simply because they are claimed as slaves." Consistent with the northern states' rights arguments of the antebellum period, Hornblower warned the "American people would not long submit" to such an expansive view of Congressional power. Although this analysis seemed to lead to the conclusion that the Fugitive Slave Act was unconstitutional, Hornblower declined "to express any definitive opinion on the validity of the act of Congress." He could avoid this grave responsibility because the case before him had been brought "in pursuance of the law of this state." However, Hornblower's position on the unconstitutionality of the federal law was unambiguous. *Opinion of Chief Justice Hornblower on the Fugitive Slave Law* at 4–5 (1851), reprinted in Paul Finkelman, ed, 1 *Fugitive Slaves and American Courts: The Pamphlet Literature* 97 (Garland, 1988).

[96] 14 Wend 507 (NY 1835).

[97] Id at 526.

> the right of the claimant, to remove one who may be a free
> native born citizen of this state, to a distant part of the union
> as a slave; and thereby to deprive such person of the benefit of
> the writ of *habeas corpus*, as well as of his common law suit to
> try his right of citizenship in the state where the claim is made,
> and where he is residing at the time of such claim.[98]

Walworth's opinion in *Jack v Martin* was not aimed at preventing
the rendition of fugitive slaves. Walworth upheld Martin's claim
to Jack and firmly supported the obligation of state officials to
return fugitive slaves, asserting that every "state officer or private
citizen, who owes allegiance to the United States and has taken
the usual oath to support the constitution" was obligated to enforce
the Fugitive Slave Clause of the Constitution.[99] Nevertheless, he
categorically denied the constitutionality of the Fugitive Slave
Law.

Before the Supreme Court, both counsel for Pennsylvania,
Thomas Hambly and Attorney General Ovid F. Johnson, cited
the case. Hambly noted that

> the question of constitutionality was debated [in *Jack v Martin*],
> and in my judgment not a single solid reason was given for that
> construction, but, on the contrary, Chancellor Walworth says,
> 'I have looked in vain among the delegated powers of congress
> for authority to legislate upon the subject,' and concludes that
> state legislation is ample for the purpose.[100]

Attorney General Johnson noted that the states were divided on
the constitutionality of the Fugitive Slave Act. He pointed out that
Commonwealth v Griffith[101] and *Jack v Martin* "exhibit[ed] a most
striking illustration of the 'uncertainty of the law.'"[102] In these
two cases "the courts were divided in opinion," while in various
Pennsylvania cases "the question did not properly arise, and the
Court, without examination, declared its opinion on the constitutionality of the act of Congress of 1793."[103]

Despite Story's reputation as a great legal scholar, he ignored the

---

[98] Id at 528.

[99] Id.

[100] *Prigg* at 584.

[101] 19 Mass (2 Pick) 11 (1823).

[102] *Prigg* at 591.

[103] Id at 591–92.

arguments of Hambly and Johnson while unblushingly distorting Walworth's opinion. Walworth found the 1793 act unconstitutional but, citing Walworth's opinion, Story wrote, "it has naturally been brought under adjudication in several states in the Union, and particularly in Massachusetts, New York, and Pennsylvania, and on all these occasions its validity has been affirmed."[104]

This statement is flatly wrong. Chief Justice Hornblower of New Jersey had found the law unconstitutional. The Pennsylvania Supreme Court, in *Prigg*, completely disagreed with Story's interpretation of the law, and of course *Jack v Martin* did not affirm the constitutionality of the 1793 law; rather, it totally rejected its constitutionality. It is hard to imagine how Story could have written this with a straight face. Determined, however, to let nothing stand in his way, he did more than ignore countervailing precedents: he rewrote them to support his own opinion. This was the Justice's second story.

IV. THE THIRD STORY: THE LIFE OF MARGARET MORGAN

The cost of Story's rewriting of constitutional history and reinterpreting the Fugitive Slave Clause would be borne mostly by black Americans, free and fugitive, who lived in the North. After *Prigg*, a master or her agent could seize any black, and if done without a breach of the peace, remove that person to the South. No state court could intervene; no state official could question the actions of the slave catcher. The facts of *Prigg* illustrate the dangers of Story's opinion.

A. THE TRAVELS AND TRAVAILS OF MARGARET MORGAN AND HER CHILDREN

When Prigg seized her, Margaret Morgan made no claim of "mistaken" identity. She was the child of people who were born slaves, and thus Prigg had at least a *prima facia* claim to her, both under the federal law of 1793 and Maryland law. Nevertheless, Morgan's life as a slave, and the circumstances of her arrival in Pennsylvania, reveal the problems caused by the Fugitive Slave Clause and the

---

[104] Id at 621.

1793 law Congress adopted to enforce it.[105] These facts also suggest that Morgan and some or all of her children may have had viable claims to freedom, under Pennsylvania law and perhaps under Maryland law. In other words, although once a slave, by 1837 Morgan may have been legitimately free; certainly "several" of her children had been born free,[106] and were not subject to the federal law of 1793. In his opinion, Justice Story glossed over these possibilities in his desire to write a sweeping nationalistic opinion striking down Pennsylvania's personal liberty law of 1826, despite the fact that the circumstances of Morgan's life underscore the necessity of such laws to protect free blacks who might be enslaved under the color of federal law.

In the early years of the nineteenth century—probably before 1812—a Maryland slaveowner named John Ashmore allowed two of his slaves—an aged married couple—to live in virtual freedom.[107] Although Ashmore never formally freed the two slaves, thereafter he "constantly declared he had set them free."[108] The two slaves raised a daughter named Margaret.[109] Because she was born in Maryland, to a slave mother, Margaret was technically Ashmore's slave, even though Ashmore never asserted any authority over her.

In 1820, John Ashmore was a sixty-year-old farmer and mill owner, with extensive land holdings in Harford County. He also owned ten slaves, although neither Margaret nor her parents were among them. However, shortly after that he began disposing of his slaves. In March 1821, the sixty-one-year-old Ashmore sold two male slaves to his neighbor Jacob Forward for eight hundred dollars.[110] By 1824, when he died, Ashmore owned only two young

---

[105] On the history of the adoption of the law, see Paul Finkelman, *The Kidnapping of John Davis and the Adoption of the Fugitive Slave Law of 1793*, 56 J Southern History 397–422 (1990).

[106] Thomas C. Hambly, *Argument of Mr. Hambly, of York, (Pa.) in the Case of Edward Prigg* 8 (Baltimore, Lucas & Dever, 1842), reprinted in Paul Finkelman, ed, 1 *Fugitive Slaves and American Courts: The Pamphlet Literature* 128 (Garland, 1988) (hereafter *Argument of Hambly* [with original page numbers and reprint page numbers in parentheses]).

[107] Information about this case comes from the printed report in *Prigg* at 608–10.

[108] *Argument of Hambly* at 8 (128) (cited in note 106).

[109] We have no record of what her last name was before she married Morgan.

[110] John Ashmore to Jacob Forward, Bill of Sale, March 6, 1821, in Harford County Historical Society manuscripts. In 1837 Forward would join Edward Prigg and Nathan S. Bemis in their quest for Margaret Morgan. Forward was one of the four men indicted for the kidnapping, but only Prigg was returned for trial. Ashmore's total slave property in 1820 is based on the US Manuscript Census, 1820, Harford County, Maryland, p 380 (also

male slaves. In May 1821, Ashmore sold his considerable real estate holdings to his daughter, Susanna Ashmore Bemis, for "the consideration of natural love and affection" and a nominal sum.[111] Three years later Ashmore died intestate. All his remaining property went to his wife, Margaret Ashmore. By this time the estate, which included no real property, was relatively small, and valued at only $509. The most valuable assets were two slave boys, Tommy, age 12, and James, age 11.[112] There is nothing to indicate that he owned, or claimed to own, a teenaged slave girl named Margaret at his death or before. At the time of his death Ashmore was living at his old home, which by this time he had deeded to his daughter, Susanna Bemis. His widow, Margaret Ashmore, continued to live there as well.[113]

Sometime after John Ashmore's death, Margaret, the daughter of his former slaves, married Jerry Morgan, a free black from Pennsylvania. They continued to live in Harford County, in the same neighborhood as Margaret Ashmore and her daughter and son-in-law, Susanna and Nathan S. Bemis. It is possible that Margaret Morgan lived with her aged parents on land once owned by John Ashmore and given to Susanna Bemis.[114] In 1830, the county sheriff, who was also the census taker, recorded Jerry Morgan as the head of a family consisting of one free black woman (Margaret) and their two "free black" children.[115] In 1832, after the death of Margaret's parents, the Morgans moved to York County, Pennsylvania, apparently with the knowledge of Margaret Ashmore and Nathan S. Bemis.

What happened next is unknown. But, in February 1837, Ashmore's son-in-law, Nathan S. Bemis, went to Pennsylvania to bring

---

noted as p 76). Ashmore's birthdate, Jan 22, 1760, is found in Bill and Martha Reamy, *St. George's Parrish Registers, 1689–1793* (Family Line Publications) 85.

[111] Deed of Conveyance from John Ashmore to Susanna Bemis, May 11, 1821, in Harford County Historical Society manuscripts. Edward Prigg was one of the two witnesses to this need.

[112] John Ashmore Inventory, Sept 28, 1824, Harford County, Register of Willis, # 1672.

[113] US Manuscript Census, 1830, Harford County, Maryland, p 387. On April 22, 1845, Margaret Ashmore manumitted her slave Jim, who she had inherited when her husband died. Nathan S. Bemis served as the "agent and attorney" for Margaret Ashmore in this transaction. "Margaret Ashmore and Negro Jim, Manumission Deed, recorded May 10, 1845." Harford County Historical Society manuscripts.

[114] This claim is made by Thomas Hambly, counsel for Pennsylvania, in his Supreme Court brief. Hambly, *Argument of Mr. Hambly* at 8 (128) (cited in note 106).

[115] US Census, 1830, Manuscript Census for Harford County, Maryland, p 394.

Margaret and her children back to Maryland. Accompanying Bemis were three neighbors, Edward Prigg, Jacob Forward, and Stephen Lewis, Jr. Prigg and Forward had long ties to the Ashmore family. Prigg witnessed John Ashmore's deed of land to his daughter and later witnessed the inventory of his estate; Forward had purchased slaves from Ashmore and Ashmore had been a witness to the will of Forward's father.[116] The four neighbors easily located Margaret Morgan and secured an arrest warrant from Thomas Henderson, a York County, Pennsylvania, justice of the peace, as required by the Pennsylvania law of 1826. A local constable then accompanied the four Marylanders to the Morgan home, arrested the family, and brought them back to Justice of the Peace Henderson. When Henderson actually saw the Morgan family, however, he refused to grant Bemis and Prigg a certificate of removal to take the Morgans back to Maryland. It was clear that Morgan's husband was a free-born native of Pennsylvania, and that at least two of her children had been born in that free state as well. Perhaps on hearing Margaret Morgan's story, Henderson concluded that the entire family was really free. Bemis and Prigg were not deterred, and without process took Margaret Morgan and her children back to Maryland. They were subsequently indicted for kidnapping, but only Prigg was returned for trial.[117]

B. THE JUSTICE'S STORY ABOUT MARGARET MORGAN

In *Prigg*, Justice Story did not tell Margaret Morgan's story. Rather, he repeated, in the barest details, the findings of the lower court. He noted that the Pennsylvania trial court had found Prigg guilty "for having, with force and violence, taken and carried away from that county to the state of Maryland, a certain negro woman, named Margaret Morgan, with a design and intention of selling and disposing of, and keeping her as a slave or servant for life, contrary to a statute of Pennsylvania, passed on the 26th of March, 1826."[118] He recounted Prigg's response "that the negro woman, Margaret Morgan, was a slave for life, and held to labour and service under and according to the laws of Maryland, to a certain

---

[116] *Bible Records of Harford County, Maryland Families*, 133, typescript in Maryland Historical Society, Baltimore. See also notes 110, 112.

[117] *Prigg* at 543.

[118] Id at 608.

Margaret Ashmore, a citizen of Maryland; that the slave escaped and fled from Maryland into Pennsylvania in 1832."[119] Almost as an afterthought, Story added that "The special verdict [of the Pennsylvania trial court] further finds, that one of the children was born in Pennsylvania, more than a year after the said negro woman had fled and escaped from Maryland."[120]

This is all Justice Story has to say about Margaret Morgan, her husband Jerry, and their children. This limited summary of facts, while not untrue, is surely misleading. The facts, as Story presents them, raise three important questions, which the Justice never addressed. First, was Morgan in fact a "slave for life" under Maryland law? Second, had Morgan in fact "escaped and fled from Maryland into Pennsylvania?" Third, what was the status of the child—and was it only one child—who "was born in Pennsylvania?"

Had Story addressed these issues he would have been unable to so easily create a right of self-help for slave hunters. He similarly might have been less able to strike down Pennsylvania's personal liberty law. In his opinion Story asserted, "we have not the slightest hesitation in holding, that, under and in virtue of the Constitution, the owner of a slave is clothed with entire authority, in every state in the Union, to seize and recapture his slave, whenever he can do it without any breach of the peace, or any illegal violence. In this sense, and to this extent this clause of the Constitution may properly be said to execute itself; and to require no aid from legislation, state or national."[121]

Because he did not consider the facts of Margaret Morgan's life, Story did not address how a state would be able to protect the liberty of its free-born citizens, such as Margaret Morgan's child. He ignored the free status of the child and the possible free status of Morgan herself. Only by doing so could he justify the right of self-help and the striking down of the state protections for free blacks who might otherwise be claimed as fugitive slaves.

C. MARGARET MORGAN'S CLAIMS TO FREEDOM

Margaret Ashmore based her claim to Morgan on the fact that Morgan's mother had never been legally emancipated, and thus

---

[119] Id at 608–09.

[120] *Prigg* at 609.

[121] Id at 613.

Morgan herself was born a slave, and continued to be owned by the Ashmores. On its face this was a valid claim. However, Morgan may have had a legitimate claim to freedom, both in Maryland and Pennsylvania. As a slave who was allowed to travel to a free state and live there with the knowledge of her master, Morgan may have become legally free.[122]

There is no evidence that anyone raised this potential claim to freedom, either in the trial court or at the appellate level. This is in part because Morgan's status was never brought before any Pennsylvania court.[123] Nevertheless, Story might have addressed these issues in his opinion, had he been interested in finding a way to uphold the Pennsylvania law. Indeed, these facts could have been enough to send the case back to trial in Pennsylvania, to determine if Morgan had in fact been free all along. After all, if Margaret Morgan was entitled to freedom under Pennsylvania law, it would not have been unreasonable for the Court to assert that she had a right to prove that freedom in a Pennsylvania court. Even if the Supreme Court had decided it could not consider Morgan's claims to freedom because she was not a party to the case, this potential claim to freedom should have alerted Story to the importance of allowing states to protect the liberty of their residents.

---

[122] As the daughter of slaves abandoned by their owner, she might have claimed some common law right to be free. Ashmore, the original owner, had clearly abandoned his claim to Margaret Morgan's parents. They lived and acted like free persons. Moreover, Ashmore seems to have never asserted any claim over Margaret. In 1832, the South Carolina courts held that "Proof that a negro has been suffered to live in a community for years, as a free man, would *prima facie*, establish the fact of freedom. Like all other *prima facie* shewing, it may be repelled, and shewn that, notwithstanding it, he is a slave, not legally manumitted, or set free. But until this is done, the general reputation of freedom would . . . establish it. . . ." *State v Harden*, 2 Spears (SC) 151 n (1832). Maryland case law appears to have been hostile to the notion that a slave could gain freedom through reputation, through something akin to adverse possession of one's self. In *Walkup v Pratt*, 5 Har and John 51, at 56 (1820), the Court held that "general reputation of the neighbourhood, that the petitioner, or his . . . maternal ancestors, were free negroes" was not admissible to prove freedom. Similarly, in 1837 the Maryland court also held that a slave was not free even though he "went at large and acted as a free man, by keeping an oyster house, and boot-black shop, and otherwise acted as a free man, his own master. . . .", *Bland v Negro Beverly Dowling*, 9 Gill and John 19 (1837). This case did not directly raise the freedom issues under consideration *Prigg*. In *Bland* the slave unsuccessfully claimed his freedom on the grounds that he had purchased it from his owner Bland.

[123] In May 1837, Margaret Morgan sued for her freedom in a Harford County court. On August 28, a jury was sworn, which two days later decided that she was still a slave. More than a dozen witnesses appeared on behalf of the defendant, Margaret Ashmore. Margaret Morgan, on the other hand, does not seem to have been represented by counsel. Docket Book, Harford County Civil and Criminal Court, 1837, in Harford County Historical Society. Margaret and her children were subsequently sold South. *Argument of Hambly* at 10 (130) (cited in note 106).

Morgan's strongest claim to freedom rested on the law of slave transit and interstate comity. By 1837, most of the North accepted the principle that a slave became free if brought into a free jurisdiction.[124] As early as 1780, Pennsylvania had accepted the principle that any slave voluntarily brought into the state became free. However, in order to preserve interstate comity, Pennsylvania also granted masters a six months grace period before freeing their slaves.[125]

Clearly Margaret Ashmore knew that Margaret had gone to Pennsylvania. Yet she did nothing to stop her or retrieve her. Indeed, she acquiesced in the actions of Margaret.[126] A Pennsylvania court could easily have found Margaret free under Pennsylvania's 1780 law on the theory that Ashmore had implicitly consented to her taking up residence in a free state and allowed her to live there for more than six months. A Maryland court might have agreed as well. In 1799 a Maryland court had upheld the freedom claim of a slave because his master had hired him to work in Pennsylvania.[127]

Morgan may also have had a claim to freedom under Maryland law. Technically Morgan was a slave because her mother was a slave, and neither had ever been formally manumitted. Maryland, like all other slave states, did not allow a master to accomplish a manumission de facto. Rather, manumissions required specific acts and actions. However, in 1837 a Maryland court seemed to imply that a slave might become free because "he appeared at all times openly, and it was notorious to his neighbors" that he resided in Pennsylvania.[128] This was analogous to the concept of adverse possession in real property law. Because Ashmore had allowed

---

[124] For a full discussion of freedom through transit, see Finkelman, *An Imperfect Union* (cited in note 18).

[125] "An Act for the Gradual Abolition of Slavery," Act of March 1, 1780, *Pennsylvania Laws, 1780*.

[126] This might be because Margaret Ashmore did not claim Margaret Morgan as her slave. She was not part of John Ashmore's estate, and considered free by the local authorities who took the 1830 census.

[127] *Negro David v Porter*, 4 Harr & McH 418 (1799).

[128] *Pocock v Hendricks*, 8 Gill and John (Md) 421 (1837). However, later that month (June 1837) the same court also held that a slave was not free even though he "went at large and acted as a free man" and had been allowed to travel to New York and work there. *Bland v Negro Beverly Dowling*, 9 Gill and John 19 (1837). Neither case directly raised the freedom issues under consideration here. *Pocock* involved a suit between two whites, while in *Bland* the slave unsuccessfully claimed his freedom on the grounds that he had purchased it from his owner Bland.

Margaret to adversely possess herself by living free in both Maryland and Pennsylvania for her entire life, she might have had a claim to freedom. The finding of the 1830 census that she was free would certainly have bolstered this claim. This reasoning, and the few Maryland cases on the issue, suggest that Margaret might have been free under Maryland law, as well as under Pennsylvania law.

D. THE CLAIM TO FREEDOM OF MARGARET MORGAN'S CHILDREN

By 1837, Margaret Morgan was the mother of a number of children. The existing record is unclear about how many she had. It is also not clear how many of these children were born in Pennsylvania,[129] and how many were born in Maryland. It was undisputed, however, "that one of the children was born in Pennsylvania, more than a year after the said negro woman had fled and escaped from Maryland."[130]

Under Pennsylvania's Gradual Emancipation Act of 1780, all children born of slave mothers in Pennsylvania after March 1, 1780 were free,[131] but could be indentured until age twenty-eight.[132] Pennsylvania courts, both before and after *Prigg*, supported the notion that any child born in the Commonwealth was free, even if the child's mother was a runaway slave.[133] Pennsylvania law furthermore prohibited the removal from the state of any minor child born to a slave.[134] Thus, under Pennsylvania law at least one, and perhaps more than one, of Morgan's children was a free person.

---

[129] "The children were born in Pennsylvania. . . .", *Prigg* at 539.

[130] Id at 609.

[131] "An Act for the Gradual Abolition of Slavery," Act of March 1, 1780, *Pennsylvania Laws, 1780,* § III, "All persons as well Negroes and Mulattoes as others, who shall be born within this state from and after the passing of this act, shall not be deemed as considered servants for life, or slaves; and that all servitude for life, or slavery of children, in consequence of the slavery of their mothers, in the case of all children born within this state from and after the passing of this act as aforesaid, shall be, and hereby is, utterly taken away, extinguished, and for ever abolished."

[132] Id at § IV.

[133] *Commonwealth v Holloway*, 2 S & R (Pa) 305 (1816); *Commonwealth v Auld*, 4 Clark (Pa) 507 (1850). This issue is discussed in Finkelman, *An Imperfect Union* at 64–65 (cited in note 18).

[134] "An Act to Explain and Amend An Act, Entitled 'An Act for the Gradual Abolition of Slavery,'" Act of March 29, 1788, *Pennsylvania Acts, 1788,* § II.

E. THE CLAIMS TO FREEDOM AND THE PENNSYLVANIA PERSONAL
   LIBERTY LAW OF 1826

If either Margaret Morgan or any of her children were entitled
to their freedom under Pennsylvania law, then Prigg had no right
to seize them and remove them from the state. Similarly, the Commonwealth of Pennsylvania had a presumptive right to protect
them from kidnapping. Shortly before the legislature adopted the
1826 law, five free black children were kidnapped from Philadelphia and sold as slaves. While three of the young boys were returned to Philadelphia after "they fell into the hands of a humane
protector" in Mississippi, the other two died during their illegal
captivity.[135]

Thus, while the 1826 law might have been used to frustrate the
return of a fugitive to a slave state, the act had been adopted to
both prevent kidnapping and avoid conflicts between Pennsylvania
and her slave-holding neighbors. At the time of its adoption, "it is
unlikely that many, except the militant antislavery people, understood that the law was subject to interpretations which would virtually deny the recovery of runaways in Pennsylvania."[136] The first
section of the 1826 act was aimed at kidnappers, not slave catchers.
This section punished anyone

> who by force and violence, take and carry away, or cause to
> be taken or carried away, and shall by fraud or false pretense,
> seduce, or cause to be seduced, or shall attempt so to take,
> carry away, or seduce any negro or mulatto from any part
> or parts of this commonwealth, to any other place or places,
> whatsoever, out of this commonwealth, with a design and in-
> tention of selling and disposing of, or of causing to be sold, or
> of keeping and detaining, or of causing to be kept and detained,
> such negro or mulatto, as a slave or servant for life, or for any
> term whatsoever. . . .[137]

If Margaret Morgan had a reasonable claim to freedom under
Pennsylvania law, then she surely had a right to try that claim under
Pennsylvania law. Even if she could not have maintained her claim,

---

[135] This is described in Leslie, *The Pennsylvania Fugitive Slave Act of 1826* at 221 (cited in
note 26).

[136] Id at 440.

[137] *Pennsylvania Act of 1826*, § 1.

Morgan's Pennsylvania-born children should have be able to prove their freedom in the courts of the state in which they were born.[138]

Certainly other blacks claimed as fugitive slaves would in fact be free. Thus, the Supreme Court should have upheld at least some parts of the Pennsylvania law, *as it related to free blacks*. In dissent Justice John McLean argued for precisely this position. Justice Story, however, writing for the majority, had no interest in protecting the liberty of Pennsylvania's substantial free black population. By striking down the Pennsylvania law, the Court seemed to leave Pennsylvania powerless to prevent the kidnapping of its own citizens.

V. The Fourth Story: The Myth of the "Triumph of Freedom"

According to his son William Wetmore Story, Justice Story "repeatedly and earnestly spoke" of his *Prigg* opinion as a "triumph of freedom."[139] Whether Story actually said this is not clear. It does not appear in any of his letters, and except for his son's assertion, there seems to be no independent evidence on the subject.[140] It seems doubtful that Story actually thought he was writing

---

[138] Authorities in Maryland privately acknowledged that Bemis, Prigg, Forward and Lewis were probably guilty of kidnapping for taking Morgan's Pennsylvania-born children to Maryland, but they nevertheless objected to the extradition of the men from Harford County. When he received a letter from the Governor of Pennsylvania indicating that there would be an extradition requisition for the four men, Thomas Culberth, the Clerk of the Governor's Council, told Maryland's governor that "The part of the case involved in the most difficulty, and danger of producing collision and excitement, relates to the children which it seems, were born in Pennsylvania. They were free by the Law of Pennsylvania, and according to my reading and understanding of the constitutional and legal provisions for reclaiming fugitives, do not come within their provisions, and, consequently, the seizing and taking of *them* away, (if Esquire Henderson or some other authorized magistrate, did not give authority) was the 'crime' of kidnapping." Yet, Culberth urged the Governor to avoid any cooperation on the issue because it was so politically sensitive in Maryland. Thom. Culberth, Clerk of Council, to His Excellency, Gov Thomas W. Veazey, March 27, 1837, Maryland State Archives; MSA NO S1075; Governor and Council Letterbook, 1834–38, pp 553–54.

[139] William Wetmore Story, ed, 2 *Life and Letters of Joseph Story* at 392 (Charles C. Little and James Brown, 1851).

[140] In his prize-winning biography of Story, R. Kent Newmyer wrote: "Upon his return to Massachusetts in the spring of 1842, he spoke of opinion in *Prigg* 'repeatedly and earnestly' to his family and friends as a 'triumph of freedom.' " Newmyer, *Justice Joseph Story*, at 372 (cited in note 1). In the note to this sentence, Newmyer cites to William Wetmore's discussion in 2 *Life and Letters* at 392 (cited in note 139), and then Newmyer writes, " 'Triumph of Freedom' was Story's phrase, not his son's." But, Newmyer provides no other evidence that it was the justice's phrase. Ordinarily, I would accept William Wetmore Story as a

an opinion that was a "triumph of freedom" in any easily recognizable way. Neither did his assertion make the opinion such a triumph. The "triumph of freedom" seems, in the end, to be just one more story, told by the justice and/or his son, to defend what was a triumph of proslavery judicial nationalism.

William Wetmore Story made the best defense he could of his father's opinion. The defense was in the end neither credible nor persuasive. Made after his father's death, it was a pathetic attempt to reverse in the court of northern public opinion the correct assessment of Story's opinion of the court as fundamentally a triumph over freedom for the South.

A. THE STORYS TELL THEIR TALE

The younger Story, himself an accomplished legal scholar,[141] defended *Prigg* as a "triumph of freedom" on three grounds.

First, William Wetmore argued that *Prigg* "was a 'triumph of freedom,' because it localized slavery, and made it a municipal institution of the States, not recognized by international law, and except, so far as the exact terms of the clause relating to fugitive slaves extend[ed], not recognized by the Constitution."[142] This was a fair summary of one of the initial premises of the opinion. Citing to *Somerset v Stewart* (1772),[143] Story declared that under "the general law of nations, no nation is bound to recognize the state of slavery."[144] Story further declared that "The state of slavery is deemed to be a mere municipal regulation, founded upon and limited to the range of the territorial laws."[145] Had Story stopped his opinion here, it would have indeed "localized" slavery.

---

good source for what Justice Story said. But William Wetmore was clearly embarrassed by his father's opinion, and by his father's attempt to hide the proslavery force of the opinion. Thus, William Wetmore edited out a key section of a letter to Senator Berrien, in which Justice Story set out a way that the South could avoid any aspects of the opinion that might make it a triumph of freedom. Newmyer's own compelling analysis of Story, combined with William Wetmore's less than honest editing of his father's papers, undercuts the credibility of William Wetmore's attribution of the "triumph of freedom" statement to the justice. See Story to Berrien Letter (cited in note 13).

[141] William Wetmore Story, *Treatise on the Law of Contracts* (Charles C. Little and James Brown, 1844).

[142] William Story, ed, 2 *Life and Letters of Story* at 392 (cited in note 139).

[143] Lofft 1 (GB, 1772).

[144] *Prigg* at 611.

[145] Id.

Second, Story's son argued that the decision favored freedom "because it promised practically to nullify the Act of Congress,—it being generally supposed to be impracticable to reclaim fugitive slaves in the free States, except with the aid of State legislation, and State authority."[146] This analysis was based on the assumption that without the active aid of state authorities—justices of the peace, sheriffs, and the like—masters would have been unable to actually remove a slave from the North. Story's assertion that the federal government had exclusive jurisdiction over fugitive slave rendition and that state officials could not be compelled by the federal government to enforce the law thus set the stage for state withdrawal from aiding in the implementation of the Fugitive Slave Clause or of enforcing the federal law. William Story's point here was again correct as far as it went. In his opinion Story conceded that there was a "difference of opinion" as to "whether state magistrates are bound to act under [the Fugitive Slave Act]," but did not decide the issue.[147] It was certainly possible to conclude, therefore, that the states could withdraw their support for the law. However, in his opinion Story also affirmed that no "difference of opinion" was "entertained by this Court that state magistrates may, if they choose, exercise that authority, unless prohibited by state legislation."[148] William Wetmore Story's argument for the "triumph of freedom" was tied to this last point. If state officials did not enforce the federal law, no one could, and thus fugitive slaves could be secure in their freedom. Some northern judges and legislators would in fact take advantage of this part of Story's opinion to withdraw their support for enforcement of the federal law. Indeed, whether Story intended the opinion to be a triumph of freedom or not, this part of the opinion allowed some northerners to shape it into such a triumph.[149]

Third, William Wetmore argued that by "giving exclusive jurisdiction to Congress, power was put in the hands of the whole people to remodel the law, and establish, through Congress, a legislation in favor of freedom; while, to permit a concurrent or exclu-

---

[146] William Story, ed, 2 *Life and Letters of Story* at 393 (cited in note 139).

[147] *Prigg* at 622.

[148] Id.

[149] Paul Finkelman, *Prigg v Pennsylvania and Northern State Courts: Anti-Slavery Use of a Pro-Slavery Decision*, 25 Civ War History 5 (1979).

sive jurisdiction to the States, would not only deprive all the free States of a voice in establishing a uniform rule throughout the country, guarded by the strictest legal processes, but would enable each slave State to authorize recaption, within its own boundaries, under the most odious circumstances, without any legal process, . . ."[150] The faithful son praised his father's opinion because "[b]y this decision, the question, as to fugitive slaves, was made a national one, and open for discussion on the floor of Congress. To the North was given a full voice on it."[151]

B. THE FAMILY STORY UNMASKED

The claims of Joseph and William Wetmore for the antislavery thrust of *Prigg* do not comport with the text of Story's opinion, his career as a judge, or his actions after the decision.

1. *The localization of slavery.* The argument that *Prigg* localized slavery is inconsistent with the essence of William Wetmore Story's very defense of the opinion and with the justice's career. As a lawyer, scholar, and judge, Story was a committed nationalist. His important *Commentaries on the Constitution*[152] was "the most influential statement of constitutional nationalism made in the Nineteenth Century."[153] One aspect of Story's nationalism was his desire to create a uniform federal common law. In *Prigg*, Story discovered a federal common law right to recapture a slave. To understand the continuity of *Prigg* with the rest of Story's jurisprudence, it is necessary to briefly examine his lifelong commitment to a federal common law.

In 1812, Story silently opposed[154] the outcome in *United States v Hudson and Goodwin*,[155] where a bare majority of the Court found that the national government could not enforce the common law of crimes. A year later, in *United States v Coolidge*,[156] Story, acting as a Circuit Justice, deftly avoided *Hudson and Goodwin* in applying

---

[150] William Story, ed, 2 *Life and Letters of Story* at 394–95 (cited in note 139).

[151] Id at 101.

[152] Joseph Story, *Commentaries on the Constitution of the United States* (Hilliard, Gray, & Co., 1833).

[153] Newmyer, *Justice Joseph Story* at 182 (cited in note 1).

[154] Id at 101.

[155] *United States v Hudson and Goodwin*, 7 Cranch (11 US) 32 (1812).

[156] *U.S. v Coolidge*, 25 F Cases 619 (CCD Mass 1813).

federal common law to admiralty cases. The Supreme Court remained unpersuaded by Story's arguments, and reversed Story's circuit court decision in *Coolidge*, on the basis of *Hudson and Goodwin*.[157] This reversal underscores Story's early commitment to a federal common law, in spite of the Court majority.

Unable to convince the Court of the importance of a federal common law, Story turned to the Congress. After *Hudson and Goodwin*, Story urged Congress to pass legislation to "give the Judicial Courts of the United States power to punish all crimes and offenses against the Government, as at common law."[158] That year Story sent a draft of such legislation to the Attorney General, and in 1818 sent a similar proposal to Senator David Daggett of Connecticut.[159] In 1825, Congress amended the federal criminal code, based on a draft that Story provided.[160] In 1842, he wrote Senator John Macpherson Berrien urging a recodification of all federal criminal law and the extension of the common law to all federal admiralty jurisdiction.[161]

Story's attempts at creating a federal common law of crimes parallel his efforts in creating a federal common law for commercial cases. In 1812, while riding circuit, Story applied general common law to a diversity case.[162] Thirty years later, in *Swift v Tyson*,[163] Story would gain the support of the Court to create a general federal common law for civil litigation. Significantly, Story wrote the opinion in that case in the same term that he wrote the Court's opinion in *Prigg*. *Swift* is the first case reported in that volume of Peters' reports, and *Prigg* is the last case reported in the volume.

---

[157] *United States v Coolidge*, 1 Wheat (14 US) 415 (1816).

[158] Story to Nathaniel Williams, Oct 8, 1812, reprinted in William Story, ed, 1 *Life and Letters of Story* at 243 (cited in note 139).

[159] Story to Daniel Webster, Jan 4, 1824, reprinted in William Story, ed, 1 *Life and Letters of Story* 435 at 437; 2 *Life and Letters* at 401 (cited in note 139). Newmyer, *Justice Joseph Story* at 103 (cited in note 1).

[160] William Story, ed, 1 *Life and Letters of Story* at 437, 439–41; 2 *Life and Letters of Story* at 403–04 (cited in note 139); "An Act more effectually to provide for the punishment of certain crimes against the United States, and for other purposes," Act of March 3, 1825, 4 *Stat* 115.

[161] Story to Berrien, Feb 8, 1842, William Story, ed, 1 *Life and Letters of Story* at 402–03 (cited in note 139); but see also Story to Berrien Letter (cited in note 13).

[162] See *Van Reimsdyk v Kane*, 28 F Cases 1062 (CCD RI, 1812), discussed in Newmyer, *Justice Joseph Story* at 100 (cited in note 1).

[163] *Swift v Tyson*, 16 Peters (41 US) 1 (1842).

Thus, *Prigg*, which nationalized slavery and made it part of a federal common law, is consistent with Story's lifelong commitment to a nationalistic approach to law. Despite his dislike for slavery, in *Prigg* he could not resist an opportunity to nationalize slavery and create a federal common law right of recaption for slaves, just as he had tried throughout his career to expand federal common law in other areas. Thus, in defending his discovery of a constitutionally protected common law right of recaption, Justice Story declared:

> We have said that the clause contains a positive and unqualified recognition of the right of the owner in the slave, unaffected by any state law or regulation whatsoever, because there is no qualification or restriction of it to be found therein. . . . If this be so, then all the incidents to that right attach also; the owner must, therefore, have the right to seize and repossess the slave, which the local laws of his own state confer upon him as property; and we all know that this right of seizure and recaption is universally acknowledged in all the slaveholding states.[164]

This is hardly a localization of slavery. On the contrary, it is a specific declaration that some aspects of the law of slavery should be imposed on the North. This dovetailed with his assertion that "the state of slavery is deemed to be a mere municipal regulation, founded upon and limited to the range of the territorial laws."[165] Having made this point in his opinion, Story then noted that the Constitution fundamentally altered this principle of law. "The [fugitive slave] clause was, therefore, of the last importance to the safety and security of the southern states; and could not have been surrendered by them without endangering their whole property in slaves. The clause was accordingly adopted into the Constitution by the unanimous consent of the framers of it; a proof at once of its intrinsic and practical necessity."[166]

Ironically, William Wetmore Story's own praise for his father's decision undercut his localization argument. William's third argument was that by making the debate over fugitive slaves "a national one," his father gave the North "a full voice on the debate."[167]

---

[164] *Prigg* at 612.

[165] Id at 611.

[166] Id at 612.

[167] William Story, ed, 2 *Life and Letters of Story* at 395 (cited in note 139).

In defending *Prigg*, William Wetmore Story explained that the opinion

> conforms to those principles of interpretation in favor of the Federal Government, which appear in his family letters, and are developed in all his other constitutional opinions. It affirms the doctrine, that the Constitution creates, not a mere confederation of States, but a government of the people, endowed with all powers appropriate or incidental to carry out its provisions, although not expressly surrendered by the States.[168]

Here the younger Story is correct. But, in recognizing his father's lifelong commitment to judicial nationalism, the son undercut his argument that *Prigg* localized slavery.

2. *The practical nullification of the federal law.* The argument for practical nullification the fugitive slave law is the strongest one in Story's favor. Indeed, the decision, in the end, did lead to a practical nullification of the federal law. After *Prigg*, many northern judges refused to hear fugitive slave cases, free state officials refused to help claimants, and some legislatures actually prohibited state support for the federal law.[169] However, it is important to make a distinction between what state officials *did* after *Prigg* and what Story intended in his decision.

It would have been completely out of character for Story to have tried to sabotage his own decision. This simply was not his style. As Robert Cover has argued, this would have been "a truly extraordinary ameliorist effort."[170] Similarly, as Kent Newmyer noted, "there are serious problems" with this analysis.[171] It is hard to believe that someone who devoted his entire life to the law—and most of it to constitutional law and the Supreme Court—would late in his career sabotage one of his most important nationalist opinions in hopes of achieving a secret goal.

Second, Story did not necessarily want to remove all state participation in the return of fugitive slaves. It is true that Story argued for exclusive federal power to legislate about fugitive slave rendition. But, Story did not rule out active, and even legislatively

---

[168] Id at 392.

[169] Finkelman, *Prigg v Pennsylvania and Northern State Courts* (cited in note 149), and Morris, *Free Men All* (cited in note 19).

[170] Cover, *Justice Accused* at 241 (cited in note 10).

[171] Newmyer, *Justice Joseph Story* at 377 (cited in note 1).

creative, state participation in the capture and incarceration of runaway slaves. He wrote:

> We entertain no doubt whatsoever, that the states, in virtue of their general police power, possess full jurisdiction to arrest and restrain runaway slaves, and remove them from their borders, and otherwise to secure themselves against their depredations and evil example, as they certainly may do in cases of idlers, vagabonds, and paupers.[172]

In other words, Story hoped the states would act as slave catchers, arresting and incarcerating fugitives until they could be claimed under the federal law by some putative master or master's agent.

Tied to this invitation for state legislative action, Story made clear his hope that state officers would enforce the federal law. He declared: "As to the authority so conferred upon state magistrates, while a difference of opinion has existed . . . none is entertained by this [C]ourt, that state magistrates may, if they choose, exercise that authority . . . ."[173] This is consistent with his career of favoring a strong national government and hoping that the states would support the federal government, especially on this issue. Story was a thoroughgoing judicial nationalist. *Prigg* could be a triumph of freedom only if northern states refused to enforce federal laws and then passed legislation in opposition to the national government.[174] But everything in Story's judicial and earlier political career suggests that he hated states' rights claims more than even slavery, because states' rights claims were even a greater threat to the Union and the constitutional nationalism he held dear. *Prigg* may have pitted Story's hostility to slavery against his lifelong commitment to constitutional nationalism. If so, his nationalism easily won.

Third, the "triumph of freedom" analysis assumes that Story not only disliked slavery, but was somehow rather a secret abolitionist. Any abolitionist thoughts Story had were surely kept secret. Story's biographer argues for the justice's "hatred of slavery" and "his sincere belief in Christian morals and his general sense of

---

[172] *Prigg* at 625.

[173] Id at 622.

[174] This would in fact happen, and would lead to northern assertions of states' rights. See the arguments of *Ableman v Booth*, 62 US (21 How) 506 (1859). See also Finkelman, *Prigg v Pennsylvania and Northern State Courts* (cited in note 149), and Paul Finkelman, *States Rights North and South in Antebellum America*, in Kermit Hall and James W. Ely, Jr., eds, *An Uncertain Tradition: Constitutionalism and the History of the South* 125–58 (Athens, Ga, 1989).

decency,"[175] which slavery offended. Surely Story disliked slavery, as did most northerners. But Story was not an abolitionist; rather, he opposed the abolitionists because their movement undermined the Union.

Fourth is the suspect source of this analysis. It does not come from Story himself, or a disinterested second party to whom Story made such a claim. Rather, the claim began with the writings of Justice Story's son, William Wetmore. The dutiful son was more committed to antislavery than his father, and may have hoped to salvage the justice's reputation by this posthumous cleansing of the interpretation of *Prigg*. As Kent Newmyer notes, when looking at the evidence there is "the suspicion that a biographer must have of an apologia written by a loving son."[176]

The remaining evidence undermining the "triumph of freedom" argument heightens these suspicions. The same evidence demolishes the third leg of the "triumph of freedom" argument: that *Prigg* provided the North with an opportunity to help shape the federal government's relationship to slavery by remodeling the law in favor of freedom. This evidence suggests both that Story's goal in *Prigg* was to nationalize fugitive slave rendition, and that his son deliberately hid information which undermined the "triumph of freedom" argument.

3. *The power to remodel the law in favor of freedom.* Technically, William Wetmore Story was right. *Prigg* opened the door for a reconsideration of the federal role in the return of fugitive slaves. An abolitionist-dominated Congress could have repealed the 1793 law without replacing it, and left slaveowners with neither state nor federal law at their disposal. Or, a more moderate Congress could have provided due process protections for free blacks, while supporting the right of masters to capture runaways. A new federal law might even have created a statute of limitations on the capture of fugitive slaves, thus protecting people like Margaret Morgan. Theoretically, Congress could have done all those things.

Realistically, all of these things were impossible. In 1842, as I have already noted, slaveholders and their northern allies domi-

---

[175] Newmyer, *Justice Joseph Story* at 373 (cited in note 1). Barbara Holden-Smith argues that "Story's antislavery reputation has been exaggerated." Holden-Smith, 78 Cornell L Rev at 1086 (cited in note 10).

[176] Newmyer, *Justice Joseph Story* at 373 (cited in note 1).

nated the American political system. One half of the U.S. Senate came from slave states. This alone made it impossible to pass any antislavery legislation. On top of this, between 1800 and 1860 every president but John Quincy Adams was neither a slaveholder, former slaveholder, nor a northern democratic doughface who owed his political survival to the South.

Eventually William Wetmore Story's hope that his father's opinion could lead to a remodeling of federal law did occur. But it was not until after 1861, when eleven slave states had left the Union and antislavery was tied to Civil War policy.

Even if the politics of mid-century America had allowed a pro-freedom remodeling of the fugitive slave law, Joseph Story did not want this to happen, and his son knew this to be true when he compiled his father's letters.

Shortly after the Court decided *Prigg*, Story wrote to Senator John Macpherson Berrien of North Carolina about various legislative matters. The letter began with a discussion of their collaboration on pieces of legislation involving federal criminal law and bankruptcy. This evidence suggests the close relationship Story had with Berrien, and thus makes his next suggestion even more important. Story then turned to a draft bill on federal jurisdiction that he had sent to Berrien. He reminded Berrien that he had suggested in that proposed bill

> that *in all cases*, where by the Laws of the U. States, powers were conferred on State Magistrates, the same powers might be exercised by Commissioners appointed by the Circuit Courts. I was induced to make the provision thus general, because State Magistrates now generally refuse to act, & cannot be compelled to act; and the Act of 1793 respecting fugitive slaves confers the power on State Magistrates to act in delivering up Slaves. You saw in the case of Prigg . . . how the duty was evaded, or declined. In conversing with several of my Brethren on the Supreme Court, we all thought that it would be a great improvement, & would tend much to facilitate the recapture of Slaves, if Commissioners of the Circuit Court were clothed with like powers.[177]

Essentially, Story presented Senator Berrien with the solution to the debate over federal exclusivity and the role of the states in enforcing the Fugitive Slave Act. The federal government would

---

[177] Story to Berrien Letter (cited in note 13).

supply the enforcement mechanism, through the appointment of commissioners, and the enforcement would be uniform throughout the nation. The fundamental problem with this idea was how to enact it in a Congress where northerners, who were at least somewhat opposed to slavery, controlled the House of Representatives. Story, the justice, had the answer for Berrien, the politician:

> This might be done without creating the slightest sensation in Congress, if the provision were made general . . . . It would then pass without observation. The Courts would appoint commissioners in every county, & thus meet the practical difficulty now presented by the refusal of State Magistrates. It might be unwise to provoke debate to insert a Special clause in this first section, referring to the fugitive Slave Act of 1793. Suppose you add at the end of the first section: "& shall & may exercise all the powers, that any State judge, Magistrate, or Justice of the Peace may exercise under any other Law or Laws of the United States."[178]

This was not the letter of a man hoping for a triumph of freedom. This was the letter of a justice committed to the aggrandizement of federal power and the return of fugitive slaves. Here he could have both.

This letter is doubly damning for Story and the "triumph of freedom" analysis. In the collection of his father's letters, Story's son reprinted the first part of this letter, which dealt with bankruptcy law, but failed to reprint the material quoted above.[179] William Wetmore Story deliberately hid the evidence which proved that his father neither thought *Prigg* was a "triumph of freedom" nor wanted it to be such. *Prigg* was a triumph of slavery, and the author of the opinion of the court knew so. He also wanted to insure that his handiwork would be implemented.

VI. Joseph Story and Judicial Nationalism

Joseph Story was never a friend of slavery. During the debates over the Missouri Compromise—more than a decade before the abolitionists appeared on the national scene—Story had spoken out against the expansion of the institution west of the Mississippi.

---

[178] Id.

[179] William Story, ed, 2 *Life and Letters of Story* at 404–05 (cited at note 139).

In the 1820s "no other New England statesmen . . . was more fearful of Southern aggression or more determined to resist it."[180] His circuit court opinion in *United States v La Jeune Eugenie*,[181] a case involving the illegal African slave trade, and his charges on the slave trade to New England grand juries,[182] "revealed Story's deep abhorrence of the slave trade and slavery."[183] In the 1830s he privately opposed Texas annexation, and secretly advised public opponents of the annexation,[184] considered it "grossly unconstitutional,"[185] and continued this opposition right up until the annexation took place in 1845. Similarly, although no supporter of the abolitionist movement, Story privately argued that the Gag Rules passed by Congress to prevent the reading of abolitionist petitions were "in effect a denial of the constitutional right of petition."[186]

As Story's best biographer has amply demonstrated, the justice "had spoken out consistently on and off the bench against slavery and the slave trade."[187] He was not an abolitionist—indeed, the Garrisonians often vilified him[188]—but he would happily have seen the institution come to an end.

Why then, did this justice from Massachusetts—who personally found slavery abhorrent—take an unnecessarily pro-slavery position in both *Prigg* and his treatise *Commentaries on the Constitution?*

The answer is rooted in Story's profound constitutional nationalism. In his defense of *Prigg*, Justice Story's son noted that the Fugitive Slave Clause "is in the national Constitution, and is a national guarantee."[189] Story himself made the same point in *Prigg*, noting that the claim to a fugitive slave was a "a case 'arising under the Constitution'" more or less obligating Congress to "prescribe

[180] Newmyer, *Justice Joseph Story* at 350–51 (cited in note 1).

[181] 46 F Cases 832 (CCD Mass, 1822).

[182] Joseph Story, *A Charge to the Grand Juries in Boston, and Providence, 1819* (Boston, 1819), reprinted in Paul Finkelman, ed, 1 *The African Slave Trade* (Garland, 1988). For the discussion of a similar charge in 1838, see Newmyer, *Justice Joseph Story* at 345 (cited in note 1).

[183] Newmyer, *Justice Joseph Story* at 348 (cited in note 1).

[184] Id at 350–51.

[185] Story to Ezekiel Bacon, April 1, 1844, in 2 *Life and Letters of Story* at 481.

[186] Story to Harriet Martineau, Jan 19, 1839, in William Story, ed, 2 *Life and Letters of Story* at 307 (cited in note 139).

[187] Newmyer, *Justice Joseph Story* at 346 (cited in note 1).

[188] Id at 345–46.

[189] William Story, ed, 2 *Life and Letters of Story* at 386 (cited at note 139).

the mode and extent in which it shall be applied, and how, and under what circumstances the proceedings shall afford a complete protection and guaranty to the right."[190] In essence, the justice believed that the Constitution required him to protect the right of masters to recover fugitive slaves. In *Prigg*, Story found that Congress had the exclusive power to regulate the rendition of fugitive slaves. This is one of the earliest examples we have in constitutional law of the preemption doctrine.[191] *Prigg* gave Story an opportunity to use this doctrine to further strengthen the national government. It was an opportunity he could not pass up. The cost of that gain was the freedom of some free blacks and fugitive slaves. But, it was a cost Story was willing to pay, as long as he could explain it by retelling in his own way the stories he told about the Constitutional Convention, the precedents of the state courts, the life of Margaret Morgan, and his own decision.

---

[190] *Prigg* at 616.

[191] Another example might be *Gibbons v Ogden*, 22 US (9 Wheat) 1 (1824). In a slightly different context, T. Alexander Aleinikoff notes a connection between "the early conflict over the scope of the commerce power" and "the explosive question of Congress's power to regulate the internal slave trade." He believes this "helps establish linkages between the nationalist opinions of Chief Justice Marshall in *Gibbons v Ogden* and Justice Story in *Prigg v Pennsylvania. . . .*" T. Alexander Aleinikoff, *A Case for Race-Consciousness*, 91 Colum L Rev 1060 at 1086–87 (1991).

LEA BRILMAYER

FEDERALISM, STATE AUTHORITY, AND THE PREEMPTIVE POWER OF INTERNATIONAL LAW

If law worked through syllogisms, the argument about to be elaborated would have to qualify as one of them:

> 1. All federal laws preempt inconsistent state law under the Supremacy Clause;
> 2. International law is federal law;
> 3. Therefore, international law preempts contrary state law.

The first premise is an unquestionable principle of constitutional law. The second is an "unquestioned" principle of the law of foreign relations.[1] The only additional ingredient needed to invalidate some particular state practice—a state's choice of law rules, for example, or the way it implements the death penalty—would seem

Lea Brilmayer is Benjamin F. Butler Professor, New York University School of Law.

Author's note: I wish to thank readers and colleagues who have contributed critical comments and helpful material: Lori Damrosch, Eleanor Fox, Hal Maier, Greg Fox, Ted Meron, Linda Silberman, Peter Spiro, Carlos Vazquez, Russell Weintraub, David Wippman, and the participants at the New York University Law School Faculty Workshop. Catherine Anderson and Eileen O'Keeffe provided much appreciated research assistance. Research support was generously provided by the Filomen D'Agostino and Max E. Greenberg Faculty Research Fund.

[1] See generally Louis Henkin, *International Law as Law in the United States*, 82 Mich L Rev 1555, 1555 (1984). Henkin uses the word "unquestioned" to refer to the reasoning of *The Paquete Habana*, 175 US 677, 700 (1900) ("international law is part of our law"), discussed at page 300 below. He then explains at greater length why international law is necessarily federal law.

to be good evidence that international law prohibits it.[2] If it's so simple, though, why are courts so erratic when it comes to reviewing state law's conformity to international legal standards? Why doesn't the conclusion automatically follow?

I say "erratic" because there are certain situations where the syllogism's force is recognized. No one doubts that treaty law trumps inconsistent state legislation.[3] There are also certain well-recognized rules of customary international law that states have recognized as binding.[4] Yet there are other sorts of cases—the majority, apparently—in which international legal arguments exist that could have resulted in invalidation of the rules of the constituent states of the Union. The problem is not that courts deciding these cases explicitly reject the power of international law to invalidate a contrary state rule; more striking is the fact that the preemption argument never seems to be discussed. Lawyers don't make it, judges don't consider it, and scholars haven't thus far intervened to ask for explanations.

In an earlier coauthored article, I addressed a parallel phenomenon.[5] For reasons that have never been explained, certain exercises of federal power overseas, namely, the application of U.S. federal law to controversies with international connections, have never been evaluated for consistency with the Due Process Clause. This is true despite the fact that precisely analogous exercises of state power over international cases have been held to due process standards.[6] The reason that these two situations are parallel is as follows. International law has been the favored vehicle for assessing the validity of applying federal law extraterritorially. Constitu-

---

[2] In this article, I will refer to the power of international law to preempt "state" practice. In international law, nations are referred to as "states." Here, however, I use the term to refer only to the constituent states of the United States; the principal actors in international law will be referred to as "nations." The same argument would of course result in preemption of the actions of counties or municipalities.

[3] See page 313 below. The most forceful argument for the different status of treaty and customary international law is surely Phillip Trimble, *A Revisionist View of Customary International Law*, 33 UCLA L Rev 665 (1986).

[4] See pages 313–14 below.

[5] Lea Brilmayer and Charles Norchi, *Federal Extraterritoriality and Fifth Amendment Due Process*, 105 Harv L Rev 1217 (1992).

[6] The due process standards applied to state international choice of law come from the Fourteenth Amendment; see, for example, *Home Insurance v Dick*, 281 US 397 (1930). For that matter, the federal exercise of international personal jurisdiction must also satisfy due process standards derived from the Fifth Amendment. See Brilmayer and Norchi at 1220.

tional due process has not been used, and in fact its potential applicability has never been considered. Conversely, as I will argue here, constitutional law has been the favored vehicle for assessing the validity of exercise of state power with international overtones. International law has not been used, and in fact (as we will see below) its potential applicability has typically been overlooked. Thus, state practices have escaped international law scrutiny just as federal practices have escaped constitutional review.

There is a superficial plausibility to this division of labor. We tend to think of the federal government as having responsibility for international relations, and to envision state governments as addressing legal issues of purely domestic concern. If we add to this assumed assignment of responsibility a tendency to see the Constitution as relevant to domestic concerns and international law as relevant to international concerns, then we come to the conclusion that the Constitution is relevant to what the states do and international law is relevant to the actions of the federal government. This conclusion is supported by the fact that international law itself does not purport to address the actions of the constituent states of a federal union; its subjects are the national states themselves.[7]

But both parts of this argument are wrong. There is no reason to exempt the federal government from due process requirements just because a case involves occurrences in other nations. International cases are also constitutional cases. And, of course, states as well as the federal government engage in actions with international consequences, even if these actions do not involve the high politics of waging war and maintaining peace. They apply their laws and assert their judicial authority over international occurrences; foreign nationals, from refugees to diplomats, are sometimes subject to state authority. Furthermore, in modern times much international law concerns itself with how a government treats its own citizens. States, in other words, cannot be considered exempt from international law on the grounds that what they do is not of international law's concern. While technically speaking, it is the federal government itself that is in violation when states transgress international legal norms, this does not mean that international legal stan-

---

[7] See, for example, *Restatement (Third) of Foreign Relations Law*, § 1, reporter's note 5; § 201 comment (g).

dards do not apply to the actions of states but only that in the eyes of the world community, it is the federal government that is left ultimately with legal responsibility.[8]

The syllogism that I opened with is fairly easy to establish. All components of the proposal that international law be employed to invalidate contrary state law are lying waiting in the case reports. The first section of the article puts together the basic preemption syllogism. In the second section, I distinguish this argument from several others that resemble it, for there are numerous ways that states run afoul of the federal power over foreign relations, and most do not involve violations of international law. But the fact that states must respect these other limits resulting from the federal power over foreign relations does not excuse state violations of international law.

The third section of the discussion identifies two doctrinal areas in which states ought to take international law arguments seriously but do not—one relating to private international law (or, "conflict of laws") and the other relating to international human rights. There are no doubt other possible applications of the argument,

---

[8] See id (federal government is legally responsible for the actions of the constituent states).

In this respect it is interesting to compare the actions of states to the actions of private individuals. There is a sense in which neither constituent states nor private individuals are the primary target of international legal norms; international law, by and large, addresses itself to the actions of the nation as a whole. Yet the situations of states and individuals are rather different. If a private individual tortures someone or commits rape, this is not a violation of international law but a crime. The reason is that only officially organized or sanctioned torture or rape is a violation of human rights. Where a constituent state tortures an individual, there is a violation of international law. True, that violation is attributed to the national government rather than the constituent states, on the grounds that international law applies to national governments and not constituent states. But there is no denying that a violation has occurred, in contrast to where the torture or rape was committed by an individual.

In the discussion below, I will sometimes refer to "states" that violate international law. It would probably be more technically correct to speak in terms of states engaging in actions that bring the federal government into violation of international law, because technically speaking the violation is the federal government's, which has failed to prevent the state violation from occurring. Yet this way of speaking is very cumbersome, and it is hard to see what difference it makes, for present purposes, whether one adopts one phrasing rather than the other.

The same problem arises where constituent states engage in actions that amount to violation of U.S. treaty obligations. While technically speaking it is the United States as a whole that has violated the treaty, it is easier to refer to the problem as one where the state has violated the treaty. Moreover, nothing apparently hinges on which phrasing is used. In particular, the fact that technically it is the United States that is in violation when a state violates the treaty norm does not mean that treaty law is not binding on the states. It clearly is, under the Supremacy Clause. See page 313 below. I am suggesting nothing more nor less for customary international law.

but these two show the potential it has for altering the course of state practice with international overtones. Finally I consider whether there might be some explanation for the disinclination to test state actions by international legal standards. The primary basis for reluctance to employ customary international law against the states is that this is a task for the federal elected branches to undertake. This objection can be met by preserving for those branches a right to reverse judicial decisions invalidating state practices. My proposed resolution is a presumption that Congress will ordinarily want the states to comply with international law unless it has explicitly stated otherwise; state law inconsistent with international law will, therefore, typically be preempted.

I. THE BASIC SYLLOGISM

Readers whose main professional attention is directed to domestic legal affairs may react to the entire argument, at the outset, with skeptical surprise. What (they might exclaim) does international law have to do with what goes on in local courts? International law (if in fact it exists—some of course deny the very meaningfulness of the concept) is something "out there," something that can be safely quarantined, and then forgotten.[9] The weakest link in the syllogism is the second premise, the claim that international legal rules have the status of federal law. There are two parts to this premise: the claim that international law has the status of *American* law, and the claim that it is American *federal* law.

The debate over the proper status to assign international law—whether it is part of American law at all—has traditionally been between "monists" and "dualists."[10] The dualist sees international and domestic law as two wholly independent systems. The fact that domestic law conflicts with international law does not have any implications for the former. Rules of international law can come to have domestic legal status, but only through their explicit adoption into "municipal" (i.e., domestic) law by the authoritative

---

[9] The question whether international law is "really law" is, of course, one of the oldest debates in the entire subject. For relatively recent treatments of the subject, see, for example, Antony D'Amato, *Is International Law Really "Law"?* 79 Nw U L Rev 1293 (1984); Louis Henkin, *How Nations Behave* at 39–87 (Columbia, 2d ed 1979).

[10] See generally, Mark Janis, *An Introduction to International Law* at 83–84 (Little, Brown, 2d ed 1993).

organs of domestic government. The monist, in contrast, sees domestic and international law as part of the same legal system. International law has superior status and invalidates contrary domestic legislation. Thus a monist would see international legal rules as limiting the power of governments (both state and federal) automatically and of their own force, while the dualist would insist on some sort of authoritative enactment before international law could be used to assess the validity of state action.

The monists have gotten much of what they want. In the oft-cited case of *The Paquete Habana*, the United States Supreme Court essentially rejected the central dualist assumption, stating:

> International law is part of our law, and must be administered by the courts of justice of appropriate jurisdiction, as often as questions of right depending upon it are duly presented for their determination. For this purpose, where there is no treaty, and no controlling executive or legislative act or judicial decision, resort must be had to the customs and usages of civilized nations.[11]

International lawyers have been quoting *The Paquete Habana* ever since. And the courts, by and large, seem to have been listening. As Henkin summarized approvingly on the occasion of the hundredth anniversary of the *Harvard Law Review*, "[i]n the eighty-seven years since *The Paquete Habana*, the Court repeatedly has emphasized that international law is the law of the land, and it has given effect to principles of customary international law as the law of the United States."[12]

The Paquete Habana involved international law applicable to actions of the federal government, but all indications are that it is at least equally relevant regarding the actions of the states. In 1940 the United States Supreme Court cited the case in upholding Florida's efforts to regulate sponge fishing outside its territorial waters, hold-

---

[11] 175 US 677, 700 (1900). There is an interpretation of the case that is supportive of the dualist position. It is that international law is of its own nature not part of domestic law, but that our legal system has adopted international law. This interpretation, while philosophically consistent with dualism, leads to exactly the same result as the monist position; it is a model of complete incorporation of international law.

[12] Louis Henkin, *The Constitution and United States Sovereignty: A Century of Chinese Exclusion and Its Progeny*, 100 Harv L Rev 853, 873 (1987). See generally, Edwin Dickinson, *The Law of Nations as Part of the National Law of the United States* (Parts I and II), 101 U Pa L Rev 26, 792 (1952).

ing that such regulation was permissible because the defendant was a Florida resident:

> International law is a part of our law and as such is the law of all States of the Union (*The Paquete Habana*, 175 U.S. 677, 700), but . . . the United States is not debarred by any rule of international law from governing the conduct of its own citizens upon the high seas or even in foreign countries when the rights of other nations or their nationals are not infringed. . . . If the United States may control the conduct of its citizens upon the high seas, we see no reason why the State of Florida may not likewise govern the conduct of its citizens upon the high seas with respect to matters in which the State has a legitimate interest and where there is no conflict with acts of Congress.[13]

The remaining question is whether customary international law is federal law. Henkin points out that this question was not definitively answered until surprisingly recently.[14] That treaties are federal is obvious from the wording of the Supremacy Clause; but that clause does not say whether customary international law is state or federal.[15] Depending on the view one takes of what makes international legal norms authoritative, Henkin argues, one might come to either conclusion. If one understood international law to be part of the common law that the various states of the union received from England after the Revolutionary War, then it was state law just as tort or contract law was. Alternatively, international law might come to govern by virtue of our independence as a sovereign nation; if so, it took as its domain the activities of the federal government. Henkin argues, moreover, that even if international law started out as state common law, the adoption of the federal Constitution would have federalized it, by referring in the text to the various international functions of the new nations as essentially federal.[16]

---

[13] *Skiriotes v Florida*, 313 US 69, 73–77 (1940).

[14] Louis Henkin, *International Law: International Law as Law in the United States*, 82 Mich L Rev 1555, 1556 (1984).

[15] The Supremacy Clause states that "This Constitution, and the Laws of the United States which shall be made in Pursuance thereof; and all Treaties made, or which shall be made, under the Authority of the United States, shall be the supreme Law of the Land; and the Judges in every State shall be bound thereby, any Thing in the Constitution or Laws of any State to the Contrary notwithstanding." US Const, Art VI, cl 2.

[16] For example, the judicial power of the United States was extended to cases arising under treaties, cases affecting ambassadors, admiralty and maritime cases, and controversies involving foreign states and their citizens. US Const, Art III, § 2. US Const, Art I, § 8, cl 10 also gave Congress the power to define offenses against the law of nations.

Prior to the decision of *Erie Railroad v Tompkins*,[17] there was no real need to characterize international law as definitively state or federal; under the jurisprudence that then prevailed, it was enough that international law was part of the general common law. *Erie Railroad*, however, forced the issue out into the open with its holding that no such general common law existed. While a few decisions treated international law as state law,[18] it came gradually to be explicitly recognized that international law must be federal. The final disposition came in *Banco Nacional de Cuba v Sabbatino*.[19] That case involved the so-called act of state doctrine, which holds that the courts of other nations will not assess the validity of official acts undertaken by a sovereign within its own territory.

The Supreme Court did not claim that international law compelled it to apply the act of state doctrine: the Court characterized the doctrine as a consequence of neither international law nor the constitutional text, but as a doctrine with "constitutional underpinnings . . . aris[ing] out of the basic relationships between branches of government in a system of separation of powers."[20] But in its explanation of why the act of state doctrine was a matter of federal law, the Court supplied the logic necessary for treating international law as federal law as well:

> [W]e are constrained to make it clear that an issue concerned with a basic choice regarding the competence and function of the Judiciary and the National Executive in ordering our relationships with other members of the international community must be treated exclusively as an aspect of federal law. It seems fair to assume that the Court did not have rules like the act of state doctrine in mind when it decided *Erie R Co v Tompkins*. Soon thereafter, Professor Philip C. Jessup, now a judge of the International Court of Justice, recognized the potential dangers were *Erie* extended to legal problems affecting international relations. He cautioned that rules of international law should not be left to divergent and perhaps parochial state interpretations. His basic rationale is equally applicable to the act of state doctrine.[21]

---

[17] 304 US 64 (1938).

[18] See, for example, *Bergman v De Sieyes*, 170 F2d 360 (2d Cir 1948).

[19] 376 US 398 (1963).

[20] Id at 421–23.

[21] Id at 425, citing Phillip C. Jessup, *The Doctrine of Erie Railroad v Tompkins Applied to International Law*, 33 Am J Intl L 740 (1939). See also Henry Friendly, *In Praise of Erie—and of the New Federal Common Law*, 39 NYU L Rev 383 (1964).

Henkin, after developing interesting theoretical arguments on both sides of the issue, reached the same conclusion: International law, obviously, was not state law. The law of nations was the law of the political community of States developed by the practice of States

For present purposes, a great deal turns on the recognition that international law is federal law as opposed to something else. Merely to say that international law is "part of our law" says little about how all of these different sorts of legal rules of "our law" are hierarchically arranged. There has been much debate about the relative status of customary international law and other varieties of federal authority. May the President violate customary international law? What do we do when customary international law conflicts with a federal statue?[22] But none of these issues need be addressed when state and international law are inconsistent, so long as the federal characterization sticks. When state and federal law conflict, it does not matter whether the state law is a product of executive, legislative, or judicial decision. It also does not matter what sort of federal law is at issue; whether it is executive, legislative, or judicial. *All* federal law trumps *all* state law. If international law enjoys that elevated status, it also will prevail.[23]

The point to be emphasized here is that employment of international legal norms to challenge state practices ought to be much

---

and modified by State treaties, and it was the United States, not the individual states, that was the relevant national entity for international purposes. Questions of international law engaged the responsibility of the United States toward other nations. It made no sense that questions of international law should be treated as questions of state rather than federal law; that they could be determined independently, finally, and differently by the courts of fifty states, and differently also by federal courts for their own, "nondiversity" purposes; that, whereas the interpretation of a U.S. treaty was a federal question to be decided finally by the Supreme Court for all courts (and domestically, at least, for the political branches as well), determinations of customary international law by state courts were not reviewable by the Supreme Court.

[22] On the relative power of customary international law and federal statute, see the *Restatement (Third) of Foreign Relations Law*, § 115, comment (d) ("It has . . . not been authoritatively determined whether a rule of customary international law that developed after, and is inconsistent with, an earlier statute or international agreement of the United States should be given effect as the law of the United States"); Jack Goldklang, *Back on Board the Paquete Habana: Resolving the Conflict Between Statutes and Customary International Law*, 25 Va J Intl L 143 (1984).

On the power of the President to override customary international law, see, for example, *Agora: May the President Violate Customary International Law?* 80 Am J Intl L 913 (1986); Michael Glennon, *Raising the Paquete Habana: Is Violation of Customary International Law by the Executive Unconstitutional?* 80 Nw U L Rev 321 (1985). Glennon, interestingly, proposes an answer that is somewhat similar to the suggestion here about how state law and customary international law should be reconciled. He claims that the President may only violate international law when so authorized by Congress; I am arguing, similarly, that the states may only violate international law when there is authorization from Congress. The difference between our two arguments is that Glennon must deal with separation of powers concerns—with the respective roles of courts, Congress, and the executive—while I need only face federalism objections. In this respect, my argument should be much the easier one to make, given the states' limited authority in the international area.

[23] That is the position of the *Restatement (Third) of Foreign Relations Law;* see, for example, § 111(1), comment (d) and reporter's note 3; § 115, comment (e).

easier than the employment of international legal norms to challenge federal practices. Attempts to use international law to challenge federal practices and legislation raise difficult questions of separation of powers, for there is substantial controversy over whether the courts as opposed to the President or Congress should have the final word on international relations. But challenging state practices and legislation raises, at most, concerns of federalism—and these are very weak when international relations are at stake. This is particularly so given that one of the primary historical reasons for granting the federal government foreign relations power was to control the states, who during the period of the Articles of Confederation had violated treaty obligations and international law with impunity.[24] Henkin did not seem to be exaggerating when he wrote, "federalism . . . appeared irrelevant to the conduct of foreign affairs even before it began to appear to be a wasting force in American life generally."[25]

II. Comparable Inhibitions on State Power in the International Arena

Our Constitution assigns to the federal government a virtual monopoly over international relations. The inhibitions on the exercise of state power in the international arena are substantial. But precisely because this is so clear, we must be careful to distinguish the argument here from a number of comparable arguments resting on similar assumptions, which have slightly different contours and

---

[24] Glennon, 80 Nw U L Rev 321, 333 n 79 (cited in note 22); Peter Spiro, *Adding Teeth to United States Ratification of the Covenant on Civil and Political Rights: The International Human Rights Conformity Act of 1993*, 42 DePaul L Rev 1209, 1223 (1993); Carlos Vazquez, *Treaty-Based Rights and Remedies of Individuals*, 92 Colum L Rev 1082, 1102-03 (1992); Charles Siegal, *Deference and Its Dangers: Congress' Power to "Define . . . Offenses Against the Law of Nations,"* 21 Vand J Intl L 865, 868 (1988); Carlos Vazquez, *The Four Doctrines of Self-Executing Treaties* (forthcoming).

See also *Boos v Barry*, 485 US 312, 322–23 (1988) (stating that as a general matter the United States has a vital national interest in complying with international law, and discussing the interest in protecting diplomats as an inadequate basis for portions of a District of Columbia statute prohibiting picketing, harassing, or intimidating foreign officials).

[25] He continues,

> Foreign relations are national relations. The language, the spirit and the history of the Constitution deny the States authority to participate in foreign affairs, and its construction by the courts has steadily reduced the ways in which the States can affect American foreign relations.

Foreign Affairs and the Constitution 228 (1972).

consequences. One might be misled into assuming that states already pay due regard to international law, simply because other sorts of limits on international exercise of state power are generally adhered to. But these other limits on the international exercise of state power are not cases in which states have been required to comply with customary international law; they are simply cases in which the states must comply with federal foreign relations policy.

There are at least five different ways in which international law might seem to limit the states, but which on closer examination involve something else. The first has to do with federal constitutional limits on what states do in the foreign relations area; the second with federal legislative preemption of state power with international consequences; the third with use of international law to interpret constitutional provisions that place restrictions on what states may do; the fourth with incorporation of international law into federal statutes; and the fifth with federal common law's reliance on international legal norms. None of these examples rebuts the general proposition that states have not been systematically required to comply with customary international law.

A. CONSTITUTIONAL PREEMPTION

The first example of doctrinal limits that might be confused with a requirement that states conform to customary international law involves federal constitutional provisions that disqualify states from acting in certain areas having international overtones. Several constitutional provisions having this feature are found in Article I, section 10,[26] which prohibits states from entering into treaties, alliances, or confederations, and from laying imposts or duties on imports or exports without the consent of Congress. Unless Congress has consented, states are also forbidden to lay any "Duty of Tonnage" or to enter into agreements with a foreign power, or to engage in war.

The thrust of all of these limitations is to restrict state power to act internationally. While sovereign nations possess the power to

---

[26] US Const, Art I, § 10: "No State shall enter into any Treaty, Alliance, or Confederation; grant Letters of Marque and Reprisal; coin Money; emit Bills of Credit; make any Thing but gold and silver Coin a Tender in Payment of Debts; pass any Bill of Attainder, ex post facto Law, or Law impairing the Obligations of Contracts, or grant any Title of Nobility."

undertake all of these activities, the states of the Union do not. Their foreign affairs are conducted, on their behalf, by the federal government.

B. STATUTORY PREEMPTION ANALYSIS

The second example of a federalism limit on what states may do in the international arena concerns the preemption of state law which conflicts with the federal government's exercise of its constitutionally granted foreign relations power. A good example can be found in the regulation of aliens. In a number of cases, state efforts to regulate aliens have been invalidated on the grounds that immigration regulation is for the federal government, and not the states.[27] Not all regulations of aliens are forbidden to the states.[28] But the difficulty in determining whether a particular statute is preempted is no different here than in any other context in which state law arguably intrudes on federal prerogatives; the question is whether the state regulations interfere with the accomplishment of the federal objectives. In addition to treatment of aliens, one well-known case preempted state laws that interfered with federal policy on the recognition of the Soviet Union and its nationalization of industry.[29] When a state strikes out on its own into the field of international relations, it risks angering other nations and attracting their wrath to the nation as a whole.[30]

There are, roughly speaking, two different ways that state laws intruding into foreign relations may be preempted. One is that

---

[27] *Takahashi v Fish and Game Commn*, 334 US 410, 420 (1948); *Hines v Davidowitz*, 312 US 52, 73 (1941).

[28] See, for example, *De Canas v Bica*, 424 US 351 (1976); *Clark v Allen*, 331 US 503 (1947); but see, *Zschernig v Miller*, 389 US 429 (1968).

[29] *United States v Pink*, 315 US 203 (1941); *United States v Belmont*, 301 US 324 (1937).

The action of New York in this case amounts in substance to a rejection of a part of the policy underlying recognition by this nation of Soviet Russia. Such power is not accorded a State in our constitutional system. . . . [T]here are limitations on the sovereignty of the States. No State can rewrite our foreign policy to conform to its own domestic policies. Power over external affairs is not shared by the States; it is vested in the national government exclusively.

Pink, 315 US at 233.

[30] Although states do not engage in large-scale diplomacy, the power of state actions to alienate American allies should nonetheless not be underestimated. See, for example, Peter Smith, *SOS Is an Insult to California Voters*, San Diego Union-Tribune (September 25, 1994), p G-3 (describing Mexican government reaction to anti–illegal immigrant initiative on California ballot).

some particular federal foreign relations policy has been adopted, and state legal rules conflict with it. But a second arises where the federal government has not committed itself to any particular foreign policy on the issue at all. State law is preempted merely because it interferes with the uniformity of federal foreign relations policy. In *Japan Line, Ltd v County of Los Angeles*, the Supreme Court invalidated a tax imposed on foreign commerce; the test imposed was whether the tax prevented the federal government from "speaking with one voice when regulating commercial relations with foreign governments."[31]

C. USING INTERNATIONAL LAW IN CONSTITUTIONAL INTERPRETATION

Two examples illustrate how international norms might be employed in constitutional interpretation. In *Burnham v Superior Court*,[32] the Court unanimously upheld "tag" jurisdiction, under which an individual who is served with process within the state is subject to its jurisdiction. Justice Scalia, for the Court, rejected as "imperious" the possibility that judges might employ "subjective" standards to invalidate a long tradition of state use of transient presence as a basis for jurisdiction. Professor Russell Weintraub, writing in response, disagreed:

> I focus on his argument that declaring transient jurisdiction unconstitutional would be "subjective" and "imperious". One way to rebut this argument would be to identify an objective basis for casting transient jurisdiction beyond the pale of civilized procedure. One such objective basis comes from the fact that the use of the defendant's temporary presence in the forum as grounds for personal jurisdiction is contrary to the consensus of civilized nations and, if used against foreigners, may violate international law.[33]

Indeed, the *Restatement of Foreign Relations Law* had explicitly concluded that tag jurisdiction was a violation of international law.[34]

The second example concerns the argument that capital punish-

---

[31] *Japan Lines, Ltd, v County of Los Angeles*, 441 US 434, 451 (1979). For an interesting list of examples in which cities and states have formulated their own foreign relations policies, see Peter Spiro, *Taking Foreign Policy Away from the Feds*, 1988 Wash Q 191 (Winter, 1988).

[32] 110 S Ct 2105 (1990).

[33] *An Objective Basis for Rejecting Transient Jurisdiction*, 22 Rutgers L J 611, 611–12 (1991).

[34] See § 421(2)(a), comment (e), reporters' notes at 310–11.

ment (at least in certain circumstances) might violate international law. *Thompson v Oklahoma*[35] dealt with execution of offenders who were less than sixteen years old at the time of their offenses. In reversing the death sentence of a youth of fifteen, the Court cited international practice:

> The conclusion that it would offend civilized standards of decency to execute a person who was less than 16 years old at the time of his or her offense is consistent with the view that have been expressed by respected professional organizations, by other nations that share our Anglo-American heritage, and by the leading members of the Western European community.[36]

In two footnotes, the Court added, "We have previously recognized the relevance of the views of the international community in determining whether a punishment is cruel and unusual"[37] and also recognized that three major human rights treaties explicitly prohibited juvenile death penalties.[38] None of those three had been ratified by the United States. Subsequently, Justice Blackmun argued in a dissent from a denial of certiorari that international practice, likewise, prohibited the execution of the mentally retarded.[39] Despite the unsteady reception of such arguments, civil libertarians have consistently asserted that the most important and successful use of international norms is to give meaning to vague constitutional provisions.[40]

---

[35] 487 US 815 (1987).

[36] Id at 830.

[37] Id.

[38] Id at 831.

[39] *Wills v Texas*, 114 S Ct 1867 (1994). This line of reasoning has since been rejected; see page 325 below.

International rights norms have also been cited in opposition to racial discrimination. See, for example, *Hurd v Hodge*, 162 F2d 233, 245 (DC Cir 1947) (Edgerton dissenting) (relying on portions of the Charter of the United Nations requiring respect for human rights and prohibiting racial discrimination); *Oyama v State of California* 332 US 633, 277 (1948) (Black and Douglas concurring). Now, of course, such challenges are more likely to be framed in terms of the Fourteenth Amendment.

[40] See, for example, Kathryn Burke, Sandra Coliver, Connie De La Vega, and Stephen Rosenbaum, *Application of International Human Rights Law in State and Federal Courts*, 18 Tex Intl L Rev 291, 322 ("Perhaps the most successful use of international human rights law in state and federal courts has been its assistance in defining rights under state and federal law"); Paul Hoffman, *The Application of International Human Rights Law in State Courts: A View from California*, 18 Intl Law 61 (1984) ("My remarks will focus on the use of international human rights law in what I consider to be the manner most likely to be accepted by California's judges; namely, to provide specific content to broad norms such as equal protection due process of law"); Anne Bayefsky and Joan Fitpatrick, *International Human Rights*

D. INCORPORATION BY STATUTE

A fourth federalism-inspired way that international law might appear to bind the states is through the incorporation of international legal standards into federal statutes.[41] One well-known case along these lines was *Filartiga v Pena-Irala*, in which the plaintiff sought damages for torture committed by Paraguayan officials in Paraguay.[42] 28 USC 1350 provided for federal district court jurisdiction over "any civil action by an alien for a tort only, committed in violation of the law of nations or a treaty of the United States." The jurisdictional grant was authorized by the federal constitutional provision giving the federal government the power "To define and punish Piracies and Felonies committed on the high Seas, and Offenses against the Law of Nations."[43]

The *Filartiga* court explicitly considered international legal norms in making the determination whether a violation of the law of nations had been alleged. It cited *The Paquete Habana* for the proposition that courts should consult international customary law as well as treaty law, and that international law was not static (so that modern rather than only ancient rules of international law had to be considered).[44] It cited numerous sources for the proposition that torture was a violation of international law.

> The prohibition is clear and unambiguous, and admits of no distinction between treatment of aliens and citizens. Accordingly, we must conclude that the dictum . . . to the effect that "violations of international law do not occur when the aggrieved parties are nationals of the acting state," is clearly out of tune with the current usage and practice of international law.[45]

Law in United States Courts: A Comparative Perspective, 14 Mich J Intl L 1, 23 (1992) (discussing ways that international law has been used to interpret American law); Jordan Paust, *On Human Rights: The Use of Human Rights Precepts in U.S. History and the Right to an Effective Remedy in Domestic Courts*, 10 Mich J Intl L 543, 650 (1989) ("It is clear that the Supreme Court, as most courts, most often utilizes human rights as legally relevant standards or juridic aids for interpretation of constitution, customary or statutory norms.").

[41] Bayefsky and Fitzpatrick at 6 (cited in note 40).

[42] *Filartiga v Pena-Irala*, 630 F2d 876 (1980). But cf *Tel-Oren v Libyan Arab Republic*, 726 F2d 774 (DC Cir 1984). Note that it is not clear that the statute in *Filartiga* really counts as a limit on state action; instead, what it is is a jurisdictional grant to the federal courts. Other examples of incorporation by statute are provided in Ralph Steinhardt, *The Role of International Law as a Canon of Statutory Construction*, 43 Vand L Rev 1103, 1110 (1990).

[43] US Const, Art I, § 8, cl 10.

[44] 630 F2d at 880–81.

[45] Id at 884.

While other courts have disagreed with *Filartiga*'s result, it has, in most respects, been approved by subsequent federal statute.[46]

E. FEDERAL COMMON LAW

International law also plays a role in shaping federal common law. International law has been employed for many years in supplying rules of decision for controversies between the states. It has been extensively relied on to fix locations for the borders between the states and to allocate water rights. In *Connecticut v Massachusetts*, for example, the Court cited international law as a source of authority to decide whether Massachusetts might divert waters from the watershed of the Connecticut river to provide water for the Boston area.

> For the decision of suits between States, federal, state and international law are considered and applied by the Court as the exigencies of the particular case may require.[47]

While early cases seemed to suggest that international law is applicable to such cases by its own force,[48] later cases have clarified that interstate boundary and water cases are decided according to federal common law.[49] International law provides a guide in determining the shape that federal common law will take.

In each of these five doctrinal areas, state options are limited in some way as a consequence of federal supremacy, and there is something "international" about the rule with which state law must comply. None of these five examples, however, is really a case of states being required to comply with international law.

In the first two cases, states are deprived of the power to conduct foreign relations, either because some activities are generally forbidden to them under the Constitution (declaring war, imposing import duties) or because federal foreign relations policy occupies a particular area. The things that the states are forbidden to do are

---

[46] Torture Victim Protection Act of 1991, Pub L No 102-256, 106 Stat 73 (1991). The new statute is not precisely analogous because it provides its own definition of torture.

[47] *Connecticut v Massachusetts*, 282 US 660, 671 (1931).

[48] See, for example, *Kansas v Colorado*, 206 US 46, 97 (1906) (citing *The Paquete Habana*); *New Jersey v Delaware*, 291 US 361, 378 (1933) (employing international principles to decide title case because "[w]hen independence was achieved, the precepts to be obeyed in the division of the waters were those of international law").

[49] *Hinderlider v La Plata River & Cherry Creek Ditch Co.*, 304 US 92, 110 (1938).

not necessarily violations of international law, however. International law does not prohibit the laying of duties; and, depending on the circumstances, it may not prohibit declarations of war. It does not mandate the act of state doctrine, which *Sabbatino* held binding upon the states as an American federal principle of foreign relations. The prohibitions on state conduct of foreign relations are thus in some respects much broader than international law would require.

Conversely, though, they are also, in some respects, narrower. American jurisprudence recognizes that Congress has the authority to violate international law;[50] and if Congress did so (e.g., by adopting a statute violating treaty obligations), then the states would presumably be required to follow Congressional directives rather than their view of what international law required.[51] The exclusion of the states from conducting foreign relations says almost nothing about the obligation of states to comply with international law.

The other three come closer to involving international law, as opposed to the conduct of foreign relations. But in none of them is international law operative directly by way of the Supremacy Clause. Where international human rights norms are used to interpret vague constitutional provisions, they serve mainly as a reposi-

---

[50] See generally *Restatement (Third) of Foreign Relations Law* § 115. While this authority is well recognized in the cases (see, e.g., *The Chinese Exclusion Case*, 130 US 581 (1889)), it does not mean that the international obligation is extinguished; a violation remains, for which the United States will be answerable in the international community. *Restatement (Third)* § 115, comment (b).

[51] Perhaps the closest link between federal supremacy in foreign relations and a requirement that states not violate international law would be as follows. Where a state does something that violates international law, this is likely to offend other nations. Thus, international law violations tend, per se, to interfere with federal foreign policy control. This argument would not apply where the violation of international law was itself required by a Congressional enactment, for then the states would simply be stepping in line with federal foreign relations policy.

However, it is not clear that a state violation of international law will inevitably have an effect on foreign relations. In particular, the cases I will examine in Part IIIA (page 315) below deal with state conduct that, even if it is a violation of international law, is unlikely to give rise to diplomatic incidents. In such cases, if state laws are to be challenged, it must be because they violate international law, not necessarily because they jeopardize federal supremacy in our relations with other countries. One way to describe the relation between these two points—violation of international law and inconsistency with federal foreign relations policy—may be that a state violation of international law is presumed to be inconsistent with federal foreign relations policy, and will be held preempted unless the federal elected branches have indicated otherwise. This approach obviates the need for a case-by-case determination of whether some particular state violation is inconsistent with federal foreign relations policy. It leads to essentially the conclusion of section IVB (page 332) below, applying the "*Charming Betsy*" presumption to state practices.

tory of wisdom on which judges faced with difficult constitutional questions may draw. If the substantive constitutional provision in question did not exist, then the international norms would not be relevant; and to the extent that different principles of constitutional interpretation point toward different interpretations of the provision, the international norms are not persuasive. Where federal common law draws on international norms, it employs them only by analogy and not as binding law. Indeed, some of the federal common law uses of international norms are distinctly different from the ways that international law itself purports to apply; international law does not purport to govern, for example, water allocation or boundary disputes between the constituent states of a federal union.[52]

It is also true that international law only addresses directly what the federal government does and technically does not purport to address the international actions of constituent states. But when we say that international law does not govern what constituent states do to one another, we mean that the international community does not care about (say) the respective water rights of California and Arizona. To say that international law does not address the respective claims of California and Mexico would, by contrast, be extremely misleading. California's appropriation of water properly belonging to Mexico does constitute a violation of international law, even if the violation is technically held against the United States as a whole, rather than California specifically. Thus it makes sense to say that international law governs states' international actions directly by way of the Supremacy Clause, even though international law does not really govern states' interstate actions except by analogy.

Statutory incorporation of international norms probably bears the closest resemblance to the direct application of international law to the states. But, as with federal common law that incorporates international legal standards by analogy, the international community has no interest in whether states violate international norms incorporated into federal statutes. Moreover, there is no general federal statute requiring states to adhere to international law. While the Alien Tort Claims Act requires courts to employ the law of nations as a rule of decision in particular sorts of cases, this is a

---

[52] See, for example, the *Restatement (Third) of Foreign Relations Law* § 1, reporter's note 5 (constituent states of the union are not states for purposes of international law).

far cry from a rule that states must comply with international law as a general matter.[53]

The question remains whether there is any case support for the syllogism I have proposed. The best evidence for the syllogism—the most apt example of its application—concerns the requirement that states comply with treaty law. The limitations imposed by treaties need not be within Congress's legislative power. In *Missouri v Holland*,[54] for example, the state complained that the Migratory Bird Treaty was an unconstitutional interference with the rights reserved to the states by the Tenth Amendment. The Court held that, even if true, this would not dispose of the treaty, which had to be evaluated as an exercise of the treaty power. But probably the best way to understand the treaty power is that the states must adhere to treaties not because international law so requires, but because by adopting a treaty the federal government is engaging in the exercise of its foreign relation power. If Congress and the executive make a decision that (say) the United States will limit its whaling in international waters so long as other nations do likewise, the states are bound to go along not because international law requires them to comply with treaty obligations, but because only Congress (not the states) can alter this federal foreign relations policy.

In fact, few instances exist in which courts have squarely relied on customary international law to invalidate the actions of the states.[55] Are there areas of state practice that conflict with international law, and which would have to be invalidated if the preemp-

---

[53] Most important, it serves primarily to provide jurisdiction to the federal courts to hear cases brought by aliens against other nations that have allegedly violated human rights.

[54] 252 US 416 (1920).

[55] See, for example, *Lareau v Manson*, 507 F Supp 1177 (D Conn 1980); *In re Alien Children Education Litigation*, 501 F Supp 544 (SD Texas 1980). Both of these cases relied on a mix of customary law and international conventions which the United States either had not signed and/or had signed but not ratified.

Another possible example would be the law of diplomatic, consular, or sovereign immunity. These topics are now mostly governed by statute or treaty; see Phillip Trimble, *A Revisionist View of Customary International Law*, 33 UCLA L Rev 665, 690 (1986). Yet there are occasional cases relying only on international customary law. See, for example, *Hannes v Kingdom of Romania Monopolies Inst.*, 260 AD 189, 20 NYS 2d 825 (NY App Div 1940), *Republic of Argentina v City of New York*, 250 NE 2d 698, 25 NY 2d 252 (1969). Prior to the adoption of the Constitution, assault on a diplomat was punishable as a common law crime. *Republic v De Longchamps*, 1 US (1 Dall) 111 (1784) (citing the law of nations, which was held to form a part of the municipal law of Pennsylvania).

See also *Peters v McKay*, 195 Ore 412, 238 P2d 225, 246 P2d 585 (1951); *Caravas v California*, 40 Cal 2d 33; 250 P2d 593 (1952) (international law applies to toll statute of limitations during time of war).

tive power of international law were taken seriously? While there may not be too many, there are definitely some.

III. Implications and Applications

When, in 1951, the Supreme Court of Oregon was faced with a dispute necessitating its making a determination of international law, it expressed dismay over the novelty of the position in which it found itself. The case turned on whether the applicable statute of limitations had been tolled during wartime; the petitioners claimed that as a matter of "common law and international law" the limitations period was suspended, regardless of the Oregon statutory provision.

> This proposition presented issues of extreme delicacy which are entirely new to the jurisprudence of this and many other states. In the entire 189 volumes of the Oregon Reports, not a single case has been digested under the heading of International Law, yet, the rule is firmly established and uniformly recognized that "International law is a part of our law and as such is the law of all States of the Union" (The Paquete Habana, 175 U.S. 677). . . . [56]

The court may have exaggerated slightly, for there are scattered pockets of state adherence to customary international law; respect for consular and diplomatic immunity provides one set of examples.[57] But this is picking nits. By and large, international law hardly puts in an appearance in the state case reports.

Why should that be so? Surely one reason is that much of international law is likely simply to be of little relevance to the states. Because the foreign affairs of the nation are conducted almost entirely by the federal government, states have fewer opportunities

---

[56] It continued,

> In essence, the rule appears to be that international law is a part of the law of every state which is enforced by its courts without any constitutional or statutory act of incorporation by reference, and while a court may be without jurisdiction to enforce international law in a given case by reason of some controlling statute, nevertheless, relevant provisions of the law of nations are legally paramount whenever international rights and duties are involved before a court having jurisdiction to enforce them.

Peters v McKay, 195 Ore 412, 424; 238 P2d 225 (1951). The court did decide to follow international law.

[57] See note 54 supra.

to run afoul of international legal norms. The resulting lack of acquaintance with international norms undoubtedly also leads lawyers to fail to recognize international legal arguments that do arise, and to fail to present them to the courts. Yet, there are some areas in which state actions have the potential to violate international law. I will discuss two: "private international law" doctrines concerning a state's right to assert its judicial authority or apply its law to ordinary civil disputes, and "public international law" norms of internationally protected human rights.

A. THE PRIVATE INTERNATIONAL LAW OF CHOICE OF LAW

When we think of the subject of conflict of laws, we tend to think primarily in terms of state common law or perhaps constitutional limitations. Conflicts courses deal with traditional choice of law theories such as Joseph Beale's "vested rights" approach, set out in the *First Restatement of Conflicts*, and with modern approaches such as governmental interest analysis, the *Second Restatement* "most significant contacts" approach, the "better law" theory, and the like.[58] An important part of the subject is devoted to the circumstances in which the Due Process Clause of the Fourteenth Amendment or perhaps the Article IV Full Faith and Credit Clause are violated. Rarely does the typical conflicts course stop to ask about the relevance of international law.[59]

That this should be the case is mildly surprising. Elliot Cheatham recognized in an early article that international law might serve as a source for choice of law rules.[60] And "long before the

---

[58] For a general description of both traditional and modern choice of law theory, see Lea Brilmayer, *Conflict of Laws: Foundations and Future Directions* (Little, Brown, 2d ed 1995).

[59] Increasingly, though, the popular casebooks on the subject include material on conflicts in the international setting and on the relevance of international law. See, for example, Roger Cramton, David Currie, Herma Kay, and Larry Kramer, *Conflict of Laws: Cases, Materials, Questions* ch 8 (5th ed 1993). What is striking, however, in light of the thesis of the present article, is the fact that such material invariable deals with the limits on federal extraterritoriality, rather than the limits on state choice of law.

Interestingly, there are occasional cases in which courts have considered applying the "one voice" rationale of *Zschernig v Miller*, 389 US 429 (1968) to limit application of state law to international cases. See, for example, *United Nuclear Corp. v General Atomic Co.*, 96 NM 155; 629 P2d 231 (1980). As we have seen in Section II of this article, however, this rationale is rather different from the argument that state choice of law in the international context must be consistent with international law.

[60] See Elliot Cheatham, *Sources of Rules for Conflict of Laws*, 89 U Pa L Rev 430, 431–33 (1941):

On the relationship of International Law to Conflict of Laws, extreme and contrasted views have been expressed. . . . As to a part of the field of jurisdiction of

adoption of the 14th Amendment," courts applied "the rules of international law to resolve questions of state law jurisdiction."[61] Speaking globally, the majority of choice of law decisions probably concern choice between the laws of two independent nations rather than between the laws of two constituent states of a single nation; such international cases present similar enough problems to intrastate cases that they would serve as a fertile source of doctrinal suggestions. While there are some respects in which choice between two states laws is rather different from the choice between the law of nations,[62] the analogies are so obvious that it is reasonable and to be anticipated that state choice of law decisions will be influenced by parallel international legal norms.

The historical role of international law in the development of American choice of law doctrine has been recognized by the Supreme Court. In *Sun Oil v Wortman*,[63] a defendant sued in Kansas challenged that state's right to apply its statute of limitations to causes of action that had no connection at all to Kansas people or activities. Under traditional choice of law theory, the application of forum statutes of limitations is considered justified because statutes of limitations are characterized as "procedural." This traditional practice has led certain states of the Union to function as havens for stale litigation that would not be entertained in any of the states with which the cause of action is factually connected. The defendants in *Sun Oil* urged the Supreme Court to recognize

---

national courts, the principles of International Law undoubtedly apply. In determining whether a nation or its representatives may be sued, and whether its property may be seized under judicial process, the courts concede the immunities from jurisdiction indicated by International Law. Further, in determining the extent of national jurisdiction over marginal waters and over American vessels in foreign waters, the limits suggested by International Law will ordinarily be followed. Where a statute is not specific on the matter its scope of application will be determined in accordance with International Law. . . . Beyond these and kindred matters, International Law as it may bear on Conflict of Laws is much less specific.

The support that Cheatham offered for one proposition—that international law would influence the interpretation of ambiguous statutes—was a federal extraterritoriality case, *U.S. v Flores*, 289 US 137 (1933), and not a state extraterritoriality case.

[61] *Baker v Baker, Eccles & Co.*, 242 US 394, 401 (1917).

[62] Particularly, the existence of Constitutional limits and the likely degree of divergence, leading to possible application of the public policy exception. The existence of treaties is also important, but here I am concerned with the customary international law aspects of conflicts.

[63] 486 US 717 (1988).

the substantive nature of statutes of limitations and restrict the forum's right to apply its own law. In dashing the defendants' hopes, Justice Scalia wrote:

> The reported state cases in the decades immediately following ratification of the Constitution show that courts looked without hesitation to international law for guidance in resolving the issue underlying this case: which State's law governs the statute of limitations. The state of international law on that subject being as we have described, these early decisions uniformly concluded that the forum's statute of limitations governed even when it was longer than the limitations period of the State whose substantive law governed the merits of the claim.[64]

Justice Scalia is not the Justice best known for deference to international legal norms.[65] But the reason for consulting international legal norms in *Sun Oil* was to interpret the language of the Full Faith and Credit Clause of the Constitution. The defendants' claim was not based on international law, nor could it have been, given that the choice was between the laws of the constituent states of the Union. Moreover, international law was relevant only for showing what states were entitled to do, not what they were forbidden to do, under the Full Faith and Credit clause. Justice Scalia explained the consultation of international law as follows:

> Obviously, judges writing in the era when the Constitution was framed and ratified thought the use of the forum statute of limitations to be proper in the interstate context. Their implicit understanding that the Full Faith and Credit Clause did not preclude reliance on the international law rule carries great weight.[66]

If application of the forum statute of limitations was consistent with international law, in other words, then it must be consistent with the Constitution, for the drafters of the original text must have assumed traditional application of lex fori acceptable.

What about the converse principle: If application of local law violates traditional international legal practice, is it for that reason

---

[64] 486 US at 724. Compare also the references to international law assumptions of the Framers in *Nevada v Hall*, 440 US 410, 418 (1979) (full faith and credit does not require states to grant immunity from suit to sister states).

[65] See, for example, his lack of interest in international practice in the death penalty cases, discussed below.

[66] 486 US at 724.

unconstitutional? Somehow it seems unlikely that the Supreme Court will rule that the Constitution incorporates traditional international law restrictions on choice of law:[67] that would force the states to comply with international choice of law rules even in their dealings with one another. But the international law choice of law rules might be recognized as having force *of its own right*, rather than by virtue of constitutional incorporation. When a court is faced with a choice between the laws of New York and France (for instance), it would—in the absence of any congressional action— have to adhere to the minimum standards set by international choice of law. *Sun Oil* does not address this possibility.

More directly on point is a case mentioned above, *Skiriotes v Florida*.[68] Skiriotes was a criminal prosecution (the defendant had been convicted of illegally harvesting sponges while using scuba gear) and is perhaps for that reason not quite typical of choice of law doctrine. But while the case held that international law was not violated by the prosecution in question (because Skiriotes was a Florida resident), the Supreme Court was quite clear about the relevance of international law to the defendant's claim that his activities could not be prosecuted because they took place outside state territorial borders.

Of course, it has long been recognized that federal extraterritoriality issues pose questions of international law. The *Restatement (Third) of Foreign Relations Law* devotes an entire chapter to the international law limits on federal extraterritoriality;[69] and long prior to the *Restatement*, the general principle had been established that the overseas reach of American law was in part a function of international law.[70] In a well-known early case dealing with the

---

[67] The trend, instead, has been to loosen Constitutional limits. For example, while at one time it was assumed that choice of law problems had unique rights answers, in a pair of cases in 1935 and 1939, the Court clearly held that in most disputes, more than one state might constitutionally apply its own law. *Alaska Packers Assoc. v Industrial Accident Commn*, 294 US 532 (1935) (place of employment may apply its law to workers' compensation case); *Pacific Employers Ins. Co. v Industrial Acc. Commn*, 306 US 493 (1939) (place of injury may apply its workers compensation law). See also *Allstate Insurance Co. v Hague*, 449 US 302 (1981), described in note 77 below, in which a very fractured Court upheld application of local law to a case with extremely attenuated connections to the forum.

[68] 313 US 69 (1940).

[69] Chapter 4, "Jurisdiction and Judgments."

[70] According to the Introductory Note to Subchapter A of Chapter 4 of the *Restatement*, "International law has long recognized limitations on the authority of states to exercise jurisdiction to prescribe in circumstances affecting the interests of other states." As a general matter, the extraterritorial reach of federal statutes has been interpreted narrowly in order

international enforcement of a foreign judgment in federal courts, the Supreme Court endorsed the general relevance of private international law to federal conflicts issues:

> International law, in its widest and most comprehensive sense—including not only questions of rights between nations, governed by what has been appropriately called the law of nations; but also questions arising under what is usually called private international law, or the conflict of laws, and concerning the rights of persons within the territory and dominion of one nation, by reason of acts, private or public, done within the dominions of another nation—is part of our law, and must be ascertained and administered by the courts of justice, as often as such questions are presented in litigation. . . .
>
> The most certain guide, no doubt, for the decision of such questions is a treaty or a statute of this country. But when, as is the case here, there is no written law upon the subject, the duty still rests upon the judicial tribunals of ascertaining and declaring what the law is, whenever it becomes necessary to do so, in order to determine the rights of parties to suits regularly brought before them. In doing this, the courts must obtain such aid as they can from judicial decisions, from the works of jurists and commentators, and from the acts and usages of civilized nations.[71]

Because Congress may override international law (even a prior treaty obligation) if it chooses to do so explicitly, the role of international law in federal conflicts cases is necessarily somewhat limited. International law is employed to interpret a federal statute if its choice of law scope is not specified. There is a presumption, typically attributed to a case known as *The Charming Betsy*, that Congress should not be assumed to have intended a violation of international law unless that conclusion is unavoidable.[72] My proposal is simply that the international law limits imputed to Congressional enactments be generally recognized as binding on the states. I will

---

to avoid inconsistency with international law. See, for example, *Lauritzen v Larsen*, 345 US 571 (1958); *Romero v International Terminal Operating Co.*, 358 US 354, 382–83 (1959); *Steele v Bulova Watch Co.*, 344 US 280, 285–86 (1952); *Vermilya-Brown Co. v Connell*, 335 US 377, 385 n 8 (1948); *McCulloch v Sociedad Nactional de Marineros de Honduras*, 372 US 10, 20–21 (1963).

[71] *Hilton v Guyot*, 159 US 113, 163 (1894).

[72] See, for example, *Murray v The Charming Betsy*, 2 Cranch 64, 118 (1804); *Weinberger v Rossi*, 456 US 25, 32 (1982); see generally, Ralph Steinhardt, *The Role of International Law as a Canon of Domestic Statutory Construction*, 43 Vand L Rev 1103 (1990).

return, below, to more detailed discussion of *The Charming Betsy* presumption and its role in regulating state conduct.

This is not the place for a detailed development of the limitations that international law places on the choice of law process. The contents of these limitations are rather controversial (although their existence is not particularly) and defy easy summarization. There are two approaches that might be taken to give more concrete content to the international law limits on state choice of law. The first is simply to transplant into state choice of law case authority from the federal extraterritoriality context. For example, in one case the Supreme Court declined to apply the Jones Act to a suit brought by a Danish worker hired while temporarily in the United States by a Danish shipping company and injured in Havana, Cuba.[73] The reason was that American law should be construed so as not to create potential conflicts with international law. While the Court did not attempt a comprehensive restatement of the principles of international law, by declining to apply United States law it certainly gave some idea of where the boundary between permissible and impermissible applications might be. Furthermore, in deciding whether to apply state law to a particular set of facts, it is not necessary to have a complete restatement of international law limits, for at a minimum the case suggests that in a comparable fact pattern, state law also should be limited to avoid clashes.[74]

Alternatively, one might place one's faith in the *Restatement of Foreign Relations Law*, controversial as its standards have been. In the context of a federal extraterritoriality case, one Justice—ironically, it was Justice Scalia—has suggested that the version of international choice of law contained in the *Restatement (Third) of Foreign Relations Law* can be treated as authoritative.[75] Roughly, the

---

[73] *Lauritzen v Larsen*, 345 US 571, 577 (1953): "By usage as old as the Nation, such statutes have been construed to apply only to areas and transactions in which American law would be considered operative under prevalent doctrines of international law."

[74] This is particularly clear where the state law on which the cause of action is based has a close analogue in federal law. For example, there are state antitrust laws just as there are federal antitrust laws. (And there are state law causes of action on antidiscrimination, securities, banking, and so forth.) To the extent that existing federal law of extraterritoriality speaks to how the federal statutes should be interpreted to avoid clashes with international law, it can be transplanted directly into the state choice of law context in international cases.

[75] *Hartford Fire Ins. Co. v California*, 113 S Ct 2891, 2920–21 (1993). While Justice Scalia wrote in dissent for this portion of the opinion, the majority opinion of Justice Souter also cited the *Restatement* with approval. 113 S Ct 2910–11.

Restatement recognizes as bases for jurisdiction the fact that activities took place within the state, that the party who seeks to avoid the law is a local resident, and that the activity in question had substantial effects within the state. There are several other bases for jurisdiction, but they are likely not to have much relevance to state choice of law disputes, dealing instead with universal criminal jurisdiction over activities such as piracy and the slave trade.[76]

This list seems expansive, and at first glance may seem to encompass any situation in which a state might reasonably be inclined to apply its law. But it would be a mistake to assume that states necessarily will stay within the limits of international law of their own accord or that federal constitutional limits will make recourse to international law unnecessary.[77] For example, the choice of law theory known as governmental interest analysis holds that it is a sufficient basis for applying local law that the result would be protection or compensation for a local resident.[78] This may be a violation of the *Restatement*'s proviso that the theory known as "passive personality" (according to which the residence of the benefiting party suffices for jurisdiction) is viewed with disfavor in international law.[79] And the so-called better law theory takes into account (as its name implies) which law is substantively better; such a criterion, also, finds no support in international law as the *Restatement* understands it.

More fundamentally, the philosophical foundations for some

---

[76] The bases for jurisdiction to prescribe are set out in § 402. Universal jurisdiction is recognized in § 404.

[77] For example, in *Allstate Insurance Co. v Hague*, 449 US 302 (1981), international law would very likely have been violated if the conflict had been between a state of the Union and a foreign nation as opposed to between two states of the Union. There, two Wisconsin residents driving vehicles registered and garaged in Wisconsin became involved in an accident in Wisconsin. The insurance contract at issue had been entered into in Wisconsin. Subsequently the decedent's wife moved to Minnesota and filed suit there. The state court's application of Minnesota law was justified on the "better law" approach. The United States Supreme Court upheld this decision against constitutional challenge on the grounds that not only had the wife moved to Minnesota after the accident, but the insurance company wrote other (wholly unrelated) policies covering Minnesota risks and the decedent had been employed in Minnesota. The accident had not occurred during the course of the decedent's employment or on his way to or from work.

[78] For a general discussion of modern choice of law theory, see Lea Brilmayer, *Conflict of Laws: Foundations and Future Directions* ch 2 (2d ed 1995).

[79] *Restatement* 402, comment (g). "The principle has not been generally accepted for ordinary torts or crimes, but it is increasingly accepted as applied to terrorist and other organized attacks on a state's nationals by reason of their nationality, or to assassination of a state's diplomatic representatives or other officials."

modern approaches are quite hostile to international legal principles. Modern choice of law theory seems to support the conclusion that it is arbitrary and irrelevant to the point of unconstitutionality whether the activities in question took place in the forum or somewhere else.[80] If this approach were to capture the fancy of a state Supreme Court (this has not happened yet), one wonders what the effect would be in international disputes, for territorial sovereignty is one of the guiding premises underlying international legal norms. It stands to reason that application of international law to state law choice of law cases with international overtones will potentially clash with the choice of law doctrines applied by many states today.[81]

B. INTERNATIONAL HUMAN RIGHTS: CAPITAL PUNISHMENT

It will strike many Americans as a strange idea that international human rights norms might have any significant applicability to state laws. We tend to think of international human rights norms

---

[80] There has been debate within the modern school whether this conclusion actually follows from its premises. See generally Brilmayer, *Conflict of Laws* ch 2 (Little, Brown, 1989). For other criticisms of modern choice of law theory on this point, see, for example, John Ely, *Choice of Laws and the State's Interest in Protecting Its Own*, 23 Wm & Mary L Rev 173 (1981); Douglas Laycock, *Equal Citizens of Equal and Territorial States: The Constitutional Foundations of Choice of Laws*, 92 Colum L Rev 249 (1942).

[81] In the previous section, I mentioned an argument made by Russell Weintraub to the effect that the Supreme Court opinion in *Burnham v Superior Court* erred in upholding jurisdiction based on transient presence without first having at least considered its pariah status in international law. In *Burnham*'s precise factual context, it is clear that international law would only be relevant as a basis for interpreting due process, for *Burnham* was an interstate, as opposed to an international, conflicts case. But Weintraub also pointed out that tag jurisdiction would probably violate international law if applied to an international dispute. His argument suggests, as I have here, that it may be something of a mistake to focus on international norms solely as a method of constitutional interpretation. They may have greater force when offered in their own right.

Another example along these lines is international taxation. The *Restatement* purports to establish international law limits on the power to tax multinational entities and events. See §§ 411–14. While the Supreme Court has on a number of occasions addressed the permissibility of state taxation of multinational corporations, it has not employed standards based on international law. Instead, challenges have been based on the Commerce Clause, the Due Process Clause, and federal supremacy in foreign relations (the "one voice" rationale).

For example, in *Barclays Bank v Franchise Tax Board of California*, 62 USLW 4552 (June 20, 1994), the Court did not cite either international law or the *Restatement*. See also *Japan Line Ltd. v County of Los Angeles*, 441 US 434 (1979). In *Barclays*, the Court held that the state taxing scheme at issue did not violate any Constitutional provision or prevent the country from speaking with one voice; the contrary result was reached in *Japan Lines*. The entire discussion, however, was phrased in terms of American domestic law. See also *United States Steel v Multistate Tax Commn*, 434 US 452 (1978); *Container Corp. v Franchise Tax Bd.*, 463 US 159 (1983); *ASARCO Inc. v Idaho State Tax Commn*, 4588 US 307 (1982).

as dealing with official state torture or disappearances, with closing down opposition newspapers, or with genocide. Such extremes are rarely found in the states of the United States, and when they are the more logical vehicle for combatting them seems to be the Constitution. Human rights proponents recognize that we are fortunate in this country not to have to worry about some of the worst excesses, and that in many respects our rights in fact *are* adequately protected by the Bill of Rights. As two prominent human rights advocates argue,

> One of the reasons why the United States is lagging in its support for international human rights treaties is the widespread—and generally accurate—attitude that U.S. civil rights and civil liberties law is more protective of individual rights than the laws of any other country, so Americans do not need these international protections.[82]

Yet there are actions taken by states that raise serious issues of international human rights.[83] One area of concern is imposition of the death penalty.

The international law status of the death penalty, as a general matter, is the subject of considerable controversy.[84] According to one author,

> [S]ince 1948 . . . there has been a clear and measurable progress towards [the] goal [of eliminating the death penalty altogether]. . . . The offenses for which the death penalty may be imposed are increasingly limited. More and more categories of individuals who may never be subjected to the death penalty are being identified. International law is setting higher and higher standards for procedural requirements which are essential to any trial in which the death penalty may be imposed subject to law. These norms have been entrenched by convention, but in many cases it can be demonstrated that they are also customary

---

[82] Paul Hoffman and Nadine Strossen, *Enforcing International Human Rights Law in the United States,* ACLU International Civil Liberties Report, ACLU International Human Rights Task Force (July 1994), p 8.

[83] Burke, Coliver, De La Vega, and Rosenbaum at 294 (cited in note 40) (outlining ways that international human rights law is more protective than the American Constitution); Hoffman at 63 (cited in note 40) (same).

[84] See generally, William Schabas, *The Abolition of the Death Penalty in International Law* (Grotius Publications Limited, 1993) (arguing that the point may not be too far in the future when capital punishment generally is recognized to be a violation of international human rights law).

in nature. These developments are, in effect, a form of partial abolition of the death penalty.[85]

There are, of course, those who believe that the death penalty in any form is a violation of international law, just as there are also those who think that it is automatically a violation of the Eighth Amendment.

On the other hand, the United States has studiously avoided committing itself to international agreements that would limit application of the death penalty, carefully crafting reservations to general human rights instruments that would otherwise restrict its freedom of action on this issue.[86] Whether the United States is bound by customary law when it has so clearly chosen not to accede to the relevant treaties is something to be determined as a matter of substantive international law.[87] Perhaps there are no relevant international limits on American application of the death penalty; perhaps the death penalty is per se a violation of international law. Or perhaps international law is violated by racially disparate application of the death penalty, or by the execution of those underage at the time of their crimes or of the mentally ill. My point is that *whatever international law requires*, it is binding on the states.

Death penalty opponents have pinned their hopes on using international law limits to influence the interpretation of American con-

---

[85] Id at 20–21.

[86] See generally, David P. Stewart, *United States Ratification of the Covenant on Civil and Political Rights: The Significance of the Reservations, Understandings, and Declarations*, 42 DePaul L Rev 1183 (1993); Joan Hartman, *"Unusual" Punishment: The Domestic Effects of International Norms Restricting the Application of the Death Penalty*, 52 U Cin L Rev 655 (1983); Lauren Kallins, *The Juvenile Death Penalty: Is the United States in Contravention of International Law?* 17 Md J Intl L & Trade 77 (1993); Richard Lillich, *The Soering Case*, 85 Am J Intl L 128 (1991).

[87] It is not fatal to international law based arguments that the nation has not signed the relevant conventions. Human rights norms, in particular, have in some cases entered the realm of customary international law as to states that have not signed the relevant international agreements. For a general description of this phenomenon, see Theodor Meron, *Human Rights and Humanitarian Norms as Customary Law* (Oxford, 1989). See also, *Restatement (Third) of Foreign Relations Law* § 102(3) ("International agreements create law for the states parties thereto and may lead to the creation of customary international law when such agreements are intended for adherence by states generally and are in fact widely accepted."); Nadine Strossen, *Recent U.S. and International Judicial Protection of Individual Rights: A Comparative Legal Process Analysis and Proposed Synthesis*, 41 Hasting L J 805, 815 (1990).

A related issue, discussed at page 340 below, is whether the failure of the United States to ratify the agreements in question should be taken as federal authorization for the states to violate international law. The issue at this point, however, is whether the norms are legally binding on the United States; and on this question, the mere failure to ratify the agreements in question is not dispositive.

stitutional norms. As noted earlier, the influence of international norms on the Eighth Amendment reached its high point in *Thompson v Oklahoma*, in which Justice Stevens cited international opinion in his opinion for a plurality of the Court, writing in a footnote that "we have previously recognized the relevance of the views of the international community in determining whether a punishment is cruel and unusual."[88] A 1989 opinion for the Court by Justice Scalia, however, categorically rejected this approach. In determining what was required by "evolving standards of decency" (a formula that he recognized to provide the standard) he wrote:

> We emphasize that it is *American* conceptions of decency that are dispositive, rejecting the contention of petitioners and their various amici that the sentencing practices of other countries are relevant. While "the practices of other nations, particularly other democracies, can be relevant to determining whether a practice uniform among our people is not merely an historical accident but rather so 'implicit in the concept of ordered liberty' that it occupies a place not merely in our mores, but, text permitting, in our Constitution as well," they cannot serve to establish the first Eighth Amendment prerequisite, that the practice is accepted among our people.[89]

This avenue of attack—using international norms to define "evolving standards of decency" under the Eighth Amendment—thus seems to be foreclosed for now.[90] Interestingly, though, what opinions such as Scalia's suggest is that the proponents of greater human rights protection may actually have a doctrinally stronger argument. *The Paquete Habana*'s syllogism is a more straightforward way to make the argument; and while there is no guarantee of its success, it could hardly fare worse than the constitutional version of the argument has.

If *The Paquete Habana*'s syllogism is adopted, then the permissibility of particular applications of the death penalty must be determined by consulting international legal norms themselves. The question must be whether it is a violation of international human

---

[88] 487 US at 830, 831 (1987).

[89] *Stanford v Kentucky*, 492 US 361, 369 (1989).

[90] While this has been seen by activists as a cause for disappointment, others, such as Judge Hans Linde, have been more positive about judicial unwillingness to decide cases directly on international human rights grounds. Hans Linde, *Comments*, 18 Intl Law 77 (1984).

rights law to execute juveniles or the mentally deficient. As I have indicated, the existence and scope of such international law limitations are likely to be controversial. Yet, rejecting these limitations on the international law grounds that they do not bind the United States would at least require a serious look at what international law requires. The Supreme Court, apparently, has never been directly confronted with this version of the argument against capital punishment. Given the Court's current mood, one hesitates to place too much hope on the likely success of this appeal. But what, one wonders, is the Court likely to say in response?

IV. The Preemptive Power of International Law: Responses

These two examples—international choice of law and capital punishment—highlight the potential international law has for altering the course of state law. Its potential, however, has been largely unrealized. Why do even human rights advocates frame things in terms of interpreting American constitutional provisions, rather than the application of customary international law itself? Why have courts hardly ever taken seriously the possibility that international law would supply a rule of decision? What is the matter with the argument that state courts are as bound by customary international law as by any other sort of federal law?

One possibility is that courts simply feel too uncomfortable with the process of identifying international customary law; that because it is somewhat vague, and because its sources are literally foreign to an American court, courts hesitate to take on the responsibility of probing its requirements. But these difficulties are not as daunting as they are made out to be. Is international law really harder to ascertain than the law of Saudia Arabia or Thailand? The courts are obliged to determine the law of other nations where the facts underlying a case have few or no local connections. And American courts determine international law for other purposes, such as allocating interstate water rights or applying certain federal statutes. Courts need not be so modest about their own abilities, and to the extent that they remain unsure about what international law requires, they need only place the burden of adequately demonstrating that international law exists on the party who would benefit from it.

If lack of confidence is not the answer, three other possibilities remain to be considered: that state courts are essentially passive when it comes to identifying international legal norms, that customary international norms need some sort of authoritative adoption before they can be binding in American courts, and that review for consistency with international law is unacceptably countermajoritarian.

The first explanation to examine is that although state courts are genuinely bound by international law, their role is an essentially passive one. While they would consider themselves bound by an authoritative statement by the Supreme Court of what international law requires, they need not take an active stand in identifying it. State courts have apparently never claimed that they can disregard international law once it has been authoritatively identified; they simply fail to take the lead in determining what international law requires. It seems clear that if the Supreme Court had already authoritatively identified some norm, they would fall in line behind. So long as the Supreme Court has not, they simply watch and wait for instructions. Such passivity would draw support from the well-known principle that the states are not entitled to intrude on the federal conduct of foreign affairs.

But states are no more excluded from pronouncing principles of international law than they are from pronouncing principles of federal constitutional law or federal statutory law. While the Supreme Court has the last word on what a federal statute or constitutional provision requires, the very words of the Supremacy Clause require state courts to apply federal law.[91] And every day, state courts apply their best understanding of federal law, even in the absence of an authoritative Supreme Court interpretation—for example, in state criminal prosecution, where many defenses and evidentary rules are federal.

In any event, the Supreme Court has been no more involved in applying international law to the states than the state courts themselves have been. Even if the states could wait for the Supreme Court's guidance before passing on the relevance of international legal norms to the infliction of capital punishment on children or the mentally deficient, the Supreme Court would have no excuse

---

[91] See, for example, *Testa v Katt*, 330 US 386 (1947) (states cannot deny their courts jurisdiction to hear cases based on federal law).

to wait. And yet the Court has not been any more willing to face the international law consequences of the death penalty than the state courts.

A second and perhaps better way of explaining the lack of interest in international law might be by arguing that it has never been authoritatively adopted into American law. This explanation would draw support from a comparison of customary international law to treaty law. Treaty law is traditionally treated with greater respect in court than is customary law. Treaties, of course, have already been through some official process of adoption, namely, their ratification.[92] This makes their norms explicitly American; they look more or less like statutes. What treaties have that customary norms seem to lack is the imprimatur of authoritative organs of decision. Indeed, even some treaties may be judicially unenforceable: only "self-executing treaties," those that were designed to take direct effect in American courts, are authoritative without additional legislative promulgation.[93] Thus, the argument would be that customary international law is similar to a treaty that is not self-executing and that has not been legislatively implemented. While it is authoritative in some respects—it creates legal obligations between states—it has no direct impact on what goes on in American courts.[94] *The Paquete Habana*'s dictum could be rephrased to run, "international law is *potentially* part of our law. . . . "

There may indeed be some intuition of this sort at work, but if so it does not stand up too well to critical scrutiny. First, there does not currently exist a recognized customary law analogue of

---

[92] On the arduous process of treaty ratification, and the legitimacy that the process bestows, see Trimble at 727 (cited in note 55).

[93] *Foster v Neilson*, 2 Pet 253 (1829). In that case, Justice Marshall stated that a treaty is

to be regarded in courts of justice as equivalent to an act of the Legislature, whenever it operates of itself, without the aid of any legislative provision. But when the terms of the stipulation import a contract—when either of the parties engages to perform a particular act, the treaty addresses itself to the political, not the judicial department; and the Legislature must execute the contract, before it can become a rule for the court.

2 Pet 253, 314. The treaty that Foster held not to be self-executing was later held to be self-executing upon examination of its Spanish language version. *U.S. v Percheman*, 7 Pet 51 (1833). On the doctrine of self-executing treaties, see generally Vazquez, *Treaty Based Rights and Remedies of Individuals* (cited in note 24 above).

[94] A treaty effectively establishes international obligations between nations regardless of whether it is not enforceable in domestic courts. See, for example, *Restatement* § 311 (3) (internal law does not vitiate consent to be bound to international agreements).

the self-executing treaty requirement.[95] Furthermore, some of the legal areas I have considered are not very good candidates for an argument that they are not self-executing: for example, if there were a choice of law treaty imposing limits on application of local law, it would probably pass the test for being a self-executing treaty.[96] The very purpose of such a treaty or convention would be to govern domestic private law disputes. Moreover, no additional requirement of authoritative promulgation has ever stood in the way of imposing international law standards on federal extraterritoriality. It is hard to see why something more would be needed to make international law authoritative in state choice of law cases given that international law is authoritative on its own in federal choice of law cases.

A. THE COUNTERMAJORITARIAN DIFFICULTY

The most convincing argument opposing the direct enforceability of international law against the states—and the most widely held—may be the third one. Only the federal elected branches have the authority to declare state laws invalid as inconsistent with international law.[97] Where the President or Congress acknowledges a norm of international law, then courts may rely on it to invalidate

---

[95] See, for example, the statements about customary international law in Henkin, *International Law as Law in the United States* (cited in note 14 above) at 1561:

> International law is not merely law binding on the United States internationally but is also incorporated into United States law. It is "self-executing" and is applied by courts in the United States without any need to it to be enacted or implemented by Congress.

Indeed, the *Restatement* suggests that even a non-self-executing treaty can sometimes preempt state law. See § 115, comment (e).

For one commentator taking the position that there ought to be some analogue to the self-executing treaty doctrine in customary international law, see Fredrick Kirgis, *May the President Violate Customary International Law? (Cont): Federal Statutes, Executive Orders and "Self-Executing Custom,"* 81 Am J Intl L 371 (1987).

[96] See, for example, *Volkswagenwerk Aktiengesellschaft v Schlunk*, 486 US 694 (1988); *Societe Nationale Industrielle Aerospatiale v United States District Court*, 482 US 522 (1987) (applying the Hague Convention on Service Abroad of Judicial and Extrajudicial Documents in Civil and Commercial Matters (Nov 15, 1965) (Hague Service Convention), 20 UST 361, TIAS No 6638.

Interestingly, though, parts of the UN Charter have been held by one state supreme court not to be self-executing. *Sei Fujii v State*, 38 Cal 2d 718, 242 P2d 617 (1952).

[97] Here, I do not consider whether the proper institution to make the decision is Congress or the President. As I have noted, there is considerable debate about the proper role of the executive and legislative branches in setting foreign policy. But nothing turns for present purposes on the respective roles of the federal elected branches.

particular exercises of state power. Until Congress does so, courts (both state and federal) have no such power. Congressional approval of international law (either through the treaty process or through statutory enactment) is both a necessary and a sufficient condition for invalidation of state law on the grounds of inconsistency with international law.[98] Where the reason for invalidation is the constitutional text, at least the American people have the ability to alter that text if they disagree with the court's interpretation. International law, in contrast, is not responsive to the American electorate and may be perceived as wholly alien and an illegitimate imposition.[99] "When the claimed fundamental rights have their source in international law, the judicial impulse to defer to the political branches is likely to be strong."[100]

International relations has traditionally been deemed a particularly difficult area for courts to second guess the President and Congress.[101] The unusually large role that the political question doctrine has played in international relations is symptomatic.[102] Similarly, the Supreme Court has held that the Constitution restrains the elected branches less in their international activities than domestically.[103] Two reasons are often given for judicial modesty: courts are thought to lack expertise in international relations, and the federal government (it is said) should be able to "speak with one voice," without the interruptions of the judiciary.[104] Yet, there is very substantial scholarly opinion to the effect that the rule of law should be taken more seriously in international relations than

---

[98] Sufficiency is established by the Offenses Clause of Article 1, § 8, cl 10 (granting Congress the power "to define and punish . . . Offenses against the Law of Nations"). The *necessity* of Congressional action is the question at issue here.

[99] Note, however, the role that state consent has traditionally played in the establishment of customary law. While consent is not as clearly expressed to customary law as to treaty law, the general idea is still that states have acquiesced in the law's formation. "The fundamental idea behind the notion of custom as a source of international law is that states in and by their international practice may implicitly consent to the creation and application of international legal rules." Mark Janis, *An Introduction to International Law* 42 (2d ed 1993).

[100] Bayefsky and Fitzpatrick, note 40 supra, at 83.

[101] The most forceful recent proponent of this point of view is Phillip Trimble, note 55 supra.

[102] See especially Thomas Franck, *Political Questions, Judicial Answers* (Princeton, 1992); Louis Henkin, *Is There a Political Question Doctrine?* 85 Yale L J 597 (1976).

[103] See, for example, *U.S. v Verdugo Urquidez*, 494 US 259 (1990) (holding that the Fourth Amendment does not apply to warrantless search by American law enforcement in Mexico).

[104] See, for example, Trimble (note 55 supra) at 713, 715.

it is, and that the courts should be the ones to see that this happens.[105]

But whatever one thinks about the propriety of judicial deference to the federal elected branches, there is no reason that such deference should be extended to the states. The problem at issue here is one not of separations of powers but of federalism. The reason for allowing federal courts to review state legislation is not that courts have some oversight role vis-à-vis legislatures, but that the federal government has an oversight role vis-à-vis the states when the subject is international relations. Whether one thinks that the reason for deference is that the federal government must be able to speak with one voice or that only the Congress (or, only the President) has sufficient experience and expertise with the realities of foreign policy, these reasons do not counsel judicial deference to the states. When fifty or more different jurisdictions potentially adopt different approaches to international issues, the reason for judicial abstention cannot be prevention of an international relations Babel.[106] And there is no reason to think that the states are more knowledgeable in international affairs than the federal courts.

The conclusion that federal courts may enforce international law against the states is fully consistent with—indeed, it reinforces—the supremacy of Congress and the executive. Much has been made of *The Paquete Habana*'s reference to executive and legislative action:

> [W]here there is no treaty, and no controlling executive or legislative act or judicial decision, resort must be had to the customs and usages of civilized nations.[107]

If, as this language suggests, customary international law does not prevail over executive and legislative acts, in what sense is international law "part of our law, . . . [which] must be administered by

---

[105] See, for example, Harold Hongju Koh, *The National Security Constitution* ch 6 (1990) ("*Why the President Almost Always Wins in Foreign Affairs: The Problem of Judicial Tolerance*"); Thomas Franck, *Political Questions, Judicial Answers* (1993).

[106] If the states are free to engage in international relations, and to undertake activities that violate international law, this raises the possibility that the same freedom may be extended to municipal governments and the District of Columbia. In addition, there would be serious issues about the power of Native American groups to conduct foreign relations on their own behalf.

[107] 175 US at 700.

the courts of justice of appropriate jurisdiction, as often as questions of right depending upon it are duly presented for their determination"?[108] The answer must be: international law can preempt the states. The stronger the case for excluding Congressional and Presidential actions from the ambit of *The Paquete Habana*, the stronger the case for the primacy of customary international law over state law. If international law is to be applied, it must be applied to *something*, and if separation of powers makes it inapplicable, then the primary domain of application must be the actions of the states.[109]

B. CHARMING BETSY AND THE STATES

Even if one decides that the predominant analysis must reflect federalism rather than separation of powers concerns, one might still want Congress and the President to play a more prominent role. Those committed to the superior expertise of the elected branches may argue that it should not be disregarded simply because the actions of the states are at issue. But Congress and the President have not been read out of the picture. For better or

---

[108] Id.

[109] The two questions are linked, of course, in one important way. If international law is federal law, it is (in the circumstances under consideration here) federal common law. Federal common law is well recognized as presenting serious problems of judicial legitimacy, for the argument can be made that only Congress is entitled to preempt the law of the constituent states. This argument is often tied to the Rules of Decision Act, although it can also be based on simple premises about the proper structuring of a federal system. See generally, Larry Kramer, *The Lawmaking Power of the Federal Courts*, 12 Pace L Rev 263 (1992).

Even commentators relatively unsympathetic to the development of federal common law recognize that foreign relations is a special case, however. The reason is precisely that foreign relations is an area in which deference to the states is not necessary, because foreign relations is a quintessential federal function. See Kramer at 288 n 84 (citing authorities).

Another version of the argument might be that it is mistaken to lump together all violations of international law, because some raise core foreign relations problems while others are on the periphery. One might, for this reason, wish to differentiate between state law impinging on the rights of consular officials and state laws providing no exception to the death penalty for the underage or pregnant women. There is no doubt that the country as a whole is likely to face much more substantial international protest if rules regulating diplomatic and consular immunities are violated than if states execute underage prisoners. In this sense, the former presents a stronger argument for preemption than the latter. It nonetheless remains the case that when states violate international human rights law, they bring the country as a whole into violation. The fact that some violations are more threatening to friendly international relations than others does not necessarily mean that only the most threatening cases are of federal concern.

worse, the Supreme Court allows the federal elected branches to violate international law if they choose to.[110] It does not follow that states likewise have the power to decide to violate international law, for our courts' separation of powers based reluctance to intervene in the former context does not carry over into the latter. But it does seem to follow that the federal elected branches could authorize the states to violate international law. If judicial modesty is motivated by separation of powers concerns, then the determinative factor should be the attitude of the federal elected branches toward the states' international law violations. And it seems plausible to presume that unless they have otherwise explicitly so provided, the federal elected branches would not want states to have that freedom.

The resolution recommended here is to reserve for the federal elected branches a role, but not to require that they affirmatively act before a court invalidates state law that violates international legal norms. Federal legislative silence should be understood as hostile to state efforts to violate international legal norms. This resolution is prompted by *The Charming Betsy*.[111] *The Charming Betsy* stands for the proposition that Congress will be presumed to have acted in accordance with international law unless the contrary conclusion is unavoidable. It is a principle of federal statutory interpretation that has been applied, among other legal areas, to federal extraterritoriality cases.[112] Translating it into the context of state violations of international law, it holds that unless otherwise explicitly so stated, Congress should be presumed not to want the states to violate international law.

Applying such a presumption to the present context makes sense because the point is that only the elected branches of the federal government should have the power to authorize a violation of inter-

---

[110] *Restatement (Third) of Foreign Relations Law* § 115; *Head Money Cases*, 112 US 580 (1884); *Whitney v Robertson*, 124 US 190 (1888); *The Chinese Exclusion Case*, 130 US 581 (1889). The fact that U.S. courts will give effect to a federal statute that is inconsistent with an earlier treaty or rule of customary international law does not mean that the international obligations of the United States are at an end; the United States will still be held responsible in international fora. *Restatement* § 115(1)(b).

[111] 2 Cranch 64. See generally, Ralph Steinhardt, *The Role of International Law as a Canon of Domestic Statutory Construction*, 43 Vand L Rev 1103 (1990).

[112] See, for example, *Lauritzen v Larsen*, 345 US 571, 578 (1958); see also cases cited in note 70 supra.

national law.[113] The presumption acknowledges the traditionally recognized power of Congress to violate international law if it clearly chooses to overstep international legal limits. But it assumes that Congress does not typically wish to do so; a fortiori, Congress typically does not wish the states to do so. This approach leaves the final word with Congress (and should for this reason be adequately reassuring that electoral branch prerogatives are protected). It does, however, operate as a restraint upon state power to violate international law, for where Congress has not addressed the issues, state law that is inconsistent with international law will be preempted.[114]

This version of *The Charming Betsy* presumption is actually a corollary of the more traditional one.[115] The reason is that where

---

[113] Compare *Benz v Compania Naviera Hidalgo*, 353 US 138, 147 (1957), where the Supreme Court declined to apply the federal Labor Management Relations Act to a controversy resulting from the picketing of a foreign ship operated by foreign seamen hired under foreign articles while it was temporarily in an American port.

> For us to run interference in such a delicate field of international relations there must be present the affirmative intention of the Congress clearly expressed. It alone has the facilities necessary to make fairly such an important policy decision where the possibilities of international discord are so evident and retaliative action so certain.

[114] Compare a suggestion made by Prof. Ralph Steinhardt, note 111 at 113 n 45. He writes, "the supremacy clause of the Constitution and the federal interest in relatively uniform interpretations of international law should support a *Charming Betsy* norm in these local contexts," referring to "interpretation of state or municipal statutes in light of international law."

Steinhardt may be suggesting essentially what is suggested here, namely, that a state statute that violates international law should be declared invalid for that reason. Given that he refers to "the interpretation" of state law, however, he seems instead to be proposing something else, namely, a precise parallel to the traditional *Charming Betsy* rule under which a clear statement of state intent to violate international law would be dispositive. Under this view, states would have the same right to violate international law as the federal government would; they would only be required to do so clearly.

The import of such a presumption is unclear, though. Interpretations of state statutes are a matter of state law, not federal law. The Supreme Court is in general not entitled to reverse a state's construction of its own statute unless that construction involves an issue of federal law. If all that is involved is using *Charming Betsy* to interpret state statutes, then the Supreme Court probably has no basis for requiring the states to go along, and the uniformity that is sought will be difficult to achieve. Such a presumption, at any rate, would operate quite differently from the presumption argued for here. Steinhardt's would (apparently) be rebuttable by the state legislature; mine would be rebutted only by a showing of what Congress wanted. His, also, would give federal courts little basis for invalidating state legislation.

[115] In one respect, it is also more persuasive than its traditional separation of powers counterpart. If one thinks that the primary issue is the intent of Congress and the President, then one could find evidence in even an ambiguous federal statute of a desire to transgress international legal norms. The search for the true intent behind the statute might seem to lead one to study the statute more deeply, rather than to consult presumptions such as the *Charming Betsy* rule. Once Congress has indicated what it wants, however obliquely, it might be thought that the presumption should be treated as rebutted. In the federalism context, however, the key desideratum is not the intended meaning of the state statute but

the constituent states of the Union violate international legal norms, the ultimate responsibility falls upon the federal government. This is true not only as a practical matter—for in the eyes of other nations, the federal government will get the blame—but as a legal matter as well. The constituent states are not themselves formal subjects of international law, and any remedies for international legal violations will be directed against the national government.[116] Thus, if Congress truly wishes to avoid international law violations (as the traditional version of the presumption would have it), then it must wish that the states not commit violations as well. Whether one sees this as a matter of the practical desire of Congress and the President to avoid international embarrassment, or as a matter of their legal inclination to abide by international legal norms, a presumption against federal violations gives rise to a presumption against state violations as well. For, state violations *are* federal violations.

This presumption that Congress would not want the states to be free to violate international law is in some respects reminiscent of judicial review under the dormant commerce clause.[117] The Commerce Clause has been interpreted not only as a source of federal legislative authority (an authority that is explicitly written into the Constitution) but also as a prohibition on certain actions by the states (a prohibition that is nowhere clearly provided). The so-called "dormant" commerce clause has been used to invalidate state laws that discriminate against or unduly burden interstate commerce.[118] But the basic regulatory authority over interstate

---

the intent of the federal elected branches; there is no reason to delve deeper into the state statute being challenged. Instead, one consults what the federal elected branches would want, and given their silence one turns to presumptions. To put it differently, where the application of a federal statute is at issue one might question whether Congress has ever been truly silent on the question of whether to violate international law, and thus doubt the propriety of a presumption with a definite substantive slant. Where the application of a state statute is at issue, its existence cannot itself be taken as evidence that Congress did in fact contemplate a violation of international law.

[116] See, for example, *Restatement (Third) of Foreign Relations Law* § 1, reporter's note 5; § 201, comment (g).

[117] US Const, Art I, § 8, cl 3. "The Congress shall have Power to regulate Commerce with foreign Nations, and among the several States, and with the Indian Tribes." "In short, the Court views the mere fact that the Constitution grants Congress the power to regulate commerce as limiting state regulation of commerce, even absent conflicting federal legislation on the subject. Hence, the dormant Commerce Clause." Amy M. Petragnani, *The Dormant Commerce Clause on Its Last Legs*, 57 Albany L Rev 1215 (1994).

[118] The concept of the dormant Commerce Clause was first suggested in the dicta of *Gibbons v Ogden*, 22 US (9 Wheat) 1, 188; 6 L Ed 23, 68 (1824).

commerce remains in Congressional hands. If Congress wishes to grant states the power to adopt legislation that would otherwise violate the Commerce Clause, it can; and it has exercised this power, for example, in the regulation of insurance.[119]

Congress has power to define and punish offenses against the law of nations, just as it has power to regulate interstate commerce.[120] If the parallel holds, it suggests that state actions that violate international law are ordinarily invalid, but that Congress has the power to ratify state violations of international law to the extent that Congress could itself effectively act in violation of international norms.[121] Since Congress can violate international law so long as it does so clearly, the states also may violate international law so long as Congress has clearly authorized such violations. There is a strong but rebuttable presumption that state violations of international law should be invalidated.

C. REBUTTING THE PRESUMPTION

The final question that remains concerns what would count as evidence sufficient to rebut the presumption. Certainly a federal statute that specifically gave the states the right to violate international law in the particular type of case at issue would count. It is hard to think of federal statutes that grant approval of state violations in so many words, though. The closest analogue would be statutes that seem to authorize federal violations of international

---

[119] McCarran-Ferguson Act, 59 Stat 34, 15 USC § 1011 et seq (1945), which suspended Commerce Clause restraints on state regulation of insurance. See generally, *Western & Southern Life Ins. Co. v State Board of Equalization of California*, 451 US 648, 655 (1981).

Similarly, in 1947 the Supreme Court held that the territorial sea and seabed resources were of sufficient importance to American international relations that the nation as a whole, rather than the states, should regulate them. *U.S. v California*, 332 US 19 (1947). Congress responded by adopting the Submerged Lands Act of 1952, which returned control over the territorial seas to the states. Submerged Lands Act of 1953, ch 65, 67 Stat 29 (1953), 43 USC §§ 1301–15 (1970). In effect, this approach results in a rebuttable presumption that areas of great importance to international relations should be dealt with by the federal government; the burden is then on Congress to overthrow that presumption.

[120] On the use of this clause generally as a basis for federal legislation, see Michael Posner and Peter Spiro, *Adding Teeth to United States Ratification of the Covenant on Civil and Political Rights: The International Human Rights Conformity Act of 1993*, 42 DePaul L Rev 1209 (1993); Charles Siegal, *Deference and Its Dangers: Congress' Power to "Define . . . Offenses Against the Law of Nations,"* 21 Vand J Trans L 865 (1988).

[121] Those who believe that the Constitution should not be read as giving Congress the leeway to violate international law would conclude from this that Congress likewise cannot bestow such power on the states.

law, and which might be read to extend a similar power to the states. The search for evidence to rebut the presumption, then, leads us to look for areas in which the states exercise power parallel to the federal government.

In such circumstances, two questions arise: whether the statute authorizes violations of international law, and if so, whether there is reason to think that Congressionally authorized international law violations are limited to exercise of federal as opposed to state authority. The first question arises because it is hard to imagine that Congress would want the states to have power to violate international law when federal statutes have been drafted not to. The second arises because even if Congress has shown an inclination to violate international law, there may be differences between exercise of state and federal power that make it unlikely that a comparable power should be extended to the states. I will briefly explore three examples of parallel state and federal powers. Two have already been mentioned: international choice of law and the death penalty. The third is the kidnapping of criminal defendants to bring them to trial. Each sheds light on the argument that Congress ordinarily does not want states to be free to violate international law.

Take first the example of the use of kidnapping to bring a criminal suspect to trial. Although there is considerable debate over the issue, there are strong arguments for the position that it is a violation of international law for one nation to kidnap criminal suspects present on another nation's territory as a means of obtaining their presence at trial.[122] I will not address the merits of this point of international law but simply assume for the sake of argument that

---

[122] See generally a remarkable series of articles by Andreas Lowenfeld: *U.S. Law Enforcement Abroad: The Constitution and International Law*, 83 Am J Intl Law 880 (1989); *U.S. Law Enforcement Abroad: The Constitution and International Law, Continued*, 84 Am J Intl Law 444, 472 (1990); *Kidnapping by Government Order: A Follow-Up*, 84 Am J Intl Law 712 (1990); *Still More on Kidnaping*, 85 Am J Intl 655 (1991).

United States v Alvarez Machain, 112 S Ct 2188, 2195–96 (1992), failed to address this issue, saying that the parties had not raised the question. Instead, the defendant had argued that the kidnapping was a violation of the extradition treaty. As stated in the brief for the respondents, "The Government resists the cumulative and evidentiary effect of these provisions [prohibiting prosecution of a defendant brought to trial by kidnapping] by denying what no party asserts. It is not necessary to find that these conventions offer independent grounds for invalidating extraterritorial abductions, only that they provide powerful evidence of the customary understanding with which the Treaty was negotiated." Brief for Respondent, *United States v Alvarez-Machain*, 17 n 13. For a general discussion of the Court's failure to address the issue, see Carlos Vazquez, *Misreading High Court's Alvarez Ruling*, Legal Times (October 5, 1992), p 29.

international law prohibits such trials. In an early case, *Ker v Illinois*,[123] the Supreme Court, nonetheless, upheld a state's right to conduct trials when jurisdiction over the defendant was obtained by such means. Is this result correct?

One explanation of the result could rest on the fact that Congress has allowed the federal government a parallel power to violate international law.[124] An evident difficulty with this argument is that the case upholding federal power came many years after the one upholding state power. The state practice that was upheld in 1886 cannot be defended on the grounds that a comparable federal practice existed, so that there was implied Congressional or executive approval of parallel international law violations by the states. *Ker v Illinois* itself, moreover, did not purport to rely on a federal tendency to commit the same sort of international violation. Yet, in one respect the Court did rely on parallel federal powers. It cited an earlier opinion holding that seizure of a vessel in violation of international law does not affect the jurisdiction of a United States court to adjudicate rights in connection with the vessel.[125] Thus the first element necessary to rebut the presumption seems to be satisfied: the federal elected branches were recognized as having a parallel power to violate international law.

The second step is more problematic. Even if the federal elected branches seem to have reserved for themselves the right to violate international law, one must still ask whether this reservation should be extended to give rise to comparable powers by the states. It is one thing for the federal government to kidnap suspects and bring them to trial in the United States. The decision to do so will probably be made by officials high enough in federal law enforcement, with sufficient awareness of international repercussions, as

---

[123] 119 US 436 (1886).

[124] See *U.S. v Alvarez Machain*, 112 S Ct 2188 (1992). As pointed out in note 122 supra, there is some doubt about the best way to interpret the *Alvarez* decision. The opinion itself clearly stated that it was addressing the treaty law issue and not the customary international law issue. The parties only addressed their arguments to the former, and not the latter. Thus, one possible aftermath of the *Alvarez* decision would be that neither the federal government nor the states would be entitled to try a kidnapped defendant, because, although doing so is not a violation of the treaty, it is a violation of international law. The argument in the text assumes that the Supreme Court would uphold such trials in the federal context, posing the question whether such trials would also be permissible when conducted by states.

[125] *Ship Richmond v United States (The Richmond)*, 9 Cranch 102 (1815), cited at 119 US 444. See also *Alvarez Machain*, 112 S Ct 2188, 2196 n 15 (1992), citing *The Richmond* and also *The Merino*, 9 Wheat 391 (1824), for this proposition.

to evidence a deliberate undertaking of the costs to friendly relations with other countries.[126] Once we recognize the federal elected branches' right to violate international law, their right to make this calculation follows.[127] But it does not follow that they have authorized the states to make that calculation. Not only would acknowledgment of a state power straightforwardly enlarge the number of kidnappings (since there would be state kidnappings in addition to federal kidnappings), but there are no assurances that states would exercise the power is as responsible a way. The reasons for federalizing foreign relations power point to the conclusion that the power to kidnap defendants in violation of international law should not be delegated to the states.[128]

Parallel federal practice, therefore, probably should not insulate state kidnappings of criminal suspects from judicial review for consistency with international law. The argument plays out somewhat differently in the other two contexts, however. In the kidnapping context, a federal assumption of the power to violate exists but it does not extend to the states. In the extraterritoriality context, in contrast, no federal assumption of the power to violate exists. In the context of the death penalty, the federal government has reserved a right to violate international law and has done so in a way that probably extends to the states.

Turn then to the problem of international choice of law. There, the assumption regarding federal enactments has been that Congress intends to observe international legal norms regarding the extraterritorial application of its own laws. Very few federal statutes actually specify their territorial reach, and in even fewer are

---

[126] As to whether this was true on the facts of *Alvarez Machain*, however, see Vazquez, note 122 supra.

[127] It should be kept in mind, however, that some commentators would distinguish between the power of Congress and the power of the executive on this issue. See sources cited in note 22 supra. The present discussion does not purport to take a stand in this controversy; the question is merely the degree to which a valid federal elected branch power to violate international law translates into a comparable power on behalf of the states. To the extent that one thinks the power of the federal elected branches is limited, one will a fortiori find comparable limits on the power of the states.

[128] These reasons include that states do not take into account the costs of an action to the nation as a whole and that they are not as experienced in the handling of foreign affairs. States, for example, do not have access to normal diplomatic channels to ascertain in advance which violations of international law would be taken most seriously by other states, and do not have the opportunity to rally international support or acquiescence for international law violations.

there serious questions about consistency with international law.[129] Typically, questions of territorial reach are decided by the courts interpreting vague statutes, and typically international law has been influential in resolving the question. Thus inconsistency between international law and the reach of federal statutes is virtually nonexistent. It would seem quite perverse to allow the states to violate international norms that Congress has consistently left in place to define the reach of its own statutory enactments.

Now compare, however, the federal attitude toward the death penalty, specifically, the legality of capital punishment when the defendant was underage or mentally deficient when the crime was committed. In the case of the death penalty, there is little evidence of federal practice one way or the other. The reason is that there have been few federal statutes providing the death penalty, and apparently no federal executions in violation of international human rights norms since the point that international law on the subject started to develop.[130] The number of federal crimes for which the death penalty is provided has recently increased,[131] but as yet there have been no executions, and a fortiori none in violation of international law.

There is other evidence, however, of a federal willingness to allow states to violate international law prohibitions on application of the death penalty. The United States has made reservations to most international legal instruments that might be interpreted to restrict capital punishment.[132] There is some controversy over whether, as a matter of international law, these reservations preclude international law limits on executions in the United States.

---

[129] For a survey of federal statutes that specify application even where connections with the United States are fairly attenuated, see Brilmayer and Norchi, note 5 supra at 1249–60. The most serious potential problems concern hijacking and antiterrorism laws. See, for example, the Hostage Taking Act, 18 USC 1203 (1988) and the Antihijacking Act, 49 USC app sec 1472n (1988). See also the Maritime Drug Law Enforcement Act, 46 USCA app sec 1903(a),(j) (West Supp 1991).

[130] As of spring 1994, the federal government had not applied the death penalty for 31 years; its imposition was permitted only for murder during aircraft hijackings and drug-related crimes. Leonard Larsen, *Federal Crime Bill Is Designed to Affect Voters, Not Criminals*, Dallas Morning News (May 2, 1994), p 13A.

[131] The new crime control bill provided the death penalty for a large number of new offenses. Otto Obermaier and Laraine Pacheco, *Crime Legislation of the 103rd Congress*, New York Law Journal (October 6, 1994), p 1 (listing 16 new offenses). Amnesty International protested the new death penalty provisions as a violation of international law. *Around the World*, Dallas Morning News (August 27, 1994), p 25A.

[132] See note 86 supra.

The mere fact that the United States has not signed a treaty does not mean that there are no international customary laws placing parallel requirements. But the fact that the United States has made reservations to such international agreements does tend to show that the federal government considers internationally questionable applications of capital punishment domestically acceptable. While the reservations may not show, in other words, that no international norm exists, they do suggest an elected branch intent to allow executions regardless.

This is only the first step in the analysis: the federal government's retention of a right to violate international law. The second step concerns whether a similar power exists on the part of the states. This is where the case for a state power to kidnap seems weak. But the question is an open one with regard to capital punishment. The very fact that federal statutes have until quite recently had few provisions for capital punishment suggests that the federal government was preserving power for the states when it made reservations to human rights treaties that might have impinged on capital punishment. Thus the federal government might be argued to have authorized states to apply the death penalty as they wish, irrespective of the strictures of international human rights law.

D. CONCLUSIONS

International law has its fans, and it has its detractors. Advocates of the international rule of law are likely to applaud the conclusion that international legal norms must be taken seriously by states and municipalities. They would probably favor most expansions of the role of international norms in taming the power and self-interest of nation states (and their constituent units) that all too often act in disregard of legal principle. Their opponents, in contrast, have an almost instinctive distaste for arguments that courts should intervene to judge the legality of international activities. Such arguments are cast as politically naive, the reckless innocence of the academy.

I have tried to steer clear of the argument that states should be bound by international law simply because international norms are good, or enlightened, or the will of the world community. Although they mostly are, and this counts as a reason to favor them, the argument that I have made is couched instead in terms of standard doctrine. It is not for states themselves but for the federal government to decide whether the states will violate international law. This is not because international law is enlightened (even though it often is), but because international law is federal law and trumps contrary state law under the Supremacy Clause. The states do not have any residual power to regulate international relations, which would require federal intrusions on this power to be narrowly construed.[133] There is no federalism-based reason that state power on this subject should be deferred to by the federal courts. Quite to the contrary, power over international relations is traditionally federal. A presumption that Congress does not want the states to violate international law, for this reason, makes enormous sense.

We started with an apparently simple syllogism about the role of international law in reviewing state legislation. As with other apparently simple lines of reasoning, a second look reveals complexities. We are left with something of a puzzle. The premises seem to be generally accepted, but the conclusions they lead to inexorably are not.

The reluctance to proceed straightaway to the conclusion

---

[133] *Guaranty Trust Co. v United States*, 304 US 126 (1938), contains language suggesting that even treaties must be narrowly construed when they seem to conflict with state statutes.

> Even the language of a treaty wherever reasonably possible will be construed so as not to override state laws or to impair rights arising under them. *United States v Arrendondo*, 6 Pet 691, 748; *Haver v Yaker*, 9 Wall 32, 34; *Dooley v United States*, 182 US 222, 230; *Nielsen v Johnson*, 279 US 47, 52; *Todok v Union State Bank*, 281 US 449, 454.

304 US at 143. But none of the cases cited by the Court supports the proposition. In fact, one of them explicitly holds the opposite—that a treaty need not be narrowly construed to avoid conflict with a state statute, because under the Supremacy Clause federal law invalidates contrary state law.

> The narrow and restricted interpretation of the Treaty contended for by respondent, while permissible and often necessary in construing two statutes of the same legislative body in order to give effect to both so far as is reasonably possible, is not consonant with the principles which are controlling in the interpretation of treaties. Treaties are to be liberally construed so as to effect the apparent intention of the parties. . . . When a treaty provision fairly admits of two constructions, one restricting, the other enlarging rights which may be claimed under it, the more liberal interpretation is to be preferred . . . and as the treaty-making power is independent of and superior to the legislative power of the states, the meaning of treaty provisions so construed is not restricted by any necessity of avoiding possible conflict with state legislation and when so ascertained must prevail over inconsistent state enactments.

Nielsen v Johnson, 279 US 47, 51–52 (1929) (citations omitted).

prompts a second look at the premises. What is the matter with them; where do they go wrong? Certainly, we are unlikely to interfere with the premise that federal law preempts contrary state law. So the problem (in the eyes of those who think there is one) must lie in the second premise, in the statement that international law is part of federal law. There is unlikely to be debate over the proposition that international law is federal law *if it is American law at all*. The characterization of international law as state law is not likely to win much support. So, the best strategy for resisting the ultimate conclusion must be to deny that customary international law is part of our law in the first place.

That path, of course, seems to be foreclosed by the ringing language of *The Paquete Habana*. Perhaps the answer is that *The Paquete Habana* is wrong, in whole or part. Perhaps the unmitigated dualist position is correct; international law simply has no consequences in domestic courts. Some would probably be glad to see *The Paquete Habana*'s dictum go on any grounds that can be made available, and would be only too glad to find one more example of the "absurd" results its logic leads to. But others of us are willing to live with the consequence that state law must be reviewed for consistency with international law. Some, in fact, could only be described as eager.

DAN M. KAHAN

LENITY AND FEDERAL COMMON LAW CRIMES

Introduction

Federal criminal law is widely believed to be marred by an
embarrassing contradiction. It is a basic axiom of federal criminal
jurisprudence that a court should adopt the "harsher" of "two rational readings of a criminal statute only when Congress has spoken
in clear and definite language."[1] More than a simple canon of construction, this principle—known as the "rule of lenity"—is considered essential to securing a variety of values of near-constitutional
stature. Narrow construction of criminal statutes, it is proclaimed,
assures citizens fair notice of what the law proscribes; it constrains
the discretion of law enforcement officials; and, most fundamentally, it embodies our legal system's "'instinctive distaste against

Dan M. Kahan is Assistant Professor, University of Chicago Law School.

Author's note: I am grateful to the Morton C. Seeley Endowment Fund at the University of Chicago Law School for financial support; to Al Alschuler, Douglas Baird, David
Currie, Richard Craswell, Neal Devins, Richard Epstein, Elena Kagan, Lawrence Lessig,
Jacqueline Ross, Stephen Schulhofer, and Cass Sunstein for comments; and to Tim Delaune
and Jennifer Wisner for research assistance.

[1] See, for example, *McNally v United States*, 483 US 350, 359–60 (1987). I will refer
generically to "lenity" as a shorthand for the rule of lenity and for its "identical twin[ ],"
Sedima v Imrex Co., Inc., 473 US 479, 491 n 10 (1985), the rule of "strict construction" for
penal legislation.

men languishing in prison unless the lawmaker has clearly said they should.' "[2]

This is the theory. But it isn't the reality. Judicial enforcement of lenity is notoriously sporadic and unpredictable.[3] As often as not, the "instinctive distaste" for extinguishing individual liberty without clear legislative warrant gives way to other tastes that can be satisfied only by broad readings of federal criminal statutes.[4] In view of the quasi-constitutional status of lenity, it is not surprising that the failure of courts to honor this rule is commonly understood to demonstrate that federal criminal jurisprudence is unprincipled or arbitrary.[5]

Is this conclusion warranted? My primary goal in this article is to explore more systematically what the failure of lenity tells us about federal criminal law. I believe it tells us a lot. The message, however, is not that federal criminal law is *un*principled but that it is *dual-*

---

[2] *United States v Bass*, 404 US 336, 349 (1971), quoting Henry J. Friendly, *Mr. Justice Frankfurter and the Reading of Statutes*, reprinted in Henry J. Friendly, *Benchmarks* 196, 209 (Chicago, 1967). See generally Cass R. Sunstein, *Interpreting Statutes in the Regulatory State*, 103 Harv L Rev 405, 471 (1989) (noting that "courts employ a clear-statement principle in favor of the 'rule of law' " and identifying lenity as "[t]he most celebrated aspect of this general idea").

[3] See, for example, *United States v Nofziger*, 878 F2d 442, 456 (DC Cir 1989) (Edwards dissenting) ("Although the rule is a widely accepted theoretical notion, my review of the nearly one hundred federal cases in which reviewing courts in the last ten years have paid lip service to the principle reveals that, almost without exception, courts have found the rule to be altogether *inapplicable* to the facts before them."); William N. Eskridge, Jr., and Philip P. Frickey, *Cases and Materials on Legislation: Statutes and the Creation of Public Policy* 665–66 (West, 2d ed 1995) (suggesting Supreme Court applies rule inconsistently); Friendly, *Benchmarks* at 209 (cited in note 2) ("One might question the utility of a rule if there are such dubieties about its exits and its entrances; the problem of deciding whether the rule may legitimately be used becomes as hard as the issue itself."); Francis A. Allen, *The Erosion of Legality in American Criminal Justice: Some Latter-Day Adventures of the* Nulla Poena *Principle*, 29 Ariz L Rev 385, 397–98 (1987) (concluding that "federal courts with fair regularity have read important new criminal legislation as constituting inappropriate objects for the rule" and that "the idea of strict interpretation has suffered significant erosion in the present century"); William N. Eskridge, Jr., *Public Values in Statutory Interpretation*, 137 U Pa L Rev 1007, 1083 (1989) (*"Public Values"*) (characterizing "invocation of the rule" as "random" and "bizarre"); compare Wayne R. LaFave and Austin W. Scott, *Criminal Law* § 2.2(d) at 109 (West, 2d ed 1986) (noting that rule is subject to numerous "generally accepted limitations").

[4] See text accompanying notes 191–203 (summarizing survey of Supreme Court case law).

[5] See, for example, *Public Values* at 1083 (cited in note 3) (characterizing application of lenity as "capricious" and suggesting that it reflects "the political preferences of the Justices"); John Calvin Jeffries, Jr., *Legality, Vagueness, and the Construction of Penal Statutes*, 71 Va L Rev 189, 199–200 (1985) ("[T]he construction of penal statutes no longer seems guided by any distinct policy of interpretation; it is essentially ad hoc."); but see Mark Kelman, *Interpretive Construction in the Substantive Criminal Law*, 33 Stan L Rev 591, 660 (1981) ("[I]ronically, the 'rule system' [conception of criminal law] is upheld only occasionally, and in a very un-rule-like fashion.").

principled. The historic underenforcement of lenity, I will argue, reflects the existence of another largely unacknowledged, but nonetheless well established, rule of federal criminal law: that Congress may *delegate* criminal lawmaking power to courts.

In the course of developing this thesis, I expect to accomplish three objectives. First, I will seek to demonstrate that federal criminal law is most appropriately viewed as a species of *federal common law*. Federal common law is commonplace in various statutory domains, including antitrust, labor law, and securities regulation.[6] In these fields, broad statutory language is understood to constitute an implicit delegation of lawmaking power to courts.[7] But the existence of delegated judicial lawmaking has never been formally recognized in federal criminal jurisprudence, a central principle of which is that there are and can be no "federal common law crimes."[8] Nonetheless, any close examination reveals that federal criminal law, no less than other statutory domains, is dominated by judge-made law crafted to fill the interstices of open-textured statutory provisions.

Delegated criminal lawmaking and lenity cannot peacefully coexist. Were a court invariably constrained to select the narrowest "rational reading" of every ambiguous criminal statute, it would be impossible for Congress to enlist the lawmaking assistance of courts through broad statutory grants. Indeed, the rule of lenity, I will argue, is best understood as a "nondelegation doctrine" in criminal law. As such, it is about as effective in constraining Congress's power to shift criminal lawmaking power to courts as the now dormant "nondelegation doctrine" is in constraining Congress's power to shift regulatory-lawmaking authority to administrative agencies.

Second, I will try to make sense of a debate now raging among Justices of the Supreme Court over the function of lenity and its

---

[6] See generally Thomas W. Merrill, *The Common Law Powers of Federal Courts*, 52 U Chi L Rev 1 (1985); Martha A. Field, *Sources of Law: The Scope of Federal Common Law*, 99 Harv L Rev 883 (1986); and Henry J. Friendly, *In Praise of Erie—and the New Federal Common Law*, reprinted in Friendly, *Benchmarks* at 155 (cited in note 2).

[7] See, for example, Merrill, 52 U Chi L Rev at 40–46 (cited in note 6).

[8] See *United States v Hudson & Goodwin*, 11 US (7 Cranch) 32, 34 (1812). Justice Stevens has come the closest to recognizing the interstitial lawmaking function that the judiciary plays in criminal law. See *United States v Kozminski*, 487 US 931, 965–66 (1988) (Stevens concurring in judgment); *McNally*, 483 US at 372 (Stevens dissenting).

relationship to other techniques of statutory construction.[9] The Court's renewed interest in lenity is surprising enough. But even more puzzling, the current lenity debate appears to involve a startling role reversal. In the main, the Court's most conservative members, including Justices Scalia and Thomas, have been lenity's most vigorous defenders, and the Court's most liberal members, including Justice Stevens and the late Justice Marshall, its most forceful detractors.[10] If commitment to lenity were truly a measure of how committed individual Justices were to the values thought to underlie the rule, why would the alignment on this issue defy the Court's familiar (if crude) ideological division on questions that pit "liberty" against "authority" in criminal law?

It is much easier to understand the current lenity debate once the rule is conceived of as a nondelegation doctrine. Justice Scalia has waged a much-heralded campaign to overthrow methods of statutory interpretation that require the exercise of normative discretion by courts.[11] His attempted rehabilitation of lenity is integral to that project as it applies to the interpretation of criminal statutes. The Court's liberal Justices, in contrast, are comfortable with delegated judicial lawmaking and for that very reason relatively unconcerned with lenity. In other words, the current debate really isn't about notice, prosecutorial discretion, individual liberty, or any of the other values conventionally associated with lenity; it is about how criminal lawmaking power should be allocated between Congress and the judiciary.

Third, I will appraise the relative merits of lenity and delegated lawmaking. The time has come, I will argue, formally to dispatch the former and openly to recognize and perfect the latter. In theory, a regime of delegated criminal lawmaking is much more efficient and more effective than one in which Congress is obliged to make criminal law without judicial assistance. In addition, there is no important tension, in theory, between delegated lawmaking and the values that are commonly thought to animate lenity. But in order for the benefits of delegated lawmaking to be realized in

---

[9] See text accompanying notes 231–61.

[10] See text accompanying notes 231–61.

[11] See generally William N. Eskridge, Jr., *The New Textualism*, 37 UCLA L Rev 621 (1990); William D. Popkin, *An Internal Critique of Justice Scalia's Theory of Statutory Interpretation*, 76 Minn L Rev 1133 (1992); Sunstein, 103 Harv L Rev at 415–18 (cited in note 2); and, Note, *"Plain Meaning": Justice Scalia's Jurisprudence of Strict Statutory Construction*, 17 Harv J L & Pub Pol 401 (1994).

practice, it is essential that rational principles for the exercise of this power be self-consciously and rationally developed. This article is intended to be a step in that direction.

My argument has five parts. Part I connects lenity to the allocation of criminal lawmaking power, showing that its primary function is to block delegation of such authority to the judiciary. Part II exposes the hidden rule of delegated criminal lawmaking and describes how courts have formally reconciled this function with lenity while assuring the supremacy of the former. Part III examines the contemporary debate over lenity in the Supreme Court. Part IV defends the abolition of lenity. Finally, Part V offers some preliminary reflections on what should take lenity's place: a theory of federal common law crimes.

I. Lenity and the Nondelegation of Criminal Lawmaking Power

Lenity is almost universally celebrated among commentators.[12] Most emphasize its nexus with due process and rule of law values like fair notice,[13] others its generic bias in favor of liberty,[14] and still others its contribution to economic efficiency.[15] Indeed, a prevalent understanding depicts lenity as one part of an integrated package of interpretive devices by which courts advance "public values" that otherwise receive insufficient attention in the legislative process.[16]

---

[12] For qualified criticisms, see generally Jeffries, 71 Va L Rev at 198–201 (cited in note 5); Paul H. Robinson, *Legality and Discretion in the Distribution of Criminal Sanctions*, 25 Harv J Leg 393, 393–96, 400–01 (1988).

[13] See, for example, Sunstein, 103 Harv L Rev at 471 (cited in note 2); *Public Values* at 1029–30 (cited in note 3); Colin S. Diver, *The Optimal Precision of Administrative Rules*, 93 Yale L J 65, 74 (1983); David L. Shapiro, *Continuity and Change in Statutory Interpretation*, 67 NYU L Rev 921, 935–36 (1992); Reed Dickerson, *The Interpretation and Application of Statutes* 208–10 (Little, Brown, 1975); Jerome Hall, *General Principles of Criminal Law* 37 (Bobbs-Merrill, 2d ed 1960).

[14] See, for example, Friendly, *Benchmarks* at 209–10 (cited in note 2); Stephen F. Ross, *Where Have You Gone, Karl Llewellyn? Should Congress Turn Its Lonely Eyes to You?* 45 Vand L Rev 561, 570–71 (1992).

[15] See Richard A. Posner, *The Federal Courts: Crisis and Reform* 283 (Harvard, 1985); Isaac Ehrlich and Richard A. Posner, *An Economic Analysis of Legal Rulemaking*, 3 J Legal Stud 257, 262–63 (1974).

[16] See William N. Eskridge, Jr., *Overriding Supreme Court Statutory Decisions*, 101 Yale L J 331, 413–14 (1991); Edward O. Correia, *A Legislative Conception of Legislative Supremacy*, 42 Case W Res L Rev 1129, 1142–43 (1992) (including lenity among canons that promote "extra-legislative polic[ies]"); but see Sunstein, 103 Harv L Rev at 471 (cited in note 2).

In fact, lenity has a slightly different and more specialized mission: to enforce legislative supremacy in criminal law. Under this view, criminal lawmaking is the prerogative of Congress and Congress alone. Lenity promotes this conception of legislative supremacy not just by preventing courts from covertly undermining legislative decisions, but also by forcing Congress to shoulder the entire burden of criminal lawmaking even when it prefers to cede some part of that task to courts. I will call this the nondelegation conception of lenity.

The nondelegation conception is not necessarily inconsistent with the public values conception of lenity, but is, I believe, more basic. It is more basic, first, because foreclosing judicial lawmaking is understood to be the primary means of securing the other values associated with lenity. Second, nondelegation is more basic because the value of legislative supremacy that it promotes is viewed as a sufficient justification for lenity. Courts apply lenity even when it is clear, for example, that strict construction is unnecessary to secure any of the other values associated with the rule.

A. STRICT CONSTRUCTION AND NONDELEGATION: A THEORETICAL OVERVIEW

Rarely emphasized by commentators,[17] the link between lenity and legislative supremacy is prominently featured in the Court's own explanation for the rule. "Because of the seriousness of criminal penalties, and because criminal punishment usually represents the moral condemnation of the community," the Court has explained, "legislatures and not courts should define criminal activity."[18] The Court's opinions, however, furnish little elaboration of how lenity promotes this form of legislative supremacy.

Perhaps the most obvious way in which lenity might be thought to promote legislative supremacy is by disciplining courts. When Congress enacts a statute, it could be understood to make a conscious and deliberate decision about where to draw the line be-

---

[17] Compare Shapiro, 67 NYU L Rev at 936 (cited in note 13); and, Dickerson, *The Interpretation and Application of Statutes* at 210 (cited in note 13), both of whom defend using lenity to regulate incidence of criminal lawmaking power. For slightly more ambivalent accounts, see Jeffries, 71 Va L Rev at 202–05 n 40 (cited in note 5) and Robinson, 25 Harv J Leg at 400–01 (cited in note 12).

[18] *United States v Bass*, 404 US 336, 349 (1971).

tween criminality and noncriminality.[19] Giving courts the discretion to select broad as well as narrow readings of ambiguous statutes creates a risk that they will exceed congressionally desired limits on criminal liability by disguising judicial definitions of crimes as mere "interpretations." Lenity combats this type of encroachment upon legislative prerogatives by constraining courts to choose the narrowest reasonable readings of ambiguous criminal statutes.

I want to suggest the possibility that lenity promotes legislative supremacy in a very different way. Under this view, lenity assures legislative supremacy in criminal law not by disciplining courts, but by disciplining Congress itself. Because lenity (in theory) requires courts to default to the narrowest reasonable reading of an ambiguous criminal statute, the canon assures that there exists no operative rule of criminal liability that lacks Congress's self-conscious and express imprimatur. Thus, lenity promotes legislative supremacy by *forcing* Congress to take the lead in the field of criminal law and to forgo judicial assistance in defining criminal obligations.

To make this claim plausible, it is necessary to understand why Congress might need this sort of discipline. Why would Congress expect or appreciate judicial assistance in making any type of law? The answer to this question derives from the function of implied delegation as a strategy for reducing the institutional cost of legislation.

Congress's power to create a regulatory universe that reflects the collective preferences of its members is subject to various constraints. Making law takes time, which is necessarily scarce in a legislature with a two-year session.[20] Making law also takes political consensus, which is difficult and time consuming to generate in a legislative body comprising hundreds of members who represent scores of diverse and competing interests.[21] Consequently, as issues multiply in number, complexity, and political sensitivity, it is inevitable that Congress will be unable to enact as much law as its members desire.

---

[19] Richard A. Posner, *Economics, Politics, and the Reading of Statutes and the Constitution*, 49 U Chi L Rev 263, 281 (1982).

[20] See Frank H. Easterbrook, *Statutes' Domains*, 50 U Chi L Rev 533, 548 (1983).

[21] Ehrlich and Posner, 3 J Legal Stud at 267 (cited in note 15); Diver, 93 Yale L J at 75 (cited in note 13).

One solution to this problem is *express* delegation of lawmaking authority. This strategy is most obvious in administrative law, where Congress frequently authorizes an agency to promulgate rules according to a general standard or set of standards.[22] "Time spent on details must be at the sacrifice of time spent on matters of broad public policy,"[23] and faced with a shortage of time Congress might willingly trade off power to specify the details for greater time to specify the policies. It is also considerably easier to generate political consensus for a delegation standard than for an operative rule of law precisely because a standard is general and does not attempt resolution of the most controversial issues.[24]

Delegated lawmaking is also likely to permit more efficient updating of legal norms. The same constraints that prevent Congress from enacting a detailed solution to a complex or controversial problem may also prevent Congress from adapting any such solution to changed circumstances. It may be significantly easier for an agency to revise its rules.[25]

To be sure, from Congress's point of view, delegated lawmaking is not a perfect solution to the limitations on its own lawmaking powers. By choosing to spend its time on "matters of broad policy" rather than on "details,"[26] Congress may achieve a greater volume of law consistent with congressional policies, but it necessarily surrenders control over the precise content of that law. Indeed, because discretion is integral to delegation, agencies will inevitably promulgate rules with which a majority of Congress disagrees; Congress must then incur the cost of overriding those rules or (more likely) simply endure them. But so long as Congress can be confident that it will approve of most of what an agency does, the cost of these occasional miscues will likely be smaller than the cost of having to forgo delegation altogether.

---

[22] See, for example, 47 USC § 303 (1988 & Supp 1993) (authorizing Federal Communications Commission to promulgate licensing regulations "as public convenience, interest, or necessity requires"); 28 USC § 994 (1988 & Supp 1993) (identifying numerous factors to guide promulgation of sentencing guidelines by United States Sentencing Commission).

[23] See generally Final Report of the Attorney General's Committee on Administrative Procedure, 77th Cong, 1st Sess 14 (1941) (Doc No 8).

[24] See Richard B. Stewart, *The Reformation of American Administrative Law*, 88 Harv L Rev 1669, 1695 (1975); Diver, 93 Yale L J at 75 (cited in note 13).

[25] See Final Report of the Attorney General at 14 (cited in note 23) (noting "danger of harmful rigidity if [solution to a complex regulatory problem] were crystallized in the form of a statute"); Louis Kaplow, *Rules versus Standards: An Economic Analysis*, 42 Duke L J 557, 616–17 (1992); but see Stewart, 88 Harv L Rev at 95 (cited in note 24).

[26] Final Report of the Attorney General at 14 (cited in note 23).

There is at least one additional technique for ameliorating the practical constraints on congressional lawmaking. Congress can enact open-textured or highly general legislation that is nonetheless directly enforceable in court. Federal antitrust law,[27] labor law,[28] and civil rights laws[29] all conform to this model. When construed "generatively"—that is, as statements of general policy to govern all foreseen and unforeseen problems within a regulatory field[30]— broadly worded statutes are necessarily more potent sources of law than are narrowly worded ones. By enacting the Sherman Act, for example, Congress created not one but scores of distinct legal obligations.[31]

Beyond this particular efficiency, open-textured statutory language presents Congress with essentially the same benefits as express delegation of lawmaking authority. Like delegations, open-textured statutes require smaller investments of time and less political consensus to enact than do extremely precise statutes.[32] And again, open-textured statutory language may facilitate more efficient updating of legal norms; the generality of these statutes means that courts can modify or overrule prior decisions without awaiting amendment of the statutory language by Congress.[33]

---

[27] See, for example, *Nat'l Soc'y of Professional Eng'rs v United States*, 435 US 679, 688 (1978) (recognizing that Sherman Act invites courts to give "shape to the statute's broad mandate by drawing on common-law tradition"); Phillip Areeda and Louis Kaplow, *Antitrust Analysis: Problems, Text, Cases* 5–6 (Little, Brown, 4th ed 1988) (suggesting that "the [Sherman] Act may be little more than a legislative command that the judiciary develop a common law of antitrust").

[28] See, for example, *Textile Workers Union v Lincoln Mills*, 353 US 448, 456–57 (1957).

[29] See *Public Values* at 1052–54 (cited in note 3) (describing case law implementing 42 USC § 1983).

[30] See *Moragne v States Marine Lines, Inc.*, 398 US 375, 392 (1970) ("[A] statute may reflect nothing more than the dimensions of the particular problem that came to the attention of the legislature, inviting the conclusion that the legislative policy is equally applicable to other situations in which the mischief is identical."); *Van Beeck v Sabine Towing Co.*, 300 US 342, 351 (1937) (Cardozo) ("There are times when uncertain words are to be wrought into consistency and unity with a legislative policy which is itself a source of law, a new generative impulse transmitted to the legal system."); and, Note, *Intent, Clear Statement, and the Common Law: Statutory Interpretation in the Supreme Court*, 95 Harv L Rev 892 (1982).

[31] See generally Herbert Hovenkamp, *Federal Antitrust Policy* § 2.1(b) (West, 1994).

[32] See Diver, 93 Yale L J at 75, 103, 106 (cited in note 13); compare *Landgraf v USI Film Products*, 114 S Ct 1483, 1494 (1994) ("It is entirely possible—indeed, highly probable—that, because it was unable to resolve the retroactivity issue . . . Congress viewed the matter as an open issue to be resolved by the courts.").

[33] Although the policy of *stare decisis* is strongest for decisions construing statutes, the Supreme Court affords less deference to statutory precedents that implement delegated lawmaking. See William N. Eskridge, Jr., *Overruling Statutory Precedents*, 76 Georgetown L J 1361, 1377–81 (1988).

But also like delegation to administrative agencies, implicit and express delegations to courts require Congress to sacrifice a significant amount of control over the precise content of legal rules. Statutes that are framed in highly general terms are incompletely specified. They do not purport exhaustively to enumerate all of their applications; rather, completion of these statutes is deferred until the moment of application.[34] This task necessarily falls on courts, which must fashion mediating rules that allow the statutory language to be brought to bear on the facts at hand.[35] For this reason, statutes such as the Sherman Act and § 301 of the Labor Act are frequently conceptualized as *implicit* delegations of lawmaking power to courts, and judicial applications of these statutes as instances of "federal common-lawmaking" rather than simple statutory interpretation.[36]

"Strict construction" would essentially defeat the implied-delegation strategy for reducing the costs of congressional lawmaking. Under a rule of strict construction, the only statutory applications that courts would enforce would be those clearly and expressly approved of by Congress. Congress would thus be forced to bear the entire cost—practical and political—of making law in the first instance and of remaking it as circumstances changed.[37] Because it forecloses Congress's tacit reliance on judicial lawmaking as a strategy for enlarging Congress's power to promulgate general policies, a rule of strict construction is tantamount to a nondelegation doctrine.[38]

---

[34] See generally Kaplow, 42 Duke L J at 616–17 (cited in note 25); Diver, 93 Yale L J at 103 (cited in note 13); Cass R. Sunstein, *Problems with Rules*, Calif L Rev (forthcoming 1995).

[35] See Correia, 42 Case W Res L Rev at 1187–88 (cited in note 16); and Ehrlich and Posner, 3 J Legal Stud at 261 (cited in note 15).

[36] See *Northwest Airlines v Transp. Workers Union*, 451 US 77, 95 (1981) ("Broadly worded . . . statutory provisions necessarily have been given meaning and application by a process of case-by-case judicial decision in the common-law tradition"); *Nat'l Soc'y of Professional Eng'rs*, 435 US at 688 (recognizing that Sherman Act invites courts to give "shape to the statute's broad mandate by drawing on common-law tradition"); Merrill, 52 U Chi L Rev at 40–46 (cited in note 6); Friendly, *Benchmarks* at 185–92 (cited in note 2).

[37] Correia, 42 Case W Res L Rev at 1131 (cited in note 16); Posner, *Federal Courts* at 219–20, 292–93 (cited in note 15).

[38] See generally Dickerson, *The Interpretation and Application of Statutes* at 206 (cited in note 13) ("Here, 'strict' means merely that the court will refrain from exercising its creative function to apply the rule announced in a statute to situations not covered by it, even though such an extension would help to advance the ulterior purpose of the statute. Here, strictness relates not to the meaning of the statute but to using the statute as a basis for judicial lawmaking by analogy with it.").

This feature of "strict construction" is hardly accidental; many influential proponents of strict construction have advocated it for the very purpose of denying Congress the economies associated with judicial lawmaking.[39] Justice Frankfurter advanced such an argument in his famous essay, *Some Reflections on the Reading of Statutes*.[40] "[W]hat courts may do with legislation," Frankfurter observed, "may in turn deeply affect what Congress will do in the future." "Loose judicial reading," he argued, "makes for loose legislative writing," which he equated with an undemocratic shift of lawmaking responsibility to the judiciary:

> In a democracy the legislative impulse and its expression should come from those popularly chosen to legislate, and equipped to devise policy, as courts are not. The pressure on legislatures to discharge their responsibility with care, understanding and imagination should be stiffened, not relaxed. Above all, they must not be encouraged in irresponsible and undisciplined use of language.[41]

It is no coincidence that Frankfurter viewed *express* delegation of lawmaking power to the judiciary as unconstitutional.[42]

Of course, Frankfurter and his allies have lost the battle against delegated judicial lawmaking. In contemporary law, there is neither a formal bar to express delegation to courts nor a global presumption in favor of strict construction. Instead there are only a series of localized "strict construction" or "clear statement" rules, which tend to operate as nondelegation doctrines within their respective fields of operation.

Such rules play a critical role, for example, in the Supreme Court's federalism jurisprudence. In lieu of identifying substantive constitutional limits on Congress's power, the Court demands incontrovertible textual warrant for statutory readings that would authorize private damages actions against the states,[43] expose the

---

[39] See, for example, Easterbrook, 50 U Chi L Rev 533 (cited in note 20); and Frank H. Easterbrook, *Legal Interpretation and the Power of the Judiciary*, 7 Harv J L & Pub Pol 87, 94 (1984).

[40] 47 Colum L Rev 527, 545 (1947).

[41] Id at 546–47.

[42] See *Lincoln Mills*, 353 US at 484 (Frankfurter dissenting).

[43] See, for example, *Pennsylvania v Union Gas Co.*, 491 US 1, 7 (1989); *Atascadero State Hospital v Scanlon*, 473 US 234, 242 (1985).

states to generally applicable regulations,[44] or displace state law in domains of traditional state concern.[45] These clear statement rules protect state interests in two ways. First, they preclude courts from participating in the creation of legal rules adverse to state interests. Because the states depend entirely on their representation in the political process to protect their essential interests,[46] the impetus for operative legal rules that disadvantage the states must, in the Court's view, be supplied entirely by Congress and not in any material way by the judiciary.[47] Second, these clear statement rules simply make it hard for Congress effectively to regulate state interests. They demand a level of foresight and consensus that predictably exceeds Congress's capacities.[48]

As a clear statement rule, lenity can be understood to produce similar effects in the domain of criminal law. Like the federalism canons, lenity also places the onus of legislating entirely on Congress. And to the extent that it is rigorously enforced, lenity, too, makes it harder for Congress to make criminal law by raising the practical and institutional cost of such legislation.

B. ILLUSTRATIONS, HISTORICAL AND CONTEMPORARY

At this point, I have defended the "nondelegation" understanding of lenity only in conceptual terms. I now want to show that

---

[44] See *Gregory v Ashcroft*, 501 US 452, 469–70 (1991).

[45] *BFP v Resolution Trust Corp.*, 114 S Ct 1757, 1764–65 (1994) (state real-property law); and, *Cipollone v Liggett Group, Inc.*, 112 S Ct 2608, 2618 (1992) (state tort law).

[46] See *Garcia v San Antonio Metro. Transit Auth.*, 469 US 528, 554 (1985).

[47] *Gregory*, 501 US at 464.

[48] The Court also insists on express textual warrant for applying a statute extraterritorially, see *EEOC v Arabian American Oil Co.*, 499 US 244, 248, 258–59 (1991), and, for statutory readings that raise substantial constitutional questions, see *Edward J. DeBartolo Corp. v Fla Gulf Coast Bldg. & Constr. Trade Council*, 485 US 568, 575 (1988). In these contexts, too, clear statement rules concentrate lawmaking responsibility in Congress and thus limit the amount of law with these particular properties. See generally Shapiro, 67 NYU L Rev at 940–41 (cited in note 13). The *Chevron* doctrine, see *Chevron, USA, Inc. v NRDC*, 467 US 837 (1984), can likewise be understood as a barrier to delegated judicial lawmaking, although one that does not concentrate lawmaking responsibility in Congress. Under *Chevron*, a court may override an agency's interpretation of the agency's organic statute only if the meaning of the statute is plain; if the statute is ambiguous, the court must defer to the agency's interpretation so long as the agency's reading is "reasonable." See id at 842–44 & nn 9–10. *Chevron* divides interpretive authority in this way on the ground that agencies are better situated than courts to exercise the lawmaking power implicitly delegated by open-textured administrative statutes. See id at 865–66.

the nondelegation view furnishes a coherent and convincing explanation of the Court's own case law. For purposes of illustration, I will focus on two decisions: *Wiltberger v United States*,[49] the 1820 decision in which the Supreme Court first applied lenity; and *United States v Kozminski*,[50] an instructive contemporary application of that rule.

1. *Wiltberger*. *Wiltberger* involved a defective statute. Section 8 of the Crimes Act of 1790 (the very first piece of criminal legislation enacted by Congress) punished murder, piracy, or mutiny committed "upon the high seas, or in any river, haven, basin or bay, out of the jurisdiction of any particular state."[51] Succeeding sections of the Act applied to related offenses, including aiding and abetting in § 8 offenses, piratic acts under the commission of a foreign sovereign, and manslaughter.[52] However, in specifying the extraterritorial reach of these provisions, the Act used formulations—including "land or seas" or simply "high seas"—that were different from, and plainly less comprehensive than, the formulation used in § 8.[53] The question in the case was whether Wiltberger could be convicted of manslaughter—which under § 12 was limited to homicides "on the high seas"—for a killing that occurred on a river in the interior of China.[54]

The Court concluded that he could not. "[I]t [wa]s almost impossible to believe," Chief Justice Marshall acknowledged, "that there could have been a deliberate intention" on the part of Congress to create the bizarre loopholes associated with reading only § 8, and not succeeding sections, to apply to offenses committed on inland waterways outside of the United States.[55] Nonetheless, invoking the rule of strict construction, Marshall denied that the Court could

---

[49] 18 US (5 Wheat) 76 (1820).

[50] 487 US 931 (1988).

[51] Crimes Act of 1790 § 8, 1 Stat 112, 113.

[52] See id §§ 9–10, 12, 1 Stat at 114–15.

[53] See id §§ 8–10, 12, 1 Stat at 113–15.

[54] See *Wiltberger*, 18 US at 94.

[55] Id at 99. Reading the statute literally, for example, resulted in the anomaly that piracy could be punished when committed on any body of water (§ 8), whereas the more serious offense of piracy under the commission of a foreign sovereign (§ 9) could be punished only when committed on the "high seas." See id. Marshall dismissed the significance of this point by noting that the scope of § 9 "is not directly before us, and we may, perhaps, be relieved from ever deciding it." Id.

legitimately remedy this defect by "engraft[ing] the words of the 8th section . . . on the 12th section":[56]

> The rule that penal laws are to be construed strictly, is perhaps not much less old than construction itself. It is founded on the tenderness of the law for the rights of individuals; and on the plain principle, that the power of punishment is vested in the legislative, not in the judicial department. It is the legislature, not the court, which is to define a crime, and ordain a punishment.[57]

Although *Wiltberger* was the first Supreme Court decision to apply strict construction, the rule did have a well established history in English law. English courts had used strict construction to repel early parliamentary efforts to enter the field of criminal law. The eighteenth century had witnessed an explosion of statutory enactments abrogating the "benefit of clergy," a doctrine that allowed courts (at their discretion) to spare defendants from capital punishment and sentence them to some lesser form of punishment.[58] By construing these statutes narrowly—indeed, in many cases, fantastically[59]—English courts were able both to temper the severity of the law and to protect the judiciary's traditional prerogatives in the administration of criminal justice.[60]

To anyone familiar only with the function of strict construction in English law, Marshall's use of the doctrine in *Wiltberger* might have seemed peculiar. Whereas in England, courts had confined strict construction to offenses punishable by death, manslaughter under the Crimes Act was punishable by only three years' imprisonment. In addition, *Wiltberger*'s invocation of strict construction obviously had nothing to do with preserving "benefit of clergy"; that doctrine was virtually extinct in the states and was completely

---

[56] Id at 94.

[57] Id at 95.

[58] John H. Langbein, *Shaping the Eighteenth-Century Criminal Trial: A View from the Ryder*, 50 U Chi L Rev 1, 37–41 (1983); J. M. Beattie, *Crime and the Courts in England, 1660–1800* 141–45 (Princeton, 1986); Jerome Hall, *Theft, Law and Society* 356–64 (Bobbs-Merrill, 1952).

[59] William M. Blackstone, 1 *Commentaries* *88; George W. Dalzell, *Benefit of Clergy in America and Related Matters* 38–39 (Winston-Salem, 1955).

[60] See Hall, *Theft, Law and Society* at 118–26 (cited in note 58).

unknown to federal law.[61] Indeed, far from using strict construction to protect judicial prerogatives from legislative interference, Marshall deployed the rule to dramatize the judiciary's *subservience* to Congress in the domain of criminal law.

For exactly this reason, however, the significance of Marshall's reliance on strict construction could not possibly have escaped anyone familiar with the relatively brief history of criminal jurisprudence in the United States. By connecting this canon to "the plain principle, that the power of punishment is vested in the legislative, not in the judicial department,"[62] Marshall unambiguously aligned strict construction with what was then the most basic tenet of federal criminal law: that federal courts lacked the power to develop a body of *common law crimes*. Chief Justice Marshall's formulation in *Wiltberger* unmistakably alluded to a parallel passage in *United States v Hudson & Goodwin*,[63] which had held that "[t]he legislative authority of the Union must first make an act a crime, affix a punishment to it, and declare the court that shall have jurisdiction of the offense" before any person could be charged with a federal offense.[64]

Hudson sprung from political and social conditions that were uniquely American. Although *Hudson* treated it "as having been long . . . settled in public opinion,"[65] the question whether federal courts could develop a body of common law crimes was in fact fiercely disputed in the early years of the Republic. The position that they could provoked resistance from Jeffersonian republicans because it was thought to entail a source of general federal common law unconstrained by the limits of Article I, § 8. It also provoked resistance from those who distrusted the judiciary as a policymaking institution.[66] As belief in the natural grounding of the common law receded, the discretionary character of judge-made criminal

---

[61] Dalzell, *Benefit of Clergy in America* at 233–68 (cited in note 59).

[62] *Wiltberger*, 18 US at 95.

[63] 11 US (7 Cranch) 32 (1812).

[64] Id at 34.

[65] Id at 32.

[66] See, for example, Gary D. Rowe, *The Sound of Silence: United States v Hudson & Goodwin, The Jeffersonian Ascendancy, and the Abolition of Federal Common Law Crimes*, 101 Yale L J 919, 942 (1992); Lawrence M. Friedman, *Crime and Punishment in American History* 63–65 (Basic Books, 1993).

law became intolerable to a wide spectrum of American legal theorists.[67] For those who subscribed to this position, "it followed that the only legitimate authority that could impose criminal sanctions was the legislature by means of statutory enactment."[68]

These lessons were clearly on Chief Justice Marshall's mind when he wrote his opinion in *Wiltberger*.[69] Marshall could have disposed of the case on the straightforward ground that the literal terms of the Crimes Act were controlling.[70] But he chose to go much further, articulating a conception of "strict construction" that excluded from statutory interpretation exactly the types of policymaking judgments associated with common law adjudication. Marshall thus rejected the suggestion that the Court enforce "the obvious intent of the legislature,"[71] because gauging Congress's intent independently of the text would require courts to make normative judgments functionally akin to lawmaking:

> We admit that it is extremely improbable [that Congress intended Section 12 of the Act to be more limited in its extraterritorial reach than Section 8]. But probability is not a guide which a court, in construing a penal statute, can safely take. We can conceive no reason why other crimes, which are not comprehended in this act should not be punished. But congress has not made them punishable, and this court cannot enlarge the statue.[72]

---

[67] Morton J. Horwitz, *The Transformation of American Law, 1780–1860* 9–19 (Harvard, 1987).

[68] Id at 16; see also Friedman, *Crime and Punishment in American History* at 64–65 (cited in note 66). Nonetheless, exactly how critical distrust of the judiciary was to the case against federal common law crimes is disputed among historians. See generally Stewart Jay, *Origins of Federal Common Law: Part Two*, 133 U Pa L Rev 1231, 1250–54 (1985). Moreover, as illustrated by the advent of the general common law of *Swift v Tyson*, 41 US (16 Pet) 1 (1842), *Hudson* cannot be viewed as reflecting a general consensus among nineteenth-century Americans that it was illegitimate in all circumstances for federal courts to engage in common-lawmaking. On the contrary, *Hudson* is probably best viewed as marking the beginning of sustained and profound dissensus in American legal culture on the appropriateness of federal judicial lawmaking.

[69] They were also clearly on the minds of other jurists who were called upon to construe the Crimes Act. See text accompanying notes 122–23 (discussing circuit court decisions refusing to enforce undefined statutory offenses).

[70] See generally John Choon Yoo, *Marshall's Plan: The Early Supreme Court and Statutory Interpretation*, 101 Yale L J 1607, 1618–21 (1992) (chronicling Marshall Court's use of "plain meaning" canon).

[71] *Wiltberger*, 18 US at 94.

[72] Id at 105.

Marshall also adamantly renounced analogical reasoning, the mainstay of common law adjudication:[73]

> It would be dangerous, indeed, to carry the principle, that a case which is within the reason or mischief of a statute, is within its provisions, so far as to punish a crime not enumerated in the statute, because it is of equal atrocity, or of kindred character, with those which are enumerated.[74]

If anything, *Wiltberger's* principle of strict construction was an even stronger vindication of legislative supremacy than was *Hudson's* prohibition on common law crimes. Both forbade the judiciary to assume significant policymaking responsibilities in the field of criminal law. But whereas the prohibition on common law crimes prevented the judiciary from exercising such power on its own initiative, the rule of strict construction foreclosed policy-laden decision making even in pursuit of congressionally approved ends. The teaching of *Wiltberger* was that Congress could not anticipate a cooperative court willing to remedy defects in legislative draftsmanship or to extend a general principle by analogical reasoning. The premise that only the legislature could legitimately define criminal offenses meant not just that Congress was *entitled* to take the lead in defining criminal law, but also that Congress was *obliged* to do so however inconvenient the consequences might be.

2. *Kozminski*. *Kozminski* involved criminal enforcement of the Thirteenth Amendment. The defendants were farmers who induced a pair of mentally retarded adults to work for them without pay by verbally berating them, isolating them from outsiders, and housing them in squalid conditions.[75] For this conduct, they were convicted of violating 18 USC § 1584, which tracks the Thirteenth Amendment's prohibition on "hold[ing]" any person "to involuntary servitude." The issue was whether a person could be "h[eld] . . . to involuntary servitude" solely through psychological coercion.

The Supreme Court answered this question in the negative. It did not rule, however, that psychologically coerced labor is not "involuntary servitude" for purposes of the Thirteenth Amend-

---

[73] See Cass R. Sunstein, *On Analogical Reasoning*, 106 Harv L Rev 741, 754 (1993).

[74] *Wiltberger*, 18 US at 96.

[75] See *Kozminski*, 487 US at 935–36.

ment itself; rather, it avoided this constitutional issue and held only that the defendants' conduct did not come within the scope of 18 USC § 1584.[76] Relying on the "time-honored interpretive guideline that uncertainty concerning the ambit of criminal statutes should be resolved in favor of lenity," the Court concluded that only physically or legally compelled labor should be deemed "involuntary servitude" for statutory purposes.[77]

The Court's application of lenity was clearly animated by nondelegation concerns. Indeed, the *very distinction* between the scope of § 1584 and the Thirteenth Amendment rested on the Court's refusal to make law in Congress's stead. The Court recognized that Congress intended to "incorporate by reference a large body of potentially evolving federal law."[78] But tying the meaning of criminal statutes to evolving judicial interpretations of the Constitution, the Court reasoned, would require the Court to engage "the inherently legislative task of defining 'involuntary servitude' through case-by-case adjudication":[79]

> It is one thing to recognize that some degree of uncertainty exists whenever judges and juries are called upon to apply substantive standards established by Congress; it would be quite another thing to tolerate the arbitrariness and unfairness of a legal system in which the judges would develop the standards for criminal punishment on a case-by-case basis.[80]

The Court used lenity to reconcile Congress's desire for criminal enforcement of the Thirteenth Amendment and the powerlessness of courts to make criminal law. The Court's solution was to read "involuntary servitude" for statutory purposes in light of "the understanding of the Thirteenth Amendment that prevailed at the time of § 1584's enactment."[81] "At that time, all of the Court's

---

[76] See id at 944, 948.

[77] Id at 952.

[78] Id at 941.

[79] Id at 951. In advancing this justification for lenity, moreover, the Court was expressly rejecting the position of Justice Stevens, who concluded that "Congress probably intended the definition [of 'involuntary servitude' in § 1584] to be developed in the common-law tradition of case-by-case adjudication, much as the term 'restraint of trade' has been construed in an equally vague criminal statute." Id at 966–67 (Stevens, joined by Blackmun, concurring in judgment).

[80] Id at 951.

[81] Id at 945.

decisions identifying conditions of involuntary servitude had involved compulsion of services through the use or threatened use
of physical or legal coercion."[82] "Whether other conditions are so
intolerable that they, too, should be deemed to be involuntary," the
Court indicated, "is a value judgment . . . best left for Congress" to
implement through its Thirteenth Amendment enforcement authority.[83]

Kozminski's use of lenity is perfectly faithful to *Wiltberger*'s rejection of policy-laden methods of interpretation. Far from facilitating
the advancement of "public values" generally, lenity allowed the
Court to construe the relevant statutes in a mechanical fashion
so that the relevant "value judgment[s]" would be made only by
Congress.

Kozminski also forcefully illustrates the "tough love" dimension
of lenity. By incorporating constitutional norms into the text of
the relevant criminal statutes, Congress had effectively invited the
Court to contribute to criminal lawmaking. The Court's use of
lenity frustrated this expectation, putting Congress in the position
of having to exercise its own Thirteenth Amendment enforcement
authority in the event that it wished to enlarge the scope of § 1584.
With lenity, Congress must take the bitter with the sweet: it is
assured a position of policymaking leadership in the field of criminal law, but is also forced to occupy that field through its own
lawmaking.

C. THE "RULE OF LAW" FICTION

Showing that the Court's case law can be explained by the nondelegation understanding does not by itself establish that this view
of lenity is the best one. I now want to take another step toward
that objective by demonstrating that lenity *cannot* convincingly be
understood as advancing "rule of law" values such as fair notice
and nonretroactivity. This view of the rule—which is heavily em-

---

[82] Id. The Court also used narrow construction to reverse the Kozminskis' convictions
for violating 18 USC § 241, which prohibits conspiracies to interfere with constitutional
rights generally. To prevent that statute from becoming a vehicle for judicial criminal
lawmaking, the Court concluded that § 241 could be used to enforce only "express terms
of the Federal Constitution" or extant judicial "decisions interpreting them." Id at 941.
Neither the text of the Thirteenth Amendment nor any previous judicial interpretation of
it had equated involuntary servitude with psychologically coerced labor. See id at 942–44.

[83] Id at 951.

phasized by the Court and by commentators alike[84]—adds essentially no weight to the nondelegation understanding.

Analytically, the "nondelegation" and "rule of law" explanations occupy much common space. To assure "fair notice" and avoid "retroactive lawmaking," a court must consider whether a particular statutory reading would enforce a rule of law that is not already clearly set forth in the text of the statute. This is the same question that a court must ask in determining whether a particular reading would amount to delegated lawmaking, which consists precisely in translating general statutory directives into legal rules not clearly specified in advance by Congress.[85]

Because the "nondelegation" and "rule of law" views overlap, it makes sense to ask which one of these views supplies the animating thrust of the rule. Does lenity preclude the exercise of delegated lawmaking in order to promote "rule of law" values, or do courts insist on "notice" and "nonretroactivity" in order to foreclose delegation? I conclude the latter because it is well known that the "rule of law" understanding is a rank fiction: lenity applies even when it is perfectly obvious that a narrow reading is unnecessary to assure notice or other rule of law values.[86]

To illustrate, consider the Court's classic decision in *McBoyle v United States*.[87] The issue in that case was whether the interstate transportation of a stolen plane violated the National Motor Vehicle Theft Act.[88] The Act applied to any "motor vehicle," which was defined as "any . . . self-propelled vehicle not designed for running on rails."[89] Writing for the Court, Justice Holmes conceded that it was "etymologically . . . possible to use the word [vehicle] to signify a conveyance working on land, water or air,"[90] but concluded nonetheless that the statute should be limited to land-moving vehicles. This narrow reading, Holmes asserted, was necessary to provide fair notice:

---

[84] See, for example, *United States v Bass*, 404 US 336, 347–48 (1971); see note 13 for commentators.

[85] See text accompanying notes 34–35.

[86] See, for example, Jeffries, 71 Va L Rev at 219–20 (cited in note 5). I will focus on "fair warning" or notice here; I address a second rule of law value, the prevention of arbitrary law enforcement, below. See text accompanying notes 292–99.

[87] 283 US 25 (1931).

[88] 41 Stat 324 (1919).

[89] Id § 2(a), 41 Stat at 324.

[90] *McBoyle*, 283 US at 26.

> Although it is not likely that a criminal will carefully consider
> the text of the law before he murders or steals, it is reason-
> able that a fair warning should be given to the world in lan-
> guage that the common world will understand, of what the law
> intends to do if a certain line is passed. To make the warning
> fair, so far as possible the line should be clear. When a rule of
> conduct is laid down in words that evoke in the common mind
> only the picture of vehicles moving on land, the statute should
> not be extended to aircraft simply because it may seem to us
> that a similar policy applies, or upon the speculation that, if
> the legislature had thought of it, very likely broader words
> would have been used.[91]

The fictional character of notice in this reasoning is barely con-
cealed. Airplane thieves, no less than murderers and other types
of thieves, are unlikely to consult statute books. Moreover, had the
petitioner in *McBoyle* done so, he would have discovered that his
conduct, whatever its status under federal law, *was* clearly illegal
under state-law theft statutes (and he almost certainly did not need
to see a statute to know that). Taken literally, the "fair notice"
argument is implausible because the broad reading rejected in
McBoyle (like the broad readings rejected in *Wiltberger* and *Kozminski*) would not have affected anyone who was honestly attempting
to conform her behavior to what she believed the criminal law
required.

The same can be said of the Court's use of lenity in *Williams v
United States*.[92] The issue in that case was whether the defendant
made "false statements" to federally insured banks when he issued
a string of bad checks as part of a check-kiting scheme.[93] The Court
conceded that it was "plausible" to view a drawer as making the
representation that he has sufficient funds to cover his check.[94] But
because there was no "evidence of congressional awareness" that
the "false statement" statute would be applied to check kiting, the
Court concluded that lenity precluded such a reading.[95] Whatever
justification there might be for this result, it cannot be the need to

---

[91] Id at 27.

[92] 458 US 279 (1982).

[93] See 18 USC § 1014 (1988 & Supp 1993) (making it a crime "knowingly [to] mak[e] any
false statement . . . for the purpose of influencing in any way the action of [a federally
insured bank]"). In a check-kiting scheme, a person writes a series of bad checks, each
presented to a bank to cover the last, thereby obtaining what amounts to an interest-free
loan. See *Williams*, 458 US at 281 n 1.

[94] See *Williams*, 458 US at 285–86.

[95] See id at 290.

give check kiters fair warning that they are breaking the law. Such individuals are consciously engaging in fraud, which the Court acknowledged to be illegal under state criminal law.[96]

These decisions demonstrate not that lenity is pointless but only that its real point—assuring legislative supremacy—is independent of the notice rationale.[97] Again, *McBoyle:* "When a rule of conduct is laid down in words that evoke in the common mind only the picture of vehicles moving on land, the statute should not be extended to aircraft simply because *it may seem to us that a similar policy applies,* or upon the speculation that, *if the legislature had thought of it,* very likely broader words would have been used."[98] Holmes here expresses the same antagonism toward analogical reasoning that Marshall expressed in *Wiltberger.*[99] Refusing to advance beyond the "picture" that the statutory text immediately "evoke[s] in the common mind" is simply a means of foreclosing the exercise of normative judgment by courts when they construe criminal statutes. Similarly, by insisting on specific "evidence" that Congress was "aware[ ]" of a particular statutory application, the Court in *Williams* assured that judges would not be called upon to extrapolate specific rules of law from general statutory language.[100]

In suggesting that the "rule of law" understanding of lenity is derivative from the "nondelegation" understanding, I do not mean to argue that rule of law values are never relevant to the interpretation of criminal statutes. I will return to this point.[101] But insofar as notice and other rule of law values do not invariably support narrow over broad readings of criminal statutes, the rule of law

---

[96] See id at 287, 290.

[97] It could be suggested, of course, that lenity secures notice in an overinclusive fashion. But because the rule could easily be limited to circumstances in which parties do look to the law for guidance, and in which their reliance on law is morally legitimate, this claim is unpersuasive. See text accompanying notes 272–87.

[98] 283 US at 27 (emphasis added).

[99] See text accompanying notes 73–74.

[100] The *Williams* dissent, in contrast, defended exactly this role for courts. Congress, Justice Marshall argued, had defined the offense in "broad" and "generic" terms because it was impossible to enumerate all of the specific means by which federally insured institutions might be defrauded; accordingly, using lenity to confine the offense to "conduct [specified] by name in the statute or described in detail in the statute's legislative history" contravened Congress's intent and created unjustifiable and unavoidable "loopholes" in the statute. *Williams,* 458 US at 293–94, 304, 305–06 (Marshall, joined by Burger, Brennan, and White, dissenting).

[101] See text accompanying notes 269–99.

understanding is necessarily an incomplete explanation for the rule of lenity, which, if enforced, would require courts to construe criminal statutes narrowly in all contexts.

II. THE HIDDEN RULE: DELEGATED CRIMINAL LAWMAKING

Lenity is commonly perceived to be underenforced.[102] Such a claim resists conclusive empirical testing. Nonetheless, the relative infrequency with which the Supreme Court invokes lenity, and the relative unimportance of the rule in cases that do invoke it, tend to confirm this perception.[103]

What accounts for the failure of the Court to take lenity seriously? One explanation is that federal criminal law is unprincipled. Judges invoke or disregard lenity in order to reach results consistent with their political or ideological preferences.[104]

I believe this explanation surrenders to skepticism much too quickly. It overlooks the possibility that lenity is underenforced not because the judiciary lacks principle but rather because it is institutionally committed to an additional principle or set of principles antagonistic to lenity. That is the hypothesis that I now want to advance. I will argue that lenity is in competition with—indeed, has been largely eclipsed by—another basic principle of federal criminal jurisprudence, a principle that has never been formally acknowledged but that is as old as lenity itself. This principle holds that Congress may delegate, and courts legitimately exercise, criminal lawmaking authority.

In this Part, I present an account of this hidden rule of delegated criminal lawmaking and its impact on lenity. I first establish the plausibility of delegated criminal lawmaking as a conceptual matter and then show how the actual performance of Congress and the judiciary conforms to this theory.

A. THEORETICAL OVERVIEW

At first blush, the proposition that Congress might want to delegate criminal lawmaking to the judiciary (or anyone else) might

---

[102] See note 3.

[103] See note 5.

[104] See note 5 and text accompanying notes 3–5.

seem implausible. By any measure, criminal statutes are among the most important species of law that Congress makes. The sanctions for criminal violations are among the most severe and most costly to administer in the entire legal system; the subject matter of criminal law concerns the electorate more than any other issue;[105] and the symbolic import of criminal law is vital to competing understandings of the nature of the American political regime.[106]

The intuition that Congress would resist dilution of its authority in this critical domain is reflected in another common understanding of lenity. This view depicts lenity as an interpretive principle that Congress itself would likely endorse. The Supreme Court itself sometimes speaks this way, defending strict construction as founded on the judiciary's "[d]ue respect for the prerogatives of Congress in defining federal crimes."[107] Some commentators also defend lenity as a reliable gauge of congressional intent.[108]

What makes this account questionable, however, is the value that Congress places on delegated lawmaking generally.[109] Far from diluting Congress's authority, delegation (whether express or implied) enlarges Congress's policymaking power by reducing the political and practical costs of legislation. And strict construction, far from implementing likely congressional preferences, constricts Congress's institutional influence by forcing it to take the time to

[105] See Dan Balz, *Democrats Ride High into '94 Primaries: Americans Doubt GOP's Ability on Key Issues, Poll Indicates,* Wash Post A1 (Mar 3, 1994) (reporting results of national opinion poll showing that "crime remains the biggest issue of concern to the public" and that "83 percent of the public believes the federal government can do much to make a difference on crime").

[106] See generally Joel Feinberg, *The Expressive Function of Punishment,* in Joel Feinberg, ed, *Doing and Deserving: Essays in the Theory of Responsibility* 102–04 (Princeton, 1970); Jean Hampton, *The Retributive Idea,* in Jeffrie G. Murphy and Jean Hampton, eds, *Forgiveness and Mercy* 134–35, 140–42 (Cambridge, 1988).

[107] *Dowling v United States,* 473 US 207, 213 (1985); see also *Williams,* 458 US at 290; *United States v Bass,* 404 US 336, 347 (1971); *United States v Universal C.I.T. Credit Corp.,* 344 US 218, 221–22 (1952).

[108] See, for example, William D. Popkin, *Law-Making Responsibility and Statutory Interpretation,* 68 Ind L J 865, 881 (1993); Posner, 49 U Chi L Rev at 280–81 (cited in note 19); Ross, 45 Vand L Rev at 570–71 (cited in note 14); Ehrlich and Posner, 3 J Legal Stud at 272–73 (cited in note 15); Shapiro, 67 NYU L Rev at 936 (cited in note 13); *Public Values* at 1029 (cited in note 3).

[109] See text accompanying notes 20–25.

reach the consensus necessary to translate general policies into specific rules of law. Congress's acceptance of the prominent role of the judiciary in shaping federal antitrust, copyright, and labor law—among other "federal common law" fields—strongly corroborates Congress's preference for a lawmaking collaboration rather than a lawmaking monopoly.

Nonetheless, it is sometimes said that this explanation for delegated lawmaking does not fit criminal law. Pointing to the various benefits supposedly associated with clarity and precision in criminal offenses, commentators sometimes argue that Congress can be "assumed to draft criminal statutes more carefully than civil statutes."[110] Under this account, lenity would implement congressional preferences by assuring that courts respect well considered legislative limits on criminal statutes.

The institutional and political dynamics of criminal lawmaking furnish little support for this account. Because Congress faces the same time constraints when it makes criminal law that it does when it makes civil law, it has the same incentive to maximize the return on its legislative investment by drafting criminal statutes broadly. A rule of construction that systematically prevents courts from filling such statutes out by analogical reasoning, from adapting such statutes to new circumstances, or from simply fixing these statutes in the face of obvious defects in draftsmanship is certain to prevent the creation of as much criminal law as Congress desires.

Congress also faces political constraints when it makes criminal law. Just like civil regulatory legislation, criminal legislation can provoke intense controversy among powerful interest groups. Such controversy makes it politically perilous for Congress to proceed and can thus block legislation.[111] Thus, in criminal lawmaking no less than civil lawmaking, Congress has every incentive to avail itself of the "'virtue of vagueness,'" resorting to highly

---

[110] Posner, 49 U Chi L Rev at 281 (cited in note 19); see Ehrlich and Posner, 3 J Legal Stud at 272–73, 277 (cited in note 15); Diver, 93 Yale L J at 77 (cited in note 13).

[111] See generally Charles R. Wise, *The Dynamics of Legislation* chs 4–5 (Jossey-Bass, 1991) (analyzing effect of interest-group politics in shaping and ultimately blocking federal criminal code reform); Louis B. Schwartz, *Reform of the Federal Criminal Laws: Issues, Tactics, and Prospects*, 41 L & Contemp Probs 1 (1977) (same); Katharine Q. Seelye, *Crime Bill Fails on a House Vote, Stunning Clinton*, NY Times A8 (Aug 12, 1994) (Democratic-sponsored legislation "foiled by a bizarre if unintended alliance among liberal blacks, conservative gun proponents and Republicans").

general language that facilitates legislative consensus by deferring resolution of controversial points to the moment of judicial application.[112]

Finally, the assumption that Congress takes greater care to specify the content of criminal statutes than other types of statutes misconceives the place of criminal lawmaking on the congressional agenda. Notwithstanding public concern with "law and order," criminal law has historically comprised a very small part of Congress's docket.[113] This is easy to explain. There is no real constituency for "simplicity, efficiency, and understandability" in criminal law.[114] Congress can effectively satisfy the public demand for criminal law by enacting isolated pieces of highly general (or even purely symbolic) criminal statutes. More detailed legislation would offer little additional reward to individual legislators and would actually detract from the amount of time Congress can devote to the concerns of highly organized interest groups, which are more likely than the public generally to reward legislators for benefits conferred and to punish them for disabilities imposed.[115]

For these reasons, it should not be surprising to discover that federal criminal law consists of just as much delegated judicial lawmaking as the recognized "federal common law" fields. Of course, the only way to determine whether this is in fact so is to look at the actual performance of Congress and the judiciary in the domain of criminal law. I now turn to this task.

B. ILLUSTRATIONS

I will document the rule of delegated criminal lawmaking in two steps. First, I will try to show just how pervasive delegated lawmaking has been and continues to be in federal criminal juris-

---

[112] Wise, *The Dynamics of Legislation* at 178 (cited in note 111). "Such a formulation allows each representative to tell his constituents that he obtained language to protect them and allows him to vote for the bill, thus preserving a majority for the bill. Congressmen know that clarity is not always required to pass a bill, but a majority is required. The courts can be left to devise an interpretation of what 'congressional intent' was." Id.

[113] See Friedman, *Crime and Punishment in American History* at 275–76 (cited in note 66).

[114] Wise, *The Dynamics of Legislation* at 317 (cited in note 111).

[115] See generally Mancur Olson, Jr., *The Logic of Collective Action* (Harvard, 1965); Michael T. Hayes, *Lobbyists and Legislators: A Theory of the Political Process* (Rutgers, 1981).

prudence.[116] Second, I will examine how this practice has shaped Congress's and the Court's respective views on the rule of lenity.

1. *Delegated criminal lawmaking at work*

a) *The Crimes Act of 1790.* Congress's implicit delegation of criminal lawmaking authority to courts began with the very first piece of criminal legislation that Congress enacted—the Crimes Act of 1790. This legislation provided for punishment of various offenses on the "high seas," in federal enclaves, and in other areas beyond the reach of state criminal law jurisdiction.[117] The offenses, however, were merely identified and not defined by the statutory text, nor did all of these offenses have clear common law antecedents.[118] The only way, then, for courts to enforce these offenses was to give them content in the course of applying them.[119]

However unproblematic court-supplied definitions for statutory offenses may have appeared to the First Congress in 1790, the practice became increasingly questionable as federal criminal jurisprudence began to take shape. By the time the Court decided *Hudson* in 1812, it was already "long . . . settled"[120] that federal courts were powerless to devise common law crimes. And after *Wiltberger* was decided in 1820, it certainly appeared to be settled that federal courts were without power to engage in what amounted to common-lawmaking in the guise of statutory interpretation. Chief Justice Marshall's use of "strict construction" was calculated to prevent

---

[116] The most obvious example is federal antitrust law, which is criminally enforceable and pervaded by common–lawmaking, see note 32. Nonetheless, civil enforcement is the norm in antitrust, and the Department of Justice reserves criminal enforcement for intentional violations of clearly established doctrines. See Areeda and Kaplow, *Antitrust Analysis* at 63 (cited in note 27). Accordingly, the significance of delegated *criminal* lawmaking in antitrust is open to dispute. To avoid that issue, I will concentrate here on offenses in which criminal prosecutions furnish either the exclusive or the primary occasions for the exercise of delegated lawmaking.

[117] 1 Stat 112. See generally Dwight F. Henderson, *Congress, Courts, and Criminals: The Development of Federal Criminal Law, 1801–1829,* 8–9 (Greenwood, 1985); and David P. Currie, *The Constitution in Congress: Substantive Issues in the First Congress, 1789–1791,* 61 U Chi L Rev 775, 828–33 (1994).

[118] See, for example, *United States v Tully,* 28 F Cases 226, 229 (CCD Mass 1812) (No 16,545) (Davis, J) (recognizing that § 8 of the statute "make[s] certain . . . acts piracy, which would not be so at common law").

[119] See, for example, *United States v Hemmer,* 26 F Cases 259 (CCD Mass 1825) (No 15,345) (defining statutory offenses of "confin[ing] the master of any ship" and "endeavor[ing] to commit a revolt").

[120] 11 US at 32.

courts from exercising at Congress's invitation the very sort of criminal lawmaking authority that courts lacked under the Constitution.[121] The Crimes Act, however, seemed to compel the exercise of this forbidden power.

A number of defendants successfully challenged Crimes Act prosecutions on this ground. Federal circuit courts were particularly reluctant to entertain prosecutions for the (undefined) statutory offenses of "mak[ing]" or "endeavor[ing] to make" a "revolt."[122] "[A]s there was no such phrase to be met with in the common law of England, to which a meaning had been affixed," these courts reasoned that "it seem[s] . . . too much like legislating to give a definition of our own."[123]

The Supreme Court, however, ultimately made short work of this position. Responding to the objection that federal courts lacked the power to enforce the offense of "endeavoring to make a revolt," the Court in *United States v Kelly*[124] stated simply: "This court is of opinion, that although the act of congress does not define this offence, it is, nevertheless, competent to the court to give a judicial definition of it."[125] The Court then proceeded to elaborate in very specific terms the *actus reus* and *mens rea* elements of the crime.[126]

Kelly supplied what was, in effect, a blueprint for the hidden rule of delegated lawmaking in federal criminal law. Through enacting incompletely specified criminal statutes, Congress could implicitly transfer lawmaking authority to the judiciary. By formulating the

---

[121] See text accompanying notes 61–74.

[122] See *United States v Sharp*, 27 F Cases 1041, 1043 (CCD Penn 1815) (No 16,264) (declining to instruct the jury because of the absence of any fixed definition "either in the common, admiralty, or civil law" and because of the court's "natural repugnance[ ] to selecting from th[e] mass of definitions" suggested by "philologists"); *United States v Bladen*, 24 F Cases 1161 (CCD Penn 1816) (No 14,606) (directing verdict of acquittal on count charging "endeavoring to make revolt"); *United States v Smith*, 27 F Cases 1246, 1247 (CCD Penn 1811) (No 16,344) (declining to instruct jury on the offense on the ground that the "court feels some difficulty" in defining it). But see *United States v Smith*, 27 F Cases 1166, 1167 (CCD Mass 1816) (16,337).

[123] *United States v Kelly*, 26 F Cases 700, 701 (CCED Penn 1825) (No 15,516) (explaining rationale of previous decisions but instructing on offense subject to Supreme Court certification), conviction aff'd, 24 US (11 Wheat) 417 (1826); see also *United States v Haskell*, 26 F Cases 207, 209 (CCED Penn 1823) (No 15,321) (noting that "[t]his court has decided that there is no legitimate or safe standard, by which to ascertain the definitions of this offence").

[124] 24 US (11 Wheat) 417 (1826).

[125] Id at 418.

[126] See id at 418–19.

mediating principles and doctrines necessary to bring these statutes to bear on real-world facts, courts could accept this grant of law-making responsibility. Conspicuous only by its absence was any acknowledgment of the tension between this lawmaking collaboration and the conception of legislative supremacy that animated *Hudson* and *Wiltberger*.[127] It was a pattern that was to be repeated time and again.

b) "Fraud." Historically, the fraud offenses—including mail fraud (18 USC § 1341),[128] wire fraud (18 USC § 1343),[129] and

---

[127] It takes little investigation, however, to solve this mystery. One jurist who, on circuit, expressed no misgivings about defining the elements of "endeavoring to make a revolt" was Justice Story. See *Smith*, 27 F Cases at 1167 (acknowledging that "[t]he language of the statute is not of very easy interpretation; and the word 'revolt' has not acquired so definite a meaning, as to be free from all doubt" but proceeding to supply a definition based on "the best consideration, which we can give the subject"). Before *Hudson*, Story had forcefully defended the position that federal courts did have the constitutional power to devise common law crimes; after *Hudson*, he took the position that Congress still could and should enact a statute authorizing federal courts to recognize federal crimes by common-lawmaking. See R. Kent Newmyer, *Supreme Court Justice Joseph Story: Statesman of the Old Republic* 100–05 (North Carolina, 1985); Rowe, 101 Yale L J at 926 (cited in note 66). By the time *Kelly* reached the Supreme Court, Story had apparently persuaded a majority of his colleagues that it was indeed appropriate for the judiciary to accept the assignment of defining statutory offenses, notwithstanding the reasoning of *Wiltberger* and other lower court decisions. Given the Marshall Court practice against dissenting opinions, see Rowe, 101 Yale L J at 929 & n 48 (cited in note 66), the absence of a dissent in *Kelly* does not imply that Story had persuaded *all* of his colleagues that the exercise of such lawmaking power was constitutional. Ironically, however, the Court's opinion in *Kelly* was written by Justice Washington, who had authored the circuit court opinions refusing to enforce "endeavoring to make a revolt" and who had certified the issue to the Supreme Court only after expressing the view that the judiciary's power to define this offense was "very questionable." 26 F Cases at 701. The definition adopted by the Court in *Kelly* was essentially the one devised by Story, compare 24 US at 418–19 with *Smith*, 27 F Cases at 1167, and in the years following *Kelly*, Story (on circuit) continued to embroider this definition in a common law fashion. See *United States v Haines*, 26 F Cases 62 (CCD Mass 1829); *United States v Barker*, 24 F Cases 985 (CCD Mass 1829); *United States v Gardner*, 25 F Cases 1258 (CCD Mass 1829); *United States v Savage*, 27 F Cases 966 (CCD Mass 1830); *United States v Morrison*, 26 F Cases 1351 (CCD Mass 1833); *United States v Cassedy*, 25 F Cases 321 (CCD Mass 1837).

[128] "Whoever, having devised or intending to devise any scheme or artifice to defraud, or for obtaining money or property by means of false or fraudulent pretenses, . . . for the purpose of executing such scheme or artifice or attempting so to do, places in any post office or authorized depository for mail matter, any matter or thing whatever to be sent or delivered by the Postal Service, or takes or receives therefrom, any such matter or thing, . . . shall be fined under this title or imprisoned not more than five years, or both." 18 USCA § 1341 (1994).

[129] "Whoever, having devised or intending to devise any scheme or artifice to defraud, or for obtaining money or property by means of false or fraudulent pretenses, . . . transmits or causes to be transmitted by means of wire, radio, or television communication in interstate or foreign commerce, any writings, signs, signals, pictures, or sounds for the purpose of executing such scheme or artifice, shall be fined under this title or imprisoned not more than five years, or both." 18 USCA § 1343 (1994).

"conspiracy to defraud the United States" (18 USC § 371)[130]—have occupied a prominent position in federal criminal law.[131] Eclipsed only by drug-distribution cases, fraud cases still comprise almost 15% of all federal prosecutions.[132]

The law of criminal fraud, moreover, clearly conforms to the model of delegated lawmaking. Connecting mail fraud[133] to other "federal common law" statutes, Justice Stevens has observed:

> Statutes like the Sherman Act, the civil rights legislation, and the mail fraud statute were written in broad general language on the understanding that the courts would have wide latitude in construing them to achieve the remedial purposes that Congress had identified. The wide open spaces in statutes such as these are most appropriately interpreted as implicit delegations of authority to the courts to fill in the gaps in the common-law tradition of case-by-case adjudication.[134]

An examination of what Congress and the courts have respectively contributed to the development of the law of criminal fraud completely bears out Stevens's view.

The incompleteness of the criminal fraud statutes is virtually inherent in their very use of the term "fraud," which has traditionally been understood to be one of the most open-ended concepts in law. Story, for example, offered this virtually limitless definition: "all acts . . . which involve a breach of legal or equitable duty . . . and [which] are injurious to another, or by which an undue and unconscientious advantage is taken of another."[135] More forthrightly, common law commentators and jurists (including Story) frequently conceded that it was impossible to define "fraud" with any real precision given the wide variety of contexts in which

---

[130] "If two or more persons conspire . . . to defraud the United States, or any agency thereof in any manner or for any purpose, and one or more of such persons do any act to effect the object of the conspiracy, each shall be fined not more than $10,000 or imprisoned not more than five years, or both." 18 USC § 371 (1988).

[131] For an historical account of the offense of conspiracy to defraud, see Abraham S. Goldstein, *Conspiracy to Defraud*, 68 Yale L J 406 (1959); for mail fraud, see Jed S. Rakoff, *The Federal Mail Fraud Statute*, 18 Duquesne L Rev 771 (1980).

[132] See *Reports of the Proceedings of the Judicial Conference of the United States: Annual Report of the Director of the Administrative Office of the United States Courts 1990*, Table D-2, 184–85 (GPO, 1991); Administrative Office of the United States Courts, *Federal Judicial Workload Statistics March 31, 1993*, Table D-2, 52–54.

[133] I will refer to wire fraud and mail fraud together as "mail fraud."

[134] *McNally v United States*, 483 US 350, 372–73 (1987) (Stevens dissenting).

[135] J. Story, 1 *Equity Jurisprudence* § 186 at 190 (10th ed 1870).

courts had found it to exist.[136] Indeed, they often refused on principle even to attempt a definition, lest it detract from the discretion of judges to adapt "fraud" to unforeseen species of deceptive behavior.[137] In embedding the term "defraud" within § 1341 and § 371, then, Congress self-consciously harnessed this engine of judicial ingenuity for purposes of criminal lawmaking.

Of course, nothing compelled federal courts to accept this assignment. They could have used strict construction to cabin the generative capacity of the concept of fraud as embodied in federal criminal statutes. In particular, courts could have tied the meaning of the mail fraud and conspiracy statutes to some finite schedule of deceptive practices that existed at the time these statutes were enacted, thereby forcing Congress to enact additional statutes to deal with any new forms of dishonesty or deception. This is the approach, for example, that the Court took in *Kozminski* to prevent 18 USC § 1584—the statute that provides for criminal enforcement of the Thirteenth Amendment—from spawning judge-made criminal rules.[138]

But courts never took that approach in construing § 1341, § 371, or the other federal criminal fraud statutes. The Supreme Court established early on that "defraud" in § 1341 and § 371 was not limited to the meaning of "fraud" at common law, in state law, or in any other independent source of law.[139] Once the statutory language was severed from these sources, moreover, it was necessarily incumbent on courts, guided only by their conception of "the evil sought to be remedied,"[140] to determine just what meaning the federal statutes *ought* to have.

For over a century, they have pursued this task with a vengeance. The wire fraud and conspiracy to defraud statutes have been applied to scores of distinct forms of misconduct—from business and consumer fraud, to securities and commodities fraud, to blackmail, to lottery schemes, to public corruption, to misappropriation of confidential information (both private and governmen-

---

[136] See, for example, id at 189; Milton D. Green, *Fraud, Undue Influence and Mental Incompetence*, 43 Colum L Rev 176, 177–79 (1943).

[137] See, for example, Story, *Equity Jurisprudence* at 189 (cited in note 135); *Clyce v Gustavus*, 39 Mo 37, 40 (1871); *McAleer v Horsey*, 35 Md 439, 451–52 (1872).

[138] See text accompanying notes 78–83.

[139] *Durland v US*, 161 US 306, 312–13 (1896); *Haas v Henkel*, 216 US 462, 479–80 (1910).

[140] *Durland*, 161 US at 313.

tal).[141] Had courts been unwilling to treat "fraud" as a generative concept, each of these applications would have required the enactment of a separate criminal statute. If anything, the criminal fraud statutes have proven even more potent as fonts of independently operative legal rules than any of the recognized "common law" statutes, including the Sherman Act.

Beyond adapting the fraud statutes to myriad forms of criminality, federal courts have also elaborated an intricate body of doctrinal principles to guide application of these statutes in various contexts. Notwithstanding the nearly identical language of these offenses, for example, the Supreme Court has concluded that mail fraud, but not conspiracy to defraud, must be aimed at divesting another party of a property interest.[142] Specifying what does and does not count as "property" for purposes of the mail fraud statute has generated even more case law.[143] In addition, federal courts have filled out the mail fraud statute by devising a cluster of special rules on the nexus between the scheme to defraud and the mailing.[144] Neither specifically contemplated by Congress nor contrary to any discernible congressional expectations, all of these doctrines, too, must be understood to be the product of federal common-lawmaking.

The leadership role of the judiciary in developing the law of criminal fraud has not disappointed Congress. Far from objecting to the failure of courts to construe these statutes narrowly, Congress has largely been content to watch the evolution of these crimes from the sidelines, intervening only intermittently to codify expansive judicial readings.[145] Indeed, the *only* significant amendment of the mail fraud statute was designed to overrule the Su-

---

[141] Rakoff, 18 Duquesne L Rev at 772–73 (cited in note 131); Goldstein, 68 Yale L J at 437–41 (cited in note 131).

[142] Compare *McNally*, 483 US at 358–59 (mail fraud) with *Haas*, 216 US at 480 (conspiracy to defraud).

[143] See, for example, *Carpenter v United States*, 484 US 19 (1987) (holding that intangible interest in confidentiality of proprietary information is property for purposes of mail fraud); see, generally, Norman Abrams and Sara Sun Beale, *Federal Criminal Law and Its Enforcement* 158–72 (West, 2d ed 1993).

[144] See, for example, *Schmuck v United States*, 489 US 705, 712–15 (1989); *United States v Maze*, 414 US 395, 397 (1974).

[145] Rakoff, 18 Duquesne L Rev at 772, 809, 816 (cited in note 131) (detailing two major amendments to the statute which codified broad judicial interpretation). See also *McNally*, 483 US at 374 (Stevens dissenting).

preme Court's decision in *McNally v United States*,[146] which had narrowly construed the mail fraud statute as inapplicable to schemes to defraud state governments of the intangible interest in honest services.[147]

Congress's willingness to defer so generously to the judiciary derives from the "updating" economies associated with delegated lawmaking. By conserving the generative character of "defraud," courts have been able to adapt the fraud statutes almost instantaneously to emerging forms of misconduct, thus sparing Congress from having to expend the institutional capital necessary to address such activity through specific legislation.[148] Commenting on this function, Chief Justice Burger characterized the mail fraud statute "as a first line of defense. When a 'new' fraud develops—as constantly happens—the mail fraud statute becomes a stopgap device to deal on a temporary basis with the new phenomenon, until particularized legislation can be developed and passed to deal directly with the evil."[149] Given the press of other concerns on the congressional agenda, however, the gap between a new application of the mail fraud statute and the enactment of specific legislation has not always been so "temporary." Often Congress has been content to leave the fraud statutes as the sole instrument of criminal punishment.[150]

Finally, it should be noted that courts have not invariably construed the fraud statutes expansively.[151] In delegating lawmaking authority, Congress necessarily authorized the judiciary to adopt the best readings of the fraud statutes, whether narrow or broad.

---

[146] 483 US 350 (1987).

[147] 18 USC § 1346 (1988) ("For the purposes of this chapter, the term 'scheme or artifice to defraud' includes a scheme or artifice to deprive another of the intangible right of honest services.").

[148] See Rakoff, 18 Duquesne L Rev at 772–73 (cited in note 131); Goldstein, 68 Yale L J at 440 (cited in note 131).

[149] *Maze*, 414 US at 405–06 (Burger dissenting).

[150] The most prominent example is the use of the fraud statutes (including the mail fraud and securities fraud provisions) to enforce various fiduciary duties in corporate and other employment settings. This use of the fraud statutes has flourished—and drawn criticism— for years without congressional efforts to enact more precise statutory rules. If anything, Congress has ratified continuing judicial leadership in this field. See note 386 (discussing aftermath of *McNally*).

[151] See, for example, *McNally*, 483 US at 359–60; *Fasulo v United States*, 272 US 620, 629 (1926); *Gradwell v United States*, 243 US 476, 485, 488–89 (1916); *Tanner v United States*, 483 US 107, 131 (1986); *Maze*, 414 US at 395.

When the Supreme Court has viewed narrow readings as best, it has sometimes (but not always) bolstered its conclusions by invoking the rule of lenity.[152] Against the background of generative interpretations of the statutes, the use of the rule in these cases understandably rings hollow; it is precisely this sort of opportunistic appearance and disappearance of the rule that fuels the skeptical conclusion that the Court's substantive criminal law jurisprudence is unprincipled.[153] Because the Court has so obviously not viewed itself as constrained in *all* circumstances to select the narrowest reasonable reading of the fraud statutes, any decision that does adopt a narrow reading is best understood as reflecting the judgment that, in the *particular* circumstances at hand, a narrow reading better promotes relevant values than does a broad one.[154] The authority to engage in ad hoc balancing of the benefits of broad and narrow readings, however, is exactly the type of normative discretion that lenity, as a nondelegation doctrine, purports to deny to courts.

c) RICO. Congress's delegation of criminal lawmaking authority to the judiciary is not a phenomenon confined to eighteenth- and nineteenth-century legislation. If anything, this practice reached its zenith in Congress's most important recent contribution to federal criminal law: the Racketeer Influenced Corrupt Organizations Act.[155]

As an account of how Congress and courts have collaborated to make criminal law, the story of RICO mirrors the stories of the Crimes Act and of the criminal fraud statutes. Like those offenses, RICO is incomplete on its face. RICO forbids any person to "conduct or participate . . . in the conduct of" any "enterprise . . . through a pattern of racketeering activity."[156] The statute defines the crucial term "enterprise" as "includ[ing] any individual, part-

---

[152] See, for example, *McNally*, 483 US at 359–60; *Tanner*, 483 US at 131; see also *Fasulo*, 272 US at 629 and *Gradwell*, 243 US at 485.

[153] See note 5 and accompanying text.

[154] Many decisions construing the fraud statutes narrowly are animated by federalism values. See, for example, *McNally*, 483 US at 360 (narrow reading of mail fraud to avoid setting federal standards of ethics for local governments); *Gradwell*, 243 US at 484 (adopting narrow reading of § 371 in order to respect "policy of . . . entrusting the conduct of elections to state laws, administered by state officers").

[155] 18 USC §§ 1961–68 (1988 & Supp 1993).

[156] Id at § 1962(c).

nership, corporation, association, or other legal entity, and any union or group of individuals associated in fact."[157] This formulation literally excludes nothing; any "individual" or any "group of individuals," however constituted, is eligible to be a RICO "enterprise." In truth, the statutory "definition" of "enterprise" is no definition at all, but only a directive to courts not to limit "enterprise" to the formally structured entities that it commonly denotes—such as corporations, partnerships, or associations.[158] But beyond conveying that "enterprise" is *not merely* one of these entities, the statute affords no clue as to *what else* an enterprise is (and, more importantly, is not). That task necessarily falls upon the courts.

The meaning of "pattern of racketeering activity" is also incompletely specified. According to the statutory "definition," this element of the offense "requires at least two acts of racketeering activity."[159] This, too, is not a genuine definition, for it states only a necessary and not a sufficient condition for finding a pattern: there must be *at least* two racketeering offenses.[160] But while the statute "assumes that there is something to a . . . pattern beyond simply the number of predicate acts involved," the text "does not identify . . . [what] these additional prerequisites" are; this, too, is for courts to work out.[161]

The incompleteness of the statutory text was no accident. Responding to the classic incentives to delegate lawmaking authority, Congress deliberately chose to frame RICO in highly general terms. Although Congress had a general idea of the evil that it wanted to combat—"organized crime," the "Mafia," "Cosa Nostra"—it found the task of defining this phenomenon to be excruciatingly complex and controversial.[162] Moreover, Congress did not

---

[157] Id at § 1961(4).

[158] See Clark D. Cunningham et al, *Plain Meaning and Hard Cases*, 103 Yale L J 1561, 1590 (1994).

[159] 18 USC § 1961(5) (1988 & Supp 1993).

[160] " '[P]roof of two acts of racketeering, without more, does not establish a pattern,' " *H. J. Inc. v Northwestern Bell Tel. Co.*, 492 US 229, 238 (1989) (quoting legislative history); see also *Sedima v Imrex Co.*, 473 US 479, 497 n 14 (1985).

[161] *H. J. Inc.*, 492 US at 238. Other key terms—such as "to conduct . . . or participate . . . in the conduct" of RICO enterprise, 18 USC § 1961(5)—were excluded from the definitions section of RICO altogether.

[162] See, for example, 116 Cong Rec 35204 (1970) (debate between Reps. Mikva and Poff).

necessarily want a precise definition of this concept; it wanted an offense broad enough to cover all forms of criminal associations functionally equivalent to classic "organized crime."[163] The solution to these problems was to use exceedingly porous language, which obviated the need to resolve conceptual difficulties and which assured that the statute would have the generative capacity to reach beyond its core application.[164]

Congress understood this drafting choice to reflect an appropriate division of labor between Congress and the judiciary. Rejecting calls to make the statutory language more precise, RICO's principal sponsor explained that the "proper legislative role [is to] examine not only individual instances, but whole problems," and thus to avoid "piecemeal legislation" by framing criminal statutes in "[c]omprehensive" terms.[165] Fitting such terms to the specific "facts of the cases before them" is the proper "role of a court."[166] In performing this task, of course, courts would necessarily be obliged to supply RICO's key terms with the operative content that Congress self-consciously avoided imparting.

Courts have adopted an interpretive posture that permits them to perform exactly this function. "RICO is to be read broadly," the Supreme Court has explained, in order to implement its "expansive language and overall approach."[167] "Congress," it has recognized, "drafted RICO broadly enough to encompass a wide range of criminal activity, taking many different forms and likely to attract a broad array of perpetrators operating in many different ways"; consequently, a "narrow construction" that confined RICO to the specific forms of criminal associations that moved Congress to enact the statute "would be counterproductive and a mismeasure of congressional intent."[168]

---

[163] See *H. J. Inc.*, 492 US at 246–48.

[164] See id; Gerard E. Lynch, *RICO: The Crime of Being a Criminal: Parts I & II*, 87 Colum L Rev 661, 685–94 (1987).

[165] 116 Cong Rec 18914 (1970) (statement of Sen McClellan).

[166] Id; see also 115 Cong Rec 9567 (1969) (statement of Sen McClellan) (suggesting that statute will afford wide remedial discretion to courts: "The ability of our chancery courts to formulate a remedy to fit the wrong is one of the great benefits of our system of justice. This ability is not hindered by the bill.").

[167] *Sedima*, 473 US at 497–98.

[168] *H. J. Inc.*, 492 US at 248–49.

Guided by this philosophy, courts have fashioned a body of RICO law every bit as rich as the judge-made law of criminal fraud. They have recognized as RICO "enterprises" not only the types of associations that Congress clearly did have in mind— primarily "mafia-infiltrated" legitimate businesses[169]—but also a wide array of other entities that Congress almost certainly did not, including wholly criminal associations,[170] corrupt local governments,[171] terrorists,[172] and even political-protest organizations.[173] In many of these settings, RICO, much like the criminal fraud statutes, operates as a "gap filler," permitting extension of federal criminal law to species of misconduct that Congress has failed to address through specific legislation.[174] In the course of translating RICO's general principles into operative rules of law, courts have also devised an elaborate set of doctrinal tests and definitions, including the "continuity plus relationship" standard for assessing whether a series of racketeering offenses constitutes a "pattern."[175]

There is no evidence that Congress views this innovative implementation of RICO as a usurpation of congressional authority to determine the boundaries of criminal liability. On the contrary, Congress has codified some of the Supreme Court's most expansive readings and has consistently rejected any proposals to limit RICO.[176] As Gerard Lynch has observed, "if RICO has evolved into something different from what Congress intended at its creation, it is difficult to escape the conclusion that Congress has looked at what has evolved, and pronounced it good."[177]

---

[169] See, for example, Lynch, 87 Colum L Rev at 678 (cited in note 164).

[170] *Turkette v United States*, 452 US 576, 587 (1981).

[171] See Lynch, 87 Colum L Rev at 734–37 (cited in note 164).

[172] See, for example, *United States v Bagaric*, 706 F2d 42, 58 (2d Cir 1983).

[173] *NOW v Scheidler*, 114 S Ct 798, 806 (1994).

[174] For example, RICO permits the prosecution of various forms of local corruption that may not be covered by any other federal statute. See Lynch, 87 Colum L Rev at 741 (cited in note 164).

[175] *Sedima*, 473 US at 497 n 14; *H. J. Inc.*, 492 US at 239. See also *Reves v Ernst & Young*, 113 S Ct 1163, 1172–73 (1993) (fashioning "operate or manage" test for construing § 1961(5)).

[176] Lynch, 87 Colum L Rev at 711 (cited in note 164); Abrams and Beale, *Federal Criminal Law and Its Enforcement* at 561 (cited in note 143).

[177] Lynch, 87 Colum L Rev at 713 (cited in note 164).

2. The disfavored status of lenity

a) Congressional disapproval. Like any other rule of strict construction, lenity raises the practical and political cost of lawmaking by preventing Congress from implicitly delegating lawmaking power to courts.[178] So if Congress does value implied delegation as much in criminal law as it does in the recognized "federal common law" fields, there should be some indication that Congress would in fact resent an uncompromising application of lenity. Such evidence is readily discoverable.

It includes Congress's express abrogation of strict construction in certain criminal statutes. Among these is RICO, which directs that "[t]he provisions of this [statute] shall be *liberally construed* to effectuate its remedial purposes."[179] This "liberal construction" clause compliments Congress's deliberate decision to obtain maximum statutory coverage by leaving RICO's key terms unspecified.[180]

Congressional antagonism toward lenity has also been reflected in various proposals for comprehensive criminal code reform. The 1977 version of this legislation would have required that all federal criminal statutes "be construed in accordance with the fair import of their terms to effectuate the general purposes of th[e] [criminal law]."[181] According to the Senate Judiciary Committee report, this rule of construction was designed to "repeal whatever vestiges remain in the Federal system of the artificial canon of 'strict construction' under which a court is obligated to adopt the narrowest possible view of the language used by Congress in a criminal statute."[182] Strict construction, the report explained, makes criminal lawmaking " 'intolerably cumbersome,' " forcing " 'the legislative draftsman . . . to anticipate every possible narrow construc-

---

[178] See text accompanying notes 37–42.

[179] Pub L No 91-452, § 904(a), 84 Stat 947 (1970) (emphasis added).

[180] See text accompanying notes 155–66; see also *United States v Russello*, 464 US 16, 27–28 (1983) (recognizing connection between liberal construction clause and congressional goals of breadth and flexibility in statutory coverage). Other criminal statutes containing "liberal construction" clauses include 21 USC § 854(d) (1988) (prohibition on drug-sale proceeds); 21 USC § 853(o) (1988) (forfeiture of drug-distribution proceeds); 18 USC § 1467(n) (1988 & Supp 1993) (forfeiture of obscenity-sale proceeds); 18 USC § 2253(n) (1988 & Supp 1993) (forfeiture of child pornography proceeds).

[181] S 1722, 96th Cong, 1st Sess, § 112(a) (Sept 7, 1979).

[182] S Rep No 605, 95th Cong, 1st Sess 23 (1977).

tion.' "[183] A 1979 proposal included a similar interpretive directive.[184]

It is true that Congress (for reasons having nothing to do with
lenity) failed to enact the 1977 and 1979 proposals[185] and has never
otherwise seen fit to enact a global "liberal construction" rule. But
it is also true that the Supreme Court has demonstrably failed to
enforce lenity.[186] Against this background, Congress's inaction by
no means supports the inference that Congress approves of that
rule of construction. Insofar as federal courts only sporadically
apply lenity, a statute enacted for the sole purpose of repealing it
would be of relatively little value and probably not worth what it
would cost (practically and politically) to enact it. Repeal *is* worth
the trouble only when Congress has already committed substantial
resources to making criminal law—in enacting RICO, for example,
or in attempting comprehensively to reform the federal criminal
code.[187] And considering how imperfectly courts enforce lenity,
even this much attention to the rule is powerful confirmation of
how intensely Congress disapproves of it.

An idea of what Congress would likely do if lenity *were* truly
enforced can be gleaned from the history of the rule in state law.

---

[183] Id (quoting Working Papers of Nat'l Commn for Reform of Federal Criminal Code
(1970)). Somewhat perplexingly, the committee report sought to distinguish "strict construction" from "lenity," which the report described as a much milder preference for narrow
readings to be adopted only if ambiguity persists after a court consults a statute's legislative
history, its purpose, and other extrinsic interpretive guides. See id at 24. As I discuss below,
this conception of lenity, which is now the dominant doctrinal formulation, nearly assures
the irrelevance of the rule as a practical matter. See text accompanying notes 202–30. By
endorsing this version of lenity, the 1977 proposal would have codified the effective judicial
repeal of lenity.

[184] See S Rep No 553, 96th Cong, 1st Sess 22–25 (1979). The 1979 proposal, however,
denounced strict construction less wholeheartedly than did the 1977 proposal. While rejecting "the artificial" version of the rule, the 1979 proposal purported to endorse a superior
version of " 'strict construction' " that it deemed consistent with reading statutes " 'in accordance with the fair import of their terms.' " Id at 22; see also id at 24 (explaining that
"automatic niggardly interpretations are to be avoided and that the search is to be directed
at discovering the 'fair import' of the statutory language in accordance with the general
purpose [of the criminal code]").

[185] See Wise, *The Dynamics of Legislation* at chs 4–5 (cited in note 111); Schwartz, 41 L &
Contemp Probs 1 (cited in note 111.

[186] See text accompanying notes 3–5.

[187] The other "liberal construction" rules likewise entered the US Code through much
larger crime bills. See Comprehensive Forfeiture Act of 1984, § 303, Pub L No 98-473, 98
Stat 1837, 2050; Anti-Drug Abuse Act of 1988, § 7522, Pub L No 100–690, 102 Stat 4181,
4499.

Unlike federal courts, state courts did aggressively enforce strict construction in the nineteenth and early twentieth centuries.[188] In response, many state legislatures abrogated strict construction universally within their criminal codes.[189] The explanation furnished by Pound and other contemporary commentators was clear: "the disinclination of courts and lawyers to give to penal statutes any wider application than the letter required" was severely constraining the power of legislators "to make improvements in the definition of old crimes."[190]

b) Judicial trivialization. As its track record in enforcing lenity confirms,[191] the Supreme Court has fully accommodated Congress's preference for broad rather than narrow readings of criminal statutes. I now want to consider the mechanism by which lenity has been rendered so largely inoperative. Obviously, the Court has never formally repudiated lenity. But it has done something nearly as effective, adopting a doctrinal formulation of the rule that poses no effective impediment to the exercise of delegated lawmaking power by courts.

On its own terms, lenity is appropriate only when a court is confronted by multiple "rational readings" of a criminal statute.[192] As the Court has repeatedly stated, "the 'touchstone' of the rule of lenity 'is statutory ambiguity.'"[193] Accordingly, the key doctrinal issue is what counts as "ambiguity" for purposes of the rule.

This question does not answer itself. In an important sense, statutory "ambiguity" is a legal construct. The "meaning" of a

---

[188] See Livingston Hall, *Strict or Liberal Construction of Penal Statutes*, 48 Harv L Rev 748, 751–52 (1935).

[189] See id at 752–54.

[190] See generally Roscoe Pound, *Criminal Justice in America* 143 (Holt, 1930); see also Hall, 48 Harv L Rev at 760 (cited in note 188); Comment, *Criminal Law and Procedure—Statutory Construction*, 32 Mich L Rev 976 (1934). This philosophy informs the American Law Institute's influential Model Penal Code, which provides that "when the language [of a Code provision] is susceptible of differing constructions it shall be interpreted to further the general purposes [of the Code] and the special purposes of the particular provision involved." See Model Penal Code § 1.02(3). The drafters deliberately rejected "[t]he ancient rule that penal law must be strictly construed, . . . because it unduly emphasized only one aspect of the problem," namely, fair notice to potential offenders, associated with statutory ambiguity. 1 American Law Institute, Model Penal Code and Commentaries, 32–33 (1985).

[191] See note 4.

[192] *McNally v United States*, 483 US at 359–60.

[193] *Bifulco v United States*, 447 US 381, 387 (1980), quoting *Lewis v United States*, 445 US 55, 65 (1980); accord, *Moskal v United States*, 498 US 103, 107–08 (1990).

statute is a function not just of the signification of words to English-speaking people generally but of the interpretive conventions shared by members of the legal culture in particular.[194] Statutory language is "ambiguous" when these conventions conflict or point in different directions.[195] Ambiguity is either avoided or resolved by giving certain of these conventions priority over others.

Decisions giving effect to lenity illustrate this point. In *Wiltberger*, the literal terms of the statute—"high seas"—plainly supported the conclusion that § 12 of the Crimes Act did not apply to manslaughter committed on an inland river.[196] The statute nonetheless became (or would have become) ambiguous when its literal terms were juxtaposed with Congress's evident purpose to punish all homicides and other serious offenses committed outside the jurisdiction of the states.[197] Chief Justice Marshall invoked "strict construction," however, to block recourse to Congress's "intent" or to the "mischief of the statute" more generally.[198] In *McBoyle*, the language of the statute—"any . . . self-propelled vehicle not designed for running on rails"[199]—was acknowledged to be literally consistent with applying the National Motor Vehicle Theft Act to stolen planes.[200] The statute became ambiguous only when Holmes juxtaposed this application with the narrower one that Congress expressly had in mind—namely, stolen automobiles. Holmes used narrow construction to block a literal reading of the text, thereby rendering the statute generatively inert. What made lenity dispositive in these cases, in sum, was the decision of the Court to give that rule priority over other interpretive conventions that create or resolve statutory ambiguities.[201]

What is distinctive of the great majority of cases, in contrast, is that they expressly give all other interpretive conventions priority

---

[194] See, for example, Sunstein, 103 Harv L Rev at 416–18 (cited in note 2).

[195] See Cass R. Sunstein, *Law and Administration after Chevron*, 90 Colum L Rev 2071, 2106 (1990).

[196] See text accompanying notes 52–57.

[197] See text accompanying notes 52–55.

[198] 18 US at 96.

[199] 41 Stat 324, § 2(a).

[200] See text accompanying notes 89–90.

[201] Compare Sunstein, 90 Colum L Rev at 2106–09 (cited in note 195) (noting that scope of *Chevron* principle depends on whether *Chevron* takes precedence to or is instead logically subsequent to other rules of interpretation).

over lenity. In a doctrinal formulation that has now become dominant, a court may properly conclude that a statute is "ambiguous" for purposes of lenity only "[a]fter 'seiz[ing] every thing from which aid can be derived,'"[202] including "the language and structure, legislative history, and motivating policies" of the statute.[203] "The rule comes into operation at the end of the process of construing what Congress has expressed, not at the beginning as an overriding consideration of being lenient to wrongdoers."[204]

Ranking lenity "last" among interpretive conventions all but guarantees its irrelevance.[205] The entire point of interpretive conventions is to avoid or resolve ambiguity. And once lenity is subtracted from the body of such conventions, the remainder do not lose their power to generate closure; after all, in civil statutory fields that do not include the rule of lenity, no interpretive games end in a tie. So if lenity invariably comes in "last," it should essentially come in never.

Even more important, ranking lenity "last" among interpretive conventions is incompatible with the function of lenity as a nondelegation doctrine. Lenity seeks to assure legislative supremacy by preventing courts from using common-lawmaking discretion to complete statutory offenses that emerge incompletely specified from Congress.[206] However, it is impossible for lenity to perform this function when it is treated as lexically subsequent to all other interpretive conventions, because many of these conventions clearly involve the exercise of normative discretion.[207]

---

[202] *United States v Bass*, 404 US 336, 347 (1971) (quoting *United States v Fisher*, 6 US 2 Cranch 358, 386 (1805); accord *Smith v United States*, 113 S Ct 2050, 2059–60 (1993); *Chapman v United States*, 500 US 453, 463 (1991).

[203] *Bifulco*, 447 US at 387; accord *Moskal*, 498 US at 108 (1990); *United States v R. LC.*, 112 S Ct 1329, 1338 (1992); *Dowling v United States*, 473 US 207, 213 (1985).

[204] *Callanan v United States*, 364 US 587, 596 (1961); accord *Albernaz v United States*, 450 US 333, 342 (1981); *Russelo*, 464 US at 303; *Gozlon-Peretz v United States*, 498 US 395, 410 (1991); *Chapman*, 500 US at 463.

[205] Compare Friendly, *Benchmarks* at 209 (cited in note 2) ("One might question the utility of a rule if there are such dubieties about its exits and its entrances; the problem of deciding whether the rule may legitimately be used becomes as hard as the issue itself.").

[206] See Part I.

[207] My claim here is not that this trivilialization of lenity logically entails the existence of delegated lawmaking. If the interpretive conventions given precedence to lenity were designed only to reveal pre-existing congressional policy choices, then courts in applying them would not be making law in any significant sense. They would be engaging in "ordinary interpretation." However, given the incompletely specified nature of many criminal statutes, and the policy-laden nature of the conventions that courts use to make sense of them, the suggestion that statutory construction minus lenity equals "ordinary interpretation" does not hold true in fact.

Ranked last, for example, lenity poses no bar to the invocation of other policy-laden rules of construction.[208] Some of these canons call for "broad" readings of particular criminal offenses, such as bribery of a federal official[209] and RICO.[210] Others—such as the principle that " '[f]ederal statutes . . . intended to fill a void in local law enforcement should be construed broadly' "[211]—expand the scope of large classes of offenses. These directives, which are understood to trump lenity, license the Court to use its own judgment in translating broad statutory language into operative rules of criminal law.

Under the dominant formulation, lenity is also powerless to prevent courts from reading criminal statutes expansively in light of congressional "intent" or "purpose."[212] Reliance on congressional intent does not always require significant normative judgments, particularly when a court consults legislative history merely to confirm that a particular statutory application was expressly contemplated (even if not expressly enumerated) by Congress. But quite frequently, courts invoke congressional "purpose" to support analogical extension of statutory language to circumstances that Congress admittedly did *not* foresee.[213] When that occurs, courts are using legislative history and other materials only to animate the normative creativity that it takes to construe statutes generatively.[214]

Examples of judicially creative uses of "purpose" to defeat lenity

---

[208] See, for example, *Albernaz*, 450 US at 342–43 (*Blockburger* rule trumps lenity).

[209] *Dixson v United States*, 465 US 482, 496, 500 n 19 (1984) (rejecting lenity and relying on "Congress's longstanding commitment to a broadly drafted federal bribery statute" to support conclusion that private corporation may be "public official").

[210] See *Sedima*, 473 US at 497.

[211] *Moskal*, 498 US at 113 (quoting *Bell v United States*, 462 US 356, 362 (1983) (Stevens dissenting)); see also *Sheridan v United States*, 329 US 379, 384 (1946); *McElroy v United States*, 455 US 642, 654–55 (1982); *Turley v United States*, 352 US 407, 417 (1957).

[212] See, for example, *Turkette*, 452 US at 587 n 10, 589–90; *Turley*, 352 US at 413–17; *United States v Brown*, 333 US 18, 25–26 (1948); *Dixson v United States*, 465 US at 496, 500 n 19.

[213] See Posner, *The Federal Courts* at 287 (cited in note 15).

[214] See *Van Beeck v Sabine Towing Co.*, 300 US 342, 351 (1937) (Cardozo) ("[A] legislative policy [may] itself [be] a source of law, a new generative impulse transmitted to the legal system."). Judge Posner has labeled this approach to statutory interpretation "the method of imaginative reconstruction." Posner, *The Federal Courts* at 287 (cited in note 15). This phrase accurately captures the creative ingredient of using statutory "purpose" to generate applications not expressly contemplated by Congress. See also Easterbrook, 50 U Chi L Rev at 539 (cited in note 20) ("To delve into the structure, purpose, and legislative history of the original statute is to engage in a sort of creation. It is to fill in the blanks.").

are legion. The issue in *Smith v United States*[215] was whether a statute that prohibited "use[ ] [of] a firearm" as part of a "drug trafficking crime"[216] applied to the exchange of a gun for drugs. The Court recognized that the statutory "phrase normally evokes an image of the most familiar use to which a firearm is put—use as a weapon."[217] But since exchanging a firearm for drugs creates the same "grave possibility of violence and death," the Court concluded that the statute could justifiably be read to cover this "use" as well, lenity notwithstanding.[218] Had the Court in *Smith* treated lenity as lexically prior to literalism—as the Court did in *McBoyle*[219]—the analogy between "using a weapon as a weapon" and "using a weapon by exchanging it for drugs" would not have sufficed to justify the broad reading.

The subordination of lenity to "purpose" likewise facilitated judicial lawmaking in *Moskal v United States*.[220] The issue was whether a genuine automobile title bearing incorrect odometer readings constituted a "falsely made, forged, altered or counterfeited securit[y]."[221] The Court acknowledged that Congress, when it selected this language, might have expressly contemplated only bogus documents fabricated by the defendant.[222] Nonetheless, the Court reasoned, inducing state agencies to produce "genuine" automobile titles "containing false information" is just as "fraudulent" as producing bogus documents and, when part of a scheme that crosses state lines, just as likely to "elude state detection."[223] Accordingly, the Court held lenity posed no obstacle to treating title washing schemes as an "*instance[]*" of the general "*class* of fraud encompassed by [the statutory] language."[224] In sum, whereas the Court in *Wiltberger* used "strict construction" to prevent courts from resorting to "the reason or mischief of a statute . . . to punish a crime not

---

[215] 113 S Ct 2050 (1993).

[216] 18 USC § 924(c)(1) (1988 & Supp 1993).

[217] *Smith*, 113 S Ct at 2054.

[218] Id at 2060.

[219] See text accompanying notes 87–91.

[220] 498 US 103 (1990).

[221] 18 USC § 2314 (1988 & Supp 1993).

[222] See *Moskal*, 498 US at 110.

[223] Id at 110–11.

[224] Id at 112.

enumerated,"[225] the Court now routinely uses the reason or mischief of a statute to identify just what crimes a statute enumerates.

When lenity is ranked last, courts are even liberated to repair statutory defects.[226] "[A]n inadvertent casualty of a complex drafting process," according to the Court, should not be permitted to displace what the "legislative history as a whole suggests" was Congress's broader aim.[227] Far from using strict construction to promote greater care in the drafting of criminal statutes,[228] the Court has identified the fact that a statute was "enacted hastily with little discussion and no hearings" as a ground *not* to assume that Congress deliberately drafted a criminal statute narrowly.[229] Lenity notwithstanding, the Court has accepted the lawmaking function of correcting the inevitable drafting errors that accompany Congress's attempt to satisfy an excessive demand for legislation.[230]

Under the prevailing doctrinal formulation of lenity, *Wiltberger* would almost surely come out the other way. Ranking lenity "last" among interpretive conventions sends the clear message that the Court is both willing and able to collaborate with Congress in the articulation of a comprehensive and effective body of federal criminal law.

III. The Contemporary Debate

In the last Part, I tried to document how the rule of lenity has been effectively overtaken by the hidden rule of delegated crim-

---

[225] 18 US at 96.

[226] See, for example, *United States v Brown*, 333 US at 24–25 (rejecting lenity on basis of congressional intent, while noting "Congress, it is true, did not cast the original Act in terms specifically relating to a situation comprehending consecutive sentences existing at the time of the escape or attempt, as more careful drafting of the Act would have required to insure achieving the object of adding independent punishment in all cases").

[227] *Taylor v United States*, 495 US 575, 589–90 (1990).

[228] See Dickerson, *The Interpretation and Application of Statutes* at 210 (cited in note 13); see also text accompanying notes 40–42 (discussing Frankfurter's defense of strict construction).

[229] *Scarborough v United States*, 435 US 563, 570 (1977); see also *Brown*, 333 US at 24 ("[Congress's] concentration upon that main aspect of the legislation apparently led it to reduced emphasis upon and care in the definition of the situations to which the Act would apply"); *Taylor*, 495 US at 589–90 & n 5; but *cf United States v Granderson*, 114 S Ct 1259, 1266–68 & n 12 (1994) (rejecting both broadest and narrowest readings of sentencing provision adopted without significant deliberation).

[230] See generally Popkin, 68 Ind L J at 876–77 (cited in note 108); Eskridge, 37 UCLA at 687 (cited in note 11).

inal lawmaking. But unless and until the Court overtly renounces lenity, the resuscitation of that canon will remain a possibility.

A campaign to resuscitate lenity is indeed underway. Over the last several Terms, a group of Justices, led by Justice Scalia, has aggressively sought to elevate the importance of the rule. Their efforts have provoked resistance from Justices who believe that lenity should not occupy a dominant position in federal criminal jurisprudence. I now want to examine this debate and show how it reflects competing views of the appropriateness of delegated criminal lawmaking.

In the course of the past few Terms, no Justice has either uniformly supported or uniformly opposed application of lenity in all cases. Nonetheless, several current and recent members of the Court can be divided into distinct "pro-" and "anti-lenity" camps, the former consisting of Justices Scalia, Kennedy, and Thomas, and the latter of Justice Stevens, and former Justices Marshall, Blackmun, and (to a lesser extent) Brennan.

The "pro" and "anti" contingents have joined issue on a number of points. They have disagreed, for example, on whether the rule should be given a categorical or contextual application. Whereas the "pro-lenity" Justices have generally been willing to apply the rule in all circumstances, "anti-lenity" Justices have advocated confining the rule to circumstances in which a narrow reading would demonstrably advance the rule's underlying purposes, and have declined, in particular, to apply the rule in circumstances in which offenders are on notice that their conduct is illegal or "wrongful," whether or not they are on notice that their conduct would violate the particular federal criminal statute at issue.[231] Another point of contention is whether lenity should be applied in civil cases involving statutes that may also be enforced criminally.[232] The general

---

[231] See, for example, *Williams*, 458 US at 304 (Marshall joined by Burger, Brennan, and White dissenting) ("There is no question that Williams, a bank president, knew that his check-kiting scheme was wrongful."); *Moskal*, 498 US at 113, 114 n 6 (Marshall) (declining to find lack of "fair notice" where defendant engaged in admittedly fraudulent scheme); *McNally*, 483 US at 375 n 9 (Stevens) ("When considering how much weight to accord to the doctrine of lenity, it is appropriate to identify the class of litigants that will benefit from the Court's ruling today. . . . [They] are people who unquestionably knew that their conduct was unlawful.").

[232] Compare *United States v Thompson/Center Arms Co.*, 112 S Ct 2102, 2109–10 (1992) (Souter) and id at 2110, 2112 (Scalia joined by Thomas concurring in judgment) with id at 2114 (Stevens dissenting). See generally Bruce A. Markell, *Bankruptcy, Lenity, and the Statutory Interpretation of Cognate Civil and Criminal Statutes*, 69 Ind L J 335 (1994).

significance of the rule in federal criminal jurisprudence has also generated biting exchanges.[233]

But the issue on which the "pro" and "anti" forces have disagreed most intensely is the relationship of lenity to other techniques of statutory interpretation. The "anti-lenity" Justices have consistently defended the dominant doctrinal formulation, under which lenity is ranked lexically subsequent to all other interpretive conventions.[234] Writing for the Court in *Moskal v United States*,[235] Justice Marshall offered this forceful elaboration:

> We have repeatedly "emphasized that the 'touchstone' of the rule of lenity 'is statutory ambiguity.'" Stated at this level of abstraction, of course, the rule "provides little more than atmospherics, since it leaves open the crucial question—almost invariably present—of how much ambiguousness constitutes . . . ambiguity." Because the meaning of language is inherently contextual, we have declined to deem a statute "ambiguous" for purposes of lenity merely because it was possible to articulate a construction more narrow than that urged by the Government. Nor have we deemed a division of judicial authority automatically sufficient to trigger lenity. If that were sufficient, one court's unduly narrow reading of a criminal statute would become binding on all other courts, including this one. Instead, we have always reserved lenity for those situations in which a reasonable doubt persists about a statute's intended scope even *after* resort to "the language and structure, legislative history, and motivating policies" of the statute.[236]

The "pro-lenity" group, in contrast, has advocated pushing lenity up to the top of the interpretive hierarchy. "If the Rule of Lenity means anything," Scalia wrote in response to Marshall's formulation in *Moskal*, "it means that the Court ought not to . . . use an ill-defined general purpose to override an unquestionably clear term of art . . . ."[237] Nor is it "consistent with the rule of lenity," Scalia has argued, "to construe a textually ambiguous penal statute against a criminal defendant on the basis of legislative his-

---

[233] See, for example, *Moskal*, 498 US at 107–08 (Marshall); id at 477 (Scalia dissenting); *Williams*, 458 US at 287–88 nn 8–9 (Blackmun).

[234] See text accompanying notes 202–04.

[235] 498 US 103.

[236] Id at 107–08 (emphasis deleted) (citations omitted) (quoting *United States v Hansen*, 772 F2d 940, 948 (DC Cir 1985) (Scalia)); see also *Williams*, 458 US at 303 (Marshall dissenting).

[237] 498 US at 132 (Scalia joined by Rehnquist, O'Connor, and Kennedy dissenting).

tory."[238] According to the "pro-lenity" Justices, lenity should take second place only to the "fundamental principle" that a word be given the meaning it plainly conveys in the "context in which it is used";[239] should that principle fail to generate a definitive reading, lenity precludes recourse to any nontextual sources that would support a broad reading of the statute.[240]

Lenity must be ranked lexically prior to other interpretive guides, the "pro-lenity" Justices have argued, in order to promote the rule's basic aims. "It may well be true that in most cases the proposition that the words of the United States Code or the Statutes at Large give adequate notice to the citizen is something of a fiction," Scalia has conceded, "but necessary fiction descends to needless farce when the public is charged even with knowledge of Committee Reports."[241] Subordinating lenity to legislative history and the general policies of a statute also undermines legislative supremacy:

> The only thing that [Congress] authoritatively adopted for sure was the text of the enactment; the rest is necessarily speculation. . . . "[T]he moral condemnation of the community" is no more reflected in the views of a majority of a single committee of congressmen (assuming, of course, they have genuinely considered what their staff has produced) than it is reflected in the views of a majority of an appellate court; we should feel no less concerned about "men languishing in prison" at the direction of the one than of the other.[242]

Expressing "doubt that *Moskal* accurately characterizes the law,"[243] Scalia has called on the Court to "acknowledge the tension

---

[238] *United States v R.L.C.*, 112 S Ct 1329, 1339 (1992) (Scalia joined by Thomas concurring); see also *Taylor v United States*, 495 US 575, 603 (1990) (Scalia concurring).

[239] *Deal v United States*, 113 S Ct 1993, 1996 (1993).

[240] Even this formulation, however, begs the question how to determine whether the text has a plain meaning. At least one member of the pro-lenity contingent, Justice Thomas, has taken care to emphasize that lenity does not prevent recourse to canons of interpretation designed to resolve that issue. See *R.L.C.*, 112 S Ct at 1341 (Thomas, J, concurring in part and in the judgment) ("although we require Congress to enact 'clear and definite' penal statutes, we also consult our own 'well-established principles of statutory construction' in determining whether the relevant text *is* clear and definite" (citations omitted)). The reason, presumably, that this approach does not dissolve into the approach favored by the anti-lenity Justices is that Justice Thomas (like Scalia) excludes legislative history, statutory purpose, and other policy-laden presumptions from the canons by which "plain meaning" can legitimately be ascertained. See id at 1342.

[241] *R.L.C.*, 112 S Ct at 1340.

[242] Id.

[243] Id at 1339.

in our precedents, the absence of an examination of the consequences of the *Moskal* mode of analysis, and the consequent conclusion that *Moskal* may not be good law."[244]

It is difficult to make sense of this debate if it is viewed through
conventional ideological lenses. The Justices who comprise the
"pro-lenity" contingent include those who are typically counted as
the Court's most "conservative" members, while the "anti-lenity"
group includes those typically described as its most "liberal." Insofar as lenity is understood to place a thumb on the individual-
liberty side of the balance, the identity of the "pro" and "anti"
contingents might seem counterintuitive.

But the contemporary debate is not the least bit counterintuitive
if it is assessed against the background of lenity as an anti-
delegation doctrine. Led by Justice Scalia, the Justices who comprise the "pro-lenity" contingent have waged an even more prominent campaign to confine statutory interpretation to the "plain
meaning" of the text. The avowed purpose of this "new textualism"
is to allocate the incidence of lawmaking power between Congress
and the judiciary.[245] By precluding reliance on legislative history,
statutory "purpose," and other nontextual sources, this method of
interpretation is intended to limit the discretion of judges to convert
their own preferences into law.[246] Even more important, textualism
prevents Congress from alienating its lawmaking authority. Echoing Frankfurter's defense of strict construction, Scalia has stressed
the Court's "obligation to conduct [its] exegesis in a fashion which
fosters th[e] democratic process"; adhering closely to "plain meaning" achieves that end by making it impossible to "obtain[ ] a particular result in this Court without making that result apparent on
the face of the bill which both Houses consider and vote upon."[247]

The effort to resuscitate lenity merely extends to criminal law
this general strategy for assuring legislative supremacy. Using len-

---

[244] Id at 1341. A plurality of the Court expressly rejected Scalia's contention that lenity
must be ranked lexically prior to nontextual interpretive conventions. See id at 1338 n 6
(Souter joined by Rehnquist, White, and Stevens).

[245] See generally, Eskridge, 37 UCLA L Rev at 648 (cited in note 11).

[246] See, for example, Antonin Scalia, *Speech on Use of Legislative History* 13–14 (delivered
at various law schools from fall 1985 to spring 1986) (transcript on file with D'Angelo
Library, University of Chicago Law School); *Public Citizen v United States Dep't of Justice*,
491 US 440, 470–71 (1989) (Kennedy concurring in the judgment).

[247] *United States v Taylor*, 487 US 326, 345 (1988) (Scalia concurring in part).

ity to bar recourse to interpretive principles that might give effect
to any result not "apparent on the face" of a criminal statute guarantees that Congress will be powerless to confer, and the Court powerless to accept, the authority to define operative rules of criminal
law. "Stretching language in order to write a more effective statute
than *Congress* devised is not an exercise *we* should indulge
in"[248]—no matter how much Congress might appreciate the
stretching.[249]

That the pro-lenity contingent values strict construction only for
its non-delegation qualities is confirmed by the short shrift that
they give to the other values traditionally associated with lenity.
The proposition that narrow construction is necessary to assure
"fair notice," according to Scalia, is a "fiction."[250] And in another
recent decision in which Scalia declined to apply the rule of lenity,
he ridiculed the suggestion that liberty-conservation alone supplied
a sufficient basis for construing a statute narrowly where a literal
reading resulted in an extraordinarily harsh sentence.[251]

---

[248] *Smith*, 113 S Ct at 2063 n 4 (Scalia dissenting); and, *Moskal*, 498 US at 132 ("[t]he temptation to stretch the law to fit the evil is an ancient one, and it must be resisted").

[249] *United States v Granderson*, 114 S Ct 1259, 1274 (1994) (Kennedy concurring in judg-ment) (lenity precludes broad reading based "upon some vague intuition of what Congress 'might . . . have had in mind' ").

[250] See text accompanying note 241. Insofar as even the pro-lenity Justices would subordi-nate lenity to textual or grammatical canons of interpretation, the notice rationale becomes even less compelling. See *R.L.C.*, 114 S Ct at 1341 (Thomas, J, concurring in part and in judgment) ("we must presume familiarity not only with the United States Code, but also with the United States Reports, in which we have developed innumerable rules of construc-tion powerful enough to make clear an otherwise ambiguous penal statute"). No one can plausibly claim that principles such as *expressio unius est exclusio alterius* or *ejusdem generis*, much less the *Blockburger* rule, are matters of common knowledge. It can plausibly be said, however, that enforcing these mechanical presumptions does not implicate the judiciary in making substantive policy judgments. Thus, whether or not using these canons to support broad statutory readings is consistent with fair notice, ranking these rules ahead of lenity is consistent with the pro-lenity Justices' concern to minimize judicial discretion and to concentrate criminal lawmaking responsibility in Congress.

[251] See *Deal*, 113 S Ct at 1999 ("[W]e need not tarry over petitioner's contention that the rule of lenity is called for because his 105-year sentence [for bank robbery] 'is so glaringly unjust that the Court cannot but question whether Congress intended such an applica-tion . . . .' "). Justice Scalia also joined the majority opinion in *Chapman v United States*, 500 US 453, 464–65 (1991), which declined to use lenity to avoid severe sentences for distribu-tion of LSD. Indeed, Scalia appears to have recognized the functional kinship between lenity and the "plain meaning" theory of interpretation only recently. As a judge on the United States Court of Appeals for the D.C. Circuit, Scalia wrote an opinion (quoted, with evident irony, in *Moskal*), in which he dismissed the rule as "atmospherics," *Hansen*, 772 F2d at 948, and as late as 1990, he wrote a law review article dismissing "strict construction" of criminal statutes as a "canard." See Antonin Scalia, *Assorted Canards of Contemporary Legal Analysis*, 40 Case W Res L Rev 581, 582 (1990).

The Justices who comprise the "anti-lenity" contingent, in contrast, are associated with a very different philosophy of statutory interpretation. They reject textualism because they reject its positivist underpinnings.[252] What unites them is a shared belief in the existence of democratically approved public values—accessible through the Court's own deliberative process—that can be used to discipline and guide the generative elaboration of statutory terms.[253] They are quite comfortable, in short, with the tradition of delegated lawmaking and with the conception of the judicial role that this tradition entails.

Ranking lenity "last" among interpretive conventions coheres perfectly with this philosophy. Were lenity to be treated as lexically prior to all other conventions, it would preclude recourse to all the sources of normative inspiration that guide delegated lawmaking. For this reason, Justice Stevens has declined to apply lenity when he has concluded that Congress "intended [a criminal statutory] definition to be developed in the common-law tradition of case-by-case adjudication."[254] Justice Marshall criticized using lenity to limit a statute to conduct that "Congress specifies . . . by name . . . or describes . . . in detail"[255] if it is "evident from the face of the statute that [it] was written broadly in order to prohibit certain *kinds* of conduct which entail specific risks or dangers";[256] implicit in this position is the premise that Congress may appropriately enlist courts to devise, in common law fashion, the applications that Congress has failed to specify or describe in detail on the face of the statute (or even the legislative history[257]).

In finally exposing this conflict to plain view, the contemporary debate has brought the story of lenity and delegated criminal lawmaking to a critical stage. Justice Scalia clearly exaggerates when

---

[252] Eskridge, *Public Values* at 1079–81 (cited in note 3).

[253] Id at 1080–81; Kathleen M. Sullivan, *Foreword: The Justices of Rules and Standards*, 106 Harv L Rev 24, 117–20 (1992).

[254] *Kozminski*, 487 US at 965–66 (Stevens concurring in judgment); see *McNally*, 483 US at 372–73 (Stevens dissenting) (declining to apply lenity to mail fraud statute on ground that "wide open spaces in statutes such as these are most appropriately interpreted as implicit delegations of authority to the courts to fill in the gaps in the common law tradition of case-by-case adjudication").

[255] *Williams*, 458 US at 305 (Marshall dissenting).

[256] Id at 302 (emphasis added).

[257] See id at 305–06.

he labels the "*Moskal* formulation" a departure from existing law;[258] contrary to Scalia's claims, the Court has repeatedly construed criminal statutes broadly on the basis of legislative history and purpose.[259] All the same, Scalia is definitely correct to characterize the Court's precedents as in "tension."[260] The tension is as old as *Wiltberger* and *Kelly*, and as recent as the decisions of this past Term.[261]

At this point, the Court surely must choose, openly and decisively, between these two rules of federal criminal jurisprudence. The debate should now shift from what the law *is* to what the law *ought* to be: should the Court facilitate Congress's practice of delegating criminal lawmaking authority to the judiciary, or should it finally enforce the promise of *Hudson* and *Wiltberger* to banish "federal common law crimes"? It is to that question that I now turn.

IV. THE CASE FOR ABOLISHING LENITY

A. OVERVIEW

Lenity should be abolished. The thrust of my argument so far is that the genuine enforcement of lenity would require that courts

---

[258] See *R.L.C.*, 112 S Ct at 1339.

[259] See, for example, *Taylor v United States*, 495 US 575 (1990) (relying on legislative history and purpose to support definition of "burglary" more expansive than common law definition); *United States v Yermian*, 468 US 63 (1984) (relying on legislative history and statutory purpose to overcome presumption of *mens rea* as to factual elements of offense); *Dixson v United States*, 465 US 482 (1984) (relying on statutory purpose to overcome ambiguity relating to whether federal bribery statute applies to bribes of private parties receiving federal grants); *Scarborough v United States*, 435 US 563, 570 (1977) (relying on legislative history to resolve ambiguity relating to nexus between possession of firearm and interstate commerce); *Turley v United States*, 352 US 407 (1957) (relying on legislative history and purpose to support definition of "stolen" more expansive than common law definition of larceny); *United States v Brown*, 333 US 18 (1948) (relying on legislative history and purpose to resolve ambiguity relating to relationship between sentence for escape and sentence for offense being served at time of escape).

[260] *R.L.C.*, 112 S Ct at 1341.

[261] Compare *Ratzlaf v United States*, 114 S Ct 655, 657–58 (1994) (invoking lenity in support of narrow construction notwithstanding "contrary indications in the statute's legislative history") and *Granderson*, 114 S Ct at 1274 (Kennedy concurring in judgment) (noting debate on lexical ranking and criticizing Court for relying on "some vague intuition of what Congress 'might . . . have had in mind' ") with *Ratzlaf*, 114 S Ct at 667 (Blackmun dissenting) ("rule should not be applied to defeat a congressional purpose that is as clear as that evidenced here") and *Granderson*, 114 S Ct at 1267 (appropriate to invoke lenity only "where text, structure and history fail to establish that the Government's position is unambiguously correct").

give that rule priority over other interpretive conventions and then mechanically select the narrowest readings of all ambiguous criminal statutes; only then would lenity be effective in blocking the exercise of delegated criminal lawmaking.[262] In this part, I will argue that such an approach to construing criminal statutes is indefensible. Lenity is completely unnecessary to assure the fair and predictable administration of criminal justice. At the same time, the allocation of lawmaking authority that the rule entails would substantially raise the cost of criminal law while reducing its effectiveness.

I want to preface my analysis, however, with two important qualifications. The first is that in attacking lenity I do not mean to advocate a mechanical rule of "broad construction." My claim is that federal criminal law works best when Congress is permitted to cede a certain portion of its criminal lawmaking power to courts. Once courts are recognized as legitimate delegated lawmakers, however, it does not follow that courts should invariably opt for broad over narrow rules of law, for in some instances narrow rules will be superior in substance to broad ones. My analysis will shed some light on when that is likely to be the case.

Nonetheless, I would resist the conclusion that I am advocating merely an appropriate narrowing of the circumstances in which lenity should be employed. The considerations that support narrow readings over broad ones are discrete and particular; they do not generalize into a single *rule* of any kind, much less one that reflects an abstract preference for the liberty of criminal defendants. Accordingly, to continue to speak as if there were a "rule of lenity"—however defined—would at best only obscure the reasons that make narrow rules of law appropriate in particular settings. At worst, pretending that narrow construction is a rule rather than an outcome that is sometimes appropriate and sometimes not will continue to induce courts to select narrow readings when good reasons for doing so are lacking.

The conclusion that I think my analysis does support is that courts should adopt the *best* readings of incompletely specified criminal statutes, whether those readings are broad or narrow— which is obviously not a "rule" in any helpful sense. Moreover, because identifying the best readings of such statutes cannot be

---

[262] See text accompanying notes 191–230.

identified with implementing choices self-consciously made by Congress, this approach is appropriately viewed as a form of delegated lawmaking.

The second qualification is that my defense of delegated criminal lawmaking by no means justifies all that federal courts can have actually done in exercising it. Many instances of judicial improvisation in the field of federal criminal law are indeed indefensible.

I will try to show, however, that such misadventures are not intrinsic to delegated criminal lawmaking. Indeed, if the great bulk of them are attributable to anything, it is to the judiciary's failure to be self-conscious about delegated lamwking and to accept the institutional responsibility that such an assignment entails for devising rules of defensible content. In an important sense, then, the cure for most of the ills associated with incompletely specified criminal statutes is not *less* common-lawmaking but *more*.

B. DELEGATION VERSUS LENITY: THE VALUES AT STAKE

I have suggested that lenity is best understood as a judicial strategy for enforcing legislative supremacy in criminal law. Yet one does not have to reject legislative supremacy in order to reject lenity. For the historical conflict between the lenity and delegated lawmaking reflects a deeper division over what respect for legislative supremacy requires.[263]

The pro-lenity position stems from an "ideal" conception of legislative supremacy, under which the judiciary is powerless to enforce any operative rule of law that Congress has not self-consciously authored. This understanding of legislative supremacy sets a standard that is even more demanding of Congress than of courts; as cases like *Wiltberger* and *Kozminski* illustrate,[264] the "ideal" conception often frustrates the will of actual legislators, since it obliges Congress to exercise all of its lawmaking authority without judicial assistance.

The anti-lenity position, in contrast, stems from a "practical"

---

[263] For discussions of the interplay between statutory interpretation and different conceptions of legislative supremacy, see generally Posner, *The Federal Courts* at 207–08 (cited in note 15); William N. Eskridge, *Spinning Legislative Supremacy*, 78 Georgetown L J 319 (1989); Correia, 42 Case W Res L Rev 1129 (cited in note 16); Popkin, 68 Ind L J 865 (cited in note 108); and Lawrence C. Marshall, *"Let Congress Do It": The Case for an Absolute Rule of Statutory Stare Decisis*, 88 Mich L Rev 177 (1989).

[264] See Part IB.

conception of legislative supremacy, under which courts are authorized to propound operative rules of law at Congress's explicit or implicit direction. Since the aim of this arrangement is to maximize the policymaking authority of actual legislators,[265] the exercise of delegated lawmaking power cannot be viewed as a judicial "usurpation" of legislative prerogatives.

The issue, then, is which of these competing conceptions of legislative supremacy should guide interpretation of criminal statutes. This question cannot be answered by resort to history or settled practice. As the prevalence of "federal common law" statutes attests,[266] the practical conception is well established. Indeed, since at least the New Deal, no serious challenge has been made to Congress's discretion to vest either agencies or courts with lawmaking authority within particular regulatory fields.[267] Nevertheless, isolated pockets of the ideal conception of legislative supremacy persist. Enforced by rules of strict construction, the inalienability of Congress's policymaking prerogatives is understood to be essential to protecting particular values within these limited domains.[268]

The contest between the ideal and practical conceptions must thus be decided according to a normative criterion: Which best advances the values at stake in federal criminal law? I will consider how lenity and delegated lawmaking affect four values in particular: the rule of law, efficiency, democracy, and federalism.

1. *Rule of law*

a) Notice. As an ingredient of the rule of law, "notice" rests on several foundations. One account stresses individual autonomy: legal obligations should be transparent so that individuals can plan their conduct with confidence and thereby maximize their liberty.[269] Other rationales emphasize collective interests. Clarity in law (particularly criminal law) is said to avoid "overdeterrence"—the social loss associated with private decisions to refrain from engaging in what is in fact lawful conduct because citizens

---

[265] See text accompanying notes 252–57.

[266] See text accompanying notes 27–31.

[267] See generally Cass R. Sunstein, *Constitutionalism After the New Deal*, 101 Harv L Rev 421, 491 (1987).

[268] See text accompanying notes 43–48 (describing Court's federalism jurisprudence).

[269] See, for example, Friedrich A. von Hayek, *The Road to Serfdom* 72 (1944); Joseph Raz, *The Rule of Law and Its Virtue*, in *The Authority of Law* 220–22 (1979).

are unable to determine the true extent of the law.[270] It is also claimed that "notice" increases the effectiveness of the law, since compliance presupposes knowledge.[271] None of these accounts justifies the preclusion of delegated lawmaking that lenity would entail.

Consider, to start, the suggestion that the "notice" afforded by lenity is essential to individual autonomy. This argument fails because it is insensitive to differences in social context that are decisive to the moral assessment of an individual's entitlement to rely on what she understands the law to be.

The individual autonomy argument works well when a court is applying a statute to conduct that sits on the boundary line between socially desirable and socially undesirable conduct. Certain federal crimes—including tax evasion,[272] securities fraud,[273] and antitrust violations[274]—are dominated by applications of this character; these laws regulate common forms of conduct that enhance social welfare and that individuals are expected and encouraged to engage in subject only to what the law prohibits. Moreover, notice here is not a fiction; in these settings individuals do in fact make substantial investments to discover their legal obligations so that they may conform their behavior to the law. Because these laws are understood to invite individuals to come right up to the line between what is a crime and what is not, obscurity as to where that line is drawn is indeed grossly unfair.[275]

But the situation is quite different when the underlying conduct is located not on the border but deep within the interior of what is socially undesirable. Many federal offenses deal with behavior

---

[270] Posner, 49 U Chi L Rev at 280 (cited in note 19).

[271] See Lon L. Fuller, *The Morality of Law* 33–94 (1964); Raz, *The Authority of Law* 226 (cited in note 269); Ehrlich and Posner, 3 J Legal Stud at 263 (cited in note 15); Diver, 93 Yale L J at 74 (cited in note 13).

[272] See *Cheek v United States*, 498 US 192, 199–203 (1991) (construing criminal tax offenses to permit mistake of law defense in order to avoid punishing socially innocent behavior).

[273] See *Dirks v Securities and Exchange Commission*, 463 US 646, 658–59 (1983) (requiring proof of breach of fiduciary duty for insider trading violations in order to shield socially desirable trading from liability); *Chiarella v United States*, 445 US 222, 232–33 (1980) (same).

[274] *United States v United States Gypsum Co.*, 438 US 422, 441–43 (1978) (reading *mens rea* requirement into Sherman Act in order to avoid chilling effect on socially desirable market behavior).

[275] See generally Stephen McG. Bundy and Einer Elhauge, *Knowledge About Legal Sanctions*, 92 Mich L Rev 261, 305 (1993).

of this character;[276] the most prominent are those that "federalize" state-law offenses carried out across interstate lines.[277] The purpose of these "interior" offenses is not so much to inform citizens of what conduct is prohibited as it is to create or increase criminal penalties for conduct that is already understood to be absolutely forbidden by independent laws or social mores.[278] That is why individuals (assuming they act with *mens rea*) do not need to consult these statutes to be put on "notice" that their conduct is unlawful.[279] In this context, a person who consciously seeks to come up to the statutory "line" without crossing it is not attempting to conform her behavior to the law, but rather to evade punishment for admittedly wrongful or illegal acts. Respect for "individual autonomy" does not justify narrow construction to accommodate this behavior, for such conduct is, by hypothesis, aimed at infringing the moral and legal rights of other parties.[280]

McBoyle is a case in point. I have already attempted to demonstrate that "fair notice" fails to explain that case as a descriptive matter: as the Court itself acknowledged, it was silly to suggest that McBoyle had consulted, or even needed to consult, the statute books to determine whether his conduct was lawful.[281] But if anything, the "fair warning" explanation grows weaker, not stronger, if we assume that he *did* carefully review the National Motor Vehicle Act before acting. The purpose of the Act was to reinforce state theft statutes, which were (and remain) difficult to enforce against crimes that span multiple jurisdictions.[282] Thus, a person

---

[276] See, for example, *United States v Feola*, 420 US 671 (1975) (assault of federal officer).

[277] See, for example, 18 USC § 1952(a)–(b) (1988) (interstate travel to distribute proceeds of state-law crimes); 18 USC §§ 1961(1), 1962 (1988) (RICO); compare 18 USC § 1951(a) (1988) (prohibiting interference with interstate commerce through robbery or extortion); 8 USC § 2314 (1988) (interstate transportation of stolen property).

[278] See text accompanying notes 91–96.

[279] See Meir Dan-Cohen, *Decision Rules and Conduct Rules: On Acoustic Separation in Criminal Law*, 97 Harv L Rev 625, 662–64 (1984).

[280] See Bundy and Elhauge, 92 Mich L Rev at 305–06, 332–33 (cited in note 275); compare Dan-Cohen, 97 Harv L Rev at 671–72 (cited in note 279) (respect for autonomy requires accommodating behavior motivated by moral duty, not behavior motivated by calculating assessment of consequences); Robert Nozick, *Philosophical Explanations* 391–92 (Harvard, 1981) (parties who knowingly attempt to exploit loopholes in laws that punish immoral acts are not deprived of fair notice when punished by retroactive laws).

[281] See text accompanying note 91.

[282] See *United States v Turley*, 352 US 407, 413–14 (1957); *United States v Dowling*, 473 US 207, 218–20 (1985).

who concluded that a plane was not a "vehicle" for purposes of the Act could have decided to steal one believing that it would be difficult for law enforcement officials to apprehend him. If the Act were thereafter construed to apply to stolen airplanes after all, this hypothetical offender would indeed be "surprised" but not "unfairly"; a thief has no legitimate expectation that he will not be caught and punished. The notion that lenity exists for the purpose of facilitating evasion of punishment for admittedly illegal behavior is difficult to credit.

The suggestion that lenity is justified to combat overdeterrence[283] displays the same fatal insensitivity to context that kills the argument from individual autonomy. The overdeterrence concern makes sense as applied to boundary readings. Because these interpretations mark the line between what is socially desirable and what is socially undesirable, they necessarily discourage something society values when (by virtue of vagueness) they induce individuals to forgo lawful activity. The overdeterrence justification makes no sense, however, in interior settings. By definition, society places no value—or even negative value—on lawful conduct that falls just short of what the law prohibits. And conduct that has either no or negative social value cannot be overdeterred. Had McBoyle, for example, decided not to steal an airplane because he feared that a court might treat a plane as a "vehicle" for purposes of the National Motor Vehicle Theft Act, society would have benefited from his caution.[284] So again, the sensible interpretive approach—distinguishing "boundary" from "interior" offenses—would be a more subtle one than lenity allows.

Individual autonomy and overdeterrence would require strict construction in both interior and boundary settings only if distinguishing one from the other defied the institutional competence of courts. There is little reason, however, to indulge this skeptical claim. In many cases, it is clear as a matter of positive law that a federal criminal statute tracks or incorporates existing legal prohibitions.[285] For other statutes, a court must consult common mores to

---

[283] See text accompanying note 270.

[284] But see Bundy and Elhauge, 92 Mich L Rev at 330 (cited in note 275) (where parties overestimate liability for socially undesirable conduct, "then a strategy of diminishing knowledge about legal sanctions (such as curbing legal advice) may be desirable to prevent the overestimations from being corrected").

[285] See text accompanying notes 276–78 and note 277.

determine whether the conduct that would be affected by a broad reading is socially approved or disapproved; but these common intuitions are no less accessible to judges than they are to other members of the community.[286] There will certainly be close calls—in which "notice" or other values might indeed justify narrow construction[287]—but even the certain prospect of these hard cases does not justify presuming that courts are incompetent to distinguish interior from boundary offenses in the vast multitude of easy ones.

In noting the distinction between interior and boundary readings, however, I do not mean to suggest that delegated lawmaking is appropriate for certain types of offenses but not for others. Indeed, some of the fields in which federal common-lawmaking is most well established, such as antitrust, are dominated by boundary readings. My claim is only that the relationship between social context and notice should inform how courts carry out delegated lawmaking.[288] As statutory readings approach the border between

---

[286] Compare *Liparota v United States*, 471 US 419, 426 (1985) (inappropriate to adopt broad reading of statute prohibiting misuse of food stamps where to do so "would be to criminalize a broad range of apparently innocent conduct") with *United States v Freed*, 401 US 601, 609 (1971) (justifying broad reading of National Firearms Act on ground that "one would hardly be surprised to learn that possession of hand grenades is not an innocent act").

[287] Determining whether an offense constitutes a border or interior offense is likely to be especially difficult when there is political dissensus on whether the underlying conduct (such as possession of any type of gun) is socially undesirable. See *United States v Staples*, 114 S Ct 1793 (1994). In that situation, narrow readings might be justified to give fair notice to the members of subcommunities (regional or otherwise) that do view the activity as socially acceptable. See id. In addition, narrow construction might be justifiable to assure that the use of criminal law to *create* social consensus on such disputed matters is attended by the requisite democratic deliberations. See id; see text accompanying notes 369–74. These rationales, however, have no application when there clearly is social consensus that the conduct to which a broad statutory reading would apply—such as theft, fraud, forgery, assault, or homicide—has no licit value.

[288] For similar reasons, I disagree with the suggestion that lenity should be viewed as applying to *malum prohibitum* but not *malum in se* offenses. See Dickerson, *The Interpretation and Application of Statutes* at 210–11 (cited in note 13); compare Eskridge and Frickey, *Cases and Materials on Legislation* at 656 (cited in note 3). If lenity truly applied to *malum prohibitum* offenses, then there would be no effective delegated lawmaking in domains such as antitrust or securities regulation. This proposition not only fails to describe the law, but also fails to set out a defensible normative prescription. Narrow interpretations might often be appropriate for *malum prohibitum* offenses; but they will not invariably be appropriate because broad readings will not invariably differ from core statutory readings in ways on which regulated parties can legitimately rely. See, for example, *United States v Naftalin*, 441 US 768, 778–79 (1978) (holding that Securities Act of 1933 prohibits frauds against brokers as well as investors, lenity notwithstanding); *United States v Yermian*, 468 US 63 (1984) (holding that 18 USC § 1001 applies to individuals who knowingly make false statements whether or not they know the statement is "in any matter within the jurisdiction" of federal agency). Likewise, broad readings might often be appropriate for *malum in se* offenses, but they will

socially desirable and socially undesirable conduct, courts should take care to fill out incompletely specified statutes with more precise operative rules. In the main, this is what they do.[289]

Finally, the objective of enhancing compliance with criminal law also fails to support the rule of lenity. If the choice is between a rule that clearly prohibits a particular form of conduct and one that does so only ambiguously, then the clear rule is indeed preferable on deterrence grounds. For in that situation, a potential offender is more likely to believe that the clear rule will be construed to cover her conduct than she is to believe that the ambiguous rule will be.[290]

But the choice between a clear rule and an ambiguous one is the wrong baseline against which to measure the effect of lenity on compliance. Lenity presupposes that the statute *is* ambiguous. In that circumstance, lenity only aggravates the problem of inadvertent noncompliance. When a potential offender believes that an ambiguous statute is likely to be construed narrowly, she is more likely to engage in conduct that in fact violates the statute than she would be if she believed the statute were likely to be construed broadly. The power of broad construction to induce actors to refrain from engaging in conduct only arguably covered by a statute is exactly why it is believed to overdeter.

Lenity could be defended as enhancing compliance with law only if it could be shown to promote the adoption of clear rules over ambiguous ones *ex ante*. It is unclear that lenity or any other rule of strict construction ever has this effect. But in any event, as I will demonstrate presently,[291] the suggestion that lenity should be used to prod Congress to enact a completely specified criminal

---

not invariably be the best. In some cases, broad readings would carry the definitions of even *malum in se* offenses across the boundary line between socially desirable and socially undesirable conduct, undermining notice and other values. See, for example, *Dowling*, 473 US at 226–27 (declining to read National Stolen Property Act to apply to materials distributed in violation of copyright in order to avoid chilling effect on legitimate copying). Courts will reach the right result for both sets of offenses only if they dispense with mechanical rules of interpretation and instead consider which readings are best in light of all the circumstances. Because this approach overtly acknowledges that courts should use normative discretion to define incompletely specified criminal offenses, it is appropriately viewed as a form of delegated lawmaking.

[289] See notes 272–74. There are well known exceptions, however. See text accompanying notes 333–41 (discussing failure of courts to be specific when they should be).

[290] See Richard A. Posner, *Economic Analysis of Law* 543 (Little, Brown, 4th ed 1992).

[291] See Part IVB2.

code grossly underestimates the cost and overstates the effectiveness of attempting completely to specify criminal law by legislation.

b) Prosecutorial discretion. Preventing "arbitrary law enforcement" is another rule of law value sometimes associated with lenity.[292] This rationale for the canon, however, is as uncompelling (descriptively and normatively) as the fair warning rationale.

Controlling prosecutorial discretion is the most important objective of vagueness doctrine,[293] the paradigmatic application of which is *Papachristou v City of Jacksonville*.[294] That case involved a "vagrancy" ordinance that prohibited conduct as amorphous and innocuous as "wandering or strolling around . . . without any lawful purpose" and "habitual loaf[ing]."[295] What was remarkable about this offense was that it purported to "make[ ] criminal" various "activities that by modern standards are normally innocent";[296] by its literal terms, the offense was located deep within the interior of what is considered socially *desirable* conduct. In effect, the ordinance was a delegation of authority to law enforcement officials to decide on the basis of unstated and unexaminable criteria who within the general population should be deemed a criminal. And there was little doubt that the criteria they were employing were entirely illicit.

Lenity typically arises in a very different context. Even when federal criminal statutes lack clear edges, their core applications ordinarily involve socially undesirable conduct. In some cases, broad readings might push these statutes across the line into the territory of the socially desirable, thus creating the danger of unfair surprise and overdeterrence. But in many others, broad readings would prohibit conduct as undesirable as the core conduct at which the statute is aimed.[297] In such circumstances, a court deciding whether to apply lenity is effectively considering whether to spec-

---

[292] See, for example, *United States v Kozminski*, 487 US 931, 952 (1988); William N. Eskridge, Jr., and Philip P. Frickey, *Quasi-Constitutional Law: Clear Statement Rules as Constitutional Lawmaking*, 45 Vand L Rev 593, 600 (1992).

[293] See *Kolender v Lawson*, 461 US 352, 358 (1982).

[294] 405 US 156 (1972).

[295] *Papachristou*, 405 US at 156 n 1.

[296] Id at 163.

[297] See text accompanying notes 51–72, 87–96.

ify an otherwise justifiable rule of law itself or to insist that the rule be specified (if at all) only by Congress.

The goal of minimizing arbitrary law enforcement does not supply a reason to prefer either judicial or congressional specification of such a rule. Again, consider *McBoyle*: the risk of prosecutorial abuse is the same whether an airplane is treated as a "vehicle" according to express statutory enumeration or instead according to judicial interpretation of a generally worded standard. Either way, moreover, the risk of abuse would be much smaller than the risk deemed intolerable in *Papachristou*, since the statute would remain limited to socially undesirable conduct.[298]

There is one way, however, in which consistent application of lenity would minimize abuse of prosecutorial discretion. A bad prosecutor can abuse even a good rule, and the possibility for doing so necessarily increases with the scope of criminal law. If the National Motor Vehicle Theft Act is made (whether by Congress or by courts) to cover planes as well as automobiles, then the bad prosecutor has that many more potential offenders against whom to act arbitrarily. Lenity raises the cost of criminal legislation by forcing Congress to specify all operative legal rules itself.[299] If imposing this cost on Congress prevents it from enacting as much criminal law as its members desire, then full enforcement of lenity would shrink the overall scope of criminal law, thereby reducing the opportunities for prosecutorial abuse.

But this is an uncompelling defense of lenity. Under this view, lenity would combat prosecutorial discretion not by seeking to prevent deliberately overinclusive laws like the vagrancy ordinance at issue in *Papachristou*, but by seeking to inhibit the creation of law generally, however clear or sensible. It would be ironic indeed if the "rule of law" supported a position this antagonistic to law itself.

2. *Efficiency*

a) Cost. Delegated lawmaking is cheaper than lenity. It simply costs less for courts to fill out general statutory directives through

---

[298] It is not "arbitrary" to go after airplane thieves because they are airplane thieves. To be sure, a prosecutor might abuse this power by relying on illegitimate criteria to single out some class of airplane thieves for prosecution. She could do the same, however, with her power to prosecute car thieves. Selective enforcement is a risk whether statutory offenses are read broadly or narrowly. Under some circumstances, this abuse of discretion itself may violate the Constitution. See generally *Wayte v United States*, 470 US 598 (1985).

[299] See text accompanying notes 37–48.

common-lawmaking than it would for Congress fully to specify all statutory applications legislatively.

Increasing the cost of legislation is intrinsic to lenity as a rule of strict construction.[300] Specifying each and every application of a statute is burdensome; Congress frees itself from this burden when it legislates in a highly general fashion, effectively specifying only a general policy that a court may then translate into multiple operative rules. The genuine enforcement of lenity would deny Congress this economy by preventing courts from giving effect to any application not expressly specified on the face of a criminal statute.

Raising the cost of criminal legislation imposes real costs on society. Congress's capacity to legislate is limited by various practical and political constraints.[301] In a complex, industrialized society, it is inevitable that the legitimate demand for legislation will outstrip Congress's unaided power to supply it. Accordingly, if Congress is denied the policymaking multiplier of implied delegation in criminal law, it will be forced either to forgo legislating in another area or to leave part of the demand for criminal legislation unmet. The social cost of lenity would be particularly apparent were courts to refuse to repair manifest errors in statutory drafting.[302] In that situation, not only would Congress be pointlessly forced to expend legislative resources, but society would be pointlessly forced to endure unregulated antisocial conduct during the time that it took Congress to fill the gap.

Showing that full enforcement of lenity would raise the cost of criminal legislation constitutes only half a proof that delegated lawmaking is a cheaper way to make criminal law than is lenity. It is also necessary to consider what costs such an allocation of lawmaking authority would impose on other actors. The burden of specification that Congress avoids by implied delegation is necessarily shifted to courts.[303] In addition, where the law is incompletely specified, private parties, too, must invest more to determine what the law is.[304]

---

[300] See id.

[301] See text accompanying notes 20–21.

[302] See generally text accompanying notes 55–57 (describing approach in *Wiltberger*) and text accompanying notes 226–30 (describing modern approach).

[303] See Kaplow, 42 Duke L J at 609–11 (cited in note 25).

[304] See id at 609–10.

The setting in which delegated criminal lawmaking takes place, however, suggests that these costs are relatively small, and less, certainly, than those associated with attempting to specify all operative rules of criminal law by legislation. Article III courts have relatively few members and are insulated from democratic politics. Consequently, decision making for them is less burdensome, practically and politically, than it is for Congress.[305] In addition, while anticipating each and every potential application of a general criminal norm—say, the prohibition on fraud—may be prohibitively time consuming for Congress *ex ante*, determining whether a particular fact pattern meets that standard *ex post* may be a relatively straightforward task for a court.[306]

Nor are these decision-making economies likely to be offset by any increase in the workload of courts associated with delegated criminal lawmaking. The volume of litigation is in part a function of uncertainty about the content of the law. Were it clearly understood, however, that courts would construe generally worded criminal statutes in a generative fashion to include all applications that are analogous to their core applications, there would be relatively little uncertainty about the reach of many statutes that might otherwise be viewed as ambiguous. There would definitely be less uncertainty than there is now, when courts are perceived to vacillate in an unpredictable fashion between narrow and broad construction.[307] Indeed, the recognized power of broad construction to overdeter[308] would promote conservation of law enforcement and judicial resources.

For similar reasons, a regime of delegated lawmaking would impose relatively small costs on private actors. Particularly if the statute creates what I have called interior offense, it should not ordinarily be that difficult for a private actor to determine whether a proposed course of action comes within a general statutory prohibition; in a world in which delegated criminal lawmaking was open and thoroughgoing, McBoyle would not have had to ponder long before concluding that airplanes were "vehicles" for purposes of the National Motor Vehicle Theft Act (assuming he bothered to

---

[305] See id at 608–09; and Ehrlich and Posner, 3 J Legal Stud at 267–68 (cited in note 15).

[306] For elaboration on this point, see text accompanying notes 310–28 (discussing loopholing).

[307] See text accompanying note 5.

[308] See text accompanying note 270.

ponder at all). Moreover, the private burden of making such a determination—including any residual uncertainty about the precise coverage of such a statute—is in fact a public benefit, since greater expenditures on deciphering the law effectively raise the cost of socially undesirable conduct.[309]

b) Effectiveness. The full enforcement of lenity would not only raise the cost of criminal lawmaking but also reduce the value of the law that is made. For an unavoidable consequence of prohibiting delegated lawmaking would be to create indefensible gaps in the law, substantially undermining its effectiveness in deterring socially undesirable conduct.

The ideal conception of legislative supremacy recognizes Congress as the sole legitimate author of operative legal rules. Lenity seeks to attain this aspiration by directing courts to assume that it has already been realized, thus forbidding them to apply any operative rule that Congress has not specifically endorsed. Accordingly, the full enforcement of lenity would be tantamount to treating all federal criminal statutes as fully specified.

This approach would render federal criminal statutes systematically underinclusive. Because what makes criminal conduct socially undesirable can often feasibly be described only abstractly—in terms only of the risks and dangers that such conduct poses—any attempt to enumerate all the forms that such conduct assumes is bound to be incomplete.[310] Consequently, by obliging a court to treat all statutes as if they were fully specified, lenity would insulate from punishment numerous forms of misconduct that Congress (understandably) lacked the foresight clearly to prohibit but that inflict the same harm as forms of misconduct that Congress has expressly banned. This consequence of lenity would reward individuals for consciously seeking out and exploiting loopholes in the law.[311]

The only way to avoid this kind of underinclusivity is to treat criminal statutes as incompletely specified. Either statutes that enumerate prohibited forms of conduct must be construed to cover analogously harmful types of conduct or the gaps in statutes that

---

[309] See Kaplow, 42 Duke L J at 603–04 (cited in note 25) (recognizing that there can be "divergences between the private and social values" of information about the law).

[310] See *Williams*, 458 US at 304–05 (Marshall dissenting).

[311] See Geoffrey C. Miller, *The Case of the Speluncean Explorers: Contemporary Proceedings*, 61 Geo Wash L Rev 1754, 1799–1800 (1993); compare Posner, *Economic Analysis of Law* at 544 (cited in note 290).

appear to be exhausted by their enumerated applications must be filled in by other broader, less completely specified prohibitions.[312] Because statutes can be viewed as incompletely specified only if Congress has expressly or implicitly left part of their content to be imparted after enactment, this solution to the problem of loopholing necessarily entails delegated lawmaking.[313] Indeed, to avoid underinclusivity, courts, too, must refrain from completely specifying their content in the course of interpreting them.

These concerns figure prominently in the judiciary's implementation of the criminal fraud statutes.[314] The mission of closing loopholes, for example, is well captured in Chief Justice Burger's depiction of the mail fraud statute as "a stopgap device to deal . . . with [a] new phenomenon, until particularized legislation can be developed."[315] In defending a conception of mail fraud flexible enough "to cope with the new varieties of fraud that the ever-inventive American 'con artist' is sure to develop," Burger echoes common law jurists, who refused to "la[y] down as a general proposition, what shall constitute fraud, or any general rule, beyond which they will not go upon the ground of fraud, lest other means of avoiding the equity of the courts should be found out."[316]

---

[312] See Ehrlich and Posner, 3 J Legal Stud at 268, 275 n 24 (cited in note 15).

[313] In theory, the delegation need not be to the judiciary. Some statutes delegate authority to administrative agencies to promulgate criminally enforceable rules of law. In the case of the Controlled Substances Act, 21 USC § 811(h) (1988), Congress delegated criminal law-making authority for the express purpose of avoiding loopholes. Congress recognized that the capacity of drug producers to alter the chemical composition of psychedelic drugs, in particular, would outstrip the capacity of Congress to enumerate with specificity the types of substances that it wished to outlaw. Accordingly, it authorized the Attorney General to promulgate a schedule of controlled substances, and to update the schedule with expedited rulemaking procedures. See generally *Touby v United States*, 500 US 160, 163 (1991).

[314] See text accompanying notes 128–54.

[315] *United States v Maze*, 414 US 395, 405–06 (1974) (Burger dissenting).

[316] Story, *Equity Jurisprudence* at 190 (cited in note 137); see also *McAleer v Horsey*, 35 Md 439, 451–52 (1872) ("[t]he common law not only gives no definition of fraud, but perhaps wisely asserts as a principle that there shall be no definitions of it, for, as it is the very nature and essence of fraud to elude all laws in fact, without appearing to break them in form, a technical definition of fraud, making everything come within the scope of its words before the law could deal with it as such, would be in effect telling to the crafty precisely how to avoid the grasp of the law"); Charles L. Black, Jr., *Law as an Art*, in Charles L. Black, Jr., *The Humane Imagination* 33 (Ox Bow Press, 1986) ("Some lawyers talk as though they thought maximum clarity always desirable even though they wouldn't have to probe very deeply to find that fraud, and fiduciary obligation, and undue influence, have been carefully isolated from exact definition, because such exact definition would simply point out safe ways of immunity, and, to the birds of prey, make the law 'their perch and not their terror.' "); and, Goldstein, 68 Yale L J at 423 n 60 (cited in note 131).

The problem of underinclusivity has also animated the Court's interpretation of the National Stolen Property Act[317] (the successor to the Motor Vehicle Theft Act). Thus, in *United States v Turley*,[318] the Court refused to limit the term "stolen" to property obtained by common law larceny.[319] "Professional thieves resort to innumerable forms of theft," the Court explained, "and Congress presumably sought to meet the need for federal action effectively rather than to leave loopholes for wholesale evasion."[320] Lest offenders "easily evade the reach of federal law,"[321] the Court has also consistently read the phrase "falsely made, forged, altered, or counterfeited" to apply to a general *"class* of fraud" and not only to the specific *"instances* of fraud" that were associated with these terms at common law or that inspired Congress's enactment of this provision of the Act.[322] In construing the Act, moreover, the Court has consistently rejected claims of lenity.

Closing loopholes also informs the Court's approach to construing RICO.[323] RICO's key terms not only emerged incompletely specified from the legislative process, but have largely remained that way in the course of judicial interpretation. The Court has disavowed readings that would confine the statute to discrete forms of criminality as "counterproductive" and contrary to Congress's intent that RICO "encompass a wide range of criminal activity, taking many different forms and [attracting] a broad array of perpetrators operating in many different ways."[324] Although attacked as

---

[317] 18 USC § 2314 (1988 & Supp 1993).

[318] 352 US 407 (1957).

[319] See id at 417.

[320] Id at 416–17. Significantly, Justice Frankfurter dissented; in his view, "the principle of lenity" precluded construing "the term 'stolen' to include every form of dishonest acquisition" unless "Congress expresses, if not an explicit, at least an unequivocal, desire" to regulate such diverse forms of misconduct. Id at 418 (Frankfurter dissenting). See text accompanying notes 40–42 (explaining Frankfurter's views on strict construction and the allocation of lawmaking authority).

[321] *McElroy v United States*, 455 US 642, 655 (1982).

[322] *Moskal*, 498 US at 109–11 (construing § 2314 to apply to genuine automobile titles bearing false odometer readings whether or not such activity constituted "false making" at common law); see *United States v Sheridan*, 329 US 379, 390 (1946) (statute applies to check forgeries "[w]hether or not Congress had [such transactions] in mind"); see also *McElroy*, 455 US at 653–54 (statute applies to checks forged after crossing state lines).

[323] See text accompanying notes 155–77.

[324] *H. J., Inc. v Northwestern Bell Telephone Co.*, 492 US 229, 248–49 (1989).

THE SUPREME COURT REVIEW

contrary to the rule of law principle of fair "notice,"[325] this approach is defensible. "Bright-line" rules on what counts as a RICO "pattern" or "enterprise" would allow offenders to make simple adjustments in their conduct in order to sidestep the statute without losing the efficiency of group criminality.

The settings in which incomplete specification makes sense as a strategy for avoiding underinclusivity share two general features. The first is that they relate to antisocial conduct that appears in heterogeneous forms. The conceptual cores of "fraud," "theft," and "organized criminality" may be easy enough to specify, but their factual instantiations are inexhaustible. Were this not the case— were there only a finite number of recurring and identifiable devices by which such harms could be inflicted—it would be possible to enumerate them exhaustively without fear of loopholing. It is exactly the infeasibility of exhaustive specification *ex ante*, moreover, that makes delegated lawmaking the most efficient means of making criminal law.[326]

The second shared feature of these settings is that they involve what I have called "interior" offenses.[327] Although the types of conduct that involve "fraud" cannot be exhaustively described, they all involve "trick, deceit, chicane, or overreaching"[328]— attributes that (in theory, at least) deprive them of any licit utility. RICO requires proof of "at least" two independent criminal offenses;[329] thus, no matter how "enterprise" and "pattern" are defined, the statute will punish only conduct independently deemed criminal and, as long as these terms are given some content, will in fact leave some manifestly undesirable conduct untouched. For boundary offenses, in contrast, the very concept of "loophole" makes no sense; all conduct that falls on the nonprohibited side of the line is, by definition, socially desirable, and the law is understood for that reason to invite parties to take account of exactly where liability terminates when planning their primary conduct.

Of course, even if society places no or negative value on a

---

[325] Id at 254 (Scalia dissenting); see Lynch, 87 Colum L Rev at 717 (cited in note 164).

[326] See generally Kaplow, 42 Duke L J at 599–601 (cited in note 25).

[327] See text accompanying notes 276–80.

[328] *Hammerschmidt v United States*, 265 US 182, 188 (1924).

[329] 18 USC § 1961(5) (1988).

particular form of conduct, the social benefit from deterring it might be less than the social cost of punishing those who engage in it, particularly if the punishment is a lengthy term of imprisonment. Narrow construction is sometimes asserted to be necessary to avoid this form of over-enforcement,[330] but this rationale for lenity is singularly unconvincing. Here the judgment of the judiciary definitely *is* inferior to that of another institutional actor, namely, the executive. Whether or not prosecutors can be trusted to show adequate respect for individual liberty, they certainly can be trusted to make the essentially political judgment of whether using a particular statute to deter some species of socially valueless conduct is worth the cost.[331] Construing a statute narrowly to avert over-enforcement not only invades the territory most efficiently occupied by prosecutorial discretion; it also needlessly denies society the deterrent effect that a broad reading of a harsh statute might have even without frequent enforcement.[332]

I have suggested that incomplete specification is efficient in theory when confined to interior offenses; nonetheless, there are well-known applications of generative criminal statutes that defy this constraint. For example, some applications of the criminal fraud statutes—including their use to regulate fiduciary obligations within corporations or between participants in securities markets—create "boundary" offenses, because they regulate what would otherwise be socially desirable commercial activity. Moreover, because RICO makes mail fraud a predicate racketeering offense,[333] this statute also has the potential to be used in some boundary contexts.[334] Sometimes courts have been sensitive to the appropriate-

---

[330] See, for example, *Rewis v United States*, 401 US 808, 813 (1971) (rejecting broad reading on ground that it would "overextend limited federal police resources"); *United States v Bass*, 404 US 336, 350 (1971) (same).

[331] See generally Frank Easterbrook, *Criminal Justice Discretion as a Regulatory System*, 12 J Legal Stud 289, 305–06 (1983).

[332] See generally Gary S. Becker, *Crime and Punishment: An Economic Approach*, 76 J Pol Econ 169, 184 (1968).

[333] See 18 USC § 1961(1)(B) (1988 & Supp 1993).

[334] See Lynch, 87 Colum L Rev at 749–50 (cited in note 164) (discussing use of RICO to prosecute white collar crimes); compare Ellen S. Podgor, *Tax Fraud—Mail Fraud: Synonymous, Cumulative or Diverse?* 57 Cincinnati L Rev 903, 923–29 (1989) (discussing use of mail fraud statute to fill in gaps in, enhance penalties for, and supply basis of RICO prosecution of tax fraud).

ness of precision in such settings.[335] But quite often, and quite unfortunately, they have not.[336]

Ironically, at least some of these miscues are a consequence of the failure of courts to acknowledge their delegated lawmaking role. Courts sometimes suggest that fashioning limiting constructions for open-textured criminal statutes would itself offend the primacy of Congress in making criminal law.[337] It is simply "beyond our power," the Supreme Court has explained, "to correct" any "defect" associated with the breadth of RICO.[338] "[R]ewriting [the statute] is a job for Congress, if it is so inclined, and not for this Court."[339]

This reasoning is indefensible once the dynamics behind delegated criminal lawmaking have been exposed. Congress drafts criminal statutes in broad terms not because it favors limitless statutory coverage, but because it is unable or unwilling to specify the full content of criminal statutes *ex ante*. The open-ended statutory definitions of RICO's key terms, for example, can be understood only as directives to courts to supply the statute with operative content.[340] Because Congress expects courts to take the lead, it is incoherent for the Court to invoke "congressional intent" to defend broad rather than narrow readings of the statute. And because it is the Court, rather than Congress, that is making the law, the Court cannot persuasively disclaim responsibility for undesirable statutory applications.[341]

---

[335] See, for example, *Dowling*, 473 US at 226–27 (declining to read National Stolen Property Act to apply to materials distributed in violation of copyright in order to avoid chilling effect on legitimate copying); *United States v United States Gypsum Co.*, 438 US 422, 441–43 (1978) (reading *mens rea* requirement into Sherman Act in order to avoid chilling effect on socially desirable market behavior).

[336] Daniel Fischel, *Payback* (forthcoming 1995); John C. Coffee, Jr., *From Tort to Crime: Some Reflections on the Criminalization of Fiduciary Breaches and the Problematic Line Between Law and Ethics*, 19 Am Criminal L Rev 117 (1981).

[337] See, for example, *United States v Culbert*, 435 US 371, 374 (1978) (declining to read a "racketeering" limitation into Hobbs Act); *Turkette v United States*, 452 US 576, 581, 586–87 (1981) (declining to limit RICO to legitimate enterprises); *United States v DiGilio*, 538 F2d 972, 978 (3d Cir 1976) ("solution to th[e] problem[s]" associated with reading federal theft statute to apply to unauthorized receipt of government information "would appear to be legislative"). See generally Abrams and Beale, *Federal Criminal Law and Its Enforcement* at 51 (cited in note 143).

[338] *H. J. Inc.*, 492 US at 249.

[339] Id.

[340] See text accompanying notes 156–66.

[341] Indeed, it is hard to take any such disclaimers at face value. Exercising what amounts in substance to common-lawmaking authority, the Court has read RICO (and other open-textured criminal offenses) narrowly when doing so has struck the Court as sensible. See,

The lesson to be drawn from this kind of confusion, however, is not that courts should invariably construe open-textured statutes narrowly; rather, it is that courts should consciously acknowledge and perfect the function of delegated criminal lawmaking. In particular, a full understanding of how delegated criminal lawmaking legitimately avoids underinclusivity should be used to generate limiting principles for the common law elaboration of criminal statutes. Courts should demand more specificity from Congress, or at least supply it themselves, as the applications of such statutes approach the border between socially desirable and socially undesirable conduct. But because the exercise of this type of judgment and discretion does not exceed the capacity of courts,[342] the benefits of making criminal statutes precise when they ought to be does not require society to endure the detriment of making such statutes precise when they ought not to be.

c) Efficiency and liberty. So far I have assumed that increasing the efficiency of criminal lawmaking is generally a good thing. It is at least possible to argue otherwise. After all, lenity "is founded on the tenderness of the law for the rights of individuals."[343] Placing a premium on the efficiency of criminal lawmaking might seem out of keeping with the " 'instinctive distaste against men languishing in prison' "[344] that the rule is understood to embody.

The answer to this objection is that a generic bias in favor of individual liberty has little to recommend it as a strategy for construing criminal statutes. The class of persons who benefit from narrow readings of federal criminal statutes includes a great many individuals who have deliberately engaged in socially undesirable conduct but who hope to avoid punishment on the basis of an unanticipated gap in the law. A rule that systematically sought to protect these individuals through narrow construction would systematically disadvantage the persons whose rights these individuals have violated. It is true that the class of persons who benefit

---

for example, *Reves v Ernst & Young*, 113 S Ct 1163 (1993) (construing phrase "to conduct . . . or participate . . . in the conduct" of RICO enterprise to require "operation or management" of enterprise); see text accompanying notes 151–54 (discussing limiting constructions of mail fraud statute). Accordingly, the Court's rejection of other proposed limiting constructions ought to be understood to reflect the judgment that the proposed limitations are inappropriate as a matter of substance.

[342] See text accompanying notes 285–87.

[343] *Wiltberger*, 18 US at 95.

[344] *Bass*, 404 US at 349 (quoting Friendly, *Benchmarks* at 196, 209 (cited in note 2)).

from narrow readings also includes some individuals who have engaged in socially tolerated or socially desirable conduct. But if courts are sensitive to the distinction between boundary offenses and interior offenses, they can easily display appropriate regard for the rights of these persons without vitiating the efficiency of delegated criminal lawmaking across the board.

William Eskridge has recently advanced a more sophisticated challenge to the kind of efficiency that I am proposing. He attributes Congress's historical failure to overrule broad readings of criminal statutes to a distortion in the political process that causes Congress to be over-responsive to the demand for severity in criminal law and under-responsive to the interests of "people accused of committing crimes."[345] Lenity, he argues, corrects this bias by reinforcing the representation of persons "too easily brushed aside in the legislative process."[346]

It is necessary, however, to examine critically the premise that Congress's tilt toward severity is a distortion. There is no neutral procedural balance in representative politics; the use of judicial review to reinforce representation for a particular class can be defended only by showing, on the basis of a substantive normative theory, that the class is entitled to receive more than what representative politics typically delivers.[347] The question that Eskridge's account puts, then, is whether "people accused of committing crimes"[348] are getting systematically less than they deserve from Congress.

Some of them might be. It is not difficult to expose the normative shortcomings of mandatory minimums for minor drug offenders,[349] life sentences without parole for all individuals convicted of three felonies,[350] or capital punishment for offenders who inadvertently

---

[345] Eskridge, 101 Yale L J at 331, 413 (cited in note 16).

[346] Id at 413, 414. For a similar account, see Ross, 45 Vand L Rev at 570–71 (cited in note 14) (justifying lenity on ground that it advances "widely held 'background values' " that receive insufficient attention in "the heat of [a] particular battle" in Congress).

[347] See Einer Elhauge, *Does Interest Group Theory Justify More Intrusive Judicial Review?* 101 Yale L J 31, 48–66 (1991); and David A. Strauss, *Corruption, Equality, and Campaign Finance Reform*, 94 Colum L Rev 1269, 1377–79 (1994).

[348] Eskridge, 101 Yale L J at 413 (cited in note 16).

[349] See, for example, 21 USC §§ 841(b), 844(a) (1988 & Supp 1993).

[350] Violent Crime Control and Law Enforcement Act of 1994 §§ 70001, 80001, Pub L No 103-322, 108 Stat 1796, 1982–86, reprinted in 1994 USCCAN.

kill postal inspectors.[351] Such measures not only appear to under-value the liberty of individual defendants, but also pay insufficient attention to efficiency, federalism, and other societal values that ought to inform federal criminal law.[352]

But lenity would not likely redress this imbalance. The problem with these statutes is not that they are ambiguous; it is that they all too clearly compel severity when the merits of severity are questionable. Unless lenity is converted into a tool for outright judicial nullification,[353] it will do little to counteract Congress's inattentiveness to the welfare of individuals charged with violating these types of laws.

The persons whom lenity does help are those charged with violating incompletely specified criminal offenses. The normative justification for reinforcing the representation of these individuals, however, is far from obvious. Again, the class of persons who would benefit from systematically narrow constructions is pervaded by those who intend to injure other, innocent individuals.[354] How would undeserved leniency for the McBoyles, the Kozminiskis, and the Wiltbergers of the world compensate for the wastefully severe punishment of those charged with minor drug offenses?

Indeed, full enforcement of lenity would likely aggravate the distortions with which Eskridge is concerned. The central object of lenity is to prevent Congress from implicitly delegating criminal lawmaking power to the judiciary. At least in theory, then, the more vigorously courts enforce lenity, the greater the pressure is on Congress to enact a fully specified criminal code. But if Congress predictably undervalues liberty, efficiency, federalism, and other worthy interests when it enacts specific criminal legislation, why is this shift in effective lawmaking authority desirable? Criminal law is more likely to reflect an appropriate weighting of the values

---

[351] Id § 60007, 108 Stat at 1971.

[352] See, for example, William Tucker, *Three Strikes and You're Dead*, American Spectator 22 (Mar 1994); Jeffrey Rosen, *Crime Bill Follies: Our Guide to the Clinton Plan*, New Republic 22 (Mar 21, 1994).

[353] This is exactly what it was in English practice. See text accompanying notes 58–60.

[354] And, again, there are others who intend to engage in conduct that is socially tolerated or desired. It seems unlikely, however, that these persons—who include securities analysts, corporate executives, and other market participants, see text accompanying notes 272–74—are really under-represented in Congress!

that Congress systematically disregards if the law is at least partially made by courts.

3. *Democracy.* The most substantial defense of lenity is that delegated criminal lawmaking is antidemocratic. If a bar on delegation makes criminal lawmaking more expensive and less effective, so be it; criminal lawmaking, under this view, is simply too vital to the experience of self-government to be taken out of the hands of society's elected representatives and placed in the hands of unaccountable judges.[355]

The democracy defense emphasizes a special nexus between criminal law and self-government. "[C]riminal punishment," under this view, "represents the *moral condemnation* of the community."[356] It not only raises the cost of satisfying particular preferences, but also self-consciously stigmatizes those preferences as deviant, thereby signaling in authoritative moral terms which values and outlooks entitle a person to respect and which to censure.[357] In this way, the contours of the criminal law—what it singles out for sanction and what it excuses; what it punishes severely and what it treats more lightly—express the political community's core ideals.[358] Accordingly, a political community that lacked democratic control over the formation of its criminal law could hardly view itself as self-governed at all. Lenity seeks to guarantee the democratic character of criminal law by assuring that "legislatures and not courts . . . define criminal activity."[359]

I do not wish to take issue with the conception of democracy that underlies this defense of lenity;[360] indeed, I accept it entirely.

---

[355] See Dickerson, *The Interpretation and Application of Statutes* at 207–10 (cited in note 13); Shapiro, 67 NYU L Rev at 944–45 (cited in note 13); compare Marshall, 88 Mich L Rev 177 (cited in note 263).

[356] *Bass*, 404 US at 348.

[357] See Feinberg, *Doing and Deserving* at 102–04 (cited in note 106); and Kenneth G. Dau-Schmidt, *An Economic Analysis of the Criminal Law as a Preference-Shaping Policy*, 1990 Duke L J 1.

[358] Feinberg, *Doing and Deserving* at 102–04 (cited in note 106); compare Hampton, *Forgiveness and Mercy* at 134–35, 140–42 (cited in note 106) (definition of crimes and severity of punishments embody implicit theories of human worth).

[359] *Bass*, 404 US at 348; see also *United States v R.L.C.*, 112 S Ct 1329, 1340 (1992) (Scalia concurring in judgment) (purpose of lenity is to "assur[e] that the society, through its representatives, has genuinely called for punishment to be meted out").

[360] I believe that such a defense of lenity is fairly implicit in many of the Court's cases applying the rule. For a scholarly treatment that comes very close to this account, see Shapiro, who defends lenity as reflecting "judicial reluctance to read a statute as extending federal criminal law in to a new sphere without a clear direction from the legislature."

I disagree, however, that this view of the relationship between criminal law and democracy entails full enforcement of lenity. Like the claim that lenity is essential to the rule of law, the claim that it is essential to democracy is much too sweeping.

To begin, delegation of criminal lawmaking need not involve congressional abdication. Even when it enacts incompletely speci-fied criminal statutes, Congress ordinarily addresses matters of sub-stantial political importance. In enacting RICO and the National Stolen Property Act, for example, Congress debated and resolved important issues relating to use of federal resources to combat state-law crimes.[361] Or consider the recently enacted Freedom of Access to Clinic Entrances Act.[362] However vague, the prohibition on "in-timidat[ing] or interfer[ing] with"[363] efforts to obtain an abortion communicates clear condemnation of those who seek to prevent a woman from exercising this right.[364] Thus, Congress's resort to implicit delegation to magnify the reach of federal criminal prohibi-tions does not invariably compromise its participation in expressing the "moral condemnation of the community."[365]

By the same token, filling out incompletely specified statutes does not invariably involve courts in this expressive function to a significant degree. Concluding that title washing was an "instance" of the "general class" of fraud prohibited by the ban on "falsely made, forged, altered, or counterfeited securities," for example, did not require the Court in *Moskal* to advance even one step be-yond the policy choices that Congress itself made when it enacted this provision of the National Stolen Property Act.[366] Similarly, it

---

Shapiro, 67 NYU L Rev at 936 (cited in note 13). Such a reluctance, he argues, reflects an appropriate "allocation of institutional responsibility between legislatures and courts." Id at 944. "If a legislature adopts imprecise language that is then used by a court to effect a change that the legislature itself would not openly have enacted, the idea of a 'partnership' is being used in a manner that subverts the democratic ideal." Id.

[361] See 116 Cong Rec 35193 (Oct 6, 1970) (defending definition of racketeering by refer-ence to local law); Organized Crime Control Act of 1969, S Rep No 91-617, 91st Cong, 1st Sess 34 (same); 58 Cong Rec 5472–73 (Sept 15, 1919) (debating interstate commerce justifi-cation for Dyer Act); and, HR Rep No 1599, 73d Cong, 2d Sess 3 (1934) (resolving interstate dimensions of disposition of stolen property in National Stolen Property Act).

[362] § 3, Pub L No 103-259, 108 Stat 694 (1994), reprinted in 1994 USCCAN.

[363] Id § 3, 108 Stat 694–97.

[364] On the imprecision of this statute, see Michael Stokes Paulsen and Michael W. McCon-nell, *The Doubtful Constitutionality of the Clinic Access Bill*, 1 Va J Soc Pol & L 261 (1994).

[365] *Bass*, 404 US at 348.

[366] See text accompanying notes 220–24.

is quite implausible to suggest that the Court in *Smith* would have enriched the Nation's democratic experience had it forced Congress to amend 18 USC § 924(c) in order expressly to prohibit the "use[ ] [of] a firearm" to *buy* drugs.[367] In sum, the democracy defense errs in assuming that Congress's delegation of criminal lawmaking authority invariably relocates the center of normative gravity to the judiciary.

This is not to say, however, that any and all such delegations respect democracy. For example, a statute that expressly directed courts to construct the criminal code from top to bottom would impoverish self-government by removing criminal lawmaking as an occasion for the democratic appraisal and reform of societal values. Accordingly, the nexus between self-government and criminal law furnishes another limiting principle to guide delegated criminal lawmaking. In performing this function, courts should ask whether a particular reading of a criminal statute would preempt rather than implement democratic deliberation on important issues, particularly when express congressional consideration is appropriate to protect other constitutional values, such as federalism.[368] In some circumstances, the answers to these questions will counsel narrow readings of a criminal statute for the very purpose of enhancing Congress's policymaking voice.

The Court's decision last Term in *Staples v United States*[369] fits this description. At issue was the *mens rea* requirement for the National Firearms Act: Should the government be required to prove that the defendant knew he possessed a weapon possessing the characteristics of a statutory "firearm" or should it be required to prove only that he knew he possessed any type of "gun"?[370]

The Court construed the statute to require the more demanding proof. There is no consensus in the United States, the Court noted, that possession of *any* type of guns is inappropriate; legal regulations and moral understandings relating to guns vary widely across

---

[367] See text accompanying notes 215–19.

[368] See text accompanying notes 43–48 (describing Court's use of "clear statement" rules to advance federalism).

[369] 114 S Ct 1793.

[370] See id at 1796, 1798. The Act itself is silent on *mens rea*. See 26 USC § 5861(d) (1988) ("[i]t shall be unlawful for any person . . . to receive or possess a firearm which is not registered to him . . . ."). The Act defines "firearm" to include a variety of weapons— including sawed-off shotguns, machineguns, and various types of explosives, see 18 USC §§ 5845(a)–(f)—but excludes a wide range of guns as well.

the states.[371] Accordingly, the broad statutory reading advanced by the government would have permitted conviction of persons who honestly believed that they were behaving morally.[372] No doubt one purpose of the National Firearms Act was to create a uniform national moral understanding about guns and to criticize and reform deviating subcommunity understandings. But to assure that Congress and not the judiciary is responsible for such reformation, the Court declined to read the statute expansively.[373]

By using narrow construction, the Court in *Staples* thus assured that judicial lawmaking would not be used to displace democratic deliberation on issues on which there is social or regional dissensus. But this rationale for construing a criminal statute narrowly does not generalize, because broad constructions do not invariably displace deliberation in the way that a broad reading of the National Firearms Act would have. Accordingly, respecting the democratic underpinnings of criminal law does not justify lenity. Indeed, the Court in *Staples* expressly disclaimed reliance on that canon.[374]

4. *Federalism.* Federalism supplies another normative constraint on the scope of federal criminal law. What conduct a state chooses to criminalize and how severely it chooses to punish it are matters critical to the experience of deliberative democracy within that state. Because federal criminal law dictates uniform, national answers to such questions, expansive readings of federal criminal law threaten to extinguish the opportunity that states have to use criminal law to express and shape local ideals. Respect for the traditional importance of criminal law to the vitality of the states as political communities is one of the primary reasons that federal criminal laws are routinely underinclusive with respect to the harms that they regulate.

As it does for other federalism interests,[375] the Supreme Court uses a clear statement rule to safeguard the primacy of the states in the field of criminal law. In theory, there must be express and unambiguous textual warrant before the Court will construe a federal criminal statute to punish "conduct readily denounced as crim-

---

[371] See 114 S Ct at 1801.

[372] See id at 1802.

[373] See id at 1804.

[374] See id at 1804 n 17.

[375] See text accompanying notes 43–48.

inal by the States."[376] The Court frequently uses this "federalism canon" in tandem with lenity.[377] Indeed, given the erratic enforcement of lenity, federalism supplies a much more convincing explanation for these and many other decisions construing criminal statutes narrowly.[378]

It seems appropriate to consider, then, whether federalism supplies a sufficient justification for lenity. If clear statement rules are an appropriate way to enforce federalism values generally, and if expansive rules of federal criminal law can threaten federalism in particular, then why shouldn't all federal criminal statutes be read narrowly to vindicate federalism values? Again, the answer is that the complete disablement of delegated lawmaking that lenity would entail is an unnecessary and counterproductive means of advancing these values.

There are at least two recurring and readily identifiable circumstances in which federalism does not support strict construction of federal criminal statutes. The first is where such statutes are used to remedy enforcement gaps in the application of state criminal laws to conduct that spans multiple jurisdictions. By hypothesis, such conduct—whether interstate transportation of stolen property[379] or interstate kidnapping[380]—cannot be regulated effectively by any one state. Accordingly, the use of federal law to fill these gaps does not displace state law. Indeed, because narrow construction in this setting would necessarily protect conduct that violates but evades state law, enforcing lenity here would clearly *disserve* state interests. In addition, insofar as violation of such statutes always presupposes the illegality of the offender's conduct under state law, these are the same contexts in which notice and overdeterrence concerns are least likely to counsel against broad readings of federal statutes. Not surprisingly, then, this is the context in which the Court has most frequently

---

[376] *Bass*, 404 US at 349–50.

[377] See *McNally*, 483 US at 359–60 (rejecting application of mail fraud statute to local governmental corruption); *Williams*, 458 US at 287, 290 (declining to apply to check-kiting scheme federal statute prohibiting false statements to federally insured savings institutions); *Bass*, 404 US at 347–48 (nexus with interstate commerce necessary to show violation of federal law prohibiting convicted felons from possessing firearms); *Rewis v United States*, 401 US at 811–12 (gambling operation frequented by persons living across state lines not a violation of Travel Act).

[378] See text accompanying notes 151–54 and note 154.

[379] See 18 USC §§ 2311–21 (1988).

[380] See 18 USC §§ 1201–03 (1988 & Supp 1993).

relaxed the requirements of lenity and the federalism canon and endorsed delegated lawmaking.[381]

The second circumstance in which federalism is not advanced by strict construction is where federal law is used to combat local corruption. This is another problem that states cannot effectively solve on their own, for corruption frequently infects the very agencies responsible for enforcing a state's anti-corruption laws.[382] Related political dynamics, moreover, have traditionally prevented Congress from enacting federal legislation aimed specifically at combating local corruption: the demand for such legislation is likely to be strongest in jurisdictions affected by corruption; yet these are the same jurisdictions in which members of Congress face the greatest risk in sponsoring legislation targeted at local political establishments. For these reasons, the problem of local corruption—which itself threatens federalism values—is likely to be most effectively addressed if courts are allowed to adapt incompletely specified federal statutes into anti-corruption offenses through a process of common-lawmaking.

The Court's attitude toward use of general statutes to combat local corruption has been ambivalent. Historically, federal courts have taken a leadership role in adapting general statutes such as the Travel Act, the Hobbs Act, and RICO to local corruption.[383] In *McNally v United States*,[384] however, the Supreme Court cited

---

[381] *Moskal*, 498 US at 107–08; *United States v Turley*, 352 US 407, 416–17 (1957); *United States v Sheridan*, 329 US 379, 384–85 (1946); see also *Perrin v United States*, 444 US 37, 42–43, 49–50 (1979). Justice Stevens has concluded that there should in fact be *two* "federalism canons" in criminal law, one calling for broad construction and the other for narrow construction: "Although federal criminal statutes that are intended to fill a void in local law enforcement should be construed broadly, I take a different approach to federal laws that merely subject the citizen to the risk of prosecution by two different sovereigns. When there is no perceivable obstacle to effective state enforcement, I believe federal criminal legislation should be narrowly construed unless it is clear that Congress intended the coverage in dispute." *Bell v United States*, 462 US 356, 362–63 (Stevens dissenting) (citations omitted).

[382] 1 *Working Papers of the National Commission to Reform Federal Criminal Laws* 54 (1970) (noting that "Federal investigation and prosecution" of local corruption "may be desirable because local law enforcement may find it difficult or awkward to proceed since local officials are involved"); John T. Noonan, Jr., *Bribes* 600–01 (MacMillan, 1984) (noting that federal prosecutors have greater ability to investigate and prosecute state and local corruption than do state prosecutors); see also Adam H. Kurland, *The Guarantee Clause as a Basis for Federal Prosecutions of State and Local Officials*, 62 S Cal L Rev 367, 377–81 (1989) (noting that enforcement of state anti-corruption laws is routinely frustrated by limits in substantive law, by local politics, and by procedural difficulties relating to venue and jurisdiction).

[383] See generally Kurland, 62 S Cal L Rev at 383–91 (cited in note 382).

[384] 483 US 350.

both lenity and federalism to reject use of mail fraud to prosecute schemes that deprive citizens of the intangible right of honest services from state or municipal officials.[385] Under my analysis, neither lenity nor federalism furnishes a persuasive basis for the Court's decision.[386]

Much remains, of course, once these two classes of statutes have been subtracted from the whole of federal criminal law. And in many of these settings, narrow construction will indeed advance federalism. This is especially likely to be so when a broad reading of a federal statute would make criminal (or punish severely) conduct that is socially tolerated (or only mildly condemned) in certain regions.[387] This is the particular circumstance in which federal law threatens the stake that states have in using criminal law to differentiate themselves as political communities. Narrow construction guarantees that states will not be stripped of this incident of self-government without an opportunity to protect their interests in Congress; it also tends to assure that Congress itself will not interfere with this state interest very often, since strict construction raises the cost and thus reduces the amount of such legislation. These are the general rationales for the use of clear statement rules as substitutes for judicially enforced limits on Congress's power to regulate state concerns.[388]

Nonetheless, even outside the contexts of interstate criminality and local corruption, there is good reason for courts not to construe federal criminal statutes narrowly in a mechanical or rule-like fash-

---

[385] See id at 359–60.

[386] If anything, the aftermath of *McNally* only confirms that Congress cannot be expected to play a meaningful role in the field of local corruption. The Court in *McNally* rejected the judicially constructed "intangible rights" theory in order to force Congress to take the lead "in setting standards of disclosure and good government for local and state officials." Id at 360. Congress did thereafter respond, but in a manner that completely sidestepped the leadership obligation that the Court tried to impose. Section 1346 of title 18 USC simply enlarges the definition of " 'scheme or artifice to defraud' " to include interfering with the "intangible right of honest services"; the effect was to "reinstate all pre-*McNally* case law pertaining to the mail and wire fraud statutes without change." 134 Cong Rec S17360-02 (daily ed, Nov 10, 1988) (statement of Sen. Biden). Thus, § 1346 shows that Congress does desire to combat local corruption, but only if it can force the judiciary to accept the burden and the responsibility to define the operative rules of law.

[387] For example, *Staples*, 114 S Ct 1793 (possession of guns); *Bass*, 404 US at 336 (same); see also *Rewis*, 401 US 808 (lottery scheme under Travel Act).

[388] See text accompanying notes 43–48; see also *Bass*, 404 US at 349–50 ("the requirement of clear statement assures that the legislature has in fact faced, and intended to bring into issue, the critical matters involved in the judicial decision").

ion. If, for example, broadly worded statutes that overlap substantially with state laws nonetheless reflect national consensus, strict construction is unnecessary to serve federalism interests. Indeed, demanding more specificity in that setting could just as easily undermine as invigorate federalism, since Congress frequently gives insufficient weight to federalism values when it enacts specifically worded legislation.[389] Again, federalism is most likely to be secured by a highly discriminating use of strict construction rather than by a formal, across-the-board prohibition on delegated lawmaking.

V. THE NEXT STEP: A THEORY OF FEDERAL COMMON LAW CRIMES

In this article, I have tried to do two things. First, I have tried to explain why the rule of lenity—the canon directing a court to select the narrowest reasonable reading of an ambiguous criminal statute—has been historically underenforced. Lenity, I have argued, conflicts with an equally basic, although largely unacknowledged, rule of federal criminal jurisprudence: that Congress may implicitly delegate, and courts exercise, the power to make criminal law. Congress faces a powerful incentive to alienate part of its lawmaking authority to the judiciary in order to reduce the practical and political cost of enacting criminal legislation. From early on, federal courts have accommodated this congressional preference by exercising what amounts to federal common-lawmaking power to fill in deliberately incomplete criminal statutes. This type of lawmaking collaboration would be impossible, however, were courts fully to enforce lenity, the very purpose of which is to prevent courts from applying any operative rule of law not specifically and clearly endorsed by Congress. Accordingly, courts have developed doctrinal strategies that subordinate lenity to the body of interpretive conventions that facilitate the exercise of federal common-lawmaking power. The contemporary debate among the Justices of the Supreme Court has finally brought into focus this antagonism between lenity and the delegation of criminal lawmaking.

Second, I have tried to justify doing away with lenity altogether. Delegated lawmaking reduces the cost of making criminal law, particularly where the harm that Congress wishes to regulate mani-

---

[389] See text accompanying notes 349–52.

fests itself in heterogeneous forms of conduct that defy advance enumeration. It also enhances the effectiveness of the criminal law by preventing the underinclusivity associated with excessive legislative specification of criminal prohibitions. Lenity is ordinarily defended as advancing a cluster of values associated with the rule of law. I have argued, however, that delegated criminal lawmaking—if properly exercised—poses no threat to these values.

Over the course of my argument, it should have become apparent that I have not attempted to do a third thing, which is to identify or defend any mechanical rule of "broad construction." Federal courts do not invariably adopt the broadest "reasonable" reading of ambiguous or open-textured statutes, nor should they. As I have suggested,[390] the rationales for delegated lawmaking furnish—or at least ought to furnish—limiting principles, under which narrow readings will at least sometimes be preferable to broad ones. Simply stated, federal criminal statutes should not uniformly be read either *narrowly* or *broadly*, but rather *appropriately* so as to carry out their purposes and to realize the full range of benefits associated with delegated lawmaking.

I believe that it is possible, though, to be much more concrete than this. Obviously, what makes for an "appropriate" reading of a criminal statute will often turn on considerations unique to that statute. Nonetheless, there are a great many issues, objectives, themes, and pathologies that relate to federal criminal statutes generally. With respect to these, it is feasible to articulate a catalogue of general principles the exercise of which would perfect the judiciary's delegated lawmaking authority. I have started to develop some of these guidelines here: broad readings are more appropriate for what I have called "interior" offenses, narrow for what I have called "boundary" ones; broad readings make more sense when the regulated conduct is heterogeneous, narrow when it is homogeneous; broad readings are more defensible if they implement preexisting social consensus, and narrow if creating such consensus would be furthered by legislative deliberation; and broad readings are more desirable when they address matters that the states cannot effectively regulate, narrow ones when federal law threatens to displace state law on issues on which there is regional diversity. But there is much more that can be said, both about these principles and about others that I have not addressed. Once completely

---

[390] See text accompanying notes 288–89, 327–28, 342, 368–74.

developed, these principles, strategies, and techniques would constitute a theory of federal common law crimes.

Federal criminal jurisprudence is in desperate need of such a theory. From its inception, the rule of delegated criminal lawmaking has existed in the dark; it has never been formally acknowledged, much less developed in the self-conscious, systematic way that delegated lawmaking has in other "federal common law" fields, such as antitrust. In this inchoate form, the judiciary's criminal lawmaking function has been rendered vulnerable to a multitude of distorting influences. One of these is the rule of lenity. Another is the "agency" theory of statutory interpretation, under which "[t]he judicial task is to discern and apply a judgment made by others, most notably the legislature."[391] Whatever the merits of the agency theory as a general conception of interpretation,[392] it is obviously tractionless in a regime in which Congress has deliberately left many important judgments to be made by courts. Delegation without a theory of how courts should exercise independent judgment is thus a recipe for incoherence.

My suggestion that there should be a theory of federal common law crimes will no doubt strike many as paradoxical—more so, even, than my suggestion that the rule of lenity should be abolished.[393] Even to those who are comfortable with the concept of federal common-lawmaking generally, it may seem that I am proposing development of a plan for a function that courts have no business performing.[394] The proposition that there are no "federal common law crimes," however, is just as much a fiction—indeed, it is really the same fiction—as the rule of lenity.[395] And it is

---

[391] Sunstein, 103 Harv L Rev at 415 (cited in note 2); see also David A. Strauss, *Common Law Constitutional Interpretation* (unpublished manuscript) (discussing "command theory" of interpretation).

[392] See Sunstein, 103 Harv L Rev at 415–41 (cited in note 2) (critiquing it).

[393] See, for example, Jeffries, 71 Va L Rev at 219–23 (cited in note 5) (criticizing "strict construction" while disavowing "common law" approach to interpretation of criminal statutes).

[394] See, for example, Guido Calabresi, *A Common Law for the Age of Statutes* 78–79 (Harvard, 1982) (noting that common law modification of criminal statutes seems to be foreclosed "because in our system criminality has required a degree of foreknowledge, and hence of forewarning, that common law methods seemed to preclude"); Merrill, 52 U Chi L Rev at 29 (cited in note 6) (depicting criminal common-lawmaking as foreclosed by "constraints of federalism and separation of powers" as reflected in *Hudson*).

[395] See Louise Weinberg, *Federal Common Law*, 83 Nw U L Rev 805, 834 (1989) ("In the United States, today, common law means judge-made law, in equity and in criminal cases no less than in actions at law."); Posner, *The Federal Courts* at 300 (cited in note 15) (recognizing "judge-made concepts of criminal law, such as the meaning of and requirements for proving

a fiction that serves no useful purpose. By insisting on treating judge-made criminal law as unthinkable, the conventional wisdom has succeeded only in making federal criminal law thoughtless. It is time for such thoughtlessness to end.

---

conspiracy," "are not less genuine examples of federal common law than [are doctrines of] admiralty").

PETER L. STRAUSS

ON RESEGREGATING THE WORLDS OF
STATUTE AND COMMON LAW

Qui tacet, consentire videtur[1]

I. Introduction—The Gottshall Case

In the early afternoon of a humid, 97 degree summer day, James Gottshall was part of a crew of mostly 50- to 60-year-old men replacing track for Conrail. Michael Norvick, the crew supervisor, pressed the men to finish the work. He discouraged observance of the scheduled breaks. Richard Johns collapsed in the heat; Norvick ordered the men back to work as soon as a cold compress had revived him. Five minutes later Johns collapsed again, the victim of a heart attack. Gottshall began 40 minutes of ultimately fruitless cardiopulmonary resuscitation on Johns, his friend for 15 years. Norvick was unable to radio for assistance because Conrail was repairing that part of its communications system; by the time he could drive for help, Johns was dead. Norvick made the men work in sight of his body, which lay covered with a sheet to await the coroner. The next day, Gottshall alleged, Norvick reprimanded Gottshall for his efforts to revive Johns, and—in the same heat and humidity—pushed the crew even harder, with three or four

Peter L. Strauss is Betts Professor of Law, Columbia University.

AUTHOR'S NOTE: Beyond the usual debts an author owes to colleagues for work developed in their midst are those I have to John Manning and Richard Pierce. Thanks are also owing to Christopher Cross for research help and to the Rockefeller Foundation, whose generosity in providing four weeks' time at their Bellagio Study and Conference Center, in the midst of humanists and far from Lexis and Westlaw, provided unparalleled opportunities for reflection on this paper.

[1] *United States v Irvine*, 114 S Ct 1473, 1483 (1994) (Scalia concurring).

hours of overtime. Within a few days Gottshall was hospitalized, suffering major depression and post-traumatic stress disorder; he continued to need treatment after his release three weeks later. He sued Conrail under the Federal Employers' Liability Act of 1908,[2] asserting that his condition was caused by its negligent infliction of emotional distress—both through Norvick's actions, and through Conrail's failure to maintain operative communications links with the work party.

FELA, like many state statutes of its time, sought to mitigate the rigor of the existing common law remedies for workplace injuries. Its general thrust was to create a federal tort remedy for railroad workers injured by their employers' negligence, under rules that significantly limited the common law defenses employers could otherwise use. While injured workers still had to show negligence, their employers could claim neither assumption of the risk nor the fellow servant defense; contributory negligence served only to reduce proportionately, not to eliminate, a worker's claim. The statute left the federal courts responsible to develop the contours of this negligence recovery. FELA neither named nor precluded "negligent infliction of emotional distress" as a cause of action. Although the Supreme Court had not had to decide whether it was available before Gottshall sued, in 1987 it had noted both that question and the fact-dependency of any answer to it.[3]

During the years before FELA, state courts had given grudging readings to statutes that sought directly to modify common law tort doctrine on injured workers' behalf. (In reaction, state reform statutes at this time predominantly took the form of worker compensation laws whose implementation was assigned to a new competitor with the courts, the administrative agency.)[4] That state court approach reflected what Roscoe Pound, writing in the same year FELA was enacted, characterized as "the orthodox common law attitude towards [a] legislative innovation[]"—to "give to it a strict and narrow interpretation, holding it down rigidly to those cases which it covers expressly."[5] Although he thought the better

---

[2] 35 Stat 65, as amended, 45 USC §§ 51–60.

[3] *Atchison T. & S.F. R. Co. v Buell*, 480 US 557, 568–70 (1987).

[4] Louis Jaffe and Nathaniel Nathanson, *Administrative Law: Cases and Materials* 133–36 (1961).

[5] Roscoe Pound, *Common Law and Legislation*, 21 Harv L Rev 383, 385 (1908).

courts were already tending to give statutes "a liberal interpretation to cover the whole field [they were] intended to cover," he hoped for the day when a statute would be treated, as well, as a source of policy for courts' analogical reasoning; they should, he believed, receive a statute "fully into the body of the law as affording not only a rule to be applied but a principle from which to reason, and hold it, as a later and more direct expression of the general will, of superior authority to judge-made rules on the same general subject."[6] The judicial attitude he decried, we now associate with the general hostility to legislative (i.e., political) change captured by the metaphor of *Lochner v New York.*[7] It would take the New Deal Court to put his more cooperative vision in place; in 1936, Harlan Fiske Stone would evoke "the ideal of a unified system of judge-made and statute law woven into a seamless whole by the processes of adjudication."[8] The "switch in time" brought not simply a retreat from substantive due process and its constitutional cousins, but also strikingly open attitudes toward statutes and the federal agencies Congress often appointed to administer them.

FELA, a beneficiary of these changing attitudes, was more successful than the initial state statutes had been in generating liberal interpretation. Responding to "the breadth of the statutory language [and] the Act's humanitarian purposes,"[9] the courts, led by the Supreme Court, accepted it as a remedy to "be developed and enlarged to meet changing conditions and changing concepts of industry's duty toward its workers."[10] That is, until Gottshall's case and a companion reached the Supreme Court from the Third Circuit. *Conrail v Gottshall,*[11] like many of the Court's statutory cases in October Term 1993, suggests a return to the treatment of statutes as commands "to be obeyed grudgingly, by construing [them] narrowly and treating [them] as though [they] did not exist for any purpose[s] other than th[ose] embraced within the strict construction of [their] words"[12]—to the formalist orthodoxy identified by Dean Pound.

---

[6] Id.

[7] 198 US 45 (1905).

[8] Harlan Fiske Stone, *The Common Law in the United States*, 50 Harv L Rev 4, 12 (1936).

[9] *Urie v Thompson*, 337 US 163, 180 (1949).

[10] *Kernan v American Dredging Co.*, 355 US 426, 432 (1958).

[11] 114 S Ct 2396 (1994).

[12] Stone, 50 Harv L Rev at 14 (cited in note 8).

Responding to the Court's 1987 invitation,[13] the Third Circuit had found "negligent infliction of emotional distress" to be a cause of action under FELA.[14] It then had to define what that cause of action was, and it considered the three principal tests state courts employ for delimiting compensable emotional harm: the first requires an actual physical impact associated with the claimed emotional harm; the second, that the plaintiff, if not actually touched, nonetheless have been immediately exposed to the danger of physical injury by the defendant's negligent conduct; and the third, that a bystander plaintiff, even if outside the zone of danger (say, watching her children play on the street from behind a second-story window), was so closely related to and so immediately engaged in observing an incident causing physical harm to another that the defendant could reasonably have foreseen her emotional injury as one direct consequence of its negligence. Since Gottshall's emotional injuries resulted from working conditions remarkable principally for their psychological stress, his chances under any of these tests were remote. Mindful of the interpretations underscoring FELA's generosity and the need for contemporaneous standards, and mindful as well of the somewhat restrictive character of the traditional state tests, the Third Circuit had articulated a fourth test, "whether the factual circumstances . . . provide a threshold assurance that there is a likelihood of genuine and serious emotional injury,"[15] an injury that the defendant could foresee. The facts of Gottshall's case, it concluded, gave the necessary assurance.

Justice Thomas wrote for the Court in reversing the Third Circuit and adopting for FELA use the more liberal of the two causes of action that had been in place in 1908, when Congress had acted. Invoking the remedial purposes of the statute, he easily found that FELA gave a remedy for "negligent infliction of emotional distress"; the problem lay in delimiting permissible actions. No jurisdiction allows recovery for all emotional harms that might be causally linked to negligence, given both the ease with which such injuries might be imagined or even falsified and the frequent remoteness of asserted causation. These factors, together with what

---

[13] *Atchison T. & S.F. R. Co. v Buell*, 480 US at 568–70 (cited in note 3).

[14] *Gottshall v Conrail*, 988 F2d 355 (1993).

[15] Id at 371.

Justice Thomas concluded was the Third Circuit's failure to respect the common law approaches established in the states, led him to reject that court's approach as too liberal—threatening "essentially infinite" liability and conversion of the railroads into "insurers of the emotional well-being and mental health of their employees."[16] He then turned to choose among the three state common law approaches. "[W]e begin with the state of the common law in 1908, when FELA was enacted."[17] Only the first two of the three established tests were then in use, and of these the more "progressive . . . zone of danger test would have been more consistent than the physical impact test with FELA's broad remedial goals."[18] The bystander test (currently adopted in some form in about half the states) "was not developed until 60 years after FELA's enactment and therefore lacks historical support"; moreover, "in most jurisdictions that adhere to it, this test limits recovery to persons who witness the severe injury or death of a close family member,"[19] a circumstance that would rarely arise in the FELA workplace. Since fourteen jurisdictions continue to use the zone of danger test, "current usage only confirms this historical pedigree."[20]

In at least two respects, Justice Thomas's opinion is a strikingly limited exercise of what he admits to be a common law judicial function; both will figure in the following pages. First, conceding the Court's formal freedom to choose, Congress's general purpose to create a broadly remedial statute, and the evident ferment and growth in state court development of the emotional distress remedy, his opinion takes a static view of what his choices were. He begins and virtually ends with the choices Congress would have had in 1908, had it focused on this question and the then content of the common law. As Justice Ginsburg's dissent for herself and Justices Stevens and Blackmun is at pains to point out, the intervening eight and one-half decades had generally been characterized by liberal judicial construction to protect railroad workers, a remedy that "would be developed and enlarged to meet changing conditions and changing concepts of industry's duty toward its

---

[16] 114 S Ct 2396, 2409 (1994).

[17] Id at 2410.

[18] Id.

[19] Id at 2411.

[20] Id at 2410.

workers."[21] Causation requirements had been relaxed, negligence enlarged, liability for industrial accidents extended without difficulty into liability for negligently caused occupational disease[22]— all as a widely remarked element of the Court's jurisprudence that attracted no correcting response from Congress. Rather than continue this line of development, focused on the hazards of work in the instrumentalities of interstate and foreign commerce, the majority tied itself to general common law doctrine as it had been developing in the states. Nor did it consider the most progressive aspects of that evolving remedy; rather, it privileged those elements of doctrine that could have been known to the enacting Congress. This is not a case in which the meaning of statutory text ("negligence") might be played off against legislative history or other contextual data from the time of enactment pointing in some other direction. The issue is understanding "negligence" in 1994, and the majority's conclusion appears to be that it should be guided by the common law choices available in 1908.

Justice Souter wrote a one-paragraph concurrence expressing for himself alone the view that the majority was choosing the appropriate *contemporary* rule under "the evolving common law," a choice he found "well within the discretion left to the federal courts under FELA."[23] Indeed, reading the majority opinion in isolation from the rest of the Term's work, one might be tempted to find its reasoning from what Congress might have chosen in 1908 more clumsy than portentious. Or perhaps one might say that it reflects a contemporary resistance to expansive tort liability that is not to be found only among some Justices of the United States Supreme Court. But a review of the rest of the Term's work reveals this element of *Gottshall* as part of a pattern of hostility to congressional output that threatens to return us to 1908 in more senses than one. Not every decision, but too many, suggest that we have entered a period of Supreme Court uncooperativeness with Congress and resistance to learning from statutes not seen since the early 1930s. Accretive change and integration of law, so characteristic of common law courts, seem no longer to be federal judges' responsibilities in dealing with statutes. The apparent rejection of Chief Justice

---

[21] Id at 2412, quoting *Kernan v American Dredging Co.*, 355 US 426, 432 (1958).

[22] *Urie v Thompson*, 337 US 163 (1949).

[23] 114 S Ct at 2412 (Souter, J, concurring).

Stone's coherence-building ideal for the federal judiciary suggests a remarkably weak, even irresponsible, vision for the federal courts. Combined with a somewhat rigid and time-bound textualism, it is also a profoundly destabilizing vision. That is the burden of the remaining pages.

This point may be sharpened, in relation to *Gottshall*, by contrasting a 1988 opinion of the Court, *Monessen Southwestern R. Co. v Morgan*,[24] that the majority identified as a precedent for its approach. In *Monessen*, the Court had reversed a lower court award of prejudgment interest to a FELA plaintiff. It had observed, in part, that recovery of prejudgment interest was generally barred in common law actions in 1908, when FELA was enacted; and it had reasoned, seeing the sweeping changes made in other remedies at the time, that this "well-established doctrine" was one that Congress had left intact. Yet the thrust of *Monessen* was that granting prejudgment interest would have unjustifiable implications for federal remedies generally. The courts had frequently decided against the award of prejudgment interest in intervening years, without congressional interference. Only six years earlier, Congress had considered but not enacted a general provision for prejudgment interest as a part of the Federal Courts Improvement Act of 1982.[25] *Monesson* thus was characterized by attention to contemporary legislative-judicial dialogue, existing FELA precedent, and implications for procedural claims; these elements were generally missing in *Gottshall*. While a dissent had criticized *Monesson*, too, for its failure fully to realize the remedial purposes of FELA, the *Monesson* majority voiced no commitment to take the common law as of the statute's enactment in 1908; rather its judgment was that the remedy Congress failed to give in 1908, Congress had affirmatively decided not to give in 1982. In *Gottshall*, Congress's only discernible signal in 1908 was a delegation to the courts to develop common law ideas of negligence to secure broadly remedial ends; and in the intervening decades Congress had stood quietly by while the courts aggressively pursued that mandate. Thus, along the principal dimension of interest here, the two cases stand in sharp contrast.

The second respect in which Justice Thomas's opinion takes a

---

[24] 486 US 330 (1988).

[25] Pub L 97-164, 96 Stat 25. See 486 US at 339 n 8, also citing the explanation of the omission at S Rep No 97-275, pp 11–12 (1981).

limited view of federal court common law function is perhaps more
subtle, but also worth noting in an introductory way; it too will
recur. Recall that in rejecting the widely adopted bystander test,
he argued in part that "in most jurisdictions that adhere to it, this
test limits recovery to persons who witness the severe injury or
death of a close family member." If this aspect of the test were
binding upon the Court, that might be an ahistorical reason for
rejecting it. But what "most" state jurisdictions do would be binding on the Court *only* if the Court itself lacks common law authority
to adapt that element to the workplace for FELA's federal purposes. It does not seem that Justice Thomas is reinvoking the "natural" common law of Holmes's "brooding omnipresence in the
sky";[26] the Court can choose, on federal principles, from among
the several possibilities that state common law resolutions offer.
The hidden premise seems to be, however, that unlike state courts,
the Supreme Court cannot properly make its own test. It is as if
Congress's delegation to the federal courts to develop common law
remedies for railroad worker injuries conveyed or recognized far
less judicial authority than a state common law court would
have—an authority necessarily dependent on what the state courts
were doing. In this respect, the Supreme Court (and by implication
the other federal courts) is not a common law court even when it
operates under delegated authority to fill gaps in federal law, under
what is undoubtedly the federal question jurisdiction. That would
be a strikingly limited view of the federal judicial function.

II. Integration and Interpretation

The focus of this article is the issue of integrating statutory
and other law. A sustantial number of statutory cases decided during October Term 1993 offered the Court a choice between treating
statutes as static, isolated instructions from higher authority, and
regarding them as part of a "unified system of judge-made and
statute law."[27] It tended to make the former choice, one that segre-
gates statutes from the common law. The argument here is that,
in the process, it diminishes both statute and common law, both
legislature and court. Integrating statutes and common law has the

---

[26] See note 114.

[27] Stone, text at note 8.

opposite effect. Legislative influence and statutes are extended when statutory policy becomes the basis for analogical reasoning to decide cases that have not been provided for. The judicial function is also augmented if the world in which judges act to promote coherence includes statutory as well as judge-made law. Thus, to include statutes implies that judges may shape their readings within the possibilities offered by the text, over time, as changing general law and the social circumstances to which it responds may suggest.

The contrast between legislation as static judgment, and legislation as an element in the continuing evolution of law's fabric, is strongly rooted in my own specialty in administrative law. One characteristic of administrative law, so intuitive that we easily lose sight of it, is that it is administered law—that we expect its dimensions constantly to change. Administrative agencies are continuing bodies with proactive responsibilities, acting under the oversight of the political branches as well as the judiciary. We anticipate that they will change course; they are in effect the preferred managers of change. In the communities they influence, their administration produces expectations about what is permissible that vary across time. Congress is watching and the President is watching; the emerging solutions frame community understandings to be generally acted upon, and can come to be taken as the governing law. In these respects, integrative approaches are of the essence. Whatever else, the agency, in *its* context, will not have encountered issues of statutory meaning freed of considerations of purpose, politics, or contemporary understandings. For those subject to or interested in the agency's work, one may be reasonably sure the situation is the same. Congress's continuing oversight assures that it legislates in the context of existing judicial and agency "law," as well as its own prior work. Similarly, agencies act in a context framed by statute and case law; and the judiciary, too, proceeds under the premise of mutual responsibility for the development of law.

The static view of statutory law is in sharp contrast. Its premise is that the elements of government work sporadically and in isolation from one another. At the beginning of this century, premises like these found expression in the idea that legislative actions in derogation of the common law were to be narrowly construed; that is, since the common law was an area for judicial responsibility, the legislature really shouldn't intrude, and if it tried to do so its actions should be given minimal impact. In many of the cases that concern this essay, the premise seems to be the obverse—where Congress has acted, it has (sole) responsibility for the elucidation of policy, and the only appropriate role of courts is to apply the policies enacted by the acting Congress, whose dimensions properly change only when Congress chooses to act again. Or, Congress may have delegated to an agency some authority to give shape to statutory language; if a court using standard tools of statutory interpretation is unable to determine what the language means, it must accept the agency's view. But in deciding in the first instance what the statutory language might mean, the court will look only to its own resources; for judges who are also formalists, those resources do not include the understandings reached by others, such as the agency initially responsible for the statute's implementation.

One way to characterize these competing views might be in terms of how they understand congressional silence. One takes from that silence implicit consent; the other understands that the burden of seeking new law has not been met by those who might propose it.[28] In a complex world characterized on all sides by information overload and large impersonal organizations that both generate information and attempt to deal with it, one would be foolish to claim that either view completely captured institutional reality. Congress is a bureaucracy of tens of thousands, and too frequently acts on legislative behemoths no member can have read; the claim that it "knows" anything is absurd. But so, too, is any claim that its actions are wholly independent of the expectations about law, however imperfect, generated by the work of courts and agencies. Legislation, including amendments to existing laws, responds to current problems. While the absence of problems makes it unlikely Congress will pass new laws, that absence hardly indicates that "law" is missing; most social conduct occurs in the shadow of already established expectations about what existing law requires or permits.

This way of understanding the choice might suggest that each

---

[28] Compare Barry K. Weingast and Mark J. Moran, *Bureaucratic Discretion or Congressional Control? Regulatory Policymaking by the Federal Trade Commission*, 91 J Pol Economics 765 (1983), making a similar point about "bureaucratic" and "congressional dominance" theories of the relationships between agencies and their congressional committees.

is inherently political—the integrative view likely to be favored by judges (and others) believing in law and expansive government, the static view by those who are more skeptical of the desirability of large government. In the one case, judicial sympathy for previous congressional judgments, expansively treated in the light of current conditions, places the burden of congressional gridlock (the difficulty in securing new legislation) on those who would oppose innovation; in the other, holding Congress to its precise dispositions places the burden of gridlock on those who want innovation. If both positions are inherently political, neither side, a priori, is entitled to the advantage; neither judicial position has greater legitimacy. We may be politically distressed that the Court is in the hands of Justices who are skeptical about government, but cannot claim that their position is any more "political," that is, unjudicial, than the integrative view would be.

That interpretation depends, however, on a crucial premise: that law emerges *only* as the product of political action, not as the product of (judicial) reason acting within the already extant framework of law, that is, not as "common law." And it also assumes that Congress will always act in the direction of enlarging government. At a given moment, Congress might opt for regulation or for deregulation—indeed, for economic regulation since the 1970s its direction has been predominantly the latter. A court sensitive to that deregulatory trend would be warranted in extending it by analogy, without entailing its own politics. In this way, an integrative approach would produce smaller rather than larger government. Refusing to do so—treating a deregulatory statute as expressing no larger judgment than its explicit terms require—would result in the judiciary leaving more government in place than would follow from its giving that statute larger effect. It is perhaps true that, in general, our explicitly political institutions have been choosing for more rather than less government over the past century; but then building on those judgments can be defended as accepting political outcomes from those authorized to reach them. "Larger government," like "smaller government," is not an inevitable consequence of integrative reasoning with statutes. Dependent on the judgments Congress has been reaching, it reflects legislative rather than judicial politics; the static approach cannot be so described.

Neither choice entails liberating judges from their subordination in ordinary law matters to legislative judgment, or resolves the question of what are the appropriate materials of interpretation. The point, well made by Professor Alexander Aleinikoff of Michigan,[29] can be illustrated by a table:

	Statutes are static, always meaning what was first enacted	Statutes acquire meaning over time, as social and legal contexts change
Formalist	Only text may be consulted, its meaning amplified by usages at the time of enactment	Only text may be consulted, but contemporary usage and intervening texts may be considered
Intentionalist	Political history, including a variety of legislative materials, may be consulted to discover the enacting legislature's intents, or, more broadly, purposes	All materials may be consulted; the court seeks the outcome that best fits contemporary law

Thus, *either* a textualist or an intentionalist may use her preferred tools in the service of giving relatively static meaning to a statute, the one free of any obligation to consider the information that political context provides to interpretation, the other seeking in evidence of purpose and political history the meaning that would probably have been assigned it by the enacting legislature. Both then expect that meaning to remain constant over the ensuing years. While the integrative choice lacks that expectation, it too is dependent on statutory language, and can be made by textualists as well as intentionalists.[30] In and of itself, it does *not* authorize a judge simply to disregard a statutory text that she thinks may have outlived its usefulness[31] or to invent policies of her own preference,

---

[29] T. Alexander Aleinikoff, *Updating Statutory Interpretation*, 87 Mich L Rev 20 (1988).

[30] A striking example is provided by a case once thought to have sounded the death knell of "plain meaning" interpretation, *United States v American Trucking Ass'n*, 310 US 534 (1940). The Court was divided, 5–4, between New Deal appointees who relied heavily on legislative history materials, and more experienced Justices who found the text controlling. A close reading of the dissent to which the latter subscribed reveals that its principal mechanism lies in understanding that text in a manner that integrates it well with other statutory elements of the law. Indeed, that characteristic is reinforced on seeing that the opinion appears under the signature of Justice Stone, see text at note 8.

[31] Compare Guido Calabresi, *A Common Law for the Age of Statutes* (Harvard, 1982); Robert Weisberg, *The Calabresian Judicial Artist: Statutes and the New Legal Process*, 35 Stan L Rev 213 (1983).

independent of those instinct in existing law.[32] The cases to be discussed are ones in which alternative understandings of the texts were available, with different results if they were treated as discrete instruments of a particular time, than if they were taken contemporaneously, as part of the evolving fabric of the general law.

Either choice, in particular judicial hands, could generate undesirable consequences for the relationship between the courts and Congress. Static approaches joined with a formal textualism, that limits judicial data to statutory words and disclaims judicial authority to make supplementary judgments, may induce prolix drafting,[33] reduce the likely useful lifespan of legislative judgments, and contribute to continuous friction between Congress and courts. An integrative approach, on the other hand, may weaken Congress's incentives to legislate and may encourage judicial adventurism. A strong belief in separation of powers seems to support the idea that judges should not treat statutes as they do the common law—if judges are not scrupulously attentive to legislative judgments, to do so risks confusing legislative with judicial authority.[34] Here, the

---

[32] That is, a judge taking an integrative approach may nonetheless regard herself as bound by the various considerations, external to herself and largely of legislative creation, that circumstances require her to integrate. The problem is just that faced by the self-aware common law judge; she is not the initiator of values, but a loyal agent of what she finds in the law as a whole, for whose evolving coherence and "fit" she is constantly responsible. Compare Nicholas S. Zeppos, *The Use of Authority in Statutory Interpretation: An Empirical Analysis*, 70 Tex L Rev 1073, 1081–84 (1992), describing "dynamic" theories as if they entailed personal responsibility for such ends as "furthering virtue in the body politic."

[33]

> The British spirit of civil liberty induced the English judges to adhere strictly to the law, to its exact expressions. This again induced the law-makers to be, in their phraseology, as explicit and minute as possible, which causes such a tautology and endless repetition in the statutes of that country that even so eminent a statesman as Sir Robert Peel declared, in parliament, that he "contemplates no task with so much distaste as the reading through an ordinary act of parliament." Men have at length found out that little or nothing is gained by attempting to speak with absolute clearness and endless specifications, but that human speech is the clearer, the less we endeavor to supply by words and specifications that interpretation which common sense must give to human words. However minutely we may define, somewhere we needs must trust at last to common sense and good faith.

Francis Lieber, *Legal and Political Hermeneutics* 20 (rev 3d ed. 1880). McNollgast, *Positive Canons: The Role of Legislative Bargains in Statutory Interpretation*, 80 Georgetown L J 705, 716 (1992), argues that "[i]nterpretive canons . . . should aid the legislative process, making it less costly for policy bargains to be struck"; judicial behavior that raises those costs, for example, by forcing the expense of anticipating and countermanding court decisions, is justifiable only on premises that disfavor legislation.

[34] See Thomas W. Merrill, *The Common Law Powers of Federal Courts*, 52 U Chi L Rev 1, 32–33 (1985).

revealing contrast may involve gap-filling rather than interpretation in the strict sense—that is, it may involve the willingness of a court to acknowledge cases not provided for by statutes and then use statutory material as a source of analogy to decide them. Unmistakably, permitting analogy from a statute to fill an acknowledged gap is friendlier to legislative authority than refusal; but unmistakably, too, it is the court that draws the analogy, risking judicial adventurism. The result may be to lead judges into a certain lack of candor about whether they are filling gaps, or simply interpreting what they pretend Congress has provided for.[35]

Yet if risks of misuse fall on either side, some characteristics of the legal environment argue strongly for integration: For citizens, law is inevitably an integral system, premised in contemporary social expectations and political judgments; a person interested in her legal obligations looks to the whole environment, not a disordered collection of fragmentary, isolated, mutually independent pieces. Legislation will inevitably be imprecise, requiring both interpretation and gap-filling; pretending otherwise increases its costs.[36] Courts are better suited than legislatures for the classic common law function of continually inventing coherence out of the materials of the law. With statutes the dominant form of law, and especially as they become more numerous, problems of aging statutory judgment will inevitably arise and need to be resolved

---

[35] On the importance of candor, see, for example, Nicholas S. Zeppos, *Judicial Candor and Statutory Interpretation*, 78 Georgetown L J 353 (1989); William N. Eskridge, Jr., and Philip P. Frickey, *Statutory Interpretation as Practical Reasoning*, 42 Stan L Rev 321 (1990); on its frequent absence, Zeppos, cited in note 32.

[36] The basic reason why statutes are so frequently ambiguous in application is not that they are poorly drafted—though many are—and not that the legislators failed to agree on just what they wanted to accomplish in the statute—though often they do fail—but that a statute necessarily is drafted in advance of, and with imperfect appreciation for the problems that will be encountered in, its application.

Richard Posner, *Statutory Interpretation—in the Classroom and in the Courtroom*, 50 U Chi L Rev 800, 811 (1983).

[O]nly rarely can statutory language be precise in conveying either policy bargains or instructions to agencies. Nature has a nasty habit of creating situations in which the applicability of a statute is unclear. But even if nature were not unkind, the meaning of statutes would still be problematic because language is inherently imprecise and because rational political actors, having numerous ways to occupy their time, would never devote the effort necessary to minimize the indeterminacy of statutory language.

McNollgast, *Legislative Intent: The Use of Positive Political Theory in Statutory Interpretation*, 57 L & Contemp Probs 3, 13 (1994). See also Aleinikoff, 87 Mich L Rev at 25 (cited in note 29).

before legislative attention can be directed to them. In the long run, finally, successful government must be a cooperative enterprise in its everyday affairs; as the years leading to the New Deal should have taught us, continuous legislative-judicial antagonism over ordinary political judgments is unsustainable.[37]

The explicit argument here, then, is about judicial responsibility—the difference between an integrative approach to legal materials and one that takes statutes as individual, isolated, and static events—and, consequently, about the evolving political dynamic between Congress and the Court. Moreover, the cases, not the literature, are the focus.[38] These pages are intended more to sketch the Court's work, to explore the factual ground, than to reason to a foundational theory of interpretation. A growing body of literature has plumbed the issues of interpretation in a theoretical way, and the reader probably has already found a good deal of tangency between the views offered here and those of younger scholars characterizing their approaches as "dynamic," "practical," "updating," and the like.[39] Admiring that work and indebted to it, I have none-

---

[37] "Ordinary political judgment" signals a limit here to matters that do not in themselves raise questions of constitutional law—whether liberties of the citizen, or structural arrangements such as underlay invalidation of the legislative veto. In that context, Woodrow Wilson's words have commanding force:

> . . . [G]overnment is not a machine, but a living thing. . . . No living thing can have its organs offset against each other as checks, and live. On the contrary, its life is dependent upon their quick cooperation, their ready response to the commands of instinct or intelligence, their amicable community of purpose. Government is not a body of blind forces; it is a body of men, with highly differentiated function, no doubt, in our modern day of specialization, but with a common task and purpose. Their cooperation is indispensable, their warfare fatal. There can be no successful government without leadership or without the intimate, almost instinctive, coordination of the organs of life and action. This is not theory, but fact, and displays its force as fact, whatever theories may be thrown across its track.

Constitutional Government in the United States 56–57 (1908). Wilson's argument may be taken as one about the limits of "separation of powers" or "checks and balances" rather than as an effort completely to refute those constitutionally embedded ideas. The challenge of constitutional government, as Madison described it, is that "you must first enable the government to control the governed; and in the next place oblige it to control itself." Federalist 51 (Madison). Wilson addresses what is required to "control the governed"—*a* government, one "law." Central to Madison's paradox is the understanding that institutional threats to that capacity are as dangerous to the constitutional ideal as are threats to produce "a gradual contentration of the several powers in the same department." Id.

[38] See also Zeppos, cited in note 32, for a valuable effort to explore the Court's statutory work empirically, over the course of a century; he found few pronounced changes in practice along the dimensions he sought to measure.

[39] For example, William N. Eskridge, Jr., *Dynamic Statutory Interpretation*, 135 U Pa L Rev 1479 (1987); Philip P. Frickey, *Congressional Intent, Practical Reasoning, and the Dynamic*

theless found it more urgent to address the Justices and their work than any academic colleagues. Nonetheless, the discussion will inevitably be caught up to a degree in the raging debates over interpretation, particularly those that concern the competitition between textual and purposive approaches to statutory texts.

Unmistakably, the recent cases enact the Court's preference that statutes be understood, where possible, from the surface meaning of their words, and the reader has sensed my discomfort with the implications of that approach, also, for legislative-judicial conflict. The Court's shift to textualism has been adeptly documented by others,[40] and is well captured in two recently published graphics. Professor Thomas Merrill of Northwestern, for example, gives the following table to illustrate the relative use of legislative history and dictionaries in statutory interpretation cases in 1981, 1988, and 1992:[41]

TEXTUALISM IN THE SUPREME COURT, 1981–92

Term	Total Statutory Interpretation Cases	Cases Making Substantive Use of Legislative Hist.	Cases Not Mentioning Legislative History	Cases Relying on Dictionaries
1981	69	69 (100%)	0 (0%)	1 (1%)
1988	71	53 (75%)	10 (14%)	9 (13%)
1992	66	12 (18%)	41 (62%)	22 (33%)

Nature of Federal Indian Law, 78 Cal L Rev 1137 (1990); Daniel A. Farber, *The Inevitability of Practical Reason: Statutes, Formalism and the Rule of Law*, 45 Vand L Rev 533 (1992); T. Alexander Aleinikoff, *Updating Statutory Interpretation*, 87 Mich L Rev 20 (1988); Edward L. Rubin, *Law and Legislation in the Administrative State*, 89 Colum L Rev 369 (1989); Cass R. Sunstein, *Interpreting Statutes in the Regulatory State*, 103 Harv L Rev 405 (1989); Zeppos, cited in note 29. Compare, however, note 32 above.

This eruption of materials on the problems of statutory interpretation, dating from the late 1980's, has been widely noted. As figures central to their development have appropriately recognized, their work is well grounded in the work of intellectual centrists of an earlier time. Farber, 45 Vand L Rev (Karl Llewellyn); William N. Eskridge, Jr., and Philip P. Frickey, *The Making of the Legal Process*, 107 Harv L Rev 2031 (1994) (Henry M. Hart, Jr., and Albert M. Sacks); see also Edward H. Levi, *An Introduction to Legal Reasoning* (1948); Stone, cited in note 8; Pound, cited in note 5.

[40] For example, the works cited in note 39. For a contrasting view founded on an optimism about the Court's seeking shared ground, that the sharp division of the past Term's work makes hard to join, see Frederick Schauer, *Statutory Construction and the Coordinating Function of Plain Meaning*, 1990 Supreme Court Review 231; Professor Merrill, in the work about to be cited in text, persuasively argues that the adamancy of Justices Scalia and Thomas respecting their preferred modes of interpretation may cloak a larger disposition to compromise over such matters on the part of other Justices.

[41] Thomas W. Merrill, *Textualism and the Future of the Chevron Doctrine*, 72 Wash U L Q 351, 355 (1994).

And a recent student note counts the number of cases referring to dictionaries in each term of Court since 1842:[42]

NUMBER OF REFERENCES[c] TO DICTIONARIES,
1842 TERM–1992 TERM

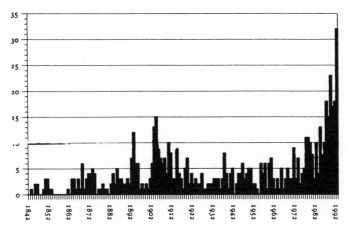

[c] Includes all cases that use the words "dictionary" or "dictionaries." Search of LEXIS, Genfed library, US file (Jan. 4, 1994).

The past Term's performance was not quite so dramatic in these terms—of forty-three cases that referred to statutory interpretation or meaning in the text of at least one opinion, sixteen also referred to a "dictionary" or "dictionaries," while a slightly larger number contained the term "legislative history."[43] And in a number of cases, some Justices appeared self-conscious about noting the ongoing disputes over the use of legislative history, sometimes narrowing but not disclaiming the appropriateness of their use.[44]

---

[42] Note, *Looking It Up: Dictionaries and Statutory Interpretation*, 107 Harv L Rev 1437, 1454 (1994).

[43] The initial search of the Lexis Genfed:US database was for "(statut! w/10 (interpret! or mean!)) and Congress! and date(aft 10/1/93)"; it was then modified (for these purposes) by adding "and dictionar!"; the modification "and (dictionar! or defin!" produced 40 results; "and legislative history," 22; "and (legislat! w/5 (purpose or inten!)," 23. Of this last group of 23, six occurrences coincided with mentions of both legislative history and dictionaries, two with mentions of dictionaries but not legislative history, 11 with mentions of legislative history but not dictionaries, and four in the absence of either. "Legislative history" and "dictionar!" appeared together in four additional opinions, in four opinions; dictionaries alone, in four opinions; and "legislative history" appears without the other terms in one opinion only.

The presence of a term doesn't show the Court's attitude or use, or whether it appeared in majority or dissent; clearly a more qualitative assessment is called for.

[44] For example, *Shannon v United States*, 114 S Ct 2419, discussed at p 471; *City of Chicago v Environmental Defense Fund*, 114 S Ct 1588, discussed at p 499.

The pages following take up most of the Term's opinions referring to issues of statutory interpretation or meaning, omitting those
that did not seem to raise the questions under discussion here.[45]
They begin with the civil and criminal cases in which only the
courts and the legislature are prominent as possible sources of
meaning, and then turn to cases in which administrative agencies
may also have spoken to the problems raised. We will find that, in
general, Court majorities did not take seriously the contributions
that settled expectations and Congress's role as a *continuing* legislative body can make to interpretation; their tendency was to take
statutes as static events. In this sense, the majorities rejected the
common law responsibility for statutes suggested long ago by Stone
and others. This phenomenon was particularly striking in the last
group of cases, in which Congress has signaled that agencies have
primary responsibility for shaping law and, as the result of those
responsibilities, agencies will have acquired a natural expertise in
the issues that complex statutes present.[46] Again, the result, in my
judgment, has been to recreate an atmosphere of virtual warfare

---

[45] For example, *United States v Irvine*, 114 S Ct 1473, from which the epigram is taken,
note 1, was an all but unanimous interpretation of the gift tax statutes and regulations.
Justice Scalia stood apart from Justice Souter's opinion for the remainder of the participating
court to insist that the dimensions of the "reasonable time" limitation on which all Justices
agreed should be derived from text, rather than policy. For the gift-giver in that case, if
not for the Congress whose work he regularly assesses, "the failure to make a reasonably
prompt disclaimer of a known bequest is an implicit acceptance." Id at 1483. *Key Tronic
Corp. v United States*, 114 S Ct 1960, is characterized by divided opinions on a statutory
issue—Justice Stevens writing for the majority and Justice Scalia for Justices Thomas and
Blackmun—but does not clearly raise the problem discussed in text. At issue was whether
a provision of CERCLA authorized recovery of attorneys' fees incurred by one responsible
party who settled its action with EPA, against other responsible parties. Justice Stevens's
opinion examines legislative history and judicial developments along with text, while Justice
Scalia contents himself with textual analysis alone; but the question is not one as to which
there appears to have been any development of a judicial or agency view over time, that
could have influenced the shape of the relevant legislative text. In *Dalton v Specter*, 114 S
Ct 1719, Justice Souter's concurrence for four prefers to ground judgment in a contextual
assessment whether Congress meant to preclude review of a Commission's actions under
the Defense Base Closure and Realignment Act than in a formal assessment of whether
those actions were "final" within the meaning of the Administrative Procedure Act, 5 USC
704, as Chief Justice Rehnquist wrote for the majority. *Posters 'n Things v United States*, 114
S Ct 1747, concerned the issue of scienter under a federal statute prohibiting the sale of
drug paraphernalia. All agreed that a scienter element was required to convict of the offense,
but Justices Scalia, Kennedy, and Thomas would have defined that element in a manner
that would give the prosecution somewhat more latitude in seeking conviction. In none of
these cases do the lines developed in the text appear to me to be particularly prominent.

[46] See Richard J. Pierce, Jr., *The Supreme Court's New Hypertextualism: An Invitation to
Cacophony and Incoherence in the Administrative State*, 95 Colum L Rev (forthcoming).

between Congress and Court that we have not witnessed since the first years of the New Deal.

III. Civil Cases

A. CONRAIL V GOTTSHALL[47]

B. HECK V HUMPHREY

Heck v Humphrey[48] possibly echoes *Gottshall's* commitment to common law readings tied to the time a statute is enacted. In this case, nine Justices agreed for varying reasons that, while his conviction remains in effect, a state prisoner has no cause of action for monetary damages under the Civil Rights Act, 42 USC § 1983, for allegedly unconstitutional conviction or imprisonment. In effect, the holding requires prisoners to secure the invalidation of their convictions by other means (such as the federal habeas corpus statute) before a Civil Rights Act cause of action can be maintained. Justice Scalia, for five Justices (the Chief Justice and Justices Kennedy, Thomas, and Ginsburg), grounded that conclusion in a study of the analogous common law cause of action for malicious prosecution, one element of which is "termination of the prior criminal proceeding in favor of the accused." Justice Souter, for Justices Blackmun, Stevens, and O'Connor, preferred to ground the outcome in what he perceived to be the appropriate relationship between § 1983 and the federal habeas corpus statute. Since the habeas statute is specifically directed at issues of legality in state criminal processes and § 1983 is a much more general form of relief, Justice Souter concluded that permitting the § 1983 action prior to an available habeas outcome would frustrate Congress's specific judgment about the manner in which relief from state convictions should be sought in federal courts.

It is striking that the Court's two former state court judges, and the three Justices who we will see most often favored integrative over static-meaning approaches to statutes during the Term, preferred to treat the case as involving the contemporary reconciliation of two federal statutes, rather than the implications for one statute

---

[47] 114 S Ct 2396 (1994); the case is discussed at p 429.

[48] 114 S Ct 2364 (1994).

(§ 1983) of a common law cause of action. Justice Souter is at pains to examine the issues in relation to what the two statutes have become at the present time, and what legislative policies would justify denying an individual federal damages "today." Thus, for him, making contemporary sense of congressional judgments was at the core; he worried that the majority's analysis would frustrate Congress's judgments by precluding § 1983 actions in cases in which habeas would not be available—for example, because state proceedings had resulted only in a fine.

The majority opinion made no specific claim that the common law action for malicious prosecution was a congressional model for § 1983; given Justice Scalia's distaste for legislative history, one would be surprised if an opinion of his rested on that kind of evidence. And the majority opinion's preference for the common law analysis may entail no necessary commitment to a static view. Section 1983, as it remarked, "creates a species of tort liability,"[49] and that arms the opinion's reference to malicious prosecution. The discussion cites contemporary as well as nineteenth-century sources as to the meaning of both § 1983 and that tort,[50] appearing to address § 1983 in the present day. What the common law action *is* for purposes of this federal action, however, appears to be dictated by external sources. The majority does not discuss it as if it were in any sense a federal tort. In relying on the "malicious prosecution" model, then, the majority hints at the subordination of the federal statute(s) to the common law.

Justice Thomas's characterization of the majority opinion, however, suggests the static view. He wrote separately to confess the Court's fault, as it were, for the situation that confronted it in this case: "it is we who have put § 1983 and the habeas statute on what Justice Souter appropriately terms a 'collision course,'" by expanding both statutes "far beyond the limited scope either was originally intended to have."[51] The rhetoric suggests that this is a regrettable state of affairs, not the expectable consequence of judicial dealings with century-old statutes. "[T]hat the Court created the tension" is the factor that makes it "proper for the Court to

---

[49] 114 S Ct 2364, 2370 (1994), quoting *Memphis Community School Dist. v Stachura*, 477 US 299, 305 (1986) and *Carey v Piphus*, 435 US 247, 257–58 (1978).

[50] 114 S Ct at 2372.

[51] Id at 2374 (Thomas concurring).

devise limitations . . . provided that it does so in a principled fashion."[52] And Justice Thomas's one stated reason for finding the majority decision principled is that its approach is "consistent with the state of the common law at the time § 1983 was enacted."[53] For him, at least, the echo of *Gottshall* is unmistakable.

C. BFP V RESOLUTION TRUST CORP.

The 5–4 split in *BFP v Resolution Trust Corp.*[54] seems to illustrate the second of the problems in *Gottshall*, that of considering federal statutes in relation to the common law and judicial responsibilities for its formation. The question concerned the bankruptcy laws, in particular, the meaning to be attributed to 11 USC § 548(a)(2). That section permits the trustee in bankruptcy to avoid transfers for which "the debtor voluntarily or involuntarily . . . received less than a reasonably equivalent value in exchange for such transfer . . . and was insolvent on the date that such transfer was made . . . or became insolvent as a result of such transfer." BFP had purchased ocean-front real estate in California, obligating itself to sizable first and second mortgages on the property. It failed to make payments on the mortgages, and the first mortgage was fore-closed. At a properly conducted foreclosure sale, the property was sold for about 60% of its alleged fair market value—an amount that repaid the first mortgage, but left insufficient surplus to repay the second mortgage, much less contribute more generally to the bankrupt's estate. The question, then, was whether this "bargain" price constituted a "reasonably equivalent value in exchange for" the mortgaged premises.

Since its revision in 1984, the Bankruptcy Act has been explicit that it applies to involuntary as well as voluntary transfers, and that "foreclosure of the debtor's equity of redemption" is a "transfer."[55] Shortly before the 1984 revisions, the Fifth Circuit, interpreting an analogous provision, had set aside a foreclosure sale that yielded 57% of estimated fair market value, stating that it thought 70% was the appropriate dividing line;[56] in enacting § 548(a), Congress

---

[52] Id.

[53] Id at 2375.

[54] 114 S Ct 1757.

[55] 11 USC § 101(54) (1988 ed, Supp IV).

[56] *Durett v Washington Nat. Ins. Co.*, 621 F2d 201 (1980).

rejected an alternative formulation that would explicitly have precluded the avoidance in bankruptcy proceedings of procedurally regular state foreclosure sales. Subsequently, the circuits divided on whether "reasonably equivalent value," in the mortgage context, referred to a price within reasonable range of what the property could have been expected to sell for on the open market (i.e., in the absence of a forced sale) or whether instead the phrase referred to a reasonable forced sale price, as would be received in a procedurally regular sale under state foreclosure law. Avoiding transfers at prices well under fair market value could provide additional resources for the bankruptcy debtor's other creditors to share and, perhaps, enlarge the debtor's estate for the fresh start that bankruptcy law promises. It would also render the title delivered at foreclosure sales somewhat less secure, arguably affronting state policies in this way.

Justice Scalia's opinion for the majority, joined by the Chief Justice and Justices O'Connor, Kennedy, and Thomas, discusses the federal statute at length, but seems to derive its principal impetus from this state policy concern, the effect of decision on the security of title resulting from foreclosure sales. As Justice Scalia sets out at some length, foreclosure sales are the result of a state common law process of development that sought to balance fairness to debtors (through participation in the proceeds of the sale) with protection to creditors and security of title. When federal bankruptcy law permitted the avoidance of fraudulent transfers, its focus was on fraud perpetrated by the debtor (also an inheritance from the common law). By contrast, the chance that a forced sale would generate an unfairly low price was dealt with by *state* law in varying ways—by state procedural requirements for such sales, including requirements to publish notice of such sales, and by state rules permitting a foreclosure sale to be set aside if it generated a price "so low as to 'shock the conscience or raise a presumption of fraud or unfairness.'"[57] The constraints of time and the seller's requirement to sell will cause a forced sale to yield a lower price than a voluntary transaction. Since the precise character of those constraints in any given case will determine just how much lower that price will be, the referent of a "reasonably equivalent value" in the federal statute cannot be to a fair market price, but must be

---

[57] 114 S Ct at 1763–64.

to the price that would be received at a forced sale held in conformity with local law.[58] Thus, for a sale held in conformity with local law, the price actually received *is* "reasonably equivalent" with that value, definitionally.

The unattractiveness of the alternative appears to have been a good part of the impulse for this conclusion. Justice Scalia could find no judicially administrable standard for a federal court to say, otherwise, what such a price could be. In a footnote, he dismissed a standard that would measure the reasonableness of the relation between forced sale price and fair market value under all the circumstances, as no different from "reasonably infinite value."[59] Before the 1984 revisions to the Bankruptcy Act, as already noted, the Fifth Circuit had set 70% of fair market value as a threshold of reasonable relationship;[60] that, Justice Scalia thought, "represent[ed a] policy determination[] which the Bankruptcy Code gives us no apparent authority to make."[61] Nor did he think the 1984 Act itself ratified the Fifth Circuit's work, despite its timing and the defeat of a measure that would have overruled it; that that Act might have modified his historical explanation, he barely considered: "absent clearer textual guidance . . . we will not presume such a radical departure."[62] The Seventh and Eleventh Circuits had more recently adopted a case-by-case "facts and circumstances"

---

[58] Justice Scalia also invoked formalist arguments in support of this position. "Reasonably equivalent value" should be given a different meaning from "fair market value," as the latter, well-known phrase appears elsewhere in the Bankruptcy Code; different formulations should be given to different wordings. This is reinforced by the practical consideration that fair market value and forced sale price will almost inevitably differ. 114 S Ct at 1761. He says that he is interpreting "reasonably equivalent" as "roughly equivalent" or "approximately equivalent" rather than "tortur[ing]" the phrase to mean "as close to [fair market value] as can reasonably be expected," because the latter would express an empty proposition—no court could decide how close that was. Id at 1762 n 4.

This last move makes the argument an equivalent of that developed in text: choice of an arbitrary figure (like the Fifth Circuit's 70%) would be beyond judicial authority; but a case-by-case factual analysis would lack governing rules. Justice Souter's dissent responded to the formalist argument by noting that "fair market value," a phrase that appears more than 150 times in federal tax legislation, appears only twice in the Bankruptcy Code (one of those times, in a tax-related section); "value," "unadorned and undefined . . . appears in more than 30 sections of the Bankruptcy Code . . . [and] is, with respect to many of them, read to mean 'fair market value.'" Id at 1768 n 1.

[59] Id at 1762 n 4.

[60] *Durrett* (cited in note 56).

[61] 114 S Ct at 1762.

[62] Id at 1764.

approach;[63] as the footnote about "reasonably infinite value" suggests, that demonstrated the unsuitability of the matter for judicial determination.

As in *Heck*, Justice Souter, for the dissenting Justices, centered his opinion on federal rather than state law and policy, statutory rather than common law development. The language of § 548(a)(2) applies to all transfers, not just those occurring as a result of foreclosure sales; in every other context it naturally refers to fair market value, as the majority conceded. Justice Souter thought giving it a special meaning in the foreclosure context both indefensible on the language and contrary to federal bankruptcy policy. From the federal perspective, assuring adequate compensation at forced sales serves important purposes, both for the bankrupt estate itself and for other creditors. Such legislative history as exists suggests that Congress had been aware of this in 1984, when it added the references to involuntary transfers that picked up foreclosure sales as a matter of federal concern. It had rejected language that would explicitly have adopted the majority's view; the language it chose tended to echo the Fifth Circuit's prior holding.[64] Not implausibly—if ironically—Justice Souter upbraided the majority for its attempt to escape the "plain effect" of these changes. Moreover, he argued, the Fifth Circuit rule had not proved embarrassing to security of title in operation, nor was there reason to think it would. Its chief effect would be to encourage bidders at forced sales to offer more than 70% of fair market value. That outcome would limit their bargain, to be sure, but do so in the service of important federal bankruptcy policies. It is hard to articulate a worthy state interest in having purchasers at foreclosure sales get unusual bargains, as against the federal policies favoring reasonable value to bankrupt estates. Nor was "case-by-case" determination, the alternative approach, an unusual judicial function as a general matter.

For a rather technical, even humdrum legal issue, the level of conflict between the two opinions is striking and the positions taken, even ironic.[65] One line of strain, wholly familiar and articulated in both opinions, is whether state property or federal bank-

---

[63] *In re Bundles*, 856 F2d 815 (7th Cir 1988); *In re Grissom*, 955 F2d 1440 (11th Cir 1992).

[64] 114 S Ct 1757, 1768 n 1; 1770 n 6; 1772 (1994) (Souter dissenting).

[65] Regarding the level of conflict, see David J. Garrow, *"Justice Souter Emerges,"* New York Times (Sept 25, 1994), Sec 6, p 36.

ruptcy policies are entitled to pride of place. Justice Scalia, widely experienced in *federal* government,[66] generates his preference for the former from the long-established prior harmony of foreclosure and fraudulent conveyance law, and the importance of security of title. Justice Souter, from a state, common law tradition,[67] reminds us that the Bankruptcy Act is a federal statute and the Supreme Court a federal court; state regulation must yield to the extent it actually conflicts with federal law, and Justice Souter argues strongly that a federal rule, once in place, will be so readily accommodated as hardly to inconvenience state interests.

In a number of respects, Justice Scalia's line of argument rests on the relatively weak stance toward federal judicial function we have already seen in *Gottshall* and *Heck*. For example, he devotes considerably more energy to his powerful exegesis of state common law development than to thoroughly working through the Bankruptcy Code, its changes and federal context. Perhaps most telling is his attitude toward the judicial fact-finding function that would be entailed in saying whether a price actually received at a foreclosure sale was fair in relation to the price that might have been expected on a voluntary sale market. *Federal* judges lack the means to make such determinations; Justice Scalia works hard to establish that § 548(a)(2) does not in terms command it. Yet he also takes reassurance from the possibility that *state* judges will perform the identical function, and may void forced sales if they conclude that the price was "so low as to 'shock the conscience of raise a presumption of fraud or unfairness.' "[68] What is it that makes this is a more acceptable judicial function at the state level? The only explanation Justice Scalia offers is that this set-aside occurs "*under state foreclosure law*, rather than fraudulent transfer law,"[69] an observation that does not much illuminate the judicial function of comparing price and value.

---

[66] Justice Scalia had served on a White House telecommunications task force, as Chair of the Administrative Conference of the United States, as Assistant Attorney General in charge of the Office of Legal Counsel, and as a judge of a uniquely national court, the United States Court of Appeals for the District of Columbia Circuit, before coming to the Supreme Court.

[67] Virtually all of Justice Souter's prior government employment had been in New Hampshire, as a state attorney, Attorney General, and the Judge of its Supreme Court before a brief tour on the United States Court of Appeals for the First Circuit.

[68] 114 S Ct at 1763–64.

[69] Id at 1763 (emphasis in original).

Perhaps this opinion, like *Gottshall* and *Heck*, reflects a reluctance to consider federal judges to be common law judges, to be officials with acknowledged law-generating authority and responsibility.[70] Common law judges—for example, state judges applying the test quoted above—often decide cases on the basis of "standards" as well as "rules." Common law emerges from the slow accretion of standard-based decisions over time. Administration of standards is common fare at trial if not at the appellate level. In his writings, Justice Scalia has argued against "standards" for federal judges; in his judgment, they can only be trusted with rules.[71] Thus the approach of the Seventh and Eleventh Circuits, intellectually indistinguishable from the state court test Justice Scalia cites, creates a fact-bound standard, inappropriate for a *federal* judge. That is the burden of the dismissive footnote about "reasonably infinite value." The alternative, a 70% test like that of the Fifth Circuit, does create a "rule"; but the creation of "rules" is the constitutional business of Congress, not the courts. The circle is closed, and the failure to accomplish the sensible federal bankruptcy policy Congress almost certainly chose (to judge, that is, by the state of the law when it acted in 1984, by what it chose to say, and by what it chose *not* to say) is certainly no responsibility of the courts. Congress should be clearer.

D. CIVIL RIGHTS ACT RETROACTIVITY

The character of judicial-legislative dialogue, and judicial responsibility for implementing legislative judgment, acquire particular importance when the legislature and the courts have already established a pattern of disagreement in a given policy area. Continuing struggles inevitably acquire political coloration and invite political responses—from the creation of administrative agencies to take over responsibilities the courts prove unwilling to implement responsibly, to court-packing plans and other pressures on the ap-

---

[70] See *Thompson v Thompson*, 484 US 174, 191–92 (1988) (Scalia dissenting).

[71] Antonin Scalia, *The Rule of Law as a Law of Rules*, 56 U Chi L Rev 1175 (1989). Compare Justice Scalia's acceptance of the obligation to use a standard, when inescapably imposed by statute, in *Harris v Forklift Systems, Inc.*, 114 S Ct 367, 372 (1993) (Scalia concurring) (while the Court's interpretation of statutory language prohibiting sexual harrassment leaves juries "virtually unguided" in deciding whether employer conduct is "egregious enough to warrant an award of damages," "I know of no test more faithful to the inherently vague statutory language than the one the Court today adopts.").

pointive processes. Interpretive techniques that stress plain language, refusing to improvise to secure congressional goals that might be demonstrated by the political history of legislation, extend those struggles if they require repeated expressions of congressional will until Congress "gets it right." That effect is even more pronounced if courts take legislative correction as only future-regarding, and are disinclined themselves to correct what are arguably *their* past errors. The burdens of securing change—and hence the opportunities for frustration and inefficiency—grow higher.

Rivers v Roadway Express, Inc.[72] and *Landgraf v USI Film Products*[73] were among the Term's more prominent cases. Mr. Rivers and a co-worker had been fired in 1986 in what they alleged to have been a racially discriminatory manner. Section 1981 of Title 42, part of the Civil Rights Act of 1866, conferred on all persons the right "to make and enforce contracts" free of racial discrimination; at the time, the United States Court of Appeals for the Sixth Circuit, where Rivers's job was, had interpreted § 1981 to prohibit racial discrimination in the administration as well as the formation of contracts of employment,[74] and the Supreme Court in dictum had appeared to approve the "well settled" conclusion in the courts of appeals "that § 1981 affords a federal remedy against discrimination in private employment on the basis of race."[75] In 1989 in *Patterson v McClean Credit Union*, however, the Supreme Court had decided that § 1981's conferral of the right was limited to contract formation, and did not apply to "conduct which occurs after the formation of a contract and which does not interfere with the right to enforce [it]."[76] The suit Rivers had brought was thus dismissed; while appeal on a related matter was pending, the Civil Rights Act of 1991 amended § 1981 to make explicit its application to "the making, performance, modification discrimination in terminating a contract of employment."[77] Rivers then argued for reinstatement of his suit.

---

[72] 114 S Ct 1510.

[73] Id at 1483.

[74] *Leonard v City of Frankfort Elec. and Water Plant Bd.*, 752 F2d 189 (1985).

[75] *Johnson v Railway Express Agency, Inc.*, 421 US 454, 459–60 (1975); see also *Runyon v McCrary*, 427 US 160 (1976).

[76] 491 US 164, 171; see Aleinikoff, cited in n 29, an essay written as *Patterson* was pending, arguing strongly for an integrative reading of § 1981.

[77] Section 101, Pub L No 102-166, 105 Stat 1071.

Ms. Landsgraf had been subjected to repeated sexual harassment by a co-worker on her production line at USI Film Products and resigned in 1986 a few days after the firm appeared to respond—albeit mildly—to her complaints;[78] after a bench trial, a district court found the harassment not so severe as to constitute a constructive discharge, and denied the equitable relief that Title VII of the Civil Rights Act of 1964 then made available. While her appeal was pending, the Civil Rights Act of 1991 established a right to jury trial and to monetary damages in such Title VII actions,[79] and she sought retrial before a jury. Both actions, then, called upon the Court to decide whether certain provisions of the Civil Rights Act of 1991 were to be retroactive in effect; in *Rivers*, the provision appears to have been enacted directly in response to the Court's unexpectedly narrow construction of the statute it amends.

The 1991 statute reflected the parlous quality of Congress's recent experience with the Supreme Court in civil rights matters, but it failed to deal directly with the retroactivity issue. Reversing earlier patterns, disagreement between the Court and Congress has become frequent in this area of the law, as the Supreme Court has announced interpretations of civil rights legislation frustrating both to civil rights plaintiffs and to a Congress that thought remedies available. A not insubstantial proportion of the Court's debates over proper approaches to legislative history and the role of "plain meaning" have arisen in that context. In one notable dissent, on the eve of the 1991 changes, Justice Stevens listed six recent opinions of the Court that had attracted congressional "correction" in civil rights legislation, upbraiding his colleagues for their seeming refusal to act in the spirit of congressional legislation, despite these consistent signals.[80] (Earlier, when the Court was more often finding merit in civil rights actions, he had reflected the other side of that coin: in 1976 he joined the Court's opinion in *Runyon v McCrary*, relying on a 1968 interpretation of § 1981 that he thought "would have amazed the legislators who voted for it" in 1866, but

---

[78] After repeated complaints, her harasser was reprimanded and transferred within the firm; she quit four days later.

[79] Rev Stat § 1977A(a), 42 USC § 1981a(a), as added by § 102 of Pub L No 102–166, 105 Stat 1071.

[80] *West Virginia Univ. Hospitals v Casey*, 499 US 83, 113–15 (1991) (Stevens dissenting).

that had become well established and "surely accords with the prevailing sense of justice today";[81] his separate opinion in *Patterson* reiterated that theme.[82]) The 1991 act was passed after Congress had failed to override President Bush's veto of the Civil Rights Act of 1990 by the slimmest of margins. The 1990 Act had been explicit about retrospectivity, enacting that its provisions should govern litigation pending at its enactment; objection to that had been among President Bush's grounds for veto. The 1991 Act omitted that explicit language and provided generally that it should "take effect upon enactment," "except as otherwise specifically provided"; the only specific provisions were two sections that provided *against* retrospective application in litigation relating to particular Supreme Court judgments among those that the Act was overturning. Neither concerned the issues in *Rivers* or *Landgraf*.

The Chief Justice assigned both of the opinions to Justice Stevens, a striking gesture given Justice Stevens's views—both the specific views noted above, and his general preference for integrative approaches to interpretation, as is reflected in these pages. As Justices Scalia (writing), Kennedy, and Thomas complained in identical concurrences filed in the two cases, the result was a mixed signal. With the concurrers' enthusiastic agreement, the majority found against retrospective application of the two provisions. The general presumption against giving legislation retrospective effect, they reasoned, must be overcome by clearly manifested congressional intent; the muddle following the President's successful veto of the 1990 legislation could not supply that manifestation. But for the majority, whether such an intent had been manifested depended on an elaborate assessment of the actual course of debates, the political situation, and the likely realities of the legislative process; for the more formal Justices of the concurrence, this was an inappropriate inquiry. Moreover, while the majority refused to apply the new legislation to cases pending at its enactment—the formal question presented—it also catalogued and indicated its acceptance of the reversals, noting in part that the new legislation had not merely restored, but expanded the causes of action involved, and had added a number of provisions that were not expres-

---

[81] *Runyon*, 427 US at 189, 191 (Stevens concurring).

[82] 491 US at 222. See text at note 99.

sive of disagreement with Supreme Court precedent.[83] The statute in *Landgraf*, enlarging the remedies available for violations of Title VII, was one of the latter.[84]

All this signaling of attentiveness to Congress's processes and stance toward the judiciary, and suggestion that *future* applications of the Act would be influenced by its spirit as well as its words, was galling to three who thought the governing principle clear. Absent a clear legislative statement in text otherwise, statutes apply only to relevant activity occurring after their effective date. It is unnecessary to say more. For them, it appears, Congress and the courts work in mutual isolation; and one may infer that (except to the extent it is expressed in unmistakably clear instructions) congressional frustration is not relevant to the courts' interpretive task. "We hear you" seems not to be an appropriate signal.

The limited statutory provisions *against* retroactivity persuaded Justice Blackmun, but none of his colleagues, that the other provisions of the act should apply to pending cases, "at least where application of the new provision would not disturb the parties' vested rights or settled expectations."[85] USI Film Products could not have imagined in 1984–86 that it was entitled to engage in sexual harassment of Ms. Landgraf; in 1986, under the well-settled court of appeals interpretation of § 1981 that seemed to have been approved by the Supreme Court, Roadway Express could not have imagined that it was entitled to engage in racial discrimination in administering Mr. Rivers's contract of employment. Justice Blackmun thought postponing the availability of new remedies, or prolonging the life of the congressionally repudiated decision in *Patterson*, could not be justified.

The majority's conclusion otherwise rested on a variety of considerations. In developing a general approach to the prospectivity question, it undertook a wide-ranging review of the Court's prior decisions in conventional common law manner and appeared to find the means—to the concurrence's considerable distaste—of preserving all.[86] In reviewing at length the contentious political

---

[83] 114 S Ct 1483, 1489 (1994).

[84] In providing the possibility of compensatory and punitive damage actions for Title VII, however, Congress eliminated one of the differences between Title VII and § 1981 relief that had armed the majority argument in *Patterson*.

[85] 114 S Ct at 1520 (Blackmun dissenting); see also 114 S Ct at 1509 (1994) (Blackmun dissenting).

[86] Two decisions, *Thorpe v Housing Authority of Durham*, 393 US 268 (1969) and *Bradley v Richmond School Board*, 416 US 696 (1974), themselves both extending remedies in civil rights

history of the measure (and its predecessor), it emphasized that the issue in this case was notorious and deliberately passed over. This review both signals Congress about its responsibilities when issues are on the table, and suggests a willingness to infer judgments that do not appear deliberately to have been withheld. In both cases, it appears to have been significant that the legislation undeniably created claims that would not have existed before its passage; it did not just revivify or expand available relief for existing claims. Thus, if the legislation had been given retrospective application here, it would have been difficult to deny its application to these new matters as well, unless by asserting a constitutional limitation—and that intellectual difficulty in itself supports a conclusion that Congress ordinarily should deal with such cases. All of this is rather supportive of, indeed premised upon, an interactive relationship in which legislature and courts learn from each other, and deal with each others' work product in a dialogic fashion.

At one point in *Rivers*, however, the majority takes a more formal stance that is worth examining. One element that makes the claim for retroactive application particularly strong, Justice Blackmun had argued, is that when trial began on Rivers's claim that he had been fired because of his race, the courts of appeals had held that § 1981 forbade racial discrimination in the administration of contracts of employment; the Supreme Court had seemed to have approved those holdings. *Patterson* later held, however, that § 1981 "does not apply to conduct which occurs after the formation of a contract and which does not interfere with the right to enforce established contract obligations."[87] In the 1991 Act, Congress unmistakably provided that § 1981 does apply to such conduct, appearing thus to return § 1981 to the meaning it had been given prior to the *Patterson* decision. To the majority, however, restoration is not simply a matter for the courts to infer judicially in response to the congressional action; it *must* be that Congress has itself enacted retrospectivity:

> *Patterson* did not overrule any prior decision of this Court; rather, it held and therefore established that the prior decisions

---

settings, marked the Court's willingness to apply to pending cases "the law in effect at the time of decision," an outcome the concurrence thought "simply misread our precedents and invented an utterly new and erroneous rule." Like its attention to legislative history, preserving those decisions might be thought to suggest to the Court's partner in dialogue, Congress, that the Court would remain attentive to the appropriateness of retroactive application even when Congress had not been explicit ("clear") about the matter.

[87] 491 US at 171.

of the Courts of Appeals which read § 1981 to cover discriminatory contract termination were *incorrect*. They were not wrong
according to some abstract standard of interpretive validity, but
by the rules that necessarily govern our hierarchical federal
court system. Cf. *Brown v Allen*, 344 US 443, 540 (1953) (Jackson, J., concurring in result). It is this Court's responsibility to
say what a statute means, and once the Court has spoken, it is
the duty of other courts to respect that understanding of the
governing rule of law. A judicial construction of a statute is an
authoritative statement of what the statute meant before as well
as after the decision of the case giving rise to that construction.[88]
Thus, *Patterson* provides the authoritative interpretation of the
phrase "make and enforce contracts" in the Civil Rights Act of
1866 before the 1991 amendment went into effect on November
21, 1991. That interpretation provides the baseline for our conclusion that the 1991 amendment would be "retroactive" if applied to cases arising before that date.

Congress, of course, has the power to amend a statute that
it believes we have misconstrued. It may even, within broad
constitutional bounds, make such a change retroactive and
thereby undo what it perceives to be the undesirable past consequences of a misinterpretation of its work product. No such
change, however, has the force of law unless it is implemented
through legislation. Even when Congress intends to supersede
a rule of law embodied in one of our decisions with what it
views as a better rule established in earlier decisions, its intent
to reach conduct preceding the "corrective" amendment must
clearly appear. We cannot say that such an intent clearly appears with respect to § 101. For this reason, and because it
creates liabilities that had no legal existence before the Act was
passed, § 101 does not apply to preenactment conduct.[89]

The formal element here is clearest in the last sentence of the
Court's footnote: "[G]iven the structure of our judicial system, the

---

[88] When Congress enacts a new statute, it has the power to decide when the statute will
become effective. The new statute may govern from the date of enactment, from a specified
future date, or even from an expressly announced earlier date. But when this Court construes
a statute, it is explaining its understanding of what the statute has meant continuously since
the date when it became law. In statutory cases the Court has no authority to depart from
the congressional command setting the effective date of a law that it has enacted. Thus, it
is not accurate to say that the Court's decision in Patterson "changed" the law that previously
prevailed in the Sixth Circuit when this case was filed. Rather, given the structure of our
judicial system, the Patterson opinion finally decided what § 1981 had *always* meant and
explained why the Courts of Appeals had misinterpreted the will of the enacting Congress.
[Court footnote; emphasis in original.]

[89] 114 S Ct at 1519–20 (emphasis in original).

Patterson opinion finally decided what § 1981 had *always* meant and explained why the Courts of Appeals had misinterpreted the will of the enacting Congress."[90] But this is a surprising characterization of "our judicial system" from a common law point of view. Justice Stevens would not normally contend that the only proper meaning for § 1981 is the meaning it had upon enactment in 1866: He had in fact taken a quite different view in joining the Court's opinion in *Runyon*[91] and in *Patterson*[92] itself; the other cases of the 1993 Term saw him, quite characteristically, regularly promoting meanings that had emerged through judicial exposition, and judicial-legislative interaction, over time. This is the characteristic common law process, which incrementally takes the law to places it previously has not been and applies those results to facts that occurred (of necessity) before the court acted. The law of product liability and the law of antitrust are both relatively stable; but both have shifted enormously since the late nineteenth century and neither still depends for its legitimacy on ideas of what it has "*always* meant." That courts are constrained to the text of statutes, as they are, does not entail treating their words as an immanent, brooding omnipresence. The existing body of statutes, no less than the existing doctrines and trends of the common law, inform contemporary judicial judgment; to insist that the statutory part is static in its content, that legislation must be taken to mean what it "*always* meant," is to rob judicially administered law of its most democratic element by subtracting the impulse to build on the policies set in motion by legislatures and restricting the building to policies generated by courts.[93]

An alternative way of understanding the situation would be to frame the question, not in terms of the retrospectivity of the 1991 Act, but as whether the Court would have been justified in overruling *Patterson*. We know from other work of the Term that the Court has not hesitated to overrule its prior interpretations of statutes even when Congress has *not* acted. Overruling has, perforce, a retrospective effect, since the Court acts in the case before it, and that case arose under—or, as in *Rivers*, at least passed through

---

[90] Id; emphasis in original.

[91] See text at n 81.

[92] See note 99.

[93] See Pound (cited in n 5), and Stone (cited in n 8).

the shadow of—the interpretation that is to be discarded. If, with the rest of law, statutes evolve, ought a court to take prompt legislative repudiation of its conclusions as a sign that it was in error? This is not a rhetorical question, and in some respects the majority opinion wrestles with its difficulties: A legislative response, even if in some respects generated by a corrective impulse, may head off in such fresh or varied directions as to sap its action of that implication. Or, the judicial action being responded to may have been entirely in line with its precedents, so that it served merely to emphasize the need to attend to a long-standing problem of policy.

But *Patterson* was itself a sharp change of direction from the body of judicial precedent that had previously developed under the aegis of § 1981. While it is certainly true, as the Court remarks, that the hierarchical nature of the judiciary established, in a formal sense, "that the prior decisions of the Court of Appeals . . . were *incorrect*,"[94] those decisions had previously reflected, and in turn served to generate, a climate of understanding respecting legal obligation in contemporary society that, until the Court acted, both had the force of law *and deprived an agreeing legislature of any need to act.* Supreme Court judgments are final, but the Court is not and need not pretend to be infallible. Observing the speed with which the law has been returned by the legislature to its prior state (and more), a court exhibiting the sensitivity Justice Stevens has generally shown to the dialogic qualities of law could easily conclude that it had been wrong in its earlier reading, and overrule it. That would not give the statute retrospective effect; what has been overruled is the earlier decision, and any fresh legislative judgments are naturally limited to future effect. It *would* avoid the embarrassment of having to apply repudiated social policy to facts that arose under other expectations, as in *Rivers*.[95]

To put the proposition this way again illuminates the sometimes strangeness of the boundary between the (common law) courts and the legislature. In *Patterson* itself, the reader may recall, the Su-

---

[94] Supra; emphasis in original.

[95] The argument is less strong for the period 1989–1991, between Patterson and the 1991 Act. During virtually all that time, however, actors were on notice that retrospective application of an explicit congressional overruling was likely; in the usual terms in which common law courts consider the fairness of retrospective application of new doctrine, no more is required.

preme Court had invited argument whether *Runyon* should be over-ruled. It unanimously decided against that step, then dividing 5–4 over the interpretation of § 1981 that defeated existing expecta-tions, and that the 1991 Act repudiated. The controlling opinion was written by Justice Kennedy; it carefully avoided saying whether *Runyon* was decided incorrectly or not, invoking instead considerations of stare decisis "that have special force in the area of statutory interpretation."[96] But it was emphatic that these con-siderations attached to the opinion, not the statute the opinion had read. "Congress may legislate . . . only through the passage of a bill which is approved by both Houses and signed by the President. Congressional inaction cannot amend a duly enacted statute."[97] It *would* be a reason to overrule even statutory precedent, the majority agreed, if "the intervening development of the law, through either the growth of judicial doctrine or further action taken by Con-gress[, has] removed or weaked the conceptual underpinnings from the prior decision or . . . rendered the decision irreconcilable with competing legal doctrines or policies," if that precedent was "a positive detriment to coherence and consistency in the law," or if, "after being ' "tested by experience, [it] has been found to be inconsistent with the sense of justice or the social welfare.' "[98] These descriptions of the proper basis for overruling even statutory precedent seem to fit the *Rivers* situation well; in *Patterson*, Justice Stevens's separate opinion had criticized the majority in just such terms:

> The Court's repeated emphasis on the literal language of § 1981 might be appropriate if it were building a new foundation, but it is not a satisfactory method of adding to the existing struc-ture. In the name of logic and coherence, the Court today adds a course of bricks dramatically askew from "the secure founda-tion of the courses laid by others," replacing a sense of rational direction and purpose in the law with an aimless confinement to a narrow construction of what it means to "make" a contract.[99]

---

[96] 491 US at 172.

[97] At 175 n 1.

[98] At 173–74, omitting citations.

[99] At 222. The concluding passage quotes Justice Stevens's opinion in *Runyon*, in turn quoting Benjamin Cardozo's *The Nature of the Judicial Process* 149 (1921), explaining his reasons for joining an opinion interpreting § 1981 in a manner he thought its drafters could not have imagined.

Petititioners seem not to have argued *Rivers* in this way; and one notes that the Chief Justice and Justice O'Connor subscribed to both Justice Kennedy's opinion in *Patterson* and Justice Stevens's opinion here. Still, to say that a prior Court interpretation is revealed to have been wrong is not the same as giving retroactive effect to a statute whose prompt enactment may contribute to that judgment; and eliding that argument tends to hide from view the important judicial responsibilities, in partnership with Congress, that Justice Kennedy's *Patterson* considerations acknowledge.

E. HOLDER V HALL

Holder v Hall,[100] a Voting Rights Act case decided on the last day of Term, captures the static quality of Justices Thomas's and Scalia's approach to statutes, their disinterest in congressional-judicial dialogue, and Justice Stevens's position at the opposite pole. A Georgia county conferred on its single elected commissioner all the county's elective authority, executive and legislative; at issue was whether this arrangement was a "standard, practice or procedure . . . which results in an abridgement or denial of the right of any citizen of the United States to vote on account of race or color," in violation of Section 2 of the Voting Rights Act of 1965.[101] Whites held a slim population majority in the county, and the contention was that choosing the single-commissioner form of government rather than a multimember "legislature" discriminated against blacks by "diluting" their vote. None but whites had been elected to (or run for) this county office, although blacks had stood for and been elected to the multimember county school board.

Vote dilution is not explicitly a violation of Section 2 or the similarly worded Section 5; both in terms appear to deal only with obstacles to physical registration and voting. Like the Civil Rights Act of 1964,[102] the Voting Rights Act was adopted just as southern resistance to civil rights legislation had been overcome; as had been the case with that Act, its supporters in Congress made no grand

---

[100] 114 S Ct 2581 (1994).

[101] 42 USC § 1973.

[102] 42 USC § 2000e-2(a) and (d); cf *United Steelworkers of America v Weber*, 443 US 193 (1979), and the continuing debate over the meaning of Title VII. The similarity is explicitly recognized in Justice Ginsburg's separate dissent, which stresses the challenge posed to the courts when congressional politics result in compromise outcomes. 114 S Ct 2581, 2624 (1994) (Ginsburg dissenting).

claims for its reach—indeed, tended to present it as its words suggested, as concerned with access to the ballot, and not proportionality of representation. A court acting in the late 60's or early 70's would have found it easier, as a technical matter, to give the Act correspondingly narrow meaning. The Supreme Court's 1969 decision in *Allen v State Board of Elections*,[103] however, broadly interpreted the language of Section 5 to reach "all action necessary to make a vote effective,"[104] including the matter of vote dilution; in 1986, the Court specifically applied Section 2 to the problem of vote dilution in its decision in *Thornburg v Gingles*.[105]

Six opinions were written in *Holder;* no more than two Justices agreed fully with any of three plurality opinions finding that the Georgia practice did not violate Section 2. Justice Thomas's opinion was one of those three;[106] Justice Stevens's, one of three dissents.[107] Most of the opinions accepted the existing case development as a starting point, and then asked whether the "dilution" concept could reasonably be applied on the facts of the case presented to the Court. As the number of opinions suggests, that task proved both difficult and controversial.

Justice Thomas took a different approach, returning to the interpretive question as an initial matter. Whether analyzing the text alone (as he emphatically prefers) or viewing the legislative history as a whole, he found it limited to obstacles to physical registration and voting—that the statute did not reach behaviors that might tend to imbalance voter influence on outcomes along racial lines, as long as the vote itself was assured. That then presented him with a question he characterized in strictly judicial terms, a question of stare decisis, whether the Court should continue to adhere to its prior decisions; and that question he thought answered by the unmanageability and inappropriately political character for judicial action of the task the Court had set for itself. The opinion was a major undertaking, substantially longer than the other five opinions

---

[103] 393 US 544.

[104] At 565–66.

[105] 478 US 30 (1986).

[106] Justices Kennedy and O'Connor also wrote.

[107] Other dissents were filed by Justices Blackmun and Ginsburg. Justice Blackmun's dissent on the merits was joined by Justices Stevens, Ginsburg, and Souter; Justice Stevens's response to Justice Thomas was also joined by all his dissenting colleagues.

combined, and this brief account can hardly capture it; its fervor may be suggested by the following:

> In my view, our current practice should not continue. Not for another Term, not until the next case, not for another day. The disastrous implications of the policies we have adopted under the Act are too grave; the dissembling in our approach to the Act too damaging to the credibility of the federal judiciary.[108]

What is striking and illustrative about the argument for current purposes is its quality of stasis. The statute is what it was on its adoption in 1965. Postenactment history is consulted only in acknowledging that stare decisis is often sound policy in matters of statutory construction, and in examining whether the past interpretations of the Court have proved refractory or unworkable (a subject about which, I wish to be clear, it appears reasonable arguments can be made).

At the center of Justice Stevens's responsive dissent are a series of intervening congressional events to which Justice Thomas does not refer:

> In 1970, one year after *Allen*, and with that case and its implications before it, Congress reenacted Section 5 without change.
> In 1975, it did so again.
> In 1982, now after over a decade of broad interpretation of the statutory references to voting "standard, practice or procedure," Congress further amended Section 2 to *extend* its application to circumstances the Court had recently found outside the statute as initially written;[109] henceforth, Section 2 was to reach invidious results as well as invidious purposes.[110]

That is, Congress's consistent pattern, in dealing with a statute of high political moment and visibility, had been to leave the Court's expansive interpretations undisturbed, and to override the limitations that the Court did find in it. These facts took the case well beyond simple congressional silence in the face of judicial interpretation; they involved reenactment, high controversy, and indeed statutory change hard to understand other than as implicit approval of judicial constructions to date.

---

[108] 114 S Ct at 2618.

[109] *Mobile v Bolden*, 446 US 55 (1980).

[110] 114 S Ct at 2626–27.

> When a statute has been authoritatively, repeatedly, and consistently construed for more than a quarter century, and when Congress has reenacted and extended the statute several times with full awareness of that construction, judges have an especially clear obligation to obey settled law.[111]

For Justice Stevens and his colleagues, the statute and the Court's interactions with Congress are organic. For Justices Thomas and Scalia, Congress's work concluded with enactment; subsequent events are relevant (if at all) only to establish the workability or not of the Court's approach to the original issue of meaning—an issue that remains open to revision in accordance with the original understanding, however expectations and general law may have changed in the interim.

F. THREE EASIER PIECES

In three civil cases decided fairly early in the Term, perhaps less difficult and in any event somewhat less adventurous in their claims on the Court, the seams between statute and case law were less evident.

In *American Dredging Co. v Miller*,[112] the Court was faced with Louisiana's statutory decision to make the doctrine of forum non conveniens unavailable in Jones Act and maritime law cases brought in its courts.[113] The frequent involvement of foreign ships and sailors gives issues of the appropriateness of American venues particular significance in admiralty. As it happened, plaintiff and defendant in this case were both domestic. Justice Scalia emphasized that tact in his opinion for a majority of six, upholding Louisiana's choice; he stressed, too, that state courts would be unable to exercise in rem jurisdiction that could result in the possibly embarrassing impoundment of a foreign vessel. Thus, Louisiana may find itself more limited in cases arising out of international commerce than the decision at first suggests.

Two strands characterize Justice Scalia's majority opinion. The

---

[111] Id at 2629.

[112] 114 S Ct 981 (1994). American Dredging was not produced by the Lexis search described above, note 43, but is mentioned at the suggestion of my colleague John Manning, who argued the case for the Solicitor General as amicus curiae.

[113] Strikingly, Louisiana made this judgment *only* for admiralty cases; the majority asserted that the propriety of this discrimination was "a question not remotely before us." 114 S Ct at 988 n 3.

first, less interesting for our purposes, applies a test for preemption in admiralty cases first articulated in 1917 and finds that Louisiana's choice is not preempted.[114] The second examines the relationship among the Jones Act (the maritime remedy for seamen under which this particular action was brought) and FELA, the more general statute also involved in *Gottshall*. The Jones Act incorporates FELA by reference, and FELA also requires state courts to apply uniform federal law; but an early decision under FELA nonetheless permitted state courts to apply their own principles of forum non conveniens.[115] "We think it evident that the rule . . . announced for the FELA applies as well to the Jones Act, which in turn supports the view that maritime commerce does not require a uniform rule of forum non conveniens."[116] The statutory judgment which the Court first found in FELA is carried through by implication at least to Jones Act litigation, without any need to see that judgment expressed in the Jones Act text.

Justice Kennedy (with Justice Thomas) dissented from this "harmonization of general admiralty law with congressional enactments,"[117] seeming to give dominant force to the Court's common law responsibilities in a setting in which they are particularly strong.[118] The admiralty jurisdiction, he thought, imposed a

---

[114] *Southern Pacific Co. v Jensen*, 244 US 205, 216 (1917). Justice Stevens, in a lone concurrence, strongly objected to unnecessarily giving life to *Jensen*, a 5–4 decision he characterized as of a piece with *Lochner v New York*, 198 US 45 (1905), in its attitude toward state legislative authority trenching on admiralty. The specific holding in *Jensen* was that New York could not apply workers' compensation remedies to a longshoreman injured in the admiralty jurisdiction; thus, the result was among those suggesting a certain judicial hostility to legislative innovations seeking to overcome the then cruelty of the common law. See text at note 3. It was in dissent here that Holmes proclaimed the necessarily "interstitial[]" quality of judicial policy-making, and that "[t]he common law is not a brooding omnipresence in the sky but the articulate voice of some sovereign or quasi-sovereign that can be identified." 244 US at 221, 222, quoted in 114 S Ct at 991, n 1 (Stevens dissenting). Is it too much to find, in this particular cleavage between Justice Scalia and Justice Stevens, some echo of a similar disinclination on Justice Scalia's part to use statutory instruction to the fullest? Note that Justice Scalia prefaces his discussion of the matter next discussed in the text, on which he and Justice Stevens agree, by characterizing it as a secondary point and observing that "[w]hile there is an established and continuing tradition of federal common lawmaking in admiralty, that law is to be developed, *insofar as possible*, to harmonize with the enactments of Congress in the field." (Emphasis added.) Id at 989. That is, separation is insisted upon and judicial primacy asserted. Admiralty is one of the few contexts in which Justice Scalia admits a common law function for federal courts. Compare note 70.

[115] *Missouri ex rel. Southern R. Co. v Mayfield*, 340 US 1 (1950).

[116] 114 S Ct at 990.

[117] Id.

[118] Id at 995.

strong, implicitly constitutional obligation of uniformity. FELA is a domestic statute; litigation about railroad activity "interposes no obstacle to our foreign relations."[119] The Jones Act makes no explicit judgment about forum non conveniens, and the Court's opinion in any event reaches the whole of admiralty jurisdiction, not just Jones Act cases. Absent assurance that foreigners could be protected from inconvenient fora, which he could not find in the majority opinion, he would not build an exception from uniformity on the basis of FELA. The worlds of statute and common law are more widely separated here—but also with an assignable reason on the merits that has its own intellectual force. It is hard to take the implication here that the exercise would be *generally* inappropriate.

Formally at issue in *Liteky v United States*[120] was the meaning to be attached to 28 USC § 455(a), which since its amendment in 1974 has required a federal judge to recuse "himself in any proceeding in which his impartiality might reasonably be questioned." Disqualification was sought on the basis of a judge's conduct of politically charged trials, and the Court was unanimous that it was not required on the facts before it. Justice Scalia wrote for the Chief Justice and Justices O'Connor, Thomas, and Ginsburg; Justice Kennedy wrote for the remainder, concurring in the result. The majority's analysis was somewhat more formal than the concurrence; the latter thought Justice Scalia emphasized too greatly doctrinal structure (whether the disqualifying impulse must come from an "extrajudicial source") and drew unwarranted limitations to the broad principle of § 455(a) from the series of specific prohibitions that is set out in § 455(b). Most striking for our purposes, however, is that both opinions were content to regard § 455 as establishing the foundation upon which judicial doctrine about disqualification would be built. The statute here was imagined as a starting point, rather than an isolated and unchanging diktat. No complaint is uttered about Congress's failure of clarity in specifying so subjective an inquiry, nor is Congress pointed out as the only proper source of any appropriate clarification. The Court builds on cases that preceded the 1974 amendment and are assumed to have in-

---

[119] Id.

[120] 114 S Ct 1147 (1994).

formed it, and on cases that followed that amendment and contribute to understanding its meaning.

Possibly the statute's concern with judicial administration underlies the ease with which all members of the Court seem able to treat it as establishing a somewhat malleable framework, rather than an unchanging specification. Disqualification may seem like it should be judicial business in the first instance, so that treating the statute as confirmatory and instructive rather than as an external command has an intuitive if unexpressed appeal. To be confirmed oneself in substantial discretion of administration is perhaps less alarming than to see that discretion awarded to another body. The minority—Justices who, save Justice Kennedy, were characteristically more wedded to integrative perspectives throughout the Term—are prepared to see Congress's instruction in less confining a way than the majority; but even the majority approaches the task with a willingness to examine context and shoulder the premises and responsibilities of continuity that were missing from much of the Term's work.

Somewhat to the same effect was *Fogerty v Fantasy, Inc.*,[121] where the question was whether courts should employ differing standards in assessing the requests of prevailing plaintiffs and prevailing defendants for the award of attorneys fees in copyright infringement actions under 17 USC § 505. Section 505 provides that "the court may . . . award a reasonable attorney's fee to the prevailing party as part of the costs," drawing no textual distinction between successful prosecutors and successful defenders of infringement actions. In earlier decisions construing essentially identical language in the Civil Rights laws, however, the Court had differentiated between plaintiffs and defendants, finding that successful plaintiffs should "ordinarily" recover attorneys' fees unless "special circumstances would render such an award unjust," but that successful defendants were not entitled to a similar presumption.[122] Those earlier decisions identified as a purpose of the Civil Rights laws the encouragement of often "impecunious" plaintiffs' actions, to vindicate congressional policies of the highest priority; and they

---

[121] 114 S Ct 1023.

[122] See 42 USC § 2000e-5(k) ("in its discretion may allow the prevailing party . . . a reasonable attorney's fee"); *Newman v Piggie Park Enterprises, Inc.*, 390 US 400, 402 (1968) (successful plaintiff's presumptive recovery); *Christianburg Garment Co. v EEOC*, 434 US 412 (1978) (successful defendants not entitled to presumptive recovery).

relied in part on legislative history supporting that understanding. The Justices were unanimous that these earlier constructions were not controlling, but they were not unanimous in their reasoning.

The Chief Justice, writing for eight members of the Court, saw a policy distinction between the two statutes that produced no embarrassment: copyright plaintiffs were no more likely to be impecunious than copyright defendants, nor did they have a special "private attorney general" role in enforcing a particularly important congressional policy. And the majority considered with some care whether the legislative history of § 505, or the prior history of the attorney's fee issue in copyright litigation, would itself support a dual standard—concluding that neither would. The premise of such inquiries into context must be that congressional action is appropriately to be understood in the framework of expectations about law that exist at the time. The questions would not have been necessary if the earlier civil rights statute, and its interpretation, had no intellectual bearing for the copyright law. Only Justice Thomas took that position, in a solitary concurrence; he stressed that straightforward attention to the text was the better analysis, would have preferred to limit if not abandon the earlier readings as error, and regretted the resulting inconsistency in construing the virtually identical language of the Copyright and Civil Rights Acts. For him, but in this case only for him, text alone, and not the context of its adoption, had bearing.

IV. CRIMINAL CASES

A. SHANNON V UNITED STATES

On the same day as the Court decided *Gottshall*, Justice Thomas, and Justice Stevens, each took a similar approach in *Shannon v United States*,[123] a criminal case in which the defendant relied alternatively on an asserted congressional-judicial interaction, and on the Supreme Court's supervisory power over federal criminal power—its common law function in that respect. At issue was whether a trial court had erred in refusing a defendant's request for a jury instruction explaining the consequences of a verdict of

---

[123] 114 S Ct 2419 (1994).

Not Guilty by Reason of Insanity under the relatively new Insanity Defense Reform Act of 1984.

Prior to 1984, no statute had governed the use or consequences of the insanity defense in federal criminal trials outside the District of Columbia. Congress had enacted such a statute for the District in 1955. In 1957, the D.C. Circuit had decided en banc that, given juries' probable unfamiliarity with the insanity defense, defendants were entitled to have juries informed about the consequences of a verdict of not guilty by reason of insanity, despite the usual unwillingness of courts to invite juries to consider the consequences of their action:

> We think the jury has a right to know the meaning of this possible verdict as accurately as it knows by common knowledge the meaning of the other two possible verdicts.[124]

This opinion was uncontroversial and had been followed for almost three decades when, in the wake of the assassination attempt on President Reagan, Congress enacted the general federal statute. The 1984 statute was generally modeled on the District Act, although many of its specific judgments were somewhat harsher toward the defense.[125] The procedure the D.C. Circuit put in place was "endorse[d]" by the Senate Committee in its report, apparently the only mention of the matter in the legislative history.[126]

Justice Thomas, writing for all but Justices Stevens and Blackmun, concluded that the defendant had no right to the instruction that he sought. The text of the new Act did not address this problem. Examining its several changes, he found that it varied sufficiently from its D.C. predecessor to make "inapplicable" the canon that when a statute with a settled construction is borrowed, its settled interpretation is presumed adopted as well. In a footnote, he added a comment that very sharply distinguishes between the

---

[124] *Lyles v United States*, 254 F2d 725, 728 (1957); Judge, later Chief Justice, Warren Burger was one of the authors of this opinion.

[125] As detailed in the majority opinion, the insanity test is more restrictively formulated. Also, a federal defendant must affirmatively establish the defense by clear and convincing evidence, not a mere preponderance; is subject to a civil hearing within 40 days, not 50; in a serious matter must show entitlement to release by clear and convincing evidence, not a preponderance; and, if then committed, will be released only when he no longer presents a substantial risk of harm to others or their property, rather than when he has ceased to be "dangerous to himself or others."

[126] S Rep No 98-225, 240 (1983), quoted in 114 S Ct at 2426.

worlds of statute and case law: since the D.C. Circuit's action had been taken under its supervisory authority over federal courts in the District rather than as an act of statutory construction as such, a "canon of *statutory construction*" would be inapplicable; "there was no 'known and settled construction' of the statute that Congress could have adopted by virtue of borrowing language from the D.C. statutory scheme."[127] But the District of Columbia's criminal bar is unlikely to have distinguished between "statutory construction" and how it knew the D.C. statute had been applied without controversy or difficulty for three decades. Nor would the Court adopt the D.C. approach judicially, fearing that "the rule against informing jurors of the consequences of their verdicts would soon be swallowed by the exceptions" if the Court adopted Shannon's argument as an exercise of its supervisory power over the federal courts.[128] And, again, the majority found force in an argument that tends to isolate the world of Congress from the world of the court: "Congress's recent action in this area counsels hesitation in invoking our supervisory powers."[129] Congress is thus credited with having chosen by not acting, when its only relevant experience— which the Court does not permit itself to know—is that judicial exercise of supervisory powers had well solved the issue.

A similarly sharp division between the two worlds is reflected in the majority's treatment of the Senate Committee Report. While acknowledging that Justices hold "differing views regarding the role that legislative history should play in statutory interpretation," Justice Thomas was "not aware of any case . . . in which we have given authoritative weight to a single passage of legislative history that is in no way anchored in the text of the statute."[130] In the abstract, one easily agrees that a "snippet of legislative history" lacking any "statutory reference point" ought to be disregarded. But here the point is tenable only if the "snippet" is itself read in isolation—if one's premise is that legislators act in the abstract, without any knowledge of or stance toward the existing body of law. Once we permit ourselves as well as the Senate to know about

---

[127] 114 S Ct at 2426 n 8 (emphasis in original).

[128] Id at 2428.

[129] Id.

[130] Id at 2426. Passages like these appear to be building a wall of defense against the future return of attention to legislative history.

the 1955 statute and its well-established and uncontroversial interpretation, the "snippet" becomes not an isolated scribble but "as
much as you could expect." There wasn't a problem requiring
legislative resolution in the context against which the Senate was
acting. To require advance legislative identification and explicit
resolution of all issues, including those that are *not* issues, is to ask
what cannot be done. Failing to anticipate what a court might insist
upon, Congress had no reason to say more than it did. Justice
Thomas's position holds as a matter of logic; it fails as a description
of events that acknowledges the continuing interaction of all the
bodies responsible for law's development, and the expectations that
interaction engenders.[131]

For Justices Stevens and Blackmun, "a rule that has minimized
the risk of injustice for almost 40 years should not be abandoned
without good reason."[132] Fears of possible unfairness to defendants
are answered by the need for defendants to request the charge; fears
that the general rule against informing jurors of the consequences of
their verdicts would be swallowed up by exceptions are answered
by the connection here to a particular statute, and by the experience of almost 40 years in the D.C. courts that no such expansion
had occurred. The Court need not simply "presume" a prior construction had been adopted by Congress, when it is evident that
construction was actually known to the legislature and was uncontroversial—indeed, they suggest, the D.C. approach was the developing trend in the states generally.

One opinion sees an abstract question, and works hard to preserve it in that frame. Indicators that might place it into a developmental context or frame the issues in dialogic terms are rejected.
For Justice Thomas in this case, Congress doesn't act in a context—
its obligations are to see to it each time that all its instructions are
clear—and neither should the Court. The other opinion is
grounded in a premise that law is developmental, that what occurs
at any moment is informed by what has gone before, by the perva-

---

[131] Compare the discussion of *City of Chicago v EDF*, discussed in text at 499. One could
add, perhaps, that in preferring what he found to be the usual treatment of this issue in
state courts over that developed in the District of Columbia, a distinctly federal jurisdiction,
Justice Thomas again reflects a preference for judicial development of law dependent on
state rather than federal sources, even when federal questions are unmistakably involved.
See text at p 436.

[132] 114 S Ct at 2428–29.

sive set of expectations against which, necessarily—their time and insight limited—humans act. And here, of course, the Court was also presented with the alternative of acting in common law mode, in the exercise of supervisory jurisdiction (as in this context that is called). For one writer, that possibility was to be evaluated by possible logical extensions of the desired holding;[133] for the other, by practical experience and the apparent trend in other jurisdictions.

B. STAPLES V UNITED STATES

Justices Thomas and Stevens again took opposed positions in *Staples v United States*,[134] but in this opinion Justice Thomas used contextual materials more freely, and in the service of finding against criminal liability; Justice Stevens was perhaps the more attentive to the statute in itself. Staples possessed a gun, originally a semiautomatic weapon, that had been modified so that it would fire repeatedly on one pull of its trigger. That modification made it a machine gun under the National Firearms Act;[135] the Act defines as an offense punishable by up to 10 years in prison the possession of a machine gun that has not been federally registered.[136] The government prosecuted Staples for failing to register the gun. The question dividing the Court was the scienter required to support his conviction. Should the jury have been instructed that it must find that Staples himself knew that the gun had been modified to make it a fully automatic weapon? Or was it enough to have been told, as in fact they were, that they must find that the gun Staples knew he had, and had not registered, had been so modified? Justice Thomas wrote for five Justices that to support

---

[133] Compare *Priestly v Fowler*, 3 Mees. & Wels. 1, 150 Eng Rep 1030 (Exch Pleas 1837); *Winterbottom v Wright*, 10 Mees. & Wels. 109 (Exch Pleas 1842), opinions by Lord Abinger long taken as caricatures of fear-ridden reasoning. Over the course of a century and a half, Lord Abinger's fears have been born out; and so, perhaps, would Justice Thomas's be. The concern is not irrelevant; yet time frame and pace are central to its legitimacy. If that change were to occur slowly, it would presumably be because of the accretion of factual circumstances demonstrating that that would be the just outcome, and in the absence of legislative reaction to the direction taken by the courts. Once again, then, the fundamental imperative here is that of stasis. Such opinions trust the future no more than they consult the past.

[134] 114 S Ct 1793 (1994).

[135] 26 USC § 5845.

[136] 26 USC § 5861(d).

conviction Staples had to have known that the gun was an automatic, and therefore his conviction must be reversed; Justices Ginsburg and O'Connor concurred in that result; Justices Stevens and Blackmun dissented, believing that the semiautomatic character of the gun together with its modification in fact were enough to establish criminal liability.

Justice Thomas's opinion is integrative in significant respects, drawing on a wide range of other opinions and statutes in reasoning to its conclusion favoring a relatively demanding scienter standard. It derives its principal thrust from propositions that might be disputed, but that plainly figure as policy threads running through the law—that the general legality of gun ownership in our society and the severity of the sentence Staples might receive argue for regarding the offense as a regulation of conduct *malum in se* rather than as an offense to public welfare. (Public welfare offenses, all agreed, do not require proving scienter in the manner the *Staples* majority required.) The text of the National Firearms Act does not answer the question of what state of mind is required for violation of its provisions; the Act is to be construed, Justice Thomas said, in light of the "background rules of the common law,"[137] but in this case *without* the dating that had characterized his opinions in *Gottshall*[138] and *Heck.*[139] In a criminal case, interpretations varying over time would raise special and important questions if their effect was to expand liability; thus, one might suppose that had the issue been presented Justice Thomas would again have been particularly interested in what the common law was on the date of enactment. Yet the tone here is quite different from those other efforts. Indeed, in a case involving hand grenades, an earlier Supreme Court opinion had directly characterized the Act as a public welfare statute, "a regulatory measure in the interest of the public safety, which may well be premised on the theory that one would hardly be surprised to learn that possession of hand grenades is not an innocent act."[140] But that case was concerned with knowledge of the registration requirement, not of the character of a hand grenade; the majority's view that the possession of guns *is* innocent in Ameri-

---

[137] 114 S Ct at 1797.

[138] Discussed in text following p 429.

[139] Discussed in text following p 447.

[140] *United States v Freed*, 401 US 601, 609 (1971), quoted in 114 S Ct at 1799.

can society—the more general proposition—thus distinguished that case, and made it permissible in these facts to invoke the more usual *malum in se* reasoning.

Justice Stevens's opinion draws on the legislative history of the Act, in particular, and on the special character of semiautomatic weapons, to support its conclusion that the "regulatory offense" approach is fully appropriate to Staples's case. Which of the two one finds more persuasive probably turns on the latter issue of characterization. In Justice Stevens's view, the majority "reaches the rather surprising conclusion that guns are more analogous to food stamps than to hand grenades";[141] Justice Thomas analogizes the equities to the Court's probable hesitation "to conclude on the basis of silence [in a statute attaching major penalties to violations of automobile emissions standards] that Congress intended a prison term to apply to a car owner whose vehicle's emissions levels, wholly unbeknownst to him, began to exceed legal limits between regular inspection dates."[142] For Justice Stevens, the guns in question are semiautomatic weapons that give notice of their special dangerousness and are not within American traditions of gun ownership; for Justice Thomas, that limitation cannot be constructed out of a statute that refers to "firearms" and then to the limited subclass of "machine guns." Within this framework of debate over characterization, however, Justice Thomas's opinion seems quite unlike many of his other efforts during the Term in its willingness to bring general considerations to bear on the interpretation of statutory text.

C. CUSTIS V UNITED STATES

In *Custis v United States*,[143] announced on the same day as *BFP*,[144] Justice Souter's common law sensibilities and attention to the actualities of rule administration failed for the second time that day to

---

[141] 114 S Ct at 1810 (Stevens dissenting). The reference is to *Liparota v United States*, 471 US 419 (1985), a case involving the *mens rea* requirement associated with food stamp offenses under a statute that, unlike the National Firearms Act (as Justice Stevens points out, id at n 15), referred to offenses committed "knowingly."

[142] 114 S Ct at 1802.

[143] 114 S Ct 1732 (1994).

[144] Discussed in text following p 449. The cases were announced May 23, 1994. Seven opinions were announced on that Monday, six of them involving at least in part the meaning of federal statutes, and splitting the Court in similar ways.

persuade a majority of his colleagues. Section 924(e) of the Armed Career Criminal Act imposes significantly enhanced penalties for persons convicted of felonies and possessing firearms if they have "three previous convictions . . . for a violent felony or a serious drug offense."[145] Custis, convicted of possessing cocaine and a firearm, had three prior state convictions for violent property offenses. The government moved to enhance his sentence under the statute. At the sentencing hearing, Custis challenged two of his prior convictions collaterally, as infected with constitutional procedural errors. The question for the Supreme Court was whether the ACCA's reference to "three previous convictions" should be understood to permit such collateral challenges.

The Chief Justice wrote for six—Justice Ginsburg now joining the *BFP* majority—that the Act does not authorize such collateral attacks. He reasoned that "the statute focuses on the *fact* of conviction."[146] Another section of the statute, § 921(a)(20), detailed what convictions counted, excluding those that had been "expunged, or set aside" or had resulted in a pardon or the restoration of civil liberties. The implication of reference to convictions *already* set aside is that those not yet impugned may be counted. In a drug offense statute, Congress had explicitly provided for collateral challenges to prior convictions that would otherwise cause sentence enhancement. And in *Lewis v United States*,[147] the Court had held it unnecessary to permit collateral challenges to convictions on which federal prosecutors premised the felony of gun possession by one previously convicted of a felony. The Court had twice held as a constitutional matter that prior convictions could not be used for sentencing enhancement; but, the Chief Justice explained, those cases involved outright denials of the right to counsel, a "unique constitutional defect" that was "jurisdictional" in character.[148] None of the flaws Custis claimed had that severity. Permitting collateral inquiry into such issues as the adequacy of representation would create practical difficulties and undermine the finality of judgments.

The first argument in Justice Souter's dissent, joined by Justices

---

[145] 18 USC § 924(e).

[146] 114 S Ct at 1736 (emphasis in original).

[147] 445 US 55 (1980).

[148] 114 S Ct at 1733.

Stevens and Blackmun, strikes a characteristic difference in tone. For him, the starting point is that the Court's two constitutional holdings were in place when § 924(e) was enacted, and were uniformly understood by both commentators and the courts of appeal to require courts generally "to entertain claims that prior convictions relied upon for enhancement were unconstitutional." After the enactment of § 924(e), the courts of appeals uniformly understood its reference to "conviction" to mean "lawful conviction"—that is, to permit collateral challenge—yet a Congress that subsequently amended § 924 with some frequency did not change its language in this respect. This more detailed view of "the contemporary legal context" within which Congress could be said and had previously been understood to have acted gave its silence about collateral challenge a different spin. Justice Souter reasoned that the legislative history of § 921(a)(20), enacted two years after § 924, showed it to have been dealing with problems arising under another section; the explicit reference to collateral attack in the drug statute, enacted in 1970, provided little information about Congress's understanding in 1984, by which time the constitutional claim to collateral relief had become well established. And *Lewis* itself carefully distinguished the earlier collateral relief cases as involving sentencing; although "a sentence-enhancement law 'depend[s] upon the reliability of a past . . . conviction,'" Congress could rationally decide to exclude all persons who had previously been convicted of felonies from lawful gun possession as "'a sweeping prophylaxis' designed 'to keep firearms away from potentially dangerous persons.'"[149] The constitutional validity of conviction was irrelevant if the statute thus served to regulate primary conduct.

Justice Souter had additional arguments in his quiver—that the statute ought to be interpreted to avoid a difficult constitutional question,[150] that the feared practical difficulties had failed to emerge in the intervening years when the courts of appeals had been permitting collateral challenges. I don't wish to suggest that the reader must be persuaded by any of them. One supposes, too, that the

---

[149] Id at 1742 (Souter dissenting), quoting 445 US at 63, 67.

[150] 114 S Ct at 1743. In particular, he deplored the reassertion of the idea of "jurisdictional" constitutional violations, one he thought had long been discredited. The distance between deprivation of one's constitutional right to counsel by utter failure to provide one and deprivation by providing one who fails to do the work is in any event not large; inadequate representation was one of Custis's claims.

opinions in the case may have been influenced by the writers' attitude toward postconviction relief, a matter quite apart from judicial
style. What seems worth remarking here, again, is the difference
in the two opinions' stance toward Congress and the job of judges.
The majority holds Congress to a standard of precision in speaking,
and is relatively indifferent to the context in which it speaks—even
when important elements of that context are of the courts' own
making. The statutory text is an abstract given; its subsequent
interpretation by the courts and the fact or absence of congressional
response are not worth mention. For Justice Souter, Congress is a
much more human institution, and its relations with the judiciary
are to be seen as interactive and dialogic. "[T]he assumption that
all omissions in legislative drafting are deliberate [is] an assumption
we know to be false."[151] Congress's actions and failures to act are
to be set in the context of the developing law of the times; the
premise here is one of shared responsibility, in which the development of judicial decision plays a significant role in assigning meaning to text and the integrative role of the judiciary is stressed.

D. HAGEN V UTAH

A case involving criminal jurisdiction over Native Americans
provided one of the Term's most thoroughly integrative opinions
for those members of the Court who—particularly in the administrative contexts we have yet to reach—were generally the most
likely to avoid inquiries into legislative history, the history of law's
application, and resulting expectations. In *Hagen v Utah*,[152] Utah's
criminal jurisdiction over a Native American accused of a drug
offense turned on whether statutes enacted in the period 1902-05
had the effect of diminishing the size of the Uintah Indian Reservation. The offense occurred on land that had been within the original boundaries of the Reservation, but that had subsequently been
opened to non-Indian settlement. State criminal law could not
apply to the acts of Native Americans occurring on reservation
lands. The fact that the land had been opened to non-Indians was
not enough in itself to establish that the reservation had been diminished. A majority of seven, Justice O'Connor writing, found
that the statutes in question worked to effect a diminution, so that

[151] Id at 1741.

[152] 114 S Ct 958 (1994).

Utah could prosecute the alleged crime; Justices Blackmun and Souter, invoking the checkered past of our national government's dealings with Indian tribes, could not find the "clear and unequivocal evidence of congressional intent to reduce reservation boundaries" prior cases required.[153]

Both opinions examined in detail the course of dealings with the Uintahs that led to the statutes in question and the records of legislative action in reaching their respective conclusions. Their disagreement over the result of this inquiry is less significant here than that both opinions undertook it. And, in contrast with the analysis often offered by Justices tending to approach statutory issues formally, Justice O'Connor credited what happened after the adoption of the statutes in question as significant for determining their meaning. She noted that the population of the apparently ceded lands was almost entirely non-Indian, that traditional Uintah administration had been limited in practice to the areas not opened for non-Indian settlement, and that Utah had regularly exercised jurisdiction over the opened lands. "This 'jurisdictional history,' as well as the current population situation . . . , demonstrates a practical acknowledgment that the Reservation was diminished; a contrary conclusion would seriously disrupt the justifiable expectations of the people living in the area."[154]

From a justice standpoint, it is somewhat perverse thus to credit behavior and results rooted in the exercise of superior force over exploited peoples, while leaving unexplored similar considerations arising from ordinary day-to-day administration of law. Justices Blackmun and Souter, who were usually more willing to credit such behavior with significance during the Term, made this irony explicit.[155] Yet one cannot escape that the premise is one argued for in this essay; like legislative history, it did not wholly disappear from the Term's work.

E. THREE HARD CASES

As with many issues of approach to judicial function, ideas such as the primacy and stability of the original text can be overcome

---

[153] Id at 971. The majority disagreed that a "clear statement" was required, but *not* that statutes must establish a congressional purpose to diminish the reservation and that doubts were to be resolved in the Indians' favor.

[154] Id at 970.

[155] Id at 971, 978, 980.

by other factors, such as attitudes toward crime. The varying opinions in three criminal decisions from the 1993 Term are illustrative; Justices who would ordinarily eschew indicators outside the text sometimes appear to be tempted by results its use produces. The special force of principles of lenity in criminal law, like the law's assertion of solicitude for Native American interests that might have been at work in *Hagen*, gives some of the Term's opinions an ironical turn.

Williamson v United States[156] promised to "clarify the scope of the hearsay exception for statements against penal interest."[157] (With four opinions supporting a remand for reconsideration—none fully the opinion of the Court—the Court seems to have fallen short of that worthy goal.) Rule 804(b)(3) of the Federal Rules of Evidence permits the introduction into evidence, as an exception to the hearsay rule, of self-inculpatory "statements."[158] The Court had to decide whether that provision reached past an accomplice's acknowledgement that he himself was carrying cocaine, to his saying that he was carrying it for the defendant. A majority of the court—Justices O'Connor, Scalia, Ginsburg, Blackmun, Stevens, and Souter—relied chiefly on textual materials to conclude that "statements" could not be taken to mean the *whole* of a suspect's conversation with authorities, but only those parts of it that were self-inculpatory. The six disagreed among themselves whether *any* part of the accomplice's narrative was likely genuinely to fit the latter description; only Justices O'Connor and Scalia concluded that some probably would. Striking for present purposes is that Justice Kennedy argued strongly for himself, the Chief Justice and Justice Thomas that collateral materials (in this case, primarily Advisory Committee notes) should be relied on to give the text a meaning that made it more likely that the accomplice's words could find use against the defendant's interest. Ordinarily, they deprecated the use of such materials; here, they failed as well to deal with the constitutional questions raised by broad admissibility of statements whose maker cannot be confronted.

---

[156] 114 S Ct 2431 (1994).

[157] Id at 2433.

[158] "Statement" is defined by Fed R Ev § 801 as "an oral or written assertion." Justice O'Connor shows by dictionary references that the definition is unhelpfully circular ("Assertion" → "declaration" → "statement"), and then argues that "the principle behind the Rule, so far as it is discernable from the text, points clearly to the narrower meaning." Justice Kennedy's concurrence, atypically for him, does not mention the textual indicator of § 801.

United States v Granderson[159] brought the Court face-to-face with imperfections in legislative process. Granderson had been convicted of a postal offense that, under the sentencing guidelines, could have resulted in at most a six-month penitentiary term; he had been placed on probation for five years. He was shortly found in possession of cocaine, and a 1988 amendment to the criminal code required the court in such a case, after a hearing, to "revoke the sentence of probation and sentence the defendant to not less than one-third of *the original sentence*."[160] The italicized language creates the problem. Other indicators give strong signals that Congress wanted the new sentence to require confinement. That would have been the natural result under the practice once followed in the federal courts. Before 1984, if probation was to be the court's choice, the sentencing court would first impose a penitentiary sentence and then suspend it for the probationary period. But passage of the Sentencing Reform Act in 1984, four years before the amendment in question, had ended that federal practice. Under that statute, probation is now a "sentence." There is no longer any "original sentence" other than the sentence of probation. What is "one-third of the original sentence"?

Justice Ginsburg, writing for five Justices,[161] was willing to improvise with "the original sentence" to rescue the apparent sense of the legislation, while the Chief Justice and Justices Scalia, Kennedy, and Thomas, in three opinions,[162] insisted on fidelity to text. Thus, glancing sideways at the size and complexity of the overall legislation, and the last-minute and largely unexplained introduction of this section as a floor amendment, the majority concluded that the statute requires at a minimum confinement for one-third of the maximum jail sentence that might initially have been imposed under the sentencing guidelines, had a jail term been chosen. In effect, they treated Congress as if it had simply forgotten the 1984 change in sentencing practice, and in 1988 had referred back to what everyone remembered sentencing practice to have been. They were willing to repair a statute that Congress had left in a state of disarray, following as best they could the indicators of

---

[159] 114 S Ct 1259.

[160] 18 USC § 3565(a).

[161] Justice Ginsburg for herself and Justices Blackmun, O'Connor, Stevens, and Souter.

[162] Justices Kennedy and Scalia wrote individually, concurring in the result; the Chief Justice, joined by Justice Thomas, wrote in dissent.

congressional purpose that could be derived from the statute and its context and measuring their success by their result—a required jail sentence, within the range that might originally have been imposed.

The four textualists insisted that "the original sentence" must refer to the sentence actually imposed, the sixty-month probation sentence, but disagreed whether the required replacement sentence was to be a minimum of 20 months *in jail*, or a minimum of 20 months on probation, with jail up to six months still possible on resentencing. Justices Kennedy and Scalia, separately concurring in the result, chose 20 months' probation; the Chief Justice and Justice Thomas chose a 20-month jail term. Both results are possible on the text, and both are extraordinary. One permits a significant amelioration rather than enhancement of sentence; while that amelioration can be controlled against, Congress cannot be imagined to have desired this interpretation. The other interpretation achieves sentence enhancement, but at the cost of offending legality; it *requires* imposition of a longer jail term, after a relatively informal hearing, than could normally have been given even after a criminal trial for drug possession followed by maximum consecutive sentences under the sentencing guidelines for the two offenses that would then have been established.[163]

Finally, *Ratzlaf v United States*, Justice Ginsburg's second opinion for the Court, also for a majority of five.[164] As a means (in part) of tracing money laundering, 31 USC § 5313 requires banks and other financial institutions to report transactions involving $10,000 or more in cash. Section 5324(3) makes it illegal, "for the purpose of evading [these] reporting requirements," to "structure . . . any transaction," and § 5322(a) states the criminal penalties applicable to anyone "willfully violating" § 5324(3) and other provisions of these reporting statutes. *Ratzlaf* concerned the problem of scienter under these statutes. Casino employees had driven Ratzlaf from bank to bank in Reno and Lake Tahoe to facilitate his cash purchase of $9,500 bank checks to meet his large gambling debt to the casino. He and they plainly knew that he was structuring his transaction

---

[163] The usual maximum sentences under the guidelines would be six months for the mail offense, one year for possession of cocaine.

[164] 114 S Ct 655. Not until her fourth opinion of the Term did Justice Ginsburg succeed in attracting the concurrence of all her colleagues, although, traditionally, a new Justice's first assigned opinion has been a unanimous one.

in order to avoid the reports that would have to be made if he paid the casino with the cash he at first brought them, or bought larger bank checks. But the jury was told it did not need to find he knew that this structuring was unlawful.

Justice Ginsburg was joined by Justices Stevens, Scalia, Kennedy, and Souter in concluding that "willfully violating" entailed that the government *did* have to make that showing. That had been the conclusion the courts of appeals had reached in prior interpretations of scienter requirements under other provisions of 31 USC referred to by § 5322(a). The majority thought people would often "structure" cash transactions for reasons other than giving some hint that they possessed cash from illegal sources—to hide it, for example, from a divorcing spouse or others who might be looking for signs of wealth. Both in its attention to general consistency and in its attention to other factual patterns proposed interpretations could affect, the majority opinion was unexceptional; arguments from text have the strongest claim in criminal cases, as it remarked, and here the text, thus illuminated, persuaded it that Congress meant to require knowledge of the unlawfulness of structuring as an element of the offense.

Justice Blackmun wrote the dissent, joined by the Chief Justice and Justices O'Connor and Thomas. With the exception of Justice Blackmun, the dissenters are among those who during the Term generally opposed the use of materials and arguments from congressional process. Yet the dissent relied on two process arguments for its conclusion that knowledge of unlawfulness need not be shown. First, it argued, § 5324 was enacted *after* the rest of the subchapter had been in place for some years, as a direct response to private structuring of transactions to avoid the desired reporting. The amendment expresses directly the element of purpose Congress wished to capture. Knowing this history of development, the dissent argued, undercuts the claim that the umbrella phrase "willfully violating" of § 5322(a), generally applicable to the subchapter, introduced an unusual requirement of knowledge here. Second, the dissent reasoned, the legislative history indicates (as the majority virtually conceded) that Congress meant to require no more than knowledge of (and purpose to evade) the reporting requirements. The text ought to be interpreted faithfully to that history. These are, of course, quite standard arguments. What is striking is to find these three Justices, perhaps especially Justice

Thomas, joining an opinion that relies so heavily on the context in which Congress acted, and on the political history of its particular actions, as its bases for understanding what Congress has said.

V. Cases Implicating the Judgment of an Administrative Agency

A. DIRECTOR, OFFICE OF WORKERS' COMPENSATION PROGRAMS V GREENWICH COLLIERIES, INC. AND HAWAIIAN AIRLINES V NORRIS

The question in *Director, Office of Workers' Compensation Programs v Greenwich Collieries*[165] was whether the Department of Labor could rule for benefit claimants, in cases arising under programs it administered, if the evidence supporting the claim was in equipoise; or, was the Department statutorily required to assign claimants the burden of ultimate persuasion (i.e., demonstration by a preponderance of the evidence). Two different programs were involved; under one, the Department had been ruling for claimants if evidence was equally balanced for more than 50 years; in the other, it had been doing so for more than 15 years. Since 1946, however, the Administrative Procedure Act has provided that "[e]xcept as otherwise provided by statute, the proponent of a rule or order has the burden of proof,"[166] and no statutory provision allocated the burden of proof under either benefit program. The question for the Court was whether this concededly applicable provision precluded the Department's pro-claimant stance.

The question may not have much practical importance. Since the "preponderance" test is satisfied by the slightest differences in proof, equipoise must be an unusual outcome. And presumably the Department could find other ways to favor claimants in considering the evidence. Yet the issue is harder than a first reading of the statute might suggest. "Burden of proof," as all the Justices recognized, is an ambiguous phrase. It might mean the burden of showing that a claim is plausible—frequently referred to as the burden of production, of going forward, or of establishing a prima facie case; or, it could mean the burden of ultimate persuasion. The Court divided 6–3; its opinions again reflect the contrast between static and developmental approaches to issues of meaning, and the usual prevalence of the former.

---

[165] 114 S Ct 2251 (1994).

[166] 5 USC § 556(d).

Justice O'Connor, for herself and five others,[167] identified the interpretive task as "ascertain[ing] the ordinary meaning of 'burden of proof' in 1946, the year the APA was enacted";[168] ultimately she concluded that "burden of ultimate persuasion" was what had been meant. This was not an easy intellectual process, and in it Justice O'Connor consulted a range of materials rather broader than those the more formal members of the Court usually seemed willing to consider—the understanding of "burden of proof" in the legal community, courts, and commentators in the years leading up to the APA's passage, and its legislative history before the Congress. Justice Souter's dissent for himself and Justices Stevens and Blackmun makes a reasonable argument that the majority reached the wrong result on its own premises, but for our purposes the more notable characteristic of the majority argument, in this respect, may have been its openness to sources beyond the text for understanding what Congress had done.

Several developments occurring *after* 1946 could be thought to bear on the section's meaning: The programs had been administered under a different understanding for years; for one of them, the Secretary plausibly claimed to have varied the APA's application by departmental rule, as the governing statute permitted. An intervening Supreme Court precedent had summarily rejected the "burden of persuasion" interpretation of § 7(c), remarking with supporting lower court citation that the section "determines only the burden of going forward, not the burden of persuasion."[169] Other Supreme Court opinions and a significant body of precedent in the lower courts built on this understanding. The majority credited none of these developments. It characterized the departmental rule in question as general in terms; the majority did "not think this regulation can fairly be read as authorizing the Department's rule and rejecting the APA's burden of proof provision"[170]—a thought that neglected both the frequently expressed obligation to defer to an agency's interpretations of its own rules[171] and the possibility that, at the time, the Secretary might not have thought she was "rejecting" what the APA provided.

---

[167] The Chief Justice and Justices Scalia, Kennedy, Thomas, and Ginsburg.

[168] 114 S Ct at 2255.

[169] *NLRB v Transportation Management Corp.*, 462 US 393, 404 n 7 (1983).

[170] 114 S Ct at 2254.

[171] See *Thomas Jefferson University v Shalala*, discussed in text at p 525.

The majority also put aside the Court's own prior construction of § 7(c), despite what it acknowledged to be "the importance of adhering to precedent, particularly in a case involving statutory interpretation."[172] It deprecated the prior interpretation as a "cursory conclusion,"[173] to which limited attention had been given in the briefs of that case. That conclusion also was in "tension" with a somewhat earlier Supreme Court interpretation of § 7(c) that had not mentioned the "burden of persuasion" approach but could be argued to support it by implication.[174] The majority did not now ask, however, whether this "tension" had been generating practical difficulties; and there appear to have been deficiencies in the briefing in *Greenwich Collieries* as well as in the earlier precedent: As the dissent remarked in a note,[175] none of the parties argued for overruling the Court's previous decision (one amicus did), and the lower courts had not considered that issue. Effectively conceding that the text of § 7(c) *could* be given either the "burden of persuasion" or the "burden of production" meaning, the only reason the majority gave for changing the law governing "burden of persuasion" in 1994 is its judgment that this is what Congress likely chose in 1946.

Justice Souter's dissent also addressed what Congress probably understood "burden of proof" to mean in 1946, but it was far more concerned with what the judiciary had done with the phrase since its adoption. The majority directly discussed only the two post-1946 Supreme Court decisions mentioned above, and did so only to set forth their doctrine. The dissent invoked 28 opinions of the courts of appeals either addressing the § 7(c) issue or supporting the application of the Department's rule in benefits claim cases; it cited as well every major treatise on federal administrative law as uncritically accepting, indeed supportive of, the "burden of production" interpretation. And it also showed how this "burden of

---

[172] 114 S Ct at 2258. Where high stakes and accompanying visibility for the Court's actions have produced strong pressures around this issue, Justice O'Connor has strongly asserted the values of stare decisis in statutory matters. Compare the discussion of *Patterson*, in the text at page 459 ff, and *Planned Parenthood of Southeastern Pennsylvania v Casey*, 112 S Ct 2791 (1992); and see Edward H. Levi, *An Introduction to Legal Reasoning* 57 (1949).

[173] 114 S Ct at 2257.

[174] *Steadman v SEC*, 450 US 91 (1981).

[175] 114 S Ct at 2263 n 4. Compare the discussion of *Central Bank of Denver v First Interstate Bank of Denver* at page 510.

production" understanding and acceptance of the Department's rule had worked its way into the Court's own jurisprudence in other cases not directly presenting the issue.[176]

If it were the highly controversial source of continuing debate, an open-and-shut question, or a matter of large practical significance, one might see a need to readdress an issue apparently put to rest on an earlier occasion; yet the Court has recently been attentive to stare decisis in such cases.[177] The burden of proof issue is none of these, and that makes all the more remarkable the majority's insouciance about ripping up a fabric of understanding the Court's actions had contributed to creating. It is not evident why the considerations underlying stability in law should be less commanding as to a matter not put forward by the parties and as to which high social stakes cannot easily be identified. The question was well settled; the issue was at best debatable even in 1946; and the only negative consequence the Court suggests arising from the existing understanding is that it would leave agencies with some discretion to allocate the burden of persuasion programmatically. This was, however, discretion they had enjoyed for the preceding decades without demonstrated inconvenience or confusion, discretion that would be granted by the alternative, permissible understanding of the language Congress employed, and discretion that would have at best marginal impact on outcomes.[178] The result is to underscore both the formally static quality of the Court's approach and its destabilizing potential. Fundamentally, the majority was concerned *only* with determining what the statute had meant in 1946. Although stare decisis might in some circumstances force the Court to swallow an intervening "error," the statute would always mean what it had meant on enactment. Common law processes could not work upon it, even within the room concededly

---

[176] Id at 2265, discussing *Ward's Cove Packing Co. v Antonio*, 490 US 642 (1989), and *Mullins Coal Co. v Director, Office of Workers' Compensation Programs, Dept. of Labor*, 484 US 135 (1987), and 114 S Ct at 2266 n 6, listing five cases in which the Court had accepted allocation of the burden of persuasion on a program-by-program basis, following "customary reference to statutory text, congressional intent, experience, policy, and relevant evidentiary probabilities."

[177] See note 171.

[178] The majority recognized that presumptions and an administrative attitude of solicitude for claimants would have the same kind of effect as the proposition that a claimant wins if, he having satisfied their burden of production, persons opposing their claim fail to persuade that it should not be granted. At 114 S Ct 2259.

left open by its text. Understandings and structures that had grown up in the interim were irrelevant to the Court's task—what the law had effectively become, a house of cards.[179]

While this style was a common one during the Term, as this essay may suggest, it was not universal. On the same day as *Greenwich Collieries*, the Court announced a unanimous opinion reflecting much greater willingness to integrate statutory and decisional materials accumulating over time. *Hawaiian Airlines v Norris*[180] required the Court to interpret a provision of the Railway Labor Act, extended to airlines in 1936, that might have preempted state law; uncontroversially identifying the question as one of congressional intent, the Court held that it did not. To reach this conclusion, Justice Blackmun's opinion considers statutory text, legislative history, and—most importantly for these purposes—the course of judicial opinions from the time of the statute's enactment as well as the relation of this issue to like issues arising under other statutes. All this appears quite unself-conscious; and it points in a direction of a unifying test that joins the preemption issue under the RLA with a similar one that had arisen under the Labor Management Relations Act. "[T]he common purposes of the two statutes, the parallel development of RLA and LMRA pre-emption law, and the desirability of having a uniform common law of labor law pre-emption support the application of the [LMRA] standard in RLA cases as well."[181]

One could hardly imagine a stronger contrast with *Greenwich Collieries*. Pre-emption is a question of congressional intent, but here one finds no suggestion that the issue was fixed as of the RLA's enactment (or its 1936 extension to airlines); the Court accepts as consistent with its idea that pre-emption is a matter for legislative determination, the idea that a test articulated under a different, later statute is the right one to apply here. It does not require any evidence of congressional action on, or even thought about, its application to the RLA. The appropriateness of the courts' creating

---

[179] For a recent, somewhat more theoretically inclined approach to these issues, see William N. Eskridge, Jr., *Post-Enactment Legislative Signals*, 57 L & Contemp Probs 75 (1994).

[180] 114 S Ct 2239.

[181] Id at 2249 n 9; to somewhat similar effect, see the Court's unanimous opinion in *Lividas v Bradshaw*, 114 S Ct 2068; see also Justice Stevens's opinion for a unanimous Court in *McDermott v Amclyde*, 114 S Ct 1461, a strictly common law matter.

a "unified system of judge-made and statute law . . . by the processes of adjudication"[182] is simply assumed.

The tendency of this approach, as Justice Stone well recognized, is to promote coherence in law, to induce stability in its administration, to reward expectations, to discourage dispute. To see where the *Greenwich Collieries* approach might lead, consider the issue of standing to challenge administrative actions. This APA issue is more controversial than "burden of proof"; it is one where the Court's "error" in departing from 1946 understandings is more readily shown; and it is one that has larger consequences. Section 10(a) of the APA[183] provided that "A person suffering legal wrong because of agency action, *or adversely affected or aggrieved by agency action within the meaning of a relevant statute*, is entitled to judicial review thereof." In 1970, the Supreme Court interpreted the italicized language as itself conferring standing on persons concretely injured by agency action, so long as the injury could reasonably be thought one the underlying statute was concerned to avoid.[184] The language can support the 1970 interpretation; that interpretation is strongly consonant with administrative law developments of the late 1960's and following that emphasized participatory values in administrative process and, in particular, greatly expanded the claims of those who were the intended beneficiaries (rather than the intended subjects) of regulation to have a part in administrative action at all levels. This judicial development was both led[185] and kept in check[186] by the Court; its general course doubtless helps to explain why the APA has not been significantly amended in the almost half century since its enactment. The judiciary has kept the APA more or less in step with developing understandings, as it has the Constitution and other important texts of general law.

If what Congress would have understood in 1946 controls, the

---

[182] Stone, note 8.

[183] 5 USC 702.

[184] *Association of Data Processing Service Organizations v Camp*, 397 US 150 (1970). From this perspective, the case adopted for APA review a public law rather than a common law model of standing, in the interesting terms suggested in Cass R. Sunstein, *Standing Injuries*, 1993 Supreme Court Review 37, 53–62. Sunstein generally criticizes *ADAPSO* for its misleading focus on "injury" as if that were independent of law.

[185] For example, in addition to *ADAPSO*, *Abbott Laboratories v Gardner*, 387 US 136 (1967), and *Citizens to Preserve Overton Park v Volpe*, 401 US 402 (1971).

[186] *Vermont Yankee Nuclear Power Corp. v NRDC*, 435 US 519 (1978).

contemporary interpretation of § 10(a) is more clearly in error than the Department of Labor approach challenged in *Greenwich Collieries*.[187] Where the ambiguity of "burden of proof" was well known in 1946, *no one* was asserting a doctrine of generalized standing to challenge agency actions for citizens intended to have been benefited by regulation and concretely injured by some failure of effort on an agency's part. Rather, Congress had passed a few particular statutes for the prominent agencies that explicitly provided participatory rights to persons who would be adversely affected or aggrieved by agency action, and these provisions had been held to authorize those persons to seek judicial review of agency outcomes that harmed their interests.[188] As it would have been understood in 1946, § 10(a) incorporated—ratified—this approach to statutes with "adversely affected or aggrieved" provisions in them. Had a general, undiscriminating grant been intended, one would expect to find it articulated and debated; those debates are not to be found,[189] and it took a quarter century, until 1970, for that interpretation to emerge. If Congress's likely understanding in 1946 of the words it employed is entitled to prevail, the following quarter century's development in administrative law—now on a matter of large significance—is in the balance.

This Court is deeply concerned with standing issues, a majority approaching them with a sensibility suggesting they would be happy for the chance to retrench.[190] Is that what *Greenwich Collieries* promises? Perhaps some or all signers of the majority opinion would find, in the standing context, that correcting the Court's earlier error in discerning what § 10(a) had meant in 1946 would have so large an effect on the general fabric of the law that stare decisis considerations would control. But even that way of putting

---

[187] The reader is entitled to know that my name was on the government's brief in *ADAPSO*, and that I argued the companion case of *Barlow v Collins*, 397 US 159 (1970) for the government; the government opposed standing in both cases. In my judgment, the Court did not act impermissibly in 1970, although it abandoned 1946 meaning; while it follows that the 1970 meaning, too, has no claim to permanence, change must be grounded in the general law and circumstances of 1994, not those of 1946.

[188] See *Associated Industries of New York State v Ickes*, 134 F2d 694 (2d Cir 1943).

[189] See *The Attorney General's Manual on the Administrative Procedure Act* 96 (1947).

[190] See Justice O'Connor's in-chambers opinion granting a stay in anticipation of a denial of standing in *INS v Legalization Assistance Project*, 114 S Ct 422 (1993); see also *Lujan v Defenders of Wildlife*, 112 S Ct 2130 (1992); Cass R. Sunstein, *What's Standing After Lujan*, 91 Mich L Rev 163 (1992).

it suggests a significant difference in stance from opinions like *Hawaiian Airlines*. It would be accompanied by expressions of regret and acceptance rather than affirmation of a judicial choice among possible meanings that had been shaped by intervening changes in law, accepted over time by Congress and by the people.[191] The Court in 1970 did not seem to imagine the APA as forever tied to 1946, until a later Congress was motivated to change it. The language Congress had used could be read and interpreted in 1970, within the general framework of law as it had developed to that point and was developing. One Court acts as Congress's partner and in the framework of development familiar to the common law; for the other, judicial development is illegitimate and statutes are fixed, static events.

B. MCI TELECOMMUNICATIONS CORP. V AMERICAN TELEPHONE AND
TELEGRAPH CO. AND NORTHWEST AIRLINES, INC. V COUNTY OF
KENT, MICHIGAN

In 1934, when the technological constraints imposed by wire transmission of telephone conversations gave AT&T a natural monopoly of interstate transmission, Congress enacted 47 USC § 203, requiring the FCC to regulate interstate telephone rates; the same section permitted the Commission "in its discretion and for good cause shown, [to] *modify* any requirement" (emphasis added) of the section imposing this requirement, except that it could not impose a longer than 120 day notice period on carriers seeking rate changes. By the 1970s, the development of microwave and satellite technologies permitted competition in interstate telephone services to develop. The same period found many economists and others vigorously criticizing rate regulation in general as an often inefficient regulatory technique, one that served to create barriers to entry into otherwise competitive markets and in other ways to keep the rates the public was charged for services above, rather than below, what they would naturally be in an unregulated market. The legal environment, as well, showed a strong deregulatory trend. Responding to these developments, the FCC used public rule making gradually to relax and then to eliminate rate-filing requirements for AT&T's new competitors (the "non-dominant

---

[191] Compare the discussion of *Patterson*, in text at page 459 ff.

carriers"). In doing so, it relied on its statutory authority to "modify" rate regulation requirements. Congress, sharply cutting back on rate regulation elsewhere in national regulation, did not alter the Commission's statutory mandate.

MCI Telecommunications Corp. v American Telephone and Telegraph Co.[192] required the Court to decide whether the FCC's action was within its authority. The thrust of Justice Scalia's opinion for five members[193] of the Court was that "modify" does not permit changes as large as these; Justice Stevens wrote for three[194] in dissent. The opinions were in one respect a duel over the use of dictionaries; in another, a dispute over the application of the Court's influential opinion in *Chevron, U.S.A., Inc. v Natural Resources Defense Council, Inc.*,[195] describing the courts' appropriate relationship to agency gap-filling on questions of law unresolved by statute.

The dictionary duel, easily caricatured, was in some respects the Term's textualist apogee.[196] For Justice Scalia, "modify" necessarily connoted incrementalism, not major change, and he supported this conclusion with dictionary evidence. The making of minor changes, without radical transformation, was a meaning dictionaries universally attached to the term. While one major dictionary had recently also included among its possible definitions "to make a basic or important change in," he regarded that inclusion— rendering "modify" a synonym of "change"—as unpersuasive, one that served to make the word more ambiguous than it had previously been. Justice Stevens expressed doubt whether dictionaries should be permitted to "substitute for close analysis of what words mean as used in a particular statutory context";[197] he argued that in the larger context the Commission's changes were only incremental. Since rate filing would still characterize the bulk of interstate tariffs, those of the dominant carrier AT&T, the general pur-

---

[192] 114 S Ct 2223.

[193] The Chief Justice and Justices Kennedy, Thomas, and Ginsburg; Justice O'Connor did not participate.

[194] Also Justices Blackmun and Souter.

[195] 467 US 837 (1984).

[196] See, e.g., Pierce, cited in note 46, which well illustrates the destabilizing potential; A. Raymond Randolph, *Dictionaries, Plain Meaning, and Context in Statutory Interpretation*, 17 Harv J L & Pub Pol 71 (1994), suggests the limits.

[197] 114 S Ct at 2236.

pose and effect of the statute would remain intact. And he pointed out that the FCC's action fit well the earliest and still primary dictionary meaning of "modify," to *limit or reduce* in extent or degree. Dictionaries consistently list the "minor change" sense Justice Scalia relied on *after* definitions suggesting limitation or reduction.

Justice Scalia's opinion in *MCI* does not appear as committed as Justice O'Connor's in *Greenwich Collieries* to the position that only direct congressional action can change the meaning of statutes. When Justice Scalia refers to dictionary definitions current when the provision became law in 1934, he calls it "perhaps gilding the lily" but "the most relevant time for determining a statutory term's meaning";[198] "large change" was not in the dictionaries then (although the primary sense of limiting or ameliorating was). Later he considers and rejects the proposition that subsequent legislative changes may have signaled congressional approval of the FCC's position; finding those changes mixed in their implication, he argues that

> We have here not a consistent history of legislation to which one or the other interpretation of the Act is essential; but rather two pieces of legislation to which first one, and then the other interpretation of the Act is more congenial. That is not enough to change anything.[199]

"Most relevant" is different from "only"; willingness to consider a consistent subsequent history implies acceptance that meaning *could* change without direct amendment. Yet that change would have to be ascribable to Congress in some sense; neither the agency's nor the court's sense of developing social and economic circumstances, and the supervening structure of law, would authorize a departure from the 1934 understanding.

Perhaps the root issue for Justice Scalia is one of delegation—a factor that has been important to him in other contexts.[200] It is not merely the largeness of the change being effected, but also that accepting it will entail accepting that an agency can be empowered to change its mandate. For Justice Stevens, author of striking passages in *Chevron* strongly endorsing delegation,[201] the FCC has "un-

---

[198] Id at 2230.

[199] Id at 2233.

[200] *Mistretta v United States*, 488 US 361, 413–27 (1989) (Scalia dissenting).

[201] 467 US at 843–44 (1984).

usually broad discretion to meet new and unanticipated problems in order to fulfill its sweeping mandate";[202] this power to "modify" is no different in kind from the Commission's responsibility to allocate licenses and otherwise act in accordance with "public convenience, interest, or necessity."[203] Justice Scalia accepts broad delegations only because he cannot imagine a judicially manageable standard for telling the good from the bad,[204] a handicap he does not face if he can plausibly construe an agency's authority in a narrow way. It is revealing in this respect that he never explains how he concludes that the New Deal Congress that so broadly empowered all the agencies it created, not just the FCC, intended here only a narrow grant of authority.

The result, in any event, is essentially formal and text-bound. Whether the FCC has rightly caught the implications of new market conditions and adapted its regulatory regime to them are not issues for the Court. "[O]ur estimations, and the Commission's estimations, of desirable policy cannot alter the meaning of the Federal Communications Act of 1934. . . . [A] whole new regime of regulation (or of free-market competition) . . . may well be a better regime but is not the one that Congress established."[205] Of course, the validity of the "but is not" clause depends on one's conclusions about the meaning of "modify," one's general estimation of the breadth of authority Congress bestowed on the Commission, and also on one's acceptance or not of agency and/or judicial authority to follow Congress's lead by using existing text to adapt law to changing circumstances. In its way, the change worked by the FCC is no different from what the Court accomplished in *Hawaiian Airlines*. Looking to the general climate of change, in regulation and in technology, it is hard to imagine that the FCC erred. The general trend of legislation, the absence of any legislative effort to correct the Commission, indeed the Commission's dogged persistence in its deregulatory course despite prior discouragement from the courts—all suggest that this was the right reading. It was one that both ancient and contemporary understandings of "modify" would permit. The insistence that Congress unmistak-

---

[202] 114 S Ct at 2234.

[203] Id at 2239 n 7.

[204] *Mistretta*, cited in note 200, 488 US at 415 ff.

[205] 114 S Ct at 2233.

ably act tends, again, to deny the coherence-building judicial function.

Northwest Airlines, Inc. v County of Kent, Michigan[206] provides a contrast with *MCI* that is not as strong as that between *Greenwich Collieries* and *Hawaiian Airlines*, but that is nonetheless suggestive. The case concerned the legality of airport user fees under both a federal statute, the Anti-Head Tax Act,[207] and the Commerce Clause of the United States Constitution. The AHTA flatly forbids states and their subdivisions from taxing persons traveling in air commerce, their carriage, or the gross receipts derived from the sale of air transportation; but as explicitly permits other forms of tax, such as property or net income tax, and, of particular importance to this litigation, also permits "collecting *reasonable* rental charges, landing fees, and other service charges from aircraft operators for the use of airport facilities." The issue the parties presented was the application of this permission to particular use charges imposed on commercial aviation by a Michigan airport; Justice Ginsburg concluded for all but Justice Thomas[208] that, applying a judicial test developed in the Commerce Clause context, the fees were "reasonable."

The contrast with *MCI* is provided by the possibility that an agency—in this case, the Department of Transportation's Federal Aviation Administration—might initially have assessed whether the fees were reasonable or not. The airlines challenging the reasonableness of Kent's charges might have initiated an action before the FAA, but did not, choosing instead to invoke a private right of action in district court. The Court might have decided that no such right of action was to be implied from the AHTA; but that question was not jurisdictional, the Court ruled, and the posture of the case made it otherwise unavailable. Similarly, the Court might have decided that the doctrine of primary jurisdiction required the district court to have referred the matter to the FAA for decision; again, the parties had failed to raise this issue.[209] In bypassing the second of these issues, the Court signaled its preference for

---

[206] 114 S Ct 855.

[207] 49 USC App § 1513.

[208] Justice Blackmun did not participate.

[209] See *New England Legal Foundation v Massachusetts Port Authority*, 883 F2d 157 (1st Cir 1989), cited by the Court, 114 S Ct at 863 n 11.

administrative treatment—recognizing that courts "are scarcely equipped to oversee [such questions] without the initial superintendence of a regulatory agency," reciting the advantages of national administration, and promising *Chevron* deference "[i]f we had the benefit of the Secretary's reasoned decision." This strongly voiced preference to have an agency give initial voice to what is "reasonable" and promise of deference to its views—perhaps the most forceful *Chevron* statement of the Term[210]—contrasts with the Court's refusal to accept agency views of the undefined "modify" in *MCI*.[211]

That contrast is underscored by Justice Thomas's lone dissent; he argued that "reasonable" failed to set a judicially administrable standard under the statute, so that the permissibility or not of the exactions in question could be decided only under the dormant Commerce Clause—an issue not developed in the case, and so requiring remand.[212] In its insistence that Congress create an administrable standard other than the "common law" standard the Court had developed under the dormant Commerce Clause, his opinion appears to reflect delegation concerns such as also seem to underlie *MCI*; it is hard for him to imagine "such unbridled discretion" for the Secretary.[213] Again, we see that, for him, what judges can do as a matter of their separately judicial capacity appears to be quite different from, and also completely isolated from, what they may do in the administration of statutes. If this is not a concern for the Justices of the *MCI majority*, perhaps that is because "modify" can be cabined in ways "reasonable" cannot;[214] or because the authority to say what is "reasonable" or not, however broad, is *not* authority to define one's own scope of regulation and so does raise delegation concerns in the same way. The Court's recognition

---

[210] See Merrill, cited in note 41.

[211] And also the agency views in the next discussed case, *City of Chicago v Envirnomental Defense Fund*, 114 S Ct 1588 (1994).

[212] Justice Thomas's argument in part reflected the origin of the AHTA in congressional disapproval of a Supreme Court opinion—the source of many of the statutes interpreted in the cases discussed in this essay. Neither he nor his colleagues, in this case, directed attention to the political or administrative history of the statute as an indicator of meaning, however.

[213] 114 S Ct at 870 (Thomas dissenting). Compare Justice Thomas's unwillingness to accept a vague regulation as establishing law in *Thomas Jefferson University v Shalala*, discussed at p 526.

[214] See Antonin Scalia, *Judicial Deference to Administrative Interpretations of Law*, 1989 Duke L J 511, 521; cf *Harris v Forklift*, discussed in note 71.

of potential partnership and of the agency's responsibility nonetheless stands in some contrast with *MCI*.

City of Chicago v Environmental Defense Fund[215] required interpretation of an amendment to a complex statute made in response to issues that had arisen in the course of its administration. The amendment had been promptly understood in a particular way by the agency responsible for the statute, a consideration that in the past has often been regarded as probative by courts attempting to decide for themselves questions of statutory meaning. In this case, however, the Court took a textualist view that essentially ignored the implications of political history and administrative signaling for judicial understanding.

The Resource Conservation and Recovery Act of 1976 (RCRA) created a much more stringent regulatory scheme for "hazardous" than for "nonhazardous" wastes. Those who generate hazardous waste are subject to handling, record-keeping, storage, and monitoring requirements;[216] the owners and operators of hazardous waste treatment, storage, and disposal facilities (TSDFs) are subject to considerably more stringent regulation.[217] RCRA does not itself identify which wastes are "hazardous," but authorizes the Environmental Protection Administration to do so by regulation.[218] Since 1980, EPA's regulations have provided that household waste and the residues of its incineration in power generation plants are not "hazardous wastes," even though a small portion of that waste stream (such as discarded batteries) would ordinarily be regarded as hazardous waste and even though the ash resulting from incineration, as a result, might if tested have met the ordinary definitions of "hazardous waste."[219] About 150 cities have been availing themselves of this exemption, including Chicago; Chicago's municipal incinerator gener-

---

[215] 114 S Ct 1588 (1994).

[216] See 42 USC § 6922; 40 CFR pt 262 (1993).

[217] 42 USC §§ 6924–25, 40 CFR pt 264 (1993).

[218] Hazardous wastes are regulated under Schedule C of the Act, 42 USC §§ 6921–34, nonhazardous wastes under Schedule D, 42 USC §§ 6941–49; EPA's authority to designate matters as hazardous or not appears in 42 USC § 6921(a).

[219] 40 CFR 261.4(b)(1). If, for example, lead or cadmium batteries formed part of the household waste stream, the lead or cadmium content of incinerator ash might exceed the EPA standards of concentration and solubility.

ates over 100,000 tons of ash annually, which it has been disposing of at landfills not licensed to receive hazardous wastes.

The 1980 regulation, however, did not exempt incinerator ash from household waste if (1) the incinerator also processed any industrial waste, and (2) the resulting ash met the usual tests of hazardousness. The exemption could be withheld even if all the added industrial waste itself was not "hazardous."[220] This created a somewhat anomalous situation, since the ash from a mixture of household waste and nonhazardous industrial waste would presumably be more dilute than ash from the household waste alone. In 1984, Congress amended RCRA by adding § 3001(i).[221] Entitled the "clarification of household waste exclusion," § 3001(i) provided that "a resource recovery facility recovering energy from the mass burning of municipal solid waste shall not be deemed to be *treating, storing, disposing of, or otherwise managing* hazardous wastes" even if, inter alia, it also burns "solid waste from commercial or industrial sources that does not contain hazardous waste" (emphasis added). EPA interpreted the new provision to ratify its regulation and eliminate the possible anomaly; thus, addition of nonhazardous industrial waste to the household waste stream would not threaten the "nonhazardous" characterization of the resulting ash, whatever its actual chemical content. The Chicago incinerator now includes some nonhazardous commercial waste in its operations.

In 1988, the Environmental Defense Fund brought a citizen's action under RCRA alleging that Chicago was in violation of its obligations respecting the "hazardous waste" it was generating. The city asserted its exemption under the EPA regulation and subsequent statute, and EPA supported the city's view. If "hazardous" means *hazardous*, the exemption Chicago relied upon is not very attractive. To be sure, the degree of hazard presented by municipal incinerator ash may be slight compared to more concentrated sources; further, mixing in ash from nonhazardous industrial sources will dilute the household waste product. Nonetheless, hazards are being generated. And one imagines that the legislative exemption for municipal facilities had its source in politics and the

---

[220] Whether this actually happened is doubtful. The Court was informed that that EPA has "never contended that the acceptance of nonhazardous commercial waste subjected any of [the facilities] to regulation." 114 S Ct at 1598 n 10 (Stevens dissenting).

[221] 42 USC § 6921(i).

realities of municipal economics, rather than scientific judgment about comparative risk. The question for the Court was whether, contrary to EPA's views, Chicago's waste was subject to hazardous waste regulation to any degree.

Justice Scalia wrote for seven Justices, all but Justices Stevens and O'Connor, finding that Chicago must be regulated as a generator if its ash met the physical standards for "hazardous waste," although not as a TSDF. Central to his analysis was the conjunction of four textual observations: first, hazardous and nonhazardous wastes are sharply distinguished in RCRA, with elaborate attention paid to protection of the environment from the ultimate disposition of the former; second, regulation of hazardous wastes and regulation of those who may come in contact with them are distinct subjects, and § 3001(i)'s exemption is directed to the facility producing the ash and not to the ash itself; third, those who merely generate hazardous waste are subject to much less stringent regulation under RCRA than those who subsequently "treat[], stor[e], dispose[e] of, or otherwise manag[e]" it; and, finally, the text of the 1984 amendment omits the word "generation." One can then construct a rational legislative judgment: municipal incinerators should be relieved of the stringent regulation attaching to those who "treat[, etc.,]" but since their processes may generate what is in fact "hazardous waste," the *incinerators* are subject to the less stringent regulatory regime governing generators and—most important—*the ash they produce*, if it has the physical characteristics of "hazardous waste," must be disposed of in hazardous waste facilities.

Considered independently of the amendment's political and administrative history, this is a credible, integrated reading of its text. The statute's dominating purpose to protect the public from the long-term consequences of carelessness in handling materials that threaten the environment is advanced, not merely acknowledged, by a reading that treats § 3001(i) as speaking to how Chicago is to be regulated under the law, rather than how the ash it produces shall be. Justice Stevens's response to the argument at this textual level was plausible, but not commanding: "Clarification of hazardous waste exclusion," the amendment's title, is directed to the exclusion of materials from the category "hazardous waste," not to the exclusion of processors from being regulated. Moreover, Chicago could be "generating" hazardous waste only if its municipal waste stream is not hazardous; but as a description of the physical sitation, if the ash is hazardous, so must the predecessor waste stream be. Finally, reading that Chicago is not to be treated as "disposing of, or otherwise managing hazardous wastes for the purposes of regulation," recipients of the ash would normally conclude they had not received "hazardous wastes." "[I]f we are to be guided only by the literal meaning of the statutory text," Justice Stevens wrote, "we must either give effect to the broad definition of hazardous waste generation and subject all municipal incinerators that generate hazardous ash to [the more stringent forms of] regulation (including those that burn pure household waste) or give effect to the exclusion that applies equally to pure household waste and mixtures that include other nonhazardous wastes."[222] On the text alone, however, and with an eye to the larger purpose of the statute, this does not seem an untoward result. Incinerators that produce physically hazardous ash will be responsible to see that it is handled by persons capable of doing so.

However strong the majority's reading might be as a construction of § 3001(i) in the abstract, it bore no resemblance to the administration RCRA had received from the outset, well before its 1984 amendment by § 3001(i), to the expectations expressed (and natural to suppose) at the time of that amendment, or to the treatment it had subsequently received. Justice Scalia was uninterested, however, whether his was the *actual* legislative judgment Congress had reached in a political sense:

> The plain meaning of this language is that . . . the facility[] is not subject to [the more extensive] regulation as a facility that treats, stores, disposes of, or manages hazardous waste. The provision quite clearly does not contain any exclusion for the ash itself.[223]

While a Senate committee report, the only available legislative evidence as to meaning, had described the exemption in terms that explicitly included "generation,"[224] that language was missing from the statute.

> [I]t is the statute, and not the Committee Report, which is the authoritative expression of the law, and the statute prominently

---

[222] 114 S Ct at 1598.

[223] Id at 1591.

[224] S Rep No 98-284, p 61 (1983), cited at 1593.

omits reference to generation. . . . The incineration here is exempt from [the more stringent form of] regulation, but subject to regulation as hazardous waste generation.[225]

It was irrelevant that EPA had consistently excused these municipal facilities *and their ash stream* from hazardous waste regulation, before as well as after the 1984 amendments; or that the amendment's history reflects not disapproval of that practice but rather (as its title suggests) the purpose to clarify and extend the exception EPA had developed. Whatever the regulation had been, the statutory text now exempted the cities only from TSDF regulation; if their ash met the physical standards, they were now generators of "hazardous waste"—whether or not they mixed nonhazardous commercial waste into their waste streams. In effect, Justice Scalia reasoned, the amendment *disapproved* the EPA regulation.[226] Any thought of deference to EPA's interpretation fell before the observation that "the most reliable guide for [reconciling the diverse purposes of legislation] is the enacted text. Here that requires us to reject the Solicitor General's plea for deference to the EPA's interpretation, which goes beyond the scope of whatever ambiguity § 3001(i) contains."[227]

While it is tempting to discuss here the misleading treatment the legislative history had in the majority's hands,[228] the opinion's ma-

---

[225] Id at 1593.

[226] Id. The EPA history was dismissed in a footnote reserving "opinion as to the validity of EPA's household waste generation regulation as applied to resource recovery facilities before the effective date of § 3001(i)." Id at n 4.

[227] Id at 1594. See Antonin Scalia, *Judicial Deference to Administrative Interpretations of Law*, 1989 Duke L J 511, 521.

[228] In the only explanation of § 3001(i) available to Congress, the Senate Committee Report had used the word "generation," that was not to be found in the statute. S Rep No 98-284, p 61 (1983), cited at 1593. The majority wrote as if the question about legislative history were whether the single mention of the word in the report could, in the abstract, make up for its absence from the statutory text. As in *Shannon v United States*, discussed at page 471, one would agree that it could not; but, also as there, the argument is a straw person. The argument from the legislative history is that the statute had been receiving a certain interpretation—established, known, relied upon by 150 cities that might be affected by the amendment. Were there indications that anyone thought Congress might be moving to increase EPA's regulation of municipal incinerators and their waste streams—a matter one might suppose would draw fire—much less that that was an announced purpose of the changes? Justice Stevens's argument is that what is in the legislative history, like the name Congress "significantly" attached to its action, "Clarification of household waste exclusion," confirms that its members had expansion rather than retraction of the existing exemption in view. "A commonsense reading of the statutory text in light of the Committee Report *and against the background of the 1980 regulation* reveals an obvious purpose to preserve, not to change, the existing rule. The majority's refusal to attach significance to 'a single word in a committee report' reveals either a misunderstanding of, or a lack of respect for, the

jor significance for the predictability and stability of law in an administrative state, in my judgment, lies in its withdrawal of attention from the elements of continuity and responsibility in regulatory regimes—in Justice Scalia's attitude toward the history over time of RCRA's provisions and EPA's administration of them. Over half a century ago, and in the same breath as it described the interpretation of statutes in justiciable controversies "[a]s exclusively a judicial function," the Supreme Court recognized in *United States v American Trucking Association*[229] at least three conventional reasons for a court to consider a responsible agency's interpretations in reaching its own conclusions about meaning:

> in any case such interpretations are entitled to great weight. This is peculiarly true . . . where the interpretations involve "contemporaneous construction of a statute by the men charged with the responsibility of setting its machinery in motion, of making the parts work efficiently and smoothly while they are yet untried and new." Furthermore, . . . [agency] interpretation gains much persuasiveness [if it is] the fact that it was the [agency] which suggested the provisions' enactment to Congress.[230]

That is, as of 1940, three propositions were well established: First, the agency is an expert reader of its statute and consequently its reading is some evidence of what Congress did. Second, when the agency is a *prompt* reader as well, the likelihood that it has understood Congress is increased; the absence of an immediate challenge or controversy both confirms that belief and contributes to establishing community expectations about legal requirements, enhancing "efficient[] and smooth[]" implementation. Finally, as a participant in the drafting process (and the subject of oversight discipline as well), an agency is well placed to know what legislation is to achieve. Note that the *American Trucking Association* Court's focus here was on accurate *judicial* interpretation, not on reasons why a court has to accept an agency's reading of an ambiguous statute once it has concluded that its meaning is not clear (*Chevron*'s "step

---

function of legislative committees. . . . What makes the Report significant is not the single word 'generation,' but the unmistakable intent to maintain an existing rule of law." 114 S Ct at 1597 and n 7 (emphasis supplied; the last two sentences quoted are from a footnote appended to the first sentence quoted). Compare *SEC v Collier*, 76 F2d 939 (2d Cir 1935) (L. Hand, J).

[229] 310 US 534 (1940).

[230] Id at 549.

two"). Like other elements of the political process that can help a court form a context in which to understand the language Congress employed, these considerations are elements that enter into the court's own initial assessment of the statute, numbered among the "traditional tools of statutory interpretation"[231] a court is to deploy at *Chevron*'s step one. In abandoning these aids to its own interpretation of that text, in my judgment, the Court significantly undercut the general stability of law.

Such an accusation warrants a few paragraphs' further explication, which should begin by acknowledging that change and stability are both ends of the law. Judicial administration of law must *always* mediate the threat that interpretations, of necessity backward-looking, will defeat expectations engendered before they occur. As law and legal institutions have become more prolix and more complex over time, however, the point at which the courts will finally speak has been delayed, and the possibility of ultimate judicial resolution has become much more remote.[232] Expectations will have been generated, and people will have had to act, without waiting on the courts. The courts have developed a variety of means for encouraging and maintaining expectation. While textualist approaches are supported in just these terms, the questions of responsibility these developments raise and their implications, as in *City of Chicago*, have not been clearly faced.

Within the traditional framework of common law, understanding the importance of reliance on current understandings has made courts chary of overrulings or even sudden departures from received traditions of analysis. Changes are constructed out of movements and trends already in place; few new rules or overrulings occur which counsel could not see looming in possibility. Statutes present harder issues in this respect—they do not have their source

---

[231] *Chevron*, 467 US at 843 n 9; see in this respect the Court's well-regarded opinion in *Skidmore v Swift & Co.*, 323 US 134 (1944), detailing the elements of agency interpretation that, "while not controlling upon the courts by reason of their authority, do constitute a body of experience and informed judgment to which courts *and litigants* may properly resort for guidance." Id at 140 (emphasis added). The resort by litigants—that is, by members of the public—occurs early in a process that may never reach the judiciary; it is encouraged by Congress, and tends to produce uniformity and acceptance of sensible administration. Justice Jackson's invocation of this reliance in *Skidmore* was hardly accidental or incidental, but a reaffirmation of the designedly central role of agencies in statutes under administration.

[232] See Peter L. Strauss, *One Hundred Fifty Cases Per Year: Some Implications of the Supreme Court's Limited Resources for Judicial Review of Agency Action*, 87 Colum L Rev 1093 (1987).

in judicial reasoning, and often enough have been passed in reaction to rather than support of judicial development of law. The challenge for the courts, seemingly met in the first half of this century, was to transcend a resulting sense of struggle with the legislatures and find means of interpretation that tended to correspond with expectations induced by the fact of passage. Courts were not interpreting statutes in the abstract, but in the midst of continuing growth and change in a legal community with ends in view and expectations about the results being produced. Putting aside for the moment the reasonable arguments that can be made of how well the legislative history tools developed for achieving these ends can still succeed in the face of changes in the legislative process, one can see how judicial attention to the political context as well as the text of legislation will have an effect similar to attention to precedent in the common law context, in bringing judicial decisions into line with social and professional expectations about what statutory text means.[233]

The administrative agency is in many respects a competitor with the courts in the formation both of public policy, and of public and professional expectations about law's course. Often enough, assignment of matters to administrative agencies amounts to a declaration of distrust in the judiciary's ability or disposition to manage the work entailed. As a practical matter, their creation means that citizens and lawyers look to agencies in the first instance for their understanding of law's demands. Judicial speaking to the same issues is significantly postponed—they must run the agency gauntlet first. People must arrange their affairs—decide, for example, whether to construct a municipal incinerator—and cannot afford to wait the five years or more it may require to get a judicial reading. The system of law requires some general confidence that ultimate judicial results will match the expectations generated today, on the basis of which such plans are, as they must be, made. Promoting that reliance is, itself, a part of the legislative scheme. And one can see without difficulty how elements such as the Court identified in *American Trucking Association* contribute to that continuity—they tend to match judicial outcomes to the predictable expectations of the community subject to the agency's jurisdiction.

---

[233] The argument is intended to concede that text is the primary source of understanding, but not that text should be read in ignorance of its provenance.

They accommodate the courts to the agency's presence and contribution, just as attention to political history accommodated courts to the emergence of statutes as the dominant mode of law creation. A judiciary that refuses to educate itself in the historical, political, and administrative context from which it emerged invites disappointing expectations the public naturally has. The arbitrariness of the outcomes, in relation to the process that generated them, invites clever argument and gaming as well; and the judiciary, with fewer colors to its palette, will inevitably produce surprising outcomes.[234]

The textualist response is that Congress and the agencies, understanding that the judiciary will limit itself to the statutory text, will respond with clearer expressions. Here again we touch a large literature of debate about the perfectibility of expression that is not necessary to repeat. Regarding the agency contribution, however, it may be appropriate to add these thoughts: First, the problem with statutes today is rarely that they are too terse, but the opposite. Many ascribe that to Congress's interaction with the agencies—its wish to see them well-instructed. Courts are not necessarily performing a public service, or generating more readily predictable outcomes, in encouraging Congress to be more verbose.[235] Second, inviting the *agencies* to rely on text alone, disregarding political background and understanding, will if successful destabilize agency administration, which is even more subject to political pressures than are the courts.[236] Third, it is hard to imagine that such an invitation would be consistently acted upon, given the different settings in which agencies and courts work. Finally, and most important in my judgment, the turn to text, even if the agencies make it, still delegitimizes their role and defeats the possibility of justified reliance on their actions. Absent some principles like those of *American Trucking*, principles wholly missing in *City of Chicago*, the agencies' efforts with the text will be no more than an interesting prelude to the judiciary's reading. They will not contribute to the generation of law; the incentives these principles provide against litigation will drop away. And, in this way, the

---

[234] See Merrill (cited in note 41), 72 Wash U L Q at 372.

[235] See Lieber, quoted in note 33.

[236] Peter L. Strauss, *When the Judge Is Not the Primary Official with Responsibility to Read: Agency Interpretation and the Problem of Legislative History*, 66 Chi Kent L Rev 321 (1990).

courts' work in the middle part of this century, accommodating themselves to agencies' as they had to statutes' intrusions on their work of law administration, will have been discarded.

The central point here is that the textualist, static approach denies the conversational, evolutionary character of the congressional-agency relationship. In relation to private conduct, judges have no difficulty in accepting such realities. Thus, Justice Scalia uttered the epigram of this essay in concurring with an otherwise unanimous opinion (the opinion, otherwise uninteresting here, turned on a Treasury Department regulation requiring the disclaimer of a trust interest within a "reasonable time" of the interest's creation, to escape gift tax):

> The justification for the "reasonable time" limitation must, as always, be a textual one. It consists, in my view, of the fact that the failure to make a reasonably prompt disclaimer of a known bequest is an implicit acceptance. *Qui tacet, consentire videtur.*[237]

Acceptance of the same "textual" justification to govern the closely watched behavior of federal agencies (and courts) administering federal statutes would have led to different results here and in many other cases.

We can perhaps imagine why Justice Scalia might argue that Congress's behavior cannot be treated in the same fashion as the taxpayer who failed to disclaim. Under the Constitution, Congress legislates only by the action of both houses with presentment to the President. Its silence cannot create legislation. This may be conceded. It only carries the day as an argument, however, if one *also* holds that the courts and the agencies are not also authorized to make law—to fill in gaps as well as to interpret—in partnership with Congress. *That* is the move, the radical segregation of the legislative from the judicial and administrative enterprise, the denial of joint effort, that is the engine of these opinions. Otherwise, we do not have to say that Congress by silence has amended the statute, as self-evidently it has not; rather, we say that the congressional silence (along with other factors) arms the interpretation that, like their other work, courts are adopting *in their own right*, attempting as best they can to pursue "the ideal of a unified system

---

[237] *United States v Irvine*, 114 S Ct 1473, 1483 (1994).

of judge-made and statute law woven into a seamless whole by the processes of adjudication."[238] In the context of their common law responsibilities, courts fill in gaps; in exercising delegated power, agencies do so as well. The proposition that they are disabled from doing so in dealing with legislation, far from obvious, is not just a reaction to recent excesses; it defeats the last century of American law.

Wouldn't one want at least to see the full course of RCRA's administration on this issue and how EPA understood both the initial statute and its 1984 amendment by § 3001(i)—and see them reflected, as well, elsewhere than in the single case before the Court? The result the *City of Chicago* majority reached may be better policy, in the abstract, than any observer could reasonably have thought Congress accomplished in 1984 (though one would want to know something about just how terrible the hazardous waste problem is, what municipal waste ashes probably contribute, and what expenses the majority's position will impose). But nothing we know suggests that it was the policy Congress sought to implement; and every political instinct tells us that, if that policy *had* been appreciated as the amendment's aim, it would have been fully discussed. Indeed, to assume that the drafter of the amendment's text knew it meant what the Court majority insisted it could only mean, is to tell this story as an abuse of legislative process, as one in which clever staff and lobbyists (in this case, for the EDF) put one over on their bosses. The bureaucratic character of today's Congress reflects itself in gargantuan texts no member has read, as well as in the materials of legislative history[239]—and will, the more so, with judicial encouragements to prolixity. The result here is strictly the Court's contribution; "the text requires it," a facade.

D. CENTRAL BANK OF DENVER V FIRST INTERSTATE BANK OF DENVER

Greenwich Collieries,[240] *MCI*,[241] and *City of Chicago* all find reflections in *Central Bank of Denver v First Interstate Bank of Denver*.[242]

---

[238] Stone, work cited in n 8.

[239] Compare *Blanchard v Bergeron*, 489 US 87, 98–99 (1989) (Scalia concurring).

[240] Discussed in text following p 486.

[241] Discussed in text following p 493.

[242] 114 S Ct 1439 (1994).

Here the issue concerned the meaning of § 10(b) of the Securities Exchange Act of 1934.[243] Section 10(b) makes it "unlawful for any person, directly or indirectly, . . . to use or employ [in security trading] . . . any manipulative or deceptive device or contrivance in contravention of such rules and regulations as the [SEC] may prescribe." Central Bank, in its role as trustee on indentures issued by a Colorado public authority to finance real property under development, arguably had aided and abetted the Authority's and the developer's violation of § 10(b). First Interstate, harmed in the financial fallout of the violations, sued Central Bank along with those directly responsible for the fraud. It invoked the private remedy given by SEC Rule 10b-5[244] on the basis of this conduct "aiding and abetting" the underlying fraud. "*Hundreds* of judicial and administrative proceedings in every circuit in the federal system"[245] had previously found that § 10(b)'s prohibition on the "use" of a device reached the secondary aiding and abetting of violations, both in connection with SEC enforcement actions and in Rule 10b-5 suits. In the lower courts, narrower questions were disputed: whether this secondary liability extended to indenture trustees who had violated none of their obligations under state law; whether the aider and abettor must have been reckless, not merely negligent. In Justice Stevens's characterization, Central Bank, the defendant in the action and the petitioner before the Court, "*assumed* the existence of a right of action against aiders and abettors, and sought review only of . . . [these] subsidiary questions . . . . But instead of simply addressing the questions presented by the parties, on which the law really was unsettled, the Court *sua sponte* directed the parties to address [the existence or not of the right of action,] a question on which even the petitioner thought the law was settled, and reaches out to overturn a most considerable body of precedent."[246]

Justice Kennedy wrote for the Chief Justice and Justices Scalia, O'Connor, and Thomas that the text of § 10(b), as enacted in 1934 and not since amended, could not support private (Rule 10b-5) liability for "aiding and abetting." After noting that the question

[243] 15 USC § 78j.

[244] 17 CFR § 240.10b-5 (1993).

[245] 114 S Ct at 1456 (Stevens dissenting) (emphasis in original).

[246] Id at 1457 (emphasis in original).

had been open since the Court had signaled its doubts in the mid-1970's, he turned to the meaning of § 10(b), on which "the text of the statute" controls. For him, it was "uncontroversial" that the text "does not itself reach those who aid and abet a § 10(b) violation. . . . [T]hat conclusion resolves the case. . . . We cannot amend the statute to create liability for acts that are not themselves manipulative or deceptive within the meaning of the statute."[247] At greater length, he also explained why a court should reach the same result even if the statute did not resolve the case: Congress in 1934 had shown no inclination to attach "aiding and abetting" liability in those cases in which it expressly created private causes of action under the securities law. Neither the general *criminal* provision on aiding and abetting,[248] nor any other source, show a general congressional purpose to establish aiding and abetting as a basis for civil liability associated with federal statutes. The 1934 Congress could not be thought to have accepted such liability as an anticipatable offshoot of general tort principles. And, finally, no post-1934 amendments to securities legislation spoke directly to the aiding and abetting question. Justice Kennedy noted that Congress had failed in the late 1950's to enact proposed legislation that would have made such liability explicit, and then, after the SEC and the courts developed that liability in the course of decision, failed to correct it; he thought neither silence persuasive. Finally, he concluded, policy considerations advanced by the SEC "cannot override our interpretation of the text and structure of the Act . . . . [I]t is far from clear that *Congress in 1934* would have decided that the statutory purposes would be furthered by the imposition of private aider and abettor liability."[249]

Thus, the static character of statutory law, which courts (and agencies) do not influence, is once again a dominant theme of the majority. The questions are what was in the statute in 1934, what attitude or understanding the Congress of 1934 might have had to

---

[247] Id at 1448.

[248] 18 USC § 2.

[249] 114 S Ct at 1454 (emphasis added). The majority appears not to have been indifferent to policy considerations; Justice Kennedy's opinion makes clear that he was aware of the argument that American liability principles, as they had developed, might be making it harder for "newer and smaller companies . . . to obtain advice from professionals." Id at 1454. But the Court's rhetorical position was not that a change in course might now be warranted; rather, it was that the SEC and private plaintiffs had, from the beginning, been relying upon absent authority.

private causes of action or secondary liability, and the like. One can argue, as Justice Stevens does in his dissent (joined by Justices Blackmun, Souter, and Ginsburg), whether the majority has correctly assessed the likely stance of Congress in 1934; Justice Kennedy makes it far more conservative and chary of administrative innovation than most historians would likely ascribe to the early New Deal Congress. But that is secondary to the static quality of the analysis generally—its hostility both to the idea of meaning evolving over time, and to ascribing significance to agency administration. The SEC's views on policy are equated with those a private party might advance; they are calls on the Court for discretionary action, rather than a reflection of assigned responsibility. Indeed, while the opinion states that it only concerns private liability under Rule 10b-5—a subject to which the Court has been increasingly hostile in recent years—its reasoning limns the permissible meaning of § 10(b), which the SEC enforces directly. The plain implication, as the dissent points out, is that the SEC can no longer bring enforcement actions based on aiding and abetting.[250] Given this reasoning, it is remarkable that the Court fails directly to confront either the SEC's authority or the implications to be drawn from the SEC's continuous pursuit of such actions under congressional oversight.[251]

For the dissent, in contrast, the central idea is the importance of respecting the shape § 10(b) and Rule 10(b)(5) has assumed over time. "While we have reserved decision on the legitimacy of the theory in two cases that did not present it, all 11 Courts of Appeals to have considered the question have recognized a private cause of action against aiders and abettors. . . ."[252] Justice Stevens might have added that the reservations were expressed in 1976 and 1977; the following 18 years of administration of the rule, without con-

---

[250] Compare the following from Skidmore, cited in note 231, describing reasons why courts should conform their interpretations in private actions to those an agency was seeking publicly to enforce: "Good administration of the Act and good judicial administration alike require that the standards of public enforcement and those for determining private right shall be at variance only when justified by very good reasons." 323 US at 140. *Skidmore*, of course, was reasoning in the opposite direction, *from* the agency's public authority rather than to conclusions what it must be.

[251] As previously noted, the opinion *does* consider the implications of proposals to Congress, and of failures to amend § 10(b) when other provisions were changed. The point here is the different one developed in the text following p 504—that during these years a body Congress had appointed to act as its agent had consistently been behaving in a certain way, and Congress had shown no disposition to correct it.

[252] 114 S Ct at 1456.

gressional reaction to the signal thus given, suggest solidified consensus, not continuing doubt, about the underlying position. "A policy of respect for consistent judicial and administrative interpretations leaves it to elected representatives to assess settled law and to evaluate the merits and demerits of changing it."[253] Here, Justice Stevens appended a footnote noting prior congressional correction of the Supreme Court's recent overruling of settled securities law—strongly suggesting that here, as in *Landsgraf* and *Rivers*,[254] the Court has been battling with Congress rather than implementing its decisions. "[W]e should . . . be reluctant to lop off rights of action that have been recognized for decades, even if the judicial methodology that gave them birth is now out of favor . . . particularly . . . because the judicially recognized right in question accords with the longstanding construction of the agency Congress has assigned to enforce the securities laws."[255] From a perspective treating Congress as a constant monitor of evolving agency and judicial interpretations, subsequent congressional actions spoke more loudly of acquiescence to Justice Stevens than to Justice Kennedy.

Justice Stevens's principal point was that the statute's meaning in 1934 was not limiting, if one could today find in its terms support for the approach that had been taken. That support is provided by the statute's reference to persons who "directly or indirectly" use manipulative devices, and by the usual openness of common law courts to building liability on such foundations as the criminal law's general extension of liability to aiders and abettors. As he had in his dissent from *Patterson* years earlier,[256] Justice Stevens ended his dissent by invoking Benjamin Cardozo's *The Nature of the Judicial Process*. The majority's refusal "to build upon a 'secure foundation . . . laid by others,'"[257] is in the service of instability and, one might add, politicization in American law.

E. NLRB V HEALTH CARE & RETIREMENT CORP. OF AMERICA

Readers who have reached this point will not doubt my unhappiness with the Term's developments. They may have questions

---

[253] Id at 1458.

[254] Discussed in text following p 454.

[255] 114 S Ct at 1460.

[256] Text at n 99 above.

[257] 114 S Ct at 1460.

about the fairness of my summarizing of what are, of necessity at the Court's level, complex issues and arguments. Surely my impatience has inflected my tone. Surely it has, although my effort has been to present the Justices' arguments in their own terms— believing this tree should fall of its own weight, and rhetorical distortion would be a disservice to my effort. In any event, the majority opinion in this workaday NLRB case may help to quell the suspicion that *I* am the one supplying the tone toward legislative effort that sometimes marks these pages.

As part of the Taft-Hartley Act of 1947, Congress adopted two definitions of who might and might not be a statutory "employee" eligible to organize that appear to be in considerable tension with one another. Section 2(3) expressly *excludes* from the category "employee" any individual employed as a "supervisor,"[258] and § 2(11) defines a supervisor as a person having "authority, in the interest of the employer," to perform a variety of tasks in relation to other employees, including the authority to "assign," "responsibly to direct," or "effectively to recommend" such action, if it "requires the use of independent judgment."[259] Section 2(12), on the other hand, expressly *includes* as statutory "employees" "professional employees," persons whose work involves "the consistent exercise of discretion and judgment in its performance."[260] Professionals' "exercise of discretion and judgment" very often includes giving assignments to other employees and directing their performance to some extent; the reader imagining the work of a lawyer in a public defender's office, for example, will easily see how this must be so. One has, then, an inevitable issue of characterization, whether professionals are excluded supervisors or included employees, on particular facts.

In *NLRB v Health Care & Retirement Corp. of America*,[261] the Court was reviewing the Labor Board's assessment of this issue for staff nurses working at nursing homes. On the one hand, the nurses are clearly professionals; on the other, management staff was on hand only during normal weekday business hours, and during the rest of the week—that is, the substantial majority of a nursing home's

---

[258] 29 USC § 152(3).

[259] 29 USC § 152(11).

[260] 29 USC § 152(12).

[261] 114 S Ct 1778 (1994).

operating hours—the nurses on duty had immediate charge of the larger number of nurses aides. The aides were the ones more likely to deal directly with patients on routine matters; they required assignment and oversight; and their conduct might have to be reported for consideration of praise or discipline. This of course was not a new issue in 1994. The Board's consistent position has been that these nurses are "professional employees" and are not "supervisors." To the Court, it argued that their direction of the aides was professional rather than managerial in character, and hence was not "in the interest of the employer" as it understood § 2(11).

Justice Kennedy wrote for the five most consistent textualists and Justice Ginsburg for the four most frequent contextualists, finding the nurses to be excluded supervisors and included professionals, respectively. While Justice Kennedy drew support from a single Supreme Court precedent excluding Labor Act coverage of a similarly conflicted situation,[262] his principal arguments drew on his understanding of Congress's action in 1947 and were indifferent to subsequent events. He took the phrase, "in the interest of the employer," to have the broad meaning that had been given it in a then-recent Supreme Court opinion whose result the Taft-Hartley Act had intended to reverse.[263] That the Board, the national body responsible in the first instance for giving shape to national labor policy, had consistently understood the phrase in a different way—even as applied to nursing homes—is dismissed; in other settings involving the "professional"-"supervisor" tension, the Board had relied on other rationales than its interpretation of "in the interest of the employer," and it was the use of that particular argument, rather than uniformity of outcome, that Justice Kennedy found significant. "[I]n almost all of those cases (unlike in cases involving nurses) the Board's decisions did not result from manipulation of the statutory phrase 'in the interest of the employer,' but instead

---

[262] *NLRB v Yeshiva University*, 444 US 672 (1980). Here, the issue was whether faculty members were "managerial employees," and the Board had argued that they acted in their own, rather than their employer's, interest.

[263] *Packard Motor Car Co. v NLRB*, 330 US 485 (1947). In contrast to Justice Ginsburg's careful survey of the legislative history, Justice Kennedy said of the legislative history only that "there is no indication that Congress intended any different meaning when it included the phrase in the statutory definition of supervisor . . . in 1947." 114 S Ct at 1782. While Congress repudiated the result in *Packard*, "we of course have rejected the argument that a statute altering the result reached by a judicial decision necessarily changes the meaning of the language interpreted in that decision." Id at 1783.

from a finding that the employee in question had not met the other requirements for supervisory status."[264] When the Act was amended in some but not these respects in 1974, the Board's interpretations were before Congress; the approving mention of these interpretations in a Committee report is not binding on the courts, "for the Constitution is quite explicit about the procedure that Congress must follow in legislating."[265] "If Congress wishes to enact the policies of the Board, it can do so without indirection."[266] These impatient words are Justice Kennedy's; assuming as they do that Congress should have known the Board was in error, they reflect a strikingly antagonistic and formal stance to the interrelation of legislative, agency, and judicial effort, and one that essentially denies the possibility of law's growth over time, or of Congress's assignment to others of responsibility in that regard.

Justice Ginsburg gave closer attention to the inherent tension between the two statutory definitions involved and the Board's primary responsibility for the Act. Within that context, she found the legislative history supported the interpretation the NLRB had given language over time, and noted the consistency of this interpretation with other well-established aspects of the Board's work. "The Board's endeavor to reconcile the inclusion of professionals with the exclusion of supervisors, in my view, is not just 'rational and consistent with the Act'; it is *required* by the Act."[267]

F. UNITED STATES DEPARTMENT OF DEFENSE V FEDERAL LABOR
   RELATIONS AUTHORITY

The dispute in *United States Department of Defense v FLRA*[268] required the Court to interrelate three somewhat disparate statutes—

---

[264] Id at 1785.

[265] 114 S Ct at 1784, quoting *American Hospital Association v NLRB*, 499 US 606, 616 (1991). In this respect, this opinion reiterates the misleading "single mention" reasoning of *Shannon*, *City of Chicago*, and *Central Bank of Denver*, discussed above at pp 471, 499, and 509. It does *not* follow from their undoubted insufficiencies as legislative acts that these events are irrelevancies for a court interpreting the phrase. That would be so *only* if the expert judgment of the agency appointed by Congress to administer the laws in the first instance, the course of interpretation over time, and its apparent acceptance by Congress had no appropriate bearing on judicial judgment on the matter.

[266] 114 S Ct at 1785.

[267] 114 S Ct at 1793 (emphasis in original), quoting *NLRB v Curtin Matheson Scientific Inc.*, 494 US 775, 796 (1990).

[268] 114 S Ct 1006.

the Federal Labor Relations Act ("the Act"),[269] the Privacy Act,[270] and the Freedom of Information Act ("FOIA").[271] Its performance reflects, again, a disinclination to take an actively integrative role. The Act, in general, seeks to bolster the position of public unions, giving them rights comparable to those enjoyed by employee representatives in the private sector; and § 7114(b)(4), in particular, requires agencies to furnish their public employee unions with data necessary for collective bargaining purposes, "to the extent not prohibited by law." Employee unions sought the names and home addresses of employees in the bargaining units they represented—a request a private employer would be required to honor under the National Labor Relations Act.[272] Under the Privacy Act, release of such personal information is prohibited unless disclosure would be "required" under FOIA.[273] And FOIA, in turn, requires agencies to comply with "any person['s]" demand for information in government possession, unless one of its exemptions applies—in this instance, its sixth exemption, for "personnel and medical files and similar files the disclosure of which would constitute a clearly unwarranted invasion of personal privacy."[274] Could one look to the Act and the focused judgment of the Federal Labor Relations Authority ("FLRA") that such disclosure was necessary for collective bargaining, in assessing the existence or not of "warrant" for invading an employee's personal privacy by disclosing her home address? Or may that invasion be "warranted" only by the sort of general considerations that might attend "any person['s]" request for this information, as assessed by a reviewing court?

Justice Thomas wrote the majority opinion finding that the information could not be disclosed. As Justice Ginsburg pointed out in a bittersweet concurrence, all courts of appeals to address this issue before 1989 had easily interpreted these three acts, in conjunction, to permit enforcement of the FLRA's judgment. Congress's labor policy choice to promote collective bargaining for federal civil ser-

---

[269] 5 USC §§ 7101–35.

[270] 5 USC § 552a.

[271] 5 USC § 552.

[272] For example, *NLRB v Associated Gen. Contractors of Cal., Inc.*, 633 F2d 766 (9th Cir 1980), cert den, 452 US 915 (1981), cited in 114 S Ct at 1017 n 9.

[273] 5 USC § 552a(b)(2).

[274] 5 USC § 552(b)(6).

vants provided a solid basis for concluding that the disclosure of home addresses to a bargaining representative was not "a clearly unwarranted invasion of personal privacy"; the disclosure placed federal unions and the federal employer in an equivalent position to unions and employers under the NLRA. "It is surely doubtful that, in the very statute bolstering federal-sector unions, Congress aimed to deny those unions information their private-sector counterparts routinely receive."[275]

Congress did not relevantly amend any of the three acts involved subsequent to these interperetations. But in 1989 the Court decided, in the context of the FOIA's similarly worded exemption for investigative files,[276] that the balancing suggested by reference to an "unwarranted invasion of personal privacy" could not consider the identity of a particular requester and the legitimacy of its needs, since the Act confers the right to information on "any person." Rather, one must justify disclosure in terms of FOIA's "core purpose" of "contributing significantly to public understanding of the operations or activities of the government."[277] Since that decision, all but one of the courts of appeal considering the matter— including a panel of the D.C. Circuit on which Justice Ginsburg had sat[278]—found that this restructured inquiry compelled the conclusion that the addresses could not be released. The general public would learn little if anything about the operation of government from their disclosure, and so in the only terms that now counted there was no warrant at all to counterbalance public employees' privacy interest in having their addresses secure from disclosure to the public.

The case provided the majority a straightforward occasion for applying its earlier precedent. FOIA gives the right to information to "any person," and gives that right in order to enhance knowledge

---

[275] 114 S Ct at 1018.

[276] 5 USC § 552(b)(7)(C) exempts law enforcement records to the extent that their production "could reasonably be expected to constitute an unwarranted invasion of personal privacy."

[277] *Department of Justice v Reporters' Committee for Freedom of Press*, 489 US 749, 775 (1989). The public's interest in knowing the contents of criminal "rap sheets" on individuals could be expected to do little to expose the operations of government, but could constitute a significant invasion of the privacy of individuals who might never have been tried for the crimes alleged on them.

[278] *FLRA v Department of Treasury*, 884 F2d 1446 (DC Cir 1989), cert den, 493 US 1055 (1990).

about government. That policies external to FOIA make a strong case for making this information available is irrelevant to a case that arises within its four corners. In one sense, the Court *is* assuming responsibility for the statute's shape; as Justice Ginsburg remarked, the "'core purpose' limitation is not found in FOIA's language," but was supplied by the Court in the particular context of disclosing information about criminal investigations; here, it is extending that reasoning.[279] Yet, "in the matter at hand, . . . it is Congress that has declared the importance of the request's purpose, and Congress that has selected a single entity—the employees' exclusive bargaining representative—as entitled to assert that purpose."[280] In its insistence that "we do no more than give effect to the clear words of the provisions we construe,"[281] in declining to accept what it describes as "respondents' ambitious invitation to rewrite the statutes before us,"[282] the majority denies its partnership with Congress. "Speculation about the ultimate goals of the Labor Statute is inappropriate"[283] where the words are clear; if the Court's interpretation creates a difference between private and public labor law that is contrary to the responsible agency's view, inexplicable as labor policy and irreconcilable with the general purposes of the Act, "Congress may correct the disparity."[284] It is not for the Court to seek the integration of statutory commands that Justice Ginsburg shows to be both available, and a fairer rendering of overall public policy attributable to Congress; it is not for the Court to pursue "the ideal of a unified system of judge-made and statute law woven into a seamless whole by the processes of adjudication."[285]

G. THREE COUNTER-EXAMPLES?

1. *John Hancock Mutual Life Insurance Co. v Harris Trust and Savings Bank. John Hancock Mutual Life Insurance Co. v Harris Trust and*

---

[279] 114 S Ct at 1019.

[280] Id.

[281] Id at 1016.

[282] Id at 1014.

[283] Id at 1016.

[284] Id.

[285] Stone, work cited in note 8. Justice Ginsburg's concurrence rests on the strength, as she reports it, of her colleagues' views and of statutory stare decisis. 114 S Ct at 1019 (Ginsburg concurring).

Savings Bank[286] was Justice Ginsburg's first opinion of the Term and the first opinion to consider issues of statutory interpretation in detail. Justice Ginsburg's cases, even when (as often) fairly closely divided, tended not to produce the rhetoric of division which concerns this essay, and that was also the case in *Hancock*. If one can find the Term's patterns here, they are in subdued form.

The Court decided, 6–3, that John Hancock's administration of certain annuity contracts subjected it to the fiduciary standards of the Employee Retirement Income Security Act of 1974, ERISA. ERISA is a complex statute, and the problem of interpretation facing the Court defies easy description. In general, ERISA makes persons responsible for managing the assets of retirement plans into fiduciaries of plan beneficiaries, with corresponding duties and limitations respecting their investment decisions. However, 29 USC § 1101(b)(2)(B) creates an exception for the assets of insurance companies who issue retirement policies, "to the extent that [a] policy or contract provides for benefits the amount of which is guaranteed by the insurer." Insurance companies are predominantly regulated by state law, which tends *not* to regard them as fiduciaries for their policy-holders; exemption from fiduciary status is thus of some importance to them. The consequence of characterizing a given plan as a guaranteed benefit plan is that the manager will be considerably freer to commingle investment funds for the plan with its general funds, to deal in securities of the employer purchasing the plan, and so on. Should Hancock's plan with the Sperry Rand Corporation, of which Harris Trust and Savings was trustee, be so characterized? Following a common insurance industry practice in administering retirement plan portfolios, the plan guaranteed the benefits a Sperry employee would receive ultimately; during the period before any particular employee retired, however, the funds contributed on her account were treated as part of the insurer's general investment pool. To the extent Hancock was successful in its investments, it built up surpluses, beyond the level its guarantees required it to pay. These surpluses and the possibility that retirees would share in them as a supplement to their defined benefits produced the question to what extent this was a "guaranteed benefit" plan. Disputes over how and on what valuations Hancock would share them with the retirement plan

---

[286] 114 S Ct 517.

in question produced the occasion for deciding whether it was a "fiduciary," and the Court held that it was. It did so in the face of contrary, but somewhat hesitant, advice from the Department of Labor and, according to the dissent, nearly 20 years of conduct based on the opposite understanding in the insurance industry as a whole.

It may be appropriate for our purposes to focus on the tools of interpretation invoked by the two opinions. In its breadth of consideration of statutory patterns, congressional process, and integration with the decision of other like questions, the majority opinion generally reflects a contextual style of analysis. For Justice Ginsburg and the majority, the important considerations were ERISA's general pattern of inclusion, and the limited ("to the extent that") way in which the statute stated the "guaranteed benefit" exclusion from the general principle of fiduciary obligation. The latter qualification held particular importance; other exclusions were stated in a much broader fashion. Similar exemptions in other, like statutes had been interpreted narrowly. In adopting the exclusion, moreover, the Senate had rejected a broader formulation, that would clearly have entitled Hancock to prevail. And prior cases, arising in analogous circumstances, tended also to suggest that "[t]o the extent that [Hancock] engages in the discretionary management of assets attributable to that phase of the contract which provides no guarantee of benefits payments or fixed rates of return, . . . [it] should be subject to fiduciary responsibility."[287]

The majority was unresponsive, however, to claims of administrative interpretation and of insurance industry practice during the first two decades of ERISA's administration. In 1975, shortly after ERISA had been enacted, the Department of Labor had taken the contrary position in an interpretive bulletin addressing another but coordinate question, whether in like circumstances an insurance company could engage in transactions involving the company whose plan it was administering. Insurance companies like Hancock administered plans like Sperry's as if they were not fiduciaries, to the extent of $332 billion,[288] without prompting a regulatory response. The Departmental bulletin, however, did not focus on the question of fiduciary status or the "guaranteed benefit" issue,

---

[287] Id at 528, quoting the opinion below, 970 F2d 1138, 1144 (2d Cir 1992).

[288] Id at 531 (Thomas dissenting).

and the majority was unpersuaded that treatment of its questions was implicit there. It also noted that in 1992 the Department of Labor had been unwilling to provide requested assistance on the precise point to the Second Circuit, pleading the complexity of the issues and the press of other business. The majority concluded that the text of ERISA would not support the interpretation the Department urged. The majority's response to the practical concerns expressed by the Department of Labor and the industry was that "we cannot give them dispositive weight" and that "administrative relief" of an unspecified character might be available.

One finds the opposite pattern in Justice Thomas's opinion for himself, Justice O'Connor, and Justice Kennedy. He begins by parsing the phrases of § 1101(b)(2)(B) in turn, and in isolation—"provides for," "the amount of which is guaranteed," and then, finally and quite briefly, "to the extent that." The history of consideration in the Senate, the unusual character of this exclusion compared with others in ERISA, overall ERISA policy, and learning from other statutes are beside the point.

> Unlike the Court, I see no need to base an understanding of [the guaranteed benefit exception] on principles derived from the interpretation of dissimilar provisions in the Securities Act of 1933 or from a sense of the policy of ERISA as a whole. The meaning of the provision can be determined readily by examining its component terms.

More surprising, Justice Thomas calls attention as well to considerations of practical impact and community expectations about what statutes mean, factors generally absent from his analyses during the Term. The majority wrote *as if* its conclusion would affect only a part of one particular insurance arrangement. Justice Thomas argues that the structure of Hancock's business assures that, in fact, the decision will have a sweeping impact on how it does business; it deals with many plans as it does with Sperry's, mingling all their funds in its general accounts up to the point at which any particular employee retires and begins to draw benefits. To apply principles of fiduciary responsibility at this stage is, as he characterizes it, to "radically alter[] the law applicable to insurance companies."[289] As a formal matter, as Justice Thomas would usu-

---

[289] Id at 535.

ally describe "law," this statement is untrue: The language of ERISA has not been changed since its enactment and had not been definitively interpreted by the Supreme Court in the interim.[290] The 1975 interpretive bulletin concerned another, although related, subject. And, an interpretive bulletin in any event does not establish binding law. If it established a shared understanding throughout the insurance industry, "[i]n reliance on [which] settled understanding" the insurance companies had been conducting their business,[291] without congressional response, that is in the framework of *this* essay a sound argument for interpreting ERISA as Hancock urged. It is, however, the kind of argument that, in other cases, the dissenters usually rejected.

2. *PUD No. 1 of Jefferson County v Washington Department of Ecology*. Under the Clean Water Act, the states and the federal government share responsibility for "restor[ing] and maintain[ing] the chemical, physical and biological integrity of the Nation's waters,"[292] and states are encouraged to develop comprehensive standards that may be more stringent than federal standards. The states may include enhancing water quality, preventing degradation, and assuring "water quality which provides for the protection and propagation of fish, shellfish and wildlife" among their goals.[293] In general, administration of the Act and approval of state standards or private initiatives that may come within its terms are the business of the Environmental Protection Agency (EPA). Section 401 of the Act[294] can bring other federal regulators into the picture, however; applicants for any federal license or permit "which may result in *any discharge* into the navigable waters" must secure from the state a certificate "that *any such discharge* will comply with [the Act]." Section 401 also provides that "any certification provided under this section shall set forth any effluent limitations *and other limitations* [under the Act or appropriate requirements of State law,]" which "shall become a condition on any Federal license or permit." An application to the Federal Energy Regulatory Commission

---

[290] Compare the civil rights retroactivity cases, discussed in the text at p 454, and the treatment of the burden of proof issue in *Director, Office of Workers' Compensation Programs v Greenwich Collieries*, discussed at p 486.

[291] 114 S Ct 535.

[292] 33 USC § 1251(a).

[293] 33 USC § 1251(a)(2).

[294] 33 USC § 1341.

(FERC) for a license to operate a hydroelectric facility is one such application. A Washington state standard sought to protect a stream's fish life by requiring a certain amount of water to be left in the stream after diversion for other uses, such as hydroelectric power generation. Does that standard qualify as an "other limitation[]"; or is it outside the statute since it concerns water *left in the river* rather than removed to generate power and then returned ("discharged")?

In *PUD No. 1 of Jefferson County v Washington Department of Ecology*,[295] Justice O'Connor, writing for seven Justices, accepted the state standard as a qualifying condition, after considering the EPA's view as embodied in its regulations and practices, and other contextual factors. Justices Thomas (writing) and Scalia found a more restrictive meaning in the statute's textual reference to "any discharge," and were unpersuaded by the course of administration the statute was said to have received at EPA. The differences were not stark. While in general the dissent appeared to be the more concerned with the limits text imposed, in one respect it gave more reflective attention than the majority to the integrative responsibilities of courts.

Justice Thomas would have left the issue of stream flow protection to be decided federally by FERC, a view that drew force from FERC's role. In licensing a proposed hydroelectric facility, FERC is required to consider "the protection, mitigation of damage to, and enhancement of fish and wildlife."[296] Section 10(a) of the Federal Power Act[297] empowers it to impose conditions, including minimum stream flow, to that end. Earlier judicial interpretations of this fish-protection authority had found that it preempted state requirements, even requirements for *higher* flows.[298] In effect, FERC must think about protecting fish, but has some discretion to prefer electricity. In *PUD*, the majority's interpretation of the Clean Water Act gives states a way to make their stream flow preferences necessary conditions of any later federal licenses, including hydroelectric licenses. The interpretation thus pretermits FERC's power to compromise between the nation's needs for electricity and its interest in fish protection.

---

[295] 114 S Ct 1900 (1994).

[296] 16 USC § 797(e).

[297] 16 USC § 803(a).

[298] *California v FERC*, 495 US 490 (1990).

The majority found no conflict between FERC and the state, since FERC had not yet acted on a license application; in arguing *amicus* for the government, the Solicitor General had represented that FERC had no objection to the stream flow condition.[299] For the dissent, this reasoning failed to make a reasonable whole of the federal statutes. If the issue was merely avoiding after-the-fact state frustration of *prior* federal determinations, the majority approach might be acceptable; if, on the other hand, Congress has given FERC the federal role of reconciling national interests in electricity supply and stream flow protection for fish, it is not responsive to observe that a policy attributable to EPA takes effect prior to FERC's opportunity to act. A holistic, integrative account of the statutes would nonetheless have to recognize FERC's primacy; such accounts are perhaps especially needed in settings of great regulatory complexity, in which Congress may often have created, out of inadvertence, arguably redundant responsibilities. Here too, then (as Justice Stevens recognized in a wry, one-paragraph concurrence), Justice Thomas appears to have departed from his more frequently static view of legislation.

3. *Thomas Jefferson University v Shalala*. *Thomas Jefferson University v Shalala*[300] divided the Court 5–4, along unusual lines, about the meaning of Department of Health and Human Services regulations implementing Medicare. Justice Kennedy's majority opinion attracted Justices Blackmun and Souter in addition to the Chief Justice and Justice Scalia; Justice Thomas's dissent was joined by Justices Stevens, O'Connor, and Ginsburg. Here the issue concerned, not the potential of conflict between two federal agencies, but the clarity with which one had provided in its regulations for matters unquestionably under its control. One problem Medicare authorities face in reimbursing teaching hospitals for their patients is that the hospital may be seeking reimbursement as a medical expense for an item that ought to be viewed as an educational expense. The problem is underscored by Congress's increasing concern to control Medicare costs generally. It surfaced here when Jefferson Medical School reexamined the accounting practices it had been following and decided it could properly claim reimbursement as medical items for some expenses it previously had been

---

[299] 114 S Ct at 1914.

[300] 114 S Ct 2381 (1994).

financing on the educational side—perhaps thus recapturing funds
it was losing to more stringent cost controls elsewhere. Jefferson
at first lost, then won, then finally lost these claims within the
Department, when the Secretary interpreted a regulation quoted
in the margin as forbidding the reimbursement.[301] Justice Kennedy, for the majority, resolved the dispute in the Secretary's favor
largely in reliance on the conventional proposition that her reasonable interpretation of her own regulation was entitled to control.[302]

Like his opinion in *John Hancock Mutual Life*,[303] Justice Thomas's
dissent mixes attention to the text with attention to the realities of
its administration. Regarding the text, his principal argument is
holistic, although motivated by a generally conservative attitude
toward the exercise of rulemaking power. The relevant language
just does not read like a rule; although appearing in CFR, it is an
explanatory "preamble," "cast in vague, aspirational terms," not
a statement of propositions that bind.[304] Reading the regulatory
language as a whole, that assessment is a commanding one.[305] And
it is reinforced by Justice Thomas's strong preference for definitive
legislative acts:

> It is perfectly understandable, of course, for an agency to issue
> vague regulations, because to do so maximizes agency power
> and allows the agency greater latitude to make law through
> adjudication rather than through the more cumbersome rule-

---

[301] Educational Activities. Many providers engage in educational activities including training
programs for nurses, medical students, interns and residents, and various paramedical spe-
cialties. These programs contribute to the quality of patient care within an institution and
are necessary to meet the community's needs for medical and paramedical personnel. It is
recognized that the costs of such educational activities should be borne by the community.
However, many communities have not assumed responsibility for financing these programs
and it is necessary that support be provided by those purchasing health care. Until communities undertake to bear these costs, the [Medicare] program will participate appropriately in
the support of these activities. Although the intent of the program is to share in the support
of educational activities customarily or traditionally carried on by providers in conjunction
with their operations, it is not intended that this program should participate in increased
costs resulting from redistribution of costs from educational institutions or units to patient
care institutions or units.

42 CFR § 413.85(c).

[302] Compare the different approach the majority took in *Greenwich Collieries*, disussed at
page 487.

[303] Discussed in text following p 519.

[304] 114 S Ct at 2390.

[305] See note 301; the precise language in issue in the case is the last sentence of the quoted
material.

making process. Nonetheless, agency rules should be clear and definite so that affected parties will have adequate notice concerning the agency's understanding of the law.[306]

"The agency has to say it clearly" resonates strongly with "Congress must say what it means; I won't look outside the text."

Justice Thomas also asserted that during the first two decades of its administration the Secretary had in fact treated his regulation as merely precatory. Its application here only served to prevent Jefferson from changing its accounting practices to conform to practices that regularly (and properly) produced reimbursement for other teaching hospitals. Here, then, Justice Thomas focused upon the actual administration and understanding respecting the Secretary's rules over time—how they seem to have been understood in the community to which they applied, what would be the practical implications of one or the other reading. As he did in *John Hancock Mutual Life*, he attaches importance here to the element of continuity in actual administration, as providing proper insight into possible meaning. That contextual element is more often missing from his address to statutory issues, and marks the most frequent divide between Justice Stevens and himself.

VI. CONCLUSION

This somewhat discursive review of the Court's work during the Term suggests that a majority of Justices, not invariably but consistently, took an essentially static and oppositional view of the task of statutory interpretation. Justices Scalia, Kennedy, and Thomas most directly, and the Chief Justice and Justice O'Connor often, tended to treat statutes as the one-time pronouncements of an independent Congress—binding so far as they imposed a meaning, but not instructive, not illuminated either by their political history or by the course of their implementation, not an invitation to judicial partnership. They seem to imagine that legislature, agencies, and courts work in isolation, as if uninformed in their own judgments by the work the others are doing and their constant, overseeing, and responsive presence. This approach reverses understandings that long predate the New Deal, about the need to

---

[306] Citing the Davis and Pierce Administrative Law Treatise in a passage making a strong quasi-delegation argument for this proposition.

accommodate the growth of statutes and administration as sources of law. It resegregates the worlds of statute and common law.

The Court was not constant in this; *Hawaiian Airlines*[307] coexisted with *Greenwich Collieries*.[308] Perhaps we have little to learn beyond the realist bromide that only results, not reasons, count.[309] Or perhaps the inconstancy is a function of judicial personality. Professor Merrill has suggested that the appearance of change in the Court's reasoning may be the result of consistent attention to the matter by only two of the Justices, Justice Scalia and Justice Thomas, who by attaching importance to methodological issues other Justices find secondary make it appear their views are more widely insisted upon than in fact they are.[310] Justice Blackmun, who wrote *Hawaiian Airlines*, was more likely than most to take integrative approaches; in a unanimous matter near the Term's end, when the most difficult controversies also remained to be resolved, the Justices may have had less time for careful scrutiny of reasoning to a result on which all had agreed. Or, possibly, we should be looking past the Justices to their law clerks; inconstancy in the intellectual premises of the Court's work may be evidence that its thirty-odd young and transient law clerks control [too] much of its workproduct. The lawyers too may bear some responsibility. Arguments do not come to the Justices perfectly shaped in each case; how particular cases are briefed and argued will influence the outcomes. Widely varying styles of advocacy (which would be encouraged by unpredictability in the intellectual premises on which the Justices appear to approach their work) both evidence and serve to enlarge the extent to which lawyering has lost a grounding in shared traditions of understanding and technique.

Yet any such "explanation" insufficiently credits, in my judgment, the seriousness with which the separatist position was, again and again, advanced. Often stated as a position about the function of Congress—what judicial approach is necessary to preserve Congress's assigned responsibilities under the constitutional separation

---

[307] Discussed in text following p 490.

[308] Discussed in text following p 486.

[309] Compare Frank H. Easterbrook, *Ways of Criticizing the Court*, 95 Harv L Rev 802 (1982).

[310] Merrill, work cited in n 41, 72 Wash U L Q at 365. In my judgment, Justice Kennedy is also persistent in emphasizing the gulf between the worlds of statute and court—the wrongness of courts taking responsibility for what is Congress's to provide.

of powers—it is equally (and inevitably) a position about the function of being a court. Five years ago, writing for himself, the Chief Justice, and Justice O'Connor,[311] Justice Kennedy had justified his general reluctance to consult legislative history in terms of the constitutional separation of powers; the strength of his view is demonstrated by its consequence, that he then had to decide a constitutional issue adversely to the statute.[312] To use legislative history to give a statute meaning beyond what its language could bear, he argued,

> creates too great a risk that the Court is exercising its own "WILL instead of JUDGMENT," with the consequence of "substituti[ng] [its own] pleasure to that of the legislative body." The Federalist No. 78, p. 469 (C. Rossiter ed. 1961) (A. Hamilton). . . .
>
> . . .
>
> . . . Where it is clear that the unambiguous language of a statute embraces certain conduct, and it would not be patently absurd to apply the statute to such conduct, it does not foster a democratic exegesis for this Court to rummage through unauthoritative materials to consult the spirit of the legislation in order to discover an alternative interpretation of the statute with which the Court is more comfortable.[313]

In *this* Term's cases, similar reasoning has been used to reject meanings that statutory language *could* bear (and meanings that for a time may have prevailed) but that the majority found unpersuasive,[314] and to reject judicial gap-filling in cases that were not directly provided for by a statute but that fall within stable expectations past precedents have promoted about its application.[315] The

---

[311] Justice Scalia was not participating in the case; Justice Thomas had not yet joined the Court.

[312] *Public Citizen v U.S. Department of Justice*, 491 US 440 (1989). The avoidance of a constitutional question, *particularly* when one's judgment will be to find against constitutionality, has long been promoted by the Justices and influential commentators, as a means of preventing unnecessary friction between the branches. See, e.g., *Ashwander v TVA*, 297 US 288, 341 (1936) (Brandeis concurring); Alexander M. Bickel, *The Least Dangerous Branch* (1962).

[313] 491 US at 471–73.

[314] For example, *BFP*, discussed at p 449; *Shannon*, discussed at p 471; *Greenwich Collieries*, discussed at p 486; *Health Care and Retirement Corp.*, discussed at p 513; *MCI Telecommunications Corp.*, discussed at p 493; *City of Chicago*, discussed at p 499.

[315] E.g., *Gotshall*, discussed at p 429; *Holder*, discussed at p 464; *Central Bank of Denver*, discussed at p 509. The concurrence in *Rivers* and *Landgraf*, discussed at p 457, is to similar effect.

Court's responsibility for separation of powers, the argument appears to be, reaches beyond the legislative history dispute. It requires the Court to promote congressional accountability for political judgments—and that means requiring Congress to make those judgments—at whatever cost to supportive collaboration between Congress and the courts.

A similar but more limited argument has long been made in support of the proposition cast aside with surprising ease in *Greenwich Collieries*[316] and, in effect, *Central Bank of Denver*,[317] that protection of congressional function requires the courts not to revisit statutory constructions once established. In 1948, for example, Edward Levi argued in his *Introduction to Legal Reasoning* that for courts freely to "*re*interpret legislation"[318] would sap Congress's political responsibility.

> If legislation which is disfavored can be interpreted away from time to time, then it is not to be expected, particularly if controversy is high, that the legislature will ever act.[319]

For Levi, however, this argument is addressed to second looks, not first ones. In the initial filling of the gap that legislation (like all use of language) inevitably leaves, Levi intends that the courts must be sympathetic to legislative purposes; "[l]egislatures and courts are cooperative lawmaking bodies."[320] That initial interpretation will set the course for the legislation; its legitimacy depends on the courts' sympathy for the democratic impulse underlying Congress's action. But

> [i]f the court is to have freedom to reinterpret legislation, the result will be to relieve the legislature from pressure. The legislation needs judicial consistency. . . . [O]nce a decisive interpretation of legislative intent has been made, and in that sense a direction has been fixed within the gap of ambiguity, the court should take that direction as given.[321]

---

[316] Discussed in text following p 488.

[317] Discussed in text following p 511. In effect because, as the majority would not consider, the interpretation had become so well established in the lower courts, over such an extensive period.

[318] At 23 (emphasis added).

[319] Id.

[320] Id.

[321] Id.

To put this another way, and generalize the argument somewhat, the "pressure" Levi is referring to appears to be pressure to move the law from some existing community understanding of it. Once it is established what legislatively created law "is" in community regard, Congress should be responsible for changing that, not the courts. But we can see, too, that this establishment can occur without the intervention of the Supreme Court—indeed, given the enormous level of judicial (and agency) business, and the very limited resources available to the Court, this is inevitable.[322] Interpretations may have become thoroughly settled in the community, the "direction . . . fixed within the gap of ambiguity," long before the Court, with its one hundred or so yearly occasions for pronouncement, reaches a matter. Even if the Court is formally free to adopt a different interpretation, because it has never before considered the issue, the direction may be so clearly set that a contrary reading would be confrontational, and inconsistent with the primary legislative responsibility for change. Just as the accretion of lower court experience presages change in the common law, a gathering body of lower court or agency interpretation, under the gaze of a responsible legislature, fixes a context of community understanding from which the Court cannot depart without raising questions of democracy.[323] It, too, may set a baseline of understanding that Congress has the responsibility to vary.

Preserving legislative responsibility also animates arguments about delegation, and thus about how ready courts should be to find that statutes present a "gap of ambiguity" they can fill. If, rather than voice policy directions, legislatures enact vacuous formulas that leave essential choices to others, shouldn't courts refuse that responsibility and find means to require the legislatures to act? Even conceding the argument, of course, requires some sensitivity to the question whether or in what respects a legislature has failed to decide in a particular instance—a question that cannot be answered by resort to artificial rules about the use of language without, again, placing the courts into possible conflict with the legislature. As Daniel Farber has persuasively remarked, this formal approach "contrasts with normal methods of communication,

---

[322] Strauss, work cited at n 232.

[323] See *Cammarano v United States*, 358 US 498, 508–11 (1959) (IRS interpretations of tax law issue in effect adopted through congressional oversight process).

which assume a cooperative listener."[324] If one can know the judgments that underlay a statute from its political history and other indicators, a decision based on formal failure to include a particular word in an operative list seems at best pedantic, at worst a symptom of struggle and uncooperativeness.[325] The inquiry whether Congress has in fact decided a matter, that is, may itself be a political one, animated by an unwillingness to find a certain kind of result; and when it is, the problem is not that *Congress* has failed to fulfill its appropriate function.

Principles of interpretation have often been defended in terms of their instructive possibilities, but the appropriate premises and limitations of judicial instruction of Congress should be kept in view. The very idea of instructing or teaching Congress suggests a hierarchical view quite inappropriate to a government of co-equal branches.[326] In a democratic society, moreover, one would anticipate premises generally supportive rather than destructive of the legislative enterprise. Levi's arguments do not suppose or seek to justify a general judicial attitude of unfriendliness toward the work of the legislature. His argument is one about the conditions most conducive to social peace, and is premised on the understanding that

> [n]ot only do new situations arise, but in addition peoples' wants change. The categories used in the legal process must be left ambiguous in order to permit the infusion of new ideas. . . . [T]he laws come to express the ideas of the community, and even when written in general terms, in statute or constitution, are molded to the specific case.[327]

The dialogue he seeks is one supposed to respect democratic values; it is not an argument for the superiority of the common law but supposes as a general endeavor judicial and legislative cooperation toward the community's preferences.

Levi, writing in 1948, assumes that the legislature speaks with a legitimately democratic voice, that its claim to having its judgments

---

[324] Daniel A. Farber, *The Inevitability of Practical Reason: Statutes, Formalism and the Rule of Law*, 45 Vand L Rev 533, 551 (1992).

[325] *City of Chicago*, discussed at p 501.

[326] See also T. Alexander Aleinikoff, *Updating Statutory Interpretation*, 87 Mich L Rev 20, 31–32 (1988); Farber, 45 Vand L Rev at 549 n 89 and 551 (cited in note 324).

[327] Levi at 4.

respected and implemented is that it utters the voice of the people in some broad sense. Both a large body of recent scholarly literature and enduring themes of contemporary politics raise difficult questions about the accuracy of that claim.[328] Should the courts agree with this broadly held perception that Congress has been captured by "faction," would that warrant their refusal to cooperate? One steps here well past the *Carolene Products* propositions that support unusual judicial interventions into politics on the ground that they may serve to unblock the political process.[329] While one sees how measures protective of speech or responsive to malapportionment may serve to reinvigorate political branches themselves blocked from self-reform, it is unclear how restrictive judicial attitudes toward legislation in general would tend to make Congress more representative. Indeed, the very fact of reasoning in this way would offend central values of the Constitution, which imagine the branches as coordinate; would appear like posing as Congress's teacher. To thus judge Congress's capacity for action is to raise a political question in the classic sense adumbrated by *Baker v Carr*:[330] "expressing lack of the respect due coordinate branches of government."[331]

Moreover, the argument presupposes that the courts would somehow remain outside politics in a government otherwise dominated by factional excess. Neither our history nor political theory warrant any such claim.[332] It was Progressive legislation enacted by new majorities on behalf of the formerly oppressed that excited judicial resistance at the turn of the century—legislation easing the obstacles to recovery for injuries suffered in the workplace, or protecting workers from unsafe or unhealthy working conditions. More recently, the Supreme Court's narrow interpretations have

---

[328] For example, Daniel A. Farber and Philip P. Frickey, *Law and Public Choice* (Chicago, 1991); Symposium: *Regulating Regulation: The Political Economy of Administrative Procedures and Regulatory Instruments*, 57 L & Contemp Probs 1 (1994); Symposium: *Positive Political Theory and Public Law*, 80 Georgetown L J 457 and 1737 (1992); Symposium: *The New Public Law*, 89 Mich L Rev 707 (1991).

[329] *United States v Carolene Products Corp.*, 304 US 144, 152–53 n 4 (1938); see, e.g., John Hart Ely, *Democracy and Distrust* (1980).

[330] 369 US at 186 (1962).

[331] Id at 210.

[332] See Edward L. Rubin, *Public Choice in Practice and Theory*, 81 Cal L Rev 1657 (1993); Daniel Shaviro, *Beyond Public Choice and Public Interest: A Study of the Legislative Process and Illustrated by Tax Legislation in the 1980s*, 139 U Pa L Rev 1, 65–68 (1990).

been visited upon legislation that expanded civil rights, provided for consumer protection, and protected bankrupts' estates. While one certainly knows that Congress sometimes enacts special interest legislation, it is hard to see these particular measures as reflecting chiefly the interests of the politically powerful. That characterization is much more easily attached to the judicial results.[333] In any competition for political legitimacy in putting into effect their political views, the judiciary has long understood, as the people have, that it comes last among the branches.

Taking seriously the separation of powers argument requires attention to an aspect that its proponents have not much discussed, but that seems implicit in some of the cases discussed in this essay: namely, what is entailed in being a "court." It is not only Congress that has a constitutional function; so does the federal judiciary. Separation of powers reasoning about Congress's role cannot properly be taken so far as to deny to the judiciary the quality and responsibility of courts. In particular, the argument here supposes the legitimacy of federal courts' common law function—that is, that it is sometimes appropriate for them to develop the law outside the realm of statutes, exercising authority of the character traditional to the English courts and to state judicial systems. That is what permits us to ask why they should do any less in the statutory context—indeed, whether they have a higher obligation to observe legislative signals as the source of policy, than their own prior reasoning.

A common law court cannot persuasively invoke, as a reason why courts should not fill out what Congress has not directly expressed, the proposition that lawmaking is only for Congress.[334]

---

[333] Aleinikoff, 87 Mich L Rev at 32, cited in note 29, considers whether formalist techniques are warranted to discipline otherwise over-adventurous "intentionalist" judges, rather than to instruct the legislature.

> But if the instances of bad-faith judging are so great that the plain meaning theorists are comfortable in their calculation, one wonders why the legislature (which after all is the injured party) hasn't taken steps to reduce bad-faith judging by writing statutes more clearly. Furthermore, if we assume such a plethora of willful judges, why should we believe that they will not similarly misuse a plain meaning approach?

If one looks to recent cases in which Congress has corrected judicial "error," as in the civil rights area, those opinions have been predominantly formalist, not intentionalist, in character. See also William N. Eskridge, Jr., *Reneging on History? Playing the Court/Congress/President Civil Rights Game*, 79 Cal L Rev 613, 675–80 (1991).

[334] This formalist argument was among those earlier and persuasively addressed in William N. Eskridge, Jr., *Dynamic Statutory Interpretation*, 135 U Pa L Rev 1479, 1497 ff (1987),

To the extent that argument depends on a wholly formal view of judicial function—the idea that judges find but do not make law—it is indistinguishable from, and no more credible than, the similar argument once made about the common law function. *City of Chicago*[335] and *BFP*[336] are good illustrations of the point. Outside the sphere of legislation, we readily see that judicial disclaimers of lawmaking are disingenuous or, at best, metaphors for the appropriateness of restraint in that function.[337]

> It is important that the mechanism of legal reasoning should not be concealed by its pretense. The pretense is that the law is a system of known rules applied by a judge; the pretense has long been under attack. In an important sense legal rules are never clear, and if a rule had to be clear before it could be imposed, society would be impossible. The mechanism accepts the differences of view and ambiguities of words. It provides for the participation of the community in resolving the ambiguity by providing a forum for the discussion of policy in the gap of ambiguity. On serious controversial questions, it makes it possible to take the first step in the direction of what otherwise would be forbidden ends. The mechanism is indispensable to peace in a community.[338]

So long as this is what judges are doing—as in the common law context—then building upon the political judgments expressed in legislation would seem, ceteris paribus, to improve the chances that the judges' inevitable resolution of "policy in the gap of ambiguity" would conform to society's wishes and thus tend toward "peace in [the] community." Indeed, this proposition lies at the heart of the arguments of Pound and Stone with which, in a sense, this article began.[339] When Pound wrote, the courts customarily elevated their common law functions over statutes, preferring the policies of the common law to the policies of statutes; the result of this self-evident struggle with state and federal legislatures was to *submerge* the views of the community in resolving "policy in the [inevitable] gap of

---

an article both germinal of much contemporary literature on the subject and self-consciously continuous with the earlier literature. See, e.g., id at 1480.

[335] Discussed in text following p 499.

[336] Discussed in text following p 449.

[337] Compare Edward Rubin, *Book Review: Interpreting Statutes: A Comparative Study*, 41 Am J Comp L 129, 131 (1993).

[338] Levi, at 1.

[339] Works cited at nn 5 and 8.

ambiguity," rather than to foster its expression. Judicial behavior was in this way destructive, not supportive, of social peace. It defeated rather than supported principles of accountability.[340]

If we were to conclude that the federal courts were not courts in this sense, then much of the preceding argument would be undercut. The Constitution, its foundational documents, and early federal judicial practice are all instinct with the understanding that the federal courts were to be courts as the English colonists and then the citizens of the states had experienced courts.[341] In areas of undoubted federal jurisdiction, such as admiralty, they have always acted as courts in the full Anglo-American sense. To be sure, *Erie R. Co. v Tompkins*[342] stands for the proposition that federal courts lack competence to generate common law independent of relevant state law in the diversity jurisdiction.[343] But that is an artifact of diversity jurisdiction, which depends on the character of the parties and assumes state law will apply. Extending that conclusion to federal question jurisdiction would be a stunning revision of constitutional understandings; it would convert the federal courts into instruments genuinely foreign to American legal traditions.[344]

Perhaps there are other ways of perceiving the occasional indica-

---

[340] To Robert Gross I owe the observation that the only actors accountable for interpretations driven by dictionaries may be their commercial publishers. The decisions legislatures actually make, as the public knows them, are not implemented. The decisions judges make are, at least ostensibly, not their own. See Muriel M. Spence, *The Sleeping Giant: Textualism as Power Struggle*, 67 So Cal L Rev 585 (1994).

[341] Compare the evocation of judicial function in David A. Strauss, *Common Law Constitutional Interpretation* (unpublished).

[342] 304 US 64 (1938).

[343] In this respect, its overruling of *Swift v Tyson*, 41 US 1 (1842), depends on a reading of *Swift* not obvious at the time it was decided, that it resolved an issue not within federal question jurisdiction. The *Swift* Court's broad insistence on the importance of uniform rules for the protection of commerce, 41 US at 18–19, might instead have been understood to invoke the federal jurisdiction over interstate commerce. One can imagine objections to invoking the Constitution in support of a necessarily federal rule; but the argument that federal courts have power to generate common law supportive of federal authority is indistinguishable in principle from the argument that they may generate principles of admiralty. Compare Thomas W. Merrill, *The Common Law Powers of Federal Courts*, 52 U Chi L Rev 1, 30, 64–65 and n 279 (1985).

[344] Thomas Merrill develops such an argument at length in the work cited in the immediately preceding note; he seems to concede, however, the bearing of the framers' expectation that the federal judiciary would be "courts." Id at 65 n 279; his essay is strongly criticized in William N. Eskridge, Jr., *Dynamic Statutory Interpretation*, 135 U Pa L Rev 1479, 1498–1501 (1987).

tions from some Justices that the Supreme Court is not a fully fledged common law court, even for federal question purposes. Might dependency on state court definitions of common law doctrine be justified on grounds of their relatively greater expertise, as they encounter such questions more often? Or as an unspoken balancing factor, given the enormity of the federal constitutional and statutory authority over the content of law for the states? Or as a reflection that the Court, with other arguably more important and in any event more distinctively federal tasks to accomplish, is simply not very adept at this function, and should not try to do it for itself? While a certain reality underlies these speculations, what also underlies them is, again, a rather aconstitutional vision of what it means to be a court in American legal culture. It may be so, in some sense, that constitutional cases are the most important element in the Court's docket, but it is nonetheless an ordinary court in our Constitution's contemplation—not a constitutional court or an administrative court, such as characterize some European systems. Indeed, we tend to think its legitimacy importantly derives from its conventional judicial function. We cannot, then, afford to let the character of its docket defeat its characteristics, without changing our Constitution. Moreover, even if the Supreme Court is in some factual sense relatively removed from ordinary judging, the lower federal courts are not. They have a steady diet of common law questions, both in the diversity jurisdiction and in the federal question jurisdiction. And the same positivistic view of the common law that underlies *Erie*—that it is simply the judge-made law of a particular political jurisdiction—makes it unthinkable that, as to *federal* questions, federal common law should be parasitic on state court choices. In making federal common law, where it is appropriate to do so, the federal courts can no more be limited by what California and North Carolina courts have chosen for their jurisdictions than are the courts of Minnesota.

Perhaps there is a sense in which this is all quite unconscious. One characteristic of formalism, often enough noted, is that it permits judges to claim—to themselves as well as to others—that they can always make decisions without drawing on their own ideas of good policy or social justice. It externalizes responsibility. Even to Justices who learned too well that formation of the common law does not work that way, common law rules can provide a similar refuge from responsibility, if they can be made to come *from some-*

place else. One no longer entertains the possibility of a single source in the heavens; but the *Erie* idea that the state courts are the necessary source in matters of diversity jurisdiction (because the questions there *are* questions of state law) is easily and perhaps unconsciously transmogrified into a more general responsibility. The common law now comes from out there, if not up there. Its federal character in these cases, and the Court's consequent responsibility for the choices that shape it, is simply ignored. Here, as in dealing with legislation by dictionary, the Court will have escaped its own responsibility.[345]

From a certain perspective, the risk of judicial politics is present, whichever approach the Justices take. In whatever fashion the Justices may interpret a statute, Congress can change that interpretation only by the concurrence of two houses and (in the usual case) acquiescence by the then President. As Professors Eskridge and Ferejohn, among others, have shown us, that in effect means that the judiciary can effectively put into place any interpretation Congress will be unable to change—a considerable degree of freedom of maneuver.[346] Even if we assume a cooperative process between courts and legislature, judicial "mistakes" will inevitably occur; but they will be mistakes made despite a posture of concern for congressional political judgment and attention to community expectations. That is the apparent story of the differences between the vetoed Civil Rights Act Amendments of 1990 and the enacted Civil Rights Act Amendments of 1991 that gave rise to the problem in *Rivers* and *Landgraf*.[347] To assert that the Constitution requires that the Congress and the Court not be cooperators, however—that the courts are obliged to honor only those instructions that are unmistakable on the "objective" surface of the text—is to free the Court of any such posture, its tools limited to the manipulable world of the text.[348] Thus one sees how the insistence on the static quality of legislation, which only Congress can correct, not only denies responsibilities for cooperation, but also plays into a rather cynically political game.

---

[345] See note 340.

[346] William N. Eskridge, Jr., and John Ferejohn, *The Article I, Section 7 Game*, 80 Georgetown L J 523 (1992).

[347] Discussed in text following p 454.

[348] Merrill, work cited in n 41.

Whatever its source, the emerging view of judging and judges' place in the political order is not only profoundly altered from that which has generally characterized our polity; it also portends rigidity and destabilization for law and its administration. The constant rising and resolution of issues through the judicial system has been a means by which law continually refits itself to social needs, reducing to that extent the need for constant legislating. Clearly enough judges sometimes err, and legislatures may then correct; or the judiciary fails to accommodate the law quickly enough to changing social circumstances and, again, legislation may do so. But the premise that legitimate change occurs only legislatively puts under constant threat all those understandings that inevitably arise—are acted upon and relied upon—in its wake. The Supreme Court hears the smallest proportion of the cases resolved by the federal system each year; its interventions are made necessarily episodic by that fact. If its task in dealing with statutes is to enforce original understandings as a majority of Justices come to see them, regardless what developments may have occurred in the interim, the prospect is more, not less, uncertainty; and this impact is heightened if the Court, in so acting, is also unwilling to educate itself about the political context within which Congress has acted—elevating, in that way, the chances of conflict over political judgments Congress has reached.

It is hard to believe that the result of this struggle will be improved performance by the legislature. First, legislation for other reasons is already assuming proportions too large for the more careful drafting the Court ostensibly invites; second, if history is any guide, the only outcome to be anticipated from the Court's formal and distant approach is a larger rather than a smaller volume of specification from the legislature.[349] Finally, and perhaps most important, even if we can imagine Congress learning from its dialog with the Court, the lesson is in one large measure perverse: While the Court *says* that it is contributing to settled expectations, that can be so only for legislation written in response to its opinions about interpretation, after those opinions have been written. But earlier legislation was written in the context of other interpretive

---

[349] Lieber, work cited in n 33. A similar argument appears in modern dress in Edward P. Schwartz, Pablo T. Spiller, and Santiago Urbiztondo, *A Positive Theory of Legislative Intent*, 57 L & Contemp Probs 51 (1994).

expectations. By failing to honor the interpretive expectations that governed Congress's action when the earlier statutes were passed, the Court teaches that today's lessons have no necessary relevance to the style of interpretation the Court will use tomorrow.

The Justices are changing the premises of our system, and not for the better. Perhaps, they will say, it is to correct for an excessively powerful view the prior generation of Justices held; but the act of deconstruction is powerful and destructive—and its premises quite outside what had until now been the shared political premises of a common law system of judging.